Taxation of Partnerships

Taxation of Partnerships

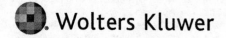 Wolters Kluwer

Legislative and other material

Telephone Helpline Disclaimer Notice

© 2016 Wolters Kluwer (UK) Limited

Wolters Kluwer
145 London Road
Kingston upon Thames
KT2 6SR
Telephone: (0) 844 561 8166
Facsimile: (0) 208 247 2638
E-mail: cch@wolterskluwer.com
Website: www.cch.co.uk

ISBN 978-1-84798-833-1

British Library Cataloguing-in-Publication Data

A catalogue record for this book is available from the British Library.

Typeset by Innodata Inc.
Printed by TOTEM, Poland, Inowrocław, 2016.

About the authors

Sarah Arnold

Sarah Arnold FCA CTA is an independent tax consultant who provides specialist tax advice via her own tax consultancy to fellow professionals providing tax and accountancy services. She additionally contributes to a number of CCH publications, including the *British Tax Reporter,* the *Weekly Tax News,* the *Red & Green* legislation volumes, *British Master Tax Guide, CCH Tax Planning* and *Hardman's Tax Rates & Tables*.

Pete Miller

Pete Miller, CTA (Fellow) is a founder member of The Miller Partnership. Pete has worked in tax for over 29 years, starting as an Inspector of Taxes in 1988, working in Birmingham and London before posts in Policy and Technical Divisions. He then worked for 11 years in 'Big 4' firms before forming The Miller Partnership in April 2011 to offer expert advice to other advisers on all business corporate tax issues.

Apart from partnerships, Pete's areas of specialist expertise include the transactions in securities rules, reorganisations, reconstructions, HMRC clearances, disguised remuneration, the Patent Box and taxation of intangible assets.

Pete speaks and writes regularly on a wide range of tax issues. Pete is also the author of a well-received textbook on company reorganisations and reconstructions and several Tax Digests, including CCH's Tax Digest on the Patent Box.

Preface

Taxation of Partnerships is designed primarily to assist practitioners in understanding tax liabilities and entitlements for all types of partnerships. It is designed to collate all relevant areas of the tax code as they apply to partnerships in order to provide practitioners with a one-stop guide to assist with the preparation of tax computations and returns for the partnership itself as well as its partners, both individual and corporate. The guide further provides guidance and information in order to assist practitioners advising on the tax consequences of transactions undertaken by partners and partnerships and providing tax planning advice thereon. The guide provides comprehensive coverage that will be relevant both to experienced practitioners and also to students and others who come to the subject for the first time.

Taxation of Partnerships is organised across three Parts. The first Part provides an overview of the different types of partnership structure; general partnerships, limited liability partnerships and limited partnerships, the legal background as well as commentary of the different types of partner.

Detailed commentary is then provided on the specific rules for calculating the chargeable gains for partners, including Statement of Practice D12 and capital gains tax reliefs including specific commentary on entrepreneurs' relief.

Part 2 covers compliance and administration matters including partnership returns, claims, enquiries and discovery provisions, penalties and powers, PAYE and National Insurance and the construction industry scheme.

Part 2 further provides extensive commentary on the computation of profits and losses of partnerships for income tax and corporation tax purposes, the allocation of profits and losses to partners and the assessment of profits to income tax and corporation tax. The respective chapters include the anti-avoidance rules for mixed partnerships, loan relationships provisions and the implications of changes in the partnership structure, mergers and demergers. Part 2 also provides commentary on aspects of the capital allowances regime that are specific to partnerships, the calculation of profits under the cash basis and corporate loans to participators rules.

Part 2 concludes with commentary on the calculation of and relief for partnership losses (income tax and corporation tax) by way of an overview of the basic rules as well as detailed commentary on restrictions on partnership losses for sideways loss relief, limited partners and members of LLPs, non-active partners, film partnerships and partnerships with mixed membership. The charging provisions in respect of avoidance involving trade losses are also covered.

Part 3 provides an overview of the special regime applicable to alternative investment funds and specific aspects of inheritance tax, stamp duty land tax and VAT that arise in connection with partnerships.

Finally the three main areas of anti-avoidance legislation relating to partnerships, the transfer of assets and income streams legislation; disguised investment management fees and carried interest provisions and the limited liability salaried members' legislation, are also covered.

The appendices provide supporting information including statements of practice, briefs and other HMRC guidance.

Sarah Arnold and Pete Miller
October 2016

Contents

About the authors   *v*
Preface   *vii*

Part 1: STRUCTURAL ISSUES   **1**

What is a Partnership?   **3**

    Introduction   3
  General partnerships   3
    Introduction   3
    Why does partnership matter?   4
    Character of a partnership   4
    Persons carrying on a business in common with a view of profit   5
    Other indicia of partnership   10
    Capacity to be a partner   11
    Family partnerships   12
    Partnership agreement   12
    Consequences of a partnership   15
    Date from which partnership exists   16
    Duration of partnership   16
    Partnership and employment   17
  Limited partnerships   19
    Limited partnerships   19
  Limited liability partnerships   20
    Introduction   20
    Legal background   20
    Limitation of liability   21
    Contrast with general partnerships   21
  Types of partner   22
    Introduction   22
    Equity partner   22
    Salaried partner   22
    Sleeping partner   23
    Limited partner   23

Contents

Taxation | 24

General and limited partnerships | 24

Formation of a partnership | **27**

Business entities | 27

Introduction | 27

Factors in deciding on a business entity | 27

Forming a general partnership | 29

Forming an LLP | 29

Changes in partnership shares | **31**

Introduction | 31

Introduction to partners' chargeable gains | 31

Limited Liability Partnerships ('LLPs') | 32

Partnership assets | 33

Admission and retirement of partners | 34

HMRC Statement of Practice: SP D12 | 35

Application of SP D12: Limited Liability Partnerships | 36

Valuation of a partner's share in a partnership asset | 37

Disposals of assets by a partnership | 38

Distribution of partnership assets in specie | 39

Changes in partnership sharing ratios | 41

Rebasing of partnership assets held at 31 March 1982 | 43

Contribution of an asset to a partnership | 44

Adjustment through the accounts (revaluation of partnership assets) | 46

Payments between partners outside the partnership accounts | 47

Transfers between persons not at arm's length | 49

Annuities provided by partnerships | 52

Mergers of partnerships | 54

Shares acquired in stages | 55

Elections under TCGA 1992, Sch. 2, para. 4 | 56

Partnership goodwill | 56

Entrepreneurs' relief on transfer of a business, 'roll-over' relief and business asset gift relief | 57

Corporate partners and intangible fixed assets | 58

Dissolution and winding up of a partnership   **61**

Introduction   61

Dissolution of a general partnership   61

Consequences of dissolution   62

Income tax on winding up a partnership   62

Capital gains tax on winding up a partnership   63

Dissolution of a limited liability partnership   65

Income tax on winding up an LLP   66

Capital gains tax on winding up an LLP   66

Tax reliefs available to partners   **67**

Introduction   67

Relief for interest payments   67

Interest payments – general   67

Limit on relief   67

Restrictions on relief   68

Qualifying purpose   69

Exclusion of double relief   70

Anti-avoidance   71

Loans to buy plant or machinery for use by a partnership   71

Loans to invest in partnership   72

Loan to invest in partnership: salaried partners   73

Loan to invest in partnership: Scottish partnerships   73

Loan to invest in a partnership: restriction on relief for
loans to invest in property partnership   74

Loan to invest in a partnership: tax reduction for
non-deductible loan interest   75

Loans to invest in film partnerships   75

Loans to invest in film partnerships: definitions   76

Loan to invest in partnership: withdrawal of relief   77

Loan to invest in partnership: replacement loans   78

Loan to invest in partnership: business successions   78

Loan to invest in partnership: ineligibility of interest:
commercial woodlands   79

Relief for interest paid: certificates from lenders   80

Contents

Capital gains tax reliefs   80

Importance of CGT reliefs to partnerships   80

Entrepreneurs' relief   80

Material disposal of business assets   81

Disposal of whole or part of a business   81

Disposal of assets after business discontinued   82

Disposal associated with material disposal   83

Restrictions on relief for associated disposals   86

Disposal by trustees   87

Restriction to relevant business assets   88

Relevant business assets: goodwill   89

Corporate partnerships and entrepreneurs' relief   91

Entrepreneurs' relief examples   93

Replacement of business assets by partners   95

Gifts of interests in partnerships or partnership assets   98

Negligible value claims by partners   98

Incorporation of partnerships   **101**

Introduction   101

Mechanisms   101

Effect of incorporation   102

Impact of incorporation   103

Incorporation relief   103

Introduction   103

Claims and elections   104

Conditions: a person who is not a company transfers
a business to a company   105

Conditions: business must be transferred as a 'going concern'   106

Conditions: whole of assets (other than cash, if desired)
are transferred to the company   107

Conditions: consideration given by the company is wholly
or party in form of its own shares issued to the transferor   108

Consequences: reduction in net gains on old assets   109

Consequences: reduction in allowable cost of shares   112

Interaction with other reliefs   114

Anti-avoidance   114

Business assets gift relief   115

Introduction 115

Effect of relief 115

Conditions for relief 116

Claims 116

Qualifying business assets 117

Agricultural land 117

Non-resident recipients 118

Actual consideration for the transfer 119

Period of non-qualifying use 119

Partial business use of building or structure 120

Interaction with other reliefs 122

Incorporation relief or business asset gift relief 123

Introduction 123

Incorporation for cash 123

Stamp Duty Land Tax and Land and Buildings Transaction Tax **125**

Basic principles 125

Meaning of 'partnership' for SDLT purposes 125

A 'see-through' analysis 125

Starting a partnership 126

Ordinary partnership transactions 127

Overview 127

Responsible and representative partners 127

Liabilities for SDLT, interest or penalties 127

Finance Act 2004 provisions 128

General 128

Scope of amended Finance Act 2003,
Sch. 15, Pt. 3 128

Partnerships chapter in the SDLT manual 129

Anti-avoidance rules 129

Application to partnerships of the s. 75A
anti-avoidance rule 130

Transfer of chargeable interest to a partnership 132

Basic statutory rule 132

Thinking behind the rule 133

Where the chargeable consideration includes rent 135

Sum of the lower proportions 135

Ascertaining the partnership shares 137

Post-transaction consideration: Finance (No. 2) Act 2005 measure 137

Election by property investment partnership to disapply para. 10 138

Summing up 139

Transfer of partnership interest 140

Basic statutory rule 140

Market rent leases 142

Exchanges of land 142

Anti-avoidance provision 143

Changes in income profit-sharing ratios 143

HMRC's response: the meaning of 'arrangements' 144

Compliance issues 146

Existence of 'arrangements': the Stamp Taxes rule of thumb 147

What is necessary to constitute the transfer of a partnership share? 147

Transfers of interest in a property investment partnership – further detail on the FA 2005 changes 149

Transfer of chargeable interest from a partnership 153

Basic statutory rule 153

Partnership share attributable to a partner 155

Transfer of chargeable interest from a partnership to a partnership 157

Application of para. 18 in a nutshell 157

Remaining provisions of Schedule 15 158

Application of exemptions and reliefs 158

The only charging provisions 158

Notification 159

Continued application of stamp duty on transfers of partnership interests 159

Interpretation: partnership share and partnership property 159

Interpretation: transfer of chargeable interest to a partnership 161

Interpretation: transfer of interest in a partnership 162

Interpretation: transfer of a chargeable interest from a partnership 162

Interpretation: market value of lease 162

Interpretation: connected persons 162

Interpretation: arrangements 163

Partnership interests held by trustees 163

Land and buildings transaction tax   163

   Overview of Sch. 17   163

   Definitions and Distinctions   165

   General provisions for chargeable interests held by partners   168

   Special rules for transactions of transfer to a partnership   172

   Special rules for transactions of transfer from a partnership   179

   Partnership and leases   184

   Property investment partnerships   185

   Application of provisions on exemptions, reliefs and notification   191

PART 2: COMPLIANCE ISSUES   **199**

Compliance and administration   **201**

   Introduction and overview   201

   Registering partners and partnerships with HMRC   201

   Partnership returns   204

   Withdrawal by HMRC of notice under TMA 1970, s. 12AA   206

   Partnership statement to be included in return   207

   Claims to be included in partnership return   207

   Amendment of partnership return by taxpayer and
correction by HMRC   208

   Relief for mistakes in the partnership tax return   208

   Partners' returns   209

   Enquiries into partnership returns   209

   Discovery and partnerships   211

   Record-keeping   212

   Penalties for failure to file a partnership return   212

   Penalties for inaccuracies in a partnership tax return   214

   Information powers   214

   Deduction of income tax   215

   Class 2 and 4 NIC   217

   PAYE and Class 1 NIC   219

   Construction industry scheme   219

Computation of firms' profits and losses   **221**

   Introduction   221

   Limited liability partnerships   222

The three-stage approach 222

Profits or losses calculated at partnership level 224

Partners to whom remittance basis applies 226

Resident partners and double taxation agreements 226

Calculation of profits and losses: general 228

Calculation of profits and losses: income tax 229

Calculation of profits and losses: corporation tax 230

Calculation of profits and losses: loan relationships 231

Calculation of profits and losses: loan relationships: determination
of debits and credits 232

Specific receipts: directors' fees received by partnerships 233

Specific deductions: expenses incurred by partners individually 233

Specific deductions: payments to partners – general 234

Specific deductions: payments to outgoing partners 236

Specific deductions: interest paid by the partnership 236

Specific deductions: rent 237

Specific deductions: service companies 237

Specific deductions: partner recruitment costs 238

Specific deductions: partner training costs 238

Specific deductions: termination payments 238

Specific deductions: partnership annuities 239

Specific deductions: costs connected with the capital
structure of a business 240

Specific deductions: deductions in relation to LLP salaried members 240

Miscellaneous computational provisions 241

Farming and market gardening 241

UK property income 241

Overseas property income 242

Jointly owned property 242

Adjustment income: change of accounting policy or tax
adjustments applied 243

Allocation of firm's profits or losses between partners **247**

Introduction 247

Allocation of income tax profits 247

Changes in the profit sharing arrangements 249

Treatment of salaries and interest on capital 250

Reallocation of notional profit/loss 251

Allocation of profits and losses to corporate partners 254

Loan relationships: Allocating loan relationship debits and credits
(and exchange gains and losses) 255

Loan relationships: lending between partners and the partnership 257

Loan relationships: lending between partners and the partnership:
tax implications 261

Loan relationships: company partners and other connections 262

Loan relationships: allocating credits and debits to the company
partner: Tax Bulletin article TB62/02 263

Treatment of exchange gains and losses 266

Company partners' shares where firm owns deeply
discounted securities 267

Charitable donations 267

Partnerships with mixed members 268

Excess profit allocation to non-individual partners 268

HMRC guidance 268

Entry conditions 269

Condition X 270

Condition Y 271

Counteraction: reallocation of profits 277

Excess profit allocation to 'individuals who are not partners'
(Anti-avoidance) 277

Counteraction reallocation of profits 279

Payments from corporate or trust partners to individual partners
(preventing double taxation) 280

Application of excess profit allocation rules to specific situations 281

Commencement 282

Mixed partnerships: practical solutions 282

Excess loss allocation 283

Assessment to income and corporation tax **285**

Assessment of partnership to tax 285

Assessment to income tax 285

Firms with trading income: concept of the notional trade or business 286

Firms with trading income: notional trades for individual partners 288

Notional trades: basis periods 289

Notional trades: basis periods – change of accounting date 290

Notional trades: basis period – start-up payments 293

Firms with trading and other source income 293

Income tax: claims for averaging of partnership profits 295

Income tax: relief for partnership annuities paid 295

Assessment to corporation tax 296

Partnership changes, merger and demergers **299**

Introduction 299

Changes in partnership: income tax overview 299

Changes in partnership: income tax treatment 300

Mergers and demergers: income tax 302

Mergers: old businesses cease and new business commences 303

Mergers: previous businesses continue as a merged joint business 303

Mergers: one business continues and the other(s) cease 305

Demergers: income tax 305

Changes in partnership: corporation tax 306

Partnership changes: special computational provisions 308

Sale of patent rights: effects of partnership changes 308

Capital allowances **311**

Overview 311

Plant and machinery allowances: annual investment allowance 312

Plant and machinery allowances: partnership changes 313

Plant and machinery allowances: partnership using property of partners 315

Plant and machinery allowances: successions 315

Plant and machinery allowances: successions election 316

Plant and machinery allowances: anti-avoidance 318

Other capital allowances: overview 319

Other capital allowances: partnership changes 319

Other capital allowances: successions 320

Other capital allowances: anti-avoidance: partners as connected persons 321

Other capital allowances: partners as connected persons: election for
alternative amount 322

Determination of market value 323

Meaning of connected person 323

Cash basis for small businesses and fixed rate deductions for expenses   **327**

Introduction and overview   327

Eligibility   328

Relevant maximum   329

Application to partnerships   329

Excluded persons   330

Effect of making an election   331

Calculating profits   332

Receipts and expenses   332

Restricting expenses   335

Expenditure normally specifically allowable   335

Loan interest   335

Transitional rules when changing accounting bases   336

Entering the cash basis   336

Leaving the cash basis   336

Election to accelerate the spreading of adjustment income on leaving the cash basis   337

Capital allowances   337

Tax relief on loans to buy plant or machinery for partnership use   337

Restriction on sideways relief and capital gains relief where cash basis applies   338

Deductions allowable at a fixed rate   338

Overview   338

Business mileage: fixed rate allowance   339

When a fixed rate allowance for business mileage is allowable   339

The amount of the deduction   339

Use of home for business purposes: flat rate deduction   340

The amount of the deduction   341

Premises used both as a home and as business premises   342

The non-business use amount   342

Corporate loans and benefits to participators   **343**

Overview   343

Application to partnerships   344

Benefits to participators   346

Losses   **349**

Overview: trading losses   349

Income tax relief against general income and gains   350

Income tax early trade loss relief   351

Income tax general restrictions on sideways relief   352

Income tax restrictions on sideways relief and capital gains relief where cash basis applies   353

Income tax restrictions on sideways relief for certain capital allowances   353

Income tax restrictions on sideways relief for specific trades   355

Income tax carry-forward trade loss relief   355

Income tax terminal trade loss relief   356

Income tax losses from trade carried on abroad   357

Corporation tax loss relief against total profits   357

Corporation tax terminal loss relief   359

Corporation tax carry-forward trade loss relief   360

Corporation tax restrictions on use of losses   360

Corporation tax restriction on transferring relief   361

Corporation tax group loss relief   362

Restrictions on trade loss relief for partners   364

Restrictions on trade loss relief for partners: background   364

Restriction on trade loss relief for partners overview   365

Income tax restrictions: key definitions   366

Income tax limit on reliefs in any tax year not to exceed cap for tax year   367

Income tax restrictions on reliefs for individual limited partners   368

Income tax restrictions on reliefs for individual members of limited liability partnerships   371

Income tax unrelieved losses brought forward (individual members of LLPs)   374

Income tax restrictions on reliefs for non-active individual partners in early tax years   374

Income tax unrelieved losses brought forward (non-active individual partners)   379

Income tax exclusion of amounts in calculating contribution to the firm or LLP   381

Income tax films   383

Income tax restriction: partnerships with mixed membership   385

Corporation tax restriction on reliefs for company limited partners   387

Corporation tax restriction on relief for company members of LLPs   389

Income tax avoidance involving trade losses   391

Income tax avoidance involving trade losses overview   391

Individuals in partnership: recovery of excess relief – overview   392

Individuals in partnership: recovery of excess relief – conditions   392

Individuals in partnership: recovery of excess relief – amount
of income treated as received   394

Individuals in partnership: recovery of excess relief – key definitions   394

Individuals claiming relief for film-related losses: introduction   396

Individuals claiming relief for film-related losses: detailed conditions   396

Individuals claiming relief for film-related losses: disposal of a right
to profits   398

Individuals claiming relief for film-related losses: key definitions   399

Individuals claiming relief for film-related losses: capital contribution   399

Individuals claiming relief for film-related losses: prevention of double
counting   401

Individuals in partnership claiming relief for licence-related
trading losses: overview   401

Individuals in partnership claiming relief for licence-related trading
losses: calculation of income chargeable to tax   402

Individuals in partnership claiming relief for licence-related trading
losses: key definitions   404

PART 3: OTHER ISSUES   **407**

Alternative investment funds   **409**

Background   409

The election for the 'special mechanism'   409

The 'special mechanism'   410

Consequences of allocating profits   410

Vesting of previously allocated profits   411

Vesting statements   412

Capital gains consequences   412

Inheritance tax   **415**

  Overview   415

  Transfer of partnership assets   415

  Transfers to partnerships   417

  Agricultural property relief   417

  Qualification for APR relief   418

  Rate of APR relief   419

  Availability of APR relief – limited partnerships   420

  Business property relief   421

Value added tax   **425**

  Registration   425

  Introduction to registration of partnerships   425

  Partnership as a separate person   426

  Registration in the name of the firm: liability for VAT   428

  Notices served on a partnership   428

  Change in circumstances: notifying HMRC   428

  Partner's VAT liability   429

  Partners' entitlement to repayments   430

  Consideration for VATable services or distribution of partners' funds?   431

  Partnerships and VAT groups   431

  Capital paid on joining partnership   431

  Transfers of partnership interests   437

  Registration of limited liability partnerships   442

  Registration of limited partnerships   443

  VAT assessments   445

  Insolvency returns   447

  VAT penalties   448

  Civil fraud penalty for partners   448

  Penalty for inaccurate information   448

  VAT on partnership transactions   449

  Capital introduced   449

  Partnership interest: purchase and disposal   449

  De-registration   450

  Input tax recovery   452

  Tripartite transactions   452

Business purpose test   453

Other legal services and fees   453

Accountancy fees   454

Partnership – cost of raising capital   455

Property ownership   456

Ownership of property: introduction   456

Property owned as 'ordinary' partnership asset   456

Property owned by some partners and included
in balance sheet   457

Property owned by some partners outside the partnership   457

Property owned by nominee company   458

Property owned by service company   458

Interest in property retained by outgoing partner   459

Ownership of property: summary   459

Property letting   459

Partnership interests   460

Opting to tax   461

Special circumstances   461

Partners providing professional services   461

Private tuition by partnership   462

Transfer of a 'Going concern'   463

Anti-avoidance: overview   **465**

Introduction   465

Disposals through partnerships   **467**

Background   467

Disposals of income streams: overview   467

Disposals of income streams: income tax provisions   468

Disposals of income streams: corporation tax provisions   471

Disposals of assets: overview   472

Disposals of assets: income tax provisions   473

Disposals of assets: corporation tax provisions   475

Disguised investment management fees and carried interest   **477**

Background   477

Disguised investment management fees (DMF)   479

Introduction   479

Contents

Charge to income tax	480
Meaning of management fee	481
Carried interest	482
Carried interest and disguised investment management fees: 'arise'	483
Carried interest: charge to capital gains tax	487
Background	487
Overview	488
Charge to capital gains tax	489
Permitted deductions	490
Exclusions from the capital gains tax charge	491
Avoidance of double taxation	491
Carried interest: consideration on disposal, etc. of right	491
Carried interest: foreign chargeable gains	492
Relief for external investors on disposal of partnership asset	492
Meaning of 'arise': deferred carried interest	493
Income-based carried interest	496
Introduction	496
Income-based carried interest	497
LLPs: Salaried members	**503**
Background	503
Structure of the legislation	504
Condition A	505
Condition B	509
Condition C	511
Date of contribution	514
Anti-avoidance	515
Consequential provisions	516
Solutions	517
Appendices	**519**
Appendix 1: SP D11 Partnership: assets owned by a partner	521
Appendix 2: SP D12 Partnerships	523
Appendix 3: SP 1/79 Partnerships: extension of Statement of Practice D12	533

Appendix 4: SP 1/89 Partnerships: Further Extension
of Statement of Practice D12   535

Appendix 5: HMRC Brief 03/08 Capital gains tax and corporation
tax on chargeable gains: contribution of assets to a partnership   537

Appendix 6: HMRC Brief 09/09 Capital gains tax: rebasing
rules Finance Act 2008 and Partnerships   539

Appendix 7: ESC D23 Relief for the replacement of business
assets: partition of land on the dissolution of a partnership   559

Appendix 8: HMRC Salaried Member Rules   561

Case Table   **621**

Legislation Finding List   **625**

Index   **647**

PART 1:   STRUCTURAL ISSUES

Chapter 1:   What is a partnership?

10-000   Introduction

This is a book about the taxation of partnerships in the UK. It is, therefore, pretty fundamental to understand what a partnership actually is, its legal status and how it is to be treated as a matter of general law.

Partnerships have been around for a very long time and have been described as being 'as old as commerce itself' (see, for example, *Partnership Law* by Mark Blackett-Ord and Sarah Haren, Fifth Edition, Bloomsbury Professional). There are records of something analogous to partnerships in 13th century records, and by the 15th century, Italian merchants had introduced the concept of commercial partnerships to Northern Europe. However, there was no legislation specific to partnerships until the Law of the *Partnership Act* 1865. This is repealed, but most of this legislation is encompassed in what is now the *Partnership Act* 1890, s. 2(3).

The scope of this book is mainly UK tax, although some international aspects will be discussed or commented upon. However, it is outside the scope to discuss the various types of non-UK entity that might be analogous to UK partnerships, or might just be taxed as such.

The UK partnerships that we will be looking at are the ordinary partnership (often called a 'general partnership'), the limited partnership and the limited liability partnership (LLP).

Legislation: PA 1890, s. 2

GENERAL PARTNERSHIPS

10-020   Introduction

An ordinary or 'general' partnership does not have a specific title, they are just partnerships. The main legislation governing these partnerships is the *Partnership Act* 1890. This defines a partnership as being 'the relation which subsists between persons carrying on a business in common with a view of profit' (PA 1890, s. 1(1)). The important point here is that the partnership legislation specifically states that a particular relationship between the parties constitutes a partnership for general UK legal purposes.

The Partnership Act does not create partnerships per se (in contrast, as we shall see, to the *Limited Liability Partnership Act* 2000), it merely describes the legal position where there is a partnership. Furthermore, the Partnership Act tells us that a partnership, as such, is not an entity; it is merely a relationship between the parties involved. The Partnership Act does not confer or suggest any formal legal persona to a partnership, in contrast, for example, to a company. This is true for England and Wales, although under Scottish law, a partnership is a legal entity, as under other civil law jurisdictions.

The *Partnership Act* 1890, s. 1(1) does not, however, apply to people carrying on a business in common in the form of a company, as this is specifically excluded by s. 1(2). This provision excludes from the scope of the Partnership Act the relationship between members of a company or association registered under UK Acts of Parliament and relating to the registration of joint stock companies, or formed or incorporated by or under any other Act of Parliament, letters patent or royal charter. So this would exclude from the concept of the partnership all limited companies, entities with corporate status through, for example, a royal charter (such as the Chartered Institute of Taxation), entities formed under specific Acts of Parliament, such as the Mersey Docks and Harbour Board, and such entities as Industrial and Provident societies, formed under the *Industrial and Provident Societies Act* 1965 (repealed by the *Co-operative and Community Benefit Societies Act* 2014, Sch. 7).

Legislation: PA 1890, s. 1

10-040 Why does partnership matter?

There are an almost infinite variety of reasons why people might argue that they either are or are not in partnership with others. From a commercial perspective, for example, a person might argue that he is not in partnership with someone else simply to avoid the obligations or liabilities that arise from that partnership. On the other hand, from a tax perspective, the argument is usually the other way, as each member of a partnership that is chargeable to income tax will have a personal allowance as well as basic and higher rate bands, so the more partners in a partnership, the less tax is payable overall. As a simple example, husband and wife partnerships are a way of maximising household income, by splitting the profits between spouses (although see the comments on the *Pauline Valentine* case, below, for a counter-example).

10-060 Character of a partnership

In England and Wales, it is not a partnership firm which carries on a trade but rather the individual partners comprising the firm. In *R v Income Tax General Commissioners, ex parte Gibbs* (1942) 24 TC 221, a firm of stockbrokers consisting of four partners took on a fifth partner during the year. The Crown contended that this constituted a cessation of the business of the firm consisting of four partners and the succession by another firm consisting of five partners. Although none of the former members had retired, a new combination resulted from the addition of a fifth member. It was held that in England a partnership firm does not carry on a trade; but rather the individuals comprising the firm. The addition of a partner constitutes a change in the person charged, both in England and Scotland, i.e. four persons jointly had ceased to carry on the trade and five persons jointly had succeeded to it.

Viscount Simon LC said (at pp. 243–244):

'Strictly speaking, it is certainly true that an old partnership cannot be regarded as "ceasing" to carry on the trade, and the new partnership cannot be regarded as "succeeding" to it when some members of the old partnership are also members of the new, and thus do not individually cease to carry on the trade at all. A, B, C and D are carrying on the trade throughout the year. How, then, can it be said that they, or any of them, have in the course of the year ceased to carry it on? If language is accurately used, a partnership firm does not carry on a trade at all. It is the individuals in the firm who carry on the trade in partnership. It is not the firm which is liable to income tax. The individuals composing the firm are so liable ...'.

In England and Wales, a partnership firm is not a separate legal persona. As Farwell LJ said in *Sadler v Whiteman* ([1910] 1 KB 868, at p. 889):

'In English law a firm as such has no existence; partners carry on business both as principals and as agents for each other within the scope of the partnership business; the firm name is a mere expression, not a legal entity, although for convenience under Order XLVIII.A it may be used for the sake of suing and being sued ... It is not correct to say that a firm carries on business; the members of a firm carry on business in partnership under the name or style of the firm.'.

10-080 Persons carrying on a business in common with a view of profit

This is an essential part of there being a partnership. If persons are not carrying on a business in common, or are not doing so with a view of profit, there cannot be a partnership.

Meaning of 'business'

For the purposes of PA 1890, s. 1(1), a business includes trades, occupations or professions (*Partnership Act* 1890, s. 45). The main ingredient, of course, is some kind of commercial activity, not something just for pleasure, whatever the extent of that activity. For example, a man whose main hobby was shooting, invited friends and relations to shoot with him and sought contributions from them to cover the costs. There was no profit element, and when an assessment to VAT was issued he successfully defended his appeal on the basis that the shooting was arranged 'for pleasure and social enjoyment and that therefore, the supplies ... were not made in the course of a business' *C & E Commrs v Lord Fisher* [1981] BTC 392.

Conversely, in another case, the lessee of a house had signed a lease which did not allow him to carry on a business on the premises. He had a charitable institution, a 'home for working girls', and provided board and lodging, regardless of whether the ladies concerned could afford payment (*Rolls v Miller* (1884) 27 Ch D 71). Lord Justice Lindley suggested that anything that was an occupation, as opposed to a pleasure, would probably fall within the category of a business and, indeed, the case was decided on this basis, i.e. that the home for working girls was, indeed, a business and the lease had been contravened.

Business in common

Apart from a business, there must also be some relationship between the parties such that they are carrying on a business in common. This has to be something more than just working together or forming a joint venture. For example, a client might require tax advice from two advisers, one to cover the corporate aspects of his business and the other to deal with issues such as personal tax and inheritance tax. In such cases, the two advisers might well work closely together in providing detailed comprehensive advice to the client, but the two advisers have not, themselves, formed a partnership.

This is reinforced by PA 1890, s. 2(2), which states that 'the sharing of gross returns does not of itself create a partnership'. In the example, the two advisers might share the gross receipts appropriately, and each will be responsible for their own expenses, etc. so merely acting together to advise the same client does not mean that they are in partnership, at best it is a form of temporary joint venture.

Conversely, if the two advisers have agreed to charge a single fee, sharing the expenses of the advice between themselves, and then splitting the net profit between them, this, according to PA 1890, s. 2(3) is 'prima facie evidence' that each is a partner in the business. In essence, and subject to the limitations in s. 2(3) (which largely reflect the *Law of Partnership Act* 1865, as already noted), once the parties agree to effectively share costs, work together jointly and split the overall profit between them, this starts to look more like a partnership.

This point is illustrated by the case of *George Hall & Son v Platt* (1954) 35 TC 440. The appellants, a firm carrying on business as farmers, and a firm of farmers and merchants entered into an agreement whereby the farmers and merchants grew a crop of carrots on land occupied by the appellants. The appellants provided horse labour, and the farmers and merchants provided seed and labour and harvested and sold the crop. Each party was to reclaim expenses out of the profits and any balance was to be divided equally.

It was held that an assessment to tax under what was then Sch. D, made jointly upon the appellants and the farmers and merchants, was correct. There was a joint venture and partnership carried on for the purpose of profit to both parties.

In *Ayrshire Pullman Motor Services and DM Ritchie v IR Commrs* (1929) 14 TC 754, Mr Ritchie bought a bus for his son-in-law to drive as his business. The son-in-law only ran the business for a few months but, after that, first Mr Ritchie's son, then various others of his children, continued the business, albeit without any kind of partnership agreement. HMRC raised assessments on Mr Ritchie, the sole owner of the business. These assessments covered the periods both before and after the signing of a Partnership Agreement in 1926. One of the provisions of this Agreement was that all the profits were to be allocated equally between the children and that Mr Ritchie had no interest in the profits of the business. His only entitlement was to 5% interest on a loan that he had made to the business.

In the Court of Session, it was held that there was a real agreement, the profits legally belonged to the children and not to Mr Ritchie, and that, for the period following the signing of the Agreement, there was, therefore, a partnership. It was recognised that there was an element of artifice in this, in that the family was well aware of the tax benefit of allocating the profits to the children and not to Mr Ritchie. Nevertheless, the Court of Session did not consider that the fiscal motive was able to nullify the Agreement. Indeed, this case is best remembered for the famous quote from Lord Clyde, the Lord President, as follows:

> 'No man in this country is under the smallest obligation, moral or other, so to arrange his legal relations to his business or to his property as to enable the Inland Revenue to put the largest possible shovel into his stores.'.

No partnership

There have been a number of cases where it was found that no partnership existed. They are generally interesting in demonstrating how important it is that the indicia of a partnership be present, before the courts will determine that one exists. Incidentally, they also demonstrate the importance of the evidence in such cases, particularly evidence given to the general or special commissioners, or nowadays the First-tier Tribunal, being the principal fact-finding bodies.

In *Dodd and Tanfield v Haddock* (1963) 42 TC 229, D asked T to finance the purchase of a lease of war damaged property. T refused and decided to acquire the lease himself, although an agreement was reached to compensate D by sharing any profit on the sale of the property. Eventually, a sale was completed, D having interviewed prospective purchasers with T's agreement.

It was held that the general commissioners could not reasonably have concluded on the findings that a joint venture existed, and it was therefore erroneous to assess D and T jointly under what was then Sch. D, Case I (i.e. as tax on business profits) on the profits of the sale.

In *Hawker v Compton* (1922) 8 TC 306, the appellant, who was the occupier of a farm, appealed against an assessment to tax under what was then Schedule B on the grounds that he occupied the farm jointly with his three sons and daughter, and that the assessment should have been made in their joint names. Although he produced evidence purporting to show the existence of a partnership, the agreement of tenancy for the farm was between the landlord and the appellant only, and he alone was the rated occupier of the farm.

It was held that the evidence presented to the court was inconsistent with the existence of a partnership and the appellant was the sole occupier of the farm. The assessment had been correctly made in his name.

In *Dreyfus v IR Commrs* (1929) 14 TC 560, the appellants were the only persons interested in the profits of société en nom collectif, a business entity under French law similar to a partnership. The société was controlled and directed from France, but had business in the UK and other countries. The société was assessed to tax in respect of the profits made by it in the UK, and super-tax assessments were made upon each of the appellants on the grounds that they were in the position of partners in a partnership.

It was held that the société was a legal person distinct from the individuals composing it and the profits were not the profits of a partnership within the meaning of the relevant tax legislation. (As an aside, we understand that many people, including HMRC, now consider that this case was wrongly decided, and that a société en nom collectif would, nowadays, be treated as a partnership.)

There is also a much more recent case involving *Valantine* ([2011] TC 01644). In this case, HMRC was contending that there was a partnership, on the basis that this gave them a greater chance of recovering unpaid tax, including PAYE and VAT. Mr and Mrs Valantine used to live in London and had been in partnership as landscape gardeners in a business that had been started by Mrs Valantine's father. Mr and Mrs Valantine separated for some time and eventually got back together on condition that they moved away from London, which they did. Mr Valantine then set up his own landscape gardening business, in which Mrs Valantine had insisted she was going to play no part whatsoever. That said, Mrs Valantine did give him some help, for example buying two vehicles which she made available for use in the business, and giving Mr Valantine some financial assistance during a period before he was able to open a bank account.

Mr Valantine did not keep particularly complete business records and had not submitted appropriate tax returns, for his own income tax, National Insurance or VAT, or in respect of PAYE and National Insurance contributions relating to employees. It was also clear that Mr Valantine had no money to pay any such liabilities and would have to declare himself bankrupt were assessments on him to stand.

HMRC's position was that, if the assistance given by Mrs Valantine was sufficient to make her a partner in the business, HMRC might be able to charge income tax and Class 4 National Insurance contributions in respect of her profit share. Furthermore, if she were a partner, she would be jointly liable for the debts of the business, such as the VAT and the unpaid PAYE and employers' NICs, so HMRC might be able to recover those liabilities, too.

The decision of the First-tier Tribunal was that Mrs Valantine was not a partner in her husband's business. Having considered the evidence, they stated that she 'was not actively engaged in the trading: she manifestly had nothing to do with the running or the management of the business; and whilst she received some cash, funded out of the profits that Mr Valantine had made, those receipts were far more realistically attributed to the reimbursement of the major items that she had paid for … than to any notion that they were jointly sharing in the partnership profits'.

If they were not sharing profits, then PA 1890, s. 2(3) could not apply and there was no partnership so HMRC's case failed.

With a view to profit

Any business carried on in common must also be carried on with a view to profit. By definition, this suggests that a partnership cannot carry on 'not for profit' activities or, rather, if persons together carry on such activities, they do not constitute a partnership under the 1890 Act. They may, of course, be able to carry on such activities as an unincorporated association, as a company (often such activities are carried out using companies limited by guarantee) or as a limited liability partnership.

The meaning of 'with a view to profit' in this context was considered in *Blackpool Marton Rotary Club v Martin* [1988] BTC 442. A members' club was set up to raise money for charities. The Inland Revenue raised assessments to corporation tax on interest and other receipts, on the basis that it was an unincorporated association. The club appealed, on the ground that it was a partnership and, hence, not liable to corporation tax. Hoffmann J (as he then was) held that it was an unincorporated association and not a partnership. The requirement of partnerships to be carried on 'with a view to profit' meant with a view to a profit accruing to the partners. The club members lacked any entitlement to profits. Per curiam, the case did not look at whether there was a view to profit per se.

Degree of activity of partners

While the existence of a partnership requires persons to be in business together with a view to profit, it is also apparently the case that a partner does not have to do anything at all, or make any contribution to the partnership to be a partner! 'There is no essential need for common capital, management, assets, facilities or firm name or for a partner to do anything at all.' Jessel MR in *Pooley v Driver* (1876) 5 Ch D 458 said 'you can have, undoubtedly, according to English law, a dormant partner who puts nothing in, neither capital, nor skill, nor anything else' (these passages are taken from *Partnership Law,* as above, 2.1). This is difficult to reconcile with the requirement that persons carry on a business together, as to carry on suggests an element of activity or involvement.

This is an interesting point which is not expanded further in the commentaries that we have seen. It sits uneasily with much of the foregoing discussion on the requirements for there to actually be a partnership. Given that a person can be a partner without doing or contributing anything at all, why was Mrs Valantine (above) not a partner when she contributed the use of vehicles and, on occasion, helped out her husband in his activities as a landscape gardener? The answer in that case may lie in the fact that there was never an intention that she be a partner and, indeed, there was a lot of background evidence as to why she did not wish to be in partnership with her husband again.

This leads us to the best answer we can give to this question, which is that the existence of partnership is down to, at least in part, the intention of the parties concerned.

If parties agree to be in partnership, even though one of them will do nothing and contribute nothing, a partnership can still exist as a result of that intention. If the parties have no intention of being in partnership, some activities or contribution by a person will not make them a partner. But if the relationship between them becomes that of being in business together with a view to profit, then a partnership might come into existence regardless of their intentions.

Legislation: PA 1890, s. 1 and 2

10-100   Other indicia of partnership

The *Partnership Act* 1890, s. 2 is a core provision in terms of setting out a series of indicia of the existence of a partnership, some of which we have already considered in the previous discussions. For example, the following do not in and of themselves create a partnership:

- joint tenancy, tenancy in common, joint property, common property or part ownership (PA 1890, s. 2(1));
- the sharing of gross returns (PA 1890, s. 2(2)).

As we have already seen, the receipt of a share of the profits of a business is *prima facie* evidence that the recipient is a partner in the business (PA 1890, s. 2(3)). However, just because a person receives a share of the profits does not necessarily make them a partner and the same is said of any payment that is contingent on or varies with the profits of a business. This is important, because otherwise payments made to a person that are somehow related to the profits of the business might make that person both a partner in the business and liable in that capacity for the debts of the business, when this is not the intention of any of the parties.

The following situations do not make the person involved a partner in the business and therefore liable as such (PA 1890, s. 2(3)(a)–(e)):

- the receipt of a debt or other liquidated amounts out of the accruing profits of a business;
- remuneration of a servant or agent by share of the profits of the business (in other words, for example, an employee might be remunerated in part by reference to the business profits, but that does not make them a partner);
- an annuity paid to the widow or child of a deceased partner, by reference to the profits, does not make the recipient a partner;
- interest payable on loans, where the interest varies according to the partnership profits, does not make the lender a partner;
- a person who receives annuities or part of the profits as consideration for the sale of goodwill of the business is not a partner.

What is particularly interesting is that the various decided cases, a few of which we have reviewed in this chapter, have not generally made reference to the *Partnership*

Act 1890, even though there are clear resonances between the decisions in those cases and that legislation.

Legislation: PA 1890, s. 2

10-120   Capacity to be a partner

This is an interesting area. Particularly with family businesses, it will often be advantageous to be able to argue that both the spouse and children are members of a partnership, in order to reduce the overall tax bill (as, for example, in the *Ayrshire Pullman* case, above).

In the main, any legal person, including companies, trustees and local authorities, may be partners in a partnership under the *Partnership Act* 1890. Indeed, there are very few persons who cannot be partners, the main exceptions being bankrupts, barristers, clergymen, disqualified company directors, drunks, foreign enemies, mental patients, disqualified professionals and English partnerships. The last case, of course, is simply because an English partnership is not a legal person. In contrast, a Scottish partnership is a legal person and can, therefore, be a member of a partnership.

A minor, an individual less than 18 years old, can become a partner and have the rights to share in profits and to bind the firm. However, there are limitations on the ability for them to contract business debts, take liability for contributions to capital, and so on, as a minor. As a result, it is often going to be commercially undesirable for a minor to be a member of a partnership.

In terms of the actual ability to be a partner, there are other considerations, particularly with respect to minors. The main one, of course, is that that person is entitled to be a partner in the particular type of business. This will very often preclude a minor from being a partner in a law firm or accountancy practice, insofar as the regulatory requirements of the appropriate institutes would not allow an unqualified person to be a member of the partnership. Conversely, Counsel has opined informally that minors certainly have the capacity to be partners in, for example, a farming partnership, or, one might surmise, a landscape gardening partnership, like that of Mr Valantine (above).

The issues are illustrated in *Alexander Bulloch & Co v IR Commrs* (1976) 51 TC 563, where a partnership carried on the business of operating off-licence shops. At a partnership meeting, it was decided to invite the children of two of the partners, aged 15 and 14, to become partners, to accept responsibility for one shop each, and to share in partnership profits. A deed of co-partnery to this effect was executed. Thereafter, the two children did routine work in the shops but did not draw salaries or shares of profits, although their shares were credited to their respective capital accounts.

The commissioners decided on the facts, including the inexperience and immaturity of the children, that they were not partners in the firm. The Court of Session held that the commissioners were entitled to reach this decision.

Legislation: PA 1890

10-140 Family partnerships

HMRC accept that it is relatively difficult for them to attack partnership profit shares between family members, as in this comment from the *Business Income Manual* at BIM72065:

> 'You cannot challenge the apportionment of profits, as you can a wage, by reference to the value of the partners' contribution to the firm's activity. It may be possible in these cases to challenge the spouse's status as a partner, but such a challenge is often very difficult to sustain. It is sometimes overlooked that there is no need for the spouse to contribute capital; or to participate in management; or, in a trading context at least, to be capable of performing the main activity of the business. Indeed, to be a partner one need not take an active part in the business at all. Where the spouse has signed a deed declaring an intention to carry on the business and the deed gives a right to share in the profits, and subsequently accounts of the business show that that person has been allocated a share of the profits, there will not usually be much chance of mounting a successful challenge.

> It is worth emphasising that a partnership is not a sham merely because it is set up to save tax, as indeed the spouse who is deserted by a partner leaving that spouse to meet the firm's liabilities may find to their cost. There will always of course be some cases which will be worth you investigating and challenging, but these are more likely to be found among those where there is no current partnership deed, and particularly where there is a clear attempt to antedate the setting up of a partnership by more than a few months. Business Tax (Technical) will be happy to advise on worthwhile cases.'

Conversely, in *Saywell v Pope* (1979) 53 TC 40, the court refused to disturb a commissioners' finding that the wives of two partners were not members of the partnership. As in the *Alexander Bulloch* case, the wives were credited with shares of profit, but did not make any drawings. Neither wife introduced any capital, or was permitted to sign cheques on the firm account. No notice of the change was given to the bank or to creditors or customers of the firm.

The taxpayers failed to discharge the burden of proving that the wives were partners in the firm.

10-160 Partnership agreement

As has already been explained, under the *Partnership Act* 1890 a partnership exists if the relationship between the persons involved is such that they are in business together with a view to profit. This is entirely independent of the question of whether there is a partnership agreement or deed. What this means is that persons might find themselves in partnership inadvertently, as they come to work more and more closely together. This might, in theory, happen in the absence of any intention or agreement for a partnership to exist, although a better view might be that the intention to be in business in common is there, without the realisation that it might then create a partnership. The *Valantine* case is an example of where such a thing might have happened, if Mrs Valantine had been more involved in the business or if the First-tier Tribunal had taken a different view of the level of activity that she did carry out.

Similarly, a partnership agreement cannot create a partnership where the actual relationship between the parties does not constitute partnership, as such. While the agreement might be one for a partnership, if the 'partners' do not, in fact, act together in such a way as to comply with PA 1890, s. 1(1), then no partnership exists, notwithstanding the existence or intentions of the partnership agreement.

For example, in *Dickenson v Gross* (1927) 11 TC 614, a farmer entered into a partnership deed with his three sons. The deed recited that he had given his sons undivided quarter-shares in his farms and stock. Contrary to the agreement, no annual accounts were kept, nor had there been any distribution of profits.

The farmer contended that profits had in effect been distributed because the 'partners' lived together as a family in his house and his sons had provision made for them. He also contended that the partnership existed because any of the parties were entitled to compel the agreement to be carried out.

It was held that the facts showed that the deed was simply set to one side and disregarded. The appeal commissioners' finding that there was no partnership in fact was upheld. Rowlatt J said (at p. 621):

> 'What they are saying is this: "There is not any partnership in fact, and there cannot be any partnership for the special purposes of Income Tax when there is no real partnership." That is what they are saying. Many people think there can be. They think by putting a bit of paper in the drawer they can make an Income Tax partnership, and they go on treating the undertaking as though it were still the sole uncontrolled property of the one person, the father, instead of a partnership.'

Conversely, a statement that an agreement does not constitute a partnership or that it begins or ends on a particular date, is not conclusive of the matter. In *Fenston v Johnstone* (1940) 23 TC 29, F wanted to purchase land for development. He introduced the owner of the land to S. There was an agreement between S and F that F be paid half of any profits received for introducing S to the site and assisting him in the development and/or sale of the site. F also agreed to bear half of any loss. The agreement contained an unqualified disclaimer of partnership. F successfully claimed that there was a partnership in existence and his share of the profit was assessable as business profits under what was then Sch. D, Case I, rather than under what was then Case VI, as maintained by the Revenue.

It was held that on a true construction of the agreement, a partnership existed. There is a rebuttable presumption that a partnership exists where there is a sharing of profits and losses, as per PA 1890, s. 2(3), and the disclaimer in the agreement could not change the character of the relationship, which was, in essence, a partnership. It therefore failed to rebut the presumption that a partnership existed.

The *Ayrshire Pullman* case (above) is quite interesting in this respect. The decision that there was a partnership related to the period following the signing of the partnership agreement in 1926. The Courts held that there was no partnership prior to the execution of the partnership agreement, which would appear to contradict our previous comments, that the existence of the partnership is independent of the agreement. Unfortunately, the case report is unclear as to the reasoning for this part of the decision. The General Commissioners had found against Mr Richie on both counts, so that they considered him to be a sole trader throughout. In overturning the decision, Lord Clyde in the Court of Session merely said that 'there is not the smallest doubt ... that until after the date of this [agreement] the profits belonged to Mr Richie ... and to nobody else.'.

As a matter of good practice, we would always recommend that any persons entering into a partnership together should have some form of partnership agreement. While this might represent an apparently quite large upfront cost, in paying a lawyer to draw up an appropriate agreement, these costs could be dwarfed by the costs of not having a partnership agreement, if the partners were to fall out. Cases we have seen include one where the partners have entered into such lengthy litigation that the sums that were the subject of the litigation were eaten up in legal fees (a situation so brilliantly lampooned by Charles Dickens in *Bleak House*, in the fictional case of *Jarndyce v Jarndyce* (Often thought to be based on *Jennens v Jennens*, a case which started in 1798 and was eventually abandoned in 1915, when the money ran out. At the time *Bleak House* was being written, the case had been running for some 55 years!)). In another case, one partner just went back to his home country, leaving the other partner in the UK being required to repay all the partnership debts out of her own pocket.

Tax is only one of the matters to be considered when a partnership agreement is drafted. Legal requirements and commercial considerations are particularly important. However, the following matters might need to be considered:

- the date of commencement, and duration of agreement;
- the accounting date;
- employment of partners' spouses (or civil partners);
- service companies or partnerships and parallel partnerships;
- partners' salaries and interest on capital;
- residence of the partnership – the place of its control, and management;
- arrangements for drawings and sharing profits and losses (both income and capital);
- whether the firm is entitled to any partners' directors fees;
- pension contributions;

- consultancy provisions for retiring partners;
- goodwill to accrue automatically to continuing partners or to be recognised on the balance sheet;
- options to purchase or buy and sell agreements for disposal of a retiring partner's interest in the business. Restraint of trade clauses. Valuation of premises on dissolution of partnership: tenanted or vacant possession?;
- use by the firm of a partner's own asset, e.g. land, and payment of rent for such use;
- a limited or unlimited partnership;
- cars to be purchased by firm for partners or purchased privately by partners.

Legislation: PA 1890, s. 1 and 2

10-180   Consequences of a partnership

The persons who have together formed a partnership are collectively referred to as a 'firm' and the firm can have a 'firm-name', which does not have to be that of the individual partners (PA 1890, s. 4(1)). Obvious examples are firms like Ernst & Young or KPMG, before they both became limited liability partnerships.

The partners in a partnership are all agents of each other and of the firm. Consequently, the actions of a partner in carrying on the firm's business will bind the firm as a matter of law (PA 1890, s. 5). This does not apply, however, if the partner concerned does not have authority to bind the partnership and the other person, i.e. the person with whom he or she is dealing, is aware that that person does not have that authority or, alternatively, that they do not know or believe that person to be a partner, in the first place.

Similarly, acts or instruments that relate to the business of the firm and are clearly intended to bind the firm will be binding on the firm and all the partners if the act or instrument is done or executed by somebody authorised to do so (PA 1890, s. 6).

The partners of a firm are jointly liable with all the other partners for the firm's debts. Joint liability simply means that every partner is liable for the whole of the partnership's debts. Hence, in the discussion on why it is sensible to have a partnership agreement (see ¶10-160), in the situation where one of the partners has absconded, the other partner was liable for all of the debts of the partnership, not just his or her proportionate share (PA 1890, s. 9).

If a partner dies, his estate is severally liable during administration for any debts and obligations of the partnership. Several liability is often referred to as proportionate liability, which gives a better indication of what this means, i.e. that the estate is only liable for the relevant proportion of the debts of the deceased partner.

In Scotland, a partner is both jointly and severally liable for the debts and obligations of the partnership.

Where matters have been conducted on the basis that a partnership exists, the onus is on the taxpayer if he wishes to assert that there was in fact no partnership. In *Phillips* [2010] TC 00276, separate legal proceedings had been concluded on the basis that there was a partnership and tax returns had been made on the same basis. The taxpayer had failed on the balance of probabilities to displace the prima facie evidence that a partnership existed for the years in question. Although the taxpayer was not a signatory on the bank account, that was not inconsistent with the existence of a partnership and it had not been proved that the taxpayer did not in general have power to bind the firm.

Similarly, in the case of *London & Essex Cleaning Services (Southern)* [2010] TC 00309, some attempt was made to argue that there was no partnership but the evidence was clearly against the contention. Partnership accounts had been prepared (showing capital accounts for the four individuals concerned) and the tribunal had no hesitation in finding, as a fact, that the business was a partnership. The legal definition seemed to encapsulate the relationship between those involved.

Legislation: PA 1890, s. 4, 5, 6 and 9

10-200   Date from which partnership exists

An important case on this point is *Waddington v O'Callaghan* (1931) 16 TC 187, where a partnership deed executed in May was expressed to be effective from the preceding January. It was held that the partnership constituted by the deed started at the date of the deed and that there was no evidence before the appeal commissioners that a partnership existed before that date. Rowlatt J said (at p. 197–198):

> 'When people enter into a deed of partnership and say that they are to be partners as from some date which is prior to the date of the deed, that does not have the effect that they were partners from the beginning of the deed. You cannot alter the past in that way. What it means is that they begin to be partners at the date of the deed, but then they are to take the accounts back to the date that they mention as from which the deed provides that they shall be partners. There is no sort of doubt at all that that is the only effect which such a deed can have. No deed can alter the past, but of course, it is quite possible that before the deed was executed the partners may in point of fact have been carrying on business in partnership which would give rise to partnership accounts and which would give rise to partnership liabilities and so on; and when the deed is executed and said to relate back to an earlier period, that means that the provisions of the deed as to the partnership rights and partnership accounts shall supersede the rights which have accrued under the partnership which de facto had existed before the date of the deed. All that is perfectly clear and perfectly simple.'.

The *Ayrshire Pullman* case (above) touched on similar issues.

10-220   Duration of partnership

In most cases, partnerships endure until the partners decide they no longer wish to work together. In some cases this can be decades, or even centuries, as in the case of some of the large UK accountancy partnerships. It is, however, also possible that a partnership might be carried on for a specified period of time, usually stated in the partnership agreement. Technically speaking this would imply that the partnership ceases to exist at the end of the fixed term.

Of course, PA 1890, s. 1(1) makes it clear that, if the relationship between the partners remains that of being in business together with a view to profit, then the partnership continues, and this continuation is referred to as 'a partnership at will' (PA 1890, s. 27(1)). A partnership at will exists where the business continues in partnership without a new agreement and the partners' rights and duties remain the same. Furthermore, any such continuance of the business by the partners is presumed to be continuation of the partnership (PA 1890, s. 27(2)).

Legislation: PA 1890, s. 1 and 27

10-240   Partnership and employment

If a person is a partner in a partnership, they cannot also be an employee of that partnership. Therefore, a partner in a partnership will not have any of the normal protections available to an employee, such as the right to redundancy pay or to compensation for unfair dismissal. However, in some circumstances an employee can be held out as a partner, which may make them liable as if they were a partner in certain circumstances.

For example, in *Nationwide Building Society v Lewis and Williams* (ChD [1997] 3 All ER 498 and CA [1998] 3 All ER 143), Mr Lewis had a law firm of which he was the sole principal. He asked Williams to join him as a 'salaried partner'. This is not a term with any specific legal meaning and, in this case, did not entitle Williams to any profit share. The building society sued Lewis and Williams as partners and Mr Williams, unsurprisingly, resisted on the basis that he was not a partner.

The High Court agreed that the relationship between them was that of master and servant, so that Williams was not, in fact, a partner of the firm. However, the High Court also held that he had effectively agreed that he should be shown as a partner on the firm's headed notepaper and was therefore liable for any negligence.

This part of the decision was reversed by the Court of Appeal, largely on the basis that the building society had not specifically relied on Mr Williams being a partner in accepting the report that had been prepared by the firm. In other words, while there may have been damage, the damage did not arise from any reliance on Mr Williams being a partner, as such.

This brings us to two principles to consider. Firstly, as noted, there is no legal meaning to the phrase 'salaried partner', and in many cases such a person will not, in fact, be a partner of the firm on first principles.

However, a person who is not a partner can still become liable through 'holding out', whereby they become liable by representing themselves, or allowing themselves to be represented, as partners in a firm. Thus, so-called salaried partners in a partnership may well be liable as partners through holding out, even though they are, strictly, employees.

It is also possible for somebody to be an employee, even though they are remunerated, wholly or partly, through a share of the partnership profits. This is explicit in the *Partnership Act* 1890, s. 14, which states that remuneration by way of sharing in the profits of a business is prima facie evidence of partnership, but the remuneration of employees by way of a share of profits does not necessarily make that employee a partner.

This point is confirmed in *Walker v Hirsh* (1884) 27 Ch D 460, where the plaintiff agreed to advance £1,500 to the firm of H & Co (the defendants) for whom he worked as a clerk. In consideration for the advance, the defendants agreed that the plaintiff should receive a fixed salary of £180 and also receive a one-eighth share of the profits and bear a one-eighth share of the losses of the firm. The agreement was determinable by four months' notice by either party. The plaintiff continued to work as a clerk for the firm, and was not presented to customers as a partner, and did not sign the firm's name on bills.

The defendants sought to determine the agreement and to remove the plaintiff from their employ. The plaintiff brought an action to wind up the partnership and moved for an injunction and receiver.

On the true construction of the agreement, it was held that the plaintiff was in the position of a servant, and no partnership existed between the parties as to entitle the plaintiff to an injunction or receiver.

As we shall see, from a tax perspective, HMRC may launch status enquiries if they consider that somebody who is holding themselves out as a partner of a partnership is, in fact, an employee.

In determining whether a person is a partner or an employee, one factor to look at is the extent to which that person is involved in the management of the business. This concept goes to the heart of persons carrying on business in common. This is not necessarily a determinative factor, but if a person is partly remunerated by salary and partly through profit share, and takes no part in the management of the business, it is more likely that the Courts would find that person to be an employee, in a master-servant relationship, rather than a partner, carrying on a business in common with the other partners.

Legislation: PA 1890, s. 14

LIMITED PARTNERSHIPS

10-260   Limited partnerships

Limited partnerships were first considered in 1879, during the drafting of what became the *Partnership Act* 1890, although the idea was not proceeded with until the *Limited Partnerships Act* 1907. The idea was to create a form of partnership where the majority of partners were only liable to the extent of the capital invested, in contrast to the unlimited liability accruing to the members of a general partnership. Limited partnerships are generally used for investment. For example, venture capital or private equity investments are very often structured as limited partnerships. Typically, a bank or other entity will set up a partnership with a subsidiary company as the general partner (which has unlimited liability) and the investors being the limited partners in the partnership.

Essentially, a limited partnership must have both limited and general partners. The general partners are liable for all the debts and obligations of the firm. Limited partners contribute capital or property to the firm when they become partners, and that is the limit of their liability in respect of the firm's debts and obligations (LPA 1907, s. 4(2)). To the extent that a limited partner withdraws any of his capital, it remains liable in respect of the firm's debts and obligations for that amount (LPA 1907, s. 4(3)).

A limited partnership must be registered, otherwise it is treated as a general partnership, with unlimited liability applying to all the partners (LPA 1907, s. 5).

The most important aspect of a limited partnership is that the limited partners are prohibited from taking any part in the management of the business (LPA 1907, s. 6(1)). If such a person does manage the business, then they become liable for all the debts and obligations of the business incurred during the period that they were managing the business, as though they were a general partner. The obvious corollary to this is that a limited partner does not have the power to bind the firm in the same way that a partner of a general partnership does. This is also made explicit in the legislation (LPA 1907, s. 6(1)).

It is interesting to note that a body corporate is expressly permitted to be a limited member of a limited partnership (LPA 1907, s. 4(4)), as there is no obvious reason why this needed to be stated. It is clear that a body corporate is entitled to be a member of a general partnership, so it is unclear why it was felt necessary to explicitly permit one to be a limited member of a limited partnership.

Apart from the specific rules introduced by the 1907 Act, limited partnerships are governed by PA 1890 in most other respects.

Legislation: LPA 1907, s. 4, 5 and 6

LIMITED LIABILITY PARTNERSHIPS

10-280   Introduction

Limited liability partnerships (LLPs) are arguably a product of globalisation. As business structures became larger and multinational in scope, they needed auditors and accounting services on a global basis. However, the sheer size of many of these multinational corporations was such that the overall level of risk to auditors and accountants was excessive, as only a small mistake could nevertheless cause damages in the tens or hundreds of millions of pounds, if not more. This meant that even the 'Big 4' accountancy firms, which also had global presence, were reluctant to take on that level of risk because of the unlimited joint liability of the partners. Even at the level of the individual jurisdictions, the size of these corporations still meant that the unlimited risk on the partners for doing work for these clients was potentially unmanageable.

The result was increasing pressure for some kind of entity through which the audit and accounting services could be provided in a way that limited the liability of the individual partners.

There are those who argue that LLPs are, therefore, the product of greed, allowing the larger accountancy firms to charge very high fees with relatively low risk to the individual partners. There may be some truth in this, of course, but the analogy seems a little unfair when one considers that the multinational corporations concerned are, themselves, creatures with limited liability, by and large, simply by virtue of being limited companies (or the equivalents in other jurisdictions).

10-300   Legal background

Whatever the rights and wrongs of the matter, the *Limited Liability Partnership Act* 2000 was the UK's response to that pressure for limited liability. Although initially embraced just by the larger accountancy firms, the LLP has become the vehicle of choice for many people working in the field of professional services (including one of the authors).

The name 'limited liability partnership' (or LLP) is, in fact, something of a misnomer, as a limited liability partnership is a body corporate, incorporated under LLPA 2000, and with many of the features of limited companies (LLPA 2000, s. 1(2)). An LLP is a legal person and can therefore carry on business on its own behalf, own assets, incur debts, and so on. Its existence is independent of its members and, as the name implies, the liability of its members is limited.

In essence, therefore, an LLP looks very like a company and, indeed, partnership law does not apply to LLPs (LLPA 2000, s. 1(5)). Instead, LLPs are largely governed by the *Limited Liability Partnerships Regulations* 2001 (SI 2001/1090) and the *Limited Liability Partnerships (Application of Companies Act 2006) Regulations* 2009 (SI 2009/1804), which apply much of the *Companies Act* 2006 and the *Insolvency Act* 1986 to LLPs.

Legislation: LLPA 2000, s. 1; SI 2001/1090; SI 2009/1804

10-320   Limitation of liability

The liability of the members of an LLP is limited to the amount of capital that they have at stake within the LLP. This includes capital contributed to the LLP, profit shares that they have not yet drawn from the LLP, any sums that the LLP agreement requires them to contribute in the case of capital inadequacy or insolvency and anything that might, under normal principles, be recoverable by an insolvency practitioner if the LLP were to be insolvently wound up.

10-340   Contrast with general partnerships

To incorporate a limited liability partnership 'two or more people associated for carrying on a lawful business with a view to profit' must subscribe to the incorporation document (LLPA 2000, s. 2(1)(a)). This immediately throws up some technical differences between membership of a general partnership (or a limited partnership) and membership of an LLP. First of all, there is an absolutely clear requirement for intent to be a member of an LLP, as you have to subscribe to the incorporation document in order to become so. This is in contrast to an ordinary partnership, where the relationship might come about accidentally, through working together ever more closely until the relationship becomes that of partnership, without any clear or deliberate intent that a partnership be formed.

Secondly, there is the reference to the requirement to carry on a lawful business. While one would not recommend this commercially, a partnership can exist for the purposes of an unlawful business. It is well established through case law that activities which contravene the law can nevertheless be businesses or trades for tax purposes (for example, *Mann v Nash* (1932) 16 TC 523 (buying and selling fruit machines) and *Southern v AB* (1933) 18 TC 59 (bookmaking)), so that tax liabilities can arise appropriately.

As with a general partnership, any legal person is able to be a member of an LLP. Again, the main restrictions are, therefore, membership by an entity that is not a legal person, such as an English or Welsh partnership, or membership where this is not permitted by the rules of the profession of the member. A prime example of this is barristers who do not operate in partnership, whether through an ordinary partnership or an LLP, under their code of conduct.

Legislation: LLPA 2000, s. 2

TYPES OF PARTNER

10-360   Introduction

Just as there are several types of partnership, so there are a number of categories of partner. From a tax perspective, these distinctions are largely irrelevant, but the legal and commercial background is still interesting.

10-380   Equity partner

This phrase is used to describe a partner who is fully entitled to share in the profits of the business and who is liable to make good a share of any losses.

Equity partners are liable to tax on the basis that they are earning business profits, even to the extent that such profits are described as 'salary'.

10-400   Salaried partner

Unfortunately, this term is not used with any great precision in practice. On the one hand, it can mean someone who is held out to be a partner but is remunerated solely by way of a fixed salary which is a deduction in arriving at profits. On the other hand, it is often used to describe a partner who is entitled to a fixed or guaranteed share of profits.

Where the individual does not contribute any capital to, or have any proprietorial interest in, the business, he or she will probably be taxable as an employee; in other words, not as a partner at all as far as tax is concerned. In such circumstances, the term 'salaried partner' is something of a non sequitur and should be avoided to prevent confusion.

In *Stekel v Ellice* [1973] 1 WLR 191, Ellice had agreed to employ Stekel for a probationary three-month period with a view to partnership. Because of uncertainties concerning amounts due to the executors of a previous partner, Ellice suggested the question of a partnership be deferred until the situation clarified. After a year, Stekel raised the question of partnership again, and after some discussion an interim agreement was reached whereby he became a 'salaried partner'. Ellice provided all the capital and took all profits.

After the agreement had been signed, the firm continued as before, except that Stekel was now held out as a partner. His salary was paid without deduction of tax. No further steps were taken towards a full partnership agreement. Some time later, there were discussions with regard to ending the partnership, and an agreement was made in theory as to how this should be affected. No steps were taken to implement it. Not long after, however, Stekel left the business, taking his clients with him and he sought to have the partnership wound up at law.

Although Stekel was described as a salaried partner, and although an agreement to enter into a partnership on certain terms might constitute a partnership, the intention of this agreement was to exclude him from any proprietary interest in the partnership and, therefore, his claim failed.

The judgment of Megarry J contains the following useful comments:

'Certain aspects of a salaried partnership are not disputed. The term "salaried partner" is not a term of art, and to some extent it may be said to be a contradiction in terms. However, it is a convenient expression which is widely used to denote a person who is held out to the world as being a partner, with his name appearing as a partner on the notepaper of the firm, and so on. At the same time he receives a salary as remuneration, rather than some share of profits, though he may, in addition to his salary, receive some bonus or other sum of money dependent on profits.

Quo ad the outside world it will often matter little whether a man is a full partner or a salaried partner; for a salaried partner is being held out as a partner, and the partners will be liable for his acts accordingly. But within the partnership it may be important to know whether a salaried partner is truly to be classified as a mere employee or as a partner.

It seems to me impossible to say that as a matter of law a salaried partner is or is not necessarily a partner in the true sense. He may or may not be a partner, depending on the facts. What must be done, I think, is to look at the substance of the relationship between the parties; and there is ample authority for saying that the question of whether or not there is a partnership depends on what the true relationship is and not on any mere label attached to that relationship. A relationship that is plainly not a partnership is no more made into a partnership by calling it one than a relationship which is plainly a partnership is prevented from being one by a clause negativing partnership.'

10-420 Sleeping partner

A term used to describe a partner who is entitled to a share of profits by virtue of contributing capital to the business but who plays no active part in the running of that business. A sleeping partner may not have his or her share of profits treated as earned income and such profits will not rank as relevant earnings for the purposes of calculating the relief for pension contributions.

A sleeping partner is not liable to Class 4 NIC on his or her share of profits, as they are not 'immediately derived' from the carrying on of a trade, profession or vocation (SSCBA 1992, s. 15(1), confirmed in HMRC's *National Insurance Manual* at NIM24520).

Legislation: SSCBA 1992, s. 15

10-440 Limited partner

A partner whose liability for the partnership debts is limited to the amount of his capital contribution. He or she will be a member of a limited partnership incorporated under the *Limited Partnership Act* 1907.

Legislation: LPA 1907

TAXATION

10-460   General and limited partnerships

Regardless of whether we have an ordinary partnership, a limited partnership or a limited liability partnership, the taxation of these entities is the same. Generally speaking, the partnership itself is not a taxable entity, although, as we shall see, it will be required to produce a tax return. However, the tax liabilities and any other duties, obligations and rights under the tax legislation accrue to the individual partners, not to the partnership as a whole.

There is a difference between English and Scottish partnerships, as already highlighted. An English partnership has no legal status and creditors must have recourse to the individual partners, who all have joint liabilities for the debts. In Scotland, however, a partnership is a separate legal entity, which means that in practice an unpaid creditor of the firm pursues the firm and not the individual partners.

From a tax perspective, this might be expected to lead to an income tax assessment on the firm, as opposed to the individual partners. However, a principle was established by Viscount Simon in the *Gibbs* case, which aims to provide for consistency between the two countries:

> 'So far as English law is concerned, it is indisputable that a partnership firm is not a single persona, though a different view obtains in Scotland, and in construing a taxing statute which applies to England and Scotland alike, it is desirable to adopt a construction of statutory words which avoids differences of interpretation of a technical character such as are calculated to produce inequalities in taxation as between citizens of the two countries.'

The practical implications of this were tested in *MacKinlay (HMIT) v Arthur Young McClelland Moores & Co* [1989] BTC 587, in which a firm of accountants sought to deduct, in calculating its partnership profits, certain sums that it had paid to various partners by way of reimbursement of relocation expenses. The question was whether there was an element of duality in the expenditure which prevented its being wholly and exclusively incurred for the purposes of the firm's profession.

The taxpayers argued that in the case of a large partnership, the interests of the partners in their capacity as partners could be severed from their personal and private interests. A benefit to a partner resulting from expenditure incurred in pursuance of a policy agreed by all partners with a view to advancing the interests of the firm could be regarded as incidental to achieving that purpose, even though in the case of an individual it could not be so regarded.

The High Court ([1986] BTC 398) took the view that expenditure, which in the case of an individual trader would be treated as serving a dual purpose, could not, even in the case of a large partnership, be treated as expenditure incurred wholly and exclusively for the benefit of the firm as a separate entity, the personal benefit to an individual partner being treated as merely an incidental effect of that expenditure.

In the Court of Appeal ([1988] BTC 110), the judgment at first instance was reversed. The court thought that where a large partnership was involved, the interests of the firm could be regarded separately from those of the individual partners.

However, the House of Lords ([1989] BTC 587) unanimously rejected the Court of Appeal's reasoning and upheld the judgment at first instance.

Chapter 2:   Formation of a partnership

BUSINESS ENTITIES

11-000   Introduction

It is clear that, when starting a business, a person will need first of all to decide what entity they will use for carrying on that business. In the context of this book, the decision is likely to be whether to use a partnership or a company and, if a partnership is chosen, whether to use a general partnership, governed by the *Partnership Act 1890*, or a limited liability partnership.

If two or more people start a business together it is likely that they will end up having created a general partnership simply by virtue of the fact that they are carrying on a business together, as pointed out in the previous chapter. This is probably the commonest form of partnership business in the UK. It is unlikely that people will find themselves in a partnership unexpectedly, as it is almost invariably the case that a decision has been made to carry on a business together. In a sense, though, in terms of the decision making process, this form of partnership is possibly the default business entity, in that no formal discussion is held as to what form the business should take; it simply ends up being a partnership because that is the simplest way to carry on business.

Legislation: PA 1890

11-020   Factors in deciding on a business entity

Regulation

Probably the main factor for a decision between whether to be a partnership (of either form) or a company is to do with regulation. A general partnership is subject to very little overt regulation, largely due to the unlimited liability borne by the partners. The reason for the substantially greater degree of regulation of limited liability partnerships and companies is, of course, to ensure that the position of creditors and other stakeholders is protected, given the limitations on the liabilities of the members themselves. The main requirements that all relevant business owners will be aware of is the requirement for companies and limited liability partnerships to submit an annual return to Companies House, along with the annual accounts for the business. A general partnership does not need to make such a return, although some form of accounts will be needed for income tax purposes.

If, therefore, compliance obligations are one of the criteria in the decision making process, we would suggest that a general partnership is by far the simplest, followed by a limited liability partnership, which has many of the general law obligations of a company, but is still taxed as if it were a partnership. A company is, therefore, the more complex from a general regulatory and compliance perspective.

Tax issues

From a tax perspective, companies are also more complicated than partnerships when considering how funds pass into the hands of the proprietors. Firstly, there can be complex tax issues arising on either the payment of remuneration (salary, bonuses, etc.) or dividends. And, secondly, the payment of remuneration itself is inherently complex. Not only must the company operate Pay As You Earn and account for National Insurance contributions on any remuneration paid, even to the owners of the business, but there is a complicated benefits code such that Pay As You Earn has to be operated in respect of actual or deemed benefits given by the company to its employees in a way that does not apply to partnerships.

Commercial issues

Obviously, commercial issues must play a part in the decision making process. At one level, one of the major advantages of partnerships is the ability for people to be admitted to the partnership, or to leave the partnership, in a relatively straightforward fashion and, as we shall see, without major tax complexities, in many cases. This applies equally to membership of general partnerships and limited liability partnerships. In contrast, it is much more difficult for somebody to become a member of a company. If they are granted shares or share options by the company there will often be an income tax charge or substantial compliance obligations or both. Alternatively, if they are required to pay for the shares, the company might have a very high value, so that the shares are expensive and the individual concerned is required to take out a large loan in order to join the business. In this context, partnerships are far more flexible than companies in terms of changes of proprietary ownership.

The limited liability aspects of membership of a limited liability partnership or of a company might be inherently more attractive to the partners, as well. This is so particularly if the partnership carries on a business which is inherently risky or where the financial consequences of error, however unlikely, might be substantial. The obvious example, already alluded to in the previous chapter, is the potential liability to the partners of a large accountancy firm when they are asked to audit a large multi-national group of companies. Clearly, if a partner in a firm might be personally liable for many billions of pounds of loss if something goes wrong, even where the error is not that of the partner herself, the attraction of limited liability in some form is immediately apparent.

It is also possible that the type of client a business is trying to attract might have an impact on the type of entity used. For example, being able to call a business Miller & Arnold Limited or Miller & Arnold LLP might be considered commercially desirable, as it looks more 'official' than just Miller & Arnold or The Miller Arnold Partnership. Perhaps more to the point, the ability to state that one is a limited liability partnership or a company is also, of course, acknowledging that the business and its proprietors are under a higher degree of regulatory control than would be the case if they were merely a general partnership.

There are, no doubt, an almost infinite number of other factors that each new business will take into account in making these decisions. One final point to bear in mind, perhaps, is the one way direction of travel. That is, a general partnership or a limited liability partnership can be incorporated to form a company in a relatively straightforward fashion (see **Chapter 6**). However, it is virtually impossible to disincorporate a company to a partnership. We make this statement, notwithstanding the availability of a disincorporation relief (FA 2013, s. 58–61): This relief is only available where the aggregate value of the land and goodwill of the business do not exceed £100,000 and, in any case, the relief ceases to be available from 31 March 2018, so its usefulness is restricted only to the very smallest of businesses and only for a very short period.

11-040   Forming a general partnership

A general partnership exists by virtue of the relationship between the parties, not by virtue of any registration process. As we have noted, however, it is unlikely that a partnership will come into existence accidentally. Cases referred to in **Chapter 1** were, of course, extreme cases, which had to be litigated, because of the uncertainty engendered by their peculiar circumstances. In the main, it is fair to say that it will almost always be the case that a general partnership comes into existence because the parties will it to be so. Taking the example above, Mr Miller and Ms Arnold will have a general partnership because they decide to start a business together, or merge their existing business interests, and not through some accident of close co-operation.

Nevertheless, it should also be clear that the partnership only exists so long as the partners are, in fact, carrying on a business together and with a view to profit. So it is not enough merely to intend to form a partnership, the business must actually be carried on in a way that complies with *Partnership Act* 1890, s. 1(1). Once again, this is very unlikely to be a problem in most cases. It is important, however, to be aware of the issue and to be able to identify and prove the partnership activities carried on by the partners, in case of challenge. This is particularly important where spouses are in partnership: as we saw in **Chapter 1**, HMRC might challenge the position if they think that a husband is only being treated as a partner to reduce the overall tax bill, rather than because he really is a partner in his wife's business.

Legislation: PA 1890, s. 1

11-060   Forming an LLP

The formation of an LLP, which is an incorporated body subject to many of the provisions of the Companies Act, is more complex. We would refer readers to document GPLLP1 on the government website which gives the relevant information and forms.

The application can be made online or by post. Once the LLP is formed, there will be a requirement to make an annual return to Companies House, and to prepare and submit formal accounts. Neither of these requirements exist for general partnerships although, of course, all partnerships are required to prepare appropriate accounts to support the relevant tax returns.

Chapter 3:   Changes in partnership shares

12-000   Introduction

When partners join or leave a partnership, the fractional ownership of each partner may change. In these cases, there is the potential for a charge to capital gains tax on every such occasion. This is supported by the legislation, but the legislation is very sparse, so we have to rely on a number of statements of practice, particularly Statement of Practice D12 on partnership gains.

Where the assets include chargeable interests in land and buildings, there may also be a charge to stamp duty land tax. In this case, there are computational rules in FA 2003, Sch. 15 to manage the charge.

Legislation: FA 2003, Sch. 15

12-020   Introduction to partners' chargeable gains

The *Taxation of Chargeable Gains Act* 1992, s. 59 provides that where two or more persons carry on a trade or business in partnership, any chargeable gains on the disposal of partnership assets are to be assessed and charged on the partners separately and any partnership dealings shall be treated as dealings by the partners and not by the firm as such. This applies throughout the UK and overrides the treatment of a partnership in Scotland as a legal person distinct from the partners.

Section 59 applies to the general and limited partners of a limited partnership as it does to partnerships formed under the *Partnership Act* 1890.

Section 59A mirrors s. 59 in respect of limited liability partnerships in that it provides that any dealings by an LLP are treated for capital gains tax purposes as dealings by the individual members. Therefore each member of an LLP to which TCGA 1992, s. 59A(1) applies is regarded as owning a fractional interest in each of the LLP's assets and not an interest in the LLP itself and any capital gains tax or corporation tax on chargeable gains due on a disposal of an asset by an LLP is charged on its members separately.

Sections 59B and 59C make further provisions in respect of the disposals of instruments which are assets of an alternative investment fund partnerships (see ¶26-120).

These are the only provisions within TCGA 1992 which specifically relate to partnerships, however, a number of statements of practice have been issued to resolve practical difficulties (see ¶12-060ff.).

Legislation: TCGA 1992, s. 59, 59A, 59B and 59C

12-040 Limited Liability Partnerships ('LLPs')

Limited Liability Partnerships: CGT provisions in detail

An LLP is a corporate body registered under the *Limited Liability Partnerships Act* 2000 or the *Limited Liability Partnerships Act (Northern Ireland) Act* 2002. In general law, it is therefore a separate legal personna from its members. The aim of the legislation is to ensure that LLPs which carry on a business with a view to profit are, in general, treated as normal partnerships for the purposes of the capital gains tax and the members are taxed on their respective shares of the partnership's assets (i.e. the LLP is fiscally transparent). In particular:

- any assets held by the LLP are treated for the purposes of chargeable gains as if they are held by the members as partners;
- any dealings by the LLP are to be treated as if they are dealings of the members as partners for the purposes of chargeable gains and not as dealings by the LLP;
- any tax due on disposals of assets held by the LLP is to be charged on the members separately (TCGA 1992, s. 59A(1), (2)).

This treatment will continue even if the LLP ceases to trade, provided that:

- the cessation of activity is only temporary; or
- the cessation is permanent and the period of winding up (which must not be associated with any tax-avoidance motives) is not prolonged unreasonably (TCGA 1992, s. 59A(3)).

However, if a liquidator is appointed, a winding up order is made by the court or similar events occur under the laws of another country, the LLP will lose fiscal transparency for chargeable gains at the same time as it loses its special income tax treatments under ITTOIA 2005, s. 863 (see ¶18-020). Thus where a liquidator is appointed or a court orders the winding up of an LLP, it will be taxed (as opposed to the partners) on any subsequent chargeable gains, as if it were a company in liquidation (TCGA 1992, s. 59A(4), (5)). However, transparency can be preserved if the winding-up is done 'informally' by settling all outstanding creditors and distributing surplus funds to the members without the appointment of a liquidator (HMRC's *Capital Gains Manual* CG27050).

Where an LLP is taxed on its gains (i.e. the members are not taxed on their shares of the partnership assets) it is taxed (or its liquidator is taxed) on any asset disposals in the same way as any other company (and it may be subject to the normal insolvency rules). Where the LLP disposes of any assets, the chargeable gains will be the responsibility of the LLP or its liquidator and will be computed as if the fiscal transparency had never applied to the LLP. As far as partners (members) are concerned, in such situations, the only asset that they will be treated as owning is their individual share in the partnership, which is treated as acquired on the day they joined the LLP. The acquisition cost for each partner of such a share will be the amount of capital contributed. The disposal proceeds of the members' shares will be the amount of any capital repaid or distributed by the liquidator (and will thus be after creditors have been settled). When an LLP loses its partnership treatment status (e.g. because of the appointment of a liquidator, etc.) no disposal of assets occurs for CGT purposes. Thus the partners of a fiscally transparent LLP which goes into liquidation are not deemed to have made a disposal of their interests in the partnership assets to the liquidator (or the LLP). Conversely, if a non-transparent LLP begins to qualify as a transparent LLP (e.g. because it begins to undertake a trade for the first time) no disposal for CGT purposes is deemed to have taken place.

Where an LLP ceases to qualify for fiscal transparency, which could be due to the appointment of a liquidator or, more unusually, the permanent cessation of a trade without such an appointment and without a speedy winding up, there are two situations where a gain may arise:

- where a member has claimed roll-over relief (see ¶14-640) by virtue of the acquisition of an interest in an asset owned by the LLP; or
- where the member has received an asset as a result of a disposal by the LLP to its members in respect of which business asset hold-over or gift hold-over relief (see ¶14-660) was claimed.

In such cases, the chargeable gain that was deferred becomes chargeable upon the cessation of trading by the LLP (TCGA 1992, s. 156A and 169A). In the case of held-over gains, these will only crystallise where the asset concerned was acquired by the member in that capacity (i.e. as a member of the LLP). Thus assets acquired by an individual member as a sole trader will not be subject to this charge.

SP D12

The capital gains tax treatment of partnerships and partnership assets is set out in SP D12, see ¶12-100. For commentary on the application of SP D12 to limited liability partnerships, see ¶12-120.

12-060   Partnership assets

By providing that, with regard to partnership dealings, partners are to be treated as owning fractional shares in each of the partnership assets, TCGA 1992, s. 59 and 59A are contrary to general law. However, they provide an equitable and practical method of apportioning gains or losses arising on the appreciation or depreciation in value of partnership assets, whether the chargeable event is the disposal of those assets by the partnership or the disposal by one of the partners of part or all of his partnership share.

In certain circumstances, difficulties may arise in establishing whether a particular asset is or is not a partnership asset. According to guidance issued to HMRC staff, it is necessary to consider the facts of the particular case, any documentary evidence and the intentions of the partners. For example, if an asset were paid for by only one partner who also took title to the asset, this would suggest that it was not a partnership asset, unless all the partners intended it to be a partnership asset, in which case HMRC would regard it as such. In the case of land or buildings to which only one partner has taken title but which it is claimed is a partnership asset, HMRC would look to see if there was evidence of a transfer of part of the title to the other partners, and if so, if it was effective under the appropriate law of property (*Capital Gains Manual*, CG27200).

The legislation relates to partnerships and is not relevant to other forms of business co-operation, such as joint ownership, joint ventures or European Economic Interest Groupings). It does, however, appear to apply equally to other forms of limited partnerships (e.g. as defined in the *Limited Partnerships Act* 1907).

Self-assessments to CGT – whether they relate to gains on partnership assets or interests in a partnership – are made by the individual partners. Assessments relate to the fiscal year in which the chargeable event occurred and the accounting year-end of the partnership and its basis periods for income tax are irrelevant. The partnership return must, if required by the notice requiring a return, include particulars of any disposal of partnership property and of any acquisition of an asset (other than certain exempt assets) by the partnership (TMA 1970, s. 12AA(7)). The individual partner's share of the total disposal proceeds is reported in the partnership statement (TMA 1970, s. 12AB(1)(b)).

Legislation: TMA 1970, s. 12AA, 12AB; TCGA 1992, s. 59, 59A

12-080   Admission and retirement of partners

In relation to partnerships, admission and retirement in themselves cause no conceptual or interpretative difficulties, but they do provide the occasion for a change in asset-sharing ratios and other disposals which are dealt with under SP D12.

Broadly, the outgoing partner disposes of his fractional share of each of the partnership assets. There may be a straight exchange or a gap between retirement of one partner and the admission of another, during which time the continuing partners take over the retiring partner's share.

Provided the arrangements for the acquisition/disposal of partnership assets are on commercial terms, partners are treated as making an arm's length bargain.

An incoming partner takes over the capital gains tax base cost of the retiring partner if there is a straight exchange, while if the share is transferred to the continuing partners, their base costs are increased accordingly.

Where there is a revaluation of partnership assets on the retirement of one of the partners, which will commonly happen in order to determine what is payable to him under the partnership agreement, or there has been an earlier revaluation, retirement will cause a change in asset-sharing ratios and therefore a charge to capital gains tax on any partner whose asset-sharing ratio falls, including the retiring partner (see ¶12-200).

Lump sums paid to partners on leaving a partnership or on a reduction in the partners share of the partnership represents consideration for the disposal of the partners whole or part share in the partnership assets. This will be subject to the rules provided by SP D12, para. 7 (see ¶12-280).

See ¶12-320 for the treatment of annuities paid to retiring partners.

12-100   HMRC Statement of Practice: SP D12

It was recognised that the statutory rules covering the application of CGT to partnerships were not sufficiently comprehensive to resolve many practical difficulties. Thus in an attempt to resolve such difficulties, and following consultation, SP D12 was issued on 17 January 1975. This statement and two later statements (SP 1/79 and SP 1/89) do not carry the force of law but have been generally accepted and followed.

In Budget 2013, the Government asked the Office of Tax Simplification (OTS) to carry out a review of ways to simplify the taxation of partnerships. The OTS published its interim report in January 2014 and its final report in January 2015. OTS concluded that as SP D12 provides a reasonable result in most circumstances, it should be left essentially as it is, but that some text should be rewritten to replace out of date language and to replace some content which was obsolete. Accordingly, a revised version of SP D12 incorporating the OTS recommendations was issued on 14 September 2015.

Previously, SP D12 had been revised and reissued on 17 October 2002, partly to confirm its application to LLPs (see below). The only significant alteration to the statement was the insertion of a new section dealing with *Partnership Goodwill and Taper Relief.*

SP D12 covers a number of different situations which are considered in the following paragraphs of this chapter:

(1)   Valuation of a partner's share in a partnership asset – ¶12-140;

(2)   Disposals of assets by a partnership – ¶12-160;

(3)   Partnership assets divided in kind among the partners (distributions in specie) – ¶12-180;

(4)   Changes in partnership sharing ratios – ¶12-200;

(5) Contribution of an asset to a partnership – ¶12-240;

(6) Adjustment through the accounts (revaluation of partnership assets) – ¶12-260;

(7) Payments outside the partnership accounts – ¶12-280;

(8) Transfers between persons not at arm's length – ¶12-300;

(9) Annuities provided by partnerships – ¶12-320;

(10) Mergers – ¶12-340;

(11) Shares acquired in stages – ¶12-360;

(12) Elections under TCGA 1992, Sch. 2, para. 4 – ¶12-380;

(13) Partnership goodwill – ¶12-400;

(14) Entrepreneurs' relief on transfer of a business, 'roll-over' relief and business asset gift relief – ¶12-420.

12-120 Application of SP D12: Limited Liability Partnerships

The enactment of the *Limited Liability Partnership Act* 2000 created, from April 2001, the concept of limited liability partnerships (as bodies corporate) in UK law. In conjunction with this, new CGT provisions dealing with partnerships were introduced in TCGA 1992, s. 59A (see ¶12-040).

TCGA 1992, s. 59A(1) compliments TCGA 1992, s. 59 by treating any dealings in chargeable assets by a limited liability partnership as dealings by the individual members, as partners for CGT purposes. Each member of a limited liability partnership to which TCGA 1992, s. 59A(1) applies has, therefore, to be regarded, like a partner in any other (non-corporate) partnership, as owning a fractional share of each of the partnership assets and not an interest in the partnership itself.

SP D12 was, therefore, extended to limited liability partnerships which meet the requirements of TCGA 1992, s. 59A(1), with the effect that capital gains of a limited liability partnership fall to be charged on its members as partners.

Accordingly, all references to a 'partnership' or 'firm' within the statement include reference to limited liability partnerships (to which TCGA 1992, s. 59A(1) applies) and all references to 'partner' includes reference to a member of a limited liability partnership (to which TCGA 1992, s. 59A(1) applies).

SP D12 confirms that, for the avoidance of doubt, the statement does not apply to members of a limited liability partnership which ceases to be 'fiscally transparent' by reason of its not being, or no longer being within TCGA 1992, s. 59A(1).

Legislation: TCGA 1992, s. 59 and 59A

12-140 Valuation of a partner's share in a partnership asset

(SP D12, para. 1)

'Market value' is the price which the assets might reasonably be expected to fetch on a sale in the open market.

For the purposes of determining the market value of a partner's share in a partnership asset for CGT purposes, it will be taken as a fraction of the value of the total partnership interest in the asset without any discount for the size of the partner's share.

Example 1

A partnership between Y and Z owns 70% of the issued share capital of X Ltd. The partners' interests in partnership assets are shared in the ratio 80:20.

The market value of the 70% shareholding as at 31 December 2015 accounting for the premium value attributable to the partnership's controlling interest in X Ltd was £100,000. The market values of the partners' interests in the 70% shareholding in X Ltd as at 31 December 2015 were:

Y: £100,000 × 80% = £80,000

Z: £100,000 × 20% = £20,000

The market value is apportioned by reference to the partners' fractional interests. No premium value is attributed to Y's larger partnership interest nor is any reduction in value attributed to Z's minority partnership interest.

(*Capital Gains Manual*, CG27250)

Leaving aside the reasonableness or otherwise of not discounting the value to reflect the size of holding, it is questionable whether the value of a partnership share reasonably approximates to the appropriate fraction of the total value of partnership assets. By reason of his share, a partner holds a fractional interest in partnership assets after they have been realised on dissolution and after all partnership liabilities have been discharged. Any member of a partnership, whose duration is undefined, has a right, subject to any agreement between the partners, to dissolve the firm at any time he pleases.

But if there is agreement that the partnership shall be terminated by mutual agreement only, which is often the case, this right is precluded and a partner cannot seek to realise the value of his partnership share through dissolution of the firm. He could assign his share, but what would an outside party pay? No person can be introduced as a partner without the consent of all existing partners, while an assignee cannot interfere in the management of the partnership business. He merely has the right to receive the share of profits to which the assigning partner would otherwise be entitled and a share of partnership assets on dissolution.

Consequently, there seems to be merit in the argument that the value of a partnership share should be discounted for the inability of partners to realise their fractional interests in the total value of partnership assets, quite apart from the matter of discounting to reflect the size of that share.

12-160   Disposals of assets by a partnership

(SP D12, para. 2)

Where a partnership disposes of an asset it owns to an outside party, each partner is treated as disposing of his fractional share of that asset for capital gains tax purposes. The capital gain or loss arising on each partner is calculated as follows:

(1)   Disposal proceeds are allocated between the partners in the ration of their share in asset surpluses at the date of disposal. Where this is not specified, the allocation follows the actual destination of the surplus as shown in the partnership accounts, having regard also to any agreement outside the accounts.

   If the surplus is not allocated between the partners and is instead put to a common reserve, regard must be had to the ordinary profit sharing ratio for the purposes of allocating disposal proceeds, in the absence of a specific asset-surplus-sharing ratio.

(2)   Acquisition costs are allocated according to the same principles (as above) but as at the date of acquisition. There may be adjustments to these allocations where there is a subsequent change in the partnership sharing ratios (see para. 4 (¶12-200)).

The guidance issued to HMRC staff also deal with the situation where there is no written agreement or any evidence for any of the above tests, in which case:

> 'each partner in England and Wales is regarded as having an equal share in the partnership assets. But in Scotland the position is that a partner's interest is determined by statute, which provides that 'on a dissolution of the firm the assets of the firm including the sums, if any, contributed by the partners to make up losses or deficiencies of capital, shall be applied in the following manner and order: 1. In paying the debts and liabilities of the firm to persons who are not partners therein; 2. In paying to each partner rateably what is due from the firm to him for advances as distinguished from capital; 3. In paying to each partner rateably what is due from the firm to him in respect of capital; 4. The ultimate residue, if any, shall be divided among the partners in the proportion in which profits are divisible.'

(*Business Income Manual*, BIM82058)

(*Partnership Act* 1890, s. 24(1) and 44)

> **Example**
>
> A partnership between Roger, Steve and Tommy purchases land for £24,000, sells it for £34,000 and throughout its ownership they share surpluses 1:2:2 respectively. Roger is treated as making a gain of £2,000, and Steve and Tommy of £4,000 each.
>
> If the partnership agreement had stated that because Steve and Tommy had actually provided £12,000 each they should share equally any surplus realised on that asset, the gain would be apportioned £5,000 to each of Steve and Tommy. In the absence of such a provision, the actual amounts contributed by partners are irrelevant in determining the capital gains tax position.

Where the partners and asset-sharing ratios do not change during an asset's ownership by the partnership, no difficulty arises in computing the gain attributable to each partner. However the base cost apportioned to a partner will not always be his fractional share of the original cost of the asset to the partnership, because since that time there may have been chargeable events, such as a revaluation of assets followed by a change in asset-sharing ratios, as a result of which the base cost to be carried forward by the partners has increased (see ¶12-260).

Where a partnership makes a part-disposal of a partnership asset to an outside party, each partner is treated as making a part-disposal of his fractional share, with any gain or loss calculated using the part-disposal rules.

Under the part-disposal rules, unless the expenditure is wholly attributable to what is disposed of or what is retained, each item of the 'base cost' of an asset is apportioned between the part of the assets disposed of and the part retained as follows. An apportionment is, for this purpose, carried out by allocating to the part disposed of the following proportion of the base cost, the remainder being allocated to the part retained (TCGA 1992, s. 42(2)):

$$\frac{A}{A + B}$$

A is the consideration for the disposal; and

B is the market value of the property which is retained.

Legislation: PA 1890, s. 24 and 44; TCGA 1992, s. 42

12-180   Distribution of partnership assets in specie

(SP D12, para. 3)

When a partnership distributes an asset in kind to one or more of its partners, a chargeable gain or allowable loss accrues to those partners who have given up their fractional share in the asset, calculated as if there had been a disposal of the whole asset to a third party at the asset's market value. Those giving up a share in the asset will accordingly have a chargeable gain or allowance loss.

Any partner receiving the asset is not regarded as disposing of his fractional share and there will be no charge on the distribution (which is logical because he clearly has made an acquisition, not a disposal). Instead, the gain is effectively deferred by reducing his CGT base cost carried forward by the amount of his gain (or increasing it by the amount of any loss). The base cost of the asset for a future disposal is, therefore, the market value of the whole asset (apportioned if more than one partner receiving the asset), less the gain (or plus any allowable loss) which would have arisen on the notional disposal).

Example

Robert, Simon and Terence are in partnership sharing asset surpluses 2:3:5. The firm transferred an asset it had acquired at a cost of £10,000 to Simon, at its market value of £25,000.

Robert and Terence make chargeable gains:

	Robert	Terence
	£	£
Disposal consideration	5,000	12,500
Less: acquisition consideration	(2,000)	(5,000)
Chargeable gain	3,000	7,500

Simon takes on a base cost of £20,500, calculated as follows:

	£	£
Market value of asset		25,000
Less: notional gain		
disposal consideration	7,500	
Less: acquisition cost	(3,000)	(4,500)
Base cost[1]		20,500

Note:

Note that Simon received a 30% share in the asset for £3,000 on its acquisition by the partnership. At the time of the distribution, he received a further 70% share for the amount equal to the disposal consideration taken into account in for Robert and Simon (i.e. market value or £17,500 being £5,000 plus £12,500). His total acquisition cost is, therefore, £20,500 (£3,000 plus £17,500).

(If the transfer to Simon had taken place prior to 6 April 2008, indexation allowance and taper relief may have had to be taken into account in calculating Robert and Terence's chargeable gains. In addition, Simon's base cost would be higher by virtue of the indexation allowance to which he would have been entitled on the notional third party sale. This would have reduced his notional gain which is deducted from the market value of the whole asset.)

12-200   Changes in partnership sharing ratios

(SP D12, para. 4)

Whenever there is a change in partnership asset-sharing ratios, for example on the admission or retirement of a partner, there is a potential charge to capital gains tax, subject to possible roll-over relief (see ¶14-640). A partner increasing his share is treated as having made an acquisition of a corresponding share of each asset owned by the partnership; similarly, a partner reducing his share is deemed to have disposed of a corresponding share of each of the partnership assets.

Disposal proceeds are taken to be a fraction (equal to the fractional share changing hands) of the balance sheet value of the asset provided there is no direct payment of consideration outside the partnership. Special computational rules apply where payments are made outside the accounts (see ¶12-280) or where the partners (including incoming partners) are connected other than by partnership (e.g. father and daughter) or are otherwise not at arm's length (e.g. aunt and nephew) (see ¶12-300).

The partner whose share in the asset reduces will carry forward a smaller proportion of the CGT base cost and a partner whose share increases will carry forward a larger proportion.

The part-disposal rules, whereby total acquisition cost is apportioned on a part-disposal of an asset (see ¶12-160) are not applicable and instead the cost of the part disposed of is calculated on a fractional basis.

Balance sheet value equals CGT base cost

Calculating the disposal by reference to the balance sheet value will produce neither a gain nor a loss where the partners' base costs are equal to the balance sheet value (see, however, ¶12-220 where the share of the asset was held by the partner at 31 March 1982).

> ### *Example*
>
> A and B carry on a business in partnership and hold equal interests in partnership assets. The partnership's assets include a freehold property that is included in the balance sheet at its acquisition cost of £500,000. The CG base costs for A and B are:
>
> A £500,000 × 50% = £250,000
>
> B £500,000 × 50% = £250,000
>
> The partners subsequently change their interests in the property to the ratio 40:60. No payments are made in respect of the change.

A is treated as having made a part disposal of a 10% interest in the property. A's disposal is calculated as:

		A
		£
Disposal consideration (BSV)	(£500,000 × 10%)	50,000
Less: acquisition consideration	(£250,000 × 10/50)	(50,000)
Chargeable gain		**No gain/no loss**

CGT costs carried forward are:

A: £250,000 – 50,000 = £200,000

B: £250,000 + £50,000 = £300,000

B is treated as having acquired his additional 10% interest for an amount equal to the disposal consideration taken into account for A.

(Example taken from *Capital Gains Manual*, CG27540)

Asset previously revalued in accounts or balance sheet value does not equal CGT base cost

Where the asset has been revalued in the partnership accounts (see ¶12-260) or a partner has transferred an asset to the partnership for an amount that is not equivalent to the CGT base cost, or where the partners' CGT base costs were determined under TCGA 1992, s. 171 rather than on cost of the asset to the partnership, the computation proceeds as follows:

Example

A and B carry on a business in partnership and hold equal interests in partnership assets. The partnership owns a freehold property that it acquired for £400,000 but which, following a revaluation, is included in the balance sheet at £600,000. The surplus on revaluation of the property, (£600,000 – £400,000) £200,000, was credited to the partners' capital accounts in the ratio 50:50.

The partners' CG base costs are:

A: £400,000 × 50% = £200,000

B: £400,000 × 50% = £200,000

The partners change their fractional interests to the ratio 40:60.

A is treated as having made a part disposal of a 10% interest in the property. A's disposal is calculated as:

		A
		£
Disposal consideration (BSV)	(£600,000 × 10%)	60,000
Less: acquisition consideration	(£200,000 × 10/50)	(40,000)
Chargeable gain		20,000

NB. A's gain is equal to the proportion of his share of the surplus on revaluation that is equivalent to the interest that has been disposed of, that is, £100,000 × 10%/50% = £20,000.

CGT costs carried forward are:

A: £200,000 – 40,000 = £160,000

B: £200,000 + £60,000 = £260,000

B is treated as having acquired his additional 10% interest for an amount equal to the disposal consideration taken into account for A.

(Example taken from *Capital Gains Manual*, CG27550.)

Legislation: TCGA 1992, s. 171

12-220   Rebasing of partnership assets held at 31 March 1982

When capital gains tax was first introduced from 6 April 1965, tax was only to be charged on gains which had arisen from that date. This was normally achieved by taking the whole gain that had arisen over the ownership of the asset and apportioning it on a time basis to determine the amount in respect of the period after 6 April 1965.

An alternative approach was for the taxpayer to elect to be treated as if the asset had been acquired at 6 April 1965 for its market value at that date. In certain cases, a deemed acquisition at 6 April 1965 was mandatory.

In 1988, the tax was 'rebased' to 31 March 1982. This time, the general rule was that, subject to a number of exceptions, assets were deemed to have been acquired at that date at market value. It was also possible for taxpayers to elect for rebasing to apply.

The exceptions to rebasing covered situations where a smaller gain or a larger loss would have arisen under the previous basis or where one basis would have produced a gain and the other a loss. This was the so-called 'kink-test' which was abolished, for capital gains tax purposes, as part of the 'simplification' of capital gains tax introduced by FA 2008.

As a result of this abolition and consequential changes, rebasing is mandatory for capital gains tax purposes (i.e. for individuals and trustees – but not for corporation tax purposes) for disposals on or after 6 April 2008. The rule is now that anyone disposing of an asset which they held at 31 March 1982 is treated as having acquired it on that date at its then market value (TCGA 1992, s. 35(1), (2)).

The implications of *Finance Act* 2008 rules for partnership assets held on 31 March 1982, including examples, are set out fully in HMRC Brief 09/09 (see **Appendix 6**).

Legislation: TCGA 1992, s. 35

12-240   Contribution of an asset to a partnership

(SP D12, para. 5 (new to version published 14 September 2015))

When SP D12 was first published in 1975, it did not address the situation where a partner contributes an asset to a partnership by means of a capital contribution. Instead, HMRC's approach was clarified in HMRC Brief 03/08. The OTS requested HMRC include this clarification in SP D12.

Where an asset is transferred to a partnership by means of a capital contribution, the partner has made a part disposal of the asset equal to the fractional share which passes to the other partners.

If the transfer is between connected persons or is otherwise than by a bargain at arm's length (see ¶12-300), the market value rule applies. Otherwise, the consideration for the part disposed will be a proportion (equal to the fractional share passing to the other partners) of the total amount given by the partnership for the asset.

The sum credited to the partner's capital account represents consideration for the disposal of the asset to the partnership. As the asset does not have a balance sheet value in the partnership accounts, it is not possible to calculate the disposal consideration by reference to SP D12, para. 4 (see ¶12-200).

Allowable costs may be apportioned on a fractional basis (as per SP D12, para. 4, see ¶12-200), rather than by reference to the statutory A/A+B formula.

Where disposal consideration (calculated on the fractional proportion of the total consideration) exceeds the allowable costs (based on the partner's CGT base cost).

Example

A and B carry on a business in partnership sharing assets in the ratio 75:25.

A transfers an asset which he acquired five years earlier for £320,000 to the partnership at its current market value of £400,000. The consideration of £400,000 is credited to his capital account. The asset is included in the balance sheet at its cost to the partnership of £400,000.

A has disposed of a 25% interest in the asset on its transfer to the partnership and has retained a 75% share by virtue of his interest in the assets of the partnership.

		A
		£
Disposal consideration	(£400,000 × 25%)	100,000
Less: acquisition consideration	(cost × A/(A+B))	
(TCGA 1992, s. 42(2))	(£320,000 × £100,000/(£100,000+£300,000))	(80,000)
Chargeable gain		20,000

Effectively, A has realised a profit of £80,000 (£400,000 – £320,000) on the transfer of the asset to the partnership, however, because he has retained a 75% interest in the asset, the gain accruing at the time of the transfer is the proportion attributable to the interest that passed to B (£80,000 × 25% = £20,000).

The CGT base costs carried forward are:

A: £320,000 – £80,000 = £240,000

B: £100,000

A's CGT base cost is based on his original cost of acquisition minus the proportion brought into charge in the CGT computation on the transfer of the asset to the partnership (and is equivalent to the original base cost × the 75% proportion A retains through his interest in the partnership). Effectively, the remainder of A's £80,000 profit on transfer of asset to the partnership is brought into charge on a subsequent disposal of the asset.

B's CGT base cost is equivalent to the disposal consideration taken into account for A.

(Example taken from *Capital Gains Manual*, CG27940)

HMRC Brief 03/08

HMRC Brief 03/08 was issued on 21 January 2008 and contained an admission that HMRC officers had been misinterpreting statement of practice SP D12 for the last 33 years.

The practice in the past had been to treat the disposal value as equal to the value of the asset as shown in the partnership balance sheet. This was understandable, as it followed the policy outlined for changes in asset-sharing ratios; the individual previously had a 100% share in the asset and after the transfer has something less.

HMRC's revised view, however, was that it was not permissible to use a proportion of the balance sheet value as 'the asset in question would not have had a balance sheet value in the partnership accounts'. By this, they presumably meant it did not have such a value before the transaction. Instead, they said 'We take the view that a sum credited to the partner's capital account represents consideration for the disposal of the asset to the partnership'. The revised view was to be applied in all future cases.

The Brief itself did not contain a definition of a 'capital contribution'. However, this could be interpreted as taking place where a partner introduces a personally-owned asset into the partnership, either on its formation or subsequently, on such terms that all partners are entitled to share in any growth in its value. Capital gains arise on disposals of beneficial ownership in chargeable assets, so, if that were the case, he had made a disposal of part of the beneficial ownership of that asset. However, if the introduction were on terms that provide for the partnership to have use of the asset but that all the surplus on its disposal remains with the introducing partner, then that would not be a 'capital contribution' and there would be no disposal of beneficial ownership because no share in any surplus on that asset has been given up.

12-260   Adjustment through the accounts (revaluation of partnership assets)

(SP D12, para. 6)

(Para. 6 was renumbered from para. 5 in the 14 September 2015 version of SP D12)

Where a partnership revalues its assets in the accounts, there will normally be an adjustment to the partners' capital accounts to reflect their share of the surplus or deficit. An upward revaluation is not of itself an occasion of charge for CGT purposes.

However, where there is a subsequent reduction in the partner's asset share ratios, this will have the effect of reducing a partner's potential liability to CGT on any future disposal of the asset. Therefore, at the time of the reduction in the sharing ratios, the reducing partner will be treated as having disposed of the fractional share (being the difference between his old share and his new share) in the partnership asset for a consideration equal to the fraction of the increased value of the asset (as per the revaluation amount).

Any partner whose asset shares increase will, correspondingly, have their CGT base cost increased by the same amount.

See ¶12-200 for the computation on a change in asset sharing ratios following an upward revaluation.

The same principles apply where the value of a chargeable asset is reduced in the balance sheet.

As a result of the potential tax charges caused indirectly by asset revaluation in the accounts, many partnerships do not formally recognise asset appreciation in their accounts even in inflationary times, but instead agreements regarding the sharing of asset surpluses or deficits are drafted with reference to memorandum accounts maintained for this purpose outside the financial statements produced by the firm.

12-280   Payments between partners outside the partnership accounts

(SP D12, para. 7)

(Para. 7 was renumbered from para. 6 in the 14 September 2015 version of SP D12)

Where, on a change in asset-sharing ratios, payments are made directly between two or more partners outside the framework of the partnership accounts, the payments are treated as part of the consideration for the disposal of the whole or part of the partner's share in partnership assets in addition to the deemed consideration based on the balance sheet value described in ¶12-200 and ¶12-260 above.

Such a payment will often be in respect of goodwill or some other asset which is not reflected in the balance sheet which has no original cost. However, if the payment is clearly payment for a share in assets which are included in the balance sheet, the partner receiving it will be able to deduct the amount of the acquisition cost relative to that share.

The partner making the payment will only be allowed to deduct the amount in the calculating of gains or losses on a subsequent disposal of his share in the asset. He will be able to claim a loss when he finally leaves the partnership, or when his share is reduced, provided he then receives no consideration or receives a lesser consideration for his share in the asset.

See also ¶12-300, for transfers between persons not at arm's length.

Example 1

A and B carry on a business in partnership and hold equal interests in partnership assets. The partnership's chargeable assets include a freehold property that cost £300,000 but which, following a revaluation, is included in the balance sheet at a value of £500,000 (with the surplus on revaluation being credited to a reserve account). The partners subsequently agree to change their fractional interests in the property to the ratio 40:60. B pays the sum of £25,000 to A for the acquisition of a further 10% interest in the property.

		A
		£
Disposal consideration		
Based on BSV	(£500,000 × 10%) £50,000	
Plus consideration from B	£25,000	75,000
Less: acquisition consideration	(£150,000 × 10/50)	(30,000)
Chargeable gain		45,000

CGT base costs carried forward are:

A: £150,000 – £30,000 = £120,000

B: £150,000 + £75,000 = £225,000

B is treated as having acquired his additional 10% interest for an amount equal to the disposal consideration taken into account for A.

(Example taken from *Capital Gains Manual*, CG27560)

Example 2

When Nigel and Oliver entered partnership as architects, the firm acquired a freehold property at a cost of £100,000. At that time, the asset-sharing ratios were 70:30 respectively. Some years later, the property was revalued in the accounts at £130,000, at which time Peter was admitted as a partner. The asset-sharing ratios were altered to 60:25:15. Peter made payments to Nigel and Oliver of £14,000 and £6,000 respectively for goodwill, which was not recognised in the firm's accounts.

Nigel's capital gains position is:

Property	£
Deemed disposal consideration (10% × £130,000)	13,000
Less: acquisition consideration (10% × £100,000)	(10,000)
Chargeable gain	3,000
Goodwill	
Chargeable gain (nil cost)	14,000
Total chargeable gain	17,000

(If these events occurred prior to 6 April 2008, taper relief and indexation allowance may be applicable.)

Oliver's position is computed similarly, with a reduction in asset-sharing of 5% rather than 10%. Peter's base costs are, in relation to the property £19,500 (£130,000 × 15%) and in relation to goodwill £20,000.

Note: see ¶12-400 for HMRC practice regarding goodwill.

12-300   Transfers between persons not at arm's length

(SP D12, para. 8)

(Para. 8 was renumbered from para. 7 in the 14 September 2015 version of SP D12)

Where there is no payment made through or outside the accounts in connection with a change in partnership sharing ratio, a CGT charge will only arise if the transaction is otherwise than by way of a bargain made at arm's length and falls, therefore, within TCGA 1992, s. 17, extended by TCGA 1992, s. 18 for transactions between connected persons.

TCGA 1992, s. 17 provides that the consideration for a disposal is taken as the market value of the asset where the acquisition or disposal of the asset is:

(1)   otherwise than by way of a bargain at arm's length; or

(2)   for a consideration that cannot be valued.

TCGA 1992, s. 18 provides that where persons are connected, the transaction is treated as other than at arm's length, and therefore market value is substituted for the consideration in computing any charge to tax.

Connected persons are defined by TCGA 1992, s. 286. Under s. 286(4), a person is connected with any person with whom he is in partnership and with the husband or wife or a relative(1) of any individual with whom he is in partnership, *except* in relation to acquisitions or disposals of partnership assets pursuant to bona fide commercial arrangements.

This treatment will also be given to transactions between an incoming partner and the existing partners.

However, where the partners (including the incoming partners) are connected other than by partnership (e.g. father and daughter) or are otherwise not at arm's length (e.g. aunt and nephew), the transfer of a share in the partnership assets may be treated as having been made at market value *unless* nothing would have been paid had the parties been at arm's length.

Where consideration of less than market value passes between partners connected other than by partnership or otherwise not at arm's length, the transfer will only be regarded as having been made for full market value if the consideration actually paid is less than that which would have been paid by parties at arm's length.

Where a transfer is treated as taking place at market value, the deemed disposal is calculated in the same way as for payments outside the accounts (see ¶12-280).

The essence of SP D12, para. 8, is, therefore, that where there is no payment in connection with a change in the partnership sharing ratio, there will only be a charge to capital gains tax if the transaction is otherwise than at arm's length, and transactions between partners will generally be treated as at arm's length unless the partners are connected otherwise than by virtue of the partnership connection (e.g. if is a family relationship also).

For commentary on apportioning market value, see ¶12-140.

Partnership assets

It could be argued that the phrase 'partnership assets' used in the connected person rules merely encompasses assets owned by the firm and not, for example, partnership shares, which in general law are separate and distinct from the former. Consistent with their interpretation of 'partnership dealings', used in provisions treating them as by the partners rather than by the firm (see ¶12-020), HMRC treat 'partnership assets' as embracing such partnership shares, which enables a uniform approach to be adopted to the disposal of partnership assets and partnership shares.

Example 1

A and B carry on a business in partnership and hold equal interests in partnership assets. They agree to change their profit sharing ratio to 60:40. The arrangement in which B disposed of part of his fractional interests in partnership assets to A was a genuine commercial arrangement and A and B are not connected persons other than by reference to TCGA 1992, s. 286(4). Therefore the transaction falls within the exception to TCGA 1992, s. 286(4) and the market value rule will not apply.

Example 2

K and L carry on a business in partnership and hold equal interests in partnership assets. K sells an asset which he owns personally to L for £6,000 at a time when its market value is £8,000. As K and L are connected persons under TCGA 1992, s. 286(4) the market value rule applies and the asset is treated as having been disposed of by K and acquired by L for a consideration equal to its market value of £8,000. The exception to TCGA 1992, s. 286(4) does not apply because the asset is not a partnership asset.

Example 3

M and N carry on a business in partnership and hold equal interests in partnership assets. They are not connected other than by means of the partnership relationship. The acquisition costs and current balance sheet values of the partnership assets were:

Freehold property £320,000

Goodwill £100,000

P is admitted to the partnership M and N agreed to change their profit sharing ratios to 25:50:25.

At the time of P's admission the market value of the partnership assets were:

Freehold property £400,000

Goodwill £120,000

M and P are connected persons under TCGA 1992, s. 286(2) as M is P's father. P did not pay any consideration to M for his acquisition of a 25% interest in partnership assets. When N acquired his 50% interest from M on admission to the partnership he made a direct payment of consideration to M. The payment by N to M on admission to the partnership indicates that M and P were not acting at arm's length. The market value rule applies in relation to the disposal of a 25% interest by M and the acquisition of a 25% interest by P. M's disposal proceeds and P's acquisition costs in respect of the 25% interest in partnership assets changing hands will be calculated at market value and their capital gains tax position is as follows:

M

	Property £	Goodwill £
Disposal proceeds (based on market value)		
(25% × £400,000)	100,000	
(25% × £120,000)		30,000
Less: acquisition costs		
£320,000 × 25%	(80,000)	
£100,000 × 25%		(25,000)
Chargeable gain	20,000	5,000

CGT base costs carried forward are:

M: Property £160,000 – £80,000 = £80,000; Goodwill £50,000 – £25,000 = £25,000

N: Property £160,000: Goodwill £50,000

P: Property £100,000: Goodwill £30,000

Example 4

A large professional partnership which consists of 40 partners including Y and Z agree to change their profit sharing ratios. Under the terms of the partnership agreement no payments are made between the partners. Y's fractional interest is increased and Z's fractional interest is reduced.

Y and Z are connected persons under TCGA 1992, s. 286(2) as they are brothers but none of the other partners are connected persons other than by virtue of the partnership relationship.

Part of the increase in Y's interest in the partnership assets is attributable to the decrease in Z's interest. As Y and Z are connected by a family relationship the market value rule would normally be applied to the extent that Z has disposed of part of his fractional interest in partnership assets to Y. However, paragraph 8 of SP D12 explains that as the facts show that the arrangement whereby no payments were made between Y and Z was a genuine commercial arrangement that applied to all of the partners the market value rule will not be applied.

(Examples taken from *Capital Gains Manual*, CG27840)

(1) 'relative' for this purpose means brother, sister, ancestor or lineal descendant.

Legislation: TCGA 1992, s. 17, 18 and 286

12-320   Annuities provided by partnerships

(SP D12, para. 9)

(Para. 9 was renumbered from para. 8 in the 14 September 2015 version of SP D12)

Where a lump sum is paid to a partner on leaving the partnership or on reduction of his share in the partnership, this represents consideration for the disposal of the whole or part share in the partnership assets and the computational rules provided by para. 7 apply (see ¶12-280).

Similarly, where the partnership buys a purchase life annuity for a partner, the treatment provided by para. 7 (see ¶12-280) applies with the measure of consideration being the actual costs of the annuity.

If the continuing partners agree to provide the retiring partner with an annuity, this amounts to consideration for the disposal of his partnership share (the capitalised value of a right to a series of payments in the nature of income not being precluded by the rule relating to amounts charged to tax as income. However, the capitalised value of the annuity will only be treated as consideration for the disposal of the retired partner's share in the partnership assets under TCGA 1992, s. 37(3), if it is more than can be regarded as reasonable recognition of the past contribution of work and effort by the partner to the partnership.

Where the annuity is provided in the form of annual payments by the firm and within the 'reasonable' limit, no charge to capital gains tax arises.

Where the partner has been in the partnership for at least ten years, an annuity will be regarded as 'reasonable' if it is no more than two-thirds of the partner's average share of the profits in the best three of the last seven years in which the partner was required to devote substantially the whole of this time to acting as a partner. In arriving at a partner's share, the partnership profits taken into account are assessable profits before deduction of capital allowances or charges. The ten-year period includes any period during which the partner was a member of another firm whose business merged with that of the present firm.

For periods of less than ten years, the fractions in the following table are applied instead of two-thirds:

Complete years in partnership	Fraction
1–5	1/60 for each year
6	8/60
7	16/60
8	24/60
9	32/60

As noted above, where the capitalised value of an annuity is in excess of the above levels, it is treated as consideration received by the retired partner for the disposal of his interest in the partnership assets. It will also be regarded as allowable expenditure by the remaining partners on the acquisition of their fractional shares in partnership assets from him.

If the capitalised value is in excess of what is 'reasonable', it is likely that only the excess will be chargeable to capital gains tax, although the statement does not make this clear.

SP 1/79

SP 1/79 extends SP D12 treatment and the circumstances in which the capitalised value of an annuity paid by a partnership to a retired partner will *not* be treated as consideration for the disposal of his share in the partnership assets to include certain cases in which a lump sum is paid in addition to an annuity.

Where the aggregate of the annuity and one-ninth of the lump sum does not exceed the appropriate fractions (set out above) of the retired partner's average share of the profits, the capitalised value of the annuity will *not* be treated as consideration in the hands of the retired partner. The lump sum, however, will continue to be so treated.

If the aggregate of the annuity and one-ninth of the lump sum exceeds the appropriate fraction, then both the lump sum and capitalised value of the annuity are treated as proceeds for the disposal of the retiring partner's share of partnership assets.

Example

Vincent retires aged 58, having been a partner for seven years and his average annual share of profits for the best three years out of the last seven is £46,000. On retirement he receives an annuity of £8,000 per annum and a lump sum of £22,500.

Maximum capitalised value not treated as consideration = £46,000 × 16/60 = £12,267

Annuity of £8,000 + 1/9 × £22,500 = £10,500

The annuity is not treated as consideration for capital gains tax purposes, but the lump sum of £22,500 is.

The lump sum will be treated as consideration as explained above, irrespective of relief for annual payments made to the retired partner. Similarly, the cost of any purchased life annuity in favour of the outgoing partner will be treated in the same manner.

Legislation: TCGA 1992, s. 37

12-340   Mergers of partnerships

(SP D12, para. 10)

(Para. 10 was renumbered from para. 9 in the 14 September 2015 version of SP D12)

HMRC treat a partnership merger in the same way that changes in partnership sharing ratios are dealt with (see ¶12-200). Each partner disposes of his share in each asset owned by his original firm and acquires a share in each asset owned by the merged firm, except in respect of assets which are transferred from the original firm to the merged firm (any disposal of such assets is determined by reference to the reduction in the partner's interest therein).

At the time of agreeing to the terms of the merger, the partners of the two different firms are not partners of each other, and therefore the arrangements would not strictly come within the exception from market value substitution on dealings between connected persons in the case of bona fide commercial arrangements (see ¶12-200). HMRC could therefore insist on using the market value of each of the firms' assets to calculate any gains or losses arising on the merger, but they do not. It may well be anyway that assets are revalued to market value in drawing up the new partnership agreement and therefore gains may arise on the change in asset-sharing ratios caused by the merger (see ¶12-260) in addition to charges where payments are made outside the accounts of the firms (see ¶12-280).

In cases where gains do arise, roll-over relief under TCGA 1992, s. 152 (in so far as the partner disposes of his share in the assets of the old firm and acquires a share in other assets put into the 'merged' firm (see ¶14-640). Where, however, consideration given for the shares in assets acquired is less than the consideration for those disposed of, relief will be restricted under TCGA 1992, s. 153.

Legislation: TCGA 1992, s. 152 and 153

12-360   Shares acquired in stages

(SP D12, para. 11)

(Para. 11 was renumbered from para. 10 in the 14 September 2015 version of SP D12)

The acquisition costs of the various assets for shares in a partnership acquired in stages wholly after 5 April 1965, will be calculated by pooling the expenditure relating to each asset.

Example

X was admitted to a partnership in 2004 at which time he acquired a 20% interest in goodwill. His interest in goodwill was increased in subsequent years:

2004	20%	Cost £100,000
2006	10%	Cost £50,000
2008	5%	Cost £35,000

The base cost of Partner X's 35% interest in goodwill for CG purposes is £185,000.

Any subsequent reduction in Partner X's interest in goodwill will be treated as a part-disposal out of the pooled expenditure.

Acquisitions pre-6 April 1965

However, the acquisition costs of the various assets for shares in a partnership acquired wholly or partly before 6 April 1965 will be determined under TCGA 1992, Sch. 2, para. 18. Accordingly, where a disposal of an asset occurs on the occasion of a reduction in a partnership's share, the disposal will be identified with shares acquired on a 'first in, first out' basis.

Where this principle appears to produce an unreasonable result when applied to temporary changes in the shares in a partnership (e.g. those occurring when a partner's departure and a new partner's arrival are separated in time), HMRC will be prepared to review the case.

Legislation: TCGA 1992, Sch. 2, para. 18

12-380 Elections under TCGA 1992, Sch. 2, para. 4

(SP D12, para. 12)

(Para. 12 was renumbered from para. 11 in the 14 September 2015 version of SP D12)

Where partnership assets disposed of are quoted securities eligible for pooling under TCGA 1992, Sch. 2, para. 4, partners will be allowed to make separate elections in respect of shares or securities held by the partnership as distinct from shares and securities held by them on a personal basis.

Each partner has a separate right of election for his proportion of the partnership securities. The time limit for the purpose of Sch. 2 runs from the earlier of:

- the first relevant disposal of shares or securities by the partnership;
- the first reduction of the particular partner's share in the partnership assets after 19 March 1968.

Legislation: TCGA 1992, Sch. 2, para. 4

12-400 Partnership goodwill

(SP D12, para. 13)

(Para. 13 was renumbered from para. 12 in the 14 September 2015 version of SP D12)

HMRC's strict view is that self-generated or 'free' goodwill (i.e. that goodwill created by the normal conduct of the partnership's business) is a 'fungible' asset. A 'fungible' asset is one which grows or diminishes as parts are acquired or disposed of but the individual parts cannot be identified separately (see *Capital Gains Manual*, CG27640 for guidance on goodwill as a 'fungible' asset). Where there is a disposal of such 'fungible' assets, the rules relating to the identification of securities are applicable.

It was recognised that the strict application of HMRC's principles regarding free goodwill could have produced difficulties in CGT computations; accordingly, indicates the situations in which partnership 'free' goodwill (and in some instances purchased goodwill) is *not* treated as a 'fungible' asset.

Para. 13 is stated to apply to acquisitions and disposals (including part disposals) of goodwill produced by a partnership if:

- the value of the goodwill is not recognised on the balance sheet; or
- the goodwill has no value placed upon it in dealings between the partners.

Para. 13 also applies to purchased goodwill if either:

- it is not recognised in the partnership balance sheet; or

- it is recognised, but only at cost price or at a written down valuation; and
- in either instance above, it is not taken into account in dealings between the partners.

In these circumstances, on a disposal for actual consideration of a partner's interest in the goodwill of the the partnership, that interest will be treated as the same asset (or in the case of a part disposal, part of the same asset) as was originally acquired by that partner when first becoming entitled to a share in the goodwill of the partnership.

Where the treatment of goodwill does not conform to the requirements of the Statement, any disposals or acquisitions should be dealt with under the rules for securities.

Partnership goodwill and taper relief (for years up to 2007–08 only)

(Former SP D12, para. 12)

Under the pre September 2015 version of SP D12, former para. 12, provided that the partners would begin to accrue taper relief from the time that they first acquire any interest in the partnership's goodwill and would continue to do so until they ceased to have any such interest. No changes would be made to a partner's accrued taper relief if there were changes to partnership sharing ratios. Thus, under this practice, a partner who started out with only a small interest in partnership goodwill would begin to accrue taper relief from the date of acquisition. If, several years later, a larger share of the goodwill was acquired, the taper relief accrued on the original acquisition would apply to the whole of the goodwill (both the original and subsequent addition). Where there was both free and purchased goodwill covered by the statement, the two types were, according to HMRC, to be kept as two separate assets for the purposes of determining taper relief entitlement.

12-420   Entrepreneurs' relief on transfer of a business, 'roll-over' relief and business asset gift relief

(SP D12, para. 14 (new to version published 14 September 2015))

Entrepreneurs' relief

The circumstances in which an individual or partner may qualify for entrepreneurs' relief are:

- the individual's business becomes a partnership;
- a partner disposes of part of the whole of a partnership business;
- a partner disposes of all or part of a fractional share in shares which are held as partnership assets.

For commentary on partnerships and entrepreneurs' relief, see ¶14-420ff.

Roll-over relief

Roll-over relief is available to individuals who are partners where the whole of the partnership business is transferred to a company as a going concern in exchange for shares.

For commentary on partnerships and roll-over relief on incorporation of a partnership business, see **Chapter 6**.

Roll-over relief may also be available to partners when there is a disposal of a partnership asset and the proceeds are reinvested in another asset which is also used for trade purposes.

For commentary on roll-over relief on replacement business assets, see ¶14-640.

Gifts of business assets

Relief for gifts of business assets is available to individual partners in partnerships which are treated as 'transparent' for tax purposes on disposals of shares in partnership assets, subject to normal conditions.

Relief for gifts of business assets is also available, subject to normal conditions, to individuals disposing of personal assets to a partnership. For tax purposes, the transferee is treated as making disposals to each of the partners who are treated as acquiring a share in the assets.

For commentary on gifts of interests in partnerships or partnership assets, see ¶14-660.

12-440   Corporate partners and intangible fixed assets

There is a special regime for the taxation and relief of gains and losses arising in respect of intangible fixed assets owned by companies (CTA 2009, Pt. 8). In many areas these rules mirror the capital gains rules, but there is no equivalent of SP D12 for corporate partners. If the partnership has intangible fixed assets of material value, this can cause issues on merging partnerships or where partners join or leave partnerships. Remember, a gain (or realisation credit) can arise on the company when another person joins or leavers a partnership of which the company is a member, so this situation does not arise only where the company itself joins or leaves.

The lack of any specific directions from HMRC in this area is a material lacuna. There are two ways to resolve the issue.

- One approach is to assume that, in the absence of any indications to the contrary from HMRC, companies should show gains and losses on intangible fixed assets as chargeable gains or allowable losses for corporation tax purposes. This is, of course, a conservative approach, as well as being potentially expensive. But the other concern is that this might be inconsistent with the approach taken by partners who are individuals, who are subject to capital gains tax on most intangible fixed assets (especially goodwill), so that SP D12 does apply to them.

- The alternative is to treat SP D12 as a statement of HMRC's view of the way in which the relevant provisions are intended to operate. Given the similarity of treatment of corporate intangible assets and chargeable assets, there is some justification for this approach, which also has the advantages of consistency of treatment between all the partners, companies and individuals, and is likely to be the less costly option!

It might also be considered prudent, particularly in larger cases, to seek HMRC's advice under the non-statutory clearance facility.

Chapter 4: Dissolution and winding up of a partnership

13-000 Introduction

The dissolution of a partnership is the term used for the termination of a partnership. This can occur by a number of methods but the main point is that the partners are then obliged to wind up the firm, settling the affairs of the firm, paying off its creditors and distributing the assets appropriately.

13-020 Dissolution of a general partnership

The *Partnership Act* 1890 states that a partnership is dissolved in the following circumstances:

- by the expiry of the term of a fixed-term partnership (PA 1890, s. 32(a));
- the termination of a specific project or undertaking for which the partnership was formed (PA 1890, s. 32(b));
- by any partner giving notice to the other partners of his or her intention to dissolve the partnership (PA 1890, s. 32(c));
- a partnership is dissolved for all of the partners on the death or bankruptcy of any partner, subject to any agreement that the partners might otherwise have made (PA 1890, s. 33(1));
- if a partner allows his share of partnership profit to be charged under the act for a separate debt, the other partners may require the partnership to be dissolved (PA 1890, s. 33(2));
- if an event occurs which makes it unlawful to carry on the partnership business, or to carry on that business in partnership, the partnership is dissolved by illegality (PA 1890, s. 34);
- a partnership may be dissolved by the courts by issuing a Decree of Dissolution on application by a partner if a partner is found to be lunatic, otherwise permanently incapable of performing his duties as a partner, has been guilty of conduct prejudicial to the carrying on of the partnership business, where it is no longer reasonably practicable for the other partners to remain in partnership with an individual who consistently breaches the partnership agreement or similarly makes it impossible to remain a partner, when the partnership can only be carried on at a loss, or in other circumstances where the court considers it just and equitable that the partnership be dissolved (PA 1890, s. 35).

It is interesting to note that none of the situations causing the dissolution of a partnership mention the situation where the partnership simply ceases to carry on any business. This is odd, because the partnership only comes into existence because there are two or more persons carrying on a business together with a view of profit (PA 1890, s. 1(1)) so when that condition ceases to be satisfied, one would prima facie assume that the partnership ceases to exist. It may be, however, that such a scenario is considered to fall into PA 1890, s. 32(b), i.e. the single undertaking of the partnership, even if that has been a long-term business, has terminated, causing dissolution by expiration.

Similarly, there is nothing in the Partnership Act referring to the incorporation of a partnership, i.e. the transfer of the business of the partnership to a company. If the partnership transfers the whole of its business to a company, it clearly ceases to carry on any business, so this probably also falls into PA 1890, s. 32(b), i.e. the single undertaking of the partnership has terminated. If the partnership transfers only part of its business to a company, the partnership will continue to exist so long as it continues to carry out the residual business, and there is no termination. Incorporation of a partnership is covered in **Chapter 6**.

Legislation: PA 1890, s. 1, 32, 33, 34 and 35

13-040 Consequences of dissolution

Once a partnership is dissolved, the partners are required to wind it up, i.e. as noted above, settle the affairs of the partnership and distribute the remaining assets amongst the partners (PA 1890, s. 39).

Legislation: PA 1890, s. 39

13-060 Income tax on winding up a partnership

From an income tax perspective, a partnership is not treated as a separate entity (ITTOIA 2005, s. 848). Instead, each partner is treated as carrying on a notional trade, so that his or her profits, gains or losses as a member of the partnership are treated as profits, gains or losses of that separate notional trade (ITTOIA 2005, s. 852(1)). This is dealt with in more detail in **Chapter 11**.

In effect, these provisions ensure that an individual is treated as starting to carry on their business when they actually start to carry on that business, which may be before they become a member of a partnership, and ceasing to carry on the business when they stop carrying on that business, which, again, may or may not be when the partnership is dissolved. In the context of the dissolution of the partnership, therefore, the income tax rules will apply as if the individual concerned has either carried on in business or has decided to stop carrying on the business at the point of the dissolution of the partnership. So the dissolution of a partnership is not necessarily treated as the cessation of a business carried on by the individual partners.

Legislation: ITTOIA 2005, s. 848 and 852

13-080 Capital gains tax on winding up a partnership

As has already been mentioned, there is very little legislation covering capital gains and partnerships. Capital gains tax on chargeable gains of a partnership is assessed and charged on the partners separately, and partnership dealings are treated as dealings by the partners and not by the firm (TCGA 1992, s. 59(1)). This means that we are effectively required to rely on SP D12, which was updated by HMRC on 15 September 2015 (the latest version incorporates material from HMRC Brief 03/08 about part disposals when assets are contributed to a partnership, as well as certain other simplifications suggested in a discussion document issued by the Office of Tax Simplification). This Statement of Practice generally applies to both ordinary partnerships and limited liability partnerships.

When an ordinary partnership is wound up, there is likely to be either a disposal of the assets, in which case Part 2 of the Statement of Practice is in point, or a distribution of the assets to the individual partners, in which case we need to look at Part 3.

Part 2, which covers disposals of assets by a partnership, will apply in the same way as to a disposal of an asset by a partnership at any time. In other words, each partner is assumed to dispose of their fractional share of the asset, in line with TCGA 1992, s. 59. This is not entirely straightforward, as the allocation of base cost between the partners might have changed due to the introduction or retirement of partners (see **Chapter 3**). So SP D12 proposes that the proceeds of a disposal be allocated between the partners on the basis of their fractional shares in the partnership assets (which may be different from their profit sharing ratios). The gains or losses on the disposal are then computed separately for each partner on the basis of their personal base costs. Where there is no separate asset sharing arrangements, the allocation of proceeds will normally follow the general profit sharing arrangements.

Example 1

Sarah and Paul are in partnership as accountants and own a building from which the practice operates. They both decide to retire, and hence dissolve the partnership and the property is sold. Sarah and Paul have always split the profits of the business on a 50:50 basis. They bought the property shortly after the business commenced for £30,000, and put £15,000 each towards the purchase. The proceeds of sale were £100,000. Clearly, therefore, the £70,000 gain is allocated £35,000 to each of them.

Suppose, instead, they were not retiring but they had decided to incorporate the business. The situation would be identical, in that the transfer of the property to the company would be a disposal and a capital gain would be computed in the same way. Of course, in this case it might be that the gain can be sheltered by the so called incorporation relief (TCGA 1992, s. 162) (see **Chapter 6**).

Example 2

Pete and Tracey form a partnership which trades as a shop selling handbags. They own the premises outright. Tracey was able to put down the initial deposit out of an inheritance, so it was agreed that the asset sharing ratio in respect of the shop would be 75% to Tracey and 25% to Pete. The profits of the business are shared 50:50.

In this case, the allocation of proceeds would, on the basis of Part 2 of SP D12, be 75% to Tracey and 25% to Pete. It is slightly harder to compute the base costs for each partner as, on a simple analysis, the base cost would be 50% each (assuming that the capital was generally paid out of the profits of the partnership), but we also have to take into account the fact that Tracey paid the deposit. HMRC's manuals at CG27350 suggest that the cost of acquisition would normally be allocated between the partners on the basis of the agreed fractional interest in the assets, which makes the computation easier, but not necessarily fairer. If we applied this simplified approach, Tracey would have 75% of the capital gain and Pete would have 25%, subject to there having been no other admissions or retirements of partners in the interim.

It is not clear either from the Statement of Practice or HMRC's Manuals, but it also seems reasonable to suggest that Pete or Tracey could insist on the actual base costs being used, on the basis of their contributions to the purchase of the asset, notwithstanding the asset sharing agreement. Suppose the shop had cost £100,000 originally and Tracey had put down a deposit of £30,000. The remaining £70,000 had been paid out of the partnership profits and, effectively, was therefore shared equally between Pete and Tracey. On that basis, Tracey's base cost would be £65,000 and Pete's would be £35,000. If the property were subsequently sold for £200,000, the proceeds would be allocated on the basis of the asset sharing arrangements, £150,000 to Tracey and £50,000 to Pete. On this analysis, Pete would have a gain of £15,000 (£50,000 minus £35,000), and Tracey would have a gain of £85,000 (£150,000 minus £65,000).

Thus, Tracey might be slightly worse off than if the overall gain of £100,000 had simply been allocated on a 75:25 basis, and might be slightly disgruntled. Pete, however, might be quite happy at only having a £15,000 gain instead of a £25,000!

Part 3 of SP D12 refers to the division of partnership assets amongst the partners, i.e. without an actual disposal outside the partnership. In this case, each partner is treated as disposing of his or her fractional share of the asset using the normal principles, except the partner who receives the asset who, of course, has not made a disposal. Instead, they have made an acquisition.

In these cases, the asset is treated as disposed of at market value, to allow a computation of the gain in respect of each partner. The partner receiving the asset will effectively enhance his base cost of the asset by the fractional shares of the market value. Statement of Practice D12 states this a slightly different way, in that it refers to the asset being rebased in that partner's hands to market value less the fractional gain on his share of the asset, which comes to the same thing.

Example 3

How does this affect our first example, above? Paul and Sarah made £35,000 gain each on disposing of an asset. Supposing, instead, they had dissolved the partnership so that Paul could retire and Sarah effectively bought him out. In that case, Paul would have the same £35,000 gain as in the previous example, as he has made a disposal. But Sarah would now own the whole asset, so her base cost would be her original £15,000 base cost plus the £50,000 market value of Paul's fractional disposal, giving a total of £65,000 base cost for when Sarah decides to sell the building. (Stating this in the terms used by SP D12, Sarah's base cost is £100,000 less the £35,000 notional gain on her fractional share, giving the same £65,000.)

Legislation: TCGA 1992, s. 59 and 162

13-100   Dissolution of a limited liability partnership

There is no equivalent for an LLP to the dissolution provisions in the *Partnership Act* 1890. Instead, as a body corporate, an LLP can only be dissolved by a winding up under the relevant provisions of the *Insolvency Act* 1986 (as applied by LLPA 2000, s. 14 and LLP Regulations 2001 (SI 2001/1090), reg. 5 and Sch. 3).

Generally, the dissolution of an LLP is started by either a winding-up order or a resolution. The LLP must then immediately cease all its activities (IA 1986, s. 87), even if it is solvent and the winding up is voluntary. The LLP is subsequently dissolved at a date depending on the specific circumstances.

- With a voluntary winding up, dissolution is three months after the final account and return have been sent to the registrar by the liquidator.
- In a compulsory winding up dissolution is three months after the registrar receives notice that the liquidator has left office and that there has been a final creditors' meeting, or three months after he receives a notice from the official receiver that the winding up is complete.

The Registrar of Companies can also strike off an LLP in the circumstances mentioned in the *Companies Act* 2006, s. 1000 or 1003, i.e. if he believes that the LLP has become moribund or if two or more designated members apply after the LLP has been dormant for at least three months.

Legislation: LLPA 2000, s. 14; SI 2001/1090; IA 1986, s. 87; CA 2006, s. 1000 and 1003

13-120 Income tax on winding up an LLP

From an income tax perspective, an LLP is also not treated as a separate entity (ITTOIA 2005, s. 848) so that each partner is treated for income tax purposes in exactly the same way as the members of an ordinary partnership (see above).

Legislation: ITTOIA 2005, s. 848

13-140 Capital gains tax on winding up an LLP

From a capital gains perspective, the same rules will generally apply as for an ordinary partnership (see above), during either a period of temporary cessation of business (TCGA 1992, s. 59A(3)(a)) or during a period of winding up following permanent cessation, as long as that period is not 'unreasonably prolonged' or connected with the avoidance of tax (TCGA 1992, s. 59A(3)(b)). This means that, if an LLP resolves to wind up and disposes of its assets, whether to third parties or by allocation amongst the partners, the same rules apply as detailed above for an ordinary partnership.

However, if the LLP is subject to a winding-up order by a Court, or if a liquidator is appointed, the LLP immediately ceases to be transparent for capital gains tax purposes (TCGA 1992, s. 59A(4)(a)). This rule also applies if a similar event occurs under the law of another jurisdiction, i.e. if there is some analogous process to a winding-up order or the appointment of a liquidator (TCGA 1992, s. 59A(4)(b)). If that happens, any further gains or losses on asset disposals by the LLP are treated as though the LLP were a company, and always had been so, so that the gains are charged to corporation tax on the entity itself, and not to capital gains tax on the individual members (TCGA 1992, s. 59A(5)(a)). The members of the LLP will then be charged to capital gains tax in the normal way on their disposals of their interests in the partnership, in effect as if they were selling shares in a company or receiving capital distributions on the winding up of a company (TCGA 1992, s. 59A(5)(b)).

Where these provisions apply, the LLP will be treated as though it had never been transparent for capital gains tax purposes, in respect of those assets. So the base cost for the disposals of any assets during a liquidation will be the original base cost of those assets to the LLP as a whole.

Legislation: TCGA 1992, s. 59A

Chapter 5: Tax reliefs available to partners

14-000 Introduction

This chapter covers various reliefs available to partners in the context of funding a partnership, or of joining or leaving partnerships. Specifically, we review the reliefs available to partners when they borrow money to join or fund a partnership, and also the capital gains reliefs.

RELIEF FOR INTEREST PAYMENTS

14-020 Interest payments – general

Relief is available for interest paid on loans used for the following qualifying purposes:

- to purchase plant and machinery for use in a partnership (see ¶14-140);
- to acquire an interest in a partnership (see ¶14-160ff.),

provided the interest is eligible for relief and a claim is made (ITA 2007, s. 383(1)).

The above purposes do not include the generality of purpose for which loans are taken out in the course of a trade or property business, as interest will normally be an allowable deduction in computing the income from that source.

Relief is given by means of a deduction, equal to the amount of the eligible interest, in calculating the individual's net income for the year in which the interest is paid (see step 2 of the calculation in ITA 2007, s. 23) (ITA 2007, s. 383(3), (4)).

Relief is subject to a number of general restrictions and conditions which are discussed below.

Legislation: ITA 2007, s. 383

14-040 Limit on relief

From 2013–14 onwards, there is a limit on the amount of income tax relief that an individual may deduct at step 2 of their income tax calculation for a tax year in relation to certain prescribed reliefs (ITA 2007, s. 24A). The limit is the greater of £50,000 or 25% of the individual's 'adjusted total income' for the tax year.

Relief for interest payments under ITA 2007, Pt. 8, Ch. 1 are specifically included in the list of reliefs subject to the limit (ITA 2007, s. 24A(6)(h)).

14-060　Restrictions on relief

Interest on overdrafts, etc.

Relief is not available for interest paid on any overdrawn account or under credit card arrangements, whatever the purpose of the borrowing (ITA 2007, s. 384(1); see also *Lawson v Brooks* [1992] BTC 53).

Interest exceeding a reasonable commercial amount

FA 2008, Sch. 22, para. 21 amended ITA 2007, s. 384 for interest paid on or after 9 October 2007, so that where interest paid on a loan in a tax year exceeds a reasonable commercial amount of interest on the loan for the relevant period, then interest representing the excess is ineligible for relief.

The relevant period is the tax year or, if the loan exists for part only of the tax year, the part of the tax year for which the loan exists (ITA 2007, s. 384(3)).

A reasonable commercial amount of interest on the loan for the relevant period is an amount which, together with any interest paid before that period (other than unrelieved interest (see below)), represents a reasonable commercial rate of interest on the loan from the date it was made to the end of that period (ITA 2007, s. 384(4)).

'Unrelieved interest' means the excess interest not eligible for relief (ITA 2007, s. 384(5)).

Restriction where arrangements to minimise risk to borrower

ITA 2007, s. 384A was introduced by *Finance Act* 2009, with effect in relation to interest paid on or after 19 March 2009 to counter avoidance schemes where arrangements were put in place that meant that there was only an insignificant risk that the investor could fail to make a profit after the availability of interest relief was taken into account.

Relief is denied if:

- the loan is made as part of arrangements which 'appear very likely to produce a post tax advantage'; and
- the arrangements seem to have been designed to reduce any income tax or capital gains tax to which the borrower (or someone like the borrower) would otherwise be liable.

Arrangements appear very likely to produce a post-tax advantage if one might reasonably assume there is no more than an insignificant risk of a 'post-tax advantage' not being produced (ITA 2007, s. 384A(2)).

This is a two-part test. It is firstly necessary to ascertain whether, within the meaning of the legislation, it is very likely that the incomings from the arrangements will exceed the outgoings on an after-tax basis. If that is the case then it is also necessary to ascertain whether the arrangements seem to have been designed to reduce income tax or capital gains tax liability that would have arisen independently of the arrangements.

The measure will thus deny relief for interest if the loan is made as part of arrangements that are certain (ignoring insignificant risk) to produce a post-tax surplus for the investor by virtue of the interest being eligible for relief, provided that the arrangement seems designed to reduce tax to which the borrower would be liable apart from the arrangements. The legislation will not catch genuine commercial investments in business where there is significant uncertainty as to whether the level of return will secure a post-tax surplus for the investor.

Restriction where cash basis applies

ITA 2007, s. 384B was inserted by FA 2013, with effect for the tax year 2013–14 and subsequent tax years as part of the introduction of the cash basis for calculating taxable profits for small businesses.

Relief is not given on a 'relevant loan' if the partnership to which the loan relates has made an election under ITTOIA 2005, s. 25A to calculate its profits on the cash basis for small businesses (see **Chapter 14**) (instead of in accordance with generally accepted accounting practice) (ITA 2007, s. 384B(1)).

A relevant loan is:

- a loan to buy plant or machinery for partnership use; or
- a loan to invest in partnership and which is not used for purchasing a share in a partnership,

(ITA 2007, s. 384B(2)).

Legislation: ITA 2007, s. 384, 384A and 384B

14-080   Qualifying purpose

A condition for interest to be eligible for relief is that it is paid on borrowings which are used for one or more of the qualifying purposes indicated above. Except in the case of loans for the purchase of plant or machinery (see ¶14-140):

- the loan must be made on the occasion of the expenditure being incurred on the qualifying purpose or within a reasonable time either before or after that expenditure; and
- the monies raised by the loan must not have been used for any other purpose prior to the expenditure for the qualifying purpose,

(ITA 2007, s. 385(2), (3)).

What is 'reasonable' depends upon the circumstances. The monies borrowed may be used to fund expenditure on a qualifying purpose which had already been incurred prior to the making of the loan (ITA 2007, s. 385(1)(b)).

Where under a sale agreement the vendor agrees to grant the purchaser a period of credit in which to pay the full amount of the purchase price, this is to be regarded as the making of a loan used by the purchaser in making the purchase (ITA 2007, s. 385(4)).

Mixed loans

These are loans which are only partly used for a qualifying purpose. Only interest paid in respect of the qualifying part is eligible for relief; the total interest paid being apportioned on the basis that the part of the loan used for qualifying purposes bears to the total loan at the time the loan was used (ITA 2007, s. 386(1), (2) and (4)).

Where a partial repayment of a mixed loan is made, it is specifically provided that from 6 April 2007 the repayment is to be treated as being applied rateably to the qualifying and non-qualifying parts, subject to the exception noted below (ITA 2007, s. 386(3)). The effect is that the proportion of the total interest qualifying for relief will remain unchanged, having been fixed at the outset. The previous legislation, ICTA 1988, s. 367(4), did not make any specific provision as to how partial repayments of mixed loans should be treated, however in practice the approach now codified was adopted.

The exception to the rule that repayments of mixed loans are to be apportioned between the qualifying and non-qualifying parts of the loan, a pro rata reduction does not apply in cases where capital is recovered from the investment financed by the qualifying part of the loan (e.g. the part used to purchase an interest in a partnership, etc.). In this case, the qualifying part of the loan is treated as having been repaid to the extent of the capital recovered (see ¶14-300).

Legislation: ITA 2007, s. 385 and 386

14-100   Exclusion of double relief

Where interest qualifies for relief as a deduction in arriving at net income for income tax purposes it cannot also qualify as a deduction for any other income tax purpose (ITA 2007, s. 387(1)).

Moreover, if, at the time when a self-assessment can no longer be varied, interest has been taken into account as a deduction in arriving at the profits of a trade or a UK or overseas property business, it is not to be allowed as a deduction in arriving at net income for the same tax year. Neither is any other 'connected' interest for that tax year. 'Connected' interest for these purposes means all the interest which can be taken into account in computing the profits and which is payable by the same person on money advanced to him, whether on one or more accounts or whether by different lenders (ITA 2007, s. 387(2)–(7)).

Legislation: ITA 2007, s. 387

14-120   Anti-avoidance

Relief is also unavailable if the interest is paid under a tax relief scheme or tax relief arrangements. A scheme is a tax relief scheme (and arrangements are tax relief arrangements) where the sole or main benefit that might be expected to accrue is the obtaining of a reduction in tax liability by means of relief under the Income Tax Acts (ITA 2007, s. 809ZG, formerly ICTA 1988, s. 787).

Legislation: ITA 2007, s. 809ZG

14-140   Loans to buy plant or machinery for use by a partnership

Relief is available where:

- an individual who is a member of a partnership (ITA 2007, s. 389(2)) pays interest on a loan which is used for capital expenditure on the provision of plant or machinery used by that partnership in carrying on a trade, profession or a property business (ITA 2007, s. 388(1), (2)(a));
- for the period of account in which the interest is paid, the partnership is entitled to capital allowances (or liable to a balancing charge) under CAA 2001, s. 264 in respect of that capital expenditure (ITA 2007, s. 388(2)(b)); and
- the interest is due and payable not later than three years from the end of the period of account in which the loan was made (ITA 2007, s. 389(3)).

The general conditions that:

- the loan must be made on the occasion of the expenditure being incurred on the qualifying purpose or within a reasonable time either before or after that expenditure; and
- the monies raised by the loan must not have been used for any other purpose prior to the expenditure for the qualifying purpose,

(see ¶14-080) are not applicable to relief under this heading (ITA 2007, s. 385(2), (3)).

Where the machinery or plant is used only partly for the trade, etc. carried on by the partnership, only that part of the total interest which it is just and reasonable to attribute to the use in the trade, is eligible for relief. Regard must be had to all the relevant circumstances and, in particular, to the extent of the use for the other purposes (ITA 2007, s. 389(4), (5)).

The predecessor legislation, ICTA 1988, s. 359(1), suggested that relief for interest paid in a period of account was dependent upon the partnership being entitled to a capital allowance for that period. Thus if a 100% first year allowance was given on the asset being brought into use, no allowance would be due in subsequent periods even though the asset may still be in use. A similar situation would arise where the whole of the capital expenditure has been relieved by allowances given in earlier periods. To avoid this interpretation, the partnership is treated as being entitled to a capital allowance for a period of account if it was so entitled in a previous period and no disposal value has yet been required to be brought into account in respect of that plant or machinery (ITA 2007, s. 388(3)).

The predecessor legislation also only referred to the partnership carrying on a trade, profession or vocation. The Tax Law Rewrite team considered that a partnership could not actually carry on a vocation and so that term was not retained in the *Income Tax Act* 2007. A more significant change was the confirmation that relief would be available where the partnership carried on a property business. There are arguments for and against saying that property businesses were always a permitted partnership activity (for the detailed arguments see the *Explanatory Notes to the Income Tax Act 2007*, Annex 1, Change 68). In view of that uncertainty, it is now specifically provided that the permitted partnership activities are the carrying on of a trade, profession or an ordinary property business.

Legislation: ITA 2007, s. 385, 388 and 389

14-160 Loans to invest in partnership

Interest is eligible for relief if it is interest on a loan to an individual used:

- to purchase a share in a partnership; or
- to contribute money to a partnership by way of capital or premium, or by way of loan, where it is used wholly for the purposes of the trade or profession carried on by the partnership; or
- in paying off another loan used for any of these purposes,

(ITA 2007, s. 398(1), (2)).

The following conditions must also be satisfied:

(1) throughout the period from the use of the loan until the interest was paid, the individual has been a member of the partnership (including a 'sleeping partner' but not a limited partner or as a member of an investment limited liability partnership (defined as one whose business, for any accounting period, is mainly the making of investments from which it derives the greater part of its income; ITA 2007, s. 399(6)). Retirement as a partner will therefore terminate any right to relief for subsequent payments of interest even if that former partner is unable to withdraw capital immediately upon leaving the partnership (HMRC Manual SAIM10290); and

(2) in that period the individual has not recovered any capital from the partnership, apart from any amount taken into account in reducing the interest eligible for relief (see ¶14-300),

(ITA 2007, s. 399(1)–(3)).

Note: the predecessor legislation, ICTA 1988, s. 362, required the money lent to the partnership to be used for the purposes of its 'trade, profession or vocation'. The reference to a 'vocation' was omitted when the legislation was rewritten for the *Income Tax Act* 2007 because it was felt that it was actually impossible for a partnership to carry on a vocation. Where, however, the business carried on by the partnership is a property business which generates income from dwelling-houses, relief is restricted (see ¶14-220) and where the business carried on by the partnership is the occupation of woodlands on a commercial basis, relief is denied (see ¶14-360). A further restriction applies where the money is invested in a film partnership (see ¶14-260), where only 40% of the eligible interest qualifies for relief (ITA 2007, s. 399(4)).

Legislation: ITA 2007, s. 399

14-180 Loan to invest in partnership: salaried partners

In Statement of Practice A33 HMRC acknowledged that the predecessor legislation extended 'to salaried partners in a professional firm who are allowed independence of action in handling the affairs of clients and generally so to act that they will be indistinguishable from general partners in their relations with clients'. That Statement has been incorporated into the *Income Tax Act* 2007 because an individual who is not a partner is treated as a partner for these purposes if:

* the partnership carries on a profession (as opposed to a trade);
* the individual is employed in a senior capacity; and
* the individual is allowed to act independently in dealing with clients and to act generally as a partner in relation to those clients,

(ITA 2007, s. 399(5)).

Legislation: ITA 2007, s. 399(5)

14-200 Loan to invest in partnership: Scottish partnerships

The *Partnership Act* 1890 applies in England, Wales and Scotland, but a few provisions specifically apply in Scotland but not in England; in particular, by s. 4(2), in Scotland a partnership is a legal person distinct from the partners of whom it is composed. This can cause some difficulties in determining who has paid and who is entitled to relief.

In the case of *Major (HMIT) v Brodie* [1998] BTC 141, Mr and Mrs Brodie were partners in a trading partnership known as the *Skeldon partnership* which, as a Scottish partnership, was a separate legal entity and was itself a partner in the *Murdoch partnership* along with a Mr Murdoch. Mr and Mrs Brodie took out a loan and introduced the capital into the Skeldon partnership, which then in turn applied it for the purposes of a farming trade carried on by the Murdoch partnership. HMRC sought to deny interest relief under the predecessor legislation, ICTA 1988, s. 362, on the grounds that the monies had not been applied for the purposes of the trade carried on by the Skeldon partnership. The Court held that a trade carried on by a partnership was carried on by the members of that partnership and by each of them. Thus in its capacity as a partner in the Murdoch partnership, the Skeldon partnership was carrying on the farming trade of the Murdoch partnership and the funds had therefore been used for the purposes of a trade carried on by the Skeldon partnership. Although this concerned Scottish partnerships, the High Court considered that the same result would arise in the case of partnerships in England and Wales.

Legislation: ITA 2007, s. 398, 399

14-220   Loan to invest in a partnership: restriction on relief for loans to invest in property partnership

Relief for interest on a loan to buy an interest in a partnership is restricted where the partnership carries on a property business and generates income from residential dwellings. Specifically, the restriction applies where the partnership business, or part of it, is carried on for the purposes of generating income from land consisting of a dwelling-house, or part of a dwelling-house, or an estate, interest or right in or over such land (ITA 2007, s. 399A(1)) but excluding furnished holiday lettings (as defined by ITTOIA 2005, Pt. 3, Ch. 6) (ITA 2007, s. 399A(9)).

Interest is to be apportioned on a just and reasonable basis where only part of the partnership business generates income from residential dwellings (ITA 2007, s. 399A(2)).

Relief is restricted for tax years 2017–18 to 2019–20 and a tax reduction is given instead in respect of the non-deductible amount (i.e. the amount in respect of which relief would otherwise be available but for the restriction) (see ¶14-240). For the tax year 2020–21 and subsequent tax years, no relief will be available and instead a tax reduction will be available for non-deductible qualifying interest payments (see ¶14-240).

The amount of (restricted) relief available is as follows:

2017–18 – 75% of the amount of relief that would be given apart from the restriction;

2018–19 – 50% of the amount of relief that would be given apart from the restriction;

2019–20 – 25% of the amount of relief that would be given apart from the restriction;

2020–21 – no relief available

(ITA 2007, s. 399A(3)–(6)).

The above restrictions are applied after the restriction (to 40%) has been applied in respect of a loan to invest in a film partnership (see ¶14-260) (ITA 2007, s. 399A(7)).

Legislation: ITA 2007, s. 399A

14-240   Loan to invest in a partnership: tax reduction for non-deductible loan interest

If for a tax year an individual would be given relief for an amount ('the relievable amount') by ITA 2007, s. 383(1) (see ¶14-020) but for ITA 2007, s. 399A (see ¶14-220), the individual is entitled to relief for the tax year in respect of that amount, calculated as the following (in effect, the amount of the tax reduction referable to the relievable amount):

$BR \times$ the relievable amount

where BR is the basic rate of income tax for the year.

(ITA 2007, s. 399B)

The tax deduction is deductible at step 6 of the calculation of the individual's income tax liability in ITA 2007, s. 23. It is, therefore, a deduction against tax, not against income, in the same way as other tax reductions such as EIS, VCT relief (ITA 2007, s. 26(1)).

Legislation: ITA 2007, s. 399A and 26

14-260   Loans to invest in film partnerships

Additional conditions are imposed on relief for an investment in a partnership where:

- that partnership carries on a trade whose profits are calculated under the special rules in ITTOIA 2005, Pt. 2, Ch. 9, relating to expenditure on the production or acquisition of films or sound recordings;
- the loan raised by the individual is 'secured on an asset or activity of another partnership' (termed the 'investment partnership') of which the individual is, or has been a member; and
- at any time of the year the proportion of the profits of the investment partnership which are liable to income tax and to which he is entitled, is less than the proportion of his contribution to that partnership's capital,

(ITA 2007, s. 400(1)).

Where these conditions are satisfied, the interest on a loan to invest in a film partnership which is eligible for relief is limited to 40% of that which would otherwise be eligible (ITA 2007, s. 399(4)). Where the restrictions for property partnerships also apply (see ¶14-220), those restrictions are applied after the restriction under ITA 2007, s. 399(4) (ITA 2007, s. 399A(7)).

These provisions were first introduced by FA 2006, s. 75 and apply in respect of payments of interest accruing on or after 10 March 2006 (ITA 2007, Sch. 2, para. 96). They are anti-avoidance measures designed to counter arrangements which seek to shelter the income from the exploitation of the film by loan interest payments. Such arrangements would involve the whole of the individual's investment in the film partnership being funded by a loan set at such a rate of interest as will be equal to the lease rental income from the film. In order to repay the borrowings, the individual invests his own capital in the investment partnership which has a non-resident corporate partner. Capital contributed to this partnership is around 75% by the corporate partner and 25% by the individuals and is invested in a financial instrument which is intended to generate the individuals a capital return sufficient to pay off the loans used to invest in the film partnership. During the life of that instrument the bulk of the income arising is due to the non-resident corporate partner but the position is reversed at the maturity of the financial instrument and the bulk of the capital is received by the individuals. By this means the individuals will have had the benefit of the trading losses of the film partnership caused by the initial expenditure on the production or acquisition of the master tapes, but the subsequent income will have been sheltered by the interest payments. The losses, which would otherwise have created a tax deferral until such time as profits were generated, have therefore been turned into an exemption.

Legislation: ITA 2007, s. 400

14-280   Loans to invest in film partnerships: definitions

A loan is 'secured on an asset or activity of another partnership' if there is an arrangement:

- whereby an asset of that partnership may be used or relied upon, wholly or partly to guarantee repayment of any part of the loan; or
- under which any part of the loan is expected to be repaid out of the assets or income of that partnership, whether directly or indirectly,

(ITA 2007, s. 400(2)).

'Partnership's capital' is interpreted in accordance with generally accepted accounting practice and any amounts lent by the partners or persons connected with them (ITA 2007, s. 400(3)). Connected persons for these purposes are:

- the individual's spouse or civil partner;
- the individual's relatives (i.e. siblings, ancestors or lineal descendants; ITA 2007, s. 994(1));
- the spouses or civil partners of the individual's relatives;
- the relatives of the individual's spouse or civil partner; and
- the spouses or civil partners of relatives of the individual's spouse or civil partner (ITA 2007, s. 400(7), s. 993(2)).

In determining at any point the amount of capital contributed to the investment partnership by the individual or those connected with him, the following are to be taken into account:

- any amount paid to acquire the interest in that partnership held at that point in time;
- any amount made available to another person (and, presumably, used by that person to acquire an interest in that partnership) so far as he has an interest in that partnership at that time;
- any amount the individual has lent to the partnership;
- any amount he has made available to another person which that person has lent to the partnership and which has not been repaid; and
- any other amounts prescribed by regulations made by HMRC,

(ITA 2007, s. 400(4)).

Legislation: ITA 2007, s. 400

14-300 Loan to invest in partnership: withdrawal of relief

The following provisions apply where relief has been claimed in respect of loans to buy an interest in a partnership (see ¶14-160).

Recovery of capital

Where, at any time after the loan is used, the individual recovers any amount of capital from the partnership, they will be treated as having at that time repaid an equal amount of the loan, whether he actually used the capital to repay the loan or not (ITA 2007, s. 406(1), (2)). As a result, the allowable interest will be reduced to such part of the total interest paid as would have been paid had the capital recovered been used to repay the loan (ITA 2007, s. 406(3), (4)).

If only part of the borrowing qualified, the capital recovered is to be set primarily against that part. If, later, the claimants do in fact repay part of their borrowing, the notional and the actual repayments should, so far as is possible, be treated as relating to the same part of the borrowing.

The individual will be treated as having recovered an amount of capital if:

(a) the individual receives consideration of that amount or value:

  (i) for the sale, exchange or assignment of part of the individual's interest in the partnership;

  (ii) for assigning a debt due to the individual from the partnership;

(b) the partnership repays that amount of a loan or advance from the individual; or

(c) the partnership returns that amount of capital to the individual,

(ITA 2007, s. 407(1)–(3)).

Where a sale or agreement is not a bargain made at arm's length, it is treated as consideration of an amount equal to the market value of the subject matter of the disposal (ITA 2007, s. 407(4)).

The conversion of a partnership into a limited liability partnership is not regarded by HMRC as a recovery of capital and therefore relief is not withdrawn in those circumstances (HMRC Manual SAIM10310).

Legislation: ITA 2007, s. 406–407

14-320   Loan to invest in partnership: replacement loans

Where relief is claimed in respect of loans to buy an interest in a partnership (¶14-160), relief will continue to be available if the original loan is repaid by the proceeds of a second loan (assuming all other conditions continue to be satisfied). The original and the replacement loan will generally be treated as a single loan (ITA 2007, s. 408).

Legislation: ITA 2007, s. 408

14-340   Loan to invest in partnership: business successions

Normally, relief would be lost where certain business reorganisations such as a business succession between partnerships or the incorporation of a partnership (because the individual would no longer be a partner). In both these scenarios the predecessor legislation did not strictly provide for a continuation of relief. However, this anomaly was remedied by concession, ESC A43, the final paragraph of which provided for continuation of relief in these circumstances, provided 'the conditions for relief would have been met if the loan had been a new loan taken out by that person to invest in the new business entity. The rules restricting or withdrawing relief where the borrower recovers any capital from the business continue to apply in the normal way.'

ESC A43 was enacted as ITA 2007, s. 409(1)–(2) and 410 as follows:

Between partnerships

Relief will continue to be available if the partnership is dissolved if the individual becomes a member (or a salaried partner) of a new partnership formed to carry on the whole or part of the undertaking of the old partnership and interest payable on the loan up to the dissolution qualified for relief. In such a case, the old and new partnerships are to be treated as if they were the same (ITA 2007, s. 409).

Incorporation

Relief also continues to be available following incorporation of a partnership, where:

- the original loan qualified for relief;
- the partnership is involved in a transaction as a result of which the individual acquires shares in or makes a loan to another company (or co-operative); and
- had the original loan been made at the time of this transaction and applied for the purchase of the shares acquired or the money lent under the transaction, it would have qualified under one of the provisions relating to close companies, employee-controlled companies or co-operatives,

(ITA 2007, s. 410(1)).

Where these conditions are satisfied, the original loan is treated as having been used for the purchase of the 'new' shares or lending money to the 'new' company or co-operative (ITA 2007, s. 410(2)).

Legislation: ITA 2007, s. 409, 410

14-360 Loan to invest in partnership: ineligibility of interest: commercial woodlands

No relief is available where the business being carried on by the partnership is the occupation of woodlands managed on a commercial basis with a view to profits (ITA 2007, s. 411(1), (5)).

Where that occupation is only part of the partnership's business, only that part of the interest which on a just and reasonable basis can be attributed to that occupation is denied relief. The attribution has to be made having regard to all relevant circumstances and, in particular, the extent of the other part of the business (ITA 2007, s. 411(2), (3)).

Legislation: ITA 2007, s. 411

14-380   Relief for interest paid: certificates from lenders

Information

A person paying interest and claiming relief under ITA 2007, Pt. 8, Ch. 1 is entitled to ask (with such request being made in writing) the lender for a statement showing:

- the date the debt was incurred;
- the amount of the debt when incurred;
- the interest paid in the tax year; and
- the name and address of the debtor.

Under self-assessment, the borrower will only normally be required to provide this information to substantiate a claim for interest relief if HMRC raise enquiries into the return or the claim. The claimant is able to obtain a certificate from the lender if he or she needs or wants to do so. Lenders do not need to issue certificates routinely.

Legislation: ITA 2007, s. 412

CAPITAL GAINS TAX RELIEFS

14-400   Importance of CGT reliefs to partnerships

Being a partner or owning assets used in a partnership business will generally bring such an individual within the scope of the various exemptions or deferment opportunities on the disposal of those assets or of part or all of the partnership share, provided all the other conditions associated with the particular relief in question are satisfied.

By far, the most important relief will be entrepreneurs' relief, but it is also important to consider:

- roll-over or hold-over relief on replacement of business assets (see ¶14-640);
- hold-over relief on gifts of business assets (see ¶14-660);
- incorporation of the partnership (see **Chapter 6**); and
- negligible value claims (see ¶14-680).

14-420   Entrepreneurs' relief

Entrepreneurs' relief was a hastily produced solution to a problem created by the Government's decision, announced in the 2007 Pre-Budget Report, to 'simplify' capital gains tax by abolishing taper relief and setting a single rate of tax at 18%. The problem was that under the taper relief regime, most business owners were expecting to pay an effective rate of only 10% on the disposal of their businesses. In order to placate the criticism which resulted, this new relief was proposed. It is largely based on the old retirement relief which was last available in 2002–03 and its effect is to preserve the effective 10% rate for businesses which applied under taper relief.

The relief provides for a lower rate of capital gains tax, upon a claim being made, in respect of 'qualifying business disposals', of which there are three:

(1)   a material disposal of business assets (by an individual);

(2)   a disposal associated with a material disposal (by an individual); and

(3)   a disposal of trust business assets (by trustees).

Legislation: TCGA 1992, Pt. V, Ch. 3, s. 169H

14-440   Material disposal of business assets

A 'material disposal' is one of business assets which have been owned for a minimum of one year and falls into one of three categories:

(1)   the whole or part of a business (see ¶14-460);

(2)   assets used in a business at the time it was discontinued (see ¶14-480); or

(3)   shares in or securities of a 'personal company' which is either a trading company or the holding company of a trading group and the individual was an officer or employee of that company or another company in the same group.

See ¶14-600 for commentary on the availability of entrepreneurs' relief on shares in companies which are partners in a partnership.

Legislation: TCGA 1992, s. 169I

14-460   Disposal of whole or part of a business

For such a disposal to qualify as a material disposal, the business must have been owned by the individual throughout the period of one year ending with the disposal (TCGA 1992, s. 169I(3)).

This relief will potentially be useful in two situations. The first is where an individual forms a partnership or joins an existing partnership, and contributes assets (including goodwill) into the partnership, as the relief can apply to the part-disposal. The second is where partnership asset-sharing ratios change, when there may be a deemed part-disposal of assets to which the relief might apply.

In the case of a partnership business, it is treated as owned by each individual who is a member of the partnership at that particular time and the disposal by an individual of all or part of his interest in partnership assets is treated as the disposal of the whole or part of the business carried on by the partnership (TCGA 1992, s. 169I(8)(b), (c)). Therefore, a partner may claim relief for:

* a disposal of the whole of their interest in the partnership – by treating it as a disposal of the whole of a business;
* a disposal of part of their interest in the partnership – by treating it as the disposal of part of a business;

- a disposal *by the partnership* of the whole or part of the partnership business – by treating the partnership as owned by the individual;

In addition, it is provided that a sole trader who takes another person into partnership, thus disposing of an interest in the assets of his business, is to be treated as disposing of a part of his business (TCGA 1992, s. 169I(8)(a)).

A point to bear in mind is that there can be the disposal of a business where there are different purchasers of the various assets; the emphasis is on the disposal by the individual, not what has been acquired by the purchasers.

A business is something more than a mere collection of assets. For the purposes of entrepreneurs' relief, it is defined as a trade, profession or vocation which is conducted on a commercial basis with a view to profit (TCGA 1992, s. 169S(1)). Thus, relief is not due where an individual or partnership sells one or more of its business assets whilst continuing with its business as before.

The requirement that there must be a disposal of a business or part of a business was also a feature of retirement relief and resulted in a string of cases before the court relating to farming, where the point at issue was whether a disposal of part of the farmland was the disposal of part of the farming business. The principles established by these cases will be relevant for entrepreneurs' relief.

Legislation: TCGA 1992, s. 169I

14-480   Disposal of assets after business discontinued

To cater for situations where an outright sale of a business is not possible, relief is also available where business is discontinued and there are subsequent disposals of the individual assets which were used in that business at the time of its cessation (TCGA 1992, s. 169I(2)(b)).

The conditions to be satisfied are:

- the business must have been owned by the individual throughout the period of one year ending with the cessation of the business; and
- the date of the disposal must be within three years of that cessation,

(TCGA 1992, s. 169I(4)).

A disposal of assets used in a partnership business which has been discontinued also qualifies as a material disposal subject to the same conditions.

HMRC have confirmed that relief will not be denied in cases where TCGA 1992, s. 28 would fix the date of disposal of assets sold by contract at a date before the cessation of trading (CIOT Guidance for members, *Entrepreneurs' Relief – Practical points*, para. 20).

Legislation: TCGA 1992, s. 169I

14-500   Disposal associated with material disposal

Where an asset used in the business of a partnership (or trading company) is owned personally by a partner (or director), relief is available for a disposal of these assets where they are associated with a material disposal (see ¶14-440).

There are four conditions to be satisfied for a disposal to qualify:

(1) either:

   (i)   condition A1A – the individual must have a partnership interest of less than 5% and must make a material disposal of business assets that consists of the disposal of his entire interest in the partnership assets, and he must have held at least a 5% interest in the partnership's assets throughout a continuous period of at least three years in the eight years ending with the date of the disposal (with no partnership purchase arrangements in place at the date of the disposal) (new TCGA 1992, s. 169K(A1A) as inserted by *Finance Act* 2016); or

   (ii) condition A1 – the individual must make a material disposal of the part of his interest in the partnership; which must be at least a 5% interest in the partnership assets (with no partnership purchase arrangements in place at the date of disposal); (TCGA 1992, s. 169K(1A)); or

   (iii) conditions A2 and A3 – the individual must make a material disposal of at least a 5% interest in the shares/securities in a company, with no share purchase arrangements in place (TCGA 1992, s. 169KA(1B)–(1D); and

(2) condition B – the individual makes the associated disposal as part of a withdrawal from participation in the business carried on by the partnership (or by the company or a fellow member of a trading group); and

(3) condition C – the asset which is the subject of the associated disposal has been in use for the purposes of that business throughout the one-year period ending with the material disposal, or, if earlier, the date on which the business was terminated; and

(4) condition D – the associated disposal must be of an asset that the individual has owned for at least three years ending with the date of the disposal but this condition only applies for assets acquired on or after 13 June 2016 (new TCGA 1992, s. 169K(4A) as inserted by *Finance Act* 2016).

(TCGA 1992, s. 169K).

Minimum disposal requirement and partnership/share purchase arrangements

The 5% specified minimum disposal requirement and restrictions over arrangements for the partner to subsequently increase his interest in the partnership were introduced by *Finance Act* 2015, with effect in relation to disposals on or after 18 March 2015 (only). This was in order to remove an unintended facility under the entrepreneurs; relief rules that enabled relief to be claimed by an individual on a disposal of a private asset used in a business without the individual permanently reducing their participation in the business by a meaningful amount. However, *Finance Act* 2015 provisions were widely criticised on the basis that they in fact prevented entrepreneurs' relief from being available in many commercial situations that were not motivated by tax avoidance. For example, the definition of 'partnership purchase agreements' would include standard accruer clauses whereby the partnership share of an outgoing partner accrues automatically to the remaining partners if the remaining partners were treated as 'connected' with the outgoing partner (i.e. as connected persons). In addition, the definition would seem to prevent relief from being available under TCGA 1992, s. 169K for family partnerships because the retiring partner would be otherwise connected with the remaining partners. It was also felt that the requirement to dispose of a minimum 5% interest impacted unfairly on individuals who had already passed on part of their holding to family members as part of a staged withdrawal from the business, but were in fact left with less than 5%. As a result, amended legislation was included in *Finance Act* 2016 and backdated to cover disposals on or after 18 March 2015, with the effect that *Finance Act* 2015 version of s. 169K is treated as never having had effect.

Partnership purchase arrangements for the purposes of conditions A1 or A1A are arrangements under which the partner or a person connected with him (e.g. spouse, civil partner, sibling or child, etc.) is 'entitled to acquire' an interest in the partnership or to increase their interest. This includes a share in the income or profits of the partnership, or a fractional share in the assets of the partnership, or an interest in such a share. However, partnership purchase arrangements do not include the material disposal itself, so that partnership succession within a family can still qualify for entrepreneurs' relief (TCGA 1992, s. 169K(1AA) as inserted by *Finance Act* 2016).

Partnership purchase arrangements for the purposes of condition B (the withdrawal from the business), are arrangements under which the partner or a person connected with him (e.g. spouse, civil partner, sibling or child, etc.) is 'entitled to acquire' an interest in the partnership or to increase their interest. This includes a share in the income or profits of the partnership, or a fractional share in the assets of the partnership, or an interest in such a share, without the exclusion of the material disposal itself. However, partnership purchase arrangements under this provision do not include arrangements that satisfy conditions A1A or A1, so ensuring that entrepreneurs' relief remains available for family successions (TCGA 1992, s. 169K(3AA) as inserted by *Finance Act* 2016).

Share purchase arrangements are arrangements under which an individual or a person connected with him (e.g. spouse, civil partner, sibling or child, etc.) is entitled to acquire shares or securities of the company or of a company which is a member of the same trading group (s. 169K(1E)).

As is the case for relevant material disposals of partnership interests, the definition of 'share purchase arrangements' on a relevant material disposal of shares or securities is also amended to ensure that the arrangements do not include the material disposal itself (TCGA 1992, s. 169K(1E), as amended by *Finance Act* 2016).

Share purchase arrangements for the purposes of condition B (the withdrawal from the business), are arrangements under which the partner or a person connected with him (e.g. spouse, civil partner, sibling or child, etc.) is 'entitled to acquire' shares or securities of the company or of a company which is a member of the same trading group. However, share purchase arrangements under this provision do not include arrangements that satisfy conditions A2 or A3, so ensuring that entrepreneurs' relief remains available for family successions (TCGA 1992, s. 169K(3BA) as inserted by *Finance Act* 2016).

Additionally, *Finance Act* 2016 inserts new subs. 169K(6A) which prevents arrangements entered into before both the material and associated disposals, and which are not connected with those disposals, from being partnership or share purchase arrangements. It ensures that pre-existing arrangements (unconnected to the material of associated disposal) for succession to a business, or ownership of shares in the event of retirement or death, will not prevent a claim to entrepreneurs' relief on an associated disposal.

An amendment is also made to TCGA 1992, s. 169K(9) to clarify that a partner's interest in the partnership's assets is to be determined by reference to his or her share in capital profits.

Minimum ownership period

Finance Act 2016 also inserts new subs. 169K(4A) which consists of a new condition which must be met in order for a disposal to be an associated disposal. The asset disposed of must have been owned by the claimant throughout the three years immediately preceding the disposal. Previously there was no requirement for any minimum ownership period (although the third condition (above) imposed a minimum period for which the asset must have been used in the business). This amendment takes effect in relation to disposals on or after 13 June 2016, so that it does not apply to disposals that qualified for entrepreneurs' relief under the rules as they stood between 18 March 2015 and the date of the publication of the new rule.

The legislation, like that for retirement relief, does not actually specify that both the material and associated disposals should take place at the same time, or indeed, in any particular order. They must, however, share the same objective: that of enabling the individual to withdraw from the business concerned. To cater for situations where a partnership (or company) ceases to trade and there is an interval between the material disposal and the associated disposal, HMRC will accept that a disposal of an asset is associated with a material disposal if the disposal of that 'associated' asset takes place:

- within one year of the cessation of a business;
- within three years of the cessation of a business where the asset has not been leased or used for any other purpose at any time after that cessation; or
- where the business has not ceased, within three years of the material disposal provided the asset has not been used for any purpose other than that of the business.

(HMRC *Capital Gains Manual* CG63995)

Under retirement relief, HMRC took the view that a withdrawal from the business required only that the individual should reduce his interest in the partnership (or holding in the company). It did not mean that he should withdraw from working in the business concerned. This view is also taken for entrepreneurs' relief (see *Capital Gains Manual* CG63995).

Legislation: TCGA 1992, s. 169K

14-520   Restrictions on relief for associated disposals

Relief for associated disposals is restricted where:

- the assets concerned have been used for the purposes of the business during only part of the individual's period of ownership;
- only a part of the asset has been so used;
- the individual was a partner (officer or employee) for only part of the period in which the assets were used for business purposes; or
- during any part of the period of ownership falling after 5 April 2008 (FA 2008, Sch. 3, para. 6) when the asset was in use for the purposes of the business, that use by the partnership (or company) was dependent upon the payment of rent (or any other form of consideration for its use: TCGA 1992, s. 169S(5)),

(TCGA 1992, s. 169P(4)).

Where these conditions are satisfied, the relief is to be restricted to an amount which is 'just and reasonable'. In other words, only the just and reasonable part of the gain is to be reduced by the relief and the balance remains taxable in full (TCGA 1992, s. 169P(1)–(3)).

In arriving at the relievable amount of the gain, consideration is to be given to the periods of time concerned in the situations in the first two bullet points, the proportion of the asset used in situations in the third and, in the final situation, the extent to which the rent paid was less than a commercial rent (TCGA 1992, s. 169P(5)).

Similar restrictions were previously applicable for both retirement and taper relief. However, whilst retirement relief was restricted where rent was paid for the use of the asset, taper relief was not.

The expanded definition of rent to include other forms of consideration will also catch situations where an enhanced partnership profit share is received in recognition of the use of the asset or where the partnership pays the interest on a loan taken out by a partner to purchase the asset concerned.

Legislation: TCGA 1992, s. 169P

14-540   Disposal by trustees

A disposal by the trustees of a settlement qualifies for entrepreneurs' relief where there is an individual who is a 'qualifying beneficiary' and the disposal is of 'settlement business assets' which comprise either:

- shares in or securities of a company; or
- assets which were previously used for the purposes of a business carried on by the qualifying beneficiary, either alone or in partnership with others,

and form part of the settled property (TCGA 1992, s. 169J(1), (2)).

Where the disposal is of assets used in a business carried on by the qualifying beneficiary:

- they must have been used for the purposes of the business throughout the period of one year ending within the three years prior to the disposal; and
- the business must have ceased (or the qualifying beneficiary ceased to be a member of the partnership carrying on the business (TCGA 1992, s. 169J(6)(b)), either on the disposal or within the preceding three years,

(TCGA 1992, s. 169J(5)).

A qualifying beneficiary is one who has an 'interest in possession' in that part of the settled property which includes the assets, shares or securities which are the subject of the disposal (TCGA 1992, s. 169J(3)).

The term 'interest in possession', in summary, means the right to enjoy the income (if any) as it arises from the settled property without having to rely upon any discretionary powers of the trustees. The most common example of an interest in possession is that of a life tenant (in Scotland, a life renter).

However, where there is at least one other beneficiary who, at what is termed the 'material time', has an interest in possession in that part of the settled property which contains the assets (shares or securities), the trustee's relief is restricted if that other beneficiary is not a qualifying beneficiary. Only what is termed the 'relevant portion' of the gain will be reduced by the relief; the remainder will be chargeable in full (TCGA 1992, s. 169O(1)–(3)).

The 'relevant portion' is the proportion that the qualifying beneficiary's interest in that part of the settled property which contains the business assets or shares concerned bears to the total interests of all the beneficiaries in that same part, including the qualifying beneficiary himself (TCGA 1992, s. 169O(4)). The qualifying beneficiary's interest for these purposes is the interest in possession by which he is a qualifying beneficiary and not any other interest he might have (TCGA 1992, s. 169O(5)).

The 'material time' is the end of the one-year period ending within the three years before the disposal throughout which the business is carried on by the qualifying beneficiary.

A claim for relief must be made jointly by the trustees and the qualifying beneficiary (TCGA 1992, s. 169M(2)) Help Sheet 275 *Entrepreneurs' Relief* contains a suitable claim form.

Trustees are not entitled to an 'allowance' of entrepreneurs' relief in the same way as individuals. Any relief given to trustees is treated as having been given to the 'qualifying beneficiary' and serves to reduce his entitlement for future disposals (TCGA 1992, s. 169N(7)).

Where there are two qualifying disposals made on the same day, one by the trustees and the other by an individual who is also a qualifying beneficiary of that trust, the trustees' disposal is to be treated as having occurred after the one made by the individual (TCGA 1992, s. 169N(8)).

The effect of these provisions is to restrict an individual's relief threshold by the relief granted to trustees of a settlement of which he is a qualifying beneficiary.

Legislation: TCGA 1992, s. 169J, 169O, 169M and 169N

14-560   Restriction to relevant business assets

Where the qualifying business disposal is one comprising the disposal of the whole or part of a business, the 'relevant gains or losses' to be taken into account in computing relief are those which arise on 'relevant business assets'. These are defined as specifically including goodwill, and:

- in the case of the disposal of a business (or part of a business) carried on by the individual or by a partnership of which he was a member (see ¶14-460); the assets used for the purposes of that business;
- in the case of a trustees' disposal (see ¶14-540) assets used for the purposes of a business carried on by a qualifying beneficiary either as a sole trader or in partnership with others;
- in the case of an associated disposal (see ¶14-500) assets used for the purposes of a business carried on by the partnership or company concerned; and
- in all cases, excluding shares, securities and other assets held as investments,

(TCGA 1992, s. 169L).

Because the relief is given for the disposal of a business rather than individual assets, the intention behind this restriction is to deny relief to those assets forming part of the business which are held as investments or are otherwise not used for business purposes. To apply the restriction to associated disposals seems unnecessary as such a disposal can only occur if the asset is in use for the purposes of the business concerned.

Legislation: TCGA 1992, s. 169L

14-580   Relevant business assets: goodwill

Finance Act 2015 introduced TCGA 1992, s. 169LA, with effect in relation to disposals on or after 3 December 2014, so as to prevent individuals from claiming entrepreneurs' relief on disposals of goodwill when they transferred the business to a related close company. The restriction did not extend to partners in a firm who did not hold or acquire any stake in the successor company, unless they were connected to participators in the company. The change was intended to prevent certain abuses involving entrepreneurs' relief. The particular mischief targeted was as described at ¶15-020, however, it was subsequently recognised that the restrictions introduced by *Finance Act* 2015 also limited the availability of relief on some transactions where there was no abuse. Accordingly, *Finance Act* 2016 amended TCGA 1992, s. 169LA so as to mitigate the disadvantage suffered by some as a result of the earlier changes. The amendments are retrospectively applied, with effect in relation to disposals on or after 3 December 2014.

Post Finance Act 2016 position

For disposals on or after 3 December 2014, TCGA 1992, s. 169LA(4) provides that goodwill is not a relevant business asset for the purposes of entrepreneurs' relief, if two requirements are satisfied. These are that the claimant (referred to as P) holds 5% or more of either the company's shares or the voting rights in the company.

If P holds less than 5% of both shares and voting rights, entrepreneurs' relief may be due. Thus retiring partners can claim entrepreneurs' relief on selling their share of the goodwill to the company.

Similarly, where a partnership business is acquired by a company in return for small shareholdings being issued to the vendors, the vendor partners can claim entrepreneurs' relief on selling their shares of the goodwill to the company.

Shares and rights held by companies and trustees (but not individuals) connected with P are also taken into account in applying these new conditions.

The original legislation in FA 2015 provided that goodwill was not a relevant business asset for the purposes of entrepreneurs' relief if the claimant was a related party in relation to the company. However, the FA 2015 rules have been repealed and replaced retrospectively by the FA 2016 rules.

(TCGA 1992, s. 169LA(1)(aa)).

Entrepreneurs' relief may also be claimed on a gain which accrues when goodwill is transferred to a close company where three further conditions given in TCGA 1992, s. 169LA(1B) are met, despite the claimant holding 5% or more of the acquiring company's shares or voting rights (TCGA 1992, s. 169LA(1A)). The three conditions are:

(1)   The individual (or related party) disposes of the whole of his or her holding in the acquiring company to another company (A) within 28 days (of the disposal of goodwill to that company); and

Where A is a close company, immediately before the end of the 28 day period;

(2)   the individual (or related party) holds less than 5% of the ordinary share capital of A (or of the ordinary share capital of any other company which is a member of the same group of companies as A); and

(3)   the individual (or related party) holds less than 5% of the voting rights in A (or in any other company which is a member of the same group of companies as A).

The purpose of these rules is to allow the incorporation of a partnership preparatory to a sale of the new company to a third party.

(TCGA 1992, s. 169LA(1B), (1C)).

Where an individual is party to anti-avoidance arrangements, the main purpose of which is to secure that the restriction by s. 169LA(4) does not apply, then s. 169LA(4) applies (to the extent that it would not otherwise do so) (TCGA 1992, s. 169LA(6), (7)).

Finance Act 2015 restrictions (superseded)

As originally introduced by *Finance Act* 2015, the restriction on goodwill being treated as a relevant business asset for the purposes of entrepreneurs' relief (TCGA 1992, s. 169LA(4)) was to apply where:

- a person disposed of goodwill as part of a qualifying business disposal directly or indirectly to a close company (a company controlled by five or fewer participators or by participators who are also directors);
- that person was a related party in relation to the close company (definitions in CTA 2009, s. 835 to apply for these purposes; i.e. that person was a participator or associate of a participator in the close company, or a participator or associate of a participator in a company that controlled or held a majority interest in the close company); and
- that person was not a retiring partner.

A retiring partner was broadly a person who was only a related party of the close company because he was associated with his fellow partners who were participators in the company and who was not a participator in the close company himself, nor were there any arrangements for him to become one. Where a partnership incorporated and one of the partners retired, any gain on the disposal of goodwill would have remained eligible for entrepreneurs' relief. The concept of retiring partner was retrospectively removed by *Finance Act* 2016.

Legislation: TCGA 1992, s. 169LA

14-600   Corporate partnerships and entrepreneurs' relief

Background

The requirements for the availability of entrepreneurs' relief on disposal of shares in a trading company are relatively straightforward. The shares must be disposed of by an individual who is an officer or employee of the company, and who holds 5% or more of the share capital of that company, together with at least 5% of the voting power. These conditions must all have been satisfied for one year to the date of disposal.

HMRC have become aware of a number of structures put in place in order to effectively allow individuals with a lower shareholding to access the entrepreneurs' relief. One such structure obviously involved some form of corporate partnership. In Diagram 5a, we see a company with a large venture capital stake and four members of the management team each with 3% of the company's shares, so that they do not qualify for entrepreneurs' relief on a disposal of that company. Conversely in Diagram 5b, the trade is now carried on in partnership between the original company, owned wholly by the venture capitalists, and by a separate company owned 25% each by the management team. The argument is that both companies are trading together, therefore both of them are trading companies, and the individual members of the management team hold sufficiently large a stake as to qualify for entrepreneurs' relief.

Diagram 5a

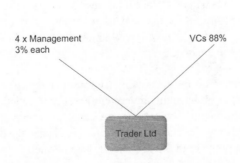

4 x Management
3% each

VCs 88%

Trader Ltd

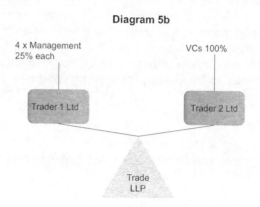

Diagram 5b

New legislation

This was clearly considered offensive by HMRC (although it has taken them seven years either to spot the problem or to decide to do something about it). As a result, *Finance Act* 2015 amended the definitions of 'trading company' and 'trading group' for entrepreneurs' relief purposes so as to exclude activities carried on by a company as a member of a partnership from being treated as trading activities (TCGA 1992, s. 4A). The amendments came into force with effect from 18 March 2015.

However, it was subsequently recognised that, whilst preventing certain abuses involving entrepreneurs' relief, the restrictions imposed by *Finance Act* 2015 had also limited the availability of relief on some disposals of shares where the shareholder had made a genuine indirect investment in a trading business carried on by a joint venture company. Accordingly, *Finance Act* 2016 retrospectively changes the meaning of 'trading company' and 'trading group' as those terms are used for the purposes of entrepreneurs' relief, with effect in relation to disposals of shares which take place on or after 18 March 2015 in order to reduce the unintended effects of the earlier changes.

Under the revised rules, activities carried on by a joint venture company may be treated as carried on by a company which holds shares in it (an 'investing company'). This attribution of activities will take place if the entrepreneurs' relief claimant has an effective interest in the joint venture company of 5% or more (effective interest being defined in terms of the claimant's directly and indirectly held shareholdings, and of the voting power he or she controls).

Similarly, activities carried on by a company as a partner in a trading firm will be treated as trading activities of that company for entrepreneurs' relief purposes subject to two requirements. The first requirement is that the claimant has an effective share of the partnership of 5% or more. The second requirement is that the claimant controls 5% or more of the voting power in the firm's corporate partners.

Legislation: TCGA 1992, s. 169S and Sch. 7ZA (as inserted by *Finance Act* 2016)

14-620   Entrepreneurs' relief examples

Disposal of whole or part of a business

Example 1

R has been an equal member of a four person trading partnership for several years. He retires completely from the partnership and disposes of his interest in partnership assets to the other partners, realising gains of £125,000. All of these gains will qualify for Entrepreneurs' Relief as they will constitute a material disposal of the whole of R's interest in the partnership.

Alternatively R may decide to work part time and agrees to reduce his partnership share to 10% from the original 25%. He sells the balance of his interests in the partnership assets to the other partners and realises chargeable gains of £75,000. R may claim Entrepreneurs' Relief because the 15% share of the partnership interests he disposed of will constitute a material disposal of part of his interest in the business of the partnership.

Example 2

F has carried on a retail business for five years. In July 2010, he takes on W as a partner. W pays £300,000 to F to enter into the partnership agreement which shares the interest in all of the business assets equally between them. The £300,000 received by F is a capital receipt in his hands which may give rise to a gain, as he disposes of a 50% interest in each of the business assets. Those gains may qualify for Entrepreneurs' Relief because F's disposal is a material disposal of part of his business to W, his new business partner.

(HMRC Manual CG63980)

Associated disposals

Example 1

W, M and S are in partnership running a chain of retail chemists. W owns one of the shops used by the business. He decides to leave the partnership and move abroad. M and S continue in partnership.

W intends at the time of leaving the partnership to sell the shop, which continues to be used by the partnership, to M. However M needs time to arrange his finances to allow the sale to proceed. W disposes of the shop to M 18 months after leaving the partnership. So the sale of the shop qualifies as an 'associated disposal' as the business does not cease, the shop continued to be used in the business and the disposal of the shop takes place within three years of W leaving the partnership.

(HMRC Manual CG63995)

Example 2

Mrs B is in business as a dairy farmer in partnership with her two sons. In 2009, she withdraws from the business and disposes of her share in the partnership to her sons who continue the business, and this gives rise to a gain that qualifies for Entrepreneurs' Relief. But the milk quota which the partnership used is owned by her personally (because originally she was a sole farmer at the time it was allocated), and she also sells this milk quota to her sons at a gain. This gain will also qualify for relief as an 'associated disposal'.

(HMRC Manual CG64000)

Example 3

On 5 April 2010, M leaves the partnership of which he has been a member for 12 years and sells his one-third partnership interest, to the remaining two partners, making a gain of £250,000. Throughout that 12 years, M has personally owned the property from which the firm has traded. For the last six of those years (since 6 April 2004), the partnership paid him a full market rent for its use. At the time he leaves the business, he also sells the property to the remaining partners, making an 'associated' gain of £100,000. He claims Entrepreneurs' Relief – all the conditions are met and there has been no previous claim.

- If no adjustment was made in respect of the rent, relief would be due on both gains totalling £350,000.

However, because for 6 of the total 12 years he was a partner a full market rent was paid to M for the business use of the property a proportion of the gain relating to the premises will not attract relief. Only the period for which rent was paid after 6 April 2008 can be taken into account. This would be two of the 12 years the property was in use for the business. A 'just and reasonable' amount in these circumstances would be:

	£	Eligible for ER £
Total gain on property	100,000	
Apportioned:		
10 years from 6 April 1998 to 5 April 2008	83,333	83,333
2 years from 6 April 2008 to 5 April 2010	16,667	
Gain on partnership interest		250,000
		333,333

If however the rent paid by the partnership to M was only two-thirds of a full market rent, the 'just and reasonable' amount must take this into account:

	£	Eligible for ER £
Total gain on property	100,000	
Apportioned:		
10 years from 6 April 1998 to 5 April 2008	83,333	83,333
2 years from 6 April 2008 to 5 April 2010 (of which 1/3 qualifies)	16,667	5,556
Gain on partnership interest		250,000
		338,889

(HMRC Manual CG64145)

14-640   Replacement of business assets by partners

Broadly speaking, where a gain accrues to a partner on the disposal of a qualifying asset and the disposal proceeds are reinvested by him in assets of a certain type, within the period 12 months before and three years after the disposal of the 'old' assets, on making a claim the gain is rolled over and the base cost of the 'new' asset is accordingly reduced (TCGA 1992, s. 152). The replacement of business assets generally is not considered in detail here and the following commentary considers its practical application to partnerships.

The relief does not, in terms, refer to partnerships, although its application to partnerships seems to be implied by the reference to a disposal or acquisition of an interest in assets used in the trade and in the terms of SP D11 and ESC D23.

The 'old' and 'new' assets must be used for the purposes of a trade carried on *by the partner*, 'trade' including a profession or vocation (TCGA 1992, s. 158(2)). There is no need for the partner to be personally acting in the conduct of the business at the time of the disposal or reinvestment, merely that he was carrying on a trade. Clearly therefore a sleeping partner (see ¶10-420) will qualify for relief.

There appear to be two differing views as to whether a limited partner is able to obtain roll-over relief: a limited partner is debarred from taking part in the management of the firm's business by the *Limited Partnership Act* 1907, s. 6(1) but it is uncertain whether this prevents such partner from carrying on the partnership trade. The better view seems to be that a limited partner can benefit from the relief. Certainly this would appear to be HMRC's view, since they consider that, for capital gains tax purposes, a limited partner is treated as is any other partner (*Capital Gains Manual*, CG27290/ CG27100). In the case of a limited liability partnership (see ¶10-280ff.), there should be no difficulty, since the partners in such an enterprise are not prohibited from being fully involved in the running of the business.

The gain may be derived from the partner's personal ownership of the asset, for example when the asset is transferred to the partnership, or may be allocated to him as a result of his fractional share in partnership assets.

The assets disposed of and acquired do not have to be used in the same trade. The trades carried on by a person either successively or at the same time are treated as if both or all were a single trade (TCGA 1992, s. 157), while it is irrelevant whether the trades are carried on outside the UK.

Example

To illustrate the extensive nature of the relief, if the Kenneth Thompson Partnership realises a chargeable gain of £30,000 on disposal proceeds of £75,000, and the three partners share asset surpluses equally, Kenneth, as one of the partners, is treated as making a gain of £10,000 on a disposal for £25,000. The alternatives open to him include:

(1) The Kenneth Thompson Partnership could reinvest the proceeds in qualifying assets for use in the trade(s) it carries on.

(2) Kenneth could purchase qualifying assets costing £25,000 for use in the partnership's trade(s).

(3) Qualifying assets costing £25,000 could be bought by Kenneth for use in a trade he carries on alone.

(4) Kenneth could join another partnership and either purchase qualifying assets for use in that partnership's trade, or the firm could purchase such assets, provided in the latter case that Kenneth's share of the acquisition cost was at least £25,000. Alternatively, he could purchase a share of the goodwill of that partnership.

A combination of these could be used to obtain relief.

On a partnership merger, roll-over relief is available to continuing partners in the new firm, inter alia, in so far as proceeds from any deemed disposal of shares in assets in the 'old' firm are reinvested in shares in assets put into, or subsequently acquired within the statutory period by, the new firm (SP D12, para. 10).

'PARTNERSHIPS

(10) Mergers

10.1. Where the members of two or more existing partnerships come together to form a new one, the CGT treatment will follow the same principles as those for changes in partnership sharing ratios. If gains arise for reasons similar to those covered in section 6 and section 7 above, it may be possible for roll-over relief under TCGA92/S152 to be claimed by any partner continuing in the partnership, insofar as he disposes of part of his share in the assets of the old firm and acquires a share in other assets put into the "merged" firm. Where, however, the consideration given for the shares in chargeable assets acquired is less than the consideration for those disposed of, relief will be restricted under TCGA92/S153.'

Notwithstanding the wording of SP D12, para. 10, any continuing partner might in fact claim relief in respect of each separate gain by reference to any reinvestment within the appropriate time scale in any appropriate asset or assets, including:

(1)   a share in one or more assets brought into the merged partnership by other firms (each asset considered separately);

(2)   a share in any asset subsequently acquired by the merged partnership;

(3)   a subsequent increase in asset surplus ratio within the merged firm reflecting the acquisition of an interest in each asset considered separately (whether or not reflected in a revaluation of assets or a payment outside the accounts); or

(4)   assets or interests in assets wholly outside the partnership.

It appears to be HMRC's view that the acceptance by a partner of a partnership asset by way of distribution in specie – say, an asset not transferred to the new firm – is not an acquisition (although this is less clear-cut than the disposal position below). If that were the case, this could not be used to roll-over the gain.

To qualify for relief, the 'old' assets must have been used and used only for the purposes of the trade. HMRC have stated that where an asset owned by a partner is used in its trade or profession by the partnership of which he is a member, roll-over relief in principle is available on the disposal of that asset. Relief is not restricted if any rent is paid by the partnership.

Practical problems can arise where assets are distributed in specie to the partners, say, on the dissolution of the partnership; here, the partner receiving the asset is not regarded as making a disposal on that occasion but his base cost for that asset is its market value at that time reduced by the gain up to the date of distribution. Roll-over relief is considered to be available where there is an *actual disposal for deemed consideration*, e.g. on a gift where consideration is deemed to be market value, but not on a *deemed disposal*, including cases where this is accompanied by a deemed reacquisition of the same asset. The recipient of the distribution in specie could not therefore claim roll-over relief in respect of his interest in the asset as a partnership asset until he actually sells the entire asset. Partners who do not receive the asset, however, are charged to CGT in respect of it at the time of the distribution; for those partners this is a 'real' disposal of the distributed asset for deemed consideration equal to their share of its then market value and potentially eligible for roll-over relief.

Business partners who acquire assets jointly – particularly husbands and wives – can encounter problems as illustrated in *Tod (HMIT) v Mudd* [1987] BTC 57. In that case, a husband sold a 100% interest in a business and, together with his wife, acquired as joint owners (75% for him and 25% for her) a property to be used in a new business. 25% of the property was physically occupied privately. It was held that the husband's roll-over relief should be calculated on the footing that his 'new asset' was a 75% share of the property, further restricted by the 25% applicable to private use; and not, as the husband contended, on the footing that he had acquired the whole interest in the 75% of the new property used for the business. To achieve that result, the acquisition would have needed to be partitioned such that the husband acquired the whole beneficial ownership of the business portion of the new premises.

Legislation: TCGA 1992, s. 152–158

14-660 Gifts of interests in partnerships or partnership assets

There is a form of deferral for gifts of business assets where the asset in question is an asset, or an interest in assets, used for the purposes of a trade, profession or vocation carried on by the claimant taxpayer (see ¶15-280). Consequently, the gift of either an interest in a partnership or of assets used by that firm would potentially qualify for relief.

Legislation: TCGA 1992, s. 165

14-680 Negligible value claims by partners

Where a person owns an asset which has become of negligible value, they may claim to be treated as though they had disposed of, and reacquired, the asset at the value stated in the claim (TCGA 1992, s. 24(2)). Clearly this claim may also be made in respect of partnership assets which have become of negligible value. In very many cases, professional partnerships may have written off goodwill in their balance sheets, on the grounds that any incoming partner would not be prepared to pay for the share of the goodwill which they acquire from existing partners and the question therefore arises as to whether a claim that the goodwill has become of negligible value could be sustained.

In cases where a claim is made in respect of partnership goodwill before a particular partner has disposed of any fractional share in the goodwill, HMRC may be expected to examine such claims very closely. They will consider, inter alia, the following matters:

- have payments been made in the past by incoming partners in respect of their acquisition of a share of the partnership's goodwill? If so, it will be necessary to identify any factors which have changed between that event and the date on which it is claimed that the goodwill is of negligible value;

- does the history of the partnership's trading activities support the claim? If not, it is unlikely that the value of the partnership goodwill, and the partner's fractional share in it, will have become negligible; and
- if the partnership dissolved, would the business survive the dissolution? If it would, then it is unlikely that the value of the partnership goodwill, and the partner's share in it, will have become negligible.

HMRC also consider that a claim that the goodwill belongs to the partnership and consequently an individual partner no longer has a share in the goodwill is not sustainable. This is because partnership goodwill is treated in the same way as any other partnership asset. Each partner is treated as owning a fractional share of the goodwill, and it is that goodwill which has to be of negligible value.

In summary, HMRC are not prepared to accept a claim that, although the partnership goodwill as a whole has value, the partner's share in it has no value because they cannot obtain payment for it from continuing or incoming partners. In cases where a claim is made that the partnership goodwill as a whole has no value, it will be a question of fact and valuation as to whether such a claim is accepted (*Capital Gains Manual* CG27725 – CG28000).

Chapter 6: Incorporation of partnerships

15-000 Introduction

There comes a point in the life cycle of many partnerships where a decision is taken to incorporate the business into a limited company. There can be a number of reasons for doing this. Historically, it was the only way for the partners to achieve limited liability, rather than them being jointly liable for the debts of the partnership under the *Partnership Act* 1890. This issue was largely ameliorated by the advent of limited liability partnerships in 2000. So it is no longer as imperative to incorporate a business when it has reached a certain size.

However, there are other commercial drivers towards incorporation and it is probably fair to say that, somewhere in that list, is the tax impact. The profits of a company are taxed at a flat rate of 20% (from 1 April 2016), with income tax on extracting profits by way of dividend at a maximum rate of 38.1% (from 6 April 2016) for those earning over £150,000, giving a maximum tax burden of 50.48% (ignoring the dividend allowance available since 6 April 2016) but this assumes profits are fully extracted as income rather than being retained and/or reinvested in growing the business or extracted by way of a capital gain on disposal, which, assuming the availability of entrepreneurs' relief and the 10% rate of tax on exit, would reduce the overall tax burden to 30%.

The profits of a partnership suffer both income tax, at up to 45%, and Class 4 National Insurance contributions on the full amount of profits arising, irrespective of whether those profits are extracted by the partners or retained and reinvested in the business. So there are definite tax advantages to incorporation.

15-020 Mechanisms

There are three main mechanisms for incorporation. The most commonly used is the transfer of the assets of a business from the partnership to a company, in return for which the company issues the shares to the partners. This method of incorporation has a specific relief associated with it, as detailed below, so that, to the extent that the consideration for the transfers of assets is the issue of shares, the transaction should be free of capital gains tax. This 'incorporation relief' is now at TCGA 1992, s. 162 and is a very old feature of the tax legislation, having been in place since 1965.

An alternative approach, if the conditions for incorporation relief are not met, is to gift the assets into the company and make a joint election that the company should inherit the base costs of the assets and the transferor partners should suffer no capital gains tax at that point. This relief, currently at TCGA 1992, s. 165 is also discussed in more detail below. It is a more restrictive relief, as it only applies to the transfer of assets used in a trade, so cannot be used for the incorporation of a business that does not amount to a trade.

Finally, for a while it was common for a trading partnership to be incorporated by selling the trade to the company. The main advantage of this was that, while the partners would suffer capital gains tax, they generally claimed entrepreneurs' relief and only paid that tax at 10%. The business transfer created a debt due from the company to the ex-partners, who were therefore able to extract post-tax profits from the company without paying any further tax. And in many cases the company was able to claim a tax deduction for the amortisation or impairment of the goodwill of the trade. This mechanism was, however, substantially restricted in its scope by changes in *Finance Act* 2015, as described below.

Legislation: TCGA 1992, s. 162 and 165

15-040   Effect of incorporation

The primary impact of incorporation is that the business that was previously carried on in a partnership is now carried on by a company owned by the same people. But what happens to the original partnership?

Effect of incorporating a general partnership

In the case of a general partnership, the effect of transferring the business out means that the partnership ceases to exist. For the purposes of the *Partnership Act* 1890, s. 1(1), a partnership is the relationship between persons carrying on a business together with a view to profit. If the business has been transferred to a company, there is no business being carried on by the original partners, so the partnership must cease to exist.

The partnership has also ceased to trade, which has both commercial and tax consequences. Thus, it will be necessary to prepare cessation accounts, to collect outstanding debts (although these may have been transferred to the company), and to pay off any final liabilities, including tax liabilities. This is why an appropriate amount of cash is generally left behind on incorporation.

Effect of incorporating a limited liability partnership

The effect of incorporating an LLP is different, as the LLP itself is a body corporate as a matter of general law. If the incorporation is carried out by simply transferring the business to the company, the LLP remains as a shell entity. Once it has dealt with all its final liabilities, including the cessation accounts, it can be formally wound up or struck off under the *Companies Act* 2006, s. 603. There is no specific requirement for this to happen, and in most cases we suspect that the shell LLP is merely left in place.

An alternative approach is for the LLP itself to be transferred to the new company. While technically more complex, this may be preferable if it is difficult to transfer the trade for wider commercial reasons, such as avoiding breaching landlord or banking covenants. An LLP must have more than one member (LLPA 2000, s. 2(1)), so the company cannot be the only member. The practical answer is to change the membership rights so that the original members of the LLP have no rights to income or capital, but the company has all the rights to income and capital. Subsequently, the trade can be hived up to the company, subject to commercial issues. The LLP then prepares cessation accounts, pays off creditors, etc. and can either be left in place or formally wound up or struck off.

In private correspondence we have seen HMRC accept that either mechanism for the incorporation of the business of an LLP is acceptable to them and, if appropriate, would qualify for the incorporation relief under TCGA 1992, s. 162.

Legislation: PA 1890, s. 1(1); CA 2006, s. 603; LLPA 2000, s. 2(1); TCGA 1992, s. 162

15-060   Impact of incorporation

Where an unincorporated business is transferred to a company, a number of tax consequences may arise. For example:

- the transfer will result in a cessation of the business and, depending upon the date concerned, may lead to more than 12 months profit being assessable for the final year of assessment, subject to overlap relief (see **Chapter 11**).
- unrelieved trading losses may be carried forward and set against director's remuneration and dividends received from the company (ITA 2007, s. 86);
- balancing adjustments can arise in respect of capital allowance claims but subject to an election under CAA 2001, s. 266 (see ¶22-100);
- the sale, if it qualifies as the 'transfer of a going concern', will be outside the scope of VAT, though the transferor should take steps to deregister (see ¶28-760);
- liability for National Insurance Class 2 contributions will cease if the transferor partners have no continuing self-employed earnings;
- the former proprietors will normally become directors and shareholders of the company and therefore chargeable to income tax on employment income and dividends; and
- liabilities to stamp duty or stamp duty land tax may arise on the transfer of the assets to the company, subject to the rules at FA 2003, Sch. 15.

Legislation: ITA 2007, s. 86; CAA 2001, s. 266; FA 2003, Sch. 15

INCORPORATION RELIEF

15-080   Introduction

The principal effect of incorporation of a partnership for capital gains tax purposes will be the disposal, by the transferors, of assets used in the business (including goodwill), and their acquisition by the company. So chargeable gains or allowable losses may accrue in respect of any chargeable assets being transferred. If the transfer qualifies for incorporation relief under TCGA 1992, s. 162 (or 'roll-over relief on transfer of business' as it is called in the legislation), the gains can be effectively rolled over into the base cost of the company's shares. This relief is available if the consideration given by the company for the business being transferred is an issue of shares by that company. In such a case, the chargeable gains which would otherwise arise may be deferred. The detailed conditions for relief are discussed at ¶15-120ff.

This relief is colloquially known as 'incorporation relief'. However, it is not a requirement that the transferee company should be newly incorporated or wholly owned by the original partners. It may already be carrying on a business and the transferor may be only a minority shareholder after the transfer.

The nature of the relief makes it a deferment, rather than an exemption, as the gain is deferred by reduction of the chargeable gain arising on the disposal of the chargeable assets of the business and a corresponding reduction in the allowable expenditure on acquisition of the shares of the company. On the subsequent disposal of the new asset, only one chargeable gain or allowable loss arises (see ¶15-200ff.).

HMRC accept that relief is due on the incorporation of a business which has been carried by on individuals in partnership with a company. The company partner is not entitled to the relief but the fact that the transfer of the business is not made wholly by persons who are not companies does not prevent the individual partners from being eligible for relief. They also accept that where not all partners take shares in the transferee company, those partners who take cash will make disposals in the normal way and those who take shares are entitled to incorporation relief if they meet the various tests in the statute (see *Capital Gains Manual* CG65700).

There are specific provisions for incorporation of a building society (TCGA 1992, s. 216) or of a friendly society (TCGA 1992, s. 217A).

Legislation: TCGA 1992, s. 162, 216 and 217A

15-100   Claims and elections

Incorporation relief is given automatically in all cases where the conditions are satisfied, without the need for a claim (TCGA 1992, s. 162(1)). However, since April 2002, the taxpayer has been able to elect for the relief not to apply (TCGA 1992, s. 162A(1)); he may, for example, prefer business asset roll-over or hold-over relief or entrepreneurs' relief (see ¶15-020). See also ¶15-240 for more detailed consideration of the possible interactions between these reliefs.

Election to disapply relief

To be effective, an election must be made within two years of the 31 January following the tax year in which the transfer occurred (TCGA 1992, s. 162A(2), (3)).

However, where the individual disposes of the whole of the shares by the end of the tax year following that in which the transfer occurs, the time limit is reduced by one year (TCGA 1992, s. 162A(4)). For these purposes, an inter-spouse/civil partner transfer is ignored but a subsequent disposal by the transferee is treated as a disposal by the transferor.

In the case of an incorporation of a partnership, each partner may make an election in respect of his share of the business transferred (TCGA 1992, s. 162A(7)).

Limitation of relief

It is important to remember that the relief is only a relief from capital gains tax. There are special rules for the transfers of other assets to which capital gains tax does not apply, such as stock or work in progress or assets on which capital allowances have been claimed.

Legislation: TCGA 1992, s. 162 and 162A

15-120   Conditions: a person who is not a company transfers a business to a company

A 'company' includes any body corporate, unincorporated association or unit trust scheme but does not include a partnership (TCGA 1992, s. 288(1)) or a limited liability partnership (TCGA 1992, s. 59A(1)). This is essentially the same definition of 'company' as applies in relation to the Taxes Acts generally. It therefore follows that relief is available to sole traders, partners and trustees or personal representatives.

There is no requirement that the recipient company be UK resident or that it be within the charge to UK tax in respect of that business following the transfer. As the gain is rolled over onto the shares held by the UK resident former proprietor, which are still within the scope of UK capital gains tax, the tax status of the company is irrelevant.

It is noteworthy that the statute refers to the transfer of a 'business' and not a 'trade'. It is generally accepted that business is something wider than a trade but there is no precise definition. It does seem clear that there must be some active involvement by the proprietor. HMRC will contest any claims that the passive holding of investments or of an investment property amount to a business (HMRC *Capital Gains Manual* CG65715).

The letting of furnished holiday accommodation in the UK on a commercial basis can be regarded as a trade for certain CGT purposes. Incorporation relief is not specified as one of those. Such businesses and property letting businesses generally may, however, qualify on general principles provided there is active involvement by the owner, rather than the appointment of a property managing agent. It will be a question of fact as to whether the activities are such as to be classed as a business. In the case of *Ramsay v R & C Commrs* [2013] BTC 1,868, the Upper Tribunal overturned the First-tier Tribunal decision in *Ramsay* [2012] TC 01871, deciding that a property letting enterprise did constitute a business. The case involved the letting of ten flats in a large house in Belfast where the taxpayer spent approximately 20 hours per week carrying out various activities, such as meeting tenants, paying electricity bills for communal areas and repairing and maintaining communal areas. In the Upper Tribunal, Mr Roger Berner decided that 'the proper approach ... is to construe "business" broadly, according to its unvarnished ordinary meaning', rather than relating to meanings given by other tax law such as for IHT business property relief or income tax. The Upper Tribunal considered six criteria, taken from the case of *C & E Commrs v Lord Fisher* (1981) 1 BVC 392, being:

(1) were the activities a 'serious undertaking earnestly pursued';

(2) were the activities a 'serious occupation';

(3) whether the activity was an occupation or function actively pursued with reasonable or recognisable continuity;

(4) whether the activity had a certain amount of substance in terms of turnover;

(5) whether the activity was conducted in a regular manner and on sound and recognised business principles; and

(6) whether the activities were of a kind which, subject to differences of detail, are commonly made by those who seek to profit by them,

and also looked at the degree of activity undertaken, to determine whether the property was a business.

Legislation: TCGA 1992, s. 59A, 162 and 288

15-140 Conditions: business must be transferred as a 'going concern'

The term 'going concern' is an unfamiliar one for direct tax purposes, although it is more common in relation to VAT. In essence, it refers to the fact that the business is transferred fully operational, so that it could be continued by the transferee without further input and without interruption. HMRC's *Capital Gains Manual* CG65710 cites a limitation identified by the court in *IR Commrs v Gordon* [1991] BTC 130 where, at p. 143, the Lord President observed that:

> 'No doubt a business cannot any longer be described as a going concern if the transferor has taken steps before the date of the transfer to prevent the transferee company from carrying on the business without interruption as it wishes after that date.'

However, earlier in his speech he held that:

> 'The phrase with which we are concerned here begins with the word "transfers". The word is used in its active sense, and it directs attention to what is transferred to the company on the relevant date by the person who is not a company. The business which he transfers to the company must be transferred to it "as a going concern". The word "as" is linked to the word "transfers" and this shows that it is the state of the business at the date of the transfer which must be considered. There is no requirement that the business shall answer to the description of being a going concern at any future date or that it shall continue to be a going concern for any period after the date of the transfer, nor is the relief said to be affected by what the transferee company may do with the business once it has been received by it. The words "going concern" do not in themselves carry any implication about what may happen in the future or about the length of time which the business must remain in that condition once it has been taken over by the transferee.'

In that case, a farming partnership agreed on 22 June 1983 to transfer its business (including farmland) to a company, the transfer taking effect on 9 September. In the interim, however, an agreement to sell the farmland to a third party was concluded on 23 August, with completion on 28 November. The company was only able to farm that land from 9 September to 28 November, but the transfer was still that of a going concern. (An additional feature of the case was that farming was a business which could be moved from one piece of land to another without being brought to an end.)

Legislation: TCGA 1992, s. 162

15-160   Conditions: whole of assets (other than cash, if desired) are transferred to the company

Assets used in the business would generally follow the business in any transfer, but in some instances, the transferor may wish to retain some assets, often freehold property. The relief, however, requires that all the assets of the business be transferred, with the possible exception of cash (TCGA 1992, s. 162(1)); therefore, the retention of any business asset, other than cash, would be fatal to a claim.

As a practical matter, if the partners do not want to transfer assets to the company, it is necessary to extract those assets from the business in advance. For example, the partners might not want the cars used in the business to be transferred to the company, to avoid the complexities of taxing car and fuel benefits. So it is important to ensure that the cars are held in the names of the individual partners, before incorporation. And it may be prudent to transfer any loans in respect of the cars into the partners' names, too. One of the authors has recently noticed that, while the car is registered in his name, the loan was in the name of the LLP, which might have caused some issues on incorporation. Other assets to consider similarly might include computers or other items of plant or machinery which the partners wish to continue to hold personally, or which might otherwise give rise to benefit in kind charges for private use.

Freehold land is a more difficult asset to manage in this context. The use of land by the partnership's business is often so closely connected to the business that the transfer of the business without the land might not be seen as a transfer of the business as a going concern. An example we have seen involved the transfer of a caravan park business to a company, where the partners wanted to retain ownership of the freehold and to rent the site to the company. In a recent VAT case, *Robinson Family Ltd* [2012] TC 02046, however, the First-tier Tribunal found that a transfer of a business constituted a transfer of a going concern for VAT purposes, despite the fact that the original business occupied the land under a freehold while the transferred business occupied it under a long lease. The Tribunal looked at the substance of the transaction and said that it was a going concern and HMRC chose not to appeal. While this case does not set precedent, being a First-tier Tribunal decision, and relates to VAT and not to direct taxes, we believe that the decision is still helpful in this context.

Although 'cash' might be said to be limited to that physically held by the business, HMRC accept that the term includes sums held in bank current and deposit accounts (HMRC *Capital Gains Manual* CG65710).

There is, however, no requirement that all liabilities should be transferred to the company and HMRC have confirmed that relief would not be precluded by the fact that some of the liabilities of the business are not taken over. Conversely, to the extent that liabilities are taken over, HMRC have agreed that this will not generally amount to consideration for the transfer (ESC D32; see HMRC *Capital Gains Manual* CG65745 and ¶15-200). Otherwise, the wording of the legislation would, in effect, defeat its policy aim (see below, relief only available to the extent that the consideration is in the form of share capital issued by the transferee company).

The First-tier Tribunal decision in *Roelich* [2014] TC 03704, emphasises that for incorporation relief to apply, there must be a 'business' (which is something wider that a 'trade', but requiring some activity on the part of the proprietor), that business must be a going concern at the point of transfer and all the assets of the business, other than cash, must be transferred. The asset transferred was a contract which provided a stream of income but did not require any activity on the part of the taxpayer. HMRC, quite understandably in the circumstances, did not regard it as a business in itself and as no further assets were apparently transferred, denied relief. The Tribunal however, despite lacking documentary evidence, found that there were other 'assets' transferred so that the whole of the assets of the taxpayer's business had been transferred. (In the authors' view, the taxpayer was very fortunate to succeed with this appeal in view of the lack of documentary evidence in support of his claim.)

Legislation: TCGA 1992, s. 162

15-180 Conditions: consideration given by the company is wholly or partly in form of its own shares issued to the transferor

It is important to distinguish between shares issued as consideration for the transfer of the business and those which are issued by way of subscription or as consideration for cash left outstanding on a loan account, as, in the latter cases, no relief would be available.

Full relief is given where the whole of the consideration for the transfer is in the form of shares. Where the shares form only part of the consideration, only partial relief is given (TCGA 1992, s. 162(4); see ¶15-200). It may therefore be possible to adjust the composition of the consideration to leave a chargeable gain sufficient to be covered by the annual exemption or brought-forward allowable losses.

Such shares as are included in the consideration are referred to as 'the new assets' (TCGA 1992, s. 162(1)).

If part of the consideration consists of a credit balance on loan or current account due by the company to the transferor, that is considered by HMRC to be effectively cash consideration and therefore some restriction of relief will be due (*Capital Gains Manual* CG65720).

There are no requirements as to the percentage shareholding in the transferee company that the transferor should have after the transfer, nor to the involvement of the former proprietor thereafter.

'Shares' include stock (TCGA 1992, s. 288(1)).

Legislation: TCGA 1992, s. 59A, 162 and 288

15-200   Consequences: reduction in net gains on old assets

The relief has the effect of reducing the net gain arising as a result of the transfer of any chargeable assets to the company (TCGA 1992, s. 162(2)). The net gain is the aggregate of the chargeable gains and allowable losses arising on the chargeable assets transferred (TCGA 1992, s. 162(2)). Obviously, there needs to be an excess of gains over losses for relief to be in point.

If there is substantial identity of control of the business before and after the transfer, the transfer may be treated as a bargain otherwise than at arm's length by virtue of the former proprietor being connected with the company, so that such gains and losses will be determined by reference to market value (see ¶12-300).

The amount of relief depends upon the extent to which the consideration is represented by the necessary share issue (see ¶15-180). By concession (ESC D32), any liabilities taken over by the company are not regarded as consideration for the transfer although, if the company agrees to meet any outstanding partnership tax liability, this will not fall within the concession and relief will be restricted. The concession applies only to business liabilities and HMRC's view is that any tax liability arising from the business transferred is a personal liability and is thus consideration for the transfer (*Capital Gains Manual* CG65745).

If the only consideration for the transfer is a share issue by the company, the whole of the net gain is reduced to nil; strictly, the more intricate calculations below must be performed but this is the intended result (TCGA 1992, s. 162(2), (4), (5)).

Example 1

Letitia carries on business as a picture framer. She transfers the business to a newly formed company on terms that the consideration for the sale is to be the market value of £86,000, satisfied by the issue to her of 80,000 £1 ordinary shares issued at a small premium.

The consideration represents the following:

	£
Stock	11,000
Debtors	2,400
Tool kit	8,000
Framing machine	14,000
Freehold shop	40,300
Goodwill	10,300
	86,000

The tool kit is tangible movable property and a wasting asset (but did not attract capital allowances), so that no chargeable gain arises. The heavy framing equipment was acquired for £20,000 and attracted machinery and plant allowances. Although Letitia and the company are connected persons, she does not elect to transfer the equipment at tax written-down value (see ¶22-100) so the disposal value to be brought into account for capital allowance purposes is the actual consideration. The freehold was acquired for £25,500.

The amount of the gain on the old assets is reduced as follows:

	£
Freehold gain (below)	14,800
Framing machine (below)	—
Goodwill gain (below)	10,300
	25,100
Less: reduction	(25,100)
	Nil

	£
Freehold	
Disposal consideration	40,300
Less: allowable expenditure	(25,500)
Chargeable gain	14,800

Framing machine	£
Disposal consideration	14,000
Less: allowable expenditure (£20,000 − £6,000)	(14,000)
Chargeable gain/allowable loss	Nil

Goodwill	£
Disposal consideration	10,300
Less: allowable expenditure	—
Chargeable gain	10,300

N.B. If this calculation was in respect of a transfer prior to 6 April 2008, indexation allowance would need to be considered.

Where the consideration is not entirely represented by shares, the amount by which such net gain is reduced is a proportion representing the extent to which the consideration for the transfer is satisfied by the shares, i.e. the reduction is as follows (TCGA 1992, s. 162(4), (5)):

$$\frac{A}{B} \times \text{the amount of the gain on the old assets}$$

'A' is the acquisition cost for capital gains purposes of the shares received as consideration; and

'B' is the value of the total consideration for the transfer of the business as a whole (not just the chargeable assets).

The value of the denominator, 'B', is unaffected by any deemed market value substitution for the purposes of the calculation of chargeable gains or allowable losses on assets transferred.

Example 2

Horace owns and runs a grocer's shop. He decides to sell his business to a rival who operates a small chain through the medium of a company. He agrees to sell his business for its market value of £124,000, taking a small cash sum (£15,000) with the balance to be satisfied by the issue of shares in the rival company. His only chargeable assets are the freehold to his shop (acquired for £50,000) to which a value of £71,400 is attributed and goodwill for which the purchaser pays £12,500. The incidental costs are £400 for the disposal of the freehold and £300 for the disposal of the goodwill. The incidental costs of acquiring the shares are put at £250.

The amount of the gain on the old assets is reduced as follows:

		£
Freehold gain (below)		21,000
Goodwill gain (below)		12,200
Amount of gain on old assets		33,200
Less: reduction (109,000 × £33,200)		(29,184)
	124,000	
Chargeable gains		4,016
Freehold	£	£
Disposal consideration		71,400
Less: allowable expenditure:		
purchase consideration	50,000	
incidental cost of disposal	400	
		(50,400)
Chargeable gain		21,000
Goodwill		£
Disposal consideration		12,500
Less: incidental costs		(300)
Chargeable gain		12,200

The reduction cannot exceed the aggregate of the allowable acquisition consideration of the new assets (TCGA 1992, s. 162(4)); if this were to be permitted, the required reduction in such amounts would leave negative consideration.

Legislation: TCGA 1992, s. 162

15-220 Consequences: reduction in allowable cost of shares

The corollary of the reduction in the gain on the old assets (see ¶15-140) is a reduction in the allowable acquisition cost of the shares issued (including incidental costs) (TCGA 1992, s. 162(3)(b)).

The cost of the shares is the total consideration given for the business as a whole (not just that of the chargeable assets) less any consideration not in the form of shares. In the majority of cases, the transferor and transferee will be connected persons (see ¶12-300) and therefore the cost will be equal to the market value of the business as a whole. The cost would normally be the value of the assets transferred less the value of the liabilities taken over by the company. Although ESC D32 (see above) applies to ignore liabilities for certain purposes, it does not operate in this context (*Capital Gains Manual* CG65745).

The overall reduction is equal to the reduction made to the gain on the old assets (TCGA 1992, s. 162(3)(a)).

If the shares issued to the transferor constitute more than one asset, the amount of the overall reduction required is apportioned between the different assets; this apportionment will require a reduction in each and every such asset (TCGA 1992, s. 162(3)(a)). This may arise if shares of different classes are issued to the transferor; in this case, the apportionment is to be made in accordance with their market value at the time they were acquired by the transferor (TCGA 1992, s. 162(3)). Market value need not necessarily equate with the value placed on the shares by the parties to the sale, but it will often do so.

Example 1

Facts as in example 2 at ¶15-200. The shares issued to Horace comprise 50,000 ordinary shares of £1 nominal value per share, taken in value at £60,000, and 24,000 preference shares of 50 pence, taken at £49,000. These figures are accepted as representing the market value of the shares at the time they are acquired by Horace.

The allowable acquisition cost of the two separate holdings of shares are:

		£
Ordinary shares		
Acquisition consideration		60,000
Incidental costs of acquisition	$\dfrac{(60 \times £250)}{109}$	138
		60,138
Less: reduction	$\dfrac{(60 \times £17,400)}{109}$	(9,578)
		50,560
Preference shares		£
Acquisition consideration		49,000
Incidental costs of acquisition	$\dfrac{(49 \times £250)}{109}$	112
		49,112
Less: reduction	$\dfrac{(49 \times £17,400)}{109}$	(7,822)
		41,290

It is unlikely that shares of the same class would constitute more than one asset; however, if this were to be the case there is no stipulated method of apportionment, so that a simple pro rata apportionment on the basis of the number of shares would appear acceptable, if desired.

Legislation: TCGA 1992, s. 162

113

15-240   Interaction with other reliefs

Roll-over or hold-over relief

Where a gain arises on the disposal of a business or part of a business to a company, the taxpayer, if he intends to acquire a further business, may be able to claim roll-over relief on that gain (see ¶14-640). HMRC are of the view that, as roll-over relief has effect by reducing the consideration for the disposal of the asset whereas incorporation relief reduces the gain on the disposal, a claim for roll-over relief will take precedence (*Capital Gains Manual* CG60210–60214). There would therefore seem to be no need to elect for incorporation relief to be disapplied in such a case.

Entrepreneurs' relief

In a situation where a sole trader or a partnership transfers a business to a company, both forms of relief are potentially available. Entrepreneurs' relief requires a claim to be made, whereas incorporation relief applies automatically unless an election is made to disapply it (see ¶15-100). Thus, if no action is taken to disapply incorporation relief, it will take precedence. Entrepreneurs' relief will therefore only be available against such gains as may not have been eliminated by incorporation relief.

Obviously if a claim is made to disapply incorporation relief, there is then no problem over precedence.

It is unlikely, however, that a transferor would want to disapply incorporation relief, following the changes made in FA 2015 (see below).

15-260   Anti-avoidance

Because incorporations involve transactions between connected persons, the 'market value rule' applies (see ¶12-300). In *Tax Bulletin* 76, April 2005, HMRC advised that they would challenge the value placed on goodwill when sold to a company on incorporation where it appeared to them to have been sold at an overvalue or where the type of goodwill purposed to have been transferred was one which they consider to be incapable of transfer.

The article also indicates the possible consequences of an excess of consideration over market value:

- taxed as earnings within ITEPA 2003, s. 62 where the overvaluation was an inducement to take up service with the company;
- in other cases, taxed as a benefit under ITEPA 2003, s. 203;
- where the above cannot apply, taxed as a distribution by the company under CTA 2010, s. 1000(1)Bff.

HMRC accept, however, that there may be occasions where, despite reasonable efforts on the part of the taxpayer (including obtaining professional valuations), the consideration is inadvertently in excess of market value. In such a case, the distribution may be 'unwound' if the taxpayer repays the excess to the company.

Legislation: ITEPA 2003, s. 62, 203; CTA 2010, s. 1000

BUSINESS ASSETS GIFT RELIEF

15-280   Introduction

Business asset gift relief, at TCGA 1992, s. 165, provides for the deferral of a chargeable gain arising on a gift of a business asset, in the form of a reduction in the base cost of the asset for the donee. This relief could be used in relation to an intended incorporation of a business as an alternative to incorporation relief. It is therefore particularly useful if the incorporation relief is not available, perhaps because the partners do not wish to transfer all of the assets of the business to the company.

Rather than the transferee company issuing shares to the partners as consideration for the transfer, the partners could gift (or partially gift) the business, or part of the business, to the company. If they are the only shareholders, as will often be the case, they will retain beneficial ownership of the business albeit indirectly through the company. To the extent that other persons are shareholders in the company, they will lose a degree of such ownership.

This is, however, a more restricted relief, as it can only be applied to gifts of assets used in a trade. Therefore, it can only be used on incorporation of a trade, not of an activity that is a business but that does not amount to a trade.

Where the relief applies, the transfer is treated as a no gain, no loss transfer for the purposes of capital gains tax. The former proprietors will be able to avoid a CGT charge to the extent that the gift relief is available. The gain, or part thereof, will effectively crystallise in the company when it disposes of the assets transferred.

Legislation: TCGA 1992, s. 165

15-300   Effect of relief

Under general capital gains principles, a transaction otherwise than at arm's length (such as a gift or an intentional sale at an undervalue) is deemed to be a disposal occurring at market value (TCGA 1992, s. 17; see ¶12-300). Where business assets gift relief applies, the deemed disposal proceeds are reduced to such an amount as will give rise to neither gain nor loss. The recipient of the asset has a corresponding acquisition cost of the assets for the purposes of a future disposal. In effect, the base cost to the company on incorporation will be the same as the base cost to the partners.

Legislation: TCGA 1992, s. 17

15-320   Conditions for relief

These are:

- there must be a disposal of an asset by an individual 'otherwise than under a bargain at arm's length' (TCGA 1992, s. 165(1)(a)). This condition is generally satisfied by the transfer of assets by partners to a company;
- the asset which is the subject of the disposal is a qualifying business asset (TCGA 1992, s. 165(2); see ¶15-360);
- the recipient must be UK resident (prior to 6 April 2013, resident or ordinarily resident), unless the asset which is the subject of the disposal is a UK residential property interest (see ¶15-400); and
- a claim must be made (TCGA 1992, s. 165(1)(b); see ¶15-340).

Relief is not, however, due:

(1)   where, on the disposal of Qualifying Corporate Bonds, a deferred gain is deemed to accrue under TCGA 1992, s. 116(10)(b); or

(2)   if a claim could be made for gift relief under TCGA 1992, s. 260 where the gift is also a chargeable transfer for inheritance tax purposes (TCGA 1992, s. 165(3)).

Legislation: TCGA 1992, s. 116, 165 and 260

15-340   Claims

The relief must be claimed, and, subject to any restrictions prescribed in the legislation, it is an 'all or nothing' claim; it is not possible to claim partial relief. However, where a number of assets are gifted at the same time, a claim may be made, or not, in respect of each asset, as desired. It is also possible to make gifts on different days and make claims in respect of only some of them.

The claim must be made by both the transferor partners and the transferee company (TCGA 1992, s. 165(1)(b)).

With effect from 1 April 2010, the time limit within which the claim must be made is four years from the end of the year of assessment. Prior to April 2010, the time limit was five years from the 31 January next following the year of assessment in which the disposal occurred. Claims can be made on the form attached to Help Sheet HS295.

In practice, the most difficult aspect of determining the held-over gain is agreeing the market value with HMRC. However, the need to agree the market value may, in most cases, be postponed until it becomes necessary to do so in order to compute a subsequent gain or loss. Under SP 8/92, HMRC will accept a claim for business assets gift relief without the need to agree the market value of the gift where the transferor and transferee jointly elect for this treatment and provide:

- full details of the asset transferred;
- its date of acquisition; and
- its allowable expenditure,

and state that they have satisfied themselves that a gain has arisen as a result of the gift.

A condition of HMRC accepting a claim on this basis is that once made it may not be subsequently withdrawn. However, if it later emerges that any information provided by either the transferor or transferee was incorrect or incomplete, the claim will be treated as invalid with the result that the gain on the disposal will become chargeable.

Where the asset was acquired before 31 March 1982 and any actual consideration is greater than the market value at that date, an immediate chargeable gain will arise on that excess. It will therefore be necessary to agree the value at 31 March 1982, although agreement of the market value at the date of gift may still be deferred (HMRC *Capital Gains Manual* CG67140).

In other cases, where a chargeable gain arises on the gift (due to restricted relief because of non-business use of the asset; see ¶15-360 and ¶15-440 or the existence of non-business assets held by companies), the statement of practice will not be applicable.

Legislation: TCGA 1992, s. 165

15-360   Qualifying business assets

To qualify for relief on incorporation, the asset must be assets, or interests in assets, used for the purposes of a trade, profession or vocation carried on by the transferor (TCGA 1992, s. 165(2)), which includes, by virtue of TCGA 1992, s. 59, members of partnerships.

Special rules apply to gifts of agricultural land (see ¶15-380) and transfers by trustees.

Whilst the term 'trade' is to have its normal meaning as for income tax (TCGA 1992, s. 288(1)), for the purposes of this relief it specifically includes the occupation of woodlands which are managed on a commercial basis with a view to profit (TCGA 1992, s. 165(9)) and the commercial letting of furnished holiday accommodation (TCGA 1992, s. 241(3), (3A); see also ITTOIA 2005, s. 323).

Legislation: TCGA 1992, s. 59, 165, 241 and 288; ITTOIA 2005, s. 323

15-380   Agricultural land

Business assets gift relief is extended to assets which are, or are interests in, property which qualifies as 'agricultural property' for inheritance tax purposes and which would not otherwise qualify for relief because the transferor does not himself farm the land (TCGA 1992, Sch. 7, para. 1(1); IHTA 1984, s. 115(2)); for commentary on agricultural property relief, see ¶27-060).

An asset will qualify for business assets gift relief if agricultural property relief:

- is given where the gift is also a chargeable transfer for inheritance tax purposes;
- would have been given if the disposal had been a chargeable transfer; or
- would have been given but for a failure of the conditions in IHTA 1984, s. 124A as to the continuing use and ownership by the transferee of a potentially exempt transfer between the date of the gift and the date of the donor's death,

(TCGA 1992, Sch. 7, para. 1(2)).

Special provisions apply to modify the relief in relation to the transfer of agricultural property by a body of trustees.

Legislation: IHTA 1984, s. 115; TCGA 1992, Sch. 7, para. 1

15-400   Non-resident recipients

To qualify for relief, the transferee company must effectively be within the charge to UK tax in respect of the asset; otherwise, there would be a loss of revenue to the Exchequer, because the held-over gain would never crystallise within the scope of UK tax. The question arises as to whether this provision complies with European legislation relating to freedom of establishment and free movement of capital.

There are also provisions to prevent relief where the recipient is a UK resident company and that company is controlled by one or more non-resident persons each of whom is connected to the transferor (TCGA 1992, s. 167(2)). Once again, this legislation may not be compliant with European law. However, it is unlikely to be an issue in most cases where a UK partnership is incorporated by gift of the business assets into a company owned by the partners. If the partners are within the scope of UK capital gains tax, then it seems highly unlikely that the company would be controlled by non-resident persons.

Emigration of donee company

A company or body of trustees becoming non-resident whilst owning the transferred asset would, under general rules, be treated as disposing of it and reacquiring it at market value, unless it is situated in the UK and the non-resident uses or holds it, etc. for the purposes of a UK branch or agency (TCGA 1992, s. 185).

Legislation: TCGA 1992, s. 167 and 185

15-420   Actual consideration for the transfer

Where actual consideration is given for the transfer (i.e. it is a sale at undervalue, rather than an outright gift) and that consideration exceeds the sums allowable as a deduction under TCGA 1992, s. 38 in computing the gain, the held-over gain is reduced by the amount of the excess (TCGA 1992, s. 165(7)).

Example

Fred transfers part of his business to his son, John, including one of his retail shops. The freehold is worth £70,000 but John pays an amount of £50,500. Fred and John claim to defer the chargeable gain arising to Fred on the disposal. The freehold had cost Fred £20,000. The incidentals costs of making the transfer are £400.

The chargeable gain is reduced as follows:

	£	£
Consideration for disposal (market value)		70,000
Less: allowable expenditure		
Cost	20,000	
Incidental costs of disposal	400	(20,400)
Gain before reduction		49,600
Less: held-over gain (£49,600 – (£50,500 – £20,400))		(19,500)
Chargeable gain		30,100

The chargeable gain therefore represents the excess of the consideration given by John over Fred's allowable costs.

To obtain full hold-over relief where there is actual consideration, it is necessary for the recipient to pay an amount which is no more than the base cost and incidental costs of the original purchase plus any enhancement expenditure.

HMRC take the view that where assets are transferred to a spouse under a court order as part of divorce proceedings, the transferee does not, by the surrender of any rights, give consideration for the transfer (*Capital Gains Manual* CG67192).

Legislation: TCGA 1992, s. 38 and 165

15-440   Period of non-qualifying use

It is a basic requirement that, to fall within the first head of relief, assets must be used for the purposes of a trade, profession or vocation carried on by the transferor, his or her personal company or a member of a trading group of which his or her personal company is the holding company. If they have not been so used throughout the period of ownership of the transferor, then, except as noted below, the held-over gain is reduced pro rata to reflect its qualifying use; this is done on a daily basis (TCGA 1992, Sch. 7, para. 5(1)).

Example

David acquires an asset for £12,000 on 15 August Year 1. He begins to carry on a trade on 23 September Year 2 and from that date, uses the asset wholly for the purposes of the trade. On 6 July Year 4, he decides to stop using the asset in his trade and gives the asset to his daughter; its value is £16,000. There are no incidental costs. The asset does not qualify for exemption.

The chargeable gain is reduced as follows:

	£
Consideration for disposal (market value)	16,000
Less: allowable expenditure	(12,000)
Gain before reduction	4,000
Less: held-over gain:	
before time apportionment time	
apportioned (651/1,045 × £4,000)	(2,492)
Chargeable gain	1,508

There is no provision which restricts the period of ownership to periods after 31 March 1982 (to which assets are rebased); it is the whole of the period since acquisition which is relevant. This contrasts with such a provision in relation to roll-over or hold-over relief. In the absence of any rule, such a construction was approved in *Richart v J Lyons & Co Ltd* [1989] BTC 337.

The pro rata reduction for non-qualifying use does not apply to certain agricultural property, which is brought within the relief by special extension (see ¶15-380).

Legislation: TCGA 1992, Sch. 7, para. 5

15-460   Partial business use of building or structure

In HMRC's view, the asset must have been in use for the purposes of a trade, etc. 'just before' it is gifted (*Capital Gains Manual* CG66950). If at any time part of a building or structure had not been so used for any 'substantial' part of the period of ownership, then, except as noted below, the held-over gain is proportionately reduced (TCGA 1992, Sch. 7, para. 6(1)). Neither statute nor HMRC's *Capital Gains Manual* offer any assistance in deciding what is substantial in this context. In connection with the same term used in the context of entrepreneurs' relief, HMRC say it means more than 20% (CG64090).

The apportionment is based on a just and reasonable fraction of the unrelieved gain attributable to qualifying use, that fraction then being applied to the held-over gain. The unrelieved gain is the chargeable gain which would otherwise have arisen. Use of this 'just and reasonable' basis permits flexibility over the method of calculation. It is arguable that numerous factors could be taken into account, although area, floor space or cubic capacities are likely to be major constituents.

Example

Dinah acquired the freehold to a piece of land on which there stood a large office building. It cost £33,000 when the acquisition took place in December Year 1. She immediately used it in her trade. She transfers it to her nephew in January Year 6 for a nominal amount of £5,000, when it is worth £50,680. Throughout her ownership of the building she has used only two of the three floors, the other being vacant for part of the time and being occupied by a tenant for the remainder. Dinah argues that a suitable apportionment would be made by a simple calculation based on the number of floors used in her trade.

	£
Consideration for disposal (market value)	50,680
Less: allowable expenditure	(33,000)
Gain before reduction	12,862
Less: held-over gain:	
use apportionment (2/3 × £12,862)	(8,575)
Chargeable gain	4,287

Any dispute over the basis of apportionment would be determined by appeal in the usual manner, although in some cases since the recipient is affected he may be joined as a party to the appeal.

Where there is also a period during the transferor's ownership during which the asset was not used for business purposes, the pro rata time apportionment is carried out before the just and reasonable apportionment (TCGA 1992, Sch. 7, para. 6(1)). In arithmetical terms, the order is irrelevant, but it is possible that the subjective nature of the just and reasonable test could be affected.

The required apportionment does not apply where the disposal is of property which would qualify for agricultural property relief for inheritance tax purposes (TCGA 1992, Sch. 7, para. 6(2): for commentary on agricultural property relief, see ¶27-060).

Legislation: TCGA 1992, Sch. 7, para. 6

15-480   Interaction with other reliefs

Annual exemption

Since the annual exemption eliminates chargeable gains altogether, whilst business asset gift relief merely defers them, it is preferable to use the former to shelter gains wherever possible. However, it is not possible to tailor a claim to business assets gift relief on a single asset so as to defer only the excess of the gain over the exemption; it is an all or nothing claim.

However, where a number of assets are gifted, each is a separate disposal and may be the subject of a separate claim to relief, or not as may be appropriate. Similarly, if a single asset can be gifted piecemeal over a number of transactions, each part will be a separate disposal. However, in the latter case it should be remembered that the values transferred by the individual transactions may be determined by reference to the value of all the 'linked transactions'.

Entrepreneurs' relief

As we shall see, entrepreneurs' relief may not be a viable alternative, following the changes in FA 2015 with effect from 3 December 2014.

HMRC's view is that if business assets gift relief is claimed in respect of all the assets gifted, there will be no chargeable gains and entrepreneurs' relief will not be in point. However, where some of the assets comprised in the disposal are not the subject of a gift relief claim, entrepreneurs' relief may still be claimed (HMRC *Capital Gains Manual* CG64137).

Roll-over relief

Where the consideration deemed to have been received for a gift is fully reinvested, a roll-over claim reduces the consideration treated as having been given for the disposal (see ¶15-280ff.). Since business asset gift relief treats the chargeable gain which would otherwise accrue as being reduced, that necessarily falls to be taken into account after the gain has been computed and the roll-over relief must take priority. The position of the donee is not affected by the roll-over relief.

Where the deemed consideration on disposal is not fully reinvested, a roll-over claim is effected by a reduction in the gain and, if not all chargeable gain, with a proportionate reduction in the chargeable gain. It is implied that the replacement relief again takes priority over the gift relief and this is the procedure usually adopted.

Where a new asset is a depreciating asset, the gain or part may be held over. The chargeable gain does not disappear, it is merely held in abeyance; since it is the gain which is the subject of relief, the interaction with the gift relief is the same as in relation to the arguments set out above.

INCORPORATION RELIEF OR BUSINESS ASSET GIFT RELIEF

15-500   Introduction

Some of the principal points to be considered are:

(1)   Business assets (other than cash – the only asset which can be retained if incorporation relief is desired) may, in part, be retained by the partners if the gift relief is used. Almost inevitably, goodwill will be transferred, otherwise assets may be retained, perhaps to avoid stamp duty land tax, stamp duty or perhaps for other reasons.

(2)   Any deferred gain will crystallise on a different event. In the case of incorporation relief, the gain will crystallise when the shareholders dispose of the shares they receive (unless a further deferral is in point). In the case of the gift relief, the gain will crystallise when the company disposes of the assets transferred (again, unless a further deferral is in point).

(3)   The value of the former partners' estates may differ. With incorporation relief, they will have substituted a holding of shares (perhaps with other consideration) for an interest in a business and its assets. With the gift relief, they may have realised a loss in the value of their estates if they do not wholly own the company, if the loss of the gifted assets outweighs any increase in value of existing shares (for inheritance tax, the gift will not be a potentially exempt transfer; if they wholly own the company, their existing shares will have risen in value in proportion to the assets gifted to the company and there should be no transfer of value).

(4)   The profile of the former proprietors' estates may differ. As a result, the rate of IHT business property relief to which they are entitled may be reduced under the gift relief. A higher rate of relief is available should there be a subsequent disposition of his shares if, broadly, they hold more than a 25% interest in the company (see ¶27-140). Further, if land and buildings or machinery and plant are retained but used in the business, a subsequent disposition of them would attract the reduced rate if they have a controlling interest, while no business property relief would be available if they have a minority interest (see ¶27-140).

15-520   Incorporation for cash

From 3 December 2014, to the extent that a person transfers goodwill when incorporating a business, entrepreneurs' relief may no longer be available (TCGA 1992, s. 169LA). This will apply to partnership incorporations from that date and incorporations of trades using this route will no longer be attractive (see ¶15-020 for the reasons this was a common route to incorporation before 3 December 2014).

Denial of entrepreneurs' relief

Where a business is sold to a close company, directly or indirectly, the goodwill is not treated as a relevant business asset for entrepreneurs' relief purposes in certain circumstances (see ¶14-580), so the 10% CGT rate may not always be available in respect of its disposal (TCGA 1992, s. 169LA, as inserted by *Finance Act* 2015 and amended by *Finance Act* 2016). A company that is not UK resident, but would be a close company if it were UK resident, is treated as a close company for the purposes of these rules (TCGA 1992, s. 169LA(5)).

In practice, this means that it is unlikely that businesses with substantial goodwill will be incorporated using this method, and people will revert to using the incorporation relief.

Anti-avoidance

If there is a disposal of goodwill, as part of a qualifying business disposal, and there are arrangements with a main purpose of ensuring that these rules do not apply, those relevant avoidance arrangements are ignored, and the rules apply, anyway (TCGA 1992, s. 169LA(6) and (7)). 'Arrangements' means any agreement, understanding, scheme, transaction or series of transactions (whether or not legally enforceable) (TCGA 1992, s. 169LA(8)).

Legislation: TCGA 1992, s. 169LA

Chapter 7: Stamp Duty Land Tax and Land and Buildings Transaction Tax

Many partnership transactions involve transfers of land or of interests in land. As a result, there may be charges to stamp duty land tax (SDLT) in the UK, or to land and buildings transaction tax (LBTT) in Scotland.

Stamp duty land tax

There are special rules within the SDLT legislation to deal with partnership transactions involving chargeable interests. These include the contributions of land and buildings into a partnership, the reallocation of ownership rights within a partnership, the extraction of assets from a partnership and the incorporation of a partnership. There are also specific rules relating to property investment partnerships.

BASIC PRINCIPLES

16-000   Meaning of 'partnership' for SDLT purposes

A 'partnership' is defined as:

- a partnership within the *Partnership Act* 1890;
- a limited partnership registered under the *Limited Partnerships Act* 1907;
- a limited liability partnership formed under the *Limited Liability Partnerships Act* 2000 or the *Limited Liability Partnerships Act* (Northern Ireland) 2002; or
- a firm or entity of a similar character to any of the above formed under the law of a country or territory outside the UK.

Legislation: FA 2003, Sch. 15, para. 1

16-020   A 'see-through' analysis

For SDLT purposes, whether or not a partnership is regarded as a legal person or as a body corporate under the law of the country or territory under which it is formed, its separate legal personality is disregarded. A chargeable interest held by or on behalf of a partnership is deemed to be held by or on behalf of the partners. Similarly, a land transaction entered into for the purposes of a partnership is deemed to be entered into by or on behalf of the partners. The partnership itself is disregarded. If there is a change in a partnership, the partnership is treated as the same partnership, provided that at least one person who was a partner before the change continues to be so after it. A partnership is not treated as either a unit trust scheme or an open-ended investment company. This see through analysis does not apply for the purposes of transactions within Pt. 3 of Sch. 15 – see ¶16-120 below.

Legislation: FA 2003, Sch. 15, para. 2, 3, 4

16-040   Starting a partnership

A partnership deed or written agreement will not generally attract SDLT (nor indeed stamp duty), at least insofar as there is no 'land transaction' as defined. The partners are simply agreeing between themselves how they will carry on business. However, if under such a document one or more of the parties agrees that land held by him is to become a partnership asset (or even perhaps, while retained by him, is to be used for the partnership business: see ¶16-720), there will be SDLT implications. Further, there may be SDLT implications where, following on (or contemporaneous with) the agreement, partners proceed to contribute land to the partnership pro rata to their existing capital shares, even though the income shares remain unchanged.

Conversion to LLP status

The transfer of a chargeable interest to a limited liability partnership ('LLP') in connection with its incorporation is exempt from charge provided three conditions are satisfied. This exemption is similar to the stamp duty exemption given under the *Limited Liability Partnerships Act* 2000, s. 12.

Conditions

The following conditions must be satisfied.

(1)   The effective date of the transaction is not more than one year after the date of incorporation of the LLP.
(2)   At the relevant time, the transferor (a) is a partner in a partnership comprised of all the persons who are or are to be members of the LLP (and no-one else) or (b) holds the interest transferred as nominee or bare trustee for one or more of the partners in such a partnership.
(3)   (a) The proportions of the interest transferred to which the persons who are all of the partners or who are to be members of the LLP are entitled immediately after the transfer are the same as those to which they were entitled at the relevant time; or (b) none of the differences in those proportions has arisen as part of a scheme or arrangement of which the main purpose or one of its main purposes is avoidance of liability to any duty or tax.

Relevant time:

The 'relevant time' is defined, in the case where the transferor acquired the interest after the incorporation of the LLP, as immediately after he acquired it, and in any other case immediately before its incorporation.

Limited liability partnership:

A limited liability partnership means such a partnership formed under the *Limited Liability Partnerships Act* 2000 or the *Limited Liability Partnerships Act (Northern Ireland)* 2002.

Legislation: FA 2003, s. 65(1), (2), (3) and (4)

ORDINARY PARTNERSHIP TRANSACTIONS

16-060   Overview

An 'ordinary partnership transaction' is one which the partnership enters into on behalf of the partners as purchaser, other than transactions within FA 2003, Sch. 15, Pt. 3. In practice, this covers transactions of purchase where the vendor is unrelated to the partnership or its members.

All the obligations and authorisations which fall on or attach to a purchaser for SDLT purposes become an obligation on or permission in relation to all the 'responsible partners'.

Legislation: FA 2003, Sch. 15, para. 6(1)

16-080   Responsible and representative partners

The 'responsible partners', in relation to a particular transaction, are those who are partners at the effective date of the transaction, together also with any person who becomes a member of the partnership after the effective date. The rule that all the responsible partners are required to act in relation to SDLT compliance matters can be displaced by the provision which allows one or more 'representative partners' to do anything required or authorised to be done by or in relation to the responsible partners instead. A representative partner is one nominated by a majority of the partners to act as their representative. Such a nomination (or its revocation) has effect only after notice of the nomination or revocation has been given to HMRC.

Legislation: FA 2003, Sch. 15, para. 6(2), 8

16-100   Liabilities for SDLT, interest or penalties

Liability to make a payment of SDLT (or interest on unpaid SDLT), or to make a payment in accordance with an assessment to recover an excessive repayment, or to a penalty (or interest on a penalty), is a joint and several liability of the responsible partners. A person who becomes a partner after the effective date of a transaction is precluded from liability for SDLT, interest on unpaid SDLT or a penalty or interest on a penalty in respect of that transaction. (Prior to 23 July 2004 an incoming partner was liable for unpaid SDLT or interest thereon in respect of a land transaction the effective date of which occurred before his admission. Therefore, there now seems little point in defining 'responsible partner' as including a person who becomes a partner after the effective date of the relevant transaction: see ¶16-080.)

Legislation: FA 2003, Sch. 15, para. 7

FINANCE ACT 2004 PROVISIONS

16-120   General

The original FA 2003 regime applied SDLT only to 'ordinary partnership transactions', that is the case where broadly a partnership enters into a land transaction. The substitution by FA 2004 of Pt. 3 of FA 2003, Sch. 15 brought within SDLT, from 23 July 2004, all remaining partnership transactions.

Very importantly, *Finance Act* 2010, s. 55 has amended FA 2003, s. 75C so as to remove the application of the rules in FA 2003, Sch. 15, Pt. 3 to the notional transaction under s. 75A–75C. This has potentially very wide consequences. Some indication of HMRC's approach is set out in the revised guidance on the application of the legislation (text below) but it still leaves considerable scope for uncertainty.

The 15% SDLT charge (and the annual ATED charge, and ATED-related CGT charge), on certain acquisitions (or holding or disposal) of high value residential property by non-natural persons, applies to partnerships in which there is a corporate member.

Legislation: FA 2003, Sch. 4A, para. 3

16-140   Scope of amended Finance Act 2003, Sch. 15, Pt. 3

Paragraphs 9–40 were introduced as new FA 2003, Sch. 15, Pt. 3. The transactions to which it applies are (expressly):

(a)   the transfer of a chargeable interest to a partnership (para. 10–13);

(b)   the transfer of an interest in a land-owning partnership (para. 14–17); and

(c)   the transfer of a chargeable interest from a partnership (para. 18–24).

An important additional charging provision, to deal with the exploitation of the SDLT rules for partnerships, was also introduced by *Finance (No. 2) Act* 2005, as Sch. 15, para. 17A. This provides for a charge on the withdrawal of money, etc. from a partnership within a three-year period after the transfer of land into a partnership under para. 10.

The rules as enacted present a significantly different regime from that first proposed in the draft clauses in 2003 (in changes largely beneficial to the taxpayer), as well as reflecting very substantial changes made to Finance Bill 2004 at report stage, in some haste it appears, with the result that there were certain acknowledged inaccuracies in the enacted provisions (some of which have since been corrected). Significant restrictions on the scope of all three heads of change were made by FA 2006 with effect from 19 July 2006. However, SI 2006/3237 and FA 2007 introduced a number of restrictive anti-avoidance provisions, largely with effect from 6 December 2006. These were further changed in FA 2008 (see below).

It should be noted that the implementation of SDLT for partnerships has not led to the abolition of stamp duty on partnership transactions. The old rules are retained with certain modifications (para. 31–33) in order to ensure that partnerships could not be used to avoid stamp duty (or SDRT).

HMRC noted that the guidance at SDLTM 34610 was incorrect in its treatment of certificates of value and revised guidance was provided.

There is some concern regarding the interaction of the rules in Sch. 15 and those in the remainder of Pt. 4 of FA 2003. It is understood that HMRC consider that the charges in Pt. 3 of Sch. 15 are self-contained and 'trump' the rules elsewhere (e.g. s. 53) in FA 2003 as regards the Pt. 3, Sch. 15 transactions.

Legislation: FA 2003, Sch. 15, para. 9–40

16-160 Partnerships chapter in the SDLT manual

At the end of March 2005, HMRC Stamp Taxes issued what were called *Partnerships for the Manual – Outline Chapters*, in draft form for comment by the professional bodies before incorporation in the Manual. Numerous changes were subsequently made in 2005, 2006, 2007 and 2008.

A later draft (spring 2009) was issued, for detailed consultation. This can be seen online at *www.gov.uk/government/collections/stamp-and-property-taxes-manuals*. It did not cover the entire scope of Sch. 15. In particular, it did not refer to or address the effect of: Sch. 15, para. 11, 17, 17A, 19, 21, 22, 25–28, 30 and 40. Nor did it deal with the interaction with s. 53 (connected company purchasers), s. 65 (incorporation of an LLP) or s. 75A (anti-avoidance).

The current guidance on Partnerships is found in the *Stamp Duty Land Tax Manual* from SDLTM 33300.

TIP

The main point for practitioners to take on board is this: No UK land transaction involving a partnership should take place before the SDLT implications have been fully considered and advised on by someone appropriately qualified. Liabilities can crop up in unexpected places. This can follow from (though is not limited exclusively to) the odd rule that an interest in a partnership is defined in terms of income (not capital) sharing ratios.

16-180 Anti-avoidance rules

Anti-avoidance rules were announced on 6 December 2006 and transitional provisions set out. Some of these came into effect on the 6 December 2006 and others from 19 July 2007 (Royal Assent to *Finance Act* 2007). The changes to Sch. 15, para. 14 were further amended by FA 2008 (retrospective to 19 July 2007). See in particular ¶16-280, ¶16-220, ¶16-560 and ¶16-640. Further changes were made to prevent unintended charges arising where there is a change in the interests of partners in a property investment partnership (see Budget Note 058). The amendment applied retrospectively from the date Royal Assent was given to FA 2007 (19 July 2007). These rules were subject to transitional provisions whereby they did not have effect in relation to:

(a) any land transaction effected in pursuance of a contract entered into and substantially performed before 2 p.m. on 6 December 2006 ('the relevant time'), or

(b) any other land transaction effected in pursuance of a contract entered into before the relevant time and which is not an 'excluded transaction'.

An 'excluded transaction' was defined as a land transaction in respect to which:

(a) at or after the relevant time the contract is varied in a way which significantly affects the land transaction (by substituting a different purchaser or altering the subject matter or the consideration);

(b) the subject matter of the land transaction is not identified in the contract in a way which would have enabled its acquisition before the relevant time;

(c) rights under the contract are assigned at or after the relevant time;

(d) the land transaction is effected in consequence of the exercise, at or after the relevant time, of any option, right of pre-emption or similar right; or

(e) at or after the relevant time there is an assignment, sub-sale or other transaction as a result of which someone other than the purchaser becomes entitled to call for a conveyance to him.

16-200 Application to partnerships of the s. 75A anti-avoidance rule

The provisions of FA 2003, Sch. 15, Pt. 3 (the special SDLT partnerships rules) do not apply to a 'notional transaction' in relation to notional transactions with an effective date on or after 24 March 2010.

HMRC issued guidance as to the scope of the anti-avoidance provisions in s. 75A and to note some of the transactions that they did not see as being normally within the scope of the anti-avoidance rules. Specifically:

'Situations where HMRC accept that S.75A is unlikely to apply

(1) X, Y and Z are individuals who decide to establish a partnership to manage their investment portfolio. They transfer investment property and cash into that

partnership at value. HMRC considers this to be a straightforward establishment of and transfer of property into a partnership.

(2) X, Y and Z are the partners of a partnership. The purpose of the partnership is to acquire and develop a large residential property into 6 flats. When the development is complete they disagree as to how to manage the completed development so the partnership is dissolved and the partnership property (the flats and any partnership monies) is divided among the partners. It is assumed here that the agreements and documents relating to creation of the partnership demonstrate that the intention was for the partnership to manage the property after development and that the dissolution of the partnership arises from an unforeseen disagreement. HMRC would not seek to apply s.75A to this situation as long as the general Stamp Duty Land Tax legislation has been applied to the creation and dissolution of the partnership.

(3) A property investment business is carried on by a company owned in equal shares by four family members. The company is to be sold to an unconnected third party. The four individuals establish a partnership to hold the properties that were held by the company but that aren't included in the sale. There is a clear commercial reason for the properties to be transferred out of the company that is to be sold to the unconnected third party.

(4) A property lettings business is carried on by three individuals X, Y and Z through a partnership. X, Y and Z consider that, commercially, the best way to continue to carry on their business is through a company. They therefore decide to incorporate the business. X, Y and Z subscribe for shares in a new company in the same proportion as their respective partnership holdings. The properties are transferred to the company.

(5) X and Y are corporate partners in a joint property-letting venture. They are unconnected except through their shares in the partnership. The partnership owns one property. Y's shareholders have accepted an offer from a third party, Z, to acquire all of its share capital. Z does not wish to continue to operate the business with X so the decision is taken to distribute the property to Y. There is a clear commercial reason for the transactions. The normal Stamp Duty Land Tax rules applied to the original acquisition of the property by the company.'

'Situations where HMRC considers that S.75A applies

(1) V agrees to sell land to X, and X agrees to sell the same land to P which is a partnership where the partners are X and persons connected to him. At the same time as the completion of the V-X contract, the X–P contract completes, this acquisition is effected by means of a "transfer of rights". X argues that no Stamp Duty Land Tax is due as his contract is disregarded by s.45, whilst P argues that no Stamp Duty Land Tax is due per Schedule 15 of FA 2003 given its connection with X. Section 75A applies because HMRC considers that the conditions of s75A 1(a) – (c) are met and that the notional transaction V-P could have been achieved in a more straight forward manner that would not have satisfied s75A(1)(c); Stamp Duty Land Tax is due on the notional consideration which is the full amount of consideration received by V.

(2) V agrees to sell land to X, and X agrees to sell the same land to P which is a partnership where the partners are X, X1 Ltd. and X2 Ltd. companies connected

to X which manage a trust for which X is the beneficiary. V and X enter an arrangement where V settles a nominal amount into X's trust, thereby creating a connection between V and X as per s.839 of ICTA 1988. The V-X contract completes and at the same time and simultaneously the X–P contract completes. X claims that no Stamp Duty Land Tax is due as his contract is disregarded by s.45 of FA 2003, whilst P claims that no Stamp Duty Land Tax is due per Schedule 15 of FA 2003 given its connection with X. Section 75A applies and the notional transaction involved is V-P Stamp Duty Land Tax is due on the notional consideration which is the full amount of consideration received by V.

Legislation: FA 2003, s. 75C(8A)

TRANSFER OF CHARGEABLE INTEREST TO A PARTNERSHIP

16-220   Basic statutory rule

Paragraph 10 applies where:

(a)   a partner transfers a chargeable interest to the partnership; or

(b)   a person transfers a chargeable interest to a partnership in return for an interest in the partnership; or

(c)   a person connected with either a partner or with a person who becomes a partner as a result of or in connection with the transfer, transfers a chargeable interest to the partnership.

It applies whether the transfer is in connection with the formation of the partnership or is a transfer to an existing partnership.

The transfer of a chargeable interest expressly includes (FA 2003, Sch. 15, para. 9(2)):

- the grant or creation of a chargeable interest;
- the variation of a chargeable interest; and
- the surrender, release or renunciation of a chargeable interest.

For land transactions effected on or after 19 July 2006 the formula for chargeable consideration was simplified to: MV × (100 − SLP)%, that is leaving out any reference to actual consideration paid (other than 'post-transaction consideration': see ¶16-320 below).

Legislation: FA 2003, Sch. 15, para. 9 and 10

16-240   Thinking behind the rule

The aim of the charging formula is to restrict the market value charge to the chargeable interest transferred to a partnership in which the owner is or becomes a partner by reference to the lower of (a) his ownership of the interest outside the partnership and (b) the combined interest of him and any connected individuals in the partnership. Partnership interests of persons connected with the transferor are assumed to belong to the transferor, but (from 6 December 2006) only if the connected person is an individual (which from Royal Assent to FA 2007 includes a particular corporate trustee). However, the interest of a partner in the same 75% group as the transferor is from 6 December 2006 included in the SLP computation – subject to the group relief clawback rules. For transactions prior to 19 July 2006, a proportion of any consideration actually given for the transfer (whether or not by connected persons) was also charged.

Significantly, however, it is income and not capital shares which are used to measure partnership shares (FA 2003, Sch. 15, para. 34(2)).

The calculation works by determining:

- which of the transferor(s) either is a partner or is connected with a partner; and
- for each of these transferor(s), the lower of the percentage of their ownership outside the partnership and that of their ownership (or that of connected persons) inside the partnership.

Where there is more than one such transferor, the proportions determined for each transferor are aggregated to determine how much remains in their ownership.

Example 1

Lady Susan Vernon transfers land worth £500,000 to a partnership comprising Lady Susan and Miss Johnson (an unconnected person). Miss Johnson has a 40% share in the partnership (both income and capital) and pays £250,000. The charge is on 40% of market value. The actual consideration is ignored.

In effect, the partnership acquiring the chargeable interest must identify what proportion of the chargeable interest changes hands (i.e. beyond the partnership interest of the transferor or persons connected with him) and it is that proportion of the market value of the interest which is charged to SDLT.

Example 2

Suppose instead, outside the partnership, Lady Susan transfers a 40% share in the land to Miss Johnson for £200,000. Miss Johnson suffers an SDLT liability at 1% of £2,000. Each then separately introduces the land into the partnership. SLP in relation to Lady Susan is 60% and in relation to Miss Johnson is 40%.

So, the chargeable consideration in relation to Lady Susan is:

40% × £300,000 = £120,000.

The chargeable consideration in relation to Miss Johnson is:

60% × £200,000 = £120,000.

Therefore the chargeable consideration for the acquisition by the partnership is:

£120,000 + £120,000 = £240,000 charged at 1%, i.e. £2,400.

So the total SDLT in this scenario (£4,400) would accordingly work out higher than in example 70A (£2,400).

Consider this third possibility:

Example 3

However, if Lady Susan and Miss Johnson were together to introduce their respective shares of land into the partnership, it appears that the only SDLT payable would be the £2,000 on Miss Johnson's initial acquisition of a 40% share. This is because, following through para. 12 defining 'the sum of the lower proportions' – see ¶16-280 below – the SLP in relation to the two partners together would be 100. Therefore there would be no charge on the market value and there is no actual consideration, assuming none withdrawn in the following three years, to be charged by para. 17A of FA 2003, Sch. 15.

It is understood that this analysis expressed above (which would apply also following FA 2006) is the one in fact applied by HMRC Stamp Taxes. On this basis, there is presumably no avoidance of SDLT to be subject to the disclosure regime.

Example 4

Mr De Courcy transfers land worth £1m into a partnership consisting of his daughter Alicia, son Reginald and his prospective son-in-law James (with whom Mr De Courcy is unconnected, at least until the marriage), for no consideration. Each partner has an equal one third income share in the partnership. The SDLT charge is based on the value of land attributable to the income share of the unconnected person James, viz. £333,333 charged at 3%, to produce an SDLT bill of £10,000.

Legislation: FA 2003, Sch. 15, para. 17A, 34

16-260   Where the chargeable consideration includes rent

In a case where rent forms all or part of the consideration for the transfer of a chargeable interest to a partnership, there is a substituted computation for the chargeable consideration. In effect, it becomes the equivalent proportion of the 'net present value' of the rent, together with the equivalent proportion of the market value of any chargeable consideration other than rent (whether or not such consideration is payable). Simplifications for a case covered by para. 11 are introduced with effect from 19 July 2006 by para. 3 of Sch. 24 to FA 2006. These embrace both (a) the formula for calculating the SDLT charge on the grant of such a lease and (b) the calculation of the charge on the net present value of any rent payable under such a lease. The 'relevant chargeable proportion' in each case becomes '(100 – SLP)%': see ¶16-280 for the SLP.

Legislation: FA 2003, Sch. 15, para. 11

16-280   Sum of the lower proportions

The SLP (sum of the lower proportions) is relevant to finding out the chargeable proportion under para. 10 for both the market value and, before 19 March 2006, the actual consideration paid. Five steps are required by para. 12, taking shares in income immediately before the transaction. Note that SLP will always be 100 in the case where the only partners entitled to income shares comprise the transferor and/or persons connected with him (who, from 6 December 2006 are individuals – which after Royal Assent to FA 2007 includes certain corporate trustees – or companies in a 75% group with the transferor).

(1)   Identify the relevant owner (or owners), *viz.* the person who immediately before the transaction was entitled to a proportion of the chargeable interest and immediately after the transaction is a partner or is connected with a partner.

In example 4, this is Mr De Courcy.

(2)   For each relevant owner, identify the corresponding partner or partners, *viz.* the partner who immediately after the transaction either is the relevant owner or is connected with the relevant owner.

In example 4, these are Alicia and Reginald.

(3)   For each relevant owner, find the proportion of the chargeable interest to which he was entitled immediately before the transaction. And apportion that proportion between any one or more of the relevant owner's corresponding partners.

It is understood that the apportionment of the chargeable interest between the corresponding partners can be made in a way which best suits the taxpayers, in the case where there is more than one possible method of apportionment. See SDLTM 33570 and the example there discussed.

In example 4, this is 100% apportioned 50/50 between the corresponding partners Alicia and Reginald.

(4) Find the lower proportion for each person who is a corresponding partner in relation to one or more relevant owners. The lower proportion is the lower of:

(a) the proportion of the chargeable interest attributable to the partner; and

(b) the partner's partnership share immediately after the transaction,

To find (a), it is:

- if he is a corresponding partner in relation to only one relevant owner, the proportion (if any) of the chargeable interest apportioned to him at Step three in respect of that owner;
- if he is a corresponding partner in relation to more than one relevant owner, the sum of the proportions (if any) of the chargeable interest apportioned to him at Step three in respect of each of those owners.

In example 4, each of Alicia and Reginald has a lower proportion of 1/3.

(5) Add together the lower proportions of each person who is a corresponding partner in relation to one or more relevant owners.

The result is the sum of the lower proportions (SLP).

In example 4, the SLP is ⅓ plus ⅓ = ⅔. So the 'relevant chargeable proportion' or RCP in relation to the market value is $(100 - 66.7) = 33.3\%$.

Step three

A change described as 'anti-avoidance' was made from 6 December 2006 by the *Stamp Duty Land Tax (Variation of the Finance Act 2003) Regulations* 2006 (SI 2006/3237), reg. 2 and Schedule, para. 2(2). When calculating the 'sum of the lower proportions' for the purposes of para. 10, 11, 18 or 19 of Sch. 15, partners who are connected with 'relevant owners' but who are not individuals are not treated as 'corresponding partners' in relation to that relevant owner. There are transitional provisions described at ¶16-180. These changes are made by FA 2007, s. 72(3), to take effect from Royal Assent.

A second change made from 6 December 2006, adding new para. 27A to FA 2003, Sch. 15, provides for a modified form of group relief on transfers of land to (but not from) partnerships (see ¶16-640 below). This is found in FA 2007, s. 72(9), with effect from Royal Assent.

A third change made from Royal Assent by FA 2007, s. 72(4) provides that a company which holds property as a trustee and which is 'connected' for tax purposes with a relevant owner only because of CTA 2010, s. 1122(6) is to be treated as an individual connected with the relevant owner. So a trustee which is a company can safely act as a partner in a partnership to which the relevant owner transfers land without an SDLT exposure.

Legislation: FA 2003, Sch. 15, para. 12

16-300   Ascertaining the partnership shares

It will not always be straightforward to determine the relevant partnership shares within 30 days after the transaction. Imagine a not uncommon scenario with say two individual partners and one corporate partner. The individual partners have fixed shares of say £50,000 each and the corporate partner the balance of the income share. Where land is transferred to the partnership during an accounting period, the income share of the corporate partner will not be known until after the year end. Presumably a land transaction return should be submitted on the basis of a provisional estimate, to be firmed up once the shares are known.

16-320   Post-transaction consideration: Finance (No. 2) Act 2005 measure

F(No. 2)A 2005, Sch. 10, para. 10 introduced a new FA 2003, Sch. 15, para. 17A *Withdrawal of money etc from partnership after transfer of chargeable interest*, with effect from 20 May 2005. The rule applies where there is a transfer of a chargeable interest to a partnership falling within Sch. 15, para. 10(1)(a), (b) or (c) and within the following three years there is a 'qualifying event' . This is defined in terms of a withdrawal from the partnership of money or money's worth which does not represent income profit. This might occur through the 'relevant person' (being the transferor and, where the transfer is within para. 10(1)(c), the transferor or a person connected with him) withdrawing capital from his capital account, reducing his interest or ceasing to be a partner. Where the relevant person has made a loan to the partnership, a 'qualifying event' means the repayment of the loan in whole or in part or a withdrawal by the relevant person from the partnership of money or money's worth which does not represent income profit.

Effect of para. 17A

Where para. 17A applies, the qualifying event is to be taken to be a land transaction which is a chargeable transaction, with the partners being the purchasers. The chargeable consideration is the value of the money withdrawn from the partnership or the amount of the loan repaid or, where following a loan there is a withdrawal of money or money's worth from the partnership, such amount of the withdrawal as does not exceed the loan. There is a limitation so that the chargeable consideration shall not exceed the market value of the land at the effective date of the land transfer, reduced by the amount previously chargeable to SDLT.

The thinking behind this new rule was possibly to catch cases where, on the face of it, there is either (a) a gift of the land or (b) where the chargeable transaction falls within the relevant threshold(s), and money tantamount to consideration is paid within the following three years. But, to be caught, there need be no connection between the original transfer of land and the subsequent withdrawal of capital. Given the removal of actual consideration from the SDLT charging formula for the transfer of land to a partnership from 19 July 2006 (see ¶16-220), it may seem somewhat anomalous that the para. 17A charging provision remains.

However, para. 17A did address certain tax avoidance schemes. For example, if A wished to sell valuable land to B, B as purchaser would ordinarily pay SDLT on the sale consideration. If instead A and B formed a partnership and A contributed the land into the partnership in return for, say, a 99% interest in the partnership (with B making a modest contribution of cash for a 1% interest), the chargeable consideration for the transfer by A would be calculated on 1% of the market value of the land. If the partnership subsequently borrowed funds against the property, the idea was that A could withdraw money from the partnership (as a withdrawal of 'capital', reducing his partnership share accordingly and thereby increasing B's partnership share). Such withdrawal, within three years, is caught by para. 17A. The three year rule corresponds to the three year clawback rule for withdrawal of group relief.

It may not always be easy, as a practical matter, to determine amounts standing to the credit of the transferor's partnership accounts which do not represent income profit. This must be an argument for ensuring that separate income and capital accounts are clearly demarcated.

Removal of double charge

A potential double charge to SDLT is removed by para. 10 of Sch. 24 to FA 2006, in the case where the same event gives rise both to a para. 17A charge and to a charge under para. 14 (transfer for consideration of interest in property investment partnership). In this case, the para. 14 charge is primary and goes to reduce any remaining charge under para. 17A, though not below nil. However, there does remain a potential double charge under para. 17A in a case where it subjects to SDLT chargeable consideration which has already been taxed under para. 10. This problem was put to HMRC Stamp Taxes, but without result.

Transition in Scotland to the Land and Buildings Transaction Tax

On 13 February 2015, HMRC published guidance (*Transitional guidance on the introduction of Land and Buildings Transaction Tax*) on applying the transitional rules to Scottish land transactions.

This included specific guidance in relation to the treatment of qualifying events under para. 17A.

Legislation: FA 2003, Sch. 15, para. 14 and 17A; FA 2006, Sch. 24, para. 10

16-340   Election by property investment partnership to disapply para. 10

Property investment partnerships can elect, under para. 12A, for para. 10 not to apply to a transfer of a chargeable interest to a property investment partnership. The effect is that the chargeable consideration is the market value of the chargeable interest transferred, and the transaction is treated as one within Sch. 15, Pt. 2 (ordinary partnership transactions).

It is only possible to make an election in relation to the transfer of a chargeable interest to a partnership that is a property investment partnership within para. 14(8). The election is irrevocable and must be included in the relevant land transaction or an amendment of that return.

Where an election under this paragraph in respect of a transaction (the 'main transaction') is made in an amendment of a land transaction return:

(a)   the election has effect as if it had been made on the date on which the land transaction return was made; and

(b)   any land transaction return in respect of an affected transaction may be amended (within the period allowed for amendment of that return) to take account of that election.

'Affected transaction' in relation to the main transaction, means a transaction to which para. 14 applied, with an effective date on or after the effective date of the main transaction.

Legislation: FA 2003, Sch. 15, para. 12A

16-360   Summing up

Putting all this together, there will be no SDLT issues to consider on land going into a partnership, provided that:

(a)   all the partners comprise the transferor and/or persons connected with him (who, from 6 December 2006 are individuals – which from Royal Assent to FA 2007 includes certain corporate trustees – subject to a modified form of group relief); *and*

(b)   no money is withdrawn by the transferor from the partnership within three years after the transaction, except as represents income profits: see ¶16-320); *and*

(c)   for transactions before 19 July 2006, no actual consideration is paid at the time: if no more than £150,000 is paid there will be compliance but no liability implications.

Subject to that, the general principle is that where land is contributed to a partnership in return for an interest in the partnership, the SDLT liability will normally be calculated by reference to the market value of the share in the land that accrues to, or is effectively transferred to, the other partners. If the person contributing the land acquires a, say, one-third interest or share in the partnership, he will generally have 'transferred' a two-thirds share to the other partners, with SDLT computed accordingly.

For transfers on or after 19 July 2006, payment of any consideration has no impact on the issue of SDLT (other than 'post-transaction consideration' amounts described at ¶16-320): see ¶16-220. Prior to this, the credit of the land to the capital account(s) of partners other than the transferor would presumably constitute a gift by the transferor, except to the extent that there was consideration. Remember that consideration would include the assumption of liability for a debt secured on the land. Equally, a change in income shares (e.g. favouring the transferor) might also constitute consideration, where 'part of the deal'. The big question to be resolved was what is 'consideration' for these purposes.

TRANSFER OF PARTNERSHIP INTEREST

16-380   Basic statutory rule

Where:

(a)   there is a transfer of an interest in a partnership, which (from 19 July 2007) is a property investment partnership; and
(b)   the relevant partnership property includes a chargeable interest, the transfer is taken to be a land transaction which is a chargeable transaction.

The purchaser is the person who acquires an increased partnership share or who becomes a partner as a result of the transfer.

Property investment partnerships

With effect from 19 July 2007, the para. 14 charge is restricted to the transfer of a chargeable interest in a 'property investment partnership'. This is one whose 'sole or main activity is investing or dealing in chargeable interests (whether or not that activity involves the carrying out of construction operations on the land in question)'. The phrase 'construction operations' is given the meaning it has in FA 2004, Pt. 3, Ch. 3. This is achieved by para. 9 of Sch. 24 to FA 2004.

The meaning of 'sole or main' has been raised with HMRC Stamp Taxes. It is understood that the expression will be given the same interpretation as is the phrase 'wholly or mainly' in IHTA 1984, s. 105(3) for the purposes of business property relief from inheritance tax: see para IHTM 25263 of the *Inheritance Tax Manual*.

These rules have been amended several times in 2006, 2007 and 2008. The relevant rules applying at the effective date need to be noted. In particular, it should be noted that the anti-avoidance provisions introduced in FA 2007 are amended retrospectively from the date Royal Assent was given to FA 2007 (19 July 2007). The legislation amended para. 14, and defines Type A and Type B transactions to which the charge applies but provides a facility to disapply the charge on entry and exit from the partnership (para. 12A).

Partnerships other than property investment partnerships

Transfers of interest in partnerships other than property investment partnerships are not generally chargeable to SDLT.

If, for example, a person buys into a partnership then there is a transfer of interest in the partnership. However, providing the partnership is not a property investment partnership (see ¶16-540 below) and there has not previously been a transfer to the partnership falling within para. 10 then the acquisition of the interest is not deemed to be a land transaction. As a result, no liability to SDLT arises, even though the partnership holds chargeable interests.

Chargeable consideration

The chargeable consideration is a proportion of the market value of the relevant partnership property. That proportion is:

(a)   if the transferee was not a partner before the transfer, his partnership share immediately after it; and

(b)   if he was a partner before the transfer, the difference between his partnership share before and after the transfer.

The 'relevant partnership property' excludes (inter alia) any interest which was transferred to the partnership in connection with the transfer and also market value leases excluded by para. 15 (see ¶16-400).

Note that, for transactions prior to 19 July 2007, the para. 14 charge was triggered whenever consideration was given for the transfer (which would include the assumption of liability).

Consider the following example.

Example 5

Edward carries on a property investment business in partnership with his wife Laura and daughter Marianne, with the partnership income shares being 50%, 30% and 20% respectively. Edward transfers a partnership interest to Laura. The partnership owns £16m of land. Laura pays Edward £50,000. Edward's partnership income share reduces to 40% and Laura's increases to 40%.

The chargeable proportion of the market value of the relevant partnership property is 10% of £16m *viz.* £1.6m, that is the difference between Laura's partnership share before and after the transfer: SDLT of £64,000 (£1.6m at 4%) is payable.

Legislation: FA 2003, Sch. 15, para. 14

16-400   Market rent leases

A 'market rent lease' is not relevant partnership property for para. 14 purposes if four conditions are met.

(1)   No chargeable consideration other than rent has been given for the grant of the lease and there are no arrangements in place at the time of the transfer for any such chargeable consideration to be given.

(2)   The rent payable under the lease as granted was a market rent at the time of the grant.

(3)   (a) the term of the lease is five years or less or (b) if the term of the lease is more than five years, there is provision for a rent review at least once every five years and the rent payable following a review is required to be market rent at the review date.

(4)   There has been no change to the lease since it was granted such that immediately after the change the rent payable is less than the market rent.

The market rent at any time is the rent which that lease might reasonably expected to fetch in the open market.

The exclusion of market rent leases from relevant partnership property is easy enough to understand, designed as it is to exclude from chargeable consideration leases which have no discernable value. A difficulty might seem to arise with agricultural leases which generally will have a term of more than five years. To qualify as a market rent review the rent must be reviewable at least once in every five years and the rent payable as a result of a review must be a market rent at the review date. This should be satisfied in the case of a continuing lease where the market rent would be that awarded by a tribunal. But, in the case of a new tenant, the market rent is likely to be higher than that set by a tribunal, *viz.* the tender rent. In those circumstances, the condition should still be satisfied on the basis that this would be the 'market rent' as defined. The above said, however, it is understood that HMRC Stamp Taxes take the view that *Agricultural Holdings Act* tenancies are less than five years.

It is perfectly possible for a commercial lease not to be a 'market rent lease' as defined by para. 15. Provision for an upwards only rent review would fail the condition 3(1) above, though it is understood that Stamp Taxes do not take the point. On the other hand, arguably the market value of a lease falling outside para. 15 is effectively nil, which probably solves the problem.

Legislation: FA 2003, Sch. 15, para. 15

16-410   Exchanges of land

Where there is an exchange of land in connection with acquiring an interest in a partnership, the interest in the partnership is treated as a major interest in land for purposes of Sch. 4, para. 5, if the relevant partnership property includes a major interest in land. These provisions relating to partitions at Sch. 4, para. 6 are disapplied.

Legislation: FA 2003, Sch. 15, para. 16

16-420   Anti-avoidance provision

The partnership share acquired in exchange for the transfer of land into a partnership may have been artificially increased. That would therefore lower the proportion of the other partners' partnership interests and the SDLT charge correspondingly. There is a deemed chargeable transaction (to counteract the SDLT advantage) when there is a readjustment to the partnership shares. Specifically, this applies where:

(a)   there is subsequently a transfer of an interest in the partnership;(b) made by the person or partner concerned in the original land transfer, and pursuant to arrangements in place at that time; and

(c)   where the transfer in (a) is not otherwise a chargeable transaction.

On 13 February 2015, HMRC published guidance (*Transitional guidance on the introduction of Land and Buildings Transaction Tax*) on applying the transitional rules to Scottish land transactions.

This included specific guidance in relation to transactions involving partnerships under para. 17.

Legislation: FA 2003, Sch. 15, para. 17

16-440   Changes in income profit-sharing ratios

Is a mere change in income profit-sharing ratios the 'transfer of an interest in a partnership'? Stamp Taxes clearly answer this question in the affirmative. However, an article by Patrick Cannon in *Taxation* of 10 March 2005 argued that this view was wrong in principle, as a matter of statutory interpretation. However, it must be considered safer to follow the HMRC interpretation.

An opposition amendment to FB 2004 in what is now para. 34(2) of Sch. 15 would have substituted capital for income-sharing ratios in determining a partner's partnership share. Quite apart from obvious difficulties where there are disparities between income and capital shares (see below), consider the possible effect of adjustments in prior salaries to a partner's total 'take' where the profit sharing ratios remain the same, even though generally these should not present a problem in the light of what is said at ¶16-460. (We are indebted for this example to Howard Paskins of Smith & Williamson.)

Example 6

Year 1

	Salary	Profit	Total	%
A		75,000	75,000	27.27%
B	50,000	75,000	125,000	45.45%
C		75,000	75,000	27.27%
	50,000	225,000	275,000	100%

Year 2

	Salary	Profit	Total	%
A		200,000	200,000	30.77%
B	50,000	200,000	250,000	38.46%
C		200,000	200,000	30.77%
	50,000	600,000	650,000	100%

The question is whether in such (not uncommon) circumstances there is an SDLT issue under para. 14. The issue is whether an increased partnership share has been acquired (in this example by A and C). The argument that consideration has not been given would be that it is only on a change in the residual income shares that there is a shift in the sharing of liabilities and consideration is given by one partner to the other(s).

However, if there were an occasion of charge in such a case and the land concerned was worth say £6m, there would be an SDLT charge (for each of A and B at 1% of £210,000 (3.5% of £6m)), unless A and C were connected with B, in which case the SDLT charge would be at 3%. To be on the safe side, unless the chargeable consideration is clearly no more than £150,000 (see ¶16-480), a provisional return should be submitted within 30 days of the earliest point at which the 'effective date' can be said to occur, with a series of claims and disclosures once the accounts are finalised (since only at that point will the precise income-sharing ratios relative to each other be determined). Happily, however, there is no SDLT charge in the circumstances of example 6 (see ¶16-460).

Legislation: FA 2003, Sch. 15, para. 14, 34

16-460   HMRC's response: the meaning of 'arrangements'

Example 6 above was put to Stamp Taxes by the Stamp Taxes Practitioners Group (STPG). The response from Stamp Taxes was that the change in overall income take arose simply because of the effect of a prior salary paid to one of the partners, even though the residual profit shares remained the same; the root cause was that the total available for distribution to the partners had increased. Happily, Stamp Taxes confirmed that, although there had been a transfer of an interest in the partnership (within the meaning of para. 36 as it was prior to 19 July 2007), consideration had not been given. This was because there had been no change either to the fixed salary or to the residual shares. The para. 14 charge would therefore not apply. They warned, however, that if there had been an amendment to the prior salary or changes to the residual shares, that might constitute consideration, with para. 14 therefore applying. However, all the circumstances have to be regarded. If in the example partner B's salary had increased to £80,000 in Year 2, leaving £190,000 (rather than £200,000) profit for each partner, although partners A and C would have received an increased share as against the previous year, they would not have given consideration for the increase (as it would not have been in direct consequence of the increased salary paid to B). It would still be as a consequence of the increased profit to be distributed (and the lower significance of salary to overall profit share). This analysis (while favourable to the taxpayer) the authors find curious.

Example 7

Year 1

	Salary	*Profit*	*Total*	*%*
A		75,000	75,000	27.27%
B	50,000	75,000	125,000	45.45%
C		75,000	75,000	27.27%
	50,000	225,000	275,000	100%

Year 2

	Salary	*Profit*	*Total*	*%*
A		90,000	90,000	25%
B	60,000	120,000	180,000	50%
C		90,000	90,000	25%
	60,000	300,000	360,000	100%

Here, there has been both an increase in salary and a change in profit share and so there would, on Stamp Taxes' interpretation, be an SDLT liability insofar as the partnership property included UK land. This time, of course, it is B's (rather than A's and C's) share of profit which has increased: there has therefore been a transfer of partnership interest from each of A and C to B. Assuming that the land in the partnership is worth £6m, the chargeable consideration would be £6m × 4.55% = £273,000, charged to SDLT at 3% to produce a liability on B of £8,190. The problem might be that things get changed the following year, with SDLT liabilities for either or both of A and C.

One practical question is whether, in a partnership which adopts the principle 'you eat what you kill', changes in residual income shares from year to year (with no question of any prior salary) are caught by para. 14 where there is land in the balance sheet (or, looking at ¶16-720), off the balance sheet but used in the partnership business. The question seems to be whether within para. 14(1)(b) (as it was prior to 19 July 2007) 'consideration is given for the transfer': if it is, a market value rule is applied. But do the additional fees brought into the partnership by the partner whose share increases constitute 'consideration' for the transfer of an interest in the partnership? If the profit allocation follows the terms of the partnership agreement, the authors would argue that no consideration is given in these circumstances, whereas a partnership decision to adopt a different basis of profit-sharing in any one year might well have brought para. 14(1)(b) into play. While the issue is not clear and requires clarification, the authors understand that, in the view of HMRC Stamp Taxes, the partnership agreement does not constitute 'arrangements'. That is, the possible problem envisaged by the paragraph does not arise.

Legislation: FA 2003, Sch. 15, para. 14

16-480   Compliance issues

The 'tidy' case of partnership changes on the accounting date should be fairly manageable, in terms of compliance, especially if the point is addressed in a timely way year on year. There remains, however, a problem illustrated by variants on example 7 above, as to whether in any given year a particular partner is a transferor or a transferee! That said, what if there are partnership changes during the year, as people come and go, and changes in income sharing are made at that point, but without knowing how the overall profit sharing for the year is going to turn out? May be the solution is to proceed as suggested below.

In the case where there is a para. 14 charge because of 'arrangements', it seems that the next year's profit allocation on the basis of assumed salary and residual income shares should be estimated, to be revised once the accounts are available. If the estimate does not exceed the notification threshold, HMRC Stamp Taxes have said that no penalty will be charged if the final figure is above the threshold. And it appears that interest may not be charged either. Some of the difficulties discussed in ¶16-440 and ¶16-460 derive from the issue as to what is the trigger date for compliance purposes in the case of the transfer of a partnership interest. It is understood that Stamp Taxes accept that the final return cannot be submitted before the date on which the partnership accounts are signed, as there is no knowing before then what the partnership interests for the period concerned are going to be. However, there remains the point about provisional returns made at ¶16-460 and example 7.

Note that, helpfully, under para. 30 of FA 2003, Sch. 15 a transaction which is a chargeable transaction under para. 14 or 17 (transfer of partnership interest) is a notifiable transaction if, but only if, the consideration for the transaction exceeds the zero-rate threshold. This means that, with non-residential land, a transaction where the chargeable consideration is (say) £140,000 is not notifiable.

Legislation: FA 2003, Sch. 15, para. 14, 17 and 30

16-500 Existence of 'arrangements': the Stamp Taxes rule of thumb

The crucial question in analysing example 7 is whether or not there are 'arrangements', whether because of clauses in the partnership agreement or indeed arrangements outside such an agreement. The practical position adopted by Stamp Taxes (hitherto, at least) seems to be that events occurring automatically under the partnership agreement and usual business facilities can be disregarded: that is, it is only circumstances resulting from a new factor which might constitute arrangements. A typical example may be the retirement of a senior partner who is paid his capital share: Stamp Taxes take the view that there could be SDLT issues where the payment is funded through additional capital subscribed by the continuing partners or by a new bank loan, but not where the payment can be made within an existing overdraft facility. However, paying out the retiring partner by instalments over a period would be caught as 'arrangements'.

Example 8

Augusta is about to retire from the family property firm. Her share in income profits is 40%, the balance being divided equally between her three children. Following a revaluation of all the partnership's assets (including land and buildings, now worth £2m), Augusta is being paid £500,000 in repayment of her capital and current accounts. The continuing partners cannot afford to pay that amount without resorting to the bank for a specific loan. The chargeable consideration for SDLT purposes, therefore, is 40% (the amount of the income share being transferred) of the market value of the land, viz. £2m, that is £800,000 on which SDLT of £32,000 will be payable by the three children.

16-520 What is necessary to constitute the transfer of a partnership share?

Changes were made to Sch. 15, para 36 by *Finance Act* 2007.

In relation to the position prior to such changes, the draft SDLT Manual stated the following:

'SDLTM 34700 Transfers under FA03/SCH15/PARA36(a)

This is the case where A (a partner) transfers (some of) his interest as partner to B (who may or may not already be a partner).

For A to transfer some of his interest as partner, that interest must be reduced after the transfer and B's interest must be increased after the transfer. Although the term 'interest as partner' is not defined, it is regarded as the cash equivalent of a partner's partnership interest. This means it is equivalent to the profit his share of the partnership entitles him to and the capital his share of the partnership entitles him to on dissolution (which may not necessarily be the same).

So, a transfer under para. 36(a) is one where the transferring partner's cash interest reduces and another persons increases as a consequence of that reduction, the comparison being made with their interests before the transaction.'

While para. 36(a) on the face of it looks very wide, it seems that Stamp Taxes may be applying a narrower meaning. This is relevant in relation to example 3 which was formerly included in the *Stamp Duty Land Tax Manual* as SDLTM 35400:

'(3) A three person equal partnership (A-B-C) has profits of £150,000 and partnership capital of £1,500,000. Partner A retires, withdrawing his capital. The partnership continues as a two person equal partnership (B-C).

This is not be a transfer under Paragraph 36(a) as the remaining partners still have the equivalent of £500,000 of net assets and with the reasonable prospect of profits declining in line with net assets, the monetary equivalent of £50,000 profits each.

This is not a transfer under Paragraph 36(b) as no-one has become a partner.

If there were arrangements in place such that B and C increased their partnership capital to allow A to withdraw his, this would be chargeable by virtue of Paragraph 14(4)(a) as these arrangements would be the purchase of (part of) A's share. For example, if the partnership only had available cash or other assets of £300,000 and B and C contributed an extra £100,000 cash each to the partnership, thus allowing A to withdraw his £500,000, this can be seen to be a purchase of £100,000 of A's interest by each of B and C. B's and C's interest in the partnership capital is now £600,000 each and thus there would be a transfer under Paragraph 36(a). In this case the chargeable consideration for each of B and C would be the difference in their profit share as a proportion of the market value of the partnership property. This difference is 16.7% of the market value of the partnership property each.

This would also apply to the case where arrangements were entered into whereby the funding of A's retirement extended of a period. In the example above, where the partnership could only afford to pay A £300,000 for his interest worth £500,000, if there were arrangements entered into whereby A retired, taking the available £300,000 with the balance being left in the partnership as a loan from A (effectively being a withdrawal of £500,000 by A with an immediate loan back to the partnership of £200,000 by A), this would be chargeable by virtue of paragraph 14(4)(a) as the only way the loan could be repaid is by B and/or C transferring cash to A. The arrangements might be that B and C left sufficient profits in the partnership over a five-year period to enable A's loan to be repaid. These arrangements would be caught as the leaving of profit in the partnership to enable repayment of the loan from A is no different to the immediate introduction of fresh capital into the partnership to achieve the same ends. The only difference is that the arrangements extend over a period.

This would also cover the position whereby B and C entered into arrangements to increase personally guaranteed loan facilities to the partnership to enable the payment to be made to A. (In other words, B and C would give/have given personal guarantees to secure a loan to the partnership and in the event that these guarantees were called upon, the funds would be non-partnership funds). This is because the guarantees, in the event of them being called in, would have the effect of increasing the partnership capital (by reducing the partnership debt from sources other than the partnership).

Again, if B and C gave A £100,000 each from assets they held outside the partnership, this would also constitute arrangements for a transfer as A would only have withdrawn £300,000 from the partnership capital leaving £1,200,000 to be split between B and C. Thus they would have entered into arrangements to facilitate the transfer of the

£100,000 of partnership capital to each of them and the transaction would be chargeable (again on 16.7% of the market value of the partnership property each).'

Analysis:

The above notes that (a) a loan back by the retiring partner, (b) increased loan facilities and (c) cash injections by the continuing partners are chargeable events. While this is correct in so far as it goes, it did not address the issue of the degree of limitation to which para. 14 may be subjected. The former Manual paragraph SDLTM 34700 also failed to address the scope of para. 29 ('the only charging provisions'), which presumably was to be divined from an examination of the numbered scenarios in the former paragraph SDLTM 35400.

In particular, the second paragraph of former SDLTM 34700 could not be right (see ¶16-420). As the expressions 'interest in a partnership' and 'interest as partner' are not defined specifically for SDLT purposes, should they not have the meaning they have in the law of partnership? The Stamp Taxes' interpretation is unclear and does not accord with the general partnership law definition. Stamp Taxes say that the terms mean the 'cash equivalent' of such an interest which apparently is taken to mean 'the profit to which the share of the partnership entitles him *and* the capital to which his share of the partnership entitles him on dissolution'. Although the manual states that the two elements may not necessarily be the same, the capital to which a partner is entitled on retirement or dissolution is likely to be the balance on his capital account plus any undrawn balance on his current account less any overdrawn balance on current account. This may well not be the same as the partner's proportionate interest in the partnership assets per the partnership agreement.

See now at ¶16-760.

Legislation: FA 2003, Sch. 15, para. 36

16-540   Transfers of interest in a property investment partnership – further detail on the FA 2005 changes

As noted, the impact of the FA 2008 changes was that where there was a transfer of an interest in a property investment partnership and the relevant partnership property included a chargeable interest, the transfer of the interest in the partnership is deemed to be a land transaction for SDLT purposes. The chargeable consideration for the transaction is taken to be a proportion of the market value of the relevant partnership property. Actual consideration is not taken into account in determining the chargeable consideration.

The purchaser under the transaction is the person who acquires an increased partnership share or, as the case may be, becomes a partner in consequence of the transfer. For a new partner, the proportion in question is the partnership share immediately after the

149

transfer. Where there is no new partner, the proportion is the difference between the partner's partnership share before and after the transfer.

Property investment partnership

A property investment partnership is defined as a partnership whose sole or main activity is investing or dealing in chargeable interests. Specifically, it is provided that whether or not a partnership carries on construction operations on the land in question does not affect its status as a property investment partnership. Hence, a partnership that is mainly in the business of property development will be a property investment partnership unless its profits derive from the construction activities. However, a partnership that rents several houses in multiple occupation as a commercial undertaking, where a significant amount of time is spent managing the tenants, collecting rents and undertaking repairs, will be a property investment partnership.

Type A and Type B transfers

Transfers of interests in property investment partnerships are divided into two types: Type A and Type B.

What is taken into account as relevant partnership property depends on whether the transfer is categorised as a Type A or a Type B transfer. Where the transfer is of Type A, most chargeable interests count as relevant partnership property. Where the transfer is of Type B, more categories of chargeable interest are *excluded* from the definition, including:

- any chargeable interest in respect of whose transfer to the partnership an election has been made under FA 2003, Sch. 15, para. 12A; and
- any chargeable interest whose transfer to the partnership was not an event within FA 2003, Sch. 15, para. 10.

Type A transfers

There are two types of Type A transfer. A transfer is a Type A transfer if it takes the form of arrangements entered into under which:

(1) the whole or part of a partner's interest as partner is acquired by another person (who may be an existing partner), and consideration in money or money's worth is given by or on behalf of the person acquiring the interest; or

    (a) a person becomes a partner;

    (b) the interest of an existing partner in the partnership is reduced or an existing partner ceases to be a partner; and

    (c) there is a withdrawal of money or money's worth from the partnership by the existing partner mentioned in paragraph (b) (other than money or money's worth paid from the resources available to the partnership prior to the transfer).

(2)   Relevant partnership property in relation to a Type A transfer of an interest in a partnership, is every chargeable interest held as partnership property immediately after the transfer, other than:

(a)   any chargeable interest that was transferred to the partnership in connection with the transfer;

(b)   a lease to which FA 2003, Sch. 15, para. 15 (exclusion of market rent leases) applies; and

(c)   any chargeable interest that is not attributable economically to the interest in the partnership that is transferred.

Type B transfers

A Type B transfer is any transfer other than a Type A transfer. For Type B transfers, relevant partnership property is every chargeable interest held as partnership property immediately after the transfer, other than:

(a)   as above;
(b)   as above;
(c)   as above;
(d)   any chargeable interest that was transferred to the partnership on or before 22 July 2004;
(e)   any chargeable interest in respect of whose transfer to the partnership an election has been made under FA 2003, Sch. 15, para. 12A; and
(f)   any other chargeable interest whose transfer to the partnership did not fall within FA 2003, Sch. 15, para. 10(1)(a)–(c).

The market rent lease exclusion

A lease held as partnership property immediately after a transfer of an interest in the partnership is not relevant partnership property for either a Type A or a Type B transfer if:

(1)   no chargeable consideration other than rent has been given in respect of the grant of the lease, and no arrangements are in place at the time of the transfer for any chargeable consideration other than rent to be given in respect of the grant of the lease;

(2)   the rent payable under the lease as granted was a market rent at the time of the grant;

(3)   the term of the lease is five years or less, or if the term of the lease is more than five years and:

(a)   the lease provides for the rent payable under it to be reviewed at least once in every five years of the term, and

(b)   the rent payable under the lease as a result of a review is required to be a market rent at the review date; and

(4)   there has been no change to the lease since it was granted which would have the effect of making the rent payable under the lease less than a market rent.

The market rent of a lease at any time is the rent which the lease might reasonably be expected to fetch at that time in the open market. A review date is a date from which the rent determined as a result of a rent review is payable.

Example 9 – Type A

A partnership, consisting of David and Eden, owns the freeholds of many houses in multiple occupation, letting them as a commercial undertaking. None of the properties were introduced by the partners: they were all acquired from unconnected third parties. The partners spend a significant amount of time managing the tenants, collecting rents and undertaking repairs and it is thus accepted that the activity amounts to a business and the partnership is a property investment partnership. Francis wishes to buy into the partnership and pays £500,000 for a 20% share in the profits of the partnership. This results in a reduction in David's and Eden's shares to 40% each.

This partnership is a property investment partnership within para. 14 and consideration is to be given for the partnership interest, so the transfer is of Type A. As a result, the transfer of the interest in the partnership is deemed to be a land transaction chargeable to SDLT and the relevant partnership property is every chargeable interest held by the partnership prior to the transfer of interest. The chargeable consideration is a proportion of the market value of the relevant partnership property, i.e. 20%.

Assuming the market value of the relevant partnership property is £1.6m, 20% is £320,000. Although Francis paid £500,000, it may be presumed that some of this reflects other commercial considerations such as responsibilities as a partner. The actual consideration given for the partnership share is ignored and the chargeable consideration for the transfer is the share acquired by the new: £320,000.

As the purchaser, Francis will be liable to pay the SDLT due on this amount.

Example 10 – Type B

Basic facts as in previous example, but instead of Francis joining the partnership, David wishes to introduce his son Jack, as a partner. He gives Jack half of his interest in the partnership – so Jack acquires a 25% interest in the profits.

Although this is a transfer of an interest in a property investment partnership, as no consideration is given and none of the other provisions in para. 14(3B) apply to make this a Type A transfer, it is a transfer of Type B. For a Type B transfer, relevant partnership property excludes any property whose transfer to the partnership did not fall to be taxed under para. 10. As all the property was purchased from parties unconnected with the partners, none of the property counts as relevant partnership property. There is, therefore, no charge to SDLT on this transfer.

Election by property investment partnership to disapply para. 10

Property investment partnerships can elect, under para. 12A, for para. 10 not to apply to a transfer of a chargeable interest to a property investment partnership. The effect is that the chargeable consideration is the market value of the chargeable interest transferred, and the transaction is treated as one within Sch. 15, Pt. 2 (ordinary partnership transactions).

It is only possible to make an election in relation to the transfer of a chargeable interest to a partnership that is a property investment partnership within para. 14(8). The election is irrevocable and must be included in the relevant land transaction or an amendment of that return.

Where an election under this paragraph in respect of a transaction (the 'main transaction') is made in an amendment of a land transaction return:

(a)   the election has effect as if it had been made on the date on which the land transaction return was made; and

(b)   any land transaction return in respect of an affected transaction may be amended (within the period allowed for amendment of that return) to take account of that election.

'Affected transaction' in relation to the main transaction, means a transaction to which para. 14 applied, with an effective date on or after the effective date of the main transaction.

Effect of election on para. 18

Where an election is made under para. 12A, para. 18 (if relevant) is also disapplied. Paragraph 18 would be relevant only if a chargeable interest was passing from a partnership to a partnership.

Legislation: FA 2003, Sch. 15, para. 12A,14(3A), (3B), (3C), (5), (5A), 15

TRANSFER OF CHARGEABLE INTEREST FROM A PARTNERSHIP

16-560   Basic statutory rule

The third set of rules, in FA 2003, Sch. 15, para. 18, apply where a chargeable interest is transferred:

(a)   from a partnership to a person who is or has been one of the partners; or

(b)   from a partnership to a person connected with a person who is or has been one of the partners.

The chargeable consideration is found much as in the case of the transfer of a chargeable interest to a partnership under para. 10, that is with the same qualification for a group transaction (where under para. 24 market value is taken) and to the extent that the chargeable consideration includes rent (under para. 19). However, (a) the time at which the income shares are measured is immediately after rather than immediately before the transaction and (b) para. 21 and 22 provide a mechanism for adjusting the partnership shares where there have been changes after 19 October 2003.

The formula for finding the chargeable consideration in a case within para. 18 is changed for transactions with an effective date on or after 19 July 2006 to: MV × (100 − SLP)%, that is removing any reference to actual consideration paid (FA 2006, Sch. 24, para. 5). Again, it is understood that this legislative change was made to reflect the previous practice of HMRC Stamp Taxes. Examples 75 and 76 should be read in that light.

A change similar to that in relation to the grant of a lease to a partnership under para. 11 (see ¶16-260) is made by FA 2006, Sch. 24, para. 6 in relation to the grant of a lease by a partnership.

And, by para. 7 of FA 2006, Sch. 24, consequential changes are made to para. 24 of FA 2003, Sch. 15 (transfer of chargeable interest from a partnership consisting wholly of bodies corporate), similar to the changes to para. 13 in the case where the chargeable interest is transferred to the partnership.

It is expressly provided in para. 18(7) that property which was partnership property before dissolution or other cessation of the partnership is treated as remaining as partnership property until it is distributed.

Sum of the lower proportions

The SLP is determined under para. 20 in much the same way as it is under para. 12 in relation to the transfer of a chargeable interest to a partnership (see ¶16-280) and, with one particular exception under Step four, where the partnership share attributable to the partner needs to be found by para. 21 (see ¶16-580).

Partners who are not connected with 'relevant owners' but who are not individuals are not treated as 'corresponding partners' in relation to that relevant owner (the *Stamp Duty Land Tax (Variation of Finance Act 2003) Regulations* 2006 (SI 2006/3237), Schedule, para. 2(5)). There are transitional provisions described at ¶16-180. The legislation for this change is in FA 2007, s. 72(7), effective from 19 July 2007. A further change made by FA 2007, s. 72(4) provides that a company which holds property as a trustee and which is 'connected' for tax purposes with a relevant owner only because of ICTA 1988, s. 839(3) and ITA 2007, s. 993 and 994 is to be treated as an individual connected with the relevant owner. So a trustee which is a company can safely act as a partner in a partnership which transfers land to the relevant owner without an SDLT exposure.

Example 11 (pre-19 July 2006)

Sophia, Dorothea and Graham are in partnership. Neither Dorothea nor Graham is connected with Sophia. The income shares are Sophia: 40%, Dorothea: 30% and Graham: 30%. The partnership was set up in June 1995 when land worth £100,000 was transferred by Sophia into the partnership. The original income shares were Sophia: 90% and each of Dorothea and Graham: 5%. The partnership income shares have been altered at various times between 1995 and 2002. The present shares have been in force since 2002. However, the capital shares remain Sophia: 90% and each of Dorothea and Graham 5%. The land is now worth £1m and Sophia, on retirement, is paying the partnership £100,000 for the withdrawal of the land.

What is the chargeable consideration? $(RCP \times MV) + (RCP \times AC)$

The chargeable consideration is split into a market value element and an actual consideration element. The market value element is applied to the RCP where the SLP needs to be established, under para. 20. In this case the relevant owner is Sophia. The corresponding partner is Sophia alone (neither Dorothea nor Graham being connected with her). The proportion of the chargeable interest to which Sophia is entitled immediately after the transaction is 100%.

The partnership share attributable to Sophia is found by para. 21. Sophia's actual partnership share on 19 October 2003 was 40%. There are no adjustments either to increase or to decrease this share under Steps two and three under para. 22 (see ¶16-580), there being no changes in Sophia's partnership share between 20 October 2003 and the day of her retirement. The lower proportion under Step four of para. 20 is therefore 40% (the lower of the chargeable interest and the partnership share). The sum of the lower proportions (SLP) is also 40%. Therefore, applying the above formula, the chargeable consideration is found as follows:

$(60\% \times £1m) + (40\% \times £100,000) = £640,000$ – as against the actual consideration paid of just £100,000.

Note: in this example the amendment of the charging formula from 19 July 2006 has little impact, in reducing the chargeable consideration by just £40,000 to £600,000.

Legislation: FA 2003, Sch. 15, para. 18

16-580   Partnership share attributable to a partner

The partnership share attributable to the partner is zero unless:

(a) the effective date of the transfer of the relevant chargeable interest to the partnership was before 20 October 2003; or

(b) the effective date was on or after that date and either ad valorem stamp duty or SDLT was paid on the transfer.

The relevant chargeable interest is that which ceases to be partnership property as a result of the transfer or, if the transaction is the grant or creation of a chargeable interest, it is the chargeable interest out of which that interest is granted or created.

In a case where either of (a) or (b) above is satisfied, the partnership share attributable to the partner is found by para. 22 as follows.

Step one

Find the partner's actual partnership share on the relevant date, which is:

- within (a) above, the later of 19 October 2003 and the date on which he became a partner;
- in a case within (b) above, the later of the effective date of the transfer of the relevant chargeable interest to the partnership and the date on which he became a partner.

Step two

To that partnership share are added any increases in the partner's partnership share which occur between the day after the relevant date and immediately before the transfer of the chargeable interest from the partnership and which 'count' for this purpose. The result is the increased partnership share. An increase counts for this purpose only where ad valorem stamp duty or SDLT has been paid on the transfer.

Step three

Deduct from the increased partnership share any decreases in the partner's partnership share which occur between the day after the relevant date and immediately before the transfer of the chargeable interest from the partnership.

The result is the partnership share attributable to the partner, but not so as to fall below zero. The partnership share will be zero if:

- in a case falling within (a) above, the partner ceased to belong to the partnership before 19 October 2003; or
- in a case within (b), the partner left the partnership before the effective date of the transfer of the relevant chargeable interest to the partnership.

> **Example 12**
>
> Philomena and Bertha are 50/50 partners and are not otherwise connected. Land is transferred out of the partnership to Claudia and Laurina in joint owners: 25% to Claudia, 75% to Laurina. Claudia is connected to Bertha but not to Philomena and Laurina is connected to no-one else. The chargeable proportion of the market value would be 75%, as this is the fraction of the property changing hands to a non-connected party (Laurina). The figure is calculated by determining the lower of Claudia's ownership outside the partnership (25%) and her ownership (through a connected party) inside the partnership (50%) to give the SLP. This represents the amount not changing hands, the balance of 75% being chargeable. (Should payment have been made in this example before 19 July 2006, 25% of that payment would also have been chargeable.)

Legislation: FA 2003, Sch. 15, para. 21, 22

16-600   Transfer of chargeable interest from a partnership to a partnership

Paragraph 23 deals with the case where there could be two possible charges, on land going in, and on land coming out, of a partnership.

Instead of the para. 10(2) and para. 18 charges, the greater of what would have been the two possible charges under those paragraphs is taken to be the chargeable consideration.

Consequential changes are made to para. 23 (by FA 2006, Sch. 24, para. 8) with effect from 19 July 2006, consequential on the changes made to para. 10, 11, 18 and 19 of FA 2003, Sch. 15.

Legislation: FA 2003, Sch. 15, para. 23

16-620   Application of para. 18 in a nutshell

Because the measure of charge to SDLT, where it arises, is on the basis of shares in income (para. 34(2)), there can be horrendous and unexpected charges to SDLT where there is a mismatch between income and capital shares and, in particular, where land comes out of a partnership to a partner on the basis of (apparently) his capital share in that land. This was the point of example 75. If on the other hand the retiring partner takes out capital other than a share in land, then as stated above there will not be an SDLT issue, unless:

(a) the case falls within para. 17A (withdrawal of money, etc.), or
(b) the consideration for the transfer of his profit share required additional financing and, following 18 July 2006, the partnership is a property-investment one.

More generally, there will be no chargeable consideration for purposes of the para. 18 charge on market value if the retiring partner's SLP is 100%, though this would be the case only if he and all partners connected with him (who, from 6 December 2006, are individuals – which from Royal Assent to FB 2007 includes certain corporate trustees) were entitled to all of the income profits before retirement. In a case where the SLP is less than 100%, it might in theory be possible to extract the land without any SDLT liability by changing the income sharing ratios to match capital entitlement for a special accounting period of say one month (though this would need to be considered against a *Ramsay*-type analysis or under anti-avoidance legislation. Second, of course, prior to 19 July 2006, to avoid an SDLT liability there had to be no actual consideration paid – or at least any consideration paid had not to exceed £150,000. For transfers of land on or after 19 July 2006, the payment of any consideration has no impact on the issue of SDLT: see ¶16-560.

Note, incidentally, that para. 18 will apply if the transferee of the land from the partnership is someone who has in the past been a partner even if he retired, say, many years ago.

Legislation: FA 2003, Sch. 15, para. 17A, 18, 34

REMAINING PROVISIONS OF SCHEDULE 15

16-640　Application of exemptions and reliefs

The exemption from SDLT in Sch. 3, para. 1 (no chargeable consideration) does not apply to these partnership transactions. Otherwise, however, SDLT exemptions will apply (subject to modification in the case of disadvantaged areas relief for transactions up to 5 April 2013; group relief; and charities relief).

The application of the group relief provisions to transfers of partnership interests was clarified to put it beyond doubt that group relief claimed on such a transfer is subject to the claw-back provisions in FA 2003, Sch. 7, para. 3.

A modification also applies to the application of charities relief to a transfer of an interest in a partnership under para. 14 or 17.

Legislation: FA 2003, Sch. 15, para. 25, 26, 27, 28

16-660　The only charging provisions

Except as charged under para. 10, 14 or 17 the acquisition of an interest in a partnership is not a chargeable transaction, notwithstanding the partnership property includes land.

Legislation: FA 2003, Sch. 15, para. 29

16-680   Notification

The transfer of a partnership interest under para. 14 or 17 is a notifiable transaction only if:

(a)   SDLT is chargeable at 1% or more;

(b)   FA 2003, Sch. 4A, para. 3 applies to the transaction.

Legislation: FA 2003, Sch. 15, para. 30

16-700   Continued application of stamp duty on transfers of partnership interests

There were two particular difficulties with these provisions as initially drawn. First, the intention behind para. 32, retaining a stamp duty liability on transfers of partnership interests irrespective of whether they hold chargeable interests in land, was to protect against avoidance through the transfer of chargeable securities within the 'wrapper' of a partnership. However, the rule failed to exempt from charge partnerships which do not own securities at all (though it was intended to do so). Second, the way in which the stamp duty charge was calculated was incorrect, so that the amount on which stamp duty was charged would be inversely proportional to the interest in the partnership transferred. For example, under the transfer of a 100% interest in a partnership, the stamp duty charge would be zero! Stamp Taxes were aware of these issues following Royal Assent to FA 2004. In relation to the first point, Stamp Taxes said that the legislation would be applied as though it provided what was intended and in relation to the second point that further action would be taken if the avoidance in question was seen to emerge.

The two deficiencies noted above were corrected by F(No. 2)A 2005, Sch. 10, para. 21, in amending para. 33 for any transaction with an effective date on or after 20 July 2005. First, it is made clear that there is no stamp duty charge in any case where the relevant partnership property does not include any stock or marketable securities. Second, in a case where the property does include such stock or securities, the consideration for the transfer is treated as the appropriate proportion of the net market value of the stock and securities immediately after the transfer.

Legislation: FA 2003, Sch. 15, para. 31, 32, 33

16-720   Interpretation: partnership share and partnership property

A person's 'partnership share' is the proportion in which he is entitled to share in the income profits of the partnership.

Paragraph 34(1) states: 'any reference ... to partnership property is to an interest or right held by or on behalf of the partnership, or the members of a partnership, for the purposes of the partnership business'. Stamp Taxes have hitherto construed this so that property owned by a partner personally held outside the partnership but made available to the partnership for its business (whether or not for consideration) would fall within the para. 34(1) definition. This is even though, on any objective measure of what is or what is not partnership property, such land would not be partnership property. This view seems to have been prompted by perceived avoidance, whatever that might be.

This view was stated in former SDLTM 35100 (a current, different reference is at SDLTM 33390) as follows:

'Partnership property is any interest or right held by or on behalf of a partnership, or the members of a partnership, for the purposes of partnership business. This means that property held by one of the partners and used for the purposes of the partnership business is partnership property. Relevant partnership property is every chargeable interest held as partnership property immediately after the transfer except:

- Chargeable interests transferred to the partnership as part of the transaction; and
- Market rent leases.'

Structures described above are common in family farming partnerships, known as a *Harrison-Broadley v Smith* arrangement (being a contractual rather than a licence arrangement), to avoid setting up an *Agricultural Holdings Act* tenancy. The point might also arise where for example the senior partner of a professional firm made his property available as the firm's office.

Example 13 – A potential horror scenario: horror happily averted

Land is owned by Janetta MacDonald, but is used by the partnership to which she belongs. Janetta dies. Her personal representatives are able to sell the land with vacant possession. If this were a chargeable transfer of land from a partnership, then they should also have submitted an SDLT return accompanied by payment of the tax within 30 days of the death on the proportion of the open market value of the land with vacant possession which was not represented by Janetta's share in partnership income. The consequences would be mind-boggling. Even if the point were picked up by the PRs, they would hardly be able to get a professional valuation or be in a position to pay the necessary tax within the 30-day period.

It was confirmed by HMRC Stamp Taxes at a meeting with the Stamp Taxes Practitioners Group on 5 October 2005, that the problem illustrated by example 13 cannot occur. This is because, within para. 18(1) of FA 2003, Sch. 15, the personal representatives of the deceased partner are not themselves a partner, nor can they be connected with a person who is or has been one of the partners. Death breaks the connection for purposes of CTA 2010, s. 1122 and ITA 2007, s. 993 and 994.

HMRC have finally accepted, as announced on 5 March 2007, that property used for the partnership business which is not partnership property under the general law will not necessarily be partnership property for SDLT purposes. Specifically, HMRC say that following a number of representations they have concluded 'that a chargeable interest owned by some but not all of the partners is not partnership property unless the partner-owners hold it on behalf of the partnership for the purposes of the partnership business' and that what was originally draft SDLTM 35100 'no longer represents [their] view'. However, HMRC Stamp Taxes have not said that the meaning of 'partnership property' for SDLT purposes is the same as under the general law. In a case where all the partners own the land (outside the partnership) and license it to the partnership, it is not clear whether HMRC would consider there may yet be possible liability and compliance obligations (which the authors would deny). Discussion on this continues.

The major outstanding issue is the SDLT analysis in the case where one of only two partners dies, thus bringing the partnership to an end. To preserve agricultural and/or business property relief from IHT in the deceased's estate, the partnership agreement will typically provide a cross option structure (that is, with 'no binding contract for sale' at the date of death). It is not clear (to the authors at least) that the transfer of actual partnership land pursuant to exercise of an option does not attract SDLT, as a situation outside the case discussed above, although HMRC Stamp Taxes have expressed the view that such a transfer is a non-event for SDLT purposes.

Legislation: FA 2003, Sch. 15, para. 34

Cases: *Harrison-Broadley v Smith* [2008] BTC 7,085; [1964] 1 All ER 867

16-740   Interpretation: transfer of chargeable interest to a partnership

Any case where a chargeable interest becomes partnership property is a transfer of a chargeable interest to the partnership.

Incidentally, if, on Stamp Taxes' original view of para. 34(1), land owned outside the partnership by a partner personally had been used by the partnership since before 1 December 2003, its introduction into the partnership now (e.g. to increase business property relief from inheritance tax from 50% to 100%) would not constitute a transfer of a chargeable interest to the partnership.

Legislation: FA 2003, Sch. 15, para. 35

16-760 Interpretation: transfer of interest in a partnership

The original position was there was a transfer of an interest in a partnership where arrangements were made either such that the partner transfers part or the whole of his interest as a partner to another person or such that a person becomes a partner and an existing partner reduces his interest or ceases to be a partner.

This provision was replaced from Royal Assent to FA 2007 (by s. 72(10)). Under the current provision: 'where a person acquires or increase a partnership share there is a transfer of an interest in the partnership (to that partner and from the other partners)'. That is, a transfer is clearly to include the *creation* of a partnership share.

Legislation: FA 2003, Sch. 15, para. 36

16-780 Interpretation: transfer of a chargeable interest from a partnership

There is a transfer of a chargeable interest from a partnership where a chargeable interest which was partnership property ceases to be partnership property or where a chargeable interest is granted or created out of partnership property and that interest is not partnership property.

Legislation: FA 2003, Sch. 15, para. 37

16-800 Interpretation: market value of lease

In determining the market value of the lease for purposes of para. 10 or 18, an obligation of the tenant is to be taken into account only if (a) it is one of those listed in FA 2003, Sch. 17A, para. 10(1) (being obligations not counting as chargeable consideration) or (b) it is an obligation to make a payment to a person.

Legislation: FA 2003, Sch. 15, para. 38

16-820 Interpretation: connected persons

The definition of connected persons in CTA 2010, s. 1122 is adopted, with the omission of s. 1122(7) (*partners connected with each other*). An amendment, from Royal Assent to FA 2007, by s. 72(11) amends the definition of 'connected persons', so that a trustee of a settlement will no longer be connected with any body corporate connected with the settlement. This is understood to be prompted by a scheme notified to HMRC Stamp Taxes under the disclosure regulations which relied on a purchaser creating a 'connection' between a property vendor and the partners of a property partnership created by trustees of the purchaser and into which the vendor sold the property.

Legislation: FA 2003, Sch. 15, para. 39

16-840   Interpretation: arrangements

Arrangements are defined as including any 'scheme, agreement or understanding, whether or not legally enforceable'.

Legislation: FA 2003, Sch. 15, para. 40

16-860   Partnership interests held by trustees

A change in definition in relation to ownership for SDLT purposes by both bare trustees and trustees of a substantive settlement is made with effect from Royal Assent to FA 2007, by s. 72(12) (see FA 2003, Sch. 16, para. 3, 4). The acquisition of a partnership interest is added to the rules relating to acquisition of a chargeable interest. This implies that a partnership interest is not a 'chargeable interest', carrying implications for partnerships which have an interest in property-owning partnerships.

Legislation: FA 2003, Sch. 16, para. 3, 4

LAND AND BUILDINGS TRANSACTION TAX

The land and buildings transaction tax applies to transactions in Scotland from 1 April 2015. It is imposed by the *Land and Buildings Transaction Tax (Scotland) Act* 2013 ('LBTT(S)A 2013'). Schedule 17 covers the application of the charge to partnerships.

16-880   Overview of Sch. 17

Scottish partnerships

Section 4(2) of the *Partnership Act* 1890 states: 'In Scotland, a firm is a legal person distinct from the partners of whom it is composed'. The definition under s. 4(2) of the 1890 Act confirms the long-standing distinction between English and Scots law, whereby a partnership under Scots law has a separate legal personality from its members. The separate legal personality conferred on a Scottish partnership has given rise to the description that a Scottish partnership is an 'opaque' structure. By contrast, an English partnership does not have a separate legal personality from its members, and is often described as 'transparent'.

This distinction defined under s. 4(2) of the 1890 Act concerns only *general* and *limited* partnerships formed under English and Scots law. The distinction is not relevant when considering a partnership formed under the LLP Act 2000.

The s. 4(2) distinction of a Scottish partnership means, among other things, that a Scottish partnership can own most assets, raise legal actions or be sued in its own name. For example, a partnership as a firm can be sequestered without the individual partners being sequestered. The converse is also true, in that the sequestration of a partner (or all of the partners) is not the sequestration of the firm.

In terms of property ownership, however, while a partnership's separate personality allows it to take title of property, for practical reasons title to heritable property is still taken in the name of the existing partners as trustees for themselves (as the current partners) and for their successors (the future partners of the firm). The reason for this practicality stems from the fact that a partnership can be dissolved, or its name changed, and as such, its legal personality lacks the necessary permanence to sustain the traditional feudal relationship between the 'superior' and the 'vassal' in the Scottish system of land tenure. Similarly, when it comes to ownership of 'incorporeal moveables' (a term reminiscent of Scots law's lineage from Roman law), it is a matter of practical necessity to have a 'corporeal owner' so that the person who is entitled to the right conferred by the 'incorporeal moveables' (such as company shares) can be identified. It means therefore that the partners, rather than the firm, are the named owners of the incorporeal moveables, albeit in their status as trustees.

Legislation: *Partnership Act* 1890, s. 4(2)

Partnerships under LBTT compared with SDLT

While an overarching aim of the LBTT legislation is to forge a closer alignment between Scots law and the taxation of land transactions in Scotland, the fact that in Scots law a partnership is a separate legal personality has not found its way into reforming how the taxation of partnerships and land transactions can be otherwise dealt with, as noted above.

In its conception, Sch. 17 of the LBTT Act bears much resemblance to Sch. 15 of FA 2003 for SDLT. While Sch. 17 has the 'benefit' of adopting the core principles of Sch. 15 for SDLT *after* all the revisions, the intrinsic complexities of partnerships under SDLT are imported into LBTT.

Legislation: LBTT(S)A 2013, Sch. 17; FA 2003, Sch. 15

The Parts to Sch. 17

The overall structure of Sch. 17 is useful to have in mind when comprehending the partnership code for LBTT. It starts with the general provisions, followed by specific provisions governing particular situations.

General provisions

- Part 1 – Overview giving summary headings of the parts
- Part 2 – General provisions of the taxation of partnerships for LBTT
- Part 3 – Defining an 'Ordinary partnership transactions' of partnership acquisition of a chargeable interest from an unconnected seller

Specific provisions

- Part 4 – Rules on the transfer of chargeable interest *to* partnerships
- Part 5 – Rules on the transfer of chargeable interest *from* partnerships

Specific applications

- Part 6 – Application of Parts 3 to 5 to leases
- Part 7 – Transactions in relation to 'property investment partnerships'
- Part 8 – Application of exemptions and reliefs to certain transactions

Interpretation

- Part 9 – Definitions of specific terms used in the Schedule

Legislation: LBTT(S)A 2013, Sch. 17, para. 1

16-900 Definitions and Distinctions

Types of partnership covered by the Act

The provisions in respect of partnership are under Sch. 17, and the types of partnerships covered by the Act are listed under para. 2 of the schedule as follows:

(a) a partnership within the *Partnership Act* 1890;

(b) a limited partnership registered under the *Limited Partnerships Act* 1907 (LP Act 1907);

(c) a limited liability partnership under the *Limited Liability Partnerships Act* 2000 (LLP Act 2000), or the *Limited Liability Partnerships Act* (Northern Ireland) 2002;

(d) a firm or entity of a similar character to any of those categorised as (a) to (c) above formed under the law of a country or territory outside the UK.

It is important to note the types of partnership governed by Sch. 17 include *foreign entities* that would be classified as a partnership under UK law. This contrasts with the taxation of partnerships for direct tax purposes, which does not extend the definition of partnerships to include foreign entities. On one level, it can be understood that the contrast in the nexus for direct taxes is with regard to the individual partner's residence as a natural person, while the nexus for a transactional tax such as LBTT is by reference to the *situs* of the land. It is immaterial therefore that a party or parties to a land transaction that falls within the scope of LBTT are foreign entities for the purpose of determining whether LBTT is chargeable. It is material, however, for determining whether the transaction should be governed by the charging provisions under Sch. 17 of the Act, if the firm is of a similar character as a type of partnership defined by para. 2.

The residence of a partnership is a question of fact and depends to a large extent on the determination of 'the place of business' of the firm. How far the foreign entity inclusion is to apply remains an area of developing guidance. Co-ownership of property with a vehicle in another jurisdiction, or the treatment for land transaction tax relating to contractual funds such as Fonds Communs de Placement (FCPs), are only two examples of what the inclusion of foreign entities in the partnership definition may entail. A detailed discussion of the implications of inclusion of foreign entities in the partnership definition is beyond the scope of this Commentary. The consultation document published by HM Treasury and HMRC in July 2014 serves as a summary of the issues involved in the taxation of partnerships for SDLT and may equally apply to LBTT; access at *www.gov.uk/government/uploads/system/uploads/attachment_ data/file/332079/Stamp_Duty_Land_Tax_rules_for_property_investment_funds.pdf.*

Legislation: LBTT(S)A 2013, Sch. 17, para. 2; FA 2003, Sch. 15, para. 1

Distinction between types of partnership

As under general UK tax law, there is no distinction within LBTT between a general partnership and a limited partnership.

On the level of whether the firm is a body corporate, however, a distinction is to be observed between:

- a *general* partnership under 1890 Act and a *limited* partnership under 1907 Act on the one hand;
- a *limited liability partnership* (LLP) under the 2000 Act on the other.

For the purpose of LBTT group relief, the critical distinction between these two categories of partnerships lies in whether the partnership is a *body corporate*. Only an LLP is capable of being considered as a body corporate and as such – under *some* forms of group structure – will not break up an LBTT group for the purpose of claiming group relief. On the contrary, a general or a limited partnership is never a body corporate, and will break up a group structure for LBTT purposes.

Legislation: LBTT(S)A 2013, Sch. 17, para. 38; *Limited Liability Partnerships Act* 2000

Terms defined under Pt. 9 to Sch. 17

The following terms are specifically defined in Pt. 9 to Sch. 17 and are useful to set out here before going into the substantive provisions.

Partnership property: an interest or right held by or on behalf of a partnership, or the members of a partnership, for the purpose of the partnership business.

Points to note:

- The provisions in Sch. 17 apply primarily to the transfer of chargeable interest which is partnership property.
- A transfer of a chargeable interest *into* or *out of* a partnership means the chargeable interest *becomes* or *ceases* to be partnership property.
- It is important therefore to the chargeable interest pertains to partnership property to establish if Sch. 17 provisions apply.

Partnership share: a person's partnership share at any time is to the proportion in which the person is entitled at that time to share in the income profits of the partnership.

Points to note:

- That the partnership share is referential to entitlement to income profits only. Entitlement to capital, or to capital profits, is not relevant for the purpose of calculation, though it would seem to be more appropriate in dealing with tax arising from transfer of capital assets. It is thought that HMRC consider the capital profit sharing ratio of the partners is more easily manipulated to avoid a tax charge.
- As regards what constitutes a partner's share of profit, it generally includes the partner's salary, his residual income profit share Income, and any interest accruing on partner loan capital (see *Green v Herzog and Others* [1954] 1 WLR 1309).
- It is not uncommon for the profit sharing ratio to vary from year to year in a partnership, depending on business brought in by an individual partner, fees earned or hours worked, and the final profit sharing ratio may be determined after the end of an accounting year. For the purpose of LBTT, it may be necessary to complete an LBTT return based on projected profit sharing and amend the return when the final ratio is determined.
- The partnership share at the effective date is to be taken to mean the sharing ratio applied to the accounting period in which the effective date falls.

Transfer of chargeable interest covers:

(a) the creation;
(b) the renunciation or release; and
(c) the variation of a chargeable interest.

Transfer of chargeable interest to a partnership: where a chargeable interest becomes partnership property.

Transfer of chargeable interest from a partnership: where

(a) a chargeable interest that was a partnership property ceases to be partnership property; or

(b) a chargeable interest created out of partnership property is not partnership property.

Transfer of chargeable interest in a partnership: where a person acquires a partnership share, or his/her partnership share increases, there is a transfer of an interest in the partnership to that partner from the other partner(s).

Connected persons: as provided under the *Corporation Tax Act* 2010, s. 1122 with the omission of:

(a) subs. (7) regarding partners connected with each other;
(b) subs. (6)(c) to (e) regarding trustee connected with settlement for the purposes of para. 12–22 of Sch. 17.

Arrangements include any scheme, agreement or understanding, whether or not legally enforceable.

Legislation: LBTT(S)A 2013, Sch. 17, para. 42–50; CTA 2010, s. 1122; RS Guidance LBTT7003

16-920   General provisions for chargeable interests held by partners

Chargeable interests treated as held by partners

As a general principle, a partnership is not regarded as a separate and distinct entity and the tax treatment is to 'look through' the partnership structure to the persons making up the partnership. Consequently, the 'transparent' treatment means, as stated under para. 3:

(a) a chargeable interest held by or on behalf of a partnership is treated as held by and on behalf of the partners;
(b) a land transaction entered into for the purposes of a partnership is treated as entered into by or on behalf of the partners,
    and not by or on behalf of the partnership as such.

The last element of para. 3(1) provision: '*and not by or on behalf of the partnership as such*' can be easily missed in the way the provision is set out.

Paragraph 3 of Sch. 17 to the LBTT Act in fact mirrors the provision under para. 2 of Sch. 15 to FA 2003 for SDLT, and under SDLT, this equivalent provision is indeed under the heading '*Legal personality of partnership disregarded*' and the SDLT heading aptly sums up the essence that the chargeable interests are treated as held by partners 'and not by or on behalf of the partnership as such'.

Legislation: LBTT(S)A 2013, Sch. 17, para. 3; FA 2003, Sch. 15, para.2

Acquisition of interest in a partnership

Under para. 4, the general position is stated that the acquisition of an interest in a partnership is *not* a chargeable transaction, and this is the case even when the partnership interest includes land.

The preposition '*in*' is important for identifying when a transaction of partnership interest falls under para. 4. A transfer of chargeable interest (where land is included) is defined under para. 48 as when a person acquires a partnership share, or a person's partnership share increases, there is a transfer of an interest in the partnership to that partner from the other partners.

The occasions when a transfer of chargeable interest in a partnership give rise to a chargeable transaction are provided for as *exceptions* to this general rule, and the exceptions are in relation to a transfer:

(a)   *to* a partnership, as provided under Pt. 4 of Sch. 17;
(b)   in pursuance of earlier arrangements under para. 17; or
(c)   of interest in property investment partnership (PIP) under para. 32.

Though para. 4 is considered a 'general' provision, it should not be taken as the default position given the number of exceptions to this general rule being applicable. The approach should be taken by first considering whether a particular transaction in acquiring an interest in a partnership falls into one of the exceptions, and only if it does not, then the general rule of it being outwith LBTT regime under para. 4 should apply.

For example, if a professional partnership also holds a sizeable portfolio of property which generates income, an assessment needs to be made to consider if the partnership may have fallen within the definition of a 'Property Investment Partnership', which may mean the exception under para. 32 applies and the acquisition of a partnership interest will not be treated as a non-chargeable acquisition under para. 4.

As a quick rule of thumb, the exceptions can be summed up as questions in the following order:

- Is the transfer to a PIP, then a potential charge to LBTT?
- If a transfer into a non-PIP, is it under the anti-avoidance rule for earlier arrangements?
- If a transfer into a non-PIP, is it caught under Part 4 special rules?

Legislation: LBTT(S)A 2013, Sch. 17, para. 4; RS Guidance LBTT7002

The continuity rule

For the general rule under para. 4 to apply, the partnership has to be the *same* partnership before and after transfer of the partnership interest.

The rule of continuity provides that a partnership is treated as the *same* partnership even when there is a change in membership so long as there is one person who was a member before the change and remains a member after the change. However, the continuity rule has to be applied in conjunction with the definition that for a partnership to exist, there must be at least two members. So if A and B leave a three-person partnership consisting of A, B and C, the partnership ceases to exist when there is only just one member C remaining. When D then joins C to form a partnership, the C and D partnership is a *new* partnership, notwithstanding the common member C. If D joins at the same time and under the same agreement as A and B leave, then the partnership has continued through the changes, as there would not be a time when C is left as the only member.

The continuity rule, of itself, is an example of the ambiguity that the taxation of partnerships in some contexts treats the partnerships as separate entities distinct from their members.

Legislation: LBTT(S)A 2013, Sch. 17, para. 5; RS Guidance LBTT7002

Unit trusts and open-ended investment companies

A unit trust scheme or an open-ended investment company is not a partnership for the purposes of the Act. As such, unit trust schemes and OEICs are taxed like companies or natural persons, and are charged to LBTT when they acquire land.

The treatment of unit trust schemes is provided under s. 45 of the Act, and of open-ended investment companies, under s. 46 of the Act. In gist, both are collective investment vehicles and are to be treated as companies for LBTT purposes, with the unit-trust or investment holders being treated as having acquired shares in the investment company. The first acquisition of a chargeable interest in land is subject to tax; that is, the purchase of a land interest that brings the asset into the portfolio of investment assets held within the collective investment vehicles. The acquisition of rights within a unit trust scheme or an OEIC by an investment holder is not a chargeable event for LBTT.

Legislation: LBTT(S)A 2013, Sch. 17, para. 6; RS Guidance LBTT5005 and 5006

Ordinary partnership transactions

An 'ordinary partnership transaction' is defined under para. 7 as a land transaction:

(a)   entered into as buyer by, or on behalf of, the members of a partnership; and
(b)   is not a transaction specifically provided for under Pt. 4–7 of Sch. 17.

Where an acquisition of a chargeable interest is an 'ordinary partnership transaction', the calculation of the LBTT payable on such a transaction is no different from the calculation if the buyer is a company or a natural person.

While ordinary partnership transactions are part of the general rules, it should not be taken as the default position, because for a transaction to be classified as 'ordinary', it must be not a transaction specifically provided for under Pt. 4–7. It would be again prudent to adopt the approach to consider whether a transaction may fall under any specific provisions under Pt. 4–7 before conclusively determine that it is an 'ordinary partnership transaction' under para. 7.

For example, embedded in all the provisions under Pt. 4–7 is the fact that there is some connection between the transferor and transferee. So, a prerequisite for an acquisition by a partnership to be 'ordinary' is that the seller in the transaction is not in any way caught by the 'connection' rules with any of the partners in the partnership.

When a partnership enters an ordinary transaction as the buyer, anything required or authorised to be done by in relation to the transaction is considered to have been required or authorised to be done by all *responsible partners*, defined as:

(a)   the persons who are partners *at the effective date* of the transaction;
(b)   any person who becomes a member of the partnership after that date.

Instead of responsible partners, a representative partner (or partners) can be nominated by a majority of the partners to act as the representative of the partnership for the purpose of the Act. Any such nomination, or the revocation of such a nomination, has effect only if given by notice to Revenue Scotland. Anything required or authorised to be done by responsible partners can be done by the representative partner, who will make the declaration required under s. 36 of the Act that the LBTT return submitted is complete and correct.

Liability to pay the LBTT on the acquisition is a joint and several liability of the responsible partners. Significantly though, recovery of LBTT is restricted to responsible partners at the date of the transaction.

Notwithstanding the definition of responsible partners includes 'any person who becomes a member of the partnership after [the effective] date' (para. 8(2)(b)), no amount of LBTT may be recovered from a person who did not become a responsible partner until after the effective date of the transaction (para. 10(2)). The liability of those who joined as partners *after* the effective date is considered to be limited to the penalties arising from any default related to the transaction occurring when they were already partners; they would not be liable for any unpaid tax or interest related to that transaction that had taken place before they became partners.

Legislation: LBTT(S)A 2013, Sch. 17, para. 7–10; RS Guidance LBTT7004

16-940 Special rules for transactions of transfer to a partnership

Circumstances for Pt. 4 special rules to apply

Under para. 12 to Pt. 4, if a transfer of a chargeable interest *to* a partnership is by:

(a) a partner;a
(b) person who becomes a partner as a result of or in connection with the transfer; or
(c) a person connected with (i) a partner, or (ii) a person who becomes a partner as a result of or in connection with the transfer.

Part 4 applies whether the transfer is:

(a) in connection with the formation of the partnership; or
(b) into an existing partnership.

A property investment partnership may elect to disapply Pt. 4 rules.

Anti-avoidance measures to treat certain events after the transfer of a chargeable interest to a partnership as land transactions under Pt. 4 as land transactions that give rise to a chargeable occasion include:

(a) if the transfer of the partnership interest is pursuant to earlier arrangements (Example 14);
(b) if money is withdrawn from the partnership after the transfer (Example 15).

Legislation: LBTT(S)A 2013, Sch. 17, para. 12, 35; RS Guidance LBTT7005

Part 4 special calculation of chargeable consideration

Where the special rules apply under Pt. 4 (and 5), the calculation for chargeable consideration is by reference to *market value* of the subject matter at the time of the transfer, and not by what money or money's worth that has actually been passed as consideration.

(1) **Chargeable consideration** *is taken to be:*

$$MV \times (100\text{-}SLP)\%$$

MV is the market value of the interest transferred
SLP is the sum of the lower proportions

The formula may look complicated, but in essence is trying to tax the proportion of ownership that is considered to have been transferred from the transferor (an existing or joining partner, or person connected with a partner) to the other partners in the partnership. The transfer gives rise to a charge in LBTT because the other partners are considered to have 'acquired' an interest as a result of the transfer.

The formula is to be understood as the transferor starts with ownership at 100% of the interest, and after the transfer into the partnership, his 100% is reduced to the extent of his overall share of interest in the partnership, represented by the SLP%. The difference between 100% ownership before the transfer and the transferor's SLP% after the transfer is the proportion of ownership that has been transferred to other partners – or the acquisition deemed to have been made by the partnership giving rise to an LBTT charge.

(1)   The Sum of the Lower Proportion (SLP)

The legislation sets out a five-step approach to ascertain the SLP:

Step one

Identify the *relevant owner*(s), being the person –

- who was entitled to a proportion of the chargeable interest immediately *before* the transfer; *and*
- who is a partner or connected with a partner immediately *after* the transfer.

Step two

For each relevant owner identify the *corresponding partner* or partners.

A corresponding partner in relation to a relevant owner is defined under para. 16 as the person who, immediately *after* the transfer, is:

(a)   a partner; and
(b)   the relevant owner or is an *individual* connected with the relevant owner;
(c)   a company is to be treated as an 'individual' connected with the relevant owner insofar as it:

- holds property as trustee; and
- is connected with the relevant owners only because of CTA 2010, s. 1122(6); (i.e. in the capacity as trustee of a settlement).

In gist, a corresponding partner is:

- the partner who is the relevant owner; **and**
- *any partners connected with the relevant owner* immediately after the transfer *who are individuals*;
- companies or any other non-individuals are not corresponding partners except as specifically provided;
- if there are no corresponding partners, then the SLP will be nil.

Step three

For each relevant owner:

(a) find the proportion of the chargeable interest to which the owner was entitled immediately before the transfer;

(b) apportion that proportion between any one or more of the relevant owner's corresponding partners.

Step four

Find the lower of the following proportions ('the lower proportion') for each corresponding partner:

(a) the sum of the proportions (if any) of the chargeable interest apportioned to the partner at Step three in respect of each relevant owner;

(b) the partner's partnership share immediately *after* the land transfer.

A comparison needs to be made between (a) and (b) and the *lower* of the two figures is the 'lower proportion'. The figure is either the proportion of the chargeable interest attributable to the partner at Step three or the partner's share immediately after the transaction, whichever is the lower.

Step five

Add together the lower proportions for each corresponding partner to arrive at the sum of the lower proportions SLP.

Legislation: LBTT(S)A 2013, Sch. 17, para. 13–16; RS Guidance LBTT7005

Example 14 – partners unconnected

Black and Green are unconnected persons who form a partnership with Black contributing the freehold premises with a market value at £1m, and Green contributing cash as capital in the sum of £250,000.

Capital and income sharing ratio is Black at 80% and Green at 20%.

Step one

The relevant owner is Black and assuming a 100% proportion ownership of the chargeable interest.

Step two

The corresponding partner is Black.

Step three

Black was entitled to 100% immediately before the transfer. As the only corresponding partner, Black is apportioned 100%.

Step four

Black's partnership share is 80%, which is lower than the 100% established at Step three.

Step five

There is only one corresponding partner, Black, whose lower proportion is 80%. No aggregation with only one corresponding partner; the SLP is 80%.

The chargeable consideration

MV × (100 − SLP)% = £1m × (100 − 80)% = £200,000.

Points to note:

- As explained earlier, the transaction is being taxed with reference to the proportion of ownership transferred from Black to Green.
- As Green's partnership share is 20%, Green is deemed to have acquired 20% of the chargeable interest from Black, and LBTT is payable on Green's 'acquisition', assessed at the market value of the premises.
- Note that the cash capital contributed by Green does not enter into the calculation at all.
- The calculation is referential to the market value of the chargeable interest; it is immaterial what the parties consider to be the 'consideration' paid by Green to acquire his partnership interest.

Example 15 – partnership with a connected company

Graham Green is the sole shareholder of his company GreenCo. Graham and GreenCo. form a limited partnership with Graham as the limited partner with 10% share and GreenCo. the general partner with a 90% share. Graham transfers a property of market value at £500,000 to the partnership.

Step one

The relevant owner is Graham with 100%.

Step two

The only corresponding partner is Graham as an *individual*.

Step three

Graham was entitled to 100% immediately before the transfer. As the only corresponding partner, Graham is apportioned 100% after the transfer too.

Step four

Graham's partnership share is 10%, which is lower than the 100% established at Step three.

Step five

There is only one corresponding partner, Graham, whose lower proportion is 10%. No aggregation needed; the SLP is 10%.

The chargeable consideration

MV × (100 − SLP)% = £500,000 × (100 − 10)% = £450,000.

Points to note:

- The transaction is being taxed with reference to the proportion of ownership transferred from Graham to GreenCo. in the partnership.
- Even though GreenCo. is connected with the relevant owner, it cannot be a corresponding partner because it is not an individual.
- GreenCo. does not fall into the exception for a company to be treated as an 'individual' under para. 16(2) either.

Example 16 – partnership with connected partners as individuals

Alder, Holly and Primrose are in partnership in the horticultural and landscaping business, sharing profits at 40%, 40% and 20%. Holly and Primrose are sisters; Alder is not related or connected to the sisters other than as a partner in business.

The partners agree to purchase a field from Garland, who is the husband of Primrose. The purchase price of the field is £250,000, while the market value is £300,000.

Step one

The relevant owner is Garland, and he owns a 100% of the property before the transfer.

Step two

The corresponding partners are Holly and Primrose because they are individuals connected with the only relevant owner Garland.

Step three

Garland was entitled to 100% of the property immediately before the transfer. There are two corresponding partners, and the sisters have chosen the apportionment at 50% to Holly and 50% to Primrose.

Step four

For Holly, her partnership share immediately after the transfer is 40%, and the apportionment to her under Step three is 50%, so her lower proportion is 40%. For Primrose, her partnership share immediately after the transfer is 20%, and her apportionment under Step three is 50%, so her lower proportion is 20%.

Step five

The sum of the lower proportions is 40% to Holly and 20% to Primrose, making a total of 60%.

The chargeable consideration

MV × (100 − SLP)% = £300,000 × (100 − 60)% = £120,000.

Points to note:

- The transaction can be interpreted as being taxed with reference to the proportion of ownership transferred to Alder.
- As Alder's partnership share is 40%, Alder is deemed to have acquired 40% of the chargeable interest. LBTT is payable on Alder's 'acquisition', assessed at the market value of the field.
- The sisters being connected to the relevant owner, the transfer results in their share of the ownership of the chargeable interest being exempt from LBTT.
- If Garland as the seller was 'unconnected' to any of the partners, the transaction would be treated as at arm's length, notwithstanding the purchase price being lower than the market value. The transaction would then be classified as an 'Ordinary partnership acquisition' under para. 7, and LBTT would then be payable on the full purchase price of £250,000.

Partnership interest transfer pursuant to earlier arrangements

As an anti-avoidance measure, the provision under para. 17 is to prevent the partnership structure from being used as a vehicle to transfer a chargeable interest free of LBTT, or with reduced LBTT paid on the transaction.

The typical arrangements covered include an understatement of the consideration on transfer, with the transferor (seller) being given the difference in consideration by shifting the value in his partnership share afterwards.

Alternatively, as the *special calculation for 'chargeable consideration'* will illustrate, an increase of partnership share of the transferor partner has the effect of decreasing the others partners' share correspondingly, thereby reducing the LBTT payable on the transfer of the chargeable interest into the partnership. But for this anti-avoidance measure, an event after the transfer of interest that adjusts the partnership share between the transferor partner and other partners would have been *a non-chargeable event* under the provision of para. 4.

The provision of para. 17 has the effect of turning the two transactions into a single transaction by linking them; the two transactions to be linked are:

(1) the transfer of a chargeable interest falling under Pt. 4;
(2) the arrangements to shift partnership share before and after the transfer of chargeable interest which would otherwise have fallen under para. 2 exemption.

The chargeable consideration is calculated as a proportion of the market value at the date of the partnership transfer; and the proportion is determined as follows:

- If the transferor is not a partner after the transfer, then it is the share of his partnership interest before the transfer.
- If the transfer is a partner immediately after the transfer, then it is the difference between his partnership share before and after the transfer.

Legislation: LBTT(S)A 2013, Sch. 17, para. 17; RS Guidance LBTT7006

Withdrawal of money after the transfer

This is another anti-avoidance measure by linking the withdrawal of money after the transfer with the original transfer that falls within the provision of Part 4, rendering the withdrawal of money as chargeable along with the original transfer.

The measure defines that if a 'qualifying event' occurs *within three years* of the original Part 4 transaction, the qualifying event:

(a) is treated as a land transaction; and
(b) is a chargeable transaction.

A qualifying event includes:

(a) A withdrawal from the partnership of money or money's worth which does not represent income profit by the relevant person, and the withdrawal can take the form of:

- withdrawing capital from the person's capital account;
- reducing the person's interest; or
- ceasing to be a partner.

(b) Where the relevant person has made a loan to the partnership:

- the repayment (to any extent) by the partnership of the loan; or
- a withdrawal by the relevant person from the partnership of money or money's worth which is not income profit.

The relevant person is referential to para. 12 definition, and refers to the person who makes the land transfer that falls under Pt. 4 rules, or the partner concerned, or a person connected with the partner.

The partners are taken to be the buyers under the transaction.

The chargeable consideration is taken to be:

(a) the value of the money or money's worth withdrawn from the partnership;
(b) the amount of loan repaid by the partnership;
(c) so much of the value of the money or money's worth withdrawn that does not exceed the amount of the loan.

There is a cap on the maximum chargeable consideration for the two transactions taken together, and is to be capped at *market value as at the effective date* of the original transfer the chargeable interest.

If the partnership happens to be a PIP, then the amount of tax payable as a result of the qualifying event is to be reduced by any amount of tax payable from the transfer for consideration of interest in the PIP.

The effect of this provision can be illustrated with a developing scenario from Example 16. Suppose the partnership did not have the ready capital to pay for the full price of £250,000 asked for by Garland, and a loan arrangement is made between the partnership and Garland for £100,000. Two years after the transfer, the partnership realised some assets and paid off the loan. The loan repayment would be caught by para. 18 provision and a chargeable event would be precipitated by the loan repayment.

Compare the above situation with the following:
(a) if the loan repayment happened after three years of the transfer, then the provision would not be triggered;
(b) if the partnership had borrowed from a bank, the repayment of the bank loan within the three years of transfer would not have triggered a charge either.

Legislation: LBTT(S)A 2013, Sch. 17, para. 18; RS Guidance LBTT7007

16-960   Special rules for transactions of transfer from a partnership

Transactions falling under Part 5 provisions

Paragraph 19 states the transactions that involve the transfer of a chargeable interest that may fall under Pt. 5 provisions are:

(1) *from* a partnership *to* a partner or connected person (para. 20);
(2) *from* a partnership *to* a partnership (para. 27);
(3) if the partnership consists entirely of bodies corporate (para. 28).

It should be noted that a transfer of a chargeable interest is in fact a disposal, and if the disposal is not to a connected party but to an unrelated third party, then Pt. 5 is not relevant. The partnership as the seller' will have no LBTT liability, and it is the third party buyer who will be accounting for LBTT on the disposal.

Part 5 only applies in relation to a disposal of chargeable interest by a partnership where the 'buyer' is a connected party: i.e. a partner (current or former) or person connected to such partner.

Legislation: LBTT(S)A 2013, Sch. 17, para. 19; RS Guidance LBTT7008–7010

Transfer from a partnership to a partner/connected person

Under para. 20 to Pt. 5, Pt. 5 applies to a transfer of a chargeable interest *from* a partnership *to*:

(a)   a person who is or has been one of the partners; or

(b)   a person who is connected with a partner (existing or outgoing).

Continuity rule in respect of partners – to benefit from the reduction on the exit of partnership property, the exiting partner must still be a member of the partnership at the effective date of the transfer. If the partner has already left the partnership, then the partnership share attributable to the outgoing partner being the transferee of the property will be reduced to zero. No reduction in LBTT payable will then result on the transfer of the partnership property to the outgoing partner.

Continuity rule in respect of partnership property – for the purpose of para. 20, property that was partnership property before the partnership was dissolved or otherwise ceased to exist, is to be treated as remaining partnership property until it is distributed.

Election to dis-apply – if the 'buyer' has elected to dis-apply Pt. 4 in respect of the transfer of a chargeable interest *into* a property investment partnership (PIP), then Pt. 5 rules are also dis-applied in respect of the transfer of the property *from* the PIP.

Legislation: LBTT(S)A 2013, Sch. 17, para. 19; RS Guidance LBTT7008–7010

Part 5 special calculation of chargeable consideration

Where the special rules apply under Pt. 5, the calculation for chargeable consideration is practically identical to the calculation applicable to a Pt. 4 transaction. However, attention needs to be given to the differences in a Pt. 4 and Pt. 5 steps taken in determining the lower proportion; for example:

- the relevant owner under Pt. 5 is referential to the ownership *after* the transfer, while Pt. 4 is referential to the ownership *before* the transfer;
- the comparison under *Step four* is to the '*partnership share attributable to the partner*' under Pt. 5 would be *before* the transfer; different from the attribution as immediately *after* the transfer under Pt. 4.

Again the reference is to *market value* of the subject matter at the time of the transfer, and the aim is to reduce the LBTT payable by the proportion that reflects the transferee's prior share in the chargeable interest held by the partnership. In other words, the tax payable is on the deemed proportion of interest 'acquired' by the outgoing partner net of what he already held before the transfer.

Chargeable consideration *is taken to be:*

MV × (100 – SLP)%

MV is the market value of the interest transferred
SLP is the sum of the lower proportions

The Sum of the Lower Proportion (SLP)

Step one

Identify the ***relevant owner***(s), being the person:

- who is entitled to a proportion of the chargeable interest immediately ***after*** the transfer; ***and***
- who was a partner or connected with a partner immediately ***before*** the transfer.

Step two

For each relevant owner identify the ***corresponding partner*** or partners. If there is no relevant owner with a corresponding partner, the SLP is nil.

A corresponding partner in relation to a relevant owner is defined under para. 24 as the person who, immediately ***before*** the transfer, was:

- a partner; and
- the relevant owner or was an *individual* connected with the relevant owner.

For these purposes, a company is to be treated as an 'individual' connected with the relevant owner insofar as it:

- holds property as trustee; and
- is connected with the relevant owners only because of CTA 2010, s. 1122(6).

Step three

For each relevant owner:

(a) find the proportion of the chargeable interest to which the owner is entitled immediately ***after*** the transfer;
(b) apportion that proportion between any one or more of the relevant owner's corresponding partners.

Step four

Find the lower of the following proportions ('the lower proportion') for each corresponding partner: (a) the sum of the proportions (if any) of the chargeable interest apportioned to the partner at Step three in respect of each relevant owner; (b) the partnership share attributable to the partner (determined in accordance with para. 25 and 26 of Sch. 17).

A comparison needs to be made between (a) and (b) and the *lower* of the two figures is the 'lower proportion'. The figure is either the proportion of the chargeable interest attributable to the partner at Step three or the partner's share immediately before the transaction, whichever is the lower.

Step five

Add together the lower proportions for each corresponding partner to arrive at the sum of the lower proportions SLP.

Legislation: LBTT(S)A 2013, Sch. 17, para. 22–26; RS Guidance LBTT7008

Example 17– partnership with connected partners as individuals

Alder, Holly and Primrose are in partnership in the horticultural and landscaping business, sharing profits at 40%, 40% and 20%. Holly and Primrose are sisters; Alder is not related or connected to the sisters other than as a partner in business.

Holly decides to take the floral horticultural business out of the partnership and to set up on her own. The partners agree that Holly will take the ground with the extensive outbuildings and greenhouses thereon in settlement of her partnership share of capital. The land and the outbuildings are valued at £200,000.

Step one

The relevant owner is Holly, and she owns a 100% of the property after the transfer.

Step two

The corresponding partners are Holly and Primrose because they are individuals connected with the only relevant owner Holly.

Step three

Holly is entitled to 100% of the property immediately after the transfer. There are two corresponding partners, and the sisters have chosen the apportionment at 50% to Holly and 50% to Primrose.

Step four

For Holly, her partnership share immediately before the transfer was 40%, and the apportionment to her under Step Three is 50%, so her lower proportion is 40%. For Primrose, her partnership share immediately before the transfer is 20%, and her apportionment under Step three is 50%, so her lower proportion is 20%.

Step five

The sum of the lower proportions is 40% to Holly and 20% to Primrose, making a total of 60%.

The chargeable consideration

MV × (100 − SLP)% = £200,000 × (100 − 60)% = £80,000.

Points to note:

- The transaction can be interpreted as being taxed with reference to the proportion of ownership Holly purchased from Alder.
- As Alder's partnership share is 40%, Alder is deemed to have sold 40% of the chargeable interest to Holly. LBTT is payable on Holly's 'acquisition', assessed at the market value of the property.
- The sisters being connected to the relevant owner, the transfer results in their share of the ownership of the chargeable interest being exempt from LBTT.

Transfers from a partnership to a partnership

Paragraph 27 is there to avoid a double charge on a transfer that is from a partnership to a partnership. If a property is transferred from partnership A to partnership B, there are two *possible* chargeable transactions:

(1)   the transfer to partnership B falling within Pt. 4 provisions;
(2)   the transfer from partnership A falling within Pt. 5 provisions.

Without para. 27, a double charge could have arisen in respect of the same transaction. Para. 27 basically provides for the LBTT payable in respect of a transfer from one partnership to another to be based on the *higher* of the two tax liabilities calculated under Pt. 4 and 5.

Legislation: LBTT(S)A 2013, Sch. 17, para. 27; RS Guidance LBTT7009

Transfers from a corporate partnership

Paragraph 28 provision applies to the situation where a chargeable interest is:

- transferred from a partnership whose members are all bodies corporate;
- to a corporate partner or partners whose aggregate of lower proportions (SLP) is 75% or more,

then the chargeable consideration is taken to be equal to the full value with any discount applied. Group relief may be available on the transfer.

If any of the chargeable consideration includes rent, then the chargeable consideration is taken to the Net Present Value of the rent over the term of the lease plus the market value of the lease.

Legislation: LBTT(S)A 2013, Sch. 17, para. 28; RS Guidance LBTT7009

16-980   Partnership and leases

Application of Pt. 3–5 to leases

Part 6 provides for the determination of the chargeable consideration when the subject matter of transfer is a lease, and *the whole or part of the chargeable consideration for the transaction is rent.*

The type of transfer covered by Pt. 6 involves the grant of:

- a chargeable interest into a partnership; or
- a chargeable interest out of a partnership.

In practice, this will cover when a partner grants a lease to a partnership (into), or a partnership grants a lease to a partner (out of).

The aim is again to reflect the economic interest the partner has within the partnership, and to reduce the LBTT chargeable on the transfer proportionately to reflect the partner's share of partnership interest.

The chargeable consideration

Instead of Market Value as the reference for the formula under Pt. 4 or 5, Pt. 6 calculation for chargeable consideration is determined as the aggregate of:

(1)   the relevant chargeable proportion of the NPV of the rent over the term of the lease; and

(2)   the relevant chargeable proportion of any consideration other than rent (i.e.: premium) and market value of the lease.

The NPV of the rent over the term of the lease is determined by the normal method.

Where premium is paid as part of consideration other than rent, the chargeable consideration needs to include consideration determined by the following formula: **(RCP × MV) + (RCP × AC)**, where:

- RCP is the relevant chargeable proportion;
- MV is the market value of the lease;
- AC is the actual consideration other than rent given.

If no premium (AC) is given, then the chargeable consideration still needs to be ascertained as RCP × MV, and is the market value of the lease if the lease were granted in the open market.

The relevant chargeable proportion

The relevant chargeable proportion is provided by para. 29 as $(100 - SLP)\%$, where SLP is the sum of the lower proportions.

The steps to be followed in determining SLP are as those set out for Pt. 4 or 5 calculations.

Legislation: LBTT(S)A 2013, Sch. 17, para. 29; RS Guidance LBTT7010

16-990   Property investment partnerships

Definition of a property investment partnership (PIP)

Part 7 of Sch. 17 governs the taxation of partnership interests in a firm classified as a PIP.

The definition of a PIP is given under para. 31, which states a PIP as:

(1)   a partnership whose sole or main activity is investing or dealing in chargeable interests, whether or not that activity involves the carrying out of construction operations on the land in question;

(2)   'chargeable interests' is to include any interest which would be a chargeable interest but for the fact that it relates to land outwith Scotland;

(3)   'construction operations' has the meaning given under *Finance Act* 2004, s. 74.

Points to note:

- The meaning of investing and dealing in chargeable interests is generally taken to mean the holding of property in order to receive rent, and/or the buying and selling of property in order to realise a gain.
- 'Chargeable interests' under para. 31(2) means any chargeable interests, wherever it is situated, and not restricted to only those chargeable interests located in Scotland.
- A firm may have other activities alongside those in investing and dealing in chargeable interests. To what extent is a firm's PIP activities to cross the threshold of the 'main activity' test is an area that needs monitoring.
- The determination of whether a firm is a PIP is an either/or decision; there is no apportionment of activities into PIP and non-PIP as such.
- The kind of 'main activity' test may involve an analysis of capital employed, income/profit derived, employee costs between the PIP and non-PIP activities to arrive at a determination.
- Once a PIP, it may be difficult to reverse the PIP status by re-balancing the activity level, as it is to be expected some permanence should be attached to such a determination to allow the correct taxation provisions to be applied to the movements in the firm's partnership share interests.
- The 'main activity' test has implications for a firm whose other activities consist in the carrying out of construction works. On the one hand, HMRC accept that a partnership whose main profits are generated from property development is not to be treated as a PIP (under SDLT). On the other hand, the reference of 'construction operations' is to ensure that a firm whose sole or main activity is that of dealing and investing in chargeable interests cannot avoid becoming a

PIP by carrying out construction operations on the land held as investment. As a corollary to being a PIP, Sch. 7 to FA 2003 restricts the availability of acquisition relief under SDLT to a PIP. Similar interpretation is likely to be adopted for LBTT.

Legislation: LBTT(S)A 2013, Sch. 17, para. 31; FA 2004, s. 74; RS Guidance LBTT7011

Transfer of interest in a PIP treated as a land transaction

The essence of a PIP definition is to catch any transfers of a PIP interest within the meaning of a chargeable transaction, as a share of partnership interest in a PIP is ultimately a share of the chargeable interests held by the PIP. An acquisition of a PIP interest is therefore traceable as an acquisition of a real estate interest of the property held by the PIP. Without the PIP provisions, the PIP structure would have allowed a chargeable acquisition of a partnership interest which is underpinned by the underlying assets to have gone 'untaxed'.

The purpose of the PIP provisions under Pt. 7 is to tax the transfer of economic ownership between partners for consideration, by taxing the transfer of a PIP interest based on the market value of the underlying chargeable assets in the proportion of the share of PIP interest acquired.

The charging provisions are set out under para. 32:

(1) where there is a transfer of an interest in a PIP, and the relevant property includes a chargeable interest;
(2) the transfer is treated as a land transaction that is chargeable;
(3) the buyer in the transaction is the person who acquires an increased partnership share, or becomes a partner as a result of the transfer;
(4) the chargeable consideration is taken to be equal to a proportion of the market value of the relevant partnership property;
(5) the proportion is determined as:

  (a) for a joining partner, the partnership share immediately after the transfer;
  (b) for an existing partner, the difference between the partnership share before and after the transfer.

Paragraph 32 then continues by classifying how the value of the relevant partnership property is to be determined. There are two types of transfers, known as Type A and Type B transfers. To determine the transfer value in a PIP share acquisition, it is therefore necessary to determine:

(1) whether the transfer is a Type A or Type B transfer; then
(2) apply the relevant list of criteria to determine the relevant partnership property, to which the proportion is to be applied.

Legislation: LBTT(S)A 2013, Sch. 17, para. 32; RS Guidance LBTT7011

Definition for Type A and Type B transfers

A Type A transfer is defined under para. 32(8) as:

(a) a transfer that takes the form of arrangements entered into under which:

   (i)   the whole or part of a partner's interest is acquired by another person (whether or not an existing partner); *and*

   (ii) consideration in money or money's worth is given by and on behalf of the person acquiring the interest; *or*

(b) a transfer that takes the form of arrangements entered into under which:

   (i)   a person becomes a partner;

   (ii) the interest of an existing partner is reduced, or an existing ceases to be a partner; *and*

   (iii) there is a withdrawal of money or money's worth from the partnership by the existing partner (other than money or money's worth paid from the resources available to the partnership prior to the transfer).

A Type B transfer is defined under para. 32(9) as any other transfer that is not a Type A transfer.

Points to note:

- The purpose of Pt. 7 is to tax a transfer of economic ownership of property between partners in a partnership (including when a person becomes, or ceases to be, a partner).
- Both types of transfers can give rise to an LBTT liability.
- The significance for the distinction between Type A and Type B transfers is for the purpose of determining whether the PIP holds relevant partnership property, as each type of transfers excludes different property interests from being relevant partnership property. Once the relevant partnership property for the transfer is determined, the value of the property can be ascertained for calculating the potential LBTT charge.
- There are *two* scenarios giving rise to a Type A transfer.
- The first scenario pertains to the acquisition of a partnership share of interest with real money. The seller of the PIP interest receives money in return of his disposal. The disposal of interest by an existing partner is matched by the acquisition of the partnership interest by the buyer. (A joining partner who introduces capital to a PIP in return for a partnership share is not a Type A transfer.)
- The second scenario occurs when a new partner joins and an existing partner's share is reduced, or ceases to be a partner. It is a transaction with share interest being acquired by the incoming partner (the buyer) and share interest being reduced or disposed of by an existing/retiring partner (the seller). However, to distinguish it from the first scenario, the consideration received by the seller does not come from the buyer, but from the withdrawal of money from the partnership.

- A typical Type B transfer is an adjustment of profit-sharing ratios between the existing partners, no consideration changed hands between the partners, and no new partners admitted.
- Another example of Type B transfer is when a partner reduces his share or leaves the partnership, and no payments are made by other partners, and no new partners are admitted.
- In relation to the parenthesis in the legislation: *(other than money or money's worth paid from the resources available to the partnership prior to the transfer)*, and a variation for the previous example, if a new partner is admitted, while the amount withdrawn by the partner reducing his share is paid out of resources available to the partnership prior to the transfer (such as previously arranged loan facilities), then that is a Type B transfer and not Type A.

Legislation: LBTT(S)A 2013, Sch. 17, para. 32; RS Guidance LBTT7011

Relevant partnership property for Type A transfer

As defined under para. 32(6), the relevant partnership property in relation to a Type A transfer is every chargeable interest held as partnership property immediately *after* the transfer, other than:

(a) any chargeable interest transferred to the partnership in connection with the transfer;a lease to which para. 33 (exclusion of market rent leases) applies; and

(b) any chargeable interest not attributable economically to the interest in the partnership transferred.

Points to note:

- Note that listing of property items is for exclusion (not inclusion).
- For further explanation for each item of property to be excluded, see below.

Legislation: LBTT(S)A 2013, Sch. 17, para. 32; RS Guidance LBTT7011

Relevant partnership property for Type B transfer

As defined under para. 32(7), the relevant partnership property in relation to a Type B transfer is every chargeable interest held as partnership property immediately *after* the transfer, other than:

(a) any chargeable interest transferred to the partnership in connection with the transfer;

(b) a lease to which para. 33 (exclusion of market rent leases) applies;

(c) any chargeable interest not attributable economically to the interest in the partnership transferred;

(d) any chargeable interest in respect of whose transfer to the partnership, a para. 35 election has been made to disapply Pt. 4 rules;

(e) any other chargeable interest whose transfer to the partnership did not fall within the meaning of Pt. 4 rules.

Points to note:

- For item (a), an example is the introduction of capital in the form of a chargeable interest being transferred by a joining partner in return for a partnership share in the PIP. Such a transfer will be taxed under Part 4 rules already, and is therefore excluded as relevant partnership property.
- Any market rent lease, see below.
- For item (c), for example, in relation to a particular property, the rights to income and gains are assigned exclusively to certain partners; the property is then not attributable to the partnership's economic interest. This kind of arrangement is common among professional or trading partnerships, where certain, (say the founding) partners 'own' the premises to the exclusion of partners who joined subsequently. Such arrangement is not common for a property interest.
- For item (d), a chargeable interest that falls under Pt. 4 rules but has elected to have Pt. 4 disapplied.
- For item (e), any chargeable interest that does not fall under Pt. 4 rules on its transfer into the partnership.
- The net effect of the exclusion list means that for a Type B transfer, the relevant partnership property will consist only of property transferred to the partnership from an existing or joining partner, or a person connected with such a partner. Also in respect of such a transfer, no para. 35 election has been made, and is not a market rent lease, and is not held solely for the benefits of certain partners.

Legislation: LBTT(S)A 2013, Sch. 17, para. 32; RS Guidance LBTT7011

Definition of market rent leases

A list of stringent conditions have to be satisfied for a lease to be classified as a 'market rent lease' and to qualify for exclusion as a relevant partnership property. The detailed provisions for these conditions are listed under para. 33 of Sch. 17.

The salient features of these conditions are:

- The lease is granted for a market rent only; i.e. no premium or arrangement for future premium.
- It must be for a term not exceeding five years, or if longer than five years, then it must provide for a market rent review at least once every five years.
- The rent review must provide for adjustment to a market rent in both directions; (an upward-only review clause will disqualify the lease as a market rent lease).
- No amendments to the terms of the lease since its first grant are allowed as an anti-avoidance measure.

Legislation: LBTT(S)A 2013, Sch. 17, para. 33; RS Guidance LBTT7011

Application of provisions about exchanges

The rules governing exchanges are under Sch. 2, para. 5. The exchange rules can apply in respect of an acquisition of partnership interest in a PIP under the provision of Sch. 17, para. 34.

If a partner acquires an interest in a PIP, and the consideration paid for that PIP interest is to transfer land *to an existing partner* (i.e. not into the partnership), for the purposes of the exchange rules, the PIP interest so acquired can be treated as a major interest in land, if the relevant partnership property of the PIP includes a major interest in land. In other words, if the relevant partnership property includes a major interest in land, then the acquisition of the PIP interest can be considered as a major interest in land by dint of this provision. The transaction, which involves the purchase of PIP interest (with a major land interest) with consideration being the transfer of land to an existing partner, meets the condition for the exchange rules to apply – i.e. the purchase of a major land interest with a major land interest.

'Relevant partnership property' in this context is similarly determined as for a Type A or Type B transfers under para. 32(6) or 32(7).

The rule on 'partition etc: disregard of existing interest' under Sch. 2, para. 6 does not apply to a transaction falling under Sch. 17, para. 34.

Legislation: LBTT(S)A 2013, Sch. 17, para. 34; RS Guidance LBTT7011

Election to disapply Part 4 rules

In a transfer of a chargeable interest into a PIP, the buyer can elect for Pt. 4 rules *not* to apply. As election to disapply Pt. 4 rules has the consequence of disapplying the rules under Pt. 5 in relation to the transfer of that chargeable interest out of the PIP.

If an election to dis-apply Pt. 4 rules means that the chargeable consideration is taken to be the market value of the chargeable interest, and the transaction is treated as an 'ordinary partnership transaction'.

The provisions to disapply Pt. 4 and 5 rules are under para. 35 of Sch. 17. For this reason, the election is referred to as a para. 35 election, and must be included in the LBTT return made in respect of the transaction into the PIP, or by amendment of that return.

A para. 35 election is irrevocable, which means if the election is made, it cannot be subsequently amended to revoke the election.

If the election is made by amendment of the 'main transaction' (i.e. the transfer into the PIP), then the election is deemed to take effect as if it had been made on the date on which the LBTT return was first made. Where a transaction is affected by a para. 35 election on the 'main transaction', the LBTT return in relation to an 'affected transaction' can be amended within the period allowed for amendment of that return.

An 'affected transaction' in relation the main transaction means a transaction:

(a) to which the rules under para. 32 (transfer of interest into PIP treated as land transaction) applied; and

(b) has an effective date on or after the effective date of the main transaction.

Legislation: LBTT(S)A 2013, Sch. 17, para. 35; RS Guidance LBTT7011

16-995   Application of provisions on exemptions, reliefs and notification

Application of exemptions and reliefs: general

The general principle in respect of the application of exemptions and reliefs to partnership transactions is under Pt. 8 to Sch. 17 (i.e. para. 37–40).

Subject to certain exceptions, partnership transactions are subject to any other provisions affording exemption or relief from LBTT. The exceptions are listed under the following paragraphs to Sch. 17:

(a) para. 37 – disapplication of Sch. 1, para. 1 exemption for land transactions for which there is no consideration;

(b) para. 38 and 39 – application of group relief to partnership transactions;

(c) para. 40 – application of charities relief.

Legislation: LBTT(S)A 2013, Sch. 17, Pt. 8, para. 36–41; RS Guidance LBTT7012

Exceptions to the application of exemption under Sch. 1, para. 1

In respect of the application of exemptions to partnership transactions, the *only* exception relates to the application of exemption under Sch. 1, para.1, which provides for a land transaction to be exempt from LBTT where no consideration is given. This exemption, is *not to apply* to transactions involving partnerships falling under:

(a) Pt. 4 rules – transfers into a partnership;

(b) Pt. 5 rules – transfers out of a partnership;

(c) para. 17 provisions – transfers of partnership interest pursuant to earlier arrangements;

(d) para. 32 provisions – transfers of interest in partnership (a PIP) treated as land transactions.

The overall effect of disapplying Sch. 1, para. 1 exemption to the list of partnership transfers under Sch. 17, para. 37 means, all transfers involving partnerships where no consideration has been given do not qualify for the exemption, *except for transfers classified as 'ordinary partnership transactions'.*

Legislation: LBTT(S)A 2013, Sch. 17, para. 37; RS Guidance LBTT7012

Group relief – key concepts on availability to partnerships

The rules governing the availability of group relief to partnerships are complex. The key concepts regarding the determination of availability are worth noting for background of this section of the Commentary.

Prerequisites for LBTT group companies

For group relief to apply, the companies concerned must be within an LBTT group. The two pre-conditions for companies to form an LBTT group are:

(1) they must be body corporate; and
(2) they must have issued share capital (75% beneficial ownership test).

The status of a partnership is relevant therefore in determining whether these two pre-conditions are met.

Ownership of chargeable interests distinguished from ownership of share capital – distinction between Sch. 10 and Sch. 17 criteria

The lens used for looking at a partnership for group relief purposes (Sch. 10) is different from the lens used to decide whether a transaction is to be taxed as a partnership transaction under Sch. 17.

Another way of distinguishing the lens to be used is to ask what concerning a partnership is being examined. For Sch. 17 purposes, the lens is used to examine the *ownership of chargeable interests*, and all partnerships are seen through as 'transparent' – to its members; the partners *are* the ultimate owners of the chargeable interest.

For group relief purposes under Sch. 10, the lens to be used is to determine if the two pre-conditions are met regarding: (1) being a *body corporate*, and (2) with ownership of *75% of issue of share capital*. In other words, instead of looking at the ownership of chargeable interests, the lens for Sch. 10 purposes is used to examine the *ownership of issued share capital*.

The status of the partnership in respect of: (a) separate legal personality, and (b) body corporate status is of importance for determining if the two pre-conditions obtain for an LBTT group to exist.

How these facets pertaining to the status of the partnership interact can be complex, but for general observations:

• A partnership is neither a body corporate, nor issues shares, and therefore cannot of itself be a group company.
• The issue about ownership of share capital where the partnership concerned has not got a separate legal personality in law, means that in identifying a group structure, the partnership can be looked through.

- If the partnership has a separate legal personality and owns shares in the company, the ownership cannot be 'looked through' and in identifying whether an LBTT group exists, such a partnership has to be included.

Partnership status re: separate legal personality and body corporate

By way of summary of what has been detailed in ¶16-900, the salient features of the partnerships under English and Scots law or formed as an LLP are as follows:

(1) English partnerships (general or limited) have no legal personality and are not bodies corporate either.

(2) Scottish partnerships (general or limited) have a separate legal personality, but do not have body corporate status.

(3) Limited liability partnerships (LLPs) have a separate legal personality and are also bodies corporate.

When does a partnership break an LBTT group

The SDLT manuals from SDLTM 34350 et al provide good examples to illustrate how partnership status affects group relief availability as regards:

(a) the separate legal personality status, as between an English and a Scottish partnership for group relief purposes; and

(b) the body corporate status, as between an English/Scottish partnership and an LLP.

Apart from the intrinsic status of the partnership concerning separate legal personality and body corporate, whether a partnership can form an LBTT group and whether its existence breaks up a group depends on two other factors:

(1) the structure of the companies and where the partnership sits within that structure; and

(2) the direction of the transfer of the chargeable interest involving the partnership.

LBTT group – English, Scottish partnerships and LLPs compared

To determine whether an LBTT group exists can involve some complex analysis, and each case must be taken on its own facts. The following serves as a summary of the general points.

(1) An English general or limited partnership is 'transparent' in relation to share ownership because it lacks a separate legal personality. By being able to look through the share ownership of an English partnership, it means:

    (a) If the corporate partners in an English partnership are members of an LBTT group, then any company that is at least 75% owned by the partnership will also be a member of the LBTT group.

    (b)   Transfers of chargeable interests between (a) the corporate partners in the English partnership, and (b) the partnership and any 75% owned company owned by the partnership can qualify for group relief.

(2)   A Scottish general or limited partnership has a separate legal personality from its members, and as such it is not 'transparent' in relation to share ownership. The share ownership by a Scottish partnership in any company cannot be looked through, so in identifying whether an LBTT group exists, the group structure has to include the Scottish partnership. However, since a Scottish partnership is not a body corporate, it cannot be a group member or a parent for LBTT purposes. The implications are:

    (a)   Any company owned by a Scottish partnership cannot be in a group with the corporate partners of the partnership.

    (b)   Transfers of chargeable interests between any of the corporate partners with a company owned by the partnership therefore cannot qualify for group relief.

    (c)   Furthermore, for not being a body corporate, a Scottish partnership cannot be a parent for its corporate partners to form a group either. Transfers between the corporate partners of a Scottish partnership therefore cannot get the benefit of group relief.

(3)   A UK LLP has a separate legal personality from its members, and as such it is not 'transparent' in relation to share ownership. For not being transparent, it means the LLP has to be included in identifying a group structure. Two factors relevant to an LLP, in respect of it being a body corporate, and in respect of its not being able to issue share capital, have the following implications:

    (a)   Even though it is a body corporate, an LLP does not issue share capital, and therefore can never qualify as a group company through the 75% ownership test. An LLP therefore can never be a *subsidiary* of a company to qualify as a group company for group relief purposes.

    (b)   The corollary is that any subsidiaries of an LLP cannot be grouped with the companies which are the corporate members of the LLP.

    (c)   However, by being a body corporate, an LLP differs from a Scottish partnership in that it can be the parent for its corporate partners which form an LBTT group. The fact that an LLP does not issue share capital is not an impediment for being the parent entity – there is no need for a *parent* entity to be 'owned' by another company through the 75% ownership test as such.

    (d)   Notwithstanding its status as a body corporate, an LLP cannot claim group relief because the ownership of chargeable interests by an LLP is still considered as held by or on behalf of its members.

    (e)   In consequence of the above, the application of group relief for an LLP is:

        (i)   Any company owned by an LLP cannot be in a group with the corporate partners of the LLP.

        (ii)   Transfers of chargeable interests between any of the corporate partners with a company owned by the partnership therefore cannot qualify for group relief.

(iii) However, for being a body corporate, an LLP can be a parent for its corporate partners to form a group. Transfers between the corporate partners of an LLP can benefit from group relief.

(iv) A transfer of a chargeable interest between companies directly and indirectly owned (i.e.: subsidiaries to company directly owned by the LLP) by an LLP as the parent entity may also qualify for group relief, subject to the 75% ownership test.

(v) A transfer by an LLP of a chargeable interest to a company within the LLP headed group cannot qualify for group relief, because the chargeable interest is deemed to be owned by the members of the LLP, and the LLP members are not in the same group as the transferee company. (Remember the important distinction between ownership for chargeable interests (Sch. 17 purposes) and ownership of share capital for different (Sch. 10 purposes).)

Legislation: LBTT(S)A 2013, Sch. 10 and 17; RS Guidance LBTT7012

Group relief – as applied to Pt. 4 partnership transactions

The claim of group relief in a partnership transfer that falls under Pt. 4 of Sch. 17 provisions can be analysed as follows:

(1) where a chargeable interest is transferred *into* a partnership *by*:

    (a) a corporate partner – i.e. a company which is a partner in the partnership; or

    (b) a company which becomes a partner of the partnership as a result of the transfer; or

    (c) a company connected to a corporate partner in the partnership, or to the company which become a corporate partner as a result of the transfer; *and*

(2) the transferor company (ACo.) and one or more of the corporate partners (say, BCo. and CLtd) are members of the same LBTT group, then:

(3) group relief can be claimed by the transferee companies (B & C), and

(4) the claim of group relief to each transferee companies is in the proportion of their partnership share; i.e. the proportion in which BCo. & CLtd are entitled to share in the income profits of the partnership.

Legislation: LBTT(S)A 2013, Sch. 10 and 17; RS Guidance LBTT7012

Group relief – types of partnership transactions to which modifications apply

The general provisions for the application of group relief are under Sch. 10 of the Act. Sch. 10 provisions apply with modifications to the following:

(1) a transaction to which Pt. 4 rules apply – i.e. a transfer of a chargeable interest into a partnership, and

(2) a transfer of interest in a partnership which is treated as a land transaction by virtue of para. 17 of Sch. 17 – i.e. transfer of partnership interest pursuant to earlier arrangements.

Note that group relief is available to both para. 17 and para. 18 transactions (deemed transaction arising on the withdrawal of money form partnership after a Pt. 4 transfer), if the following condition is met:

- that the transfer of chargeable interest is between members of the same LBTT group;
- that means all the transferee corporate partners are members of the same group as the transferor company;
- since all the partners in the partnership are treated as the buyers under both para. 17 and 18 scenarios.

The modifications to Sch. 10 do not single out para. 18 for their application, but that does not mean that para. 18 transactions cannot qualify for group relief; it means that the modifications do not apply to para. 18 transactions.

Legislation: LBTT(S)A 2013, Sch. 17, para. 38; RS Guidance LBTT7012

Group relief – modification pertaining to withdrawal provisions

The modifications to Sch. 10 under para. 38(2) pertain largely to the withdrawal of group relief that has been claimed. The conditions for withdrawal for a partnership transaction are in essence the same as those for the general/main provisions for group relief withdrawal, and the main modifications are in relation to the reference terms.

Group relief is withdrawn in part or in full, if a partner who was a partner at the effective date ('the relevant partner') of the transaction that had been exempt by virtue of a claim of group relief ('the relevant transaction') ceases to be a member of the same group as the seller (i.e. the transferor) *before the end of the period of 3 years beginning with the effective date of the transaction.*

Legislation: LBTT(S)A 2013, Sch. 17, para. 38; RS Guidance LBTT7012

Group relief – modification pertaining to calculating SLP

For a transfer of chargeable interest into a partnership under Pt. 4 rules, the determination of SLP (para. 14) has the reference that a corresponding partner must be an 'individual', thereby disqualifying a company as a corresponding partner.

The exception to this general rule is given under para. 16(2), whereby a company holding property as a trustee, or is connected with the relevant owner only because of CTA 2010, s. 1122(6) (i.e. in a capacity as trustee of a settlement), is to be treated as an 'individual'.

The modification under **para. 39** has the effect of being another exception to this general rule. The conditions for para. 39 to apply are:

(a)   a company ('the connected company') would have been a corresponding partner of a relevant owner ('the original owner') but for the fact that general rule under para. 16 that connected persons only if they are individuals; and

(b)   the connected company and the original owner are members of the same group.

Where the conditions under para. 39 are met, SLP is calculated to include the 'connected company' as a corresponding partner, thereby reducing the overall charge for the calculation of Pt. 4 chargeable consideration.

By way of an example for illustrating when para. 39 modification applies:

* Andrew and Alex are in partnership with Alpha Ltd.
* Beta Ltd transfers a chargeable interest into the partnership.
* Alpha Ltd and Beta Ltd are wholly owned by Omega Ltd.
* Omega Ltd is owned by the parents of Andrew and Alex.
* The transfer from Beta Ltd to the partnership is a Part 4 transfer as Beta Ltd is connected to Andrew and Alex and Alpha Ltd.
* However, Alpha Ltd is not a corresponding partner to the relevant owner Beta Ltd because (a) it is not the relevant owner, and (b) nor an 'individual' connected to the relevant owner.
* But Alpha and Beta are group companies through meeting the 75% ownership test by Omega.
* Paragraph 39 modification applies; SLP is calculated by treating Alpha Ltd as a corresponding partner.

Legislation: LBTT(S)A 2013, Sch. 17, para. 39; RS Guidance LBTT7012

Application of charities relief to partnership transactions

If the conditions for Sch. 13 charities relief are met, then the relief applies to all partnership transactions with the modification applicable to:

(1)   a transfer of an interest in a property investment partnership; or

(2)   a transfer of a partnership interest pursuant to earlier arrangements.

Charities relief is available to the applicable transfer on the condition that:

(1)   *every* chargeable interest held as partnership property that forms the subject matter of the transfer;

(2)   *must* be held for qualifying charitable purposes immediately after the transfer.

Legislation: LBTT(S)A 2013, Sch. 17, para. 40; RS Guidance LBTT7012

Notification

Paragraph 41 is provided in respect of the following types of transfer:

(1)   para. 17 – transfer of partnership interest pursuant of earlier arrangements; or

(2)   para. 32 – transfer of partnership interest in a PIP treated as land transaction (Type A/Type B transfer).

Either para. 17 or 32 transaction is a notifiable transaction if (*but only if*) the consideration for the transaction exceeds the nil rate band.

For the purpose of determining whether the nil rate band is exceeded, the consideration for a transaction is taken to be:

(a)   the chargeable consideration; or

(b)   the total of the chargeable consideration for all the linked transactions if the transaction is one of a number of linked transactions.

Legislation: LBTT(S)A 2013, Sch. 17, para. 41; RS Guidance LBTT7012

PART 2: COMPLIANCE ISSUES

Chapter 8: Compliance and administration

17-000 Introduction and overview

The special income tax rules affecting partnerships are contained in ITTOIA 2005, Pt. 9, beginning at s. 846. Those rules introduce the term 'firm' to denote, for tax purposes, the persons carrying on a trade in partnership. The provisions apply 'expressly' to trades but (unless there is an express or implied indication to the contrary) also apply to professions and, for certain purposes, to other businesses. Those purposes are the calculation and allocation of profits and losses, partners to whom the remittance basis applies and certain UK resident partners affected by double taxation agreements.

The general income tax rule, subject only to express or implied exceptions, is that a firm is not to be regarded as an entity that is separate and distinct from the partners. This is the case even where (as in Scotland) the partnership has its own legal identity (BIM82205). However, the HMRC guidance states that for the purposes of taxing third party (agency) income, a partnership is treated as a separate entity.

17-020 Registering partners and partnerships with HMRC

Every new partnership must be registered with HMRC. The partnership must choose a nominated partner to be responsible for managing the partnership's tax returns and keeping business records.

Both the partnership and its members must be registered. If the partners are individuals, they must register for self assessment and if the partner is a company, it must register with HMRC for corporation tax.

Registering the partnership

- Online at *www.gov.uk/government/publications/self-assessment-register-a-partnership-for-self-assessment-sa400*.
- Download and fill in form SA400 at *www.gov.uk/government/publications/self-assessment-register-a-partnership-for-self-assessment-sa400*.

Note that LLPs and LPs do not need to complete form SA400 as they will be automatically registered for self-assessment through their Companies House registration.

Form SA400 must be completed by the nominated partner. This is the partner who has been nominated by the partnership to receive and submit the partnership returns.

Registering the partners

Individual partners: use form SA401:

www.gov.uk/government/publications/self-assessment-register-a-partner-for-self-assessment-and-class-2-nics-sa401

Non-individual partners (company's or trusts): use form SA402:

www.gov.uk/government/publications/self-assessment-register-a-partner-for-self-assessment-if-theyre-not-an-individual-sa402

Use of schedules to register multiple partners for self-assessment and National Insurance

By individual agreement with Central Agent Authorisation Team (CAAT), a spreadsheet can be used to notify changes if the number of new partners warrants it, if the partnership is already in existence and all new partners already have a unique taxpayer reference (UTR) and are registered for Class 2 NICs.

The spreadsheet should be entitled 'Partners who already have a UTR and are already registered for Class 2 NICs joining this partnership' and contain the following information:

- name of partnership for HMRC purposes (as recorded at Companies House if applicable);
- address of partnership for HMRC purposes (as recorded at Companies House if applicable);
- the partnership's unique taxpayer reference (UTR);

And for each partner:

- surname;
- first name;
- date of birth;
- address;
- NINO;
- UTR;
- date of joining partnership.

LLPs and British Venture Capital Association (BVCA) cases

A spreadsheet with the SA401/SA402 information may be submitted to CAAT but must be in the format specified at SAM100137 and signed by the nominated partner.

There are four different spreadsheets covering four different scenarios and they should be kept as separate spreadsheets:

- Investment partnership UK resident individuals;
- Investment partnership UK resident 'other entity';

- Investment partnership non-UK resident individuals;
- Investment partnership non-resident 'other entity'.

The spreadsheets must contain the following information:

- name of the partnership;
- address of the partnership;
- partnership Unique Taxpayer Reference (UTR).

Information for each partner varies depending upon the category of partnership, see SAM100137.

Overseas aspects of partnership registration for SA

If a partnership's business is carried on wholly or partly in the UK or if land in the UK owned by the partnership is rented out, it will need to register and obtain a UTR. Likewise, if a foreign entity is a member of a UK partnership, it will also need a UTR. Note: There may also be a need to notify for other tax purposes.

Foreign partnerships – all activities entirely outside UK

Provided there is **no** UK presence or activity, there is currently no requirement for any partnership to register with HMRC.

A UK resident partner of a foreign partnership not required to register for SA

Where there is no requirement to register the foreign partnership for self-assessment, a UK resident partner will need to enter their own UTR as the partnership reference number – currently box 2 on the partnership pages of the return for an individual. This will facilitate inclusion of their share of the foreign partnership profits on the partnership supplementary pages of the SA100.

Authorising an agent

www.gov.uk/government/publications/tax-agents-and-advisers-authorising-your-agent-64-8

Where to send completed forms

All forms should be sent to:
HM Revenue & Customs
National Insurance contributions and Employer Office
Self-employment and self-assessment registrations
Benton Park View
Newcastle upon Tyne
NE98 1ZZ

Deadlines

The partnership and/or individual partners must be registered by 5 October in the business' second tax year to avoid a penalty.

Example

If you start a partnership or become a partner during the 2016–17 tax year, you must register before 5 October 2017.

New partners joining

The above forms should be completed as and when a new partner joins the partnership.

Other material: SAM100135ff.; *www.gov.uk/register-for-self-assessment/self-employed*

17-040   Partnership returns

A partnership is not treated as a tax-paying entity but individual partners, whether corporate or not, must include their partnership shares in their own self-assessment returns.

In order to establish the amount chargeable to income tax or corporation tax on each partner, and the amount of tax due, an officer of Revenue and Customs may employ either or both of the two powers outlined below (TMA 1970, s. 12AA(1)–(3)):

(1)   give notice to the partners, requiring a person identified in accordance to the rules given with the notice, to make a return for a period specified in the notice, by a date specified in the notice, and to deliver with it such accounts, statements and documents relating to information contained in the return as may reasonably be required in pursuance of the notice; and

(2)   give notice to any partner, reasonably requiring him or her to make returns and deliver documents as in (1). Notices may be given to single partners, or separate notices may be given to each partner or such partners as the officer thinks fit (TMA 1970, s. 12AA(3)).

The partnership tax return includes all information required to calculate the profits arising from any partnership business in the accounting periods covered by the return, including any claims (such as capital allowances) that must be taken into account when calculating the profits of that trade. In addition it includes details of any partnership investment income.

The partnership tax return also needs to include details of the profit allocation in force for the accounting periods covered by the return.

As with the return made by individuals, the amounts included must take into account any relief, allowance or repayment of tax for which a claim is made, as well as tax already deducted at source and for tax years up to 2015–16, tax credits on dividends.

Each return is to include the name, residence (address or 'registered office' in the case of a company) and tax reference of all partners involved in the period, and a declaration by the person making it that it is to the best of his knowledge correct and complete (TMA 1970, s. 12AA(6), (10)). In addition to the above, the returns are, if the notice so requires, to include details of capital gains on disposals of partnership property calculated as if the partnership were itself liable to tax, along with particulars relating to any acquisitions of partnership property (as under TMA 1970, s. 12(2), 12AA(7)).

Flexibility is permitted in the types of accounts and statements which may be required for different periods and from different types of partnership (TMA 1970, s. 12AA(8) and (9)). Partnerships with a turnover in excess of £15m and CT partnerships (those with only company partners) are required to submit full accounts and computations, rather than completing the standard accounts information on the return form.

Filing deadlines

Where the partnership includes one or more individuals and the notice to file is issued at the normal time, the filing date is 31 October after the end of the tax year for a paper partnership return and 31 January following the end of the tax year for an electronic return. Where the notice to file is issued after 31 July but before 31 October following the end of the year of assessment, the filing deadline will be three months after the issue of the notice for a paper return and 31 January following the end of the tax year for an electronic return. Where the notice to file is issued after 31 October, the deadline will be three months following the issue date for both paper and electronic returns (TMA 1970, s. 12AA(4)–(4E)).

Where a partnership includes a company, the filing date is set by reference to the period covered by the return. This will normally be nine months after the end of the period for a paper return and 12 months after the end of the period for an electronic return. However, where the notice to file is issued more than nine months after the end of the period, the filing deadline will be three months after the date of issue for both paper and electronic returns (TMA 1970, s. 12AA(5)–(5E)).

Different combinations of filing deadlines may exist in the case of a mixed partnership:

- where the accounting date of a mixed partnership falls on or between 6 April and 31 January in any tax year, the filing date for the partnership return will be 31 October following the tax year for a paper return and 31 January for an electronic return (these dates satisfy both s. 12AA(4A) and (4B) for the individual partners and s. 12AA(5A) and (5B) for the corporate partners);
- where the accounting date of a mixed partnership falls on or between 1 February and 5 April in any tax year the filing date for the partnership return will be nine months after the end of that date for a paper return and 12 months after for

an electronic return. This will also satisfy both s. 12AA(4A) and (4B) for the individual partners and s. 12AA(5A) and (5B) for the corporate partners.

However, in the latter case, the individual partners will be required to file their own personal tax returns before the partnership return is required. HMRC guidance at SALF503 states that:

> 'In such cases it may be that the partnership tax return can be completed and submitted before the formal filing date, but where this is not possible, the partner will have to include an estimate of his or her share of partnership profits in the tax return, and then correct it when the final figure becomes available'.

Appointment of a successor

Where the partner responsible for the partnership return is no longer available to carry out these duties, the relevant partners may appoint a successor. 'Relevant partners', for this purpose, are those who were partners in the period covered by the return (or the personal representatives of those partners). Nomination must be by a majority of the relevant partners, and is only effective once it has been notified to an officer of HMRC. Similarly, a revocation of the nomination is only effective once notified. Where there is no nomination, and the notice to make a return is issued to the partners, rather than to a specific partner, the successor will be chosen using the rules accompanying the return. Where there is no nomination and the notice to make a return is issued to a specific partner, the successor will be nominated by an officer of HMRC (TMA 1970, s. 12AA(11)–(13)).

Legislation: TMA 1970, s. 12AA

17-060   Withdrawal by HMRC of notice under TMA 1970, s. 12AA

With effect in respect of returns for the tax year 2012–13 and subsequent tax years, HMRC will withdraw a notice to file a return, on request in certain circumstances, where they agree a self assessment return is not required and cancel any late filing penalty already issued in respect of the outstanding return. Requests must be made within two years beginning with the end of:

- the period in respect of which the return is required in the case of a partnership which includes one or more companies; or
- the relevant year of assessment in the case of any other partnership.

In the case of any partnership, HMRC may agree an extended period with the partner in exceptional circumstances.

Legislation: TMA 1970, s. 12AAA

17-080   Partnership statement to be included in return

Every return under TMA 1970, s. 12AA (see ¶17-040) is to include a 'partnership statement' of the following for the tax year, or for each period of account ending within the period covered by the return (TMA 1970, s. 12AB(1)):

(1)   the amount of the partnership's income or loss from each source on the basis of the information in the partnership return and taking into account claims to relief and allowances under TMA 1970, s. 42(7) (see ¶17-100) included in the return;

(2)   on the same basis, the consideration received by the partnership on each disposal of a partnership asset;

(3)   the amount of income tax deducted at source suffered by the partnership;

(4)   the partnership's entitlement to any tax credit under CTA 2010, s. 1109 (in the case of corporation tax) and ITTOIA 2005, s. 397(1) or 397A(1) (in the case of income tax).

The statement must also show each partner's share of the above amounts. Thus, a partner will be able to abstract the relevant figures in order to complete the personal return.

Legislation: TMA 1970, s. 12AB

17-100   Claims to be included in partnership return

Partnership claims under provisions specified in TMA 1970, s. 42(7) are to be made in partnership returns under TMA 1970, s. 12AA where a notice to make a return has been issued, and otherwise by a nominated partner (TMA 1970, s. 42(6)). The specified claims are:

- payments under certified schemes for rationalising industry which are not repayments of contributions (ICTA 1988, s. 570);
- cancellation of certificates for schemes to rationalise industry (ICTA 1988, s. 571(4));
- claims for capital allowances (CAA 2001, s. 3);
- election for certain machinery or plant to be treated as short-life assets (CAA 2001, s. 83);
- disposal of short-life asset to connected person (CAA 2001, s. 89);
- election for 'single ship pool' not to apply (CAA 2001, s. 129);
- deferment of first-year allowance (ships) (CAA 2001, s. 131);
- deferment of balancing charge (ships) (CAA 2001, s. 135);
- expenditure incurred by equipment lessor (CAA 2001, s. 177);
- expenditure incurred by incoming lessee (transfer of allowances) (CAA 2001, s. 183);
- successions to trades (connected persons) (CAA 2001, s. 266);
- succession to trades where no election made under s. 266 above (CAA 2001, s. 268);
- election to treat grant of long lease as a sale (former CAA 2001, s. 290);
- balancing allowances made in respect of mining structures, etc. (former CAA 2001, s. 355);

- balancing events (agricultural buildings) (former CAA 2001, s. 381);
- sales without change of control or between connected persons (CAA 2001, s. 569);
- election for cash basis for small businesses (ITTOIA 2005, s. 25A);
- election for herd basis (ITTOIA 2005, s. 111(1); CTA 2009, s. 109(1));
- election for herd basis where all or majority of herd slaughtered (ITTOIA 2005, s. 126(2); CTA 2009, s. 124(2));
- election for herd basis where assessment for relevant chargeable period concluded (ITTOIA 2005, s. 129(2); CTA 2009, s. 127(2));
- valuation of work in progress at discontinuance of profession or vocation (ITTOIA 2005, s. 185);
- disposal of know-how (ITTOIA 2005, s. 194; CTA 2009, s. 178);
- under-used holiday accommodation averaging elections (ITTOIA 2005, s. 326; CTA 2009, s. 268); and
- delayed remittance of foreign securities (ITA 2007, s. 668 and 669).

Legislation: TMA 1970, s. 42

17-120 Amendment of partnership return by taxpayer and correction by HMRC

HMRC have nine months from the delivery of the statement to correct obvious errors (the 'repair' process). The correction has no effect if the person notified of it rejects the correction, by notice, within 30 days.

A partner is also entitled to amend the partnership return, within 12 months of the filing date (31 January following the end of the year of assessment or three months beginning with the date of notice where notice is given after 31 October following the year of assessment).

Once it is amended or corrected, HMRC must make consequential amendments to the individual partners' return(s) (TMA 1970, s. 12ABA and 12ABB).

Legislation: TMA 1970, s. 12ABA, 12ABB

17-140 Relief for mistakes in the partnership tax return

The partnership also has the right to claim that the amount paid or liable to be paid in accordance with the self-assessment of one or more of the partners is excessive by reason of a mistake in the partnership return. Any such claim must be made no later than four years after the end of the relevant tax year.

Legislation: TMA 1970, s. 33 and Sch. 1AB

17-160   Partners' returns

An individual's return is to include his share of any partnership income, losses, tax (i.e. tax deducted at source), tax credit or charge (TMA 1970, s. 8(1B)). These figures will be derived from the relevant partnership statement. A partnership statement is relevant if it is for a period which includes all or part of the tax year or its basis period (TMA 1970, s. 8(1B) and (1C)).

Companies which are in partnership must include their shares of the partnership income, loss, consideration, tax, credit or charge as shown in relevant partnership statements, into their own Corporation Tax Self Assessment returns (FA 1998, Sch. 18, para. 12). A 'relevant statement' is any statement which covers a period including the company's return period, or any part of the company's return period. Return periods for companies are defined in FA 1998, Sch. 18, para. 5.

As each partner is individually responsible for their own tax, it is possible for one partner to settle their affairs even though a fellow partner has failed to deliver a return, or has a return under enquiry.

There is no joint liability for the tax due on partnership profits and if a particular partner fails to pay the tax due on their share of the profits, HMRC are only able to seek recovery from that partner alone.

Legislation: FA 1998, Sch. 18, para. 12; TMA 1970, s. 8(1B), (1C)

17-180   Enquiries into partnership returns

HMRC are entitled to enquire into any partnership tax return, any amendment to the return or a partnership claim (or amendment to a claim) made outside a return within the normal enquiry time limits and subject to the same enquiry procedures as for individual returns, claims etc.

HMRC must issue a notice of enquiry:

- within 12 months from the date the return was delivered, if delivered on or before the filing date;
- before the quarter day next following the first anniversary of the day the return was delivered, if the return was delivered late; and
- before the quarter day next following the first anniversary of an amendment to a return.

Quarter days are 31 January, 30 April, 31 July and 31 October.

Except where a return is amended, or further amended, a return can only be subject to one enquiry.

A notice of enquiry into a partnership return automatically extends to the partners' own tax returns without separate notice being required. This is the case even if the time limit for opening an enquiry into a partner's own return has already passed. However, the deemed enquiry only relates to the partnership aspects of the partner's return and any enquiries into any other aspect of the partners' return must be the subject of a separate enquiry under TMA 1970, s. 9A (for individual partners) or FA 1998, Sch. 18, Pt. IV (for corporate partners).

HMRC have undertaken to notify partners where an enquiry under TMA 1970, s. 12AC has been opened into a partnership return although this is a matter of good customer service and the notice itself does not serve any statutory function.

All partners' tax returns remain open until the partnership enquiry is complete.

This section does not mean that other (non-partnership) aspects of a partner's tax return are automatically under enquiry. The non-partnership aspects of a partner's tax return can only be reviewed if a separate enquiry is opened under TMA 1970, s. 9A (or, where the time limit for such a notice has passed, if the 'discovery' rules apply). Similarly, the completion of an enquiry into one part of the tax return (for example, the partnership income) has no consequence for any separate enquiry into the other part (the non-partnership income).

An enquiry into an individual partner's tax return does not automatically open up the partnership return for enquiry.

The nominated partner (or any successor) will be responsible for dealing with the enquiry and keeping the other partners informed of its progress.

Amendment during enquiry

Amendments made whilst an enquiry is in progress do not take effect until the enquiry has been completed and the closure notice issued, unless the amendment is taken into account in the content of the closure notice or HMRC conclude the amendment is incorrect.

Alternative Investment Fund firms

Where a partnership has made an election under ITTOIA 2005, s. 863H (election for special provision for alternative investment fund managers to apply, see ¶26-020), an officer of HMRC may by notice require the firm to supply such information as is reasonably required for the purposes of the operation of legislation in ITTOIA 2005, s. 863H–863L in relation to the alternative investment firm and its members. The information must be provided within such reasonable time as is specified.

Referral of questions to the tribunal during enquiry

The nominated partner (or successor) may jointly with HMRC refer a question regarding the subject matter of an enquiry to the tribunal for determination (TMA 1970, s. 28ZA).

Completion of an enquiry into a partnership return

The rules applying to the closure of an enquiry into a partnership return mirror those for closing an enquiry into an individual's return.

An enquiry is treated as complete when an officer of the Board issues the nominated partner with a closure notice which states his conclusions and makes any amendment that is required to the partnership return (or confirms that no amendment is required).

Where a partnership return is amended, HMRC must notify all of the partners of the amendment required to their individual or company return(s) and to make such amendments as is necessary to give effect to the amendments to the partnership return.

The nominated partner has a right of appeal against any conclusions stated in the closure notice or any amendment of the partnership return on completion of the enquiry, however, the partners have no right of appeal to the tribunal in respect of the corresponding amendments to their own tax returns.

The nominated partner may also apply to the tribunal for a direction requiring a closure notice be issued within a specified period, which the tribunal must give unless there are reasonable grounds for the closure notice not being issued within a specified period.

Legislation: TMA 1970, s. 12AC, 12AD, 12ADA, 28ZA, 28B, Sch. 1A, para. 5(1)

17-200   Discovery and partnerships

Discovery assessments must be made on the partners not the partnership, however, specific rules apply in relation to partnerships.

A partnership return may be amended where HMRC discover that:

- profits have been omitted from the partnership statement;
- profits included are, or have become, insufficient;
- reliefs or allowances claimed by the representative partner are or have become excessive.

Where such a discovery is made, HMRC must amend the partners' own returns to give effect to the amendments to the partnership return.

The right of appeal against any such amendment rests with the representative partner.

The conditions under which a discovery may be made mirror those for individuals. Briefly, these require either:

- the circumstance mentioned in the bullets above to have been brought about carelessly or deliberately by the representative partner or a person acting on his behalf; or

- at a time when HMRC cease to be entitled to give notice of enquiry into the partnership return or upon closure of an enquiry into the return, the officer could not be reasonably expected on the basis of information available to him before that time to be aware of the circumstance listed in the bullets above.

Legislation: TMA 1970, s. 30B

17-220   Record-keeping

The same requirements regarding the making and keeping of documents as apply to individuals' returns apply to partnership returns.

Records must normally be retained:

- in the case of persons carrying on trades, professions or businesses, the fifth anniversary of the 31 January following the tax year (or, in the case of companies, the sixth anniversary of the end of the accounting period); and
- in any other case, the second 31 January following the tax year.

In the case of a business (including the business of letting a property) records that must be kept include records of:

- all receipts and expenses;
- all goods purchased and sold.

A penalty of up to £3,000 may be charged for each failure to keep or to preserve adequate records in support of a tax return.

Legislation: TMA 1970, s. 12B

17-240   Penalties for failure to file a partnership return

Tax years 2010–11 onwards

A penalty is payable by every 'relevant partner' where the 'representative partner' or their 'successor' fails to submit a partnership tax return (as required under TMA 1970, s. 12AA(2)(a) or (3)(a)).

A 'relevant partner' is a person who was a partner in the partnership at any time during the period in respect of which the return was required. The 'representative partner' is the person required to file the partnership return.

Penalty	£
Late return	£100 (each partner)
3 months late	Daily penalties £10 per day up to maximum 90 days (each partner)
6 months late	£300[1]
12 months late	£300[1]

Note

(1) As a partnership does not have a tax liability, the statutory tax-geared percentage cannot apply so each relevant partner will be liable to the minimum penalty of £300 (FA 2009, Sch. 55, para. 5 and 6). The increased penalties under para. 6 for deliberately withholding information do not apply to the partnership return. This is because the higher penalty is based on the liability that would have been shown in the return.

Special reduction

HMRC may reduce a penalty if they think it right because of special circumstances. Special circumstances do not include ability to pay or the fact that a potential loss of revenue from one taxpayer is balanced by a potential overpayment from another (FA 2009, Sch. 55, para. 16).

Appeals

An appeal against a penalty for failing to file a partnership return on time may be brought only by the nominated (representative) partner or their successor. Any such appeal is treated as a composite appeal made on behalf of all the relevant partners and the nominated partner is treated as if he or she were the partner liable to each penalty. The nominated partner can appeal against HMRC's decision that a penalty is payable and/or against the amount of the penalty payable (FA 2009, Sch. 55, para. 20).

There is no obligation to pay the penalty before an appeal against it is determined (FA 2009, Sch. 55, para. 21).

The First-tier Tribunal may affirm or cancel HMRC's decision that a penalty is payable and affirm HMRC's decision or substitute for HMRC's decision another decision that HMRC had the power to make with regard to the amount of the penalty payable.

In substituting a decision, the tribunal may take special circumstances into account to the same extent as HMRC (i.e. same reduction from a different starting point) or to a different extent but only if HMRC's decision on special circumstances was flawed.

Reasonable excuse

Liability to a penalty does not arise where the nominated partners satisfies HMRC or the tribunal that there is a reasonable excuse for the failure. In this respect:

- an insufficiency of funds is not a reasonable excuse unless attributable to events outside the partner's control;
- reliance on any other person to do anything is not a reasonable excuse unless the nominated partner took reasonable care to avoid the failure;
- where the nominated partner had a reasonable excuse but that excuse has ceased, they are treated as having continued to have the excuse if the failure is remedied without unreasonable delay after the excuse ceased.

Legislation: FA 2009, Sch. 55

17-260 Penalties for inaccuracies in a partnership tax return

Where an inaccuracy in a partnership return, statement or declaration in connection with a partnership return, or accounts in connection with a partnership return gives rise to an understatement in a liability to tax, or false or inflated loss, or a false or inflated repayment claim, and the inaccuracy was careless or deliberate, each partner is liable for a penalty calculated by reference to the additional tax each partner is required to pay as a result of the inaccuracy.

Where penalties are determined on two or more partners any appeal against the determination of a penalty must be made by the nominated partner or his successor. An appeal made by the nominated partner will be a composite appeal against the determination of each penalty.

Legislation: FA 2007, Sch. 24, para. 20

17-280 Information powers

The provisions at FA 2008, Sch. 36, para. 1 enables an officer of HMRC to require a person to provide information or documentation where that information is reasonably required for the purposes of checking that person's tax position.

FA 2008, Sch. 36, para. 2 enables an officer to require a third party to provide information or documentation where that is reasonably required for the purposes of checking the tax position of a person whose identity the officer knows. Such a notice can be issued only if it has been approved by the First-tier Tribunal (FTT), or is subject to the agreement of the taxpayer to whom it relates (para. 3(1)).

FA 2008, Sch. 36, para. 5 extends this third party information power to enable an officer to obtain information or documentation reasonably required for checking the tax position of a person or a class of persons whose identity he does not know. A notice under para. 5 can be issued only with the approval of the First-tier Tribunal. Before giving its approval, it is necessary for the tribunal to be satisfied, amongst other things, that the person or persons to whom the notice relates have failed, or may fail, to comply with their obligations under the Taxes Acts or the *Value Added Tax Act* 1994, and that the failure is likely to have led to, or will be likely to lead to 'serious prejudice to the assessment and collection of tax' (para. 5(4)).

FA 2008, Sch. 36, para. 5A, extends HMRC's powers to request information from a person about another person (or class of persons) whose identity can be ascertained. A notice served pursuant to para. 5A may only be issued if:

(a) the information is reasonably required to check the taxpayer's tax position;
(b) the taxpayer's identity is unknown but sufficient information is held from which the identity can be ascertained;

(c)   an officer has reason to believe that the person will be able to ascertain the taxpayer's identity from the information held and the person obtained relevant information about the taxpayer in the course of a business; and

(d)   the information cannot readily be ascertained by other means from the information already held.

'Relevant Information' is defined as all or any of the taxpayer's name, last known address and date of birth.

Application to partnerships

FA 2008, Sch. 36, para. 37 makes specific provisions in relation to partnerships:

Where a partnership tax return or claim or election has been made by any of the partners in respect of a chargeable period, the restriction in para. 21 (restrictions where taxpayer has made a return) has effect as if each partner had made a return for that period (para. 37(2)).

Where a third party notice is given to someone who is not a partner to check the tax position of one or more of the partners the notice only needs to state this and give the partnership's registered name; it is not necessary to name each partner (para. 37(3)).

Where a third party notice is given to a non-partner, relating to the tax position of one or more of the partners, a copy of the notice and a summary of reasons need only be given to one of the partners but the rule in para. 30(2) (no right of appeal in relation to a taxpayer's statutory records) applies to the statutory records of each of the partners (para. 37(4)).

Where a third party notice is given to one partner to check the tax position of another partner paragraphs 3(1) (approval of notices by tribunal or with agreement of the taxpayer) and 4(1) (copying third party notices to taxpayer) do not apply (para. 37(5)). However, the partner receiving the third party notice may appeal on any grounds (except in relation to statutory records), rather than being limited to the ground that it would be unduly onerous to comply with the notice or requirement (para. 37(5)).

HMRC is not required to obtain tribunal approval for a notice to one partner to check the tax position of another whose identity is not know, however, it may choose to do so and appeal is again permitted on any grounds (except in relation to statutory records) (para. 37(6)).

Legislation: FA 2008, Sch. 36

17-300   Deduction of income tax

ITA 2007, Pt. 15 imposes a duty to deduct sums representing income tax from certain payments, such as yearly interest. Although partnerships are usually regarded as transparent, this is not the case for deduction of income tax purposes and the partnership itself is deemed to be the 'person' to whom the legislation applies.

Therefore, the collection rules in ITA 2007, Pt. 15, Ch. 16 apply to partnerships so that the partners need not report the tax deducted at source separately and similarly, where a payment is made to a partnership within the scope of Pt. 15, the payer deducts tax on the whole of the payment and does not need to fragment the payment among the partner or consider whether the obligation to deduct arises in respect of each partner separately. This also means that partnerships are within the scope of the exceptions within ITA 2007, s. 930 in respect of 'excepted payments'.

Yearly interest

Where a partnership which has a company partner makes a payment of yearly interest it must deduct from the amount of the interest income tax at the savings rate for the tax year in which the payment is made (ITA 2007, s. 874).

The rate of deduction is to be the basic rate in force for the year in which the payment is made and the deduction is to be made by the person making the payment (ITA 2007, s. 874(2)).

Exceptions from the duty to deduct

A number of exceptions are provided which seek to prevent an overlap of obligations or the unnecessary deduction of amounts which would only have to be repaid. These exceptions relate to payments of interest made and apply in relation to partnerships as they apply in relation to companies:

- by a building society unless it is compensation treated as a payment of yearly interest under s. 874(5A) (ITA 2007, s. 875);
- by a 'deposit-taker', where it is already under a duty to deduct tax from the payment, or would be, but for a specific exemption (ITA 2007, s. 876);
- in respect of a 'UK public revenue dividend' (ITA 2007, s. 877);
- by a 'bank' in the ordinary course of its business unless it is compensation treated as a payment of yearly interest under ITA 2007, s. 874(5A) (ITA 2007, s. 878);
- by any person on an advance from a bank if the person beneficially entitled to the interest is within the charge to corporation tax in respect of that interest at the time it is paid, or (from 19 July 2011) is a bank that would be within the charge to corporation tax as respects the interest apart from CTA 2009, s. 18A (ITA 2007, s. 879);
- by any person on an advance from a building society (ITA 2007, s. 880);
- by the National Savings Bank (ITA 2007, s. 881);
- by a company where that interest is paid on a 'quoted Eurobond' (ITA 2007, s. 882);
- by an individual on a loan to buy a life annuity where the interest qualifies for a tax reduction under ICTA 1988, s. 369 by virtue of s. 365 (ITA 2007, s. 883);
- by any person where the interest is chargeable to income tax as 'relevant foreign income' (as defined by ITA 2007, s. 989) (ITA 2007, s. 884);
- by a dealer in financial instruments who is authorised by the *Financial Services and Markets Act* 2000 and the payment is made in the ordinary course of that person's business (ITA 2007, s. 885);

- by a 'relevant entity' (a 'recognised clearing house', a 'recognised investment exchange' or an EEA or third country central counterparty) if they are carrying on business providing 'central counterparty clearing services' and the interest:

    (a)   is paid in the ordinary course of that business, on margin or other collateral deposited with it by users of that service (ITA 2007, s. 886(1)); or
    (b)   is deemed to have been paid under the repos provisions in respect of contracts made as a provider of those services (ITA 2007, s. 886(2));

- by a registered society to a person whose 'usual place of abode' is in the UK where the interest is in respect of any mortgage, loan, loan stock, deposit or to a shareholder of the society in respect of that person's holding in its share capital (ITA 2007, s. 887(1));
- by virtue of the *Late Payment of Commercial Debts (Interest) Act* 1998 (statutory interest) which implies a contractual term for the payment of statutory interest in respect of qualifying debts (ITA 2007, s. 888); and
- on a payment of interest on a qualifying private placement (a security which represents a loan relationship to which a company is a party as debtor and which is not listed on a recognised stock exchange and in relation to which such other conditions as the Treasury may specify by regulations are met) (ITA 2007, s. 888A, with effect from 1 January 2016).

Legislation: ITA 2007, Pt. 15, Ch. 16, s. 874

17-320   Class 2 and 4 NIC

Individual (non-corporate) partners are liable to Class 2 and 4 NICs on their own share of the trade or profession carried on by the partnership and each partner is charged separately.

Class 2 and 4 contributions are also payable on the taxable profits of sleeping partners and inactive limited partners (from 2013–14). HMRC initially did not regard sleeping partners and inactive limited partners as being liable for Class 2 or 4 NICs as they were not regarded as gainfully employed for the purposes of Class 2 contributions (SSCBA 1992, s. 2(1)(b)) and the profits of sleeping partners and inactive limited partners did not derive immediately from the trade, profession or vocation so were not liable to Class 4 NICs (SSCBA 1992, s. 15). However, HMRC has recently reviewed its interpretation and now considers that sleeping partners and inactive limited partners are (and have always been) liable to pay both Class 2 and 4 NICs. This is because

Class 2

- *'employment' as defined in section 122 of the Social Security Contributions and Benefits Act 1992 includes business and section 1(1) of the Partnership Act 1890 provides that 'Partnership is the relation which subsists between persons carrying on a business in common with a view of profit'; and*
- *section 2(1)(b) of the Social Security Contributions and Benefits Act 1992 imposes no requirement that partners have to be active in the business.*

Class 4

- *in order for there to be a partnership for the purposes of the Partnership Act 1890, all the partners (whether General or Limited Partners) are 'carrying on a business in common with a view of profit'; and*
- *section 15 of the Social Security Contributions and Benefits Act 1992 imposes no requirement that partners have to be active in the business.*

HMRC have indicated that it will not seek to recover historic liabilities but will enforce its revised interpretation with effect from the 2013–14 tax year and subsequent tax years. However, whilst HMRC will not seek to enforce liabilities for previous tax years it will offer the opportunity for partners to make voluntary payments of Class 2 and 4 NICs in order to secure contributory benefit entitlements. They must pay both Class 2 arrears and any associated Class 4 NICs, if their profits over the relevant period exceed the Class 4 lower profits threshold.

At Budget 2015, the Government announced its intention to abolish Class 2 NICs and reform Class 4 NICs to introduce a new benefit test. At Budget 2016, the Government confirmed that Class 2 NICs will be abolished from April 2018 (NICs Bill).

Class 4

The starting point for calculation of profits chargeable to Class 4 National Insurance is as calculated for income tax purposes. However, a number of reliefs are permitted:

- under and in the manner provided by ITA 2007, s. 64 and 72 (set-off of trade losses against general income), but only where the loss arises from activities the profits of which would be brought into account for the purposes of Class 4 contributions;
- under and in the manner provided by ITA 2007, s. 83 (carry-forward of loss against subsequent profits); and
- under and in the manner provided by ITA 2007, s. 89 (carry-back of terminal losses).

Reliefs that do not apply for Class 4 purposes include:

- personal reliefs under ITA 2007, Pt. 3, Ch. 2 and 3 (personal allowance, blind persons allowance and tax reductions for married couples and civil partners);
- payments to trade unions (ITA 2007, s. 457);
- payments to police organisations (ITA 2007, s. 458);
- relief for interest (ITA 2007, s. 383);
- carry forward or carry back of certain interest as loss under ITA 2007, s. 88 and 94.

Reliefs that are allowed for Class 4 purposes include:

- payments under ITA 2007, s. 383 (relief for interest payments) being payments for which income tax relief is or can be given;
- payments from which sums representing income tax must be deducted under ITA 2007, s. 900(2) (commercial payments made by individuals); ITA 2007,

s. 903(5) (patent royalties); and ITA 2007, s. 906(5) (certain royalties etc. where usual place of abode of owner is abroad);

- so much of any payment from which a sum representing income tax must be deducted under ITA 2007, s. 910(2) (proceeds of a sale of patent rights: payments to non-UK residents) as is equal to the amount referred to in that provision as 'the chargeable amount'; or
- payment from which a sum representing income tax must be deducted as a result of a direction under ITA 2007, s. 944(2) (tax avoidance: certain payments to non-UK residents),

so far as the payment is incurred wholly or exclusively for the purposes of any relevant trade, profession or vocation.

Relief is given by way of deduction from or set-off against profits chargeable to Class 4 contributions for the year in which the payments are made, with any excess carried forward and deducted from or set off against the profits of later years in priority to relief for payments in later years.

Legislation: SSCBA 1992, s. 2(1)(b), 15, Sch. 2, para. 4

17-340 PAYE and Class 1 NIC

A partnership with employees is an employer for PAYE purposes and responsible for operating PAYE on salaries and benefits paid to and provided for employees. NB. Partners salaries are not subject to PAYE because they are not employees.

The partnership will also be liable to secondary Class 1 NICs on employees' salaries (excluding profits allocated to partners who are not employees and do not receive employment income).

Business successions

The 'PAYE succession' rules can apply to a transfer of a business from a general partnership to an LLP if the old partnership and new LLP agree that the PAYE scheme can continue with the new LLP taking over the responsibility for operating the scheme (SI 2003/2682, reg. 102). Otherwise, the new LLP will commence a new PAYE scheme and the old partnership will need to cease its PAYE scheme and issue forms P45 to all employees.

Legislation: SI 2003/2682; SSCBA 1992

17-360 Construction industry scheme

The Construction Industry Scheme (CIS) requires contractors to deduct tax from payments made to subcontractors unless the subcontractor has applied to HMRC to receive payments gross (if certain criteria are satisfied).

A partnership may register as a subcontractor by using form CIS304 (Partnership registration) which is available at *www.gov.uk/government/publications/construction-industry-scheme-partnership-registration-cis304.*

In order to gain gross payment status under CIS, the partnership must satisfy the three conditions:

- **the business test:** the business must be able to show us that it is carrying out construction work in the UK or providing labour for such work, and is run through a bank account;
- **the turnover test:** a partnership can take the standard test and have net construction turnover equal to or exceeding the threshold in the 12 months preceding the date of application (this is the £30,000 threshold multiplied by the number of partners that are individuals and in relation to each company member of the partnership, the number of 'relevant persons' (a company's 'relevant persons' are its directors and, if it is 'close', any beneficial owners of shares) associated with that company); or the partnership can take the alternative test and have a net construction turnover equal to or exceeding £100,000 in the 12 months preceding the date of application;
- **the compliance test:** the compliance history of each partner is considered for the previous 12 months and (disregarding certain specified failures) each partner must have: submitted all self-assessment returns and CIS returns; supplied any information to do with the partnership and partners tax that has been requested; paid by the due dates any PAYE tax and NICs due as an employer; and paid by the due dates any deductions due as a contractor in the construction industry.

Business successions

Where a sole trader or partnership becomes a company the new business must register for CIS and apply for gross payment status before it can be paid without CIS deductions being made. The new company may use the 'Inherited Receipts' test based on previous turnover to satisfy the turnover test.

Legislation: SI 2005/2045

Chapter 9: Computation of firms' profits and losses

18-000 Introduction

The main computational rules that apply specifically to partnerships are located in ITTOIA 2005, Pt. 9 (for income tax purposes) and CTA 2009, Pt. 17 (for corporation tax purposes).

A partnership is not to be regarded for tax purposes as an entity separate and distinct from the partners (ITTOIA 2005, s. 848; CTA 2009, s. 1258). This means that the partnership itself is not assessed to income or corporation tax and has no liability to tax.

Instead, there is a 'look through' the partnership to the persons making up the partnership, which is why partnerships are described as 'transparent' for tax purposes. It is the individual partners (whether individuals or companies) who are assessed to either income tax or corporation tax on their respective share of the partnership profits, income and gains via their income tax or corporation tax self-assessment returns.

This treatment applies to all types of partnerships, including those with separate legal personality such as Scottish partnerships or limited liability partnerships.

However, some legal obligations and rights remain with the partnership. For instance although income is charged on each partner separately rather than on the partnership, the partnership is still required to make a return of partnership income and an allocation of that income between each partner (see ¶17-040).

The special provisions in ITTOIA 2005, Pt. 9 and CTA 2009, Pt. 17 set out the approach to be taking in computing partnership profits, allocating those profits to the partners and assessing those profits to income and corporation tax.

The results in a three-stage approach:

(1) calculate the partnership profits;

(2) allocate the profits between the partners;

(3) assess the partner to income or corporation tax on his/its allocated share.

There is only one exception to this general rule which is where income is received on behalf of a third party (agency); HMRC have indicated that the partnership will continue to be treated as a separate entity for this purpose. Thus, if there were a requirement to deduct tax, this would be required of the partnership rather than the individual partners.

Legislation: ITTOIA 2005, s. 847–848; CTA 2009, s. 1258

18-020　Limited liability partnerships

An LLP which is registered under the *Limited Liability Partnership Act* 2000 is, in law, a body corporate and a separate entity apart from its members.

However, the tax provisions of ITTOIA 2005, s. 863 and CTA 2009, s. 1273 ensure that an LLP carrying on a business with a view to profit will be treated inter alia for the purposes of income tax and corporation tax (including capital gains) in the same way as a non-limited liability partnership (i.e. the partners will be taxed on their shares of the partnership's profits and gains as described in this chapter) despite its strict legal status as a body corporate.

Once a liquidator is appointed to an LLP (for the purposes of a formal winding up) it loses partnership treatment and becomes subject to tax as if it were a company in liquidation.

18-040　The three-stage approach

In *R & C Commrs v Vaines* [2016] BTC 502, the Upper Tribunal (UT) examined the basis for assessing partners to tax on partnership profits, in the context of a deduction claimed by a partner on his self-assessment income tax return for a personal expense incurred (see further commentary at ¶18-240).

The UT referred to the earlier case of *MacKinlay (HMIT) v Arthur Young McClelland Moores & Co.* [1989] BTC 587, in which the 'three stages' in the assessment to tax of a partnership's profits were endorsed by the House of Lords noting particularly, that Vinelott J said:

> 'Before turning to those cases I should, I think, say something about the way in which partnership profits are assessed to tax. There are, in effect, three stages. First the profits of the firm for an appropriate basis period must be ascertained. What has to be ascertained is the profits of the firm and not of the individual partners. That is not, I think, stated anywhere in the Income Tax Acts, but it follows necessarily from the fact that there is only one business and not a number of different businesses carried on by each of the partners. The income of the firm for the year is then treated as divided between the partners who were partners during the year to which the claim relates— the year of assessment—in one of the many senses of that word … That is the second stage. The tax payable is then calculated according to the circumstances of each partner …When the tax eligible in respect of each share of the partnership income has been ascertained the total tax payable is calculated. Section 152 (formerly Rule 10 of the Rules applicable to Cases I and II of Sch D) provides that the total sum so calculated is to be treated as "one sum … separate and distinct from any other tax chargeable on those persons … and a joint assessment shall be made in the partnership name." That is the third stage.'

The UT note that the relevant legislation at the time of this case was ICTA 1970, s. 152 which became ICTA 1988, s. 111 and pre-dated self-assessment and the rewrite of ICTA 1988 into the present acts. The relevant provisions in *Vaines* were the provisions of ITTOIA 2005, therefore, the UT consider the income tax provisions only, however, it should be noted that most of these provisions are mirrored in CTA 2009.

The UT note that ICTA 1988, s. 111 in its original terms provided that:

'111. Where a trade or profession is carried on by two or more persons jointly, income tax in respect thereof shall be computed and stated jointly, and in one sum, and shall be separate and distinct from any other tax chargeable on those persons or any of them, and a joint assessment shall be made in the partnership name.'

Section 111 was concerned with the joint assessment of partnership profits in the firm's name. The manner of assessment for partners changed with the introduction of self-assessment (together with a switch from the preceding to the current year basis as part of the process). ICTA 1988, s. 111 was replaced by a new s. 111 containing 13 subsections that are now found spread across a number of sections in Pt. 9 of ITTOIA but notably s. 848, 849, 850 and 852.

Note: ITTOIA 2005, s. 848 is mirrored by CTA 2009, s. 1258, as rewritten from ICTA 1988, s. 111(1). Corresponding provisions for companies were originally provided by ICTA 1988, s. 114 which was rewritten into CTA 2009, s. 1259 (mirrors ITTOIA 2005, s. 849) and s. 1262 (mirrors ITTOIA 2005, s. 850). ITTOIA 2005, s. 852 has no corresponding corporation tax provision because it relates to the assessment of the partnership profits to income tax (basis period rules) whereas companies are assessed to corporation tax.

The First-Tier Tribunal in *Vaines* [2013] TC 02965 had concluded that there had been a material change in the relevant legislation since that in place in 1980 when Vinelott J and Lord Oliver analysed the position. The FTT contrasted the position as it existed before the introduction of self-assessment when a partnership was treated for income tax purposes, under ICTA 1988, s. 111, as 'an entity which is separate and distinct from those persons' who carried out the trade or profession in partnership with the present position under ITTOIA 2005, s. 848 [CTA 2009, s. 1258], that a partnership is not to be regarded for income tax purposes as separate and distinct from the partners.

In allowing the deduction claimed by Mr Vaines for on his self-assessment tax return against his partnership profits for the personal expense, the FTT accepted that the effect of the legislation was that post self-assessment, it was the partners who were treated as carrying out the trade and not the firm itself and that each partner was carrying on a trade albeit collectively with others and accordingly his profits are taxed on him individually.

The UT, however, disagreed finding that whilst the manner of 'assessment' for partners had changed with the introduction of self-assessment in that partners were assessed individually rather than the assessment being made at partnership level, the basic (three-stage) approach in making the assessment had not changed.

'the basic approach adopted by section 111 is still evident from those 25 provisions of Part 9: in particular, the actual trade is the trade carried on by the partners collectively (s.111(2)), the profits of the actual trade are then shared among the partners according to their interest for the period (s.111(3)) and the concept of a "deemed trade or profession" (now the "notional trade or profession") is then introduced for the purposes of assessing each partner to tax in respect of his share by reference to the correct basis period (s.111(4)).'

'In this respect section 111(1) ICTA (following self-assessment) and section 848 ITTOIA … [CTA 2009, s. 1258] … do no more than state the general proposition of English law (that is applicable in taxing United Kingdom partnerships generally, notwithstanding the different position under Scots law for Scottish partnerships) that a partnership is not a separate entity and that the partners are each carrying on the partnership's trade in common. That is the statutory expression of the situation that exists at the first of Vinelott J's stages (which, as Vinelott J noted, was at that time nowhere stated in the Act).'

'As Lord Oliver indicated, a partnership was treated *for assessment purposes* as if it were separate from the partners and was assessed in its own name notwithstanding its "transparent" nature as a matter of the general law. But as he also noted, there was nothing to justify a conclusion that it could be treated as a separate entity at stage one of the analysis for the purpose of deciding whether certain personal expenses of two partners were deductible in computing the partnership's profits … ; in other words, stage one at the time in effect reflected an unwritten rule that now appears in section 848 ITTOIA' [and CTA 2009, s. 1258]

The concept of the 'notional trade' for income tax purposes (ITTOIA 2005, s. 852) at the third stage of the computational process is discussed further at ¶20-040).

In terms of the first two stages in the computation process, the provisions of ITTOIA 2005 which are rewritten from ICTA 1988, s. 111(2), (3), ITTOIA 2005, s. 849(2) and 850(1), correspond to CTA 2009, s. 1259(3) and 1262(1) and, therefore, the same basic three-stage approach applies equally to partnerships with corporate partners as those with individual partners.

18-060   Profits or losses calculated at partnership level

Partnerships have no tax liability but the profits or losses are nevertheless calculated at partnership level before being apportioned among the partners.

However, as profits are assessed to tax at partner level, the computation at partnership level must reflect the individual circumstances of the partner to be assessed, i.e. whether the partner will be subject to income tax or corporation tax and whether the partner (individual or company) is UK resident or not resident.

Where all partners are either individuals or companies with the same residency position, only one computation will be required. Where there is a mix of partners and/or non-resident partners, a number of computations will need to be performed in order to calculate the profits to be apportioned to each partner.

The legislation achieves this by providing special rules for calculating the profits or losses of a partnership which carries on a trade, profession or business.

ITTOIA 2005, s. 847 and CTA 2009, s. 1257 provide that persons carrying on a trade in partnership are referred to collectively as a 'firm' and the subsequent sections make provision for calculating the firm's profits or losses and allocating them between the partners. Although the provisions are expressed to apply to trades, they apply also to professions and businesses that are not trades (unless otherwise indicated) (ITTOIA 2005, s. 847 and CTA 2009, s. 857) so include partnerships with investment business as well.

The rules are further extended to cover any other income or losses of a firm to which s. 849 and 850 applies (i.e. firms carrying on a trade or business) by ITTOIA 2005, s. 851 which provides that those sections apply as if references to the profits or losses of the trade were references to other income or losses. The extension applies irrespective of whether the income is taxed, untaxed or the category in which the source of the income falls. In other words, the approach to calculating partnership trading or business profits, applies to all categories of profits and other income (although the basis of assessing the different sources may differ – see **Chapter 11**).

UK resident individual partners

For individual partners, profits or losses will be calculated following normal income tax rules. Where the individual is UK resident, the profits or losses are calculated as if the firm were a UK resident individual (ITTOIA 2005, s. 849(2)).

This means for partners who are resident in the UK, it will be necessary to include profits arising anywhere in the world.

Non-resident individual partners

Where the individual is non-resident, the profits or losses are calculated as if the firm were a non-UK resident individual (ITTOIA 2005, s. 849(3)).

This means for non-resident partners, only profits arising in the UK are to be counted.

Partners becoming resident or ceasing to be resident and split year treatment

Section 849(2) and (3) provide for profits to be calculated for 'a period of account'. It is, however, possible for a partner to be both resident (for one tax year) and non-resident (for another) within a single period of account. In such a case, the firm's profit has to be calculated twice to arrive at the partner's share of the profits.

Where split year treatment applies to any partner, a non-resident calculation will be required for the overseas part of the year (ITTOIA 2005, s. 849(3A)).

UK resident companies

If the partner is a UK resident company, the profits or losses are calculated as if the trade (or business) were carried on by a UK resident company (CTA 2009, s. 1259).

Non-resident companies

If the partner is a non-UK resident company, profits or losses are calculated as if the trade (or business) were carried on by a non-resident company (CTA 2009, s. 1259).

Effectively, a non-resident partner is limited to his share of the profits of the part of the trade carried on in the UK, where the partnership carries on a trade partly in the UK and partly outside the UK and a non-resident company's share is treated as arising from a trade carried on by it through a UK permanent establishment.

Legislation: ITTOIA 2005, s. 847, 849, 851; CTA 2009, s. 1257 and 1259

18-080   Partners to whom remittance basis applies

Where a partnership carries on a trade (profession or business) wholly or partly outside the UK and the control and management of the trade is outside the UK, then any partner who is eligible for the remittance basis under ITA 2007, s. 809B (claim for remittance basis to apply), 809D (application without a claim where unremitted foreign income and gains under £2,000) or 809E (application of remittance basis without claim: other cases) will be taxed on the remittance basis on his share of the profits of the trade (profession or business) arising outside the UK.

The partner's share of profits of the trade (profession or business) arising in the UK is calculated following the normal rules under ITTOIA 2005, s. 849–856. However, his share of the profits of the partnership's trade arising outside of the UK is treated as 'relevant foreign income' and charged on remittance under ITTOIA 2005, s. 832 (see also ITTOIA s. 830(4)).

Note: this treatment only applies if the partnership firm carries on a trade wholly or partly outside of the UK, and control and management of the trade is outside of the UK.

Legislation: ITTOIA 2005, s. 830, 857

18-100   Resident partners and double taxation agreements

Where a UK resident individual or company is a partner in a firm which either resides outside the UK or carries on a trade which is controlled and managed outside of the UK and where the operation of a double tax treaty prevents the income of that firm from being chargeable to UK tax (i.e. the double tax treaty relieves the income from UK tax) the partner is, nevertheless, liable to income tax or corporation tax (as the case may be), on their share of the firm's income (ITTOIA 2005, s. 858(1) and (2), CTA 2009, s. 1266(1) and (2)).

If the partner's share of the income of the firm includes a qualifying distribution made by a UK resident company (and for income tax purposes, is chargeable to tax under ITTOIA 2005, Pt. 4, Ch. 3), the partner (and not the firm) is entitled to a share of the tax credit corresponding to their share of the distribution, irrespective of the double tax treaty provisions (i.e. tax credit is given to the partner in proportion to his share of the distribution) (ITTOIA 2005, s. 858(3); CTA 2009, s. 1266(3)).

Both provisions ensure that a UK resident partner's share of the income of a foreign firm remains liable to UK tax even though the income of the firm as a whole is exempt from UK tax in accordance with a double taxation agreement. They are based on ICTA 1988, s. 112(4) and (5) and s. 115(5).

The provisions were introduced following the case of *Padmore v IR Commrs* [1989] BTC 221. In that case, the Court of Appeal decided that the exemption from UK tax for the profits of a Jersey firm that the business profits article of the UK/Jersey double taxation arrangements firm provided extended to the share of the profits arising to a UK resident individual. Sections 112(4) and (5) and 115(5) were enacted in 1987 to remove the exemption.

For UK tax purposes, if it is necessary to consider where a firm is resident, the question is likely to be decided by the place where the firm's business is controlled and managed. But it is possible that, under foreign law, a firm may be considered to be resident elsewhere, for example, by reference to where the firm was established. Therefore, subsection (1) (of both ITTOIA 2005, s. 858 and CTA 2009, s. 1266) uses both the 'control and management' test and the 'resides' test.

Although the intention of the former s. 115(5) and (5A) was to preserve the partner's chargeability to tax following the case of *Padmore v IR Commrs* [1989] BTC 221, there was concern that the legislation could have been interpreted as denying the partner any relief under a double tax treaty. This has been corrected in the rewrite, which states clearly that 'the partner is liable to corporation or income tax on the partner's share of the income of the firm despite the arrangements' (arrangements being the double tax treaty) (subsection (2) of both ITTOIA 2005, s. 858 and CTA 2009, s. 1266). This makes it clear that the section does no more than remove any exemption under a double taxation arrangement. It does not deny other reliefs, such as tax credit relief.

Subsection (3) (of both ITTOIA 2005, s. 858 and CTA 2009, s. 1266) deals with UK tax credits. A double taxation arrangement may give a non-UK resident 'person' an entitlement to payment of a tax credit on a distribution by a UK company. This subsection makes it clear that, where that 'person' is a firm, only a UK resident partner has the entitlement.

Legislation: ITTOIA 2005, s. 858; CTA 2009, s. 1266

18-120   Calculation of profits and losses: general

Trading (profession or business) profits

The following steps should be taken when establishing the taxable profits in respect of a partnership trade:

(1) ascertain the profit of the trade computed in accordance with generally accepted accounting principles (GAAP) (ITTOIA 2005, s. 25; CTA 2009, s. 46);

(2) adjust the accounting profit in accordance with any specific tax rules applicable, under income tax provisions for individuals and company tax provisions for companies, giving effect to any claims or elections made; then

(3) allocate a share of the adjusted profits to the partners in accordance with the profit sharing arrangements during the accounting period (see **Chapter 10**).

The partnership's profit or loss for any accounting period is calculated initially leaving out of account capital allowances or balancing charges and these are subsequently deductible as part of the tax adjustments (step (2) above) applying according to whether the calculation is being performed for income or corporation tax purposes.

Capital allowances

Capital allowances are claimed by the partnership and computed at the partnership level and are given as an expense in computing the amount of the partnership's profits (TMA 1970, s. 42(6)). Therefore, the profits allocated to each partner are the profits net of capital allowances (see ¶17-100 re claims and elections by partnerships). The claim must be made by the partnership, not by the individual partner.

For details on the calculation of capital allowances for partnerships, see **Chapter 13**.

Other claims and elections

Other claims and elections that affect the computation of partnership profits and losses must be claimed by the partnership through the partnership return (TMA 1970, s. 42). See ¶17-100 for a full list of claims and elections to be included on the partnership return.

Other income or losses

Other income or losses are calculated according to the rules applicable to the particular source of the income.

Legislation: TMA 1970, s. 42; ITTOIA 2005, Pt. 2, Ch. 3, s. 25; CTA 2009, Pt. 3, Ch. 3, s. 46

18-140   Calculation of profits and losses: income tax

Trading profits

Normal rules apply for calculating the trading (profession or business) profits of a partnership.

Profits are calculated by reference for a period of account (i.e. the accounting period of the partnership) and in accordance with generally accepted accounting principles (GAAP).

However, as an alternative to calculating profits in accordance with GAAP, partnerships can elect to use the cash basis of accounting provided all of the partners are individuals. Limited liability partnerships and partnerships with corporate partners are not eligible for the cash basis.

Because partnership profits or losses are calculated at partnership level, before allocation between the partners, where a partnership uses the cash basis, each partner's share will be based on the profit or loss calculated using the cash basis regardless of whether the individual partner is eligible or chooses to use the cash basis in respect of any of their other trading activities. For further commentary on the cash basis, see **Chapter 14**.

Adjustments for income tax purposes follow normal income tax rules.

In calculating the profits of a trade (profession or business) for income tax purposes, no account is to be taken of any losses for another period of account (ITTOIA 2005, s. 849). See **Chapter 16** for relief for partnership losses.

Other income

Where a partnership has any source(s) of non-trading income ('other income') the amount of any other income or losses is determined in exactly the same way as trade, profession or business profits are determined (i.e. as if the partnership were an UK resident individual or non-resident individual according to the status of the individual partner).

This rule applies regardless of whether the income is taxed income, or untaxed income, and irrespective of the category in which the source of other income falls. But it only applies to income, not chargeable gains.

The legislation provides for this treatment by applying ITTOIA 2005, s. 849 and 850 (which primarily apply to firms with trading profits), as if references to the profits or losses of a trade were references to other income or losses (ITTOIA 2005, s. 851).

Normal computational rules apply according to the particular source of the income in question.

Legislation: ITTOIA 2005, Pt. 2; s. 849, 851

18-160 Calculation of profits and losses: corporation tax

Trading (or business) profits

The calculation of trading (or business) profits or losses for an accounting period is to be made in accordance with generally accepted accounting principles (GAAP) (CTA 2009, s. 46).

Tax adjustments similarly follow normal rules but loan relationship debits and credits are specifically excluded from the calculation (see below) (CTA 2009, s. 380(2)).

There are two further exceptions to normal computation rules provided for by CTA 2009, s. 1260. In addition, special rules apply with regard to accounting periods of partnerships (CTA 2009, s. 1261). See below.

Exceptions to normal practice

In calculating the partnership's trading profits or losses for an accounting period, no account is to be taken of any losses for another accounting period (CTA 2009, s. 1260(1)). Without this provision, it would otherwise be possible for losses brought forward to be deducted before the (net) profits are allocated to the partners, therefore, s. 1260(1) makes clear that losses are not taken into account in the calculation of the firm's profit or loss to be allocated to the partners.

In addition, no interest paid or other distribution made by the firm is to be treated as a distribution for the purposes of CTA 2009, s. 1305(1) (which denies a corporation tax deduction in respect of a dividend or a distribution) (CTA 2009, s. 1260(2)). This ensures that interest paid by the firm cannot be disallowed in calculating the firm's profit or loss by virtue of being treated as a distribution by CTA 2010, Pt. 23, Ch. 2. CTA 2009, s. 1260(2) is based on former ICTA 1988, s. 114(1)(a) which provided that in calculating the partnership's trading profits or losses 'references to distributions' should not apply.

Accounting periods

In establishing the accounting period of a partnership for the purposes of calculating its trading profit or loss for corporation tax purposes, it is to be assumed that the partnership is a company (the deemed company) (CTA 2009, s. 1261(1)).

The deemed company is assumed to be UK resident but for the purposes of determining the accounting periods by reference to which profits are to be calculated under CTA 2009, s. 1259 (see ¶18-060), the residence of the deemed company is to be taken to be the same as the partner's (CTA 2009, s. 1261(2)(a) and (6)).

The deemed company is assumed to:

(1) acquire a source of income (first accounting period begins) on the date the trade first begins to be carried on in partnership by persons including a company

(where the trade had not previously been carried on in partnership with any corporate partner);

(2)   cease to trade (accounting period ends) on the date when no company carries on the trade in partnership (where the trade had previously been carried on in partnership by persons including a company);

(3)   ceases to trade and immediately afterwards starts to trade (accounting period ends and another accounting period begins) on the occurrence of a change of persons carrying on the trade where a corporate partner is replaced with another corporate partner but there is no corporate continuity (in that no corporate partner was a partner both before and after the change).

Subject to the exceptions noted above, normal rules apply (with corporation tax being calculated and charged by reference to accounting periods (CTA 2009, s. 8(2)) with the rules on when an accounting period begins and ends set out in CTA 2009, Pt. 2, Ch. 2).

Loan relationships

In calculating the profits of a partnership as if it were a company under CTA 2009, s. 1259, debits and credits arising from a money debt, or any loan relationship that would be treated as arising from that money debt (such as interest on trade debts) are excluded (CTA 2009, s. 380(2)).

Instead, gross credits and debits are calculated separately for each partner by calculating the gross credits and debits and apportioning them between the partners (see ¶18-180 and ¶19-120).

Legislation: CTA 2009, Pt. 3, Ch. 3, s. 46, 380(2), 1257, 1259, 1261

18-180   Calculation of profits and losses: loan relationships

Specific computational provisions are required to deal with loan relationships where a partnership has one or more corporate partners. This is because income from debt is treated in different ways for individuals and companies and different types of company may get different treatment under the loan relationships rules.

The provisions apply where a trade, profession or business is carried on by persons in partnership where any of those persons is a company and a 'money debt' is owed by or to the firm (s. 380(1)).

A 'money debt' is a debt that may be settled by

- the payment of money; or
- transferring the rights to settlement of another money debt; or
- the issue or transfer of any share in any company.

(CTA 2009, s. 301).

A 'debt' exists where one party has a **legal obligation** to transfer cash, goods or services to another. If the creditor has no legal right to the consideration, there is no debt.

To ensure that companies bring in the appropriate credits and debits relating to loan relationships and facilitate the application of the connected company rules, debits and credits in relation to:

- the money debt; or
- any loan relationship that would be treated as arising from that money debt (such as interest on trade debts)

are excluded from the calculation of profits (CTA 2009, s. 380(2)).

Instead, these are brought into account in accordance with the rules prescribed by CTA 2009, Pt. 5, Ch. 9 which provides for:

- determination of credits and debits by company partners: general,
- company partners using fair value accounting,
- lending between partners and the partnership,
- treatment of exchange gains and losses, and
- company partners where firm owns deeply discounted securities.

(CTA 2009, s. 380(3) and (4)).

Legislation: CTA 2009, s. 301, 380

18-200   Calculation of profits and losses: loan relationships: determination of debits and credits

The debits and credits to be brought into account for each partner in respect of each of its accounting periods are calculated separately for each partner as follows:

- the money debt owed by or to the partnership is treated as if it were owed by or to the company partner; and
- as if it were so owed for the purposes of the trade, business or profession which the company partner carries on.

(CTA 2009, s. 381(1), (2)).

If the money debt arises from a transaction for the lending of money, the company partner is treated as having a loan relationship (CTA 2009, s. 381(3)).

Not all money debts arise from the lending of money. For example, trade debts do not arise from lending money.

Anything done by or in relation to the partnership in connection with the money debt is to be treated as done by or in relation to the company partner (CTA 2009, s. 381(4)).

> ### Example
>
> ABC partnership lends £100,000 to D Ltd.
>
> The members of ABC partnership are:
>
> - Mrs A;
> - B Ltd;
> - C Ltd.
>
> The loan carries interest at 10% per annum.
>
> For the purposes of their respective tax calculations, B Ltd and C Ltd are each treated as being the creditor in a £100,000 loan relationship. Each company will have gross credits of £10,000, the interest accruing on the loan.
>
> Having calculated the gross credits and debits, these are then allocated to each partner according to the profit sharing ratios (CTA 2009, s. 381(5)–(7)) (see ¶19-120).

18-220   Specific receipts: directors' fees received by partnerships

As a general rule, fees received by a partner in his capacity as a director of a separate limited company are assessed on him individually as earnings from an office or employment. However, if the fees are (under the partnership agreement) pooled to be shared amongst the partners and form only a small part of the partnership profits and the directorship is a normal incident of the profession and particular practice of the partnership, the fees may be treated as part of the partnership income and taxed accordingly. This treatment is dealt with by ESC A37 and is referred to in the *Business Income Manual* at BIM40351.

The concession is not automatic and the partners must give a written undertaking not to make a tax deduction under the PAYE system even if in the relevant year of assessment the partner is no longer a director or the director is no longer a member of the partnership.

18-240   Specific deductions: expenses incurred by partners individually

Expenditure incurred by the partners in respect of partnership business must be claimed on the partnership return; it is not possible for partners to make supplementary claims in their own tax returns for expenses or capital allowances. This is because revenue expenditure incurred by a partner only qualifies for relief if it is made wholly and exclusively for the purposes of the partnership business.

HMRC guidance (at BIM82075) goes on to make the following comment in this respect:

'This does not mean that expenditure incurred by a partner can only be relieved if it is included in the partnership accounts. You may accept adjustments for such expenditure in the tax computations included in the partnership return providing the adjustments are made before apportionment of the net profit between the partners. You should not accept any deductions for expenses from the net profits allocated to a partner.'.

In *Vaines* [2013] TC 02965, the First-tier Tribunal (FTT) allowed a claim by Mr Vaines in his self-assessment tax return for a deduction against his partnership profits. Mr Vaines had made a payment under a compromise agreement to release him from all claims by a bank in respect of his former partnership and sought to deduct the expense from his share of the profits from his current partnership. The FTT allowed the claim on the basis that the payment was incurred wholly and exclusively for the purposes of the profession or trade that Mr Vaines was carrying on as an individual. The Upper Tribunal (UT), however, in *R & C Commrs v Vaines* [2016] BTC 502 overturned the FTT's decision finding that the trade that was being carried on was the partnership's trade as carried on in common by all the members and not by Mr Vaines alone and as such, his payment fell to be deducted, if at all, in the context of the partnership's trade and not as the FTT supposed by reference to Mr Vaines' circumstances alone. The payment in question was not borne by the current partnership and the FTT's conclusion that Mr Vaines' purpose in making the payment was 'to preserve and protect his professional career or trade' indicated that this was a personal expense, directed at resolving Mr Vaines' situation; it was not one that was related to the professional activities of his current partnership. The payment was not made wholly and exclusively for the purposes of the trade of the current partnership but to enable Mr Vaines to be secure in the knowledge that he could continue as a member of that partnership. The wholly and exclusively condition was not satisfied and no deduction could be claimed.

'It is the profits of the trade carried on collectively that has always been recognised as the subject matter of computation and charge … It is in the context of the partnership trade conducted collectively that Mr Vaines must justify the deduction of his payment.'

18-260 Specific deductions: payments to partners – general

Payments to partners will generally be treated as a distribution of profits unless the payment can be shown to be wholly and exclusively for the purposes of the partnership's business. If the payment does represent an expense incurred wholly and exclusively for the purposes of the partnership business, a deduction may be claimed.

In *MacKinlay (HMIT) v Arthur Young McClelland Moores & Co.* [1989] BTC 587, the House of Lords held that payments by a partnership of removal expenses when a partner was required to move from one of the firm's branches to a branch in another part of the country were not deductible in calculating the partnership profits.

The deduction had been allowed by the Court of Appeal. The Court of Appeal had considered that the 'collective purpose' of the partnership as a separate entity in making the payments was solely for business purposes, and taking into account the large number of partners, the firm having suggested that the position of a partner in a firm of such a size was analogous to the position of an employee.

Lord Oliver of Aylmerton stated:

'My Lords, for my part, I am unable to accept that the purpose of 'the partnership,' considered as if it had a separate legal identity, and the purpose of the individual partners for whose benefit the payment enured can be segregated in this way. I cannot, with respect to the Court of Appeal, resist the conclusion that they allowed themselves to be confused and led astray by a number of extraneous factors which do not, as a matter of analysis, have any legal significance. In the first place, they appear to have been influenced by the sheer size of the partnership in the instant case and to have considered that a large partnership falls in some way to be treated differently from a small partnership, so that an element of personal benefit may fall to be taken into account in the case of a small firm but ignored in the case of a large firm (see Slade L.J., [1988] BTC 110 at p. 122). It is true that *Slade* L.J. rests this distinction on the ground of the greater ease with which an inference of a confusion of private and collective motive may be drawn in the case of the smaller firm – presumably on the footing that in a large firm a great many of the partners will not, in practice, know anything about the payment and therefore cannot be said to be affected by the purpose of the recipient. But there can surely be no difference in principle. Partners are partners, however numerous; and mere numbers cannot in itself justify an attribution of a "collective purpose" unjustified in the case of a small partnership.'

'An employee has no interest in the property or profits of the firm and anything paid to him by way of additional remuneration for acting as an employee and to secure his continued loyalty to the firm cannot easily fail to be deductible as an expenditure exclusively for the purpose of the firm's business ... A partner, on the other hand, whether he be senior or junior is in a quite different position. What he receives out of the partnership funds falls to be brought into account in ascertaining his share of the profits of the firm except in so far he can demonstrate that it represents a payment to him in reimbursement of sums expended by him on partnership purposes in the carrying on of the partnership business or practice ...'

'However attractive, therefore, the employer/employee analogy may seem at first sight, it is not one from which, on analysis, I feel that I can derive any assistance. One is, accordingly, brought back, first, last and all the time to the question whether an expenditure upon a partner's removing expenses can be said to be laid out not just partly but exclusively for the purposes of the partnership business. That cannot, in my judgment, be answered simply by ascertaining what was the motive with which the move was undertaken. It is inescapable as it seems to me, that the expenditure, motivated no doubt by the fact of moving house, which in turn was motivated by the desire to put the partner concerned in a better position to further the interests of the firm, was an expenditure serving and necessarily and inherently intended to serve the personal interests of the partner in establishing his private residence for himself and his family and it cannot be said to be exclusively for the purposes of the partnership practice.'

18-280 Specific deductions: payments to outgoing partners

Two related cases, *Morgan; Self* [2009] TC 00046 addressed the question of how to treat certain payments made to partners who had been asked to withdraw from a firm of chartered accountants. The firm in question paid out the partners' shares of profits, calculated to the date of withdrawal, but also made a further payment equivalent to the share of profits to which the partners would be entitled for 12 months. The dispute concerned the tax treatment of those further payments, the retiring partners arguing that they were not payments of profits but payments that should have been deducted by the partnership in computing its taxable profits. The First-tier Tribunal rejected the taxpayers' argument.

> 'In deciding whether payments made by a partnership to an individual partner were profits of the firm, or expenditure which should be deducted from the profits, it was necessary to decide whether the payments were received by the individual partner in his capacity as a partner in the firm and whether that was "the very justification for the receipt". What an individual partner receives out of the partnership funds was part of his share of the profits unless he could demonstrate that it represents a payment to him in reimbursement of sums expended by him on partnership purposes or an entirely collateral payment made to him otherwise that in his capacity as a partner. Finally, in considering the contractual documents, it is necessary to bear in mind that the meaning of words does not always depend upon the words used.'

> 'In the present case, it was clear that the partners were carrying on business in partnership and that the terms of the partnership were binding on each partner. The constitutional documents indicated that payments made to partners leaving the firm could include both special allocations of profits as well as profits calculated by reference to the points basis and the accounts confirmed that the further payments made to retiring partners were in fact made out of profits. It was true that the constitutional documents referred to additional or further payments made within the context of the compulsory retirement of partners whereas both taxpayers had withdrawn without a compulsory retirement notice. However, the evidence was that the payments made to partners who withdrew by consent were calculated on the basis that, if consent was withheld, a compulsory retirement notice would be given on the same financial terms. Accordingly, the provisions of the constitutional documents, considered in the light of the facts surrounding the retirement of both taxpayers, pointed very strongly to the conclusion that in fact the further payments were made out of profits. The further payments were made to the taxpayers in their capacity as partners and were payments of profits chargeable to income tax accordingly. They were not amounts which should have been deducted by the firm in computing its profits.'

18-300 Specific deductions: interest paid by the partnership

Interest is an allowable deduction if it is incurred wholly and exclusively for the purposes of the business.

Where a partner borrows money personally to acquire an asset which is then used by the partnership without charge but with the interest on the loan being paid by the partnership and charged in the partnership accounts, the interest paid will normally be an allowable deduction. Where there is some non-business use of the asset or where the amount of interest payable exceeds an ordinary commercial charge for the use of the asset, the amount of interest allowed may be fully or partially restricted. The amount of the restriction will represent a distribution of profits to the partner.

Interest paid to a partner on their capital account is not an allowable deduction as it represents an allocation of profit to the partner.

Interest deductions will also be restricted where the partnership's borrowings are used to fund a partner's overdrawn capital account (i.e. where the partner has taken drawings in excess of capital contributions and profits earned).

18-320   Specific deductions: rent

Rent paid by a partnership to one of the partners for property used in the business is an allowable deduction provided the amount paid reflects a commercial rate.

In *Heastie v Veitch & Co* (1934) 18 TC 305, a fair rent paid to the senior partner in a firm of chartered accountants for the use and occupation of premises owned by the senior partners and from which premises the partnership business was carried on, was held to be deductible.

HMRC manuals at BIM38110 comment:

> 'The Master of the Rolls, Lord Hanworth explained that the rent was deductible notwithstanding that it was paid to a partner. There was nothing to show that the rent was uncommercial. The property was used for the purpose of the firm's profession and the fact that the recipient was a partner made no difference.'

Legislation: ITTOIA 2005, s. 34; CTA 2009, s. 54

18-340   Specific deductions: service companies

Often service companies are set up by partnerships to provide services such as the provision of staff, office and administration, advertising and marketing, etc. Where the service company receives a commercial return for its services, no difficulties arise and the costs will be deductible in the partnership accounts. However, anti-avoidance provisions apply to prevent obtaining a lower tax charge or increased loss relief from the manipulation of profit allocations between company and individual partners (see ¶19-280ff.).

Other material: HMRC *Partnerships Manual* PM30700

18-360   Specific deductions: partner recruitment costs

Costs of recruiting new partners and replacing existing partners are allowable deductions on the basis that the firm is paying a fee to recruit a fee earner who will generate profits for the firm. However, in certain circumstances, recruitment costs may instead be treated as capital (rather than revenue) expenditure. Such circumstances include:

- where the admission of the partner has a fundamental impact on the structure of the firm's business and is more than just expansion;
- where the partner is recruited as part of the acquisition of a business; or
- where the new partner's capital contribution is a material factor in their recruitment.

Other material: HMRC *Partnership Manual* PM30800

18-380   Specific deductions: partner training costs

Where costs are incurred on training and development courses attended by partners that merely update the partners' existing skills and professional expertise, the costs will be allowable deductions. However, where the training results in new expertise or knowledge (such as a completely new specialisation or qualification), such expenditure will be capital if what is acquired can be viewed as an identifiable asset of sufficient substance and endurance. See *Dass v Special Commissioner* [2006] BTC 866.

18-400   Specific deductions: termination payments

Payments made to partners on leaving the partnership will not normally be allowable deductions but will usually be treated as an allocation of profits by way of an additional profit share.

As noted at ¶18-280, in *Morgan; Self* [2009] TC 00046, two partners were asked to withdraw from a partnership and in addition to their share of the profits they each received a further sum equivalent to 12 months profit. The partners argued that the further payments received by them did not constitute profits of the firm and so were not chargeable to income tax under former ICTA 1988, s. 18 (former Sch. D, now within ITTOIA 2005, Pt. 2, Ch. 2; CTA 2009, s. 35) and secondly that the further payments should have been deducted by the firm in computing the amount of its profits under former ICTA 1988, s. 74 (now ITTOIA 2005, Pt. 2, Ch. 4; CTA 2009, Pt. 3, Ch. 4).

The First-tier Tribunal (FTT) found that the further payments were made to the taxpayers in their capacity as partners and were not entirely collateral payments made to them otherwise than in their capacity as partners. Accordingly, the further payments were payments of profits and so chargeable to income tax under ICTA 1988, s. 18. They were not amounts which should have been deducted by the firm in computing its profits under s. 74.

However, in *AB* [2011] TC 01527 a chartered accountant and tax adviser argued that payments made to her on her ceasing to be partner in two accountancy firms (positions she held consecutively) were compensation for her adverse treatment and not profit shares subject to income tax. The FTT found that one of the payments was compensation notwithstanding that it had been treated as profit share in the partnership accounts but the other payment was profit share. The FTT observed the same passage from the *Morgan; Self* decision as set out at ¶18-280.

In terms of the first payment, this was found to be compensation because the only interpretation that could be placed on the agreement between the appellant and her former firm was that the firm had been unwilling to make any admission but recognised that she had been unfairly treated and compensation had to be paid; against the background of an employment tribunal claim which was withdrawn in consequence of the payment. As far as the second payment was concerned, however, the Retirement Agreement and the letter which preceded it both described the payment made as a share of profit: it was offered and accepted as such and that same agreement expressly contemplated a quite separate compromise of claims, and in due course she received a further payment of £50,000 as compensation for her unfair treatment. Accordingly, no part of the earlier payment represented compensation.

18-420   Specific deductions: partnership annuities

Annuity payments made by current partners to a retired partner may be charged in the partnership's profit and loss account. Such payments should be added back in the tax computation.

ITA 2007, s. 900 provides for income tax to be deducted at source on qualifying annual payments made in connection with the individual's trade, profession or vocation.

The individual partners will obtain income tax relief for the payments through their own self assessment returns, see ¶20-180.

Tax relief not available

Where the obligation to pay the annuity has been assumed as part of the consideration for the acquisition of a partnership business tax relief for the expense will not be available.

In *Parnalls Solicitors Ltd* [2010] TC 00261, the First-tier Tribunal decided that the payment of a lump sum by a company which acquired a business from a firm of solicitors to a retired partner did not constitute a tax deductible expense for the purposes of calculating the profits chargeable to corporation tax.

The treatment of the lump sum payment which replaced a contractual obligation to make a recurring payment was determined by the nature of the payment it replaced. In this case, as the obligation to pay the former partner's annuity was assumed as part of the consideration for the acquisition of the partnership business the payment of the annuity would have been capital expenditure.

Legislation: ITA 2007, s. 900

18-440 Specific deductions: costs connected with the capital structure of a business

Costs, expenses or fees incurred on the acquisition, alteration or enhancement of the ownership structure of a business are disallowed as capital expenditure for tax purposes. Examples include:

• forming, varying or dissolving a partnership;
• negotiating a merger between companies or partnerships;
• the incorporation of a partnership's business (to a limited company);
• a partnership becoming a limited liability partnership (LLP);
• defending against a petition to wind up a company.

For fees to be deductible, they need to be 'revenue' in character and satisfy the 'wholly and exclusively' requirement in ITTOIA 2005, s. 34(1)(a) or CTA 2009, s. 54(1)(a).

Costs in connection with the capital structure of a partnership are excluded by the above provisions.

In *C Connelly & Co v Wilbey (HMIT)* [1992] BTC 538 an accountancy partnership was dissolved. The Commissioners and the courts dismissed the partners' claim that the costs of dissolving the practice be allowed. The legal expenses had not been expended wholly and exclusively for the purposes of the partnership trade, but had been incurred to protect one partner's interests.

Legislation: ITTOIA 2005, 34(1)(a); CTA 2009, s. 54(1)(a)

18-460 Specific deductions: deductions in relation to LLP salaried members

Where an individual member of an LLP is treated for income tax purposes as employed under a contract of service under ITTOIA 2005, s. 863A(2) (see **Chapter 22**), the LLP is entitled to a deduction for the deemed salary (including tax and National Insurance) paid in calculating its profits for tax purposes under ITTOIA 2005, s. 849 or CTA 2009, s. 1259, subject to, in particular, the wholly and exclusively rule (ITTOIA 2005, s. 34; CTA 2009, s. 54) in the same way as any other such business payment but also the capital expenditure rule in ITTOIA 2005, s. 33; CTA 2009, s. 53, the business entertainment and gifts rule in ITTOIA 2005, s. 45; CTA 2009, s. 1298 and social security contributions rule in ITTOIA 2005, s. 53; CTA 2009, s. 1302.

(ITTOIA 2005, s. 94AA; CTA 2009, s. 92A)

Legislation: ITTOIA 2005, s. 33, 45, 53, 94AA, 863A(2), 849; CTA 2009, s. 53, 92A, 1259, 1298, 1302

MISCELLANEOUS COMPUTATIONAL PROVISIONS

18-480   Farming and market gardening

'Farming' and 'market gardening' in the UK is treated for income and corporation tax purposes as the carrying on of a trade or part of a trade (whether or not the land is managed on a commercial basis and with a view to the realisation of profits) and all farming in the UK carried on by a person, other than farming carried on as part of another trade, is treated for income and corporation tax purposes as one trade (ITTOIA 2005, s. 9; CTA 2009, s. 36).

This is subject to one exception for corporation tax purposes that excludes from this treatment farming or market gardening carried on by an insurance company on land which is an asset of its long-term insurance fund.

This is so regardless of whether there is one farming trade or several and whether the farms are adjacent or located far apart in the UK.

A farming trade carried on by a partnership, other than as carried on as part of another trade, is also treated as one trade but the farming carried on by the partnership firm (and treated as one trade) is not included in any farming trade of any partner outside the firm (ITTOIA 2005, s. 859(1); CTA 2009, s. 1270(1)).

18-500   UK property income

In most cases all the various types of income from land and property in the UK are treated as parts of the same, single rental business. It does not matter how many properties the taxpayer has, or how many different types of income from land and property. This means that normally all the rental business receipts and expenditure can be lumped together and, hence, that the expenses on one property can be deducted from the receipts of another (ITTOIA 2005, s. 264; CTA 2009, s. 205).

Where a UK property business is carried on by a partnership, the partnership's transactions are similarly treated as the same single rental business but each partner's share of the profits or losses arising from the partnership's rental business cannot be added or subtracted from any partner's rental business profits or losses (outside the firm).

If taxpayers are in more than one partnership, each is dealt with as a separate rental business and the profits of one can't be set against the losses of another (ITTOIA 2005, s. 859(2); CTA 2009, s. 1270(2)).

18-520 Overseas property income

Similarly, an 'overseas property business' consists of every business which a person carries on for generating income from land outside the UK *and* every transaction which the person enters into for the purpose of generating income from such land otherwise than in the course of such a business (ITTOIA 2005, s. 265; CTA 2009, s. 206).

Where an overseas property business is carried on by a partnership, the partnership's transactions are again treated as the same single rental business but each partner's share of the profits or losses arising from the partnership's overseas rental business cannot be added or subtracted from any individual's overseas rental business profits or losses (ITTOIA 2005, s. 859(3); CTA 2009, s. 1270(3)).

18-540 Jointly owned property

Joint letting does not, of itself, make the activity a partnership. A distinction needs to be drawn between:

- income derived from property held by a partnership (see above) in which case the income does not belong to the individual partner in his personal capacity and is not part of his own rental business; and

- income derived from property which is jointly owned in circumstances which do not amount to partnership, in which case the individual joint owner does receive his share of the income in his personal capacity, and it does form part of his own rental business.

Usually, there won't be a partnership and the taxpayer's share from the jointly owned property will be included as part of their personal rental business profits.

Where the joint owners are husband and wife, or civil partners, profits and losses are treated as arising to them in equal shares unless:

- both entitlement to the income and the property are in unequal shares; and
- both spouses, or civil partners, ask their respective tax offices for their share of profits and losses to match the share each holds in the property.

Other material: HMRC Manual PIM1030

18-560   Adjustment income: change of accounting policy or tax adjustments applied

A change in the way profits are calculated for tax purposes may have the effect that:

- some income might fall out of account;
- some otherwise allowable expenses might not be relieved;
- some income might be taxed twice; or
- some allowable expenses might be deducted twice.

There are therefore special rules to counter such effects. The provisions for income tax purposes are contained within ITTOIA 2005, Pt. 2, Ch. 17 in respect of trading income and ITTOIA 2005, Pt. 3, Ch. 7, in respect of a property business. For corporation tax purposes, the relevant provisions are within CTA 2009, Pt. 3, Ch. 14 with regard to the profits of a trade and CTA 2009, s. 261 and 262 in respect of a property business. The income tax and corporation tax provisions are essentially mirror provisions.

The rules apply when, from one period of account to the next, a trader or company changes the basis on which the trading profits are calculated for tax purposes (as that term is defined) from one valid basis to another valid basis (i.e. both the old and the new basis accord with the law or practice that are applicable in relation to the periods respective before and after the change. The practice applicable means the accepted practice as to how profits should be calculated for income or corporation tax purposes).

A person changes the basis on which profits of a trade are calculated for income tax purposes if the person makes:

- a change of accounting policy (i.e. from using UK GAAP to using generally accepted accounting practice in accordance with international accounting standards, and vice versa); or
- a change in the tax adjustments applied.

A 'tax adjustment' is any adjustment required or authorised by law in calculating profits of a trade for income or corporation tax purposes and 'a change in the tax adjustments applied' does not include changes made to comply with amending legislation that was not applicable to the previous period but does include a change resulting from a change of view as to what is required or authorised by law or as to whether any adjustment is so required or authorised) (ITTOIA 2005, s. 227; CTA 2009, s. 180).

Giving effect to adjustments

The amount of the adjustment is to be calculated under or by reference to ITTOIA 2005, s. 231 (s. 330(1) and CTA 2009, s. 182 (CTA 2009, s. 262(1)).

Once calculated, the adjustment is treated as a receipt or expense in calculating the profits of the trade or property business.

For corporation tax purposes, the receipt or expense is treated as arising on the first day of the first period of account for which the new basis is adopted (CTA 2009, s. 181, 262).

For income tax purposes, the receipt or expense is treated as arising on the last day of the first period of account for which the new basis is adopted. For loss relief purposes, an adjustment receipt is treated as part of the profits for the tax year in which tax is charged on it. (ITTOIA 2005, s. 232–233; 333–334).

However, in the case of a change of basis affecting the calculation of trading stock (as applicable) or depreciation, the receipt or expense is not brought into account until the asset to which it relates is realised or written off (ITTOIA 2005, s. 235; CTA 2009, s. 184; 262(5)). In addition, the general rule is subject to ITTOIA 2005, s. 234 and CTA 2009, s. 183 (no adjustment for certain expenses previously brought into account) (ITTOIA 2005, s. 330(4); CTA 2009, s. 262(6)).

Application to partnerships

Where a business is carried on in partnership, the amount of any adjustment is computed, for corporation tax purposes, as if the partnership were a UK resident company or UK resident firm.

The general rule is that each partner's share of the adjustment charge is calculated according to the profit-sharing arrangements in force for the 12 months prior to the date of the change of basis.

Where there is a change in the persons carrying on a trade, etc., this does not prevent the adjustment income rules applying as long as there is at least one person (income tax purposes) or company (corporation tax purposes) who carries on the trade both before and after the change.

Similarly, a change where at least one person continues to carry on the trade does not constitute the permanent cessation of the trade for income tax purposes (ITTOIA 2005, s. 860).

(CTA 2009, s. 1267; ITTOIA 2005, s. 860).

It is possible to elect for the adjustment income to be spread over six periods of account (1/6th per period of account starting with the first period to which the new basis applies). An election must be made:

- for income tax purposes, on or before the first anniversary of the normal self-assessment filing date for the tax year in which the change of basis occurs (ITTOIA 2005, s. 237); and
- for corporation tax purposes, within 12 months of the end of the first accounting period to which the new basis applies.

Any election concerning the spreading of the adjustment charge must be made jointly by all those who were partners in the 12 months preceding the change of basis (ITTOIA 2005, s. 860(5); CTA 2009, s. 1268(2)).

Legislation: ITTOIA 2005, Pt. 2, Ch. 17 and Pt. 3, Ch. 7, s. 860; CTA 2009, Pt. 3, Ch. 14 and s. 261–262 and 1267–1269)

Chapter 10: Allocation of firm's profits or losses between partners

19-000 Introduction

The trade (profession or business profits) of the partnership are computed at partnership level and are then allocated to the individual partners in order to facilitate the assessment being made on the partners individually (see **Chapter 9**).

Profits to be allocated to individual partners will have been calculated in accordance with income tax rules. Profits to be allocated to corporate partners will have been calculated in accordance with corporation tax rules. Where there are non-resident partners, additional calculations may have been made in order to calculate the profits on a 'non-resident' basis either following income tax rules for individual non-resident partners or following corporation tax rules for non-resident corporate partners.

Profits should be allocated to individual partners following the procedure prescribed by ITTOIA 2005, s. 850–850B (see ¶19-020). Interest on capital and salaries paid to partners are treated as prior profit allocations (see ¶19-060).

Profits should be allocated to corporate partners following the procedure prescribed by CTA 2009, s. 1262–1264 (see ¶19-100).

These procedure is essentially the same for both allocations of profits to individuals and to companies.

Where there is a mix of individual and corporate partners, further rules apply at s. 850C–850E and CTA 2009, s. 1264A. These are known as the 'mixed partnership rules' and are anti-avoidance provisions introduced by FA 2014.

Legislation: ITTOIA 2005, s. 850–850E; CTA 2009, s. 1262–1264A

19-020 Allocation of income tax profits

The basis of allocation is the commercial profit sharing arrangements that are in force during the period of account (ITTOIA 2005, s. 850).

Although ITTOIA 2005, s. 850 refers to 'profits or losses of the trade', it is extended to include profits or losses of a profession or business that is not a trade (so includes investment business) by ITTOIA 2005, s. 847.

If the partnership business comprises two or more sources of trading income, the profits from each source should be allocated separately to each partner.

Other income or losses of partnerships with trading (profession or non-trading income) being allocated under these rules is also allocated using this method also (ITTOIA 2005, s. 851).

Example 1

Anna, Barbara and Carol have been in partnership for many years. They prepare accounts to 30 April each year. The accounts for the year to 30 April 2015 show a profit of £21,000. Profits and losses are shared equally.

The partnership profits are allocated as follows:

	Anna	*Barbara*	*Carol*	*Total*
	£	£	£	£
Profits allocated 1:1:1	7,000	7,000	7,000	21,000

Allocation where different bases apply: UK resident and non-resident partners

---

Example 2

Mr Adams, a UK resident, and Mrs Brown, a non-resident, are in partnership. The partnership's worldwide trade profits amount to £20,000 and included in that sum is its UK profit of £15,000. Partnership profits are shared equally. Two tax computations are required:

Computation for resident partner

Step 1	Trade profits		£20,000
Step 2	Allocation	Mr Adams	£10,000
		Mrs Brown	£10,000
Step 3	Profit assessable on	Mr Adams	£10,000

Computation for non-resident partner

Step 1	Trade profits		£15,000
Step 2	Allocation	Mr Adams	£7,500
		Mrs Brown	£7,500
Step 3	Profit assessable on	Mrs Brown	£7,500

19-040   Changes in the profit sharing arrangements

Where the profit sharing arrangements change during the basis period, this is reflected in the allocation for tax purposes.

Example 3

Ian and Peter have for several years traded in partnership. Their accounts for the year to 31 December 2015 show a profit of £16,000. Profits and losses are shared equally until 31 March 2015. From 1 April, profits and losses are shared in the ratio 7:9.

Profits are allocated in accordance with the profit sharing arrangements in force during the year to 31 December 2015 as follows:

Three months to 31 March 2015

Profits for period:

$3/12 \times £16,000 = £4,000$

Allocated 1:1 as follows:

	£
Ian ($1/2 \times £4,000$)	2,000
Peter ($1/2 \times £4,000$)	2,000
	4,000

Nine months to 31 December 2015

Profits for period:

$9/12 \times £16,000 = £12,000$

Allocated 7:9 as follows:

	£
Ian ($7/16 \times £12,000$)	5,250
Peter ($9/16 \times £12,000$)	6,750
	12,000

Thus, profits for the year to 31 December 2015 are allocated as follows:

	Ian	*Peter*	*Total*
	£	£	£
1/1/15 – 31/3/15	2,000	2,000	4,000
1/4/15 – 31/12/15	5,250	6,750	12,000
Total	7,250	8,750	16,000

Legislation: ITTOIA 2005, s. 850

19-060   Treatment of salaries and interest on capital

In England and Wales (unlike Scotland), a partnership is not a legal entity. Therefore, a partnership cannot enter into a contract of employment with an equity partner and an equity partner cannot be the employee of the remaining partners. If, therefore, an equity partner is, under the terms of the partnership agreement, entitled to a salary or wage, he is merely entitled to an allocation of profits prior to the general division among the partners.

Salaries paid to an equity partner are therefore not deductible in determining the partnership profits (or losses). Rather, they are merely an allocation of profits prior to the general division among the partners in accordance with the other profit sharing arrangements.

Example 4

Tom, Dick and Harry prepare accounts to 31 December each year and share profits and losses in the ratio 3:2:1. In a given year, the partnership made a profit of £85,000. Tom received a salary of £4,000 and Harry received a salary of £3,000.

The partnership profits are allocated as follows for the year:

	Tom	Dick	Harry	Total
	£	£	£	£
Salaries	4,000	–	3,000	7,000
Balance of profits				
(£85,000 – £7,000 = £78,000)				
distributed 3:2:1	39,000	26,000	13,000	78,000
	43,000	26,000	16,000	85,000

Interest paid on partners' capital accounts is treated as an allocation of profit in the same way as the salaries in the above example.

Example 5

Jane, Jean and Beth set up in partnership, with Jean contributing capital of £20,000 and Beth £30,000. Interest on capital is paid at 5% per annum. Jane receives a salary of £5,000 and Jean receives a salary of £10,000. For the year to 31 December in a given year, the accounts show a profit of £50,000. Profits and losses are allocated in the ratio 2:3:5.

The allocation of profits for the year is as follows:

	Jane	*Jean*	*Beth*	*Total*
	£	£	£	£
Salaries	5,000	10,000	–	15,000
Interest on capital	–	1,000	1,500	2,500
Balance allocated 2:3:5	6,500	9,750	16,250	32,500
Net allocated	11,500	20,750	17,750	50,000

Legislation: ITTOIA 2005, s. 850

19-080   Reallocation of notional profit/loss

The allocation process outlined at ¶19-020 above could, in some circumstances, produce a spurious result whereby the firm has a profit calculated under s. 849 but, in allocating that profit on the basis of the firm's profit sharing arrangements under s. 850, one or more partners could be allocated an aggregate (or notional) profit in excess of the actual profit made by the firm, whereas the remaining partners would be allocated an aggregate or notional 'loss'. This might arise where, for example, partnership salaries are allocated as a first charge on profits.

For income tax (and corporation tax) purposes the allocation of profit or loss between partners must result in a straight apportionment of the actual profit or loss made by the partnership. Therefore, if the initial allocation using the commercial profit sharing arrangement for all the partners produces a mixture of notional profits and losses, the actual partnership profit or loss must be reallocated between the profit making or loss making partners only. This reallocation is made in proportion to the notional profit or loss initially allocated to those partners.

Example 1

George, Jack, Eileen and Ian set up in partnership, with profits and losses allocated in the ratio 5:2:2:1. For the year to 30 September, the firm made a s. 849 (income tax) profit of just £6,000. George and Eileen each received 'salaries' of £8,000.

The partnership profits for the self-assessment are initially allocated under s. 850 as follows:

	George £	Jack £	Eileen £	Ian £	Total £
Salaries	8,000	–	8,000	–	16,000
Balance of profit distributed 5:2:2:1	(5,000)	(2,000)	(2,000)	(1,000)	(10,000)
Initial allocation	3,000	(2,000)	6,000	(1,000)	6,000

As there is no real loss for tax purposes to be allocated to any partner, Jack and Ian are therefore treated as having neither a profit nor a loss (ITTOIA 2005, s. 850A(1)), whilst the profits allocated to George and Eileen are reduced proportionally to bring their total down to the firm's s. 849 profit. In effect, the notional loss is reallocated between George and Eileen in proportion to the notional profit originally allocated to them, i.e. 3,000:6,000 or 1:2. The final position is thus as follows:

	George £	Jack £	Eileen £	Ian £	Total £
Salaries	8,000	–	8,000	–	16,000
Balance distributed 5:2:2:1	(5,000)	(2,000)	(2,000)	(1,000)	(10,000)
Initial allocation	3,000	(2,000)	6,000	(1,000)	6,000
Reallocation of notional loss 1:2	(1,000)	2,000	(2,000)	1,000	–
Net allocated	2,000	–	4,000	–	6,000

A similar situation arises if the partnership makes a loss under s. 849 and the initial allocation under s. 850 results in one or more partners being allocated a notional profit or if the aggregate notional loss allocated to the remaining partners exceeds the actual s. 849 loss made by the partnership (ITTOIA 2005, s. 850B).

This principle was upheld by a special commissioner in *PDC Copyprint (South)* (1997) Sp C 141. In that case, the partnership agreements provided for two of the equity partners, who were regarded as being the managers of the business, to be entitled to salaries expressed as a first charge upon the net trading profits. In the event, the salaries were paid regardless of the profitability. No PAYE was operated on the salaries. The other equity partners, who had little active involvement with the business, sought to increase their loss relief claims for certain years by the salaries paid. Although the report of the judgment is unclear, this claim was presumably on the grounds that the salaries were costs of operating the business. They could not have been appropriations of profit, for no profit arose in those years.

The special commissioner held that the losses must be computed in accordance with the Taxes Acts, which prohibit the deduction of partners' salaries in computing taxable profits. It was not open to partners to inflate their loss claims by the payment of salaries to one or more of their number.

Example 2

Alan, Beatrice and Cassandra are in partnership. Alan is entitled to a salary of £4,400, and profits/losses are shared Alan 25%, Beatrice 25% and Cassandra 50%. The partnership makes a loss of (£1,600). The partnership loss is initially allocated as follows:

	Alan	Beatrice	Cassandra	Totals
Salary	£4,400	Nil	nil	£4,400
Balance of loss	(£1,500)	(£1,500)	(£3,000)	(£6,000)
Net Allocated	£2,900	(£1,500)	(£3,000)	(£1,600)

In this case the commercial profit sharing arrangement produces a spurious result. A notional profit of £2,900 has been allocated to Alan whilst Beatrice and Cassandra have been allocated an aggregate notional loss of (£4,500).

Therefore the actual partnership loss must be reallocated between the loss making partners. The re-allocation is in proportion to the notional loss initially allocated to each partner, i.e. in the ratio

$$\frac{(£1500)}{(£4500)} : \frac{(£3000)}{(£4500)} \quad \text{or} \quad 33.3\% : 66.7\%$$

	Alan	Beatrice	Cassandra	Totals
Net Allocated	£2,900	(£1,500)	(£3,000)	(£1,600)
Percentage	(nil)	(33.3%)	(66.7%)	(100%)
Reallocated	nil	(£533)	(£1,067)	(£1,600)

Legislation: ITTOIA 2005, s. 850A, 850B

19-100 Allocation of profits and losses to corporate partners

The basic rule is that a company member of a partnership is allocated its share of the partnership's trading profit or loss of an accounting period (calculated as if the partnership was a company, see ¶18-160), together with its share of any qualifying charitable donations paid by the partnership and its share of any loan relationship debits and credits (see below), in accordance with the partnership's profit-sharing arrangements during that period (CTA 2009, s. 1262).

Example 1

A UK resident partnership has two corporate partners, Company A and Company B. Profits are shared equally. Accounts for the year ended 30 April show profits of £21,000.

The partnership profits are allocated as follows:

	Company A	*Company B*	*Total*
	£	£	£
Profits allocated 1:1	10,500	10,500	21,000

Allocation where different bases apply: UK resident and non-resident partners

---

Example 2

A UK partnership has two corporate members; Company A – a UK resident and Company B – a non-resident. Profits are share equally. The partnership's worldwide profits amounted to £10,000 of which £7,500 was earned in the UK.

Computation for resident partner

Step 1	Trade profits		£10,000
Step 2	Allocation	Company A	£5,000
		Company B	£5,000
Step 3	Profit assessable on	Company A	£5,000

Computation for non-resident partner

Step 1	Trade profits		£7,500
Step 2	Allocation	Company A	£3,750
		Company B	£3,750
Step 3	Profit assessable on	Company B	£3,750

> **Example 3**
>
> Williams and partners have been in business for many years and draw up accounts to 31 December each year. The partners of the firm are Mr Williams and Mr Bryan (individuals) and Nut Tree Ltd (a company). They share in profits in the ratio 1:1:2. The profits of Williams and partners up to 31 December 2015 are £48,000. Nut Tree Ltd's share is £24,000. Nut Tree Ltd has accounting periods from 1 August to 31 July. Nut Tree Ltd's share of the profits is divided between the corresponding accounting periods, i.e. 5/12ths of the profits (£10,000) are attributed to the accounting period ending 31 July 2016 and 7/12ths of the profits (£14,000) are attributed to the accounting period ending 31 July 2015.

Profit-making period in which some partners have a loss, or vice versa

Although the allocation of profit follows the commercial profit sharing arrangement the use of this arrangement alone might produce a spurious result. For instance it would be possible to have an allocation in which one or more partners are allocated an aggregate (but notional) profit greater than the actual profit made by the partnership, and the remaining partners are allocated an aggregate (but notional) loss.

In the same way as applies for income tax purposes, for corporation tax purposes the allocation of profit or loss between partners must result in a straight apportionment of the actual profit or loss made by the partnership. If the initial allocation using the commercial profit sharing arrangement for all the partners produces a mixture of notional profits and losses, it will be necessary to reallocate the actual partnership profit or loss between the profit making or loss making partners alone. This re-allocation is made in proportion to the notional profit or loss initially allocated to those partners (CTA 2009, s. 1263 and 1264). For examples on how these rules are to be applied, see ¶19-080.

Legislation: CTA 2009, s. 1262, 1263 and 1264

19-120   Loan relationships: Allocating loan relationship debits and credits (and exchange gains and losses)

The legislation applying to loan relationships and company partners can be found at CTA 2009, Pt. 5, Ch. 9.

Loan relationship debits and credits (arising from a money debt or any loan relationship that would be treated as arising from that money debt (such as interest on trade debts) are excluded from the calculation of profits for allocation to corporate partners (CTA 2009, s. 380(2)).

Instead, each company partner is treated as if it had a separate loan relationship equal to its apportioned share (per the partnership profit-sharing agreement as it would have been applied by CTA 2009, s. 1262) of the firm's total loan relationships and brings its 'own' debits and credits into account (CTA 2009, s. 380(3) and 381) (effectively by calculating the gross credits and debits and apportioning them between each partner).

Calculation of gross credits and debits is covered at ¶18-180ff.

Example 1

ABC partnership lends £100,000 to D Ltd.

The members of ABC partnership, and their profit shares, are:

- Mrs A 20%;
- B Ltd 60%;
- C Ltd 20%.

The loan carries interest at 10% per annum.

Each company will have gross credits of £10,000, the interest accruing on the loan.

Having arrived at the gross credits and debits, each company partner is then allocated with their 'appropriate share' of the total credits and debits determined as above but without any reduction for the fact that the debt is treated as owed by or to each partner (CTA 2009, s. 381(5)).

A partner's 'appropriate share' is the share that would be apportioned to it on the assumption that the debits and credits are apportioned in accordance with the partnership's profit sharing ratio (CTA 2009, s. 381(6), (7)).

Example 2

The gross credit calculated at Example 1 is then shared between the company partners, so that:

- B Ltd brings in a credit of £6,000;
- C Ltd brings in a credit of £2,000.

Mrs A is chargeable to income tax and will compute her profits under the income tax rules.

Company partners using fair value accounting

Where the partnership uses fair value accounting, then the company must use that too in arriving at the credits and debits to be brought into account by the company partner (CTA 2009, s. 382).

Additional special provisions are required:

- in the situation where a company partner controls (alone or together with connected parties) the firm and is one party to a money loan and the firm in which it is a partner is the other, i.e. the partner lends money to, or borrows it from, the firm. Then CTA 2009, s. 383 apples the connected parties rules at CTA 2009, Pt. 5, Ch. 5 (see ¶19-140);

- where the rules relating to exchange gains and losses included in a company's statement of recognised gains and losses would normally come into play, they are not generally applied to company partners, except where FOREX gains and losses are allocated to the partnership's statement of recognised gains and losses, statement of recognised income and expense, statement of changes in equity or statement of income and retained earnings (carried to a reserve in the firm's accounts) (CTA 2009, s. 384, see ¶19-220); and

- where a firm holds a relevant discounted security, in respect of which each partner is treated for the purposes of bringing debits and credits into account as beneficially entitled to the share of the security as if all partners were companies and the security were apportioned in the shares in partnerships profit sharing ratio (CTA 2009, s. 385, see ¶19-240).

Legislation: CTA 2009, s. 380–385

19-140   Loan relationships: lending between partners and the partnership

A partner may lend money to the partnership, and the partnership may lend to a partner.

CTA 2009, s. 383 provides the rules for determining whether a company partner controls a partnership in circumstances where a money debt exists between the partnership and a company partner.

Section 383 applies where the money debt owed by or to the partnership arises from a transaction for the lending of money and conditions A, B and C are met. See further below for transactions not from the lending of money.

If there is such a money debt the rules in CTA 2009, Pt. 5 apply accordingly for the purposes of calculating the debits and credits arising (see ¶18-200).

The three conditions are as follows:

A.   If the debt is owed by the firm, the company partner stands in the position of creditor and has a creditor relationship, and if the debt is owed to the firm, the company partner stands in the position of a debtor and has a debtor relationship;

B.   The company partner 'controls' the firm either alone or taken together with one or more company partners 'connected' with the company partner (definitions of 'control' and 'connected company partners', as below);

C.   The company partner is treated (under s. 381(3) (see ¶18-200)) as if it had:

(a)   a debtor relationship which corresponds to the creditor relationship mentioned in condition A above; or

(b)   a creditor relationship which corresponds to the debtor relationship in condition A above.

(CTA 2009, s. 383(2)–(4)).

In other words, where the company partner has lent money to the partnership, it will be both:

- creditor (as the individual lender); and
- debtor (for its share of the debt owed by the partnership).

Conversely, where the company partner has borrowed from the partnership, it will be both:

- debtor (as the individual borrower); and
- creditor (for its share of the debt owed to the partnership).

The company will, therefore, need to bring into account credits and debits for the same loan relationship.

Example 1

The members of ABC partnership, and their profit shares, are:

- Mrs A 20%;
- B Ltd 60%;
- C Ltd 20%.

C Ltd lends the partnership £10,000, carrying interest at 10% per annum.

Each company (as partner) will have gross debits of £1,000, the interest accruing on the loan. This is then shared between the company partners, so that:

- B Ltd brings in a debit of £600;
- C Ltd brings in a debit of £200.

But C Ltd is also the creditor, and will bring in a credit of £1,000 for the interest accrued on the loan.

Condition B: control of the partnership

For the purposes of determining whether any company partner (together with connected company partners) 'controls' a partnership, control is defined by CTA 2010, s. 1124(2) as:

- in relation to a partnership, the right to a share of more than half the assets or more than half the income of the partnership;

(CTA 2009, s. 1124(2) as applied by CTA 2009 s. 383(8)).

Condition B: connected company partners

For the purposes of condition B and treatment of lending arrangements between partners and the partnership, control of the partnership is determined by considering the company partner itself together with any 'connected' company partners.

A company partner is connected with another at any time if one **controls** the other or both are under the control of the same person (CTA 2009, s. 383(7)).

Control for these purpose (determining connected company partners) is defined by CTA 2009, s. 472 as:

- power to secure the affairs of the company are conducted in accordance with the person's wishes by means of holding shares or voting power or as a result of powers conferred by the articles of association of any company (excluding trading shares), and

in the case of a partnership, any property rights or powers held or exercisable by the partnership are treated as apportioned between the partners in the profit sharing ratio (excluding the general partner of a limited partnership which is a collective investment scheme).

(CTA 2009, s. 472 as applied by CTA 2009, s. 383(8)).

Example 2

H Ltd owns 100% of the shares in both B Ltd and C Ltd.

The members of ABC partnership, and their profit shares, are:

- Mrs A 30%;
- B Ltd 50%;
- C Ltd 20%.

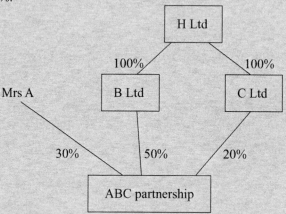

Each partner has lent £50,000 to the partnership. This lending is not performing an equity function (see further commentary below).

B Ltd and C Ltd are under the common control of H Ltd and are therefore connected. Because of this connection, the interests of B Ltd and C Ltd can be combined. Together they are entitled to 70% of the partnership profits, so both B Ltd and C Ltd **control** the partnership.

B Ltd controls the partnership together with C Ltd.

C Ltd controls the partnership together with B Ltd.

Lending arrangements

Where the partner is a company partner, the loan may be a true lending arrangement or it may be more in the nature of equity. A loan which is not quasi-equity is likely to be a loan relationship. Factors to consider in determining whether the loan is of an equity nature or lending arrangement include:

- the terms of the partnership agreement and whether the partnership can repay the loan without the departure of the lender, or the dissolution of the partnership;
- the accounts treatment and whether the debt is shown in the partnership accounts as a normal creditor or as partnership capital;
- the terms of the loan agreement and whether this reflects normal commercial rates for interest and terms of repayment.

A loan from a company partner to a partnership that is not quasi-equity is likely to be a loan relationship.

Legislation: CTA 2009, s. 383, 472

19-160 Loan relationships: lending between partners and the partnership: tax implications

Where conditions A–C (see ¶19-140) apply, there is taken to be a connection between the company partner and each company partner (including the company partner itself) that has a debtor or creditor relationship under Condition C as a result of one of them having control of the other for the purposes of s. 466(2)) and the provisions of CTA 2009, Pt. 5 apply accordingly.

In other words, where a company partner controls a partnership, it is treated as connected to all company partners including itself for the purposes of CTA 2009, Pt. 5.

This means that the partner:

- must use the mandatory accruals or amortised cost basis;
- cannot have relief for impairment losses;
- gets no relief for interest until paid unless corresponding credits are brought in;
- debits on relevant discounted securities are not brought into account until redemption unless corresponding credits are brought in;

for all its debtor and creditor relationships with the partnership (and so with the other company partners.)

Example 1

In example 2 at ¶19-140, both B Ltd and C Ltd control the partnership, and each have lent it £50,000.

The partnership is struggling, so each partner writes off £25,000 of the loan.

Both B Ltd and C Ltd will treat the loan relationship as a:

- creditor relationship in their own accounts;
- debtor relationship from the point of view of the partnership.

Each loan relationship is a connected party loan relationship for the purpose of CTA 2009, Pt. 5, Ch. 5.

So each partner will:

- bring in credits from the creditor relationship on the amortised cost basis;
- assume that the debt will be paid in full, so bring in no debit for impairment;
- compute the gross credits and debits of the partnership also on the amortised cost basis, before taking its share.

Legislation: CTA 2009, s. 383, 466

19-180   Loan relationships: company partners and other connections

In addition to the specific provisions relating to lending arrangements between the company partner and the partnership, CTA 2009, Pt. 5 contains other provisions which could affect the calculation of debits and credits on loan relationships where the company partner has a connection to another company.

Where a company stands in the position of debtor or creditor (directly or indirectly) with another connected company, it is treated as having a connected company relationship (CTA 2009, s. 348).

CTA 2009, s. 466 provides the basic definition of 'connected' as being where:

- A controls B;
- B controls A; or
- A and B are both controlled by the same person.

CTA 2009, s. 467 extends the CTA 2009, s. 466 definition of connection where partnerships are involved by providing a 'look through' rule, so that where:

- a partnership includes a company (company partner); and
- the partnership lends to or borrows from another company (not a company partner),

the question as to whether there is a connection between any two companies for the purposes of the provisions which apply s. 466 and how far any amount is to be treated in a particular way as a result of their being or not being such a connection, is to be determined by treating the company partner as the party to the loan relationship, not the partnership, to the extent of its appropriate share (which is the amount which would be apportioned to the partner in accordance with the firm's profit sharing arrangements)

(CTA 2009, s. 467).

Control is defined by s. 472 as:

- power to secure the affairs of the company are conducted in accordance with the person's wishes by means of holding shares or voting power or as a result of powers conferred by the articles of association of any company (excluding trading shares), and in the case of a partnership, any property rights or powers held or exercisable by the partnership are treated as apportioned between the partners in the profit sharing ratio (excluding the general partner of a limited partnership which is a collective investment scheme)

(CTA 2009, s. 472).

The implications of there being a connected company relationship are as follows:

- credits and debits in respect of connected company relationships are to be determined on an amortised cost basis of accounting (CTA 2009, s. 349);
- debits in respect of impairment losses and releases are prevented from being brought into account, subject to exceptions (CTA 2009, s. 354–357);
- credits in respect of the release of debts or the reversal of impairments are excluded from being brought into account, subject to exceptions (CTA 2009, s. 358–360);
- debits in relation to interest which is not paid or is paid late are treated as not accruing until paid in some cases (including loans to close companies by participators) (CTA 2009, Pt. 5, Ch. 8)

Extended definition of connection: example

GF Ltd and HD Ltd are partners in a partnership that owns 90% of the shares in LJ Ltd. GF Ltd is entitled to 40% of the profits or losses of the partnership and HD Ltd is entitled to 60%. By attributing the shares in LJ Ltd according to their interest in the profits or losses of the partnership:

- GF Ltd effectively owns 36% of LJ Ltd and is not connected to LJ Ltd;
- HD Ltd effectively owns 54% of LJ Ltd, has control and therefore is connected.

Legislation: CTA 2009, Pt. 5, Ch. 5, 6, 8, s. 466, 467, 472

19-200   Loan relationships: allocating credits and debits to the company partner: Tax Bulletin article TB62/02

Difficulties in apportioning debits and credits between company partners may occur where the partnership and company partner account in different currencies. This was dealt with by a Tax Bulletin article in October 2002 (TB62/02). Although the TB refers to the original legislation in FA 1996, most of these provisions were rewritten into CTA 2009, Pt. 5, Ch. 9 (as indicated) and the bulletin is still relevant in relation to the operation of CTA 2009, s. 381(2)–(4), former FA 1996, Sch. 9, para. 19(4)).

The text of TB62/02 is set out as follows:

'FA 2002 inserted a new paragraph 19 into Schedule 9 FA 1996 [now CTA 2009, s. 380-385] to deal comprehensively with cases where a company is a member of a partnership and a money debt (which includes a loan relationship) is owed by or to the partnership. Each company partner computes separately loan relationship debits and credits arising on the money debt.

For this purpose paragraph 19(4) Schedule 9 [now CTA 2009, s. 381(2)-(4)] deems that the money debt is owed by or to the company partner, and that everything done by the partnership in relation to the debt has been done by the company.

The company then computes the debits and credits ('the gross debits and credits') that arise from applying the loan relationships rules to this deemed situation. The company partner brings into account a proportion of these gross debits and credits, the proportion being determined by reference to the partner's interest in the partnership.

We have been asked whether paragraph 19(4) [now s. 381(2)-(4)] means that you effectively ignore the existence of the partnership. The question arises in two circumstances:

• the company partner and the partnership have different accounting dates, or
• the functional currency of the partnership differs from that of the company partner. For example, a company that prepares accounts in sterling may have an investment in a partnership that prepares financial statements in US dollars.

Our view is that paragraph 19(4) requires the company partner to imagine itself as 'standing in the shoes' of the partnership. The company is not required to substitute its own accounting date, or its own functional currency, for that of the partnership.

Case law on deeming provisions shows that the application of a 'statutory fiction' should be carried only so far as is necessary for the purposes of the statute. The purpose of the deeming exercise in paragraph 19(4) [now s. 381(2)-(4)] is to compute the debits or credits accruing to the company partner, in a way that takes account of the particular circumstances of that company. There is no need, in doing this, to pretend that the partnership does not exist at all.

Example 1 illustrates how a company partner's loan relationships debits and credits are calculated where its accounting date differs from that of the partnership. Example 2 illustrates the computation where the partnership has a different functional currency.

Example 1

X Ltd is a trading company with an accounting date of 31 December. It is a partner in a partnership P, which prepares accounts to 31 March. It does not account for its investment in P on a mark to market basis.

On 1 May 2003, the partnership acquires a zero coupon bond (issued by an unconnected company). The partnership accounts for the bond on an accruals basis. Its accounts show a credit of £50,000 in the year to 31 March 2004 in respect of accrued discount on the bond, and a similar credit of £80,000 in the year to 31 March 2005.

X Ltd is entitled to 50% of the profits of P in the year to 31 March 2004, but to only 25% in the year to 31 March 2005.

Step 1 – calculate gross credits

Under paragraph 19(4) [now s. 381(2)–(4)], the 'gross credits' are computed as if the zero coupons bond were a creditor loan relationship to which X Ltd is a party for the purposes of its own trade. The company must account for this deemed loan relationship on an authorised accruals basis (paragraph 19(10)).

[Note: para. 19(10) was omitted by FA 2004, s. 52 and Sch. 10, para. 35(2) and repealed by FA 2004, s. 326 and FA 2004, s. 326, Pt. 2(6) while para. 19(11) [now CTA 2009, s. 382] was amended so as to require companies with interests in partnerships which are fair valued to follow fair value accounting for their share of the partnership profits.]

 X Ltd (and any other company partner) computes 'gross credits' for periods of account ending on 31 March.

X Ltd therefore has gross trading loan relationship credits of £50,000 in the year to 31 March 2004, and £80,000 in the year to 31 March 2005.

The company is not required to work out the discount that would accrue on the bond in year ended 31 December 2003, or subsequent accounting periods.

Step 2 – compute the 'appropriate share' of gross credits for each AP of X Ltd

Paragraph 19(6) [now CTA 2009, s. 381(6)–(7)] says that apportionment of gross credits between partners is to be according to the shares that would be found by S114(2) ICTA88 [now CTA 2009, s. 1262(1), (2), (4) and 1265(1) and (2)]. Although paragraph 19(2) [now CTA 2009, s. 380(2), (3)] disapplies s. 114(1) ICTA88 [now across various sections within CTA 2009] where loan relationships are concerned, the apportionment rules in s. 114(2) continue to apply, including the provision for apportioning profits or losses to the corresponding accounting periods of the company.

X Ltd's apportioned credits are £25,000 (50% × £50,000) for the year to 31 March 2004, and £20,000 (25% × £80,000) for the year to 31 March 2005.

X Ltd will therefore need to time-apportion these sums between its own accounting periods, and bring in:

Year ended 31 December 2003: 275/366 × £25,000 = £18,784

Year ended 31 December 2004: (91/366 × £25,000) + (275/365 × £20,000) = £21,284

Example 2

Y plc is entitled to 40% of the profits of a partnership, Q. Y plc accounts in sterling; partnership Q accounts in dollars. Both Y plc and Q prepare accounts to 31 December. Y plc uses the closing rate/net investment method to translate its investment in the partnership, using an average exchange rate for the year to translate its share of Q's profit into sterling.

In the year to 31 December 2004, Q borrows $5 million from a bank. The bank is not connected with Y plc or any other company partner. Interest of $200,000 is payable on the loan during the period.

During the year the partnership sold goods to a customer for €10,000. The invoice remained unpaid at the year end. Q translated the trade debt into dollars at the year end, bringing into its accounts an exchange gain of $500.

Step 1 – calculate gross debits and credits

The gross debits and credits are calculated in the functional currency of the partnership. Paragraph 19(10) [not rewritten – see note above] requires an authorised accruals basis to be used. Thus there is a debit of $200,000 in respect of the loan interest. Section 100(1) [now CTA 2009, s. 479(1), (2), (3), 480(1), 481(4)] and (2) [now CTA 2009, s. 481(1), (2), (3)] FA96 also requires exchange differences on the Euro trade debt (which is a money debt, but not a loan relationship) to be accounted for under the loan relationships rules. This gives rise to a gross credit of $500.

Step 2 – apportion gross debits and credits to the company partner

Since Y plc is entitled to 40% of partnership profits, it must bring into account a debit of $80,000 and a credit of $200 (or a net amount of $79,800). In accordance with s. 94AB(1) and (2) FA93 [now CTA 2010, Pt. 2, Ch. 4], this is translated into sterling at the rate used in Y plc's accounts to translate the partnership profits. If the average rate used is, say, $1.6/£, Y plc would show a loan relationship debit of £49,875 (79,800 divided by 1.6) in its tax computations.

Similar principles apply where a partnership is a party to a derivative contract (paragraph 49 Sch 26 FA 2002 [now CTA 2009, s. 619–620]).

Other material: Tax Bulletin TB 62/02

19-220   Treatment of exchange gains and losses

Exchange gains or losses are generally treated in the same way as any other profit or loss from a loan relationship for tax purposes (CTA 2009, s. 328) on the basis on which they are reflected in the company's accounts in accordance with generally accepted accounting standards (CTA 2009, s. 307) but subject to certain exclusions including where the exchange gain or loss arises as a result of the translation of the assets, liabilities, income and expenses of all or part of the company's business from the functional currency of the business, or that part of the business, into another currency, and has been recognised as an item of other comprehensive income (CTA 2009, s. 328(3)).

'Assets, liabilities, income and expenses' and 'item of other comprehensive income' each having the meaning that it has for accounting purposes (CTA 2009, s. 328(3A)).

However, the exclusion in s. 328(3) is not generally applied to company partners, except where FOREX gains and losses are allocated to the partnership's statement of recognised gains and losses, statement of recognised income and expense, statement of changes in equity or statement of income and retained earnings (CTA 2009, s. 384(2)).

Accordingly, unless the exchange gain or loss is so recognised, a company partner must bring credits and debits into account under CTA 2009, Pt. 9 (CTA 2009, s. 384(3)).

Legislation: CTA 2009, s. 384

19-240   Company partners' shares where firm owns deeply discounted securities

Where a partnership holds a deeply discounted security, each partner is treated as beneficially entitled to the share of the security specified as if all of the partners were companies and the security were apportioned in the firm's profit sharing arrangement (CTA 2009, s. 385).

Deeply discounted security is defined by ITTOIA 2005, s. 430.

A 'deeply discounted security' is created if, at the time of issue, the amount payable on redemption or maturity exceeds the issue price by more than one-half of 1% of the amount payable on redemption for every year (or part-year) of the security's life, or 30 years if that is less (ITTOIA 2005, s. 430).

Prior to *Finance Act* 2015, timing of relief in respect of discounts on debt issued to UK companies by a connected company in a non-qualifying territory was postponed until the security was redeemed (former CTA 2009, s. 407).

Section 407 was omitted by FA 2015, s. 25(2)(c), with effect in relation to debtor relationships entered into by a company on or after 3 December 2014, and in relation to debtor relationships entered into by a company before 3 December 2014, where the relevant period (within the meaning of CTA 2009, s. 407) begins on or after 1 January 2016, subject to the transitional provisions in FA 2015, s. 25(9)–(14).

Legislation: CTA 2009, s. 385

19-260   Charitable donations

Charitable donations are to be allocated in accordance with the partnership's profit-sharing arrangements during the accounting period (CTA 2009, s. 1262(2)).

Legislation: CTA 2009, s. 1262

PARTNERSHIPS WITH MIXED MEMBERS

19-280   Excess profit allocation to non-individual partners

A mixed member partnership is a partnership or LLP which has both individual members and non individual members (typically companies but can include trusts or other entities).

The allocation of the partnership's taxable profit or allowable loss for any accounting period is to be in accordance with the firm's profit-sharing arrangements for that period, subject to the provisions of ITTOIA s. 850A and 850B and CTA 2009, s. 1263 and 1264 which reallocate the firm's result to ensure that no partner can have a profit or loss greater than that which accrued to the firm (see ¶19-080).

Despite those provisions, however, it was possible to manipulate the commercial allocation of profits under ITTOIA 2005, s. 850 by the use of a corporate partner controlled by an individual partner. Profits could be diverted to the company from the individual and thus be liable only to corporation tax, rather than the higher income tax rates. Conversely, in a loss situation, the company's share of the loss might be diverted to the individual to gain greater loss relief.

In order to counter these tactics, legislation was brought in by *Finance Act* 2014, with effect from 5 December 2013 except certain provisions (s. 850C(8)(b), (18)(b) and (19)) which come into force on 6 April 2014. The legislation does not apply to mixed membership partnerships in which the individual and non-individual partners are genuinely acting at arm's length and not intending to secure a tax advantage. The legislation aims to treat the individual as the recipient of the entire profits.

Legislation: ITTOIA 2005, s. 850C

19-300   HMRC guidance

HMRC published guidance on these new rules on 27 March 2014, which can be found at *www.gov.uk/government/publications/mixed-membership-partnership-aifms-and-asset-disposal-rules-legislation-day-technical-note-and-guidance*. This guidance supersedes the version originally published with the draft Finance Bill clauses in December 2014, but does not yet appear to have been incorporated into any of the HMRC Manuals.

The guidance contains HMRC's views of the way the legislation is intended to operate and has many examples, some of which are used in this Chapter. It should be noted, however, that HMRC's views of the meaning and operation of the legislation may not always be correct and practitioners should not be afraid to view the guidance critically and to challenge HMRC's approach, where necessary.

Other material: *www.gov.uk/government/publications/mixed-membership-partnership-aifms-and-asset-disposal-rules-legislation-day-technical-note-and-guidance*

19-320   Entry conditions

The rules apply where, for a 'relevant period of account';

- a partnership must make a profit as computed under ITTOIA 2005, s. 849 (see ¶18-060);
- an individual, 'A', must have a profit share or no profits allocated to him for the period under ITTOIA 2005, s. 850 or 850A;
- a 'non-individual' partner 'B' (e.g. a corporate body such as a company or limited liability partnership, or, indeed a body of trustees) has been allocated a profit, (for ease of reference, in the rest of this commentary we will refer to this partner as a 'company or trust'); and
- one of two conditions, X or Y, is met (ITTOIA 2005, s. 850C).

A non-individual for these purposes is effectively defined as any partner of the firm that is not an individual (ITTOIA 2005, s. 850C(6)). The non-individual partner will usually be a company but it is also possible for the non-individuals to be, say, a trust, although for there to be a tax saving the trust would prima facie have to be resident outside the UK, as UK trusts generally pay tax at higher marginal rates than individuals.

Conditions X and Y, broadly, consider whether the profits allocated to B are a deferred profit of A or whether A has power to enjoy those profits.

The effect of the legislation applying is that A's profit share is increased, on a just and reasonable basis, by the amount that one might reasonably consider to be A's deferred profit allocated to B, or profits allocated to B that A has the power to enjoy (ITTOIA 2005, s. 850C(4)). If B is subject to UK income tax or corporation tax, B's profit share is reduced by a corresponding amount (ITTOIA 2005, s. 850C(5) and CTA 2009, s. 1264A) depending on whether B pays income tax or corporation tax.

Condition X: that it is reasonable to suppose that the profit share of the company or trust includes amounts which represent the individual's 'deferred profit', and, as a consequence, his profit share and the 'relevant tax amount' are both less than they would have otherwise been; or

Condition Y:
- the company or trust's profit share exceeds the 'appropriate notional profit';
- the individual has the power to enjoy that profit share, and;
- it is reasonable to suppose that part at least of that profit share is attributable to the individual's 'power to enjoy' and both the individual's profit share and the 'relevant tax amount' are lower than they would have been in the absence of that power.

(ITTOIA 2005, s. 850C(1)–(3))

Legislation: ITTOIA 2005, s. 850C

19-340   Condition X

Condition X requires that it be reasonable to suppose that B's profit share includes or comprises amounts that represent deferred profits of the individual member or members and, as a result, the profit share for the individual or individuals is reduced, as is the overall tax bill (ITTOIA 2005, s. 850C(2)).

Deferred profits

While the concept of a deferred profit of the individual appears quite straightforward, it is further defined as including 'any remuneration or other benefits or returns' which would be provided to A but has been deferred including remuneration, etc. which would only accrue to A on the meeting of conditions whether or not these might ever be met (ITTOIA 2005, s. 850C(8)(a)). This means, for example, where profits are held by a corporate member of a partnership to be distributed in due course to the individual partners, as and when their profit share has been determined, perhaps in the light of future events, it is not possible to defer the taxation of those profits in this way (except for special rules for alternative investment finance managers (AIFMs), see **Chapter 17**).

HMRC's guidance (at example 1) refers to a deferred remuneration scheme, involving Kate, who is a member of XYZ LLP. She is awarded a bonus that is conditional upon the successful outcome of a project she has been involved in. In the interim, the bonus is initially allocated to XYZ Corporate Member Ltd. HMRC's view is that this is a deferred profit arrangement, to which the new rules will apply, so that the profit is treated as Kate's profits immediately. The fact that the award of the profit share is conditional upon a future event does not alter the position.

However, it should be noted that there does not appear to be any mechanism whereby Kate can claim back any tax if the profit share is not eventually awarded to her. If her profit share in a future period is reduced in a commensurate manner, the position might unwind that way. Otherwise, it may be necessary to claim an adjustment on the basis of cases such as *IR Commrs v Gardner Mountain & D'Ambrumenil, Ltd.* (1) (1947) 29 TC 69 or the more recent Upper Tribunal decision in *R & C Commrs v Martin* [2014] BTC 527.

It is also possible for profits to be allocated to a corporate member that represent the deferred profits of more than one member, possibly all the members of the partnership, with a view to allocation at a later date. These will be allocated to the individuals on a just and reasonable basis in such cases, on the basis that these profits, too, satisfy condition X (ITTOIA 2005, s. 850C(8)(b)).

HMRC's example 2 demonstrates this in the hypothetical Y LLP, with 50 individual members and a corporate member. In the first part of the example, it is suggested that the profits allocated to the corporate member will be tracked according to each individual's profit entitlement for the year and those profits will be made available to them to draw when they retire. In such cases, the tracked amounts will be chargeable on them under ITTOIA 2005, s. 850C(4).

In the second part of the example, the amount any partner can take on retirement will be a matter for discussion at that time. In that case, the profits must be allocated for assessment on the individuals on a just and reasonable basis, as required by ITTOIA 2005, s. 850C(8)(b).

Reduction of tax

An important point to note is the requirement that the overall result must be a reduction in the overall tax charge. Specifically, the 'relevant tax amount' must be less than it would have been, as a result of the deferred profit arrangements (ITTOIA 2005, s. 850C(2)(b)). The relevant tax amount is the sum of the tax that would have been paid by the individual and non-individual members on their income as members of the firm (ITTOIA 2005, s. 850C(9)). It is assumed that this does not take National Insurance contributions into account, as these are not generally considered to be tax.

This means that partnerships involving UK trusts are unlikely to be caught, simply because UK trusts invariably pay income tax at the highest possible rate, currently 45%, so it is unlikely that there would be any tax saving.

Similarly, even with a corporate member, allocating profits to a limited company (and subsequently withdrawing the profits by way of dividend) may not trigger Condition X, particularly following the abolition of the dividend tax credit and increase in rates of income tax on dividend income from 6 April 2016. It is, therefore, important to check the numbers before assuming that Condition X applies. If Condition X does not apply, because there is no overall tax saving, then Condition Y cannot apply, either, as it has an identical requirement.

Legislation: ITTOIA 2005, s. 850C

Cases: *R & C Commrs v Martin* [2014] BTC 527

19-360   Condition Y

Condition Y must be considered even if Condition X is not in point.

Condition Y looks for an excess of the company or trust's profit share over what would be an 'appropriate notional profit'.

Entry conditions

Condition Y has four components (ITTOIA 2005, s. 850C(3)):

- B's share must exceed the 'appropriate notional profit';
- A must have the power to 'enjoy' the profit share attributed to B;
- it must be reasonable to suppose that the whole or part of the profit share allocated to the non-individual is attributable to the fact that the individual or individuals can 'enjoy' those profits; and
- the profit shares of the individuals and the overall tax charge must be lower than they would be if A could not 'enjoy' the profit share of B (this is identical to the requirements of Condition X).

The essence of Condition Y is to permit a non-individual member to have a profit share related to the commercial contribution that it makes to the earning of those profits. In genuine arm's-length cases, it is likely that there will be no restriction on the profits allocated to the non-individual member.

The appropriate notional profit

The 'appropriate notional profit' is the aggregate of the 'appropriate notional return on capital' and the 'appropriate notional consideration for services' (ITTOIA 2005, s. 850C(10)).

Appropriate notional return on capital

The appropriate notional return on capital is defined as being the return on capital which the non-individual member could reasonably expect for their contribution to the partnership, calculated by reference to the time value of money at a commercial rate of interest, and taking all the circumstances into account (ITTOIA 2005, s. 850C(11)(a) and (12)). Subtracted from this amount is any amounts actually received by the non-individual in respect of that contribution. In other words, the profit share that can be allocated to the non-individual member is a reasonable rate of interest on the capital less any interest actually paid by the firm as such.

The contribution to the firm to be taken into account is given by ITA 2007, s. 108 (ITTOIA 2005, s. 850C(13)), and is the amount of capital which the non-individual member has contributed, less amounts previously received or drawn back, amounts that B draws out or receives back within five years of the relevant time, amounts that the member is entitled to receive or draw back whilst still a member of the firm, or amounts which may be reimbursed to the firm. This effectively forces the non-individual member to have a capital account with the partnership, alongside any current account it may have, on which it is not entitled to draw, in order to establish a contribution on which a reasonable rate of return might be allocated.

HMRC's example on this point is example 3. It refers to a company, B Ltd that has invested £10,000 in ABC LLP and is not paid any interest on this amount. ABC LLP apparently is able to borrow from the banks at an interest rate of 2%, because it is a good borrower, so HMRC tell us that 2% is an appropriate commercial rate of interest to apply to the capital contribution from the company, so that the appropriate notional return in this context to the corporate member would be £200 per year.

However, this would seem to be an absurd answer. It is highly likely that a loan to an LLP by the banks is, for example, secured on personal assets of the individual members, or indeed on assets of the partnership itself, and it is generally given on very formal and prescriptive terms, in return for the relatively low rate of interest (during 2014 and 2015 actual business interest rates far exceeded the rate used in HMRC's example). In contrast the contribution by the company to the firm is likely to be unsecured, not payable within any particular period of time albeit notionally probably repayable on demand, such that it might be perfectly reasonable to suggest a much higher rate of interest on the basis that the risk associated with an unsecured loan with no specific repayment terms is much greater.

HMRC's example would, therefore, appear to be incorrect on any sensible analysis.

Appropriate notional consideration for services

The 'appropriate notional consideration for services' is the arm's-length consideration which the non-individual would receive for any services that it provides to the firm during the relevant period, on the assumption that it is not a partner in the firm, less any amounts actually received for such services (ITTOIA 2005, s. 850C(15) and (16)). HMRC's guidance suggests that this will usually only involve the cost to the non-individual in providing those services plus a modest mark-up, although HMRC evidently also accept the possibility of an arm's-length charge for services.

HMRC's example 5 involves a corporate member of a farming LLP which has a general trade of leasing equipment to farms. HMRC accept that the appropriate notional consideration for services provided by that company as a member of the partnership would be the arm's-length consideration that it would charge third parties for the same services provided to them.

In example 6, HMRC have a farming partnership where the corporate member of the partnership owns some of the land from which the farming trade is carried out. No other services are provided in the example, and no rent is actually paid. It is accepted that the appropriate notional consideration for services would be the arm's-length rent for the land.

If a market value rent were being paid, this would be the company's recompense for the use of the land and there would be no appropriate notional consideration for services.

Case study 1: two siblings were farming some land in partnership with their father's Will Trust. The non-individual in that case was a UK resident trust, which meant that there was no reduction in the tax bill by virtue of sums allocated to the trust, as it paid income tax at the highest possible rate on consideration received, so the new legislation would not have been invoked.

Where services are also provided by a member of the firm as well as by the non-individual, the services are to be ignored (ITTOIA 2005, s. 850C(17)).

HMRC's example 4 has ABC LLP with B Ltd as a corporate member providing advertising services for the LLP. The work is actually carried out for B Ltd by an individual, A, who is also a member of the partnership. In these circumstances, the contribution is ignored and there is no appropriate notional consideration for services.

The contrast with example 5, above, is that the services in example 5 are genuinely provided by the company, which has a real trade apart from its membership of the partnership.

The power to enjoy

Condition Y only applies if A has the power to 'enjoy' B's profit share. There are several parts to this test.

An individual partner has the power to enjoy the profit share of a company or trust if:

- he is connected with the company or trust (as defined by ITA 2007, s. 993);
- he is party to arrangements (widely defined and regardless of their enforceability), the main purpose or one of the main purposes of which is to secure that an amount included in a company partner's profit share is subject to corporation tax rather than income tax and also where the aim is to access a relief only available to corporation tax payers; or
- any of the 'enjoyment conditions' is met in respect of any part of the company or trust's profit share (with references to the individual including any person connected to that individual, other than the company or the trustees themselves).

(ITTOIA 2005, s. 850C(18))

Connection

A can 'enjoy' B's profit share, if A is connected with B (ITTOIA 2005, s. 850C(18)(a)), within the meaning of the standard definition of connection in ITA 2007, s. 993.

For these purposes, s. 993(4), that states that persons are connected if they are in partnership, is ignored. Given the nature of these provisions overall, all members of mixed partnerships would be connected with each other by virtue of s. 993(4), so, unless it is necessary to ignore the provision in looking at whether persons are connected for these purposes, A would always have the power to enjoy these profit shares under such circumstances!

> **Case study 2:** The scenario (which mirrors HMRC's example 11) was a situation where two dentists decided to go into partnership. Prior to that, one of them, Jemima, operated as a sole trader and the other operated through a limited company, Puddleduck Ltd. If they went into partnership, they would be a mixed partnership, with an individual and a company carrying on a dental practice. However, at least in the context of connection, since Jemima was not connected with Puddleduck Ltd, there was no question of this test of enjoyment applying to this partnership.

Arrangements to secure corporation tax treatment

The second enjoyment test is whether A is party to arrangements which have a main purpose to secure that B's profit share is chargeable to corporation tax, not income tax, or is subject to the corporation tax rules rather than the income tax rules (ITTOIA 2005, s. 850C(18)(b)). Arrangements, as always in these sorts of provisions, 'includes any agreement, understanding, scheme, transaction or series of transactions (whether or not legally enforceable)' (ITTOIA 2005, s. 850C(19)).

HMRC's guidance explains that this is targeted at schemes designed to allocate profits to corporate partners that can then access specific reliefs to reduce their corporation tax liabilities, such as R&D allowances, amortisation of goodwill, etc. The guidance does not contain any examples, although it does state that this provision does not postulate any economic connection between the parties.

It is noticeable that this provision is very widely drawn. If we refer to the example of Jemima and Puddleduck Ltd, both will be party to arrangements to ensure that an appropriate proportion of the profit accrues to Puddleduck Ltd. But, of course, we are only likely to be looking at this test if the amount of profit allocated to Puddleduck Ltd were in excess of the appropriate notional profit, which is itself unlikely.

Enjoyment conditions

Finally, we need to see if any part of B's profit share is subject to any of the enjoyment conditions (s. 850C(18)(c)).

The enjoyment conditions in respect of the company or trust's (B) profit share (or part thereof) are that:

- it is dealt with in such a way that, at some time, it will enure for the benefit of the individual (A), whether in the form of income or otherwise;
- it is received or accrued so as to increase the value of assets held by A or for his benefit;
- A receives or becomes entitled to receive a benefit of any kind out of the profit share, however indirectly;

- on the exercise of a power by any person, A becomes entitled to beneficial enjoyment of the profit share; or
- A is able to control the application of the profit share, in whatever manner and however indirectly.

(ITTOIA 2005, s. 850C(20)–(21))

In the above enjoyment tests, A is to be read as including any person connected with A (apart, of course, from B) (ITTOIA 2005, s. 850C(21)).

These enjoyment tests are taken directly from the legislation relating to the transfer of assets abroad. They essentially refer to any way in which A is advantaged or potentially advantaged by the receipt or accrual of profits to the non-individual member of a partnership.

Taking a company wholly owned by an individual, for example:

- any profit received by or accrued to the company increases the value of that company, which is an asset owned by the individual, satisfying s. 850C(20)(b);
- the individual could exercise his power at any time to vote a dividend from the company, so satisfying s. 850C(20)(d);
- as the 100% shareholder, the individual can control the application of the company's profit share, satisfying s. 850C(20)(e).

Conversely, looking at Case study 2 above, Jemima has no interest in or power over Puddleduck Ltd, so she satisfies none of the enjoyment conditions.

HMRC's example 14 is helpful in explaining when the enjoyment conditions would not apply.

The example involves an LLP comprising three individuals and X Plc. One of the individuals owns shares in X Plc as part of a share portfolio, and other received shares under an incentive scheme when she used to work for X Plc. There are no arrangements by which those individuals can benefit from the profit share of X Plc and it would not be reasonable to suppose that the small shareholdings by those individuals have in any way influenced the profit share that X Plc is allocated.

It might be true to say that profits allocated to X Plc have the potential to increase the value of the shares held by the two individuals, but the example highlights the fact that this must still link in with the other tests for condition Y to apply. In other words, it is not reasonable to suppose that the profits are allocated to X Plc because the individuals had any power to enjoy those profits because their small shareholdings would not give them such power over X Plc. Therefore, the guidance states that HMRC would not consider condition Y to apply in these circumstances.

Legislation: ITTOIA 2005, s. 850C

19-380   Counteraction: reallocation of profits

To counteract the mischief targeted by these provisions, A's profit share must be increased by the amount that it is reasonable to suppose was allocated to B as either A's deferred profit, or attributable to A's power to enjoy the excess over the appropriate notional profit. The increase in A's profit share is determined on a just and reasonable basis (ITTOIA 2005, s. 850C(4)). There can be no double counting, so that it is not possible to increase A's profit by an amount of deferred profit and again because that profit exceeds the appropriate notational profit. And the amount of increase in A's profit share by virtue of its power to enjoy cannot exceed the excess over the appropriate notional profit for B.

Also to avoid double taxation, if B is an income tax payer its taxable profits under ITTOIA 2005, s. 850–850B are to be reduced by amounts that are just and reasonable to take into account the increase in profits to A (ITTOIA 2005, s. 850C(5)).

Where B pays corporation tax, CTA 2009, s. 1264A has the same effect in adjusting the profits calculated under CTA 2009, s. 1262–1264, making such adjustments as are just and reasonable to take into account the increase of profits charged on A under s. 850C(4).

If the accounting periods of the company are not co-terminus with that of the partnership, adjustments of the corporation tax profits are to be made for all accounting periods in which the relevant period of account falls (CTA 2009, s. 1264A(2)(b)).

Legislation: ITTOIA 2005, s. 850C; CTA 2009, s. 1264A

19-400   Excess profit allocation to 'individuals who are not partners' (Anti-avoidance)

There is a separate set of provisions (at ITTOIA 2005, s. 850D), which apply where a partnership consists only of non-individuals, with the persons who might otherwise have been partners acting through those non-individuals. Typically, this would be a partnership of companies each wholly owned by an individual who one might assume would otherwise have been a partner, directly.

Gateway provisions

These provisions apply if (ITTOIA 2005, s. 850D(1)):

(a)   an individual, A, personally performs services for the firm at any time during a period of account;

(b)   if A had been a partner throughout the period of account, A would have had a profit under the calculation under ITTOIA 2005, s. 849;

(c)   a non-individual partner, B, has a share of that profit, calculated according to s. 850 and, if relevant, ITTOIA 2005, s. 850A (ITTOIA 2005, s. 850D(7));

(d)   it is reasonable to suppose that A would have been a partner in the firm but for the provisions at ITTOIA 2005, s. 850C (see ¶19-280ff.);

(e)   one of conditions X or Y is met.

Condition X: that it is reasonable to suppose that the profit share of the company or trust includes amounts which represent the individual's 'deferred profit';

Condition Y:

  – the company or trust's profit share exceeds the 'appropriate notional profit';
  – the individual has the 'power to enjoy' that profit share, and;
  – it is reasonable to suppose that part at least of that profit share is attributable to the individual's 'power to enjoy'.

(ITTOIA 2005, s. 850D(1)–(3))

The terms 'deferred profit', 'appropriate notional profit' and 'power to enjoy' have the same meanings as described in ¶19-340 and ¶19-360.

It is assumed that condition (d), above, is met if A is a member of a partnership associated with the firm during the relevant period of account (ITTOIA 2005, s. 850D(8)). An associated partnership is one which is a member of the firm or is a member of another partnership which is associated with the firm (ITTOIA 2005, s. 850D(9)).

In the above provisions, partnership includes a limited liability partnership

(ITTOIA 2005, s. 850D(10)).

Avoidance of ITTOIA 2005, s. 850C

The critical requirement of s. 850D is in subsection (1)(d), the requirement that it be reasonable to suppose that A would have been a partner directly, had it not been for the mixed partnership provisions at ITTOIA 2005, s. 850C. This has a number of interesting consequences. Firstly, any partnership set up in this way before the provisions were enacted, or at least before any of the detail was announced, cannot be caught. A person cannot be said to have set up a structure, as described by ITTOIA 2005, s. 850D, in order to avoid anti-avoidance rules that did not exist at the time the partnership was set up.

Since the legislation came into force on 5 December 2013, albeit only with effect from 6 April 2014, it appears that this means that structures in place by 5 December 2013 are grandfathered.

This is borne out by HMRC's example 29, where the individual members of a firm decided to replace themselves with wholly owned corporate members, instead. HMRC suggest that, even though implementation was not until 12 December 2013, the agreement to do so prior to the publication of the new rules means that s. 850D could not be invoked.

Case study 3: There are a number of commercial structures, often relating to various kinds of fund management, which are invariably partnerships made up only of companies, often wholly owned by brokers or small grounds of brokers. This seems to be the standard commercial structure for a number of these fund management arrangements. Therefore, even if such a structure were set up today, these structures are more likely to be set up purely for the commercial benefits, and not because of the existence of the provisions at ITTOIA 2005, s. 850C and, accordingly, s. 850D should not apply to such structures.

Conditions X and Y

Conditions X and Y are identical to the eponymous conditions in s. 850C (ITTOIA 2005, s. 850D(2), (3), (12) and (13)).

Legislation: ITTOIA 2005, s. 850D

19-420   Counteraction reallocation of profits

Where these conditions are satisfied, the individual is to be treated as a partner in the firm throughout the relevant period of account and his share of the profit of the firm is to be such part of the company or trust's profit share as, on a just and reasonable basis, may be supposed to be attributable to his 'deferred profit' or his 'power to enjoy'.

However, the amount attributable to his 'power to enjoy' is not to exceed;
- the excess of the company or trust's profit share over the 'appropriate notional profit', less
- any increase in that profit share by virtue of the individual's 'deferred profit'.

Again, there is to be no double taxation, such that A can only be allocated a maximum of the excess profits allocated to B over the appropriate notional profit and cannot be charged on both that and an amount of those profits treated as being deferred profits of A.

A's profit share calculated in this way is charged to income tax under the income tax rules for the tax year in which the relevant period of account of the partnership ends. (ITTOIA 2005, s. 850D(4)).

Also to avoid double taxation, if B is an income tax payer its taxable profits under ITTOIA 2005, s. 850–850B are to be reduced by amounts that are just and reasonable to take into account the increase in profits to A (ITTOIA 2005, s. 850D(5)).

Where B pays corporation tax, CTA 2009, s. 1264A has the same effect in adjusting the profits calculated under CTA 2009, s. 1262–1264, making such adjustments as are just and reasonable to take into account the increase of profits charged on A under s. 850D(4). If the accounting periods of the company are not coterminous with that of the partnership, adjustments of the corporation tax profits are to be made for all accounting periods in which the relevant period of account falls (CTA 2009, s. 1264A(2)(b)).

Legislation: ITTOIA 2005, s. 850D; CTA 2009, s. 1264A

19-440 Payments from corporate or trust partners to individual partners (preventing double taxation)

Where adjustments have been made under ¶19-380 or ¶19-420 for tax purposes, the taxable profits will have been allocated in a way which differs from the way the partners have actually shared profits for a period of account. Thus amounts that have actually been received by the company or trust partner have been taxed on the individual partner.

If that individual then extracted profits from their company, this would probably be charged to income tax as a distribution from the company. There are, however, provisions in place to prevent such double taxation (ITTOIA 2005, s. 850E).

Where there has been allocation of profits to the individual member or members under s. 850C(4) or 850E(4) and:

- there is an agreement in place relating to the company or trust partner's (B) profit share under which that partner makes a payment out of its 'excess profit share' (being the amount by which the individual's profit share has been increased); and
- the payment is not made under any arrangements whose main purpose, or one of its main purposes, was the obtaining of a tax advantage (as defined by CTA 2010, s. 1139) for any person, then for income tax purposes:
  - the payment is not income of the recipient;
  - the payment is not taken into account in calculating any profits or losses of B or otherwise deducted from any income of B; and
  - the payment is not to be regarded as a distribution.

(ITTOIA 2005, s. 850E(1)–(2)).

Arrangements include any agreement, understanding, scheme, transaction or series of transactions (whether or not legally enforceable) (ITTOIA 2005, s. 850E(3)).

It is notable that 'arrangements' is defined while 'agreement' is not. The wording, however, is similar to that for payments for group relief (CTA 2010, s. 183), and HMRC have been known to insist that there be some evidence of an agreement to make such payments before accepting that a payment for group relief is to be ignored for tax purposes. So, where taxpayers decide to follow this approach with mixed partnerships, a formal agreement might be advisable.

Legislation: ITTOIA 2005, s. 850E

19-460   Application of excess profit allocation rules to specific situations

Private equity investment

In some cases an outside investor, such as a private equity fund will become a partner, directly or indirectly and inject capital into the firm. If they chose to do so through a corporate vehicle then it may make the firm a mixed membership partnership, but the excess profit allocation rules will not apply as the individual members do not meet the power to enjoy requirement.

Pseudo share schemes

The question has been raised over how the mixed membership partnership legislation applies to schemes that are intended to mimic the effect of a share scheme for employees. Unlike a partnership (including a Scottish partnership) which is simply a relationship between persons, an LLP is a body corporate and can be distinguished from its members. The LLP is governed by the LLP agreement. In some cases, the LLP agreement provides for the LLP to have something comparable to the share capital in a limited company. Other schemes involve buying shares in a limited company linked to the LLP. The excess profit allocation rules will apply where a non-individual member receives a profit share that is used to:

- buy shares of 'units' that are intended as rewards for individual members;
- buy shares or units back from individual members.

International structures

A number of LLPs form part of structures that cross international boundaries. A UK LLP (which is not of itself a mixed membership partnership) may establish a foreign LLP to ring fence an overseas venture. The members of the foreign LLP may be the UK LLP and some or all of the UK LLP's own members. The foreign LLP is a mixed membership partnership because one of its members is not an individual (and the fact that some individual members of foreign LLP may be non-UK resident does not make it a mixed membership partnership). However, even though the foreign LLP may be a mixed membership partnership, the mixed membership legislation is unlikely to apply because the profits of foreign LLP that are allocated to UK LLP are in turn allocated to the members of UK LLP. The relevant tax amount is not lower as a result of the structure.

Legislation: ITTOIA 2005, Pt. 9

19-480 Commencement

The new legislation officially came into force on 5 December 2013, but essentially only affects tax liabilities for periods of account beginning on or after 6 April 2014, subject to the transitional provisions.

The mixed partnership rules at ITTOIA 2005, s. 850C and 805D have effect for periods of account beginning on or after 6 April 2014, with appropriate impact in respect of ITTOIA 2005, s. 850E and CTA 2009, s. 1264A (FA 2014, Sch. 17, para. 12(1)).

If a period of account of a firm straddles 6 April 2014, the period must be split into two notional accounting periods, and the new legislation applied to the period from 6 April 2014 to the end of the period of account (FA 2014, Sch. 17, para. 12 and 13(3) and (4)).

Legislation: FA 2014, Sch. 17, para. 12 and 13

19-500 Mixed partnerships: practical solutions

Incorporation

The most common solution has been to incorporate the business, usually into the existing corporate partner. Prior to announcements made on 3 December 2014, it was often the case that individuals would sell their business to the newly incorporated company, rather than using the incorporation relief at TCGA 1992, s. 162 so as to create a debt outstanding from the company, representing the value of the business transferred in. If that business was a trade, the vendor (i.e. the individual members of the partnership) would only pay capital gains tax at 10%, assuming they qualified for the entrepreneurs' relief. However, to the extent that the assets sold for the company constitute goodwill, entrepreneurs' relief will no longer be available, following the changes in *Finance Act* 2015 (see ¶14-580).

Consequently, more recent incorporations have used the incorporation relief at TCGA 1992, s. 162. Incorporation by transferring the rest of the trade or business to the existing corporate member might not be seen as strictly qualifying for relief under TCGA 1992, s. 162, as that provision strictly requires that the whole of the business be transferred to a company, which cannot be possible if the company already owns part of the business. HMRC responded to the Chartered Institute of Taxation on this point, however, in May 2014, just after the legislation came into effect. They 'would, subject to all the other conditions being satisfied, accept that section 162 can apply to the individual members where an LLP transfers its business to the corporate member in exchange for shares in the corporate member. TCGA 1992, s. 59A(1)(b) treats any dealings by the LLP as those of its members so the transfer of its business by an LLP will be treated as a transfer by its members'.

This advice specifically related to LLPs. However, it is noted that TGCA 1992, s. 59(1)(b) is worded in a very similar way, in respect of ordinary partnerships, to s. 59A, which applies to LLPs and it is, therefore, anticipated that HMRC would take a similar view in respect of the incorporation of such partnerships.

The only difficulty that might arise is where the partnership includes property or, indeed, is perhaps a property investment partnership. In those cases, it is important to ensure that the relevant conditions in FA 2003, Sch. 15 are satisfied to prevent a charge to Stamp Duty Land Tax arising.

Continue with existing structure

The alternative option is to take no restricting action and accept that the individual will be taxed on the profits of the partnership but able to extract funds later from a corporate partner, relying on ITTOIA 2005, s. 850E so that no subsequent tax charge arises. In such cases, it is advisable that a formal agreement is put in place between the corporate member and the individual or individuals, so that HMRC cannot challenge the efficacy of such arrangements on the basis that there is no agreement.

Amend partnership agreement

A third option is to amend the partnership agreement, so that the corporate member has no rights to profits in the partnership. There is no requirement in the *LLP Act* 2000 for a person who is a member of an LLP to also be entitled to share in the profits or capital of that partnership. This point is a little more difficult for ordinary partnerships, as the partnership exists only so long as the relationship between the parties described in the *Partnership Act* 1890, s. 1(1) is in place: 'persons carrying on a business in common with a view of profit'. If the corporate member no longer has any rights to share in any profits, gains or capital or the partnership, and is completely inactive, and contributes no capital to the partnership, it could be suggested that the company and the individual are not carrying on a business in common. This is a difficult legal point, however, if it were not the case that a business was being carried on in common, then a partnership between a company and an individual would effectively dissolve if the corporate member's share is reduced to nothing. So it might be preferable either to incorporate the business completely, or to incorporate an LLP, first, before reducing the company's share to nil.

Legislation: TCGA 1992, s. 59, 59A and 162; *Partnership Act* 1890, s. 1

19-520   Excess loss allocation

The mixed partnerships rules introduced by FA 2014 are also designed to prevent the excess allocation of losses to high taxed individual partners, rather than to low taxed non-individual partners. The provisions are targeted at partnerships including companies, where the allocation of losses to individuals could save tax at up to 45%, in contrast to the 20% rate for corporation tax. HMRC's guidance explains that:

'In a typical case, arrangements are made between a company and wealthy individuals, where the individuals will contribute funding to a business venture in return for the losses generated in the early years of the partnership, perhaps through capital allowances. The losses will be less valuable to the company than to the individuals, who are taxable at higher income tax rates. When the business becomes profitable, the individual members will have their contribution returned and they will withdraw from the partnership.'

The main provision for trading losses is at the *Income Tax Act* 2007, s. 116A, which provides that if in a tax year, an individual, A, makes a loss in trade as a partner in a firm and A's loss arises wholly or partly, directly or indirectly in consequence of, or otherwise in connection with, relevant tax avoidance arrangements, then no relevant tax relief may be given for A's loss (ITA 2007, s. 116A(1) and (2)). The provisions fall with ITA 2007, Pt. 4, Ch. 3 'Restrictions on Trade Loss Relief for Certain Partners' and are discussed further in **Chapter 16**, see ¶25-320ff.

An identical rule preventing excess loss allocation to partners who are not individuals in a UK property business or an overseas property business in a mixed partnership is provided in s. 127C which is also discussed further in **Chapter 16**, see ¶25-540.

Legislation: ITA 2007, s. 116A, 127C

Chapter 11: Assessment to income and corporation tax

20-000 Assessment of partnership to tax

As a partnership is not to be regarded for tax purposes as an entity separate and distinct from the partners; (ITTOIA 2005, s. 848; CTA 2009, s. 1258), it is the partners (individual or company) who are assessed to tax on partnership profits and other income. **Chapter 9** and **10** discuss the computation of partnership profits and allocation of those profits to the individual or corporate partners. Both these stages take place at partnership level and are included in the partnership self-assessment tax return.

The third stage in the process is to assess the partners to income or corporation tax in respect of their allocated share of profits and other income (and to claim relief for losses where appropriate).

Individual partners are assessed to income tax in respect of their allocated share of the partnership profits and other income through their self-assessment returns.

Corporate partners are assessed to corporation tax in respect of their allocated share of the partnership profits and other income through Corporation Tax Self-Assessment returns.

Legislation: ITTOIA 2005, s. 848; CTA 2009, s. 1258

20-020 Assessment to income tax

The basis of assessment to income tax of partnership profits and other income depends on whether the partnership has trading profits and whether the income is taxed or untaxed income.

Firms with trading profits

Trading income: Special basis period rules apply to trading profits allocated to individual partners which treat the share of trade profits allocated to each partner as having been derived from a separate 'notional trade', which that partner carries on alone (ITTOIA 2005, s. 853) (see ¶20-040ff.).

Untaxed income or relievable losses from other sources: Where a partnership carries on a trade and has untaxed income or relievable losses from other (non-trading) sources, the special basis period rules also apply to the partner's allocated share of untaxed other income or losses. The provisions treat any shares of untaxed income as if they are the profits accruing to a trade, the 'notional business', carried on by the partner alone (ITTOIA 2005, s. 854–856) (see ¶20-140).

Note: The 'notional business' rules only determine the basis period for any loss and the loss relief rules appropriate to the particular type of loss determine the way in which it can be relieved.

Taxed income: Although calculated and allocated to partners using the same rules as for trading (and other) income, there are no special basis period rules applying to taxed income. This is assessed on an actual basis (6 April to 5 April) as if the income had arisen to the partner from a personal source rather than from the partnership.

Note: This rule only applies to taxed income other than trading income. Any trading receipt which has had tax deducted at source (e.g. tax suffered under the Construction Industry Scheme) is assessed under the rules applicable for trading income with credit for the tax deducted given for the tax year in which it is deducted.

Firms without trading profits (investment business)

There are no special basis period rules applicable to firms that do not carry on a trade or profession.

Although profits or losses are computed and allocated in the same way as trading or other income, (i.e. calculated under s. 849 as if the partnership were an individual and according to the residence status of the individual partner and allocated under s. 850, according to the profit-sharing arrangements in place during the period), an actual (6 April to 5 April) basis of assessment applies as for individuals.

Legislation: ITTOIA 2005, s. 853–856

20-040   Firms with trading income: concept of the notional trade or business

Profits are computed at partnership level and each individual's share of profits or losses is computed in accordance with his interests in the partnership during that period. Accordingly, the partners are bound by the date to which the partnership prepares accounts. The accounting periods for each partner's notional business corresponds to the partnership accounting periods.

However, each partner is *assessed* on his trading profit (or loss) as if it arose from a separate 'notional trade'. Each partner with trading profits and other untaxed income or relievable losses other than trading profits or losses is also *assessed* on the other income or losses as if it arose from a separate 'notional business' carried on by the individual partner.

The notional trade or business as a concept which exists for the purposes of assessment only was confirmed by the Upper Tribunal (UT) in *R & C Commrs v Vaines* [2016] BTC 502. In the earlier case before the First-tier Tribunal

(FTT), the FTT had allowed Mr Vaines (a partner in an LLP) a deduction for personal expenses (although related to a former partnership business) against his allocated share of his current partnership profits on the basis that the combined effect of the various provisions in ITTOIA 2005, Pt. 9, certainly since the introduction of personal self-assessment, was that 'it is the partners who are treated as carrying out the trade and not the firm itself ... [so] that each partner is carrying on a trade albeit collectively with others and accordingly his profits are taxed on him individually'. The expense was a payment to preserve and protect Mr Vaine's professional career (his trade) and was not capital in nature and could, therefore, be justified as 'wholly and exclusively' incurred by Mr Vaines by reference to 'his' trade. The UT, however, overturned the FTT's decision finding that there was only one trade being the trade carried on by the partners in common and it was by reference to that trade that the expense must be justified. The expense was nothing to do with the business of Mr Vaine's current partnership and was not incurred 'wholly and exclusively' for the purposes of that trade.

The UT noted that the starting point for the assessment of trading profits was provided by ITTOIA 2005, s. 5 which charged to income tax the profits of a trade, profession or vocation. A UK resident individual was chargeable to tax wherever the trade was carried on (s. 6(1)) and the person liable for the tax was the person receiving or entitled to the profits (s. 8). Section 7 provides that tax is charged on the full amount of the profits of the tax year and that these are the profits of the basis period for the tax year (s. 7(2)). The UT further noted that the basis period rules were provided by ITTOIA 2005, Pt. 2, Ch. 15 and the normal basis period rules operate by reference to the date in the tax year by reference to which 12-month accounts are drawn up (s. 198(1) ITTOIA) with specific rules to cover the situation in which a person has started or ceased (or is treated as starting or ceasing) to carry on a trade. Whilst there were particular rules for applying this framework of computation and assessment to partnerships, as a general observation, it was the full amount of the profits of the trade for the basis period that were charged to tax each year. The UT further noted that s. 849 (calculation of firm's profits) referred to 'a firm carries on a trade' and the application to LLP's by s. 863(1)(a), treating activities carried on by an LLP 'as carried on in partnership by its members' did nothing to indicate that it was Mr Vaines was carrying on the trade alone 'in fact, quite the opposite.'

> 'The concept that there is one trade carried on by the partners in common (or by the members as partners) is consistent with the idea that it is the profits of the trade that are charged to tax, albeit that the scope of that charge may depend upon the residence of the persons who from time to time are carrying it on. The profits of that one trade are computed and charged and section 850 then provides the natural link to the partners who are chargeable in respect of them according to the LLP's profit-sharing arrangements for the period.

> 'If each partner was to be treated as carrying on his or her "notional trade" as a general matter, it might raise the question whether a partner could adjust the deemed profits of the notional trade (being the allocated share of the partnership's profits). However, it is plain from section 852 ITTOIA (and section 111(4) ICTA before it) that the "notional trade" is a construct designed for the purposes of the basis period rules only.

Thus, the concept of a "notional trade" is, as we have explained, to enable Mr Vaines to self-assess tax on his share of the profits of the partnership trade by reference to the correct basis period.

It is, however, as the language of the Act recognises, a notional trade only for the purposes of assessment. The actual trade remains that of the partners collectively and it is the profits of that collective trade that must be computed before being allocated or shared among partners to provide each partner's share of the profit that is the profit of their notional trades for the purposes of their self-assessment.'

Legislation: ITTOIA 2005, s. 852

20-060   Firms with trading income: notional trades for individual partners

For each tax year in which a firm carries on an actual trade, each partner's share of trading profits (or losses) is treated as profits (or losses) of a notional trade carried on by the partner alone (ITTOIA 2005, s. 852). This fictional trade created by the legislation has a number of consequences, considered below.

Start of notional trade

A partner is normally treated as starting to carry on the notional trade at the time of becoming a partner in the firm but the notional trade cannot begin before the start of the actual trade (ITTOIA 2005, s. 852(2)).

If, however, the partner has been carrying on the trade as a sole trader before it is carried on by the partnership then the date on which the actual trade began is treated as the date on which the notional trade began (ITTOIA 2005, s. 852(3)).

End of notional trade

A partner is normally treated as ceasing to carry on the notional trade at the time of ceasing to be a partner in the firm or (if earlier) at the time when the firm permanently ceases to carry on the trade. However, if the partner continues to carry on the trade as a sole trader after it is carried on by the partnership then the date on which the actual trade ceases is treated as the date on which the notional trade ceases (ITTOIA 2005, s. 852(4), (5)).

Legislation: ITTOIA 2005, s. 852

> **Example**
>
> Mary and Albert are in business as partners. In April, Albert leaves the partnership and in July, Elizabeth joins Mary in partnership. The same trade is carried on throughout.
>
> There is no discontinuance of the business either in April when Albert leaves or in July when Elizabeth joins, as, in both cases, Mary continues to carry on the business both before and after the change.
>
> Albert's notional business ceases in April when he leaves the partnership and Elizabeth's notional business commences in July when she joins the partnership.

Change of notional trade on becoming or ceasing to be resident

A special rule applies if the firm is carrying on the actual trade wholly or partly outside the UK and a partner starts or ceases to be resident in the UK. In such a case, the partner whose residence status changes is treated, at the time of change of residence, as permanently ceasing to carry on one notional trade and as beginning another (ITTOIA 2005, s. 852(6)).

This rule does not stop the partner from carrying forward a loss from before the change of residence and setting it against a profit arising after that change (ITTOIA 2005, s. 852(7)).

Legislation: ITTOIA 2005, s. 852

20-080　Notional trades: basis periods

In computing the business profits of the partnership, the normal basis period rules for business profits (or losses) apply (ITTOIA 2005, s. 853(1)). Thus when a partner joins a partnership, he is chargeable:

(1)　for the first year, on his share of the profits for the period from the date he joined the partnership to the following 5 April;

(2)　for the second year, on whichever of the five possible bases applies:
   (i)　If the business ends in year 2, the basis period for that second year will be the period from 6 April at the start of the second year to the date of cessation of trading (ITTOIA 2005, s. 202(2)). This may be referred to as an 'actual basis'.
   (ii)　If the accounting date in year 2 falls less than 12 months from commencement (and assuming the trade does not cease in the second year) the basis period will be the first 12 months of trading (ITTOIA 2005, s. 200(2)). This will always mean that profits for a certain period of time (from the date on which the trade starts to 5 April at the end of the first year) will be taxed twice in both the first year and the second year. These

profits are known as 'overlap' profits and, briefly, are eligible for relief on certain changes of accounting date or on cessation of the business.

(iii) If the accounting date in year 2 falls not less than 12 months from commencement (and assuming the trade does not cease in the second year) the basis period will be the 12-month period ending with the accounting date in the tax year (under the general rule under ITTOIA 2005, s. 200(3)).

(iv) If there is a change of accounting date in year 2 and accounts are drawn up to more than one date then only the latest of the dates is to be treated as an accounting date for the purpose of working out the basis periods (ITTOIA 2005, s. 197(2)). If that later date falls at least 12 months from the start of trading, the basis period is the 12 months to that date. If not, then the basis period is the 12 months from commencement.

(v) If there is no accounting date in year 2 (and no cessation of trade in the year) then the tax year itself is the basis period (ITTOIA 2005, s. 200(4)). This is sometimes referred to as an 'actual basis'.

(3) for subsequent years, his share of the profits for the 12-month accounting period ending in that year.

Each partner will be entitled to his own amount of overlap relief, which will vary from partner to partner.

Where a partner leaves a partnership, the basis of assessment for the final year is the sum of his share of profits for the period from the accounting date in the previous year to the date he leaves the partnership.

Legislation: ITTOIA 2005, s. 197, 200, 202, 853

20-100 Notional trades: basis periods – change of accounting date

Any change of accounting date or any accounting change of the partnership's trade also applies to each individual partner (ITTOIA 2005, s. 853(2)). Where there is a change of accounting date, the partnership must apply the rules for a change of accounting date as if it were an individual.

Main rule

The main rule is that where there is a change from an old to a new accounting date, the change occurs in the earlier of:

• the first tax year in which accounts are drawn up to the new date; or
• the first tax year in which accounts are *not* made up to the old date.

This means that an accounting date change may be recognised in a tax year in which no accounts are made up (ITTOIA 2005, s. 214(1)).

Change of accounting date in third year

A particular rule sometimes applies if there is a change of accounting date in the third tax year in which a business is carried on (ITTOIA 2005, s. 215). A change of accounting date may occur in the third tax year even if no accounts are in fact drawn up to a date in that tax year. The rule will only apply if the accounting date (or deemed accounting date where accounts are drawn up to a particular day rather than date) falls more than 12 months after the end of the basis period for the previous (i.e. second) tax year. Where this condition is met, the basis period for the third year will run from the day after the end of the basis period for the second year and will end on the new accounting date in the year.

This rule will not apply if, in that tax year, the person ceases permanently to carry on the trade (in which the basis period begins immediately after the basis period for the previous tax year and ends on the date of the permanent cessation of the trade (ITTOIA 2005, s. 202(1))).

Change of accounting date in later year

Different rules apply where there is a change of accounting date after the third year. Once more, this rule will not apply if, in that tax year, the person ceases permanently to carry on the trade (see above).

There are three possible ways in which the basis period may need to be calculated. These depend on whether the conditions of ITTOIA 2005, s. 217 are met or not. Those conditions are:

(1)   The person carrying on the trade must give notice to HMRC of the change. Notice must be given in the tax return which must be submitted within the statutory time limit (ITTOIA 2005, s. 217(2)). It is, therefore, possible for a person to change the date for accounting purposes but retain the original date for tax purposes by not giving notice.

In the case of a partnership, one partner may be nominated to give the required notice and to appeal against a decision that the change is not made for bona fide commercial reasons (ITTOIA 2005, s. 853(3)).

(2)   The period of account ending with the new accounting date cannot be longer than 18 months. This test is usually applied to the period ending with the accounting date in the tax year in which the change of date takes place but if there is no accounting date in that year, then the test is applied to the period of account ending with the new accounting date in the first tax year in which the accounts are drawn up to the new date.

(3)   Either:
    (i)   there has been no change of accounting date recognised for tax purposes within the five years preceding the year in which the current change takes place; or

(ii) the change is made 'for commercial reasons' (as defined in ITTOIA 2005, s. 218 and in respect of which obtaining a tax advantage is not a commercial reason) and the notice of change sets out those reasons (ITTOIA 2005, s. 217(6)).

Conditions for change met: new date less than 12 months from end of previous basis period

If the conditions of ITTOIA 2005, s. 217 are met and the new accounting date falls less than 12 months from the end of the basis period for the previous year the basis period will be given by the general rule in ITTOIA 2005, s. 198. As such, the basis period will be the 12-month period ending with the new accounting date (ITTOIA 2005, s. 216(2)).

Conditions for change met: new date more than 12 months from end of previous basis period

If the conditions of ITTOIA 2005, s. 217 are met and the new accounting date falls more than 12 months from the end of the basis period for the previous year the basis period will run from the day after the end of the basis period for the previous tax year and will end with the new accounting date (ITTOIA 2005, s. 216(3)).

Conditions for change not met

If the conditions of ITTOIA 2005, s. 217 are not met then the change of accounting date is ignored and the basis period will continue to be the 12-month period ending with the old accounting date (ITTOIA 2005, s. 216(4)). This would be the case, for example, if the trader failed to give due notice to HMRC of the change of accounting date (as this is one of the conditions for recognising a change).

In the case of new partners, the commencement rules are applied in order to determine a basis period, with the modification that the accounting date is taken to be the old, rather than the new, accounting date.

Example

Alan and Brian are in partnership, having always made up their accounts to 31 December. On 1 March 2015, Charles is admitted to the partnership. Accounts are made up to 30 June 2015, and 30 June is then retained as the accounting date. All the necessary conditions of ITTOIA 2005, s. 217 are satisfied.

Alan and Brian's position is as follows:

Tax year	Basis period	Statutory reference
2014–15	year ending 31 December 2014	ITTOIA 2005, s. 198(1)
2015–16	12 months to 30 June 2015	ITTOIA 2005, s. 198(1)
2016–17	year ending 30 June 2016	ITTOIA 2005, s. 198(1)

Charles's position is as follows:

Tax year	Basis period	Statutory reference
2014–15	1/3/15–5/4/15	ITTOIA 2005, s. 199
2015–16	1/3/15–29/2/16	ITTOIA 2005, s. 200(2)
2016–17	year ending 30 June 2016	ITTOIA 2005, s. 198(1)

Thereafter, Charles's basis period will be governed by ITTOIA 2005, s. 198, unless there is a subsequent qualifying change of accounting date. He will also be entitled to overlap relief in respect of the profits which have been taxed more than once.

Legislation: ITTOIA 2005, s. 197, 200, 202, 214–218, 853

20-120   Notional trades: basis period – start-up payments

Special rules apply to the interaction of overlap relief and certain 'start-up' payments. These rules provide that if a person carrying on a trade receives a business start-up payment in a period which falls within two basis periods, and the payment is not a lump sum, then the payment is brought into account in calculating the profits of the trade of the first period (and is not brought into account in calculating the profits of the trade of the second basis period).

Those same rules are applied in the case of a partner (ITTOIA 2005, s. 853(4)) so that:

- the requirement in ITTOIA 2005, s. 207(1)(a) (that the start up payment is received in a period which falls within two basis periods) becomes a requirement that the partner's share of the firm's profits, so far as attributable to a business start-up payment, falls within two basis periods; and
- the reference in s. 207(2) to the payment is a reference to any part of the partner's share of the firm's profits which is so attributable.

Legislation: ITTOIA 2005, s. 207, 853

20-140   Firms with trading and other source income

Untaxed income or relievable losses from other sources in respect of firms which have trading income is treated in the same way as trading income and is allocated according to the profit-sharing arrangements during the basis period (ITTOIA 2005, s. 854–856). This is achieved by treating untaxed income as if it were profits or gains of a 'notional business' which commences when the individual becomes a partner and ceases when he ceases to be a partner.

All shares of untaxed income are therefore assessed using the same basis periods, and overlap relief is pooled between those sources. Each separate source of untaxed income is treated as continuing until the notional business is treated as permanently discontinued. This means that no commencement or cessation rules are required for individual sources of untaxed income.

For these purposes, 'untaxed income' is defined to include any income from which income tax has neither been deducted nor treated as paid or deducted, but excluding dividends or other distributions taxable under ITTOIA 2005, Pt. 4, Ch. 3 (Dividends, etc. from UK resident companies, etc.).

Example

The trading partnership of Bert and Fred has always made up accounts to 31 December, until it changes its accounting date by drawing up accounts for the six months to 30 June 2014. The following amounts of untaxed interest have been received by the partnership:

Date of receipt	Amount £
30 June 2012	500
31 December 2012	600
30 June 2013	620
31 December 2013	590
30 June 2014	700
31 December 2014	510
30 June 2015	630

The assessments will be as follows:

Tax year	Basis period	Amount £
2012–13	year ending 31/12/12	1,100
2013–14	year ending 31/12/13	1,210
2014–15	12 months to 30/6/14	1,290
2015–16	year ending 30/6/15	1,140

In addition, Bert and Fred will each have overlap relief in respect of their share of the £590, which has been assessed in both 2013–14 and 2014–15.

The accounts basis of assessment applies only whilst the associated trading business is carried on by a partnership (ITTOIA 2005, s. 854(1)(a)) – thus, the notional business is deemed to commence whenever a partnership is first formed, and is deemed to cease when a partnership is permanently dissolved.

Overlap relief

The notional business rules only determine the basis periods for shares of untaxed income. Therefore, in the absence of any rule to the contrary, each source of untaxed income would have an associated overlap profit that could only be relieved by set off against income from that same source.

There is therefore a special rule which provides that any amount by which the overlap relief exceeds the profits of the partner's notional business is deducted in calculating the partner's income for the tax year (ITTOIA 2005, s. 856).

Losses

As far as losses are concerned, the notional business only determines the basis period for the loss – it does not require the amount of the loss to be computed using trading income rules. The loss relief rules appropriate to the particular type of income determine the way in which the loss can be relieved.

Legislation: ITTOIA 2005, s. 854–856

20-160   Income tax: claims for averaging of partnership profits

Where the qualifying trade, profession or vocation is carried on in partnership, averaging claims may be made by each individual partner in respect of his or her share of partnership profits. It is not necessary for all of the partners to make a claim.

The partnership profits should therefore be allocated to the individual partners before averaging takes place.

A partnership change does not affect the availability of relief to any individual who was carrying on the trade both before and after the change.

Legislation: ITTOIA 2005, s. 221

20-180   Income tax: relief for partnership annuities paid

As noted at ¶18-420, annuity payments paid by partners to a retired partner are added back in the calculation of partnership profits for tax purposes where payments have been charged to the partnership's profit and loss account.

Payments are allocated to the partners in accordance with the partnership's profit sharing ratio (see ¶19-020) and the current partners receive income tax relief under ITA 2007, s. 448 through their own self-assessment tax returns.

ITA 2007, s. 448 gives tax relief to an individual who makes an annual payment from which tax must be deducted.

Annuities paid by LLP

Where the annuities are payable by a partnership which has incorporated as an LLP and the obligation to pay the annuity arose before becoming an LLP, entitlement to income tax relief depends on whether the obligation has been transferred to the LLP.

- If the obligation has been transferred to the LLP, all current members (including incoming members) assume part of the obligation and will be entitled to income tax relief.
- Where the obligation is not transferred to the LLP and the members of the old partnership continue to pay it, they will be entitled to income tax relief for their share of those payments until such time as they cease to be a member of the LLP or until the business originally carried on by the old partnership ceases, whichever is the earlier. In this situation, incoming partners have no obligation to pay the annuity.

Legislation: ITA 2007, s. 448

20-200   Assessment to corporation tax

The company is chargeable to corporation tax as though the amounts allocated to it in relation to the partnership arose in the carrying on of a trade by the company during the accounting period.

Where the accounting period of the company does not coincide with that of the partnership, the company's share of partnership profits and deductions are apportioned to the company's accounting period or periods (CTA 2009, s. 1265). HMRC guidance is that this will normally be done on a time basis unless a more accurate basis can be found (HMRC *Company Taxation Manual* CTM36510).

The extent to which the company may be entitled to relief in respect of such amounts allocated to it against its other income and profits and the extent to which it may claim relief for losses and deductions relating to its other activities against the income from the partnership will depend on the nature of its other activities. If the company carried on some other trade as well as the partnership trade, it will be a question of fact whether the two trades are to be treated as the same trade or as separate trades. This will in turn affect the availability of relief for losses incurred in other accounting periods.

Return periods

Where a partnership has both individual members and company members, return periods follow normal rules in respect of taxed and untaxed income (see ¶20-140). However, partnerships comprising only company members within the charge to corporation tax should return details of all classes of income, taxed and untaxed, for the partnership's accounting period or periods ending in the tax year (HMRC *Partnership Manual* PM40210).

Legislation: CTA 2009, s. 1265

Chapter 12: Partnership changes, merger and demergers

21-000 Introduction

Changes in the composition of a partnership can occur in a number of different situations:

(1) some or all of the partners may change with the business continuing;

(2) two or more businesses may combine;

(3) a single business may be split into one or more parts.

The impact for income tax purposes of such changes is that one or more or all of the partners may be treated as ceasing to carry on their notional trade or business and one or more or all of the partners may be treated as starting to carry on a new notional trade or business. Alternatively, the change may have no effect on the notional trade or business basis periods for some partners or may affect them only to the extent that there is a change in the accounting reference date as a result. For further details, see ¶20-080ff.

For corporation tax purposes, the calculation of profits of the deemed company (see ¶18-160) to be apportioned between corporate members will usually be unaffected by any changes in the persons carrying on the business with profits being time-apportioned between those companies who are partners according to the profit sharing ratio in force at any given time. However, where there is a complete change in companies carrying on a business in partnership (with no corporate continuity) or when the business stops being carried on by any company in partnership, this will trigger a cessation of the trade or business of the deemed company. For further details, see ¶18-160.

Legislation: ITTOIA 2005, Pt. 9; CTA 2009, Pt. 17

21-020 Changes in partnership: income tax overview

Partnership successions and the effect, for income tax, of a change in the ownership of a trade, profession or vocation was originally prescribed by ICTA 1988, s. 113. The income tax treatment and application of s. 113 for partnership mergers and demergers was further the subject of a Press Release and Statement of Practice (SP 9/86) dated 10 December 1986.

ICTA 1988, s. 113 applied to trade profits but was extended to property businesses by ICTA 1988, s. 21B. It ensured that a trade was treated as ceasing when there was a change in the persons carrying it on and was required by virtue of the fact that some rules in ICTA 1988 were expressed in terms of the commencement and cessation of a trade rather than the position of the person carrying on the trade. Upon the rewrite of ICTA 1988 into ITTOIA 2005, the rewritten basis period rules (contained in ITTOIA 2005, Pt. 2, Ch. 15 and which are applied to partnerships by virtue of s. 853(1) in respect of trading profits and s. 854 in respect of other untaxed income or losses) are expressed in terms of the persons carrying on the trade and, accordingly, there was no need for a special rule deeming there to be a cessation where the trade is carried on by a successor. When a person starts or ceases to carry on a trade, the trade commences or ceases (see ¶20-060).

In most cases, the rule in ICTA 1998, s. 113 is explicit in the rewritten provisions that a change in the persons carrying on a trade is to be treated as a cessation, however, in some cases, where there is no explicit indication that s. 113(1) applied to treat the trade as ceasing, it has been incorporated as part of the rewrite to make it clear that the trade is not treated as ceasing unless there is a complete change in the persons carrying it on. The effect of s. 113(1) is, therefore, retained as part of ITTOIA 2005, s. 77, 79, 173 and 182 but s. 113 is otherwise repealed.

Although SP 9/86 was written in terms of the taxation provisions as they applied prior to the introduction of the current year basis and rewrite of the commencement and cessations provisions which were previously in the *Income and Corporation Taxes Act* 1988, the general principles set out in the Statement of Practice continue to apply where there is a merger/demerger after the introduction of the current year basis. These are covered at ¶21-060.

Legislation: ITTOIA 2005, Pt. 2, Ch. 15, s. 853 and 854

Other material: SP 9/86

21-040 Changes in partnership: income tax treatment

Where there is a complete change in the composition of the partnership, taxable profits are calculated as if the trade had been permanently discontinued, even where the trade continues under new ownership. Where this is the case, the partnership is treated as if the trade had been permanently discontinued and a new one set up and commenced at the date of the change. The normal rules relating to commencements and cessations of trade apply.

Where there is only a partial change in ownership so that one or more persons carrying on the trade before the change (either alone or in partnership) continue to carry on the trade after the change (either alone or in partnership), there is no deemed discontinuance. There is no provision to elect for a deemed discontinuance.

Commencement and cessation rules apply individually to partners who join or leave the partnership (which can be by retirement or death). These are discussed at ¶20-060.

Example 1

Terry and June set up in business as landscape gardeners. They continue in business for two years, at which time the landscape gardening business is taken over by their daughter Julie and her husband Mike.

There is a deemed discontinuance of the business at the end of that two-year period, as there is a complete change in the composition of the partnership on that date.

A deemed cessation under these rules is not to be confused with an actual change in the trade.

Example 2

Timmy and Jane set up in business as landscape gardeners. They continue in business for two years, at which time Timmy retires. From that date, they stop the gardening activity but Jane starts to carry on a trade with her daughter Janet, providing cream teas. Although Jane was working both before and after the change, there has been a real cessation of the gardening trade and the commencement of a new trade of providing teas.

Example 3

Peter commences trading on 1/7/2012 and produces accounts to 30/6/2013 and then to 30/6/2014:

- During the period 1/7/2012 to 30/6/2014 Peter is a sole trader.
- Trading income arising from his business is chargeable under normal basis period rules.
- All other income arising in the business is chargeable on a tax year (6 April to 5 April) basis, including any such income arising in the period 6/4/2014 to 30/6/2014.

On 1/7/2014, Peter's two sons Harry and George join the business as partners:

- The formation of the partnership has no effect on Peter's notional trade basis periods.
- The notional business of all three partners commences on 1/7/2014.
- The notional trades of Harry and George commence on 1/7/2014.
- The basis periods for the notional businesses of all three partners are found using trading income basis period rules as if a trade commenced on 1/7/2014. Therefore the basis period for shares of untaxed income in 2014–15 is the 9 months to 5/4/2015 and for 2015–16 is the 12 months to 30/6/2015. The 9 months to 5/4/2015 is a period of overlap
- The basis periods for the notional trades of Harry and George Bailey are found using the same rules as for their notional trade.

On 30/6/2015 Peter retires, leaving his two sons to carry on the business:

- Peter's retirement triggers a cessation (including the rules for overlap relief) in both his notional trade and notional business.
- But the change in the membership of the partnership has no effect on the basis periods used by either Harry or George.

On 30/6/2016, the partnership between Harry and George is dissolved and George continues to carry on the business on his own:

- Harry's departure triggers a cessation (including the rules for overlap relief) in both his notional trade and his notional business.
- The dissolution of the partnership has no effect on the notional trade basis periods used by George.
- But George's notional business is deemed to cease on 30/6/2016 and from that date, any other untaxed income arising in the business is assessed on a tax year (6 April to 5 April) basis.

Legislation: ITTOIA 2005, s. 852–856

21-060 Mergers and demergers: income tax

Where two businesses which have been carried on under different ownership are brought together and continue to be carried on under common ownership there are a number of possibilities as to how these arrangements will be regarded for tax purposes:

- the previous businesses cease and a new business commences;
- the previous businesses continue as a merged joint business;
- one business continues and the other(s) ceases.

SP 9/86 provides the tax treatment of the various outcomes which are to be determined as a question of fact. In summary, SP 9/86 provides that:

Mergers

(1) Where the new business created is entirely different to the two previous businesses, both existing businesses will cease and a new business will commence (see ¶21-080);

(2) Where the activities of the two businesses are similar and the new business has essentially the same characteristics of both former businesses, the existing businesses will continue as a merged joint business (see ¶21-100);

Demergers

(3) When a business carried on in partnership is divided up, and several separate partnerships are formed, the business will have ceased unless one of the businesses carried on after the division is sufficiently large in relation to the rest

so as to be recognisably 'the business' previously carried on (see ¶21-140 for further commentary on demergers).

Where one of the businesses simply acquires the trade and assets of the other, the new merged business may simply be an enlarged version of one of the businesses, in which case, one business continues and the other ceases (see ¶21-120).

Other material: SP 9/86

21-080 Mergers: old businesses cease and new business commences

Where both original businesses cease and an entirely new business commences, normal cessation rules apply to the existing businesses and normal commencement rules apply to the new business. The consequences are:

(1) Individual partners in the two existing businesses will crystallise their overlap relief in relation to both their 'notional trade' in terms of their trading profits and their 'notional business' (if they have one) in terms of their other untaxed partnership income;

(2) Any trading losses arising in the year of cessation are dealt with as terminal losses (see ¶25-160);

(3) Any trading losses brought forward which cannot be used under the terminal loss provisions are lost.

Legislation: ITTOIA 2005, s. 77(5), 79(2), 173(3), 182(2), 246(3)(4), 258(1), (2), 353(2), (3), 361(1), (2), and 860(1) and (2).

21-100 Mergers: previous businesses continue as a merged joint business

Where the activities of the previous businesses are similar in nature, the activities of the merged business may have the same essential characteristics of both previous businesses. The new business must be capable of being described as a single business otherwise no merger has taken place and the existing businesses are simply continuing under common ownership. The new business may be an enlarged version of one or other of the previous businesses in which case, the new business will have succeeded to either or both previous businesses.

Where the new business has the same accounting date as the previous businesses, the partners will continue to be taxed on trading profits arising from the notional trade and other untaxed income arising from the notional business under normal rules as if the existing business had just continued.

Where the new business has a different accounting date, however, the partners will be taxed on the profits from the notional trade or notional business in the same way as if there had been a change of accounting date (see ¶20-100).

As the business is deemed to continue this means that the tax treatment of any trading losses brought forward is unaffected.

Example

Two firms, Ark and Wright, merge on 1 January 2015.

Ark previously prepared accounts to 30 June. Wright previously prepared accounts to 31 December.

The new firm, Arkwright, will prepare accounts to 30 June.

The partners' basis periods will be as follows:

2013–14 (year prior to merger)

Ark partners: 12 months to 30 June 2013

Wright partners: 12 months to 31 December 2013

2014–15 (year of merger)

Ex-Ark partners: 12 months to 30 June 2014

Ex-Wright partners: 12 months to 31 December 2014

2015–16 (year following merger)

The new partnership accounting date applies

Ex-Ark partners: 12 months to 30 June 2015

(NB: this will comprise the profits of Ark from 1 July 2014–31 December

2014 and of Arkwright from 1 January 2015–30 June 2015)

Ex-Wright partners: 12 months to 30 June 2015

(NB: there is a change of accounting date for each partner from

31 December – 30 June and an overlap in the basis period, as follows:

2014–15: 1 January 2014 to 31 December 2014

2015–16: 1 July 2014 to 30 June 2015)

Therefore, profits chargeable will comprise Wright from 1 January 2014 to

31 December 2014 × 6/12 plus Arkwight from 1 January 2015 to 30 June 2015.

The 'overlap profit' is the profit of the period 1 July 2014 to 31 December 2014 and is based solely on the share of profit allocated as a member of Wright.

Legislation: ITTOIA 2005, s. 852–856

21-120 Mergers: one business continues and the other(s) cease

The owners of one of the previous businesses may simply acquire the trade and assets of another business. Where this is the case, the 'merged' business is simply and enlarged version of one of the previous businesses.

The acquiring business (and its partners)

The acquiring business continues and the existing partners in that business continue to be taxed on their share of the new businesses profits as if the existing business had continued. If the accounting date for the new business is different, the partners are taxed on the profits from the notional trade or notional business in the same way as if there had been a change of accounting date (see ¶20-100).

The acquired business (and its partners)

The acquired business ceases to exist and the partners are subject to normal cessation rules in relation to that business (see ¶20-080).

Normal commencement rules will apply to the previous partners in the acquired business in relation to their profits going forward arising from the new partnership business.

Legislation: ITTOIA 2005, s. 852–856

21-140 Demergers: income tax

Where a business is split (demerged) into two separate parts then normal cessation rules apply to the original business and normal commencement rules apply to the new business. A person cannot succeed to part of a business so there can be no deemed continuance of any part of the original business.

If, however, one of the separate partnerships formed on a demerger carries on the same business as the original partnership (and this is a question of fact) then the continuation basis will automatically apply to that partnership. This may be the case where one business has retained a large number of customers and assets.

Farmers

ITTOIA 2005, s. 9(2) and 859, requires that all the farming carried on by a partnership or body of persons is to be treated as one trade (see ¶18-480).

In deciding whether a farming partnership can demerge, however, it may be necessary to consider whether the partnership has in fact carried on more than one farming trade (although deemed to be one trade by the legislation). A change in partnership personnel is not treated as discontinuance if at least one member of the old partnership continues in business under the new one.

Legislation: ITTOIA 2005, s. 9 and 859

21-160   Changes in partnership: corporation tax

The corporation tax provisions relating to partnerships involving companies were provided by ICTA 1988, s. 114–116. Section 114 is rewritten as CTA 2009, s. 1259 and provides that where any partner in a firm is a company within the charge to corporation tax, profits are to be determined as if the partner were a UK resident or non-UK resident company (the deemed company). Under ICTA 1988, s. 114, the deemed company continued for so long as the trade was carried on by persons in partnership and any of those person was a company, and without regard to any change in the persons carrying on the trade except that a change in the persons engaged in carrying on the trade was to be treated as the transfer of the trade to a different company if there continued to be a company so engaged after the change, but not a company that was so engaged before the change.

In other words, the deemed company only existed during the life of the partnership. A company was treated as ceasing to carry on a business when that company takes another person into partnership (because the deemed company then carries on the business) and the deemed company was treated as ceasing to carry on a business when the partnership business is taken over by a company on its own. The deemed company calculation was only affected by a change in the persons carrying on the business when there was no continuity of any company carrying on the business both before and after the change, in which case, the change was to be treated as the transfer of the business to a different company.

This remains the case under the rewritten provisions in CTA 2009. The occasions on which a company is treated as ceasing to carry on a business are now set out in the rules to which they are relevant (see s. 77(5), 80 and 162(3)). They also appear in this Part in s. 1267(3) and (4) and 1271(3) (see ¶18-560 and ¶21-180).

CTA 2009, s. 1261 provides the rules the commencement and cessation to trade of the deemed company and is based on ICTA 1988, s. 114. The concept of an accounting period of a firm is used in s. 1259 for the calculation of the firm's profit or loss (see ¶18-060) and s. 1261 makes provision for determining the accounting period.

An accounting period begins when a company first carries on the trade in partnership and ends when the last company leaves a firm or if the company continues to carry on the trade, when that company no longer does so in partnership (CTA 2009, s. 1261(2)(b), (c), (3) and (4)).

The deemed company calculation is otherwise only affected by any changes in the persons carrying on the trade where there is no 'corporate continuity' between the members of the firm before and after the change; that is no single company continuing to carry on the trade after the change that carried it on before the trade.

In this situation, the accounting period of the deemed company ends and the deemed company is treated as ceasing to trade and then a new accounting period begins and the deemed company is treated as starting to trade immediately afterwards (CTA 2009, s. 1261(2)(d) and (5)).

The trade is treated as being transferred to a different company with the result that balancing charges may arise for capital allowance purposes. CTA 2009, s. 162 will apply regarding the valuation of trading stock on a discontinuance of a trade (s. 162(3)); s. 188–196 and 280–285 in respect of post cessation receipts and deductions.

Other than as above, the usual rules about an accounting period ending on a date to which the firm makes up accounts and about an accounting period ending on the expiration of 12 months apply without being specifically mentioned in this section.

Example 1

Blue Box Ltd is a company and Mr White and Mr Black are individuals. Blue Box Ltd, Mr White and Mr Black are in partnership. Blue Box Ltd ceases to be a partner and is replaced by Green Door Ltd (another company). This is treated as a transfer of a trade to a different company.

Example 2

Alpha Ltd, Beta Ltd and Gamma Ltd are all companies in partnership. Alpha Ltd ceases to be a partner but Beta Ltd and Gamma Ltd continue in partnership. This change is not treated as a transfer of the trade to a different company.

A company's share in the profits and losses of any accounting period is calculated according to its entitlement during that period. Corporation tax is charged as if that share was derived from a trade carried on by the company alone in its corresponding accounting period or periods (CTA 2009, s. 1262: see ¶19-100).

Accordingly, where there is no deemed discontinuance of the trade of the deemed company, any company joining or leaving a partnership is assessed by reference to its share of the profits for the period prior to leaving or post joining and any companies continuing in the partnership are unaffected by the change.

Where there is a deemed discontinuance, separate calculations will be required for the accounting period prior to the change and the accounting period after the change and profits apportioned to the companies who were partners during each accounting period respectively.

Legislation: CTA 2009, s. 1261, 1262

PARTNERSHIP CHANGES: SPECIAL COMPUTATIONAL PROVISIONS

21-180 Sale of patent rights: effects of partnership changes

Income tax is charged on profits from sales of the whole or part of any patent rights under ITTOIA 2005, s. 587. The profit to be taxed is defined in the legislation (ITTOIA 2005, s. 588) to be the amount of any capital sum comprised in the sale proceeds, less deductible costs. For corporation tax purposes, the corresponding charge is under CTA 2009, s. 912 with the profits taxed defined in s. 913.

Income or corporation tax is charged on profits from sales of the whole or part of any patent rights as if those profits were income, even though the proceeds are capital in nature. The fact of charging a capital profit as if income runs counter to normal tax principles and a form of spreading of the tax charge operates to mitigate the effect. The detail of the spreading rules depends on whether or not the seller is resident in the UK.

For UK resident sellers, the normal rule is that one-sixth of the sale proceeds are taxed in the year of receipt, with a further one-sixth in each of the next five years but it is possible to elect to be taxed in full in the year of receipt of the proceeds. The treatment of non-resident sellers is reversed, with the normal rule that the whole amount is taxed in the year of receipt but an election is possible to spread the charge over six years.

In the case of a partnership, there may be one or more partner changes during the six-year period of profit spreading. If the conditions set out below are met, any outstanding charges following a partner change are simply taxed on the person or persons who are carrying on the trade at the later date (ITTOIA 2005, s. 861; CTA 2009, s. 1271). Such amounts are then charged as if the subsequent business proprietor(s) had at all times been carrying on the trade, and as if everything done to or by any predecessors in carrying on the trade had been done to or by those subsequent proprietors. The relevant conditions are as follows:

Tax must be charged under ITTOIA 2005, s. 587 or CTA 2009, s. 912 on the proceeds of sale of patent rights and the rules for spreading over six years must apply (ITTOIA 2005, s. 861(1); CTA 2009, s. 1271(1)).

The partnership condition

The trader must have been a firm (i.e. a partnership) at the time of sale of the patent rights.

Continuity condition

There must have been a change in the persons carrying on the trade at some point in the tax spreading period but at least one person or the company who carried on the trade before the change must continue to do so after the change (ITTOIA 2005, s. 861(3); CTA 2009, s. 1271(3)).

Partnerships: effect of later cessation of trade

Where the ITTOIA 2005, s. 861 or CTA 2009, s. 1271 rules (immediately above) have applied on the occasion of a partnership change, the subsequent partners step into the shoes of those who originally sold the patent rights. The position is further complicated if one of those subsequent partners then comes in turn to cease permanently to carry on the trade.

If, at the time of the later change, at least one person/company who was carrying on the trade before the change continues to carry it on thereafter, then (subject to the conditions being met) ITTOIA 2005, s. 861 or CTA 2009, s. 1271 can operate once more to transfer the liability to the person or persons carrying on the trade after the later change. However, if there is no continuation (as no person carrying on the trade before the change continues to do so afterwards) then any remaining tax charge crystallises in the tax year in which the cessation occurs (ITTOIA 2005, s. 862; CTA 2009, s. 1272).

The sharing of the charge is determined according to the profit-sharing arrangements immediately before the cessation (if necessary, allocating an appropriate share to the personal representatives of a partner who has died).

Further income tax provisions

The partners facing the charge may elect that the additional charge be recalculated. If they do so, the charge is reduced to the amount that would have been payable if the amount that would have been charged in later years were instead spread equally between the tax years starting with the receipt of the sale proceeds (or instalment) and ending with the tax year of cessation.

The election must be made by 31 January some 22 months after the end of the tax year in which the cessation occurs.

Deduction of tax from payments to non-UK residents

The rules in ITTOIA 2005, s. 588 and CTA 2009, s. 913 and also the making of any election under ITTOIA 2005, s. 591(2) or 592(2) or CTA 2009, s. 914–917 do not affect the amount which must be deducted and assessed under ITA 2007, s. 910. No repayment of, or of any part of, the tax deducted is made for any year unless and until it is ascertained that the tax ultimately to be paid for that year is less that the tax paid (ITTOIA 2005, s. 595, 596; CTA 2009, s. 919 and 920).

Legislation: ITTOIA 2005, s. 862–862; CTA 2009, s. 1271–1272

Chapter 13:   Capital allowances

22-000   Overview

Capital allowances are calculated and given for:

- a period of account (for income tax purposes); or
- an accounting period of a company (for corporation tax purposes).

A **period of account** is any period for which trading, professional or vocational (shortened to trading below) accounts are made up.

Accounting period has the same meaning for capital allowances as it has for corporation tax.

Where a business is carried on in partnership, capital allowances are calculated and claimed at partnership level on the partnership return.

This is the case whether the assets are partnership property or are owned by one or more of the partners but used in the partnership's business (subject to an exception where a formal leasing agreement exists between the partner and the partnership).

Partnership profits and losses are calculated according to the status of the partners and whether these are individuals or companies, with separate computations where there are both individual and company partners (see **Chapter 9**). Capital allowances are computed as part of the income tax or corporation tax adjustments to arrive at taxable profits for income tax purposes or corporation tax purposes and are, therefore, deducted before profits are allocated to the partners with the result that the profits allocated to partners are net of capital allowances (see ¶18-120).

Normal computational provisions apply to the calculation of capital allowances for partnerships, however, there are a number of provisions which are specific to or of relevance to partnerships and which are covered in the rest of this chapter, as follows:

(1) Plant and machinery allowances:

- Annual investment allowance (see ¶22-020);
- Partnership changes (see ¶22-040);
- Partnership using partners' property (see ¶22-060);
- Partnership successions and associated election (see ¶22-080);
- Anti-avoidance provisions (see ¶22-120).

(2) Other allowances (see ¶22-140ff.).

See also ¶22-240 for determination of market value, where applicable, and the definition of 'connected persons' for capital allowance purposes at ¶22-260.

Legislation: CAA 2001, s. 2, 6

22-020 Plant and machinery allowances: annual investment allowance

The annual investment allowance (AIA) is available to businesses in respect of 'qualifying AIA expenditure'. This is defined as:

- expenditure incurred by a qualifying person on or after the relevant date (1 April 2008 for corporation tax purposes and 6 April 2008 for income tax purposes); and
- that is not excluded by the general exclusions in CAA 2001, s. 38B.

(CAA 2001, s. 38A(1)–(2)).

A 'qualifying person' is defined as:

(a) an individual;
(b) a partnership of which all the members are individuals; or
(c) a company,

(CAA 2001, s. 38A(3)).

This means that partnerships are only eligible to claim the allowance if all the members are individuals. A partnership of which a company is a member is not a 'qualifying person' within s. 38A and so cannot claim AIA.

A partnership which includes another partnership as a member, e.g. an LLP, is also not a qualifying person for AIA purposes.

HMRC manuals at CA23082 comment that:

> '… Both trusts and mixed partnerships were similarly excluded from the definition of a "business" for the purposes of the previous 40% or 50% FYA for SMEs CA23170. Dawn Primarolo MP, who was then Financial Secretary to the Treasury, said in the relevant Standing Committee debate in 1997 that:
>
> > "… Incredibly complex rules would be required to bring them in, which would open possible abuses of tax-driven options that the hon. Gentleman would deprecate".
>
> Similar considerations influenced the decision not to include trusts or mixed partnerships as a "qualifying person" for AIA purposes. One of the main objectives underlying the AIA is the aim of keeping the rules as simple as possible, while safeguarding the AIA from abuse through fragmentation and the artificial creation of multiple allowances. In broad terms, the current rules provide that each business is entitled to one AIA, but in order to guard against fragmentation, "related" businesses that are controlled by the same person must share one AIA. It would have been extremely complex to have devised rules to decide who controls a business held by trustees, or to devise rules about "related" businesses and "control" that would, for example, have encompassed businesses controlled by both individual and corporate partners in a mixed partnership at the same time.'

Legislation: CAA 2001, s. 38A

Other material: HMRC *Capital Allowances Manual* CA23082

22-040   Plant and machinery allowances: partnership changes

As a general principle, a change in the persons carrying on a qualifying activity in partnership is ignored for the purposes of claiming plant and machinery allowances, as long as the change does not have the effect that all the partners permanently cease to carry on the trade or other qualifying activity (CAA 2001, s. 263).

For plant and machinery allowances, most partnership changes are not treated as a cessation and instead, the present partners step into the shoes of their predecessors. These rules apply where:

(1)   a qualifying activity has been set up and is carried on in partnership;

(2)   there has been a change in the persons carrying on the qualifying activity; and

(3)   where the activity is a trade or property business, either:

    (i)   (for income tax) a person carrying on the business immediately before the change continues to carry it on after the change;

    (ii)   (for corporation tax) a company carrying on the business in partnership immediately before the change continues to carry it on in partnership after the change,

(CAA 2001, s. 263).

In other words, a change in the persons carrying on a qualifying activity in partnership is ignored unless:

- the old and new partnerships have no single person or company in common; or
- the qualifying activity is treated by ITTOIA 2005, s. 18 (company ceasing to be within charge to income tax in respect of a trade) or ITTOIA 2005, s. 362 (company ceasing to be within charge to income tax in respect of a property business) as permanently ceasing to be carried on by a company; or
- the qualifying activity is treated as discontinued under CTA 2009, s. 41.

Where there is a complete change in the partners carrying on the qualifying activity, see ¶22-080.

Where conditions for partnership changes to be ignored are met, any annual investment allowances, first-year allowances or writing-down allowances are made to the 'present partners' (CAA 2001, s. 263(3)), defined to mean the person(s) for the time being carrying on the qualifying activity. The amount of any such allowance is calculated as if the present partners had at all times been carrying on the qualifying activity, and as if everything done to or by their predecessors in carrying on that activity had been done to or by the present partners (CAA 2001, s. 263(3), (4)).

Any balancing allowance or charge is made to or on the partners at the time of the event that triggers that allowance or charge. The amount is calculated as if the partners at the time of the event had at all times been carrying on the qualifying activity, and as if everything done to or by their predecessors in carrying on that activity had been done to or by the partners at the time of the event (CAA 2001, s. 263(5), (6)).

For these purposes only, the normal definition of 'qualifying activity' (CAA 2001, s. 15) applies, except that the term does not here include an office or employment. All other activities listed in CAA 2001, s. 15(1) are included even if the profits or gains they generate are not chargeable to tax (CAA 2001, s. 263(2)).

Corporation tax law rewrite

The mechanics of achieving the statutory effects referred to above were changed somewhat with the rewrite of the corporation tax legislation in 2010. Everything in the *Capital Allowances Act* 2001 is, for corporation tax purposes for accounting periods ending on or after 1 April 2010, subject to the modifying provisions of CTA 2010, Pt. 22, Ch. 1 (CAA 2001, s. 560A: transfers of trade without a change of ownership). CTA 2010, s. 940A specifies the trade transfers to which CTA 2010, Pt. 22, Ch. 1 applies, imposing an ownership condition and a tax condition. CTA 2010, s. 948 then specifies that where those conditions are met, the *Capital Allowances Act* 2001 has effect subject to the following:

'948(2) Any allowances or charges are to be made to or on the successor if such allowances or charges would have been made to or on the predecessor had the predecessor continued to carry on the transferred trade.

948(3) A transfer of assets from the predecessor to the successor does not of itself give rise to any allowances or charges if:

(a) the transfer of the assets is made on the transfer of the transferred trade, and

(b) the assets are in use for the purposes of that trade.

948(4) For the purpose of determining the amount of the allowances or charges mentioned in subsection (2) to be made to the successor:

(a) the successor is to be treated as if it has been carrying on the transferred trade since the predecessor began to do so, and

(b) anything done to or by the predecessor is to be treated as having been done to or by the successor.'.

This general principle is, however, subject to CTA 2010, s. 949 (dual-resident investing companies) and to s. 950 (transfers of trades involving business of leasing plant or machinery). Furthermore, the general principle does not apply to cases governed by CAA 2001, s. 561 (transfer to company in another member state) or by s. 561A (transfer during formation of *Societas Europaea* by merger).

Legislation: CAA 2001, s. 15(1), 263; CTA 2010, s. 940A, 948

22-060   Plant and machinery allowances: partnership using property of partners

Capital allowances are available in respect of plant or machinery owned by a partner but used in the partnership trade (CAA 2001, s. 264). Where, however, one partner owns an item of plant and lets it to the partnership, or otherwise receives a payment from the partnership that is deductible in calculating the profits of the trade, then the partner or partners owning the item in question are not treated as using it for the purposes of a trade. As such, no allowances will be due to them under the partnership rules (CAA 2001, s. 264(4)).

Where relief is due as above, capital allowances are given to (and balancing charges made on) the partnership rather than the individual partner (CAA 2001, s. 264(2)). Claims must be made in the partnership return, a point known to be of practical difficulty in some large professional partnerships where the partners are too busy to attend diligently to their personal tax affairs.

Where ownership of an item of plant or machinery that is used for the purposes of a qualifying activity carried on by a partnership passes from one partner to another within a single partnership, no disposal value is to be brought into account provided the item continues to be used after the sale for the purposes of the qualifying activity. This applies whether the item is sold or given to the acquiring partner (CAA 2001, s. 264(3)).

Legislation: CAA 2001, s. 264

22-080   Plant and machinery allowances: successions

Where there is a complete change in the partners carrying on a qualifying activity for capital allowance purposes, this is treated as a 'succession' under CAA 2001, s. 265.

A succession for capital allowances purposes occurs where a person succeeds to a qualifying activity previously carried on by another person and where the qualifying activity is a trade or property business, there is no single person (for income tax purposes) or single company (for corporation tax purposes) who carries on the activity both before and after the succession (CAA 2001, s. 265(1)–(1B)).

Where there remains at least one person carrying on the activity both before and after the succession, see ¶22-040.

A qualifying activity is defined as per CAA 2001, s. 15(1) but excluding an office or employment even if any profits or gains from it are not chargeable to tax. (CAA 2001, s. 265(5)).

Where there is a 'succession' to a qualifying activity, assets transferred will normally be deemed to be sold at open market value (CAA 2001, s. 265(2)) (although where the transfer is between connected persons, an election may be made for the transfer to take place at tax written down value, see ¶22-100).

The deemed sale applies to 'relevant property' which is defined as any property which:

'(a) immediately before the succession, was owned by the predecessor and was either in use or provided and available for use for the purposes of the discontinued qualifying activity, and

(b) immediately after the succession, and without being sold, is either in use or provided and available for use for the purposes of the new qualifying activity.'

(CAA 2001, s. 265(3)).

The inclusion of the words 'and without being sold' in the definition of relevant property as the subject matter of the deemed sale means that deemed sale at market value does not apply where assets are actually sold.

The assets must also be used for the purposes of the relevant qualifying activity both before and after the succession (CAA 2001, s. 265(3)).

No first-year allowance or annual investment allowance are given to the new owner (s. 265(4)).

Legislation: CAA 2001, s. 265

22-100 Plant and machinery allowances: successions election

Where there is a succession to a qualifying activity and predecessor and successor are connected persons, an election may be made (under CAA 2001, s. 266) to transfer the assets at their tax-written down value, i.e. at a value which produces no balancing adjustment either way (per CAA 2001, s. 267).

Where an election is made, the actual sales price or transfer figure will be ignored and the successor will calculate future capital allowances or balancing charges 'as if everything done to or by the predecessor had been done to or by the successor' (CAA 2001, s. 267(4)). The election may be made irrespective of whether the plant or machinery has actually been sold or transferred (CAA 2001, s. 266(3)).

This means that where assets are in a pool they are transferred at the pool value.

The conditions for making an election are:

- there is a succession between connected persons;
- both the predecessor and the successor are within the charge to UK tax on the profits of the qualifying activity;
- the successor is not a dual resident investment company (as defined in CTA 2010, s. 109);

- an election is made by notice to a Revenue officer within two years of the date of the succession, whether or not any plant or machinery has actually been sold or transferred); and
- CAA 2001, s. 561 (transfer of UK trade to a company in another member state) does not apply

(CAA 2001, s. 266)

For these purposes, the predecessor and successor are connected with each other if any of the following conditions are met, connected persons are defined as:

- they would be treated as connected persons under CAA 2001, s. 575 (NB s. 575 does not lend itself to simplification, so reference should be made to that definition as required; see ¶22-260);
- one of them is a partnership and the other has the right to a share in that partnership (i.e. a right to a share of the assets or income of the partnership);
- one of them is a body corporate and the other has control over that body;
- both of them are partnerships and another person has the right to a share in both of them (i.e. a right to a share in the assets or the income of the partnerships);
- both of them are bodies corporate, or one of them is a partnership and the other is a body corporate, and (in either case) another person has control over both of them.

In other words, the parties will be connected if they are so connected within the terms of CAA 2001, s. 575, or if there is common control or in the case of a partnership, they have at least one person in common.

Where an election is made certain provisions do not have effect:

- CAA 2001, s. 104E (disposal value in connection with special rate expenditure);
- CAA 2001, s. 108 (effect of disposal to connected person on overseas leasing pool); and
- CAA 2001, s. 265 (general provisions about successions) do not apply (but see below re a restriction on this provision at CAA 2001, s. 267A).

Restriction on effect of election: corporation tax

There is a restriction on the effect of an election (CAA 2001, s. 266) where the transferor and transferee both carry on a business of leasing plant and machinery (CAA 2001, s. 267A). The restriction applies for corporation tax purposes only.

The restriction applies if:

(1) on any day ('the relevant day'), a person ('the predecessor') carries on a business of leasing plant or machinery;

(2) another person ('the successor') succeeds to the business on the relevant day; and

(3) the predecessor and the successor make an election under CAA 2001, s. 266.

In such a case, neither CAA 2001, s. 266(7) (which disapplies s. 104E, 108 and 265 (disposal value in connection with special rate expenditure, effect of disposal to connected person on overseas leasing pool and general provisions about successions) nor s. 267 (effect of election under s. 266) have effect in relation to any plant or machinery which, in determining whether the business is a 'business of leasing plant or machinery' on the relevant day, falls within either CTA 2010, s. 387(7) (if the business is carried on otherwise than in partnership) or within CTA 2010, s. 410(6) (if the business is carried on in partnership).

(Note that this wording was changed from 23 March 2011. Before that date, the test was whether the plant or machinery in question was qualifying leased plant or machinery.)

The definition of the term 'business of leasing plant or machinery' depends on whether or not the business is carried on in partnership. If it is not so carried on, then the term is defined in accordance with CTA 2010, Pt. 9, Ch. 3. If the business *is* carried on in partnership, then the definition is in accordance with CTA 2010, Pt. 9, Ch. 4.

Legislation: CAA 2001, s. 266, 267, 267A

22-120 Plant and machinery allowances: anti-avoidance

Restrictions on allowances apply in respect of transactions:

- between connected persons (CAA 2001, s. 214);
- to obtain a tax advantage (CAA 2001, s. 215); or
- a sale and leaseback transaction (where the buyer leases the asset back to the seller or to a person connected with the seller (CAA 2001, s. 216).

In such cases, the purchaser cannot obtain any first-year allowances and the amount on which he will be able to claim writing-down allowances is restricted to the disposal value that the vendor has to bring into account. The restrictions are provided by CAA 2001, s. 217, 218, 218ZA, 218A.

For sale and leaseback transactions, the buyer and seller can elect for a relaxation of the restrictions (CAA 2001, s. 227–228). The restrictions generally do not apply to sale and finance leaseback transactions (which are treated as long-funding leases under CAA 2001, Pt. 2, Ch. 6 and 6A) with the exception of to certain sale and finance lease backs arrangements where the lessor does not bear the greater part of the risk that the lessee's obligations under the lease will not be met, in respect of which CAA 2001, s. 225 provides that no capital allowances are available.

Partners fall within the definition of 'connected persons' (see ¶22-260).

22-140   Other capital allowances: overview

The provisions relating to other allowances that are specific to partnerships or of relevance to partnerships have limited ongoing application (due to the repeal of parts of the CAA 2001 to which they relate). In summary, provisions relating to other allowances are contained in:

(1) **Partnership changes and successions** (CAA 2001, Pt. 12, Ch. 4, see ¶22-160ff.):

These provisions set out similar rules to those set out at ¶22-040ff. in respect of partnership changes and successions in respect of allowances other than plant and machinery, research and development and assured tenancy allowances.

Effectively, these provisions will now only apply to mineral extraction allowances, know-how and patent allowances (for individuals) and dredging allowances, and business premises allowances where still available;

(2) **Anti-avoidance: partners as connected persons** (CAA 2001, s. 567–570, see ¶22-200):

These provisions apply specifically for business premises renovation allowances (where still available), mineral extraction allowances, research and development allowances and if still available, assured tenancy allowances and provide for sales to be treated as taking place at market value unless an election for an alternative amount is made.

Legislation: CAA 2001, Pt. 12, Ch. 4 and s. 568–570

22-160   Other capital allowances: partnership changes

CAA 2001, Pt. 12, Ch. 4 sets out special rules that apply to partnerships, successions and transfers for capital allowance purposes except for plant and machinery allowances (see ¶22-040ff.), research and development allowances and assured tenancy allowances (CAA 2001, s. 557).

The rules are similar to those set out at ¶22-040ff. in respect of plant and machinery allowances.

As with plant and machinery allowances, a change in the persons carrying on a relevant activity in partnership is ignored for the purposes of claiming capital allowances (other than those allowances specifically excepted from these rules, as noted above), provided the change does not have the effect that all the partners permanently cease to carry on the relevant activity (CAA 2001, s. 558).

Where there is a complete change in the partners carrying on the activity, see ¶22-180.

Accordingly, partnership changes are generally not treated as a cessation and instead, the present partners step into the shoes of their predecessors. These rules apply where:

(1) a relevant activity has been set up and is carried on in partnership;

(2) there has been a change in the persons carrying on the relevant activity; and

(3) either:

(i) (for income tax) a person carrying on the relevant activity immediately before the change continues to carry it on after the change;

(ii) (for corporation tax) a company carrying on the relevant activity in partnership immediately before the change continues to carry it on in partnership after the change,

(CAA 2001, s. 588(1)–(1A)).

Following a succession, capital allowances are calculated as if the persons carrying on the relevant activity before and after the transfer were the same persons and allowances are computed as if the relevant activity had at all times been carried on by that same person (CAA 2001, s. 558(3), (4)).

Relevant activity is defined as a trade, property business, profession or vocation (CAA 2001, s. 558(5)).

Legislation: CAA 2001, s. 557–558

22-180 Other capital allowances: successions

Where there is a complete change in the partners carrying on a relevant activity for capital allowance purposes, this is treated as a 'succession' under CAA 2001, s. 559.

The provisions applicable for capital allowances purposes *other than* plant and machinery, research and development and assured tenancy allowances (CAA 2001, s. 557) are similar to those for plant and machinery allowances, as set out at ¶22-080.

The succession rules apply where there is a 'succession' to a 'relevant activity' and either:

• for income tax purposes, no person carrying on the trade or property business immediately before the succession continues to carry it on after the succession; or

• for corporation tax purposes, no company carrying on the trade or property business in partnership immediately before the succession continues to carry it on in partnership after the succession, (CAA 2001, s. 559(1)–(1A)).

A relevant activity for these purposes is defined as a trade, property business, profession or vocation (CAA 2001, s. 559(5)).

Where the succession rules apply, the property is deemed to be sold at open market value (CAA 2001, s. 559(2)).

The property is defined as:

'(a) immediately before the succession, was in use for the purposes of the discontinued relevant activity, and

(b) immediately after the succession, and without being sold, is in use for the purposes of the new relevant activity.'

(CAA 2001, s. 559(3)).

As with plant and machinery allowances, the inclusion of the words 'and without being sold' in the definition of relevant property as the subject matter of the deemed sale means that deemed sale at market value does not apply where assets are actually sold.

The property must also be in use for the purposes of the relevant activity both before and after the succession (CAA 2001, s. 559(3)).

No initial allowance is given to the new owner (CAA 2001, s. 559(4)).

22-200   Other capital allowances: anti-avoidance: partners as connected persons

A partner may be a connected person in relation to a partnership of which he is a member, meaning that special rules for transactions between connected persons may apply. These are provided for at CAA 2001, s. 567 and 568 and apply for the following purposes:

- CAA 2001, Pt. 3A: Business premises renovation allowances;
- CAA 2001, Pt. 5: Mineral extraction allowances;
- CAA 2001, Pt. 6: Research and development allowances; and
- CAA 2001, Pt. 10: Assured tenancy allowances.

(CAA 2001, s. 567(1)).

The legislation specifically does not apply to capital allowances on plant or machinery. See ¶22-120 for commentary relating to plant and machinery allowances.

Sales treated as at an alternative amount

Where allowances on an asset are calculated individually, that is where there is no pooling; the owner of an asset could create a balancing allowance by selling an asset to a connected person for a nominal amount. Accordingly, to prevent this, the legislation treats a sale of property not at market value as being at market value (subject to any election for tax written down value, see ¶22-220) where:

- the control test is met; or
- the tax advantage test is met.

(CAA 2001, s. 568).

The **control test** is met where:

- the buyer is a body of persons over whom the seller has control;
- the seller is a body of persons over whom the buyer has control;
- both the buyer and seller are bodies of persons and another person has control over both of them; or
- the seller and buyer are connected persons.

(CAA 2001, s. 567(2)).

Connected persons are defined by CAA 2001, s. 575 (see ¶22-260).

In deciding whether the control test is met what matters is control at the time of sale.

A body of persons includes a partnership (CAA 2001, s. 567(3)).

The tax advantage test is met if it appears that the sole or main benefit which might be expected to accrue from:

(a) the sale; or
(b) transactions of which the sale is one, is the obtaining of a tax advantage by all or any of the parties under any provision of the CAA 2001, except Pt. 2 (plant and machinery allowances).

Legislation: CAA 2001, s. 567, 568

22-220 Other capital allowances: partners as connected persons: election for alternative amount

Where either the control test is met (see ¶22-200) or there is a transfer treated as a sale by CAA 2001, s. 573 (exchange of property, etc.) then provided the tax advantage test is not met (see ¶22-200), the parties to a sale of property may elect for the sale to be treated as being at an alternative amount (to the market value that would otherwise apply by virtue of CAA 2001, s. 567) (CAA 2001, s. 570).

The alternative amount is the lower of market value and:

- if the sale is relevant for the purposes of Pt. 10 (assured tenancy allowances), the residue of the qualifying expenditure immediately before the sale;
- if the sale is relevant for the purposes of Pt. 5 (mineral extraction allowances), the unrelieved qualifying expenditure immediately before the sale;
- if the sale is relevant for the purposes of Pt. 6 (research and development allowances):

  (i)   in a case where an allowance under Pt. 6 is given for the expenditure represented by the asset sold, nil;

  (ii)   in any other case, the qualifying expenditure represented by the asset sold.

(CAA 2001, s. 569(3)).

Where an election is made CAA 2001, s. 569(1) does not apply to a sale which is a relevant sale for the purposes of CAA 2001, Pt. 3A (business premises renovation allowances (CAA 2001, s. 570(1)).

An election may not be made if it means that a relevant allowance or charge will not be capable of falling to be made or if the buyer is a dual resident investing company (CAA 2001, s. 570(2)).

If the sale is relevant for the purposes of Pt. 10 (assured tenancy allowances), no election under CAA 2001, s. 569 may be made unless, at the time of the sale or any earlier time, both the seller and the buyer are or have been approved bodies (as defined in CAA 2001, s. 492) (CAA 2001, s. 570(4)).

An election under CAA 2001, s. 569 must be made by notice to an officer of Revenue and Customs not later than two years after the sale (CAA 2001, s. 570(5)).

Legislation: CAA 2001, s. 569 and 570

22-240   Determination of market value

Where it is necessary to determine market value, if it is material as regards the liability of two or more persons, the matter will be decided by the tax tribunal as if it were an appeal but each person concerned is entitled to be a party to the proceedings on the application for the tribunal to determine the matter (CAA 2001, s. 564(2)).

Legislation: CAA 2001, s. 564(2)

22-260   Meaning of connected person

The definition of 'connected person' for capital allowances purposes is provided by CAA 2001, s. 575 as set out below:

'575 Meaning of "connected" persons

575(1) For the purposes of this Act whether a person is connected with another is determined in accordance with this section unless otherwise indicated.

575(2) An individual ("A") is connected with another individual ("B") if–

(a) A is B's spouse or civil partner,
(b) A is a relative of B,
(c) A is the spouse or civil partner of a relative of B,
(d) A is a relative of B's spouse or civil partner, or
(e) A is the spouse or civil partner of a relative of B's spouse or civil partner.

575(3) A person, in the capacity as trustee of a settlement, is connected with–

(a) any individual who is a settlor in relation to the settlement,
(b) any person connected with such an individual,
(c) any close company whose participators include the trustees of the settlement,
(d) any non-UK resident company which, if it were UK resident, would be a close company whose participators include the trustees of the settlement,
(e) any body corporate controlled (within the meaning of section 574) by a company within paragraph (c) or (d),
(f) if the settlement is the principal settlement in relation to one or more sub-fund settlements, a person in the capacity as trustee of such a sub-fund settlement, and
(g) if the settlement is a sub-fund settlement in relation to a principal settlement, a person in the capacity as trustee of any other sub-fund settlements in relation to the principal settlement.

575(4) A person who is a partner in a partnership is connected with–

(a) any partner in the partnership,
(b) the spouse or civil partner of any individual who is a partner in the partnership, and
(c) a relative of any individual who is a partner in the partnership.

But this subsection does not apply in relation to acquisitions or disposals of assets of the partnership pursuant to genuine commercial arrangements.

575(5) A company is connected with another company if–

(a) the same person has control of both companies,
(b) a person ("A") has control of one company and persons connected with A have control of the other company,

(c) A has control of one company and A together with persons connected with A have control of the other company, or

(d) a group of two or more persons has control of both companies and the groups either consist of the same persons or could be so regarded if (in one or more cases) a member of either group were replaced by a person with whom the member is connected.

575(6) A company is connected with another person ("A") if–

(a) A has control of the company, or

(b) A together with persons connected with A have control of the company.

575(7) In relation to a company, any two or more persons acting together to secure or exercise control of the company are connected with–

(a) one another, and

(b) any person acting on the directions of any of them to secure or exercise control of the company.'

Legislation: CAA 2001, s. 575

Chapter 14: Cash basis for small businesses and fixed rate deductions for expenses

23-000 Introduction and overview

From April 2013, eligible businesses can elect to calculate profits for tax purposes on the cash basis rather than in accordance with generally accepted accounting practice. Additionally, from 2013–14, certain business can choose to claim fixed rate deductions for certain expenses (see ¶23-360ff.).

The 'cash basis for small businesses' means that small businesses can elect to be taxed on the basis of the cash that passes through their books, rather than having to do calculations designed for bigger or more complex businesses based on generally accepted accounting practice (ITTOIA 2005, s. 25A).

The cash basis is available to self-employed sole traders and those in partnership with other individuals if their turnover is less than the VAT registration threshold at the end of the tax year or double the VAT registration threshold at the end of the tax year for Universal Credit recipients. Businesses will be able to continue to use the scheme until their receipts exceed double the VAT registration threshold (ITTOIA 2005, s. 31B).

The scheme is available for businesses that are conducting a trade, profession or vocation, i.e. those businesses which would otherwise be charged to tax under ITTOIA 2005, Pt. 2 (ITTOIA 2005, s. 31E(1)). (NB Rules apply for the purposes of a profession or vocation as they do for a trade, unless otherwise stated and references to a trade, and to related words, should be read accordingly.)

Certain businesses are not allowed to use the cash basis, such as partnerships where not all the partners are individuals, limited liability partnerships, Lloyd's underwriters, businesses with a herd basis or profit averaging election, businesses that have claimed business premises renovation allowance, businesses that carry on a mineral extraction trade and businesses that have claimed a research and development allowance (ITTOIA 2005, s. 31C).

The rules concerning the tax treatment of some specific trades are also disapplied under the cash basis, these include dealers in securities, ministers of religion and waste disposal (ITTOIA 2005, s. 148K).

Use of the cash basis is optional, but once a business has elected to use the cash basis, they will be obliged to continue to use it until either they are no longer eligible under ITTOIA 2005, s. 31A or there has been a change in circumstances so that it is more appropriate for profits to be calculated in accordance with generally accepted accounting practice and the business elects to calculate profits in that way (ITTOIA 2005, s. 31D).

Key aspects of the cash basis are that:

- receipts include money received for non-durable assets;
- allowable payments are those expenses paid wholly and exclusively for the trade, including payments for non-durable assets;
- in general, expenditure on business assets that would have qualified as plant and machinery (if the business had not been in the cash basis) is an allowable deduction (but not expenditure on cars). Expenditure on cars can either be relieved under normal principles (i.e. capital allowances for the acquisition cost and a revenue deduction for running costs) or, alternatively fixed allowances for business mileage can be used (see ¶23-380);
- interest payments are allowed up to a limit of £500 (see ¶23-200); and
- business losses are only able to be carried forward to set against future profits of the same trade and are not able to be carried back or set off 'sideways' against other income or capital gains (ITA 2007, s. 74E). The only exception is that where a trade has ceased losses can be set against profits of the same trade for the year of cessation and the three years prior to the year of cessation (for commentary on terminal loss relief, see ¶25-160).

The cash basis does not change the way a business should account for VAT. VAT-registered businesses using the cash basis can either record business receipts and payments excluding or including VAT. If VAT inclusive figures are used, the net VAT payments to HMRC should be recorded as expenses and net repayments from HMRC as receipts.

23-020 Eligibility

A person can make an election for the profits of their trade to be calculated on the cash basis under ITTOIA 2005, s. 25A instead of in accordance with generally accepted accounting practice if certain conditions are met (ITTOIA 2005, s. 31A).

The conditions are:

A: The aggregate cash basis receipts of each trade carried on by the person during the relevant tax year must not exceed any 'relevant maximum' – see ¶23-040.

B: Where the person is either an individual who controls a firm or a firm controlled by an individual:

  (a) the aggregate of the cash basis receipts of each trade, profession or vocation carried on by the individual or firm during that tax year does not exceed any relevant maximum applicable for the tax year; and

  (b) the firm or the individual has also made an election under s. 25A for that tax year.

C: The person must not be an excluded person – see ¶23-080.

Legislation: ITTOIA 2005, s. 25A, 31A

23-040   Relevant maximum

There is a relevant maximum for the purposes of s. 31A if any of three conditions, A to C, are met:

A: a person did not make a cash basis election for the previous tax year;
B: the aggregate cash basis receipts of each trade carried on by the person during the previous tax year is greater than twice the VAT registration limit at the end of that tax year; or
C: the person is either an individual who controls a firm or a firm controlled by an individual, the aggregate of the cash basis receipts of each trade carried on by the individual or the firm during the previous tax year is greater than an amount equal to twice the VAT registration limit at the end of that previous year.

If a relevant maximum applies, the amount of the relevant maximum is:

- the VAT registration limit at the end of the tax year (so for 2016–17 this is £83,000); or
- where the person is a universal credit claimant in the tax year, double the VAT registration limit at the end of the tax year.

If the basis period (see ¶20-080ff.) for the tax year is less than 12 months, the VAT registration limit is proportionately reduced.

A 'universal credit claimant' means a person who is entitled to universal credit under the *Welfare Reform Act* 2012, Pt. 1 or any similar provision made for Northern Ireland.

Legislation: ITTOIA 2005, s. 31B

23-060   Application to partnerships

The relevant maximum is applied to the aggregate of cash basis receipts of each trade carried on by a person during the tax year. For a sole trader, this means aggregating the receipts from all trades carried on.

Partnerships without a controlling partner

Partnerships without a controlling partner are effectively treated as a separate person and are eligible to use the cash basis if the partnership cash basis receipts do not exceed the relevant maximum amount. This is irrespective of whether the individual partners have other trades and irrespective as to whether the individual partners claim the cash basis in respect of any other trades.

If the individual partners wish to claim the cash basis in respect of any other businesses (excluding the partnership), only the cash basis receipts of their separate sole trades are aggregated to establish whether the relevant maximum is exceeded and it does not matter whether the partnership also uses the cash basis or not.

Partnerships with a controlling partner

Partnerships with a controlling partner, however, must take into account the cash basis receipts of any other business carried on by the controlling partner in determining whether the relevant maximum is exceeded. If the maximum is exceeded, neither the partnership business nor the other businesses carried on by the controlling partner may use the cash basis. If the maximum is not exceeded (receipts are less than or equal to the relevant maximum amount), the partnership or the other businesses may elect to use the cash basis, however, if an election is made, all of the businesses, including the partnership business, must use the cash basis and both the partnership and the controlling partner must elect to use the cash basis.

A controlling partner is a partner entitled to more than half of the assets or income of the partnership. Where two partners own a partnership equally, there is no controlling partner.

Example

Tessa and Justin are 50/50 partners in a landscape gardening partnership.

The partnership's cash basis receipts for the year ended 5 April 2016 are £76,000.

Tessa has a separate sole trade dealing in rare orchids, and her cash basis receipts for the same period are £45,000.

Justin also has a separate sole trade as a florist. Cash basis receipts of this business to 5 April 2016 are £90,000.

Neither Tessa nor Justin claim Universal Credit.

The landscape gardening partnership can elect to calculate its profits using the cash basis, as the partnership receipts do not exceed the VAT registration threshold for the tax year. As there is no controlling partner, it is not necessary to take into account Tessa's or Justin's receipts from their sole trading activities.

Since Tessa's sole trade receipts do not exceed the threshold, she can also elect to use the cash basis to calculate her profits from her orchid trade. She can use the cash basis even if the partnership elects not to.

Justin's sole trade receipts mean that he is ineligible to use the cash basis. He must use generally accepted accounting practice to calculate the profits of his florist trade.

Legislation: ITTOIA 2005, s. 31A

23-080   Excluded persons

A person will not be able to elect to use the cash basis if they are an excluded person.

The following are excluded persons:

- a partnership which had a partner who was not an individual at any time during the basis period for the tax year (e.g. a partnership with a corporate partner);

- a partnership which was a limited liability partnership at any time during the basis period for the tax year;
- an individual who was a Lloyd's underwriter at any time during the basis period for the tax year;
- a person who has made a herd basis election under ITTOIA 2005, Pt. 2, Ch. 8 for the tax year;
- a person who has made a claim under ITTOIA 2005, s. 221 for profits averaging for the tax year (for creative works, farmers and market gardeners);
- a person who has within the previous seven years obtained a business premises renovation allowance under CAA 2001, Pt. 3A;
- a person who has carried on a mineral extraction trade at any time during the basis period for the tax year;
- a person who has at any time obtained a research and development allowance under CAA 2001, Pt. 6 in respect of qualifying expenditure incurred by the person and the person owns an asset representing the expenditure.

Legislation: ITTOIA 2005, s. 31C

23-100   Effect of making an election

The cash basis is optional, but once a business has elected to use the cash basis they will be obliged to continue to use it until either they are no longer eligible under ITTOIA 2005, s. 31A or there has been a change in circumstances so that it is more appropriate for profits to be calculated in accordance with generally accepted accounting practice and the business elects to calculate profits in that way (ITTOIA 2005, s. 31D). Exactly what constitutes 'changes in circumstances' is not detailed in the legislation, but at BIM70055, HMRC give the examples of a business that is expanding and wishes to claim more than £500 interest deductions or a business that wishes to claim 'sideways' loss.

If a person's cash basis election ceases to have effect for one of the above reasons, it does not prevent that person making a cash basis election for a subsequent tax year.

An election to calculate partnership profits using the cash basis must be made on the partnership return (see ¶17-100). Where there is a controlling partner, the controlling partner must also elect to use the cash basis.

Non-controlling individual partners may elect to use the cash basis in respect of any other trades. An election applies to every trade, profession and vocation carried on by that person except in respect of the partnership business.

A person who has made a cash basis election is not able to claim capital allowances (nor be subject to any charge) other than in respect of a car (CAA 2001, s. 59).

Legislation: ITTOIA 2005, s. 31D

23-120 Calculating profits

There are two steps to calculating profits on the cash basis. Firstly, calculate the total trade receipts received in the basis period for the tax year and secondly, deduct the total expenses of the trade paid during the basis period of the tax year (subject to any adjustments required or allowed by law). The basis period for a tax year is normally the 12 months to the date the accounts are made up to in that tax year. For commentary on basis periods, see ¶20-080ff.

According to HMRC, 'the business can treat income as received and expenses as paid at the date of its choosing, as long as the treatment is consistent. For example, an expense may be paid when a card payment is made, or on the date that entry is shown on the bank statement' (BIM70005).

Where a partnership uses the cash basis, each partner's share will be based on the profit or loss calculated using the cash basis regardless of whether the individual partner is eligible or chooses to use the cash basis in respect of any of their other trading activities.

Legislation: ITTOIA 2005, s. 31E

23-140 Receipts and expenses

Generally, the rules about expenses and receipts are the same as for businesses preparing accounts in accordance with generally accepted accounting practice, other than being on a paid and received basis.

There are specific rules about receipts that apply only to businesses using the cash basis.

Capital receipts

If expenditure was incurred in acquiring, creating or improving an asset and this has been deducted either in full or in part in calculating profits under the cash basis, or would have been deducted if the business had made a cash basis election at the time the expenditure was paid, the following receipts must be included in calculating the business's profits:

- any proceeds arising from the disposal of the asset or any part of it;
- any proceeds arising from the grant of any rights in respect of, or any interest in, the asset; and
- any damages, insurance or other compensation received in respect of the asset.

Where only part of the expenditure incurred in acquiring, creating or improving an asset has been or would have been brought into account the receipt is proportionately reduced.

Where an asset ceases to be used for the purposes of the trade, the market value of the asset must be included as a receipt.

Where the non-business use of the asset materially increases, the relevant proportion of the asset's market value must be included as a receipt (an example of how this works in practice is included in BIM70020).

(ITTOIA 2005, s. 96A)

Value of trading stock on cessation of trade

Where a person within the cash basis permanently ceases to carry on a trade in a tax year the value of any trading stock at the time of cessation must be included as a receipt in calculating the profits of the trade for the tax year.

The value is to be determined on a just and reasonable basis.

If there is a change in the persons carrying on a trade no trading stock adjustment will be required as long as a person carrying on the trade immediately before the change continues to carry it on after the change.

(ITTOIA 2005, s. 97A)

Value of work in progress on cessation of profession or vocation

Where a person within the cash basis permanently ceases to carry on a profession or vocation in a tax year, the value of any work in progress at the time of cessation must be included as a receipt in calculating the profits of the profession or vocation for the tax year.

The value is to be determined on a just and reasonable basis.

If there is a change in the persons carrying on a profession, no work in progress adjustment will be required as long as a person carrying on the profession immediately before the change continues to carry it on after the change.

(ITTOIA 2005, s. 97B)

Industrial development grants

Where a business using the cash basis receives an industrial development grant, they are not able to benefit from the exemption available to other businesses where the grant is towards the cost of specified capital expenditure (ITTOIA 2005, s. 105(2A)).

Non-commercial transactions

Where there is a difference between the amount brought into account in respect of a transaction and the amount that would be brought into account, if the transaction was at arm's length, then the amount which must be brought into account is a just and reasonable amount.

This does not apply to transactions involving capital receipts (see above) nor to gifts to charity.

(ITTOIA 2005, s. 106Aff.)

Other trade profit rules

Businesses within the cash basis are not able to use any of the following rules, claims, elections and reliefs to calculate their profits:

- herd basis rules (ITTOIA 2005, Pt. 2, Ch. 8);
- sound recordings (ITTOIA 2005, Pt. 2, Ch. 9);
- telecommunication rights (ITTOIA 2005, Pt. 2, Ch. 10);
- long funding leases (ITTOIA 2005, Pt. 2, Ch. 10A);
- dealers in securities etc. (ITTOIA 2005, s. 149–154A);
- relief in respect of mineral royalties (ITTOIA 2005, s. 157);
- lease premiums etc.: reduction of receipts (ITTOIA 2005, s. 158);
- ministers of religion (ITTOIA 2005, s. 159);
- mineral exploration and access (ITTOIA 2005, s. 161);
- payments by persons liable to pool betting duty (ITTOIA 2005, s. 162);
- intermediaries treated as making employment payments (ITTOIA 2005, s. 163 and 164);
- managed service companies (ITTOIA 2005, s. 164A);
- waste disposal (ITTOIA 2005, s. 165–168);
- cemeteries and crematoria (ITTOIA 2005, s. 169–172ZE);
- changes in trading stock (ITTOIA 2005, Pt. 2, Ch. 11A);
- deductions from profits unremittable amounts (ITTOIA 2005, Pt. 2, Ch. 13);
- disposal and acquisition of know-how (ITTOIA 2005, Pt. 2, Ch. 14);
- averaging profits of farmers and creative artists (ITTOIA 2005, Pt. 2, Ch. 16);
- compensation for compulsory slaughter of animal (ITTOIA 2005, Pt. 2, Ch. 16ZA); and
- oil activities (ITTOIA 2005, Pt. 2, Ch. 16A).

Legislation: ITTOIA 2005, s. 31E, 96A, 97A, 97B, 105(2A), 106Aff.

23-160 Restricting expenses

The following rules restricting deductions do not apply to businesses using the cash basis:

- capital expenditure (ITTOIA 2005, s. 33);
- bad and doubtful debts (ITTOIA 2005, s. 35);
- unpaid remuneration (ITTOIA 2005, s. 36 and 37);
- employee benefit contributions where profits are calculated before the end of the nine month period (ITTOIA 2005, s. 43);
- car hire (ITTOIA 2005, s. 48–50B); and

There are specific expense restrictions that apply only to businesses using the cash basis:

(1) capital expenditure can only be deducted if the expenditure would have qualified for plant and machinery capital allowances and is not expenditure on a car (ITTOIA 2005, s. 33A);

(2) employee benefit contributions can only be deducted if they have been paid in the taxable period (ITTOIA 2005, s. 38(2A));

(3) interest paid on a loan is specifically disallowed under ITTOIA 2005, s. 51A(1), but this is subject to ITTOIA 2005, s. 57B;

(4) contributions to agents' expenses under a payroll deduction scheme will only be allowed for expenses which have been incurred (ITTOIA 2005, s. 72(2A)); and

(5) expenses of setting up a SAYE or CSOP option scheme are only allowable for expenses actually paid (ITTOIA 2005, s. 94A(4)).

Legislation: ITTOIA 2005, s. 32A

23-180 Expenditure normally specifically allowable

The following rules allowing expenses do not apply to businesses using the cash basis:

- tenants under taxed leases (ITTOIA 2005, s. 60–67); and
- replacement and alteration of trade tools (ITTOIA 2005, s. 68).

Legislation: ITTOIA 2005, s. 60–68

23-200 Loan interest

Where a deduction for loan interest would be disallowed under ITTOIA 2005, s. 51A(1) (see ¶23-160) or because (and only because) it is not an expense wholly and exclusively for the trade, a deduction is allowed of up to £500.

If a deduction is also claimed for incidental costs of obtaining finance under ITTOIA 2005, s. 58 the maximum deduction for both these expenses together is £500.

This £500 limit does not apply to payments of interest on purchases, provided the purchase itself is an allowable expense, as this is not cash borrowing. However, if the item purchased is used for both business and non-business purposes, only the proportion of interest related to the business usage is allowable.

Legislation: ITTOIA 2005, s. 56A

23-220 Transitional rules when changing accounting bases

ITTOIA 2005, Pt. 2, Ch. 17 deals with adjustment income where a person changes the basis on which he calculates the profits of his trade. These rules apply to business entering or leaving the cash basis.

Legislation: ITTOIA 2005, s. 227A

23-240 Entering the cash basis

Where a person enters the cash basis for a tax year, any expenditure that is unrelieved qualifying expenditure for capital allowances purposes at the end of the period before the business starts using the cash basis (apart from for cars) and would qualify as a deduction within the cash basis is allowable as a deduction in calculating the profits of the trade in the first year of using the cash basis and the pool is reduced to zero (unless the assets are not fully paid for).

Any existing car pool remains and continues to operate.

Where assets (other than cars) are not fully paid for and the amount paid exceeds the capital allowances given the difference is deductible for the purposes of calculating profit under the cash basis. Where the amount paid is less than the capital allowances given the difference is a receipt.

Legislation: ITTOIA 2005, s. 227A

23-260 Leaving the cash basis

Where a person leaves the cash basis and he has adjustment income as a result, this adjustment income will automatically be spread equally over six tax years (ITTOIA 2005, s. 239A). It is possible to elect to accelerate the charge.

Legislation: ITTOIA 2005, s. 239A

23-280   Election to accelerate the spreading of adjustment income on leaving the cash basis

A person can accelerate their adjustment income by making an election under ITTOIA 2005, s. 239B. The election must be made by the first anniversary of the self-assessment filing date for the tax year and must specify the amount to be treated as income arising in the tax year.

If an election is made under ITTOIA 2005, s. 239B, the spreading in the future years is calculated as if the amount of adjustment income were reduced by the amount given by the following formula:

$$A \times \frac{6}{T}$$

where:

A is the additional amount treated as arising in the tax year for which the election is made, and

T is the number of tax years remaining after that tax year in the period of six tax years referred to in ITTOIA 2005, s. 239A.

Legislation: ITTOIA 2005, s. 239A

23-300   Capital allowances

Where a person enters the cash basis for a tax year, any expenditure that is unrelieved qualifying expenditure for capital allowances purposes and would qualify as a deduction within the cash basis is allowable as a deduction in calculating the profits of the trade under the cash basis unless the assets are not fully paid for.

Where assets (other than cars) are not fully paid for and the amount paid exceeds the capital allowances given the difference is deductible for the purposes of calculating profit under the cash basis. Where the amount paid is less than the capital allowances given the difference is a receipt.

Legislation: ITTOIA 2005, s. 240B–240D

23-320   Tax relief on loans to buy plant or machinery for partnership use

From 2013–14 onwards, no tax relief is available for interest paid on a loan taken out by a partner to buy plant or machinery that would qualify for relief under ITA 2007, s. 388 (see ¶14-140) if the partnership has elected to be taxed on the cash basis.

Additionally, no tax relief is available for interest paid on a loan taken out by a partner to invest in a partnership that would qualify for relief under ITA 2007, s. 398 (see ¶14-160) if the partnership has elected to be taxed on the cash basis unless the loan is used for purchasing a share in a partnership (i.e. relief is denied for loans which contribute money to a partnership by capital or premium for use in the trade, or advance money to a partnership for use in the trade, or repay an earlier loan).

Legislation: ITA 2007, s. 384B

23-340   Restriction on sideways relief and capital gains relief where cash basis applies

Where the cash basis is used to calculate losses, no sideways relief or capital gains relief is available. Losses can only be carried forward against profits of the same trade or where the trade has ceased to be used against profits of the same year or previous three years.

Legislation: ITA 2007, s. 74E

DEDUCTIONS ALLOWABLE AT A FIXED RATE

23-360   Overview

From 2013–14, unincorporated businesses (more specifically self-employed individuals and partnerships where all the partners are individuals (ITTOIA 2005, s. 94C) can choose to use any of the following 'simplified expenses' deductions when computing business profits:

- fixed allowances for business mileage (instead of deductions for actual expenditure incurred purchasing, maintaining and running vehicles, apportioned between business and private use) (ITTOIA 2005, s. 94Dff.: see ¶23-380ff.);
- a flat rate to calculate expenses relating to business use of home (instead of deductions for expenditure incurred, apportioned between business and private use) (ITTOIA 2005, s. 94H: see ¶23-440ff.); and
- a three-tier banded rate to calculate the adjustment of private use of business premises (instead of deductions for expenditure incurred, apportioned between business and private use) (ITTOIA 2005, s. 94I: see ¶23-480ff.).

These simplified expenses were introduced alongside the cash basis (see ¶23-000ff.), but calculating expenses under these rules is entirely optional for businesses using the cash basis and any unincorporated business (excluding partnerships where any of the partners are not individuals) can use them whether or not they have chosen to use the cash basis.

Legislation: ITTOIA 2005, Pt. 2, Ch. 5A

23-380 Business mileage: fixed rate allowance

From 2013–14, unincorporated businesses can choose to deduct fixed allowances for business mileage instead of claiming deductions for actual expenditure incurred. The legislation specifically excludes any partnership in which one or more of the partners is not an individual (for example, a corporate partner) at any time during the period from benefitting from these rules (ITTOIA 2005, s. 94C). The rules apply to professions and vocations as they do to trades (ITTOIA 2005, s. 94B).

Legislation: ITTOIA 2005, s. 94B, 94C

23-400 When a fixed rate allowance for business mileage is allowable

If an unincorporated business would be allowed to deduct expenditure in calculating the profits of its trade, or would be were it not capital expenditure, on a vehicle which is used for the purposes of the trade, and is not an excluded vehicle (see below), the business can use the fixed rate allowance in respect of the qualifying expenditure (ITTOIA 2005, s. 94D(1), (2) and (3)).

An 'excluded vehicle' is a car, motor cycle or goods vehicle that is used for the purposes of the trade that is either:

- a car, motor cycle or goods vehicle on which the person carrying on the trade has at any time claimed capital allowances (ITTOIA 2005, s. 94E(2)); or
- a motor cycle or goods vehicle on which any expenditure incurred acquiring the vehicle has been deducted in calculating profits under the cash basis (ITTOIA 2005, s. 94E(3)) (for commentary on the cash basis, see ¶23-000ff.).

If a fixed rate allowance is claimed, no other deduction is allowed in respect of the qualifying expenditure, either in that period or any other period and only a fixed rate allowance deduction is allowed in respect of the relevant vehicle in any later period (ITTOIA 2005, s. 94D(4)). Given that once a fixed allowance for business mileage has been used for a particular vehicle, it will not be possible to change the basis in subsequent tax years, it is important that any decision to use this basis is carefully considered.

Legislation: ITTOIA 2005, s. 94D, 94E

23-420 The amount of the deduction

The amount of the deduction is the 'appropriate mileage amount' (ITTOIA 2005, s. 94D(5)).

The 'appropriate mileage amount' is calculated as the number of miles of business journeys driven by a person using the vehicle in the period multiplied by the rate applicable for that kind of vehicle. The rate applicable for cars and goods vehicles is

45p per mile for the first 10,000 miles and 25p per mile after that. For motor cycles the rate is 24p per mile, irrespective of the number of miles travelled.

The rates and bands are set out in ITTOIA 2005, s. 94F(2) and the Treasury may by regulations amend the rates or rate bands (ITTOIA 2005, s. 94F(6)).

Per HMRC Guidance (BIM75005), 'the mileage rate covers the costs of buying, running and maintaining the vehicle, such as fuel, oil, servicing, repairs, insurance, vehicle excise duty and MOT. The rate also covers depreciation of the vehicle'. However, incidental expenses of business journeys such as tolls, congestion charges and parking fees and the business proportion of the finance element of a hire purchase or finance lease can be claimed in addition to the mileage rate.

Given that this simplified expense is based on business miles travelled, it is vital that accurate business mileage records are maintained to support any claim.

Legislation: ITTOIA 2005, s. 94D, 94F

Other material: HMRC BIM75005

23-440   Use of home for business purposes: flat rate deduction

From 2013–14, unincorporated businesses can choose to make a flat rate deduction for use of home for business purposes instead of claiming deductions for actual expenditure incurred (ITTOIA 2005, s. 94H).

The legislation specifically excludes any partnership in which one or more of the partners is not an individual (for example a corporate partner) at any time during the period from benefitting from these rules (ITTOIA 2005, s. 94C). However, *Finance Act* 2016 introduces amendments to clarify how the rules should otherwise be applied for partnerships in respect of the use of home, ensuring that partnerships can fully access the provisions. The amendments will come into effect for the 2016–17 and following years.

The rules apply to professions and vocations as they do to trades (ITTOIA 2005, s. 94B).

If an incorporated business would be allowed to deduct expenditure in calculating the profits of its trade in respect of the use of home for business, it can use the flat rate deduction (ITTOIA 2005, s. 94H(1) and (2)).

Legislation: ITTOIA 2005, s. 94B, 94C, 94H

23-460   The amount of the deduction

The deduction is based on the amount of time spent working at home.

The deductible amount for an accounting period is the sum of the applicable amounts for each month, or part of a month, in the period (ITTOIA 2005, s. 94H(3)).

The applicable amount for a month, or part month, is:

- £10 – where the number of hours worked at home per month is 25 or more but less than 51;
- £18 – where the number of hours worked at home per month is 51 or more but less than 101; and
- £26 – where the number of hours worked at home per month is 101 or more.

The rates and bands are set out in ITTOIA 2005, s. 94H(4) and the Treasury may by regulations amend the rates or rate bands (ITTOIA 2005, s. 94H(6)).

The 'number of hours worked' means the number of hours spent wholly and exclusively on work done by the person, or any employee of the person, in the person's home wholly and exclusively for the purposes of the trade (ITTOIA 2005, s. 94H(4)). HMRC's view, as expressed at BIM75010, is that this means hours spent wholly and exclusively on 'core business activities' in the home. With core business activities comprising the provision of goods and/or services, the maintenance of business records and marketing and obtaining new business.

If the person has more than one home, those homes are treated as a single home for the purposes of calculating hours worked.

If businesses choose not to use the standard deduction they can claim an allowable portion of actual expenses.

HMRC state that in their view in respect of use of home for business purposes flat rate deduction 'the monthly flat rate includes all household running costs, such as heat, light, power, telephone and broadband/internet costs' (BIM75010). They also advise that for businesses not using the flat rate deduction for business use of home, then 'where private use of telephone/internet costs does not form a significant proportion of the service use, we will accept that the full amount of expenditure can be claimed'.

Where a person claims a flat rate deduction, they are still able to claim a separate deduction for fixed costs such as council tax, insurance and mortgage interest (BIM75010).

Legislation: ITTOIA 2005, s. 94H

23-480 Premises used both as a home and as business premises

From 2013–14, unincorporated businesses can choose to make a fixed rate adjustment where premises are used as a home, but are mainly used as business premises, instead of claiming deductions for actual expenditure incurred (ITTOIA 2005, s. 94I).

The legislation specifically excludes any partnership in which one or more of the partners is not an individual (for example a corporate partner) at any time during the period from benefitting from these rules (ITTOIA 2005, s. 94C). However, *Finance Act* 2016 introduces amendments to clarify how the rules should otherwise be applied for partnerships where business premises are also a home, ensuring that partnerships can fully access the provisions. The amendments will come into effect for the tax year 2016–17 and subsequent years.

The rules apply to professions and vocations as they do to trades (ITTOIA 2005, s. 94B).

To calculate the deduction allowable where business premises are used as a home, you start with the total amount of expenses and then deduct the 'non-business use amount'.

Legislation: ITTOIA 2005, s. 94B, 94C, 94I

23-500 The non-business use amount

The non-business use amount is based on the number of relevant occupants in the premises. A 'relevant occupant' means an individual (including a child and/or non-paying guest) who occupies the premises as a home or stays at the premises otherwise than in the course of the trade at any time during that month (ITTOIA 2005, s. 94I(6)).

The non-business use amount for an accounting period is the sum of the applicable amounts for each month, or part of a month, in the period (ITTOIA 2005, s. 94I(4)).

The applicable amount to be subtracted from the actual expenses is calculated as:

- £350 per month for a single person occupying the property privately;
- £500 per month for two people occupying the property privately; or
- £650 per month for three or more people occupying the property privately.

The rates and bands are set out in ITTOIA 2005, s. 94I(5) and the Treasury may by regulations amend the rates or rate bands (ITTOIA 2005, s. 94I(7)).

If businesses choose not to use the standard adjustment, they can claim an allowable portion of actual expenses.

Legislation: ITTOIA 2005, s. 94I

Chapter 15: Corporate loans and benefits to participators

24-000 Overview

The loans to participators rules have been around for as long as corporation tax and are designed to prevent the avoidance of tax by taking loans from companies, rather than dividends or salary which would trigger a charge to income tax on the individual receiving the dividend or salary.

The loans to participators legislation prevents this form of abuse by imposing a tax charge on the company for as long as any loan remains outstanding. The charge under s. 455 is 32.5% from 6 April 2016 (previously, 25%) of the amount loaned or advanced. However, where all or part of the loan has been repaid, or released or written off, relief is given from the tax charge (CTA 2010, s. 458(2)).

The charge to corporation tax

The charge arises where a close company makes a loan or advance of money to an individual who is a participator in the company, or to an individual who is an associate of such a participator (CTA 2010, s. 455(1)). Where such a loan is made, the company is required to pay an amount equal to 32.5% (from 6 April 2016, previously 25%) of the loan or advance, as if it were an amount of corporation tax chargeable on the company for the accounting period in which the loan or advance is made (CTA 2010, s. 455(2)). This mechanism of charging ensures that the sum concerned is treated in all ways as if it were a corporation tax charge on the company, so that there is no need for separate compliance procedures, etc. The tax is generally due and payable nine months and one day after the end of the accounting period (CTA 2010, s. 455(3)).

For these purposes, a loan or advance is also deemed to arise whenever a participator incurs a debt to the close company or a debt due from that person to someone else is assigned to the close company (CTA 2010, s. 455(4)).

Definitions

Close company

A close company is a company controlled by five or fewer participators or by any number of directors who are participators (CTA 2010, s. 439(2)). Alternatively, if five or fewer participators, or any number of director participators, are entitled to receive the greater part of the assets of the company were it to be wound up, the company is also close (CTA 2010, s. 439(3)).

Participator

In general terms, a participator is a shareholder in a company. However, the legislation extends the definition well beyond mere shareholders to include anyone with the sorts of rights that might be associated with a shareholding, even if they do not hold shares, and the sorts of rights associated with being a loan creditor, even if they are not actually loan creditors, and also includes rights which they may be entitled to acquire (s. 454(1) and (2)).

Associate

The loans to participators legislation also covers loans to associates of participators, which is another widely drawn concept. At its simplest, an associate of a participator includes any relative (spouse, civil partner, parent, remoter forebear, child or remoter issue, or any sibling (CTA 2010, s. 448(2)) or business partner (CTA 2010, s. 448(1)(a)). Trustees of certain settlements are also included (CTA 2010, s. 448(1)(b)–(d) as well as other companies with an interest in any company that is subject to a trust (s. 448(1)(d)–(e), personal representatives of a deceased persons estate which includes interest in share or obligations of a company as well as other companies with an interest in those shares or obligations(CTA 2010, s. 448(1)(f) and (g)).

Legislation: CTA 2010, s. 439, 448, 455, 458

24-020 Application to partnerships

Where a close company makes a loan or advance to a partnership (including an LLP) in which all of the partners/members are relevant persons and at least one of the partners/members is a participator in the company, then the other partners/members are likely to be associates of a participator. The loan is therefore to relevant persons and the loan or advance is within CTA 2010, s. 455.

Prior to the announcement on Budget Day 2013, it was widely held that the loans to participators rules did not apply where the loan was made to a limited liability partnership (LLP) which a participator of a close company was also to be a member of.

The view taken by many advisers was that a loan to a participator, given the definition of both participators and associates, did not include a loan to an LLP. The main thrust of the argument was that the LLP is a separate legal entity, being a body corporate, and it is not to be identified with the individuals or other legal persons who from time to time make up its membership.

By contrast, with an ordinary partnership (under the *Partnership Act* 1890), which is not a body corporate and does not have status as a legal person, it would have been more likely that, from a legal viewpoint, the loan by the company would be treated as a loan to its participators, on the basis that the legal approach would also be to look through the partnership to its members.

But the status of the LLP as a body corporate and separate legal person meant that the loan by the company was not, therefore, a loan to its participators.

The FA 2013 changes

HMRC say that they held a different view. Be that as it may, for loans or advances made on or after 20 March 2013, the date of the Budget announcement, the loans to participators rules were extended so that they now apply to loans to an LLP or other partnership, one or more of the partners in which is an individual who is a participator in the company or an associate of an individual who is a participator in the company (CTA 2010, s. 455(1)(c)). There are two points that are immediately noteworthy.

- The loan in Example 1, involving Flopsy, Mopsy and Cottontail, should not be caught by the new rules, if it were made before 20 March 2013. Any further loan would be caught by the new legislation. If substantial amendments were made to the terms of the current loan, it is possible that these would, in and of themselves, constitute the making of a new loan, which might be caught by the new rules.
- The other important feature is that HMRC have, to some extent, focused on pre-20 March 2013 loans to LLPs and challenged these as being loans to participators. While this does not appear to have become a campaign by HMRC, it must be noted that HMRC insisted and continues to insist that the extension of the loans to participators rules to encompass loans to LLPs is no more than clarification of the rules and is not, in their view, any form of extension. In other words, HMRC consider that loans to LLPs were always caught.

Planning

Example 1

The effect of the new rule will be to charge an amount under CTA 2010, s. 455(3) in the circumstances shown in Example 1. In the post-FA 2013 environment, such a structure would definitely carry a charge, and it would be necessary to undertake some form of planning to prevent that arising. The obvious planning, of course, would be to form another limited company, rather than an LLP, to make the acquisition. Loans to another close company are not caught by the loans to participator rules generally although, in some cases, a charge might be imposed by CTA 2010, s. 459.

Problem areas

Example 2

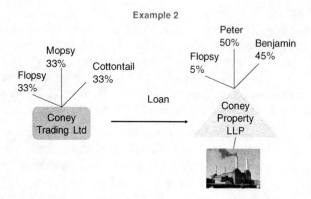

One of the problem areas with the rules arises in the situation shown in Example 2. In this case, Flopsy, the relevant participator has a one-third holding in the close company but only a small interest in the LLP. The loan is made on commercial terms and under purely commercial arrangements and the other members of the LLP are not members of the company. But they are associates of the relevant individual who is also a member of the close company, as they are Flopsy's business partners (s. 448(1)(a)). So a completely commercial loan made by a close company to a generally unrelated LLP will be caught by these arrangements in cases where, as here, a person is a minority participator in the company and a minority member of the LLP. This does seem to be a somewhat draconian result, and one which is arguably unrelated to the mischief that these rules are meant to prevent.

Legislation: CTA 2010, s. 448, 455

24-040   Benefits to participators

Background

Another new rule that came into force on 20 March 2013, which is not specifically targeted at partnerships. However, in the discussion documents relating to this new legislation, the main example given by HMRC of what they saw as abusive behaviour was shown in Example 3.

Example 3

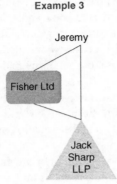

An individual, Jeremy, forms a company, Fisher Ltd. Together, they then form Jack Sharp LLP. There are many sensible commercial reasons for these structures. For example, the individual might wish to have the protection of limited liability status in law. There is no such thing as a limited liability sole trader, so the only way to achieve this is to form a partnership with another person and, in many cases, this is best achieved by the use of a company which is already wholly owned by the relevant individual.

Another commercial reason in the professional world might be the ability to use the logos and designations of a professional body. For example, until recently, if the individual was a member of the Chartered Institute of Taxation, then the LLP would be entitled to refer to itself as a firm of chartered tax advisers and use the CIOT logo. However, if the individual was in partnership with another individual who had no professional qualifications, the LLP was not entitled to use the logo or designation. So there are strong commercial reasons for setting up these structures.

The mischief HMRC were concerned about can be explained by assuming that the intended split of partnership profits was 20% to Jeremy and 80% to Fisher Ltd. If the LLP made £100,000 profit in a period, Jeremy would be entitled to draw £20,000 of the profits and the company would be entitled to draw £80,000. HMRC were concerned about situations where Jeremy might draw, say, £30,000 and the company not draw any profits. While the company has effectively funded Jeremy's overdrawn account, by not drawing its own profits, there is clearly no loan to a participator, as the company has not made a loan or advance to Jeremy, and nor has Jeremy incurred a debt to the company. He may have incurred a debt to the partnership, but that is not the same thing. So HMRC took the view that this sort of scenario should be the subject of a charge similar to that in CTA 2010, s. 455, and the relevant legislation is now in CTA 2010, s. 464A.

The FA 2013 legislation

The new rule requires a close company to be party to tax avoidance arrangements, as a result of which a benefit is conferred on an individual who is a participator in the company or an associate of such a participator (CTA 2010, s. 464A(1)). The rules apply whether that benefit is conferred directly or indirectly. Tax avoidance arrangements are arrangements whose main purpose, or one of the main purposes, is the avoidance or reduction of a charge under CTA 2010, s. 455, or the obtaining of relief or increased relief from tax on that section, or any other tax advantage for the participator or associate (CTA 2010, s. 464A(6)). So it can be seen that the charge is very widely drawn, and is certainly not restricted to the scenario outlined in Example 3.

Indeed, one might argue that that scenario is not caught by the new rules as it might be perfectly acceptable for Jeremy to overdraw from the LLP and one might argue that Fisher Ltd is not, itself, party to the arrangements. It is not clear how this argument would sit with HMRC, who would almost certainly dispute the position, but neither is it clear that the example they gave of the mischief that they were trying to prevent is resolved by this new legislation.

If the benefit itself either gives rise to a tax charge on the company under s. 455, or alternatively gives rise to an income tax charge on the individual (as would be the case for salary or dividends), then there is no application of this new rule (CTA 2010, s. 464A(2)).

Otherwise the charge is essentially identical to that of s. 455, being 32.5% (from 6 April 2016, previously 25%) of the value of the benefit conferred 'as if it were an amount of corporation tax chargeable on the company for the accounting period in which the benefit is conferred' (CTA 2010, s. 464A(3)). There is no explanation as to how the value of the benefit is to be determined, although in most cases it is assumed that the benefit will be in the form of cash or amounts otherwise easily identified. The tax is due nine months and one day after the end of the relevant accounting period (CTA 2010, s. 464A(4)), again the same as under s. 455.

As might be expected, relief is to be given if the company is paid in respect of the benefit ('the return payment'), so long as the company gives no consideration for the return payment (CTA 2010, s. 464B(2)). If the return payment is made prior to the due date for the corporation tax under s. 464A, the return payment reduces or eliminates the charge. If the return payment is made later than the due date, a repayment of tax paid is due nine months and one day after the end of the accounting period in which the appropriate payment is made (s. 464A(4) and (5)). The relief must be claimed within four years of the end of the financial year in which the return payment is made (CTA 2010, s. 464B(3)).

Legislation: CTA 2010, s. 464A–464B

Chapter 16:   Losses

25-000   Overview: trading losses

Partners are entitled to loss relief in respect of their share of partnership losses in the same way as other traders. Consequently, the income tax and corporation tax loss relief provisions applying for the relief of business losses generally are in point.

Computation of partnership losses is covered at **Chapter 9**, allocation of losses to partners (and reallocation where appropriate) is covered at **Chapter 10**.

Once the partnership loss has been established and allocated among the partners each individual partner or corporate partner must claim their/its own loss relief.

Individual partners: income tax relief

Broadly, the options available to an individual partner are:

- relief against general income (ITA 2007, s. 64–70): see ¶25-020);
- relief against chargeable gains (ITA 2007, s. 71) see ¶25-020);
- early years loss relief (ITA 2007, s. 72–74) see ¶25-040;
- relief against future profits from the same business (ITA 2007, s. 83–88): see ¶25-140; or
- terminal trade loss relief (ITA 2007, s. 89–94): see ¶25-160.

Company partners: corporation tax relief

Broadly, the options available to a company partner are:

- relief against total profits (CTA 2010, 37–38) (see ¶25-200);
- terminal loss relief (CTA 2010, s. 39–42) (see ¶25-220);
- relief against future profits from the same trade (CTA 2010, s. 45): see ¶25-240; or
- group loss relief (CTA 2010, Pt. 5): see ¶25-300.

Restrictions on loss relief for partners

A number of restrictions apply to trade losses incurred by partners. These include restrictions for:

- limited individual and company partners (ITA 2007, s. 103A, 103C–105, 113A and 114; CTA 2010, s. 56–58): see ¶25-400 and ¶25-560;
- individual and company members of limited liability partnerships (ITA 2007, s. 103C, 103D, 107–109, 113A and 114; CTA 2010, s. 59–61): see ¶25-420 and ¶25-580;

- non-active individual partners in early tax years (ITA 2007, s. 103B–103D and s. 110–114): see ¶25-460;
- individual partnerships who have exploited films (ITA 2007, s. 115): see ¶25-520;
- individual partners of a mixed membership partnership (ITA 2007, s. 116A): see ¶25-540.

Legislation: ITA 2007, Pt. 4; CTA 2010, Pt. 4 and Pt. 5

Other material: HMRC Briefs 18/07 and 19/07

25-020   Income tax relief against general income and gains

Where a trader, etc. sustains a loss in a tax year, he may claim relief from income tax against his general income in:

- the same tax year (ITA 2007, s. 64(2)(a));
- the preceding tax year (ITA 2007, s. 64(2)(b)); or
- both years (ITA 2007, s. 64(2)(c)).

Relief may not be given more than once for a loss or the same part of a loss.

A person with income tax losses may not have any other income against which to set those losses (or may have insufficient income to absorb the full amount of the losses). Such a person may be able to treat the unused part as an allowable loss for capital gains tax purposes (ITA 2007, s. 71; TCGA 1992, s. 261B and 261C).

Claims

Any claim to relief under ITA 2007, s. 64 must specify whether the loss is to be deducted in calculating the person's income for the loss-making year, for the previous year, or for both. If the claim relates to both years, the claimant must specify the year for which a deduction is to be made first (ITA 2007, s. 64(3), (4)). If a person makes a claim to set the loss against income of one of those years, he may subsequently make a further claim to set the unused part of the loss against income of the other year (s. 64(5)). However, once a claim is made in respect of a loss, all the available loss must be used subject to the claimant having sufficient income, before any part of the loss can be used in another year under another provision.

The claim must be made by the first anniversary of the normal self-assessment filing date for the year in which the loss is incurred (ITA 2007, s. 64(5)).

Relief is *not* restricted to preserve any unused personal allowance, so a loss claim may have the effect that some or all of the personal allowance is wasted (ITA 2007, s. 65(1)). This is the case even if a claim is made to offset the loss against income of two tax years.

It is possible that two separate claims may be made against income of the same year, in which case, the legislation requires that effect must be given to the loss sustained in the earlier year before that sustained in the later year (ITA 2007, s. 65(3)).

Restrictions on relief

Relief is restricted in various circumstances:

- for trades that are considered 'uncommercial' (ITA 2007, s. 66);
- for farming or market gardening ('hobby farming' (ITA 2007, s. 67–70);
- general restrictions on relief (ITA 2007, s. 74ZA–74D): see ¶25-060;
- restriction on the relief and early trade losses relief where cash basis applies (ITA 2007, s. 74E): see ¶25-080;
- restrictions on the relief and early trade losses relief in relation to capital allowances (ITA 2007, s. 75–79): see ¶25-100); and
- restrictions on those reliefs in relation to ring fence income (ITA 2007, s. 80): see ¶25-120.

See ¶25-180 for a restriction that applies (by virtue of ITA 2007, s. 95) to the offset of losses against capital gains where the trade is carried on wholly outside the UK.

Limit on relief

From 6 April 2013, the amount of income tax relief that an individual can set against his total income is capped, with one of the reliefs affected being that for trade loss relief against general income (ITA 2007, s. 65(1)). The limit is the greater of £50,000 or 25% of the individual's 'adjusted total income' for the tax year (ITA 2007, s. 24A).

Legislation: ITA 2007, s. 24A, 64, 65

25-040   Income tax early trade loss relief

A special relief ('early trade losses relief') applies to losses sustained in the tax year in which a trade is first carried on, or in any of the next three tax years. Such losses may be carried back and set against the claimant's income in the three tax years preceding that in which the loss was sustained (ITA 2007, s. 72).

The loss is set against the individual's net income for the three tax years before the year in which the loss is made, the loss being set against the claimant's income in earlier years before later years (ITA 2007, s. 73). As with other loss reliefs, it is not possible to apportion the loss for use over a number of years, so as to leave personal reliefs and allowances intact.

A claim must be made by the first anniversary of the normal self-assessment filing date for the year in which the loss is incurred (ITA 2007, s. 72(3)).

Restrictions on relief

Relief is restricted in various circumstances:

- restrictions on the relief unless trade is commercial, etc. (ITA 2007, s. 74);
- general restrictions on relief (ITA 2007, s. 74ZA–74D): see ¶25-060;
- restriction on the relief and trade loss relief where cash basis applies (ITA 2007, s. 74E): see ¶25-080;
- restrictions on the relief and trade loss relief against general income in relation to capital allowances (ITA 2007, s. 75–79): see ¶25-100; and
- restrictions on those reliefs in relation to ring fence income (ITA 2007, s. 80): see ¶25-120.

Limit on relief

From 6 April 2013, the amount of income tax relief that an individual can set against his total income is capped, with one of the reliefs affected being that for trade loss relief in first four years of trade (ITA 2007, s. 73). The limit is the greater of £50,000 or 25% of the individual's 'adjusted total income' for the tax year (ITA 2007, s. 24A).

Legislation: ITA 2007, s. 24A, 72–74

25-060　Income tax general restrictions on sideways relief

The term 'sideways relief' is used to refer to:

- relief for trade losses against general income: see ¶25-020; and
- early trade losses relief: see ¶25-040,

(ITA 2007, s. 60(4)).

No relief for tax-generated losses

There is a complete denial of sideways relief or capital gains relief for losses incurred by an individual or partner in certain circumstances. This complete denial of relief applies where:

- the person carries on a trade, profession or vocation (the 'relevant activity') in the tax year, either alone or in partnership;
- he or she incurs a loss in the relevant activity in that tax year; and
- the loss arises (directly or indirectly) 'in consequence of, or otherwise in connection with, relevant tax avoidance arrangements' (ITA 2007, s. 74ZA(1)).

Relevant tax avoidance arrangements is defined to cover arrangements to which the person is a party 'the main purpose, or one of the main purposes, of which is the obtaining of a reduction in tax liability by means of sideways relief or capital gains relief' (ITA 2007, s. 74ZA(3)). The concept of 'arrangements' is in its turn widely defined, to cover 'any agreement, understanding, scheme, transaction or series of transactions (whether or not legally enforceable)' (ITA 2007, s. 74ZA(4)).

This restriction does *not* apply, however, to any loss to the extent that it derives from qualifying film expenditure (see ¶25-520) (ITA 2007, s. 74ZA(5)).

Case law

The First-tier Tribunal (FTT) case of *Acornwood LLP* [2014] TC 03545 (known unofficially as Icebreaker 2), involved arrangements entered into by several partnerships for the acquisition and exploitation of intellectual property rights. For the one individual who entered into arrangements after 21 October 2009, and therefore to whom the provisions in ITA 2007, s. 74ZA applied, the FTT were satisfied that the individual 'knew that profits, in the true sense, were unlikely and that, absent a tax advantage, this was not a prudent investment since he was much more likely than not to lose the money paid in from his own resources', they were also satisfied that 'his primary motive for joining the partnership was to secure sideways relief; no other plausible conclusion is possible'. Therefore even if the scheme had worked to secure sideways loss relief for the partnerships' members, which the FTT concluded it substantially did not, this individual would have been denied sideways loss relief by virtue of ITA 2007, s. 74ZA.

Legislation: ITA 2007, s. 60(4), 74ZA

Cases: *Acornwood LLP* [2014] TC 03545

25-080   Income tax restrictions on sideways relief and capital gains relief where cash basis applies

For 2013–14 tax years onwards, certain businesses can elect to use the 'cash basis for small businesses' (see ¶23-000ff.). Where the cash basis is used to calculate losses no sideways relief or capital gains relief (see ¶25-020) will be given to the person for the loss (ITA 2007, s. 74E).

Legislation: ITA 2007, s. 74E

25-100   Income tax restrictions on sideways relief for certain capital allowances

Trade leasing allowances

'Sideways relief' is not given to an individual for losses from 'trade leasing allowances' unless the individual carrying on the trade meets a time commitment test. The purpose of the rule is to deny the more generous reliefs available for trading losses if the transaction is, in reality, a form of investment rather than trading as such.

A 'trade leasing allowance' is a plant and machinery allowance in relation to expenditure that is incurred:

- on the provision of plant or machinery for leasing in the course of a trade; or
- on the provision for the purposes of a trade of an asset that is not leased but that nevertheless generates royalties or licence fees by virtue of rights granted by the individual in connection with the asset,

(ITA 2007, s. 75(2), (3)).

The denial of relief is not imposed if the individual meets the time commitment test. This test is met if two conditions are met:

(1) Condition A is met if the individual carries on the trade (alone or in partnership) for a continuous period of at least six months, beginning or ending in the tax year basis period in which the loss was made.

(2) Condition B is met if the individual gives substantially the whole of his time to carrying on the trade (alone or in partnership) either for a continuous period of at least six months beginning or ending in that basis period (if the individual starts and/or ceases to carry on the trade in that tax year) or throughout the loss-making basis period (in any other case).

Where ITA 2007, s. 75 applies, so much of any loss deriving from the capital allowances can only be set against the profits of the same trade.

It will be accepted that an individual devotes substantially the whole of their time to carrying on a trade if the time they spend on it is equivalent to the full-time working week.

HMRC indicate (in *Business Income Manual* BIM85730) that they will not accept that an individual devotes substantially the whole of their time to carrying on a trade if they:

- are in full-time employment;
- run another business; or
- spend less than 30 hours a week carrying on the trade.

Restrictions re first year allowances and annual investment allowances

Sideways loss relief is not available for so much of a loss that is derived from an annual allowance or a first year allowance in either of the following circumstances (ITA 2007, s. 76):

Restriction re leases: partnerships with companies

Where a person carries on a qualifying activity in partnership with a company and the partnership incurs expenditure on plant or machinery for leasing. Sideways loss relief is also denied where arrangements are made for the qualifying activity to be carried on in a partnership either before or after the first year allowance or annual investment allowance is incurred. This ensures that an individual cannot start a leasing business, incur the expenditure and claim loss relief where arrangements have been made for a company to join the qualifying activity later on (ITA 2007, s. 77).

Arrangements to reduce tax liabilities

Where the individual carries on or will carry on the qualifying activity in partnership, or capital allowances were given on an asset which is transferred to a connected person or sold at a price below market value, and a scheme or arrangements are made of which the sole or main benefit that might be expected to arise to the individual from the transaction under which the expenditure was incurred is the obtaining of a reduction in tax liability by means of sideways relief (ITA 2007, s. 78). The legislation refers to a 'qualifying activity' which is wider than a trade. A qualifying activity as defined in CAA 2001, s. 15 includes also property businesses, management of investment companies, special leasing, mines and quarries (as well as employment or office).

Legislation: CAA 2001, s. 15; ITA 2007, s. 75–79

25-120   Income tax restrictions on sideways relief for specific trades

Sideways relief is only available against a person's ring fence income (defined as income arising from oil extraction activities or oil rights) to the extent that the loss arises from oil extraction activities or oil rights (ITA 2007, s. 80).

Sideways loss relief is restricted where the trade carried on by the individual consists of or includes the exploitation of films (see ¶25-520) (ITA 2007, s. 82).

Additionally, a stand-alone charge to income tax arises under ITA 2007, s. 796–803 (see ¶25-600ff.) if the individual made a loss in a trade consisting of or including the exploitation of films (whether carried on alone or as a partner in a firm) for which sideways relief is claimed and where non-taxable consideration is received for a disposal of a right to profits from the trade, or where losses claimed become greater than the contribution to the trade and there has been any disposal of rights to profits from the trade (ITA 2007, s. 82).

Legislation: ITA 2007, s. 80, 82, 796–803

25-140   Income tax carry-forward trade loss relief

Losses sustained by a trader (including a person carrying on a profession or vocation) may be carried forward and set against the income of the *same* trade (only) in subsequent tax years (ITA 2007, s. 83). Relief is only available if the loss has not already been wholly relieved in any other way (ITA 2007, s. 83(1)(b)) may be available to carry forward either because no claim was made under any other loss provision or because relief under such other provision was insufficient to absorb the full amount of the losses in question (ITA 2007, s. 83(2)). Relief against trading profits for a loss brought forward under this provision takes priority over any other reliefs against those profits (ITA 2007, s. 83(4)).

Legislation: ITA 2007, s. 83

25-160   Income tax terminal trade loss relief

Where a loss in a trade, profession or vocation is sustained during the 12 months prior to the date on which a trade, etc. is discontinued, it may be carried back and set against earlier profits of the same trade (ITA 2007, s. 89). Such losses are referred to in the legislation as 'terminal losses', and are given special treatment because it is clearly not possible to carry them forward as normal.

Terminal losses are trading losses sustained in the 'terminal loss period' (ITA 2007, s. 90(1)). This is the final 12 months of trading but is divided into two parts:

(1)   the period starting on 6 April prior to the cessation and ending on the date of cessation (ITA 2007, s. 90(1)(a)); and

(2)   the part of the preceding tax year falling within the 12 months to the cessation date (ITA 2007, s. 90(1)(b)).

The terminal loss includes the whole of any unused overlap relief. Any overlap relief is taken into account in calculating the loss (if any) that is made in the period from 6 April preceding the date of cessation to that cessation date (i.e. the loss referred to in (1) above and is ignored in making the calculation of any terminal loss arising in the preceding tax year (ITA 2007, s. 90(5)).

Periods of account of the notional trade are for these purposes taken to be the periods of account of the actual trade. In calculating the loss, it is necessary to look to the partner's individual share of the profit or loss of the actual trade for the period of account (ITA 2007, s. 90(6)).

Once a claim has been made for terminal loss relief, the loss is set first against any trading profits (from the same trade) of the year of cessation. Any remaining loss is then set against profits from the trade of the preceding year, then of the year before that and finally of the year before that (ITA 2007, s. 91). In other words, relief is given, so far as possible, against the profits of later years before earlier years.

If there is a remaining loss that is not fully exhausted in that way, then the excess may be the subject of an alternative claim to relief, for example in being set against general income, but obviously subject to the conditions applying to such other relief.

Trade-related interest or dividends

A trader may have a terminal loss that cannot be wholly relieved due to insufficiency of profits, and also interest or dividends that would have formed part of his business profit had they not been charged to tax in another way. In such cases, the interest or dividends are treated for these purposes as if they were trading profits, and relief is given accordingly (ITA 2007, s. 92).

Carry back of interest payments as losses

Where a payment of interest on a loan to buy plant or machinery for use in a partnership, or on a loan to invest in a partnership (see ¶14-140; ¶14-160) is made wholly and exclusively for the purposes of a trade, etc. carried on at least partly in the UK, and full relief cannot be given because of an insufficiency of income in the tax year in which the payment was made, it may be treated for the purposes of claiming terminal loss relief as a trading loss made in the trade at the date of payment (ITA 2007, s. 94).

Legislation: ITA 2007, s. 89–94

25-180 Income tax losses from trade carried on abroad

Relief is restricted where a loss is sustained in a trade, profession or vocation carried on wholly outside the UK (ITA 2007, s. 95). Restrictions apply to:

- sideways relief (see ¶25-020 and ¶25-040);
- trade income relief (encompassing both carry-forward trade loss relief (see ¶25-140) and terminal trade loss relief (see ¶25-160); and
- relief under TCGA 1992, s. 261B (use of trading loss as a CGT loss: see ¶25-020).

More specifically:

- sideways relief for the loss is available only against the person's 'qualifying foreign income';
- trade income relief is available only against the person's 'qualifying foreign trade income'; and
- relief under TCGA 1992, s. 261B does not apply in relation to the loss.

For these purposes, and subject to the caveat below, 'qualifying foreign trade income' means the profits of any trade, profession or vocation carried on wholly outside the UK. Qualifying foreign income includes both qualifying foreign trade income and any income falling within ITEPA 2003, s. 23, 355, 575, 613, 615, 631 or 635 (foreign employment or pension income).

The terms 'qualifying foreign income' and 'qualifying foreign trade income' do not include any income charged to income tax in accordance with ITTOIA 2005, s. 832 (relevant foreign income charged on the remittance basis).

Legislation: ITA 2007, s. 95

25-200 Corporation tax loss relief against total profits

On the making of a claim, a company which has made a trading loss for an accounting period can set the loss against its total profits for that accounting period (CTA 2010, s. 37(3)(a)). This is referred to as sideways relief.

A company's total profits for an accounting period are the sum of its income chargeable to corporation tax and its chargeable gains for that period, both after taking account of any relief due (CTA 2010, s. 4(3)).

A claim for sideways relief cannot be restricted to leave some profits chargeable. Where the loss for a period equals or exceeds the total profits for that period, a claim for sideways relief can only be made in respect of the amount of the loss which reduces the total profits to nil. Where losses remain after sideways relief has been given, a claim can be made to carry the excess amount back and/or forward (see ¶25-240).

Sideways relief for trade losses is given *after* relief for a current year non-trading deficit on loan relationships (CTA 2009, s. 461(6)(a)) but *before*:

- relief for a non-trading deficit on loan relationships which has been carried back (CTA 2009, s. 462 and 463);
- relief for qualifying charitable donations (CTA 2010, s. 189(2); this order of set-off also applying for charges on income); and
- group relief (CTA 2010, s. 137(4) and (5)).

Carry back

If losses remain **after** a claim for sideways relief has been made, relief against the total profits of earlier periods can also be claimed (CTA 2010, s. 37(3)(b)). Relief by way of carry-back can only be claimed after sideways relief has been claimed; it is not possible to forgo or restrict sideways relief in order to maximise the relief which can be claimed against the profits of earlier periods. It is also not possible to restrict a carry-back claim to preserve losses; if a claim is made, it must be made in respect of the whole of the loss with only the excess amount being carried forward.

A loss can only be carried back to a period if the loss-making trade was carried on in that period and if it was not carried on wholly outside the UK (CTA 2010, s. 37(6)). It should be noted that the requirement is for the trade to be carried on in that period and not throughout it.

Trade losses can only be carried back against previous accounting periods so far as they fall within the period of 12 months ending immediately before the loss-making period begins, subject to three exceptions:

(1) where the loss is incurred in the 12 months immediately preceding the cessation of the trade (see ¶25-220);

(2) where the loss is incurred in an accounting period ending after 23 November 2008 and before 24 November 2010; and

(3) where a loss arises as a result of the special 100% capital allowances due under CAA 2001, s. 163 for the decommissioning costs of offshore machinery and plant used in a North Sea oil extraction/exploitation ('ring fence') trade.

Relief is given on a LIFO basis, meaning that the loss is carried back to the first accounting period to precede the loss period, then to the next earlier period and so on, so long as the earlier periods are within the required period.

Where group relief is claimed, this is given *before* relief for trading losses which have been carried back from a later period (CTA 2010, s. 137(4)(a) and (5)(a)).

Claims

Loss relief claims can be made within two years of the accounting period in which the loss is incurred.

Restrictions

For general restrictions on company loss relief, see ¶25-260.

Legislation: CTA 2010, s. 37

25-220   Corporation tax terminal loss relief

Where a company's trade ceases, and a trading loss is incurred in an accounting period which began no more than 12 months before the date of cessation, the loss in respect of that period can be carried back three years (CTA 2010, s. 39). Where an accounting period ends, but does not begin, in the 12-month period ending with the date of cessation, a proportion of the trading loss incurred in that accounting period can be carried back three years. The proportion of the loss to be carried back in this manner is to be calculated on a time basis. The remainder of the loss can be carried back in the usual way. The rules applying to the carry-back of losses one year apply as if the words 'three years' were substituted for the words 'twelve months'.

Partnership losses (and profits) for corporation tax purposes are calculated on the assumption that the partnership is a company (the deemed company) (CTA 2009, s. 1261(1)). The deemed company is assumed to:

(1)   cease to trade (accounting period ends) on the date when no company carries on the trade in partnership (where the trade had previously been carried on in partnership by persons including a company);

(2)   ceases to trade and immediately afterwards starts to trade (accounting period ends and another accounting period begins) on the occurrence of a change of persons carrying on the trade where a corporate partner is replaced with another corporate partner but there is no corporate continuity (in that no corporate partner was a partner both before and after the change).

(CTA 2009, s. 1261(2)(c), (d), (4) and (5)).

Legislation: CTA 2009, s. 1261; CTA 2010, s. 39

25-240 Corporation tax carry-forward trade loss relief

Relief for a trading loss is available against income of the same trade in succeeding accounting periods (CTA 2010, s. 45). Relief may also be available against interest or dividends on investments where there are insufficient trading profits in the later period, but only where those amounts would be brought into account as trading receipts were they not taxed under another head of charge (CTA 2010, s. 46).

Relief is given automatically; there is no requirement to make a claim.

The loss is deducted from future income of the trade in the earliest accounting period for which trading profits (from the same trade) exist. The amount carried forward is the balance unused by any claim under CTA 2010, s. 37 (i.e. against profits of the loss-making period and earlier periods; see ¶25-200). To the extent that the next available period of trading profit does not absorb the whole of the loss, the balance carries forward to the following period of trading profit and so on until the loss is completely relieved.

Relief for losses carried forward is given against trading income and not total profits as is the case for sideways relief and carry-back relief. It is therefore given before reliefs against total profits including relief for a current year non-trading deficit on loan relationships (CTA 2009, s. 461(5)).

Companies going into partnership

Where a trading company takes another person into partnership and continues to carry on the same trade, losses incurred by the company in the trade before the formation of the partnership may be set-off under CTA 2010, s. 45 against the company's share of the partnership trading income.

Legislation: CTA 2010, s. 45

25-260 Corporation tax restrictions on use of losses

A number of restrictions apply in respect of company losses:

- relief for claims made under CTA 2010, s. 37 (sideways and carry-back relief for trade losses) may be restricted where there has been a qualifying change and a main purpose of that change was to give rise to a claim, or increased claim, for relief (the 'transfer of deductions' anti-avoidance rules) (CTA 2010, Pt. 14A);
- trade loss relief (under CTA 2010, s. 37, 42 and 45) may be restricted where the ownership of a company has changed in proximity to a major change in the nature or conduct of the business (CTA 2010, Pt. 14);
- trade loss relief (under CTA 2010, s. 37) is not available where the trade is carried on wholly outside the UK (CTA 2010, s. 37(5));

- trade loss relief (under CTA 2010, s. 37) is not available where a trade is not conducted on a commercial basis and with a view to making profits (CTA 2010, s. 44);
- trade loss relief (under CTA 2010, s. 37) may be restricted where losses are incurred in respect of a farming or market gardening trade (CTA 2010, s. 48);
- trade loss relief (under CTA 2010, s. 37) is only available against ring fence income to the extent that the loss arises from oil extraction activities or from oil rights (CTA 2010, s. 304(1));
- where a non-resident company receives interest, dividends or royalties, which are tax-exempt under double taxation arrangements, receipts are not to be excluded from profits of the trade so as to give rise to a loss deductible under CTA 2010, s. 37 or 45 (CTA 2010, s. 54);
- relief under CTA 2010, s. 37 will not be available in respect of any losses made in a trade of dealing in commodity futures where the company has carried on the trade as a partner in a partnership if arrangements have been entered into with the sole or main purpose of securing relief under CTA 2010, s. 37 (CTA 2010, s. 52);
- where losses are incurred on the writing off a government investment (CTA 2010, s. 91)
- in respect of agreements to forgo tax relief (FA 2009, s. 25);
- in respect of companies carrying on a leasing business (CTA 2010, s. 53);
- in respect of a film production company (CTA 2009, Pt. 15); and
- where a trading loss is attributable in whole or part to capital allowances, the capital allowance loss-buying rules may apply to restrict the ways in which the loss can be utilised (CAA 2001, Pt. 2, Ch. 16A).

Legislation: CAA 2001, Pt. 2, Ch. 16A; FA 2009, s. 25; CTA 2009, Pt. 15; CTA 2010, s. 37, 44, 45, 48, 52, 53, 54, 91, 304, Pt. 14A

25-280   Corporation tax restriction on transferring relief

The provisions contained in CTA 2010, Pt. 22, Ch. 3 are designed to prevent a company adjusting its share in the profits or loss of a partnership by means of a payment.

These provisions apply to a company (A) which carries on a trade in partnership and where there are arrangements under which:

(a)   in relation to all or part of A's share in the loss of the partnership company, A, or a person connected with A, receives any payment or other benefit (excluding, in certain instances, payments made in respect of group relief); or

(b)   in relation to all or part of A's share in the profits or loss of the partnership, another partner, B, or a person connected with B, receives any payment or other benefit,

(CTA 2010, s. 959).

Arrangements may be in writing or otherwise and may be part of the terms of the partnership or otherwise (CTA 2010, s. 962).

Where such arrangements exist in an accounting period of the partnership, the partner company A is to a large extent treated as carrying on the partnership trade in isolation and consequently it has only limited rights to certain reliefs, as follows:

- the company can only set off its share of any partnership loss or charges on income for that period against its share of partnership profits;
- the company cannot set off its loss from any other trade against its share of profits from the partnership for that period; and
- the company cannot set off against its share of the partnership profits for that period contained in its total profits any relief not relating to the partnership,

(CTA 2010, s. 960).

These provisions apply to any share of the company in partnership profits that are assessable to corporation tax under or by virtue of any provision to which CTA 2010, s. 1173 (miscellaneous charges) applies as if the company's share were attributable to trading profits or loss of the partnership from a trade (CTA 2010, s. 961(1) and (2)); presumably a separate distinct trade). In such cases, any capital allowances available on leased plant or machinery otherwise than in the course of a trade which would normally be deductible from income under the lease are treated as trading expenses of *that* trade (CTA 2010, s. 961(3)).

To determine a company's share in partnership profits or loss for the purposes of these provisions, the partnership profits are computed according to the normal rules (¶18-160 above) applicable to company partnerships.

Legislation: CTA 2010, s. 958–962

25-300 Corporation tax group loss relief

Where a company has a loss or other amount for a period, and it is part of a group or is owned by, or is a member of, a consortium, that loss can be surrendered as group relief.

For group relief purposes, two companies are members of the same 'group' of companies if one is a 75% subsidiary of the other or both are 75% subsidiaries of a third company (CTA 2010, s. 152). It is no longer necessary for all members of a group to be UK resident although group relief is only available for losses of non-UK resident companies in restricted circumstances.

A company is owned by a consortium if:

(1)   it is not a 75% subsidiary of any company; and

(2)   at least 75% of its ordinary share capital is beneficially owned by other companies each of which beneficially owns at least 5% of that capital (the other companies being the 'members of the consortium'),

(CTA 2010, s. 153(1) and (2)).

A claim for group relief can be made by a company (the 'claimant company') in respect of an accounting period (the 'claim period') where:

- another company (the 'surrendering company') has losses or other amounts ('surrenderable amounts') for an accounting period (the 'surrender period');
- the 'group condition' or one of three consortium conditions is met;
- there is a period (the 'overlapping period') which is common to the claim period and the surrender period; and
- the surrendering company consents to the claim.

Group relief is given to the claimant company by deduction from its total profits of the claim period. This deduction is to be made after all other available deductions save for:

(1)   relief for a trading loss of a later period under CTA 2010, s. 37;

(2)   relief for capital allowances of a later period under (special leasing); and

(3)   relief for a non-trading deficit of a later period under CTA 2009, s. 389 or 459.

(CTA 2010, s. 137(1), (4)–(6); for these purposes too, it must be assumed that the company has claimed all relief available to it for the claim period under CTA 2010, s. 37 or CAA 2001, s. 260(3).)

The basic rule is that the amount of group relief which can be claimed is limited to the lower of:

(1)   the unused part of the surrenderable amounts; and

(2)   the unrelieved part of the claimant company's available total profits for the claim period.

(CTA 2010, s. 138).

Legislation: CTA 2010, Pt. 5

RESTRICTIONS ON TRADE LOSS RELIEF FOR PARTNERS

25-320 Restrictions on trade loss relief for partners: background

For many years, there have been rules to restrict the tax relief available to partners who sustain tax losses. The Revenue had lost a case (*Reed v Young* [1986] BTC 242) in which substantial losses had been claimed by a partner. The Crown argument was that as this was a limited partnership and the taxpayer was a limited partner, the loss she had sustained was limited to the amount for which she could have been legally liable if the creditors of the partnership had chosen to recover from the partnership the amounts which were owing to them. This Revenue argument was rejected at every stage of the appeals process. In the House of Lords, it was held that the assessment of tax on the individual partners of the limited partnership had to be by reference to their respective shares as set out in the partnership deed and had no necessary relation to what might ultimately turn out to be the proportions in fact, in which the partner was called on to contribute to payment of the partnership debts. The partnership's trading losses were conceptually quite distinct from the debts and liabilities of the firm and from the assets available to meet them. The taxpayer had sustained the losses she claimed beyond the amount of the capital which she had contributed and was entitled to tax relief on the full amount.

Legislation was therefore introduced (formerly ICTA 1988, s. 117, 118) to counter the use of such losses, the effect of which (as since amended) is to impose restrictions on the amount of relief against other income available to limited partners in respect of losses sustained in connection with a trade carried on by a limited partnership. The restrictions provided by former ICTA 1988, s. 117 and 118 imposed a limit on the amount of loss relief available to a limited partner to the amount 'contributed to the trade as capital'. These rules apply for income tax and corporation tax and are described at ¶25-340ff.

Further legislation was introduced by *Finance Act* 2004 to restrict income tax loss relief for non-active partners, non-active members of LLPs and partners exploiting films. A Revenue press release at the time the rules were originally introduced (February 2004) stated that they were designed to 'tackle avoidance schemes that exploit relief for trading losses from partnerships' and it was claimed that they 'will not therefore affect genuine traders who actively run their own trade'. However, the scope of the rules is actually broader than initially suggested.

Legislation: ITA 2007, Pt. 4, Ch. 3; CTA 2010, Pt. 4, Ch. 3

25-340   Restriction on trade loss relief for partners overview

Restrictions for individual and company partners

The restrictions are now contained in ITA 2007, Pt. 4, Ch. 3 (starting at s. 102) and CTA 2010, Pt. 4, Ch. 3 (starting at s. 55). The legislation identifies two types of partner that are potentially affected by the rules:

- limited partners (see ¶25-400 and ¶25-560);
- members of limited liability partnerships (see ¶25-420 and ¶25-580);

Further income tax provisions

Additionally, for income tax purposes, the rules extend to:

- non-active partners (see ¶25-460).

ITA 2007, Pt. 4, Ch. 3 also:

- restricts the amount of relief that may be given for any loss made by a partner in a firm if the trade consists of or includes the exploitation of films (see ¶25-520) (s. 115); and
- provides for no relief to be given for a loss made by an individual in a trade carried on by the individual as a partner in a firm in certain cases where some or all of the loss is allocated to the individual rather than a person who is not an individual (see s. 116A).

In certain circumstances, an income tax charge may also be imposed:

- to recover excess relief for losses made by individuals carrying on a trade in partnership (see ¶25-620ff.) (s. 791–795);
- in relation to individuals claiming relief for film-related trading losses (see ¶25-700ff.) (s. 796–803);
- in relation to individuals carrying on a trade in partnership claiming relief for licence-related trading losses (see ¶25-820ff.) (s. 804–809).

Professions and vocations

The rules contained in ITA 2007, Pt. 4, Ch. 3, headed 'restrictions on trade loss relief for certain partners', do *not* apply:

- to professions and vocations; or
- to persons other than individuals.

(This interpretation is confirmed in para. 331 of the *Explanatory Notes* to the *Income Tax Act* 2007.)

Legislation: ITA 2007, Pt. 4, Ch. 3; CTA 2010, Pt. 4, Ch. 3

25-360   Income tax restrictions: key definitions

The following definitions apply for the purposes of these loss restriction provisions.

Sideways relief

The term 'sideways relief' is defined (ITA 2007, s. 103(1)) to refer to:

- relief for trade losses against general income; and
- early trade losses relief.

(The definition is thus identical to that used for the purposes of giving loss relief generally: see ¶25-060.)

Capital gains relief

For these purposes, the term 'capital gains relief' is defined (ITA 2007, s. 103(2)) to mean the treatment of a loss as an allowable loss for the purposes of TCGA 1992, s. 261B (use of trading loss as a CGT loss). Capital gains relief may then be given for a loss when it is so treated. See, generally, ¶25-020.

Firm

The legislation uses the term 'firm', which it defines for these purposes in accordance with ITTOIA 2005, Pt. 9. See, in particular, ITTOIA 2005, s. 847, which states that:

'persons carrying on a trade in partnership are referred to collectively as a "firm"'.

Limited partner

The legislation identifies three ways in which an individual may be treated as a limited partner (ITA 2007, s. 103A, introduced by *Finance Act* 2007 but deemed always to have had effect).

First, an individual will be so treated if he carries on a trade as a limited partner in a limited partnership registered under the *Limited Partnerships Act* 1907.

An individual will also be treated as a limited partner if he carries on a trade as a partner in a firm who in substance acts as a limited partner in relation to the trade. He is treated as falling within this category if:

- he is not entitled to take part in the management of the trade; but
- he *is* entitled to have any liabilities (or those beyond a certain limit) for debts or obligations incurred for the purposes of the trade met or reimbursed by some other person.

The third way in which an individual may be treated as a limited partner is if he carries on a trade jointly with other persons and, under the law of a territory outside the UK:

- he is not entitled to take part in the management of the trade; and
- he is not liable beyond a certain limit for debts or obligations incurred for the purposes of the trade.

For the application of this third part of the definition, references in the legislation to the individual's firm are read as references to the relationship between the individual and the other persons with whom he carries on the trade jointly.

For the purposes of the legislation in ITA 2007, Pt. 4, Ch. 3, the term 'limited partner' is defined specifically to refer to an individual (even though it is possible for others (e.g. a limited company) to be a limited partner under the terms of the *Limited Partnerships Act* 1907).

Contribution to the firm

Some care is needed with this expression, as it is variously defined for different parts of the relevant legislation. For the purposes of:

- ITA 2007, s. 104 (restriction on reliefs for limited partners), the term is defined at s. 105: see ¶25-400;
- ITA 2007, s. 107 (restriction on reliefs for members of LLPs), the term 'contribution to the LLP' is defined at s. 108: see ¶25-420; and
- ITA 2007, s. 110 (restriction on reliefs for certain non-active partners), the term is defined at s. 111: see ¶25-460.

The fact that the legislation looks at the contribution to the *firm* (as opposed to the *trade*) represents a change to the law introduced at the time of the rewrite.

Legislation: ITA 2007, s. 103, 103A

25-380 Income tax limit on reliefs in any tax year not to exceed cap for tax year

General principle

There is a general cap on the amount of loss relief that may be claimed in certain circumstances (ITA 2007, s. 103C). These rules are intended to prevent individuals from using partnerships to generate losses that can be offset against their other taxable income or capital gains. The changes were announced on 2 March 2007 (in HMRC Brief 18/07) and broadly apply from that date.

The cap is imposed where an individual carries on one or more trades:

(1) as a non-active partner in a firm during a tax year; or

(2) as a limited partner in a firm at any time in that year,

and where the individual makes a loss in any of those trades. The term 'affected loss' is given to that loss.

A cap of £25,000 is placed on the amount of sideways relief and capital gains relief that the individual may claim for the affected loss (after applying all the other restrictions made under ITA 2007, Pt. 4, Ch. 3). See ¶25-360 for the definition of sideways and capital gains relief.

When does the restriction apply?

The restriction initially applies in relation to any loss made by an individual in a trade in 2007–08 or any subsequent tax year. However, there are two exceptions to this rule.

Exceptions

Films

The further restriction described above did not apply to so much of any affected loss as derived from qualifying film expenditure (as defined at ITA 2007, s. 103D: see ¶25-520).

Losses set against profits of same trade

The further restriction described above does not apply to restrict sideways relief for a loss that is set against profits of the same trade.

Lloyd's

In ITA 2007, s. 103C, the term 'trade' is defined to exclude a trade that consists of the underwriting business of a member of Lloyd's (within the meaning of FA 1993, s. 184).

Legislation: ITA 2007, s. 103C

25-400   Income tax restrictions on reliefs for individual limited partners

Loss relief may be restricted where, in a given tax year ('the relevant tax year'), an individual sustains a loss in a trade he is carrying on as a limited partner in a firm (ITA 2007, s. 104). The restriction applies to 'sideways relief' (against the individual's other income) and to 'capital gains relief'; see ¶25-360 for definitions of both of these terms. There is no restriction on the right to carry the loss forward and set it against future profits from the same trade.

The method of restricting the relief requires an understanding of three key terms (each considered in greater detail below):

- 'relevant relief';
- 'recovered relief'; and
- 'the individual's contribution to the firm'.

The legislation then states that the sum of (a) the amount of relief given as a result of the loss claim and (b) the total amount of all other relevant relief given, less (c) the total amount of recovered relief, must not exceed the individual's contribution to the firm as at the end of the basis period for the relevant tax year (ITA 2007, s. 104(4)).

This is arguably not the most helpful solution found by those involved with the rewritten legislation of the *Income Tax Act* 2007. A person looking at these rules is likely to need to calculate the maximum amount of relief that can be claimed for a given loss. Turning the formula round, this maximum figure can be expressed as follows:

- the individual's contribution to the firm as at the end of the basis period for the relevant tax year; plus
- the total amount (if any) of recovered relief; less
- the total amount (if any) of all other relevant relief given.

The reference to the basis period (rather than the tax year itself) and the reference to the contribution to the firm rather than to the trade, are both minor changes to the legislation introduced as part of the tax law rewrite process that led to the enactment of the *Income Tax Act* 2007.

Relevant relief

The term 'relevant relief' is used (ITA 2007, s. 104(5)) to mean sideways or capital gains relief (see, in each case, ¶25-360) that is given to the individual for a loss made in the relevant trade:

- in a tax year at a time during which the individual carries on that trade as a limited partner; or
- in an 'early tax year' during which the individual carries on that trade as a 'non-active partner' (see, in each case, ¶25-460).

See below for cases where the firm is carrying on more than one trade.

When the legislation was rewritten into the *Income Tax Act* 2007, the inclusion of losses used as capital losses was made more explicit (*Change 13*). Transitional rules in ITA 2007, Sch. 2, para. 27ff. confirm that certain losses used under the pre-ITA rules are treated in the same way.

Recovered relief

This term refers to any income treated as received by the individual under ITA 2007, s. 792 (recovery of excess relief) in relation to claims for relief for losses made in the relevant trade (see ¶25-620) (ITA 2007, s. 104(6)).

See below for cases where the firm is carrying on more than one trade.

> ### Example
>
> Smith is a limited partner in a farming partnership and has contributed a net £8,000 to the capital of the firm. His share of the firm's adjusted trading loss in the first year is £12,000. In a simple case, this is his contribution to the firm.
>
> Thus, Mr Smith can only claim a total of £8,000 of relief against other income. The balance of £4,000 (being £12,000 – £8,000) is available for carry-forward.

More than one trade

It is possible, of course, that the firm will be carrying on other trades in addition to the relevant trade that has given rise to the loss claim.

In such a case, the amount of 'relevant relief' is calculated in relation to all such other trades (as well as the relevant trade), and all such amounts are aggregated. In the same way, the amount of any recovered relief is calculated by including claims for losses made by the individual in other trades, as well as in the relevant trade (ITA 2007, s. 104(7)).

Contribution to the firm

Although the legislation does not talk of 'steps' in this context, the clearest way of showing how the 'contribution to the firm' is to be calculated for the purposes of ITA 2007, s. 104 is as follows. In each case, references to profits or losses are to such amounts as calculated in accordance with generally accepted accounting practice (before any adjustments made for tax purposes) (ITA 2007, s. 105(9)).

Step 1

Take the amount that the individual has contributed to the firm as capital, including the individual's share of any profits of the firm to the extent that such profit share has been added to the firm's capital (ITA 2007, s. 105(2)–(3)).

Step 2

Deduct from the figure in Step 1 any amount that the individual:

- has previously drawn out or received back;
- is or may be entitled to draw out or receive back at any time when the individual is carrying on a trade as a limited partner in the firm; or
- is or may be entitled to require another person to reimburse to the individual.

For these purposes, the concept of 'drawing out or receiving back' is interpreted to cover cases in which an amount is so drawn or received either directly or indirectly, but does not include any amount that is chargeable to income tax as trading profits by virtue of its being drawn out or received back (ITA 2007, s. 105(4)–(5)).

Step 3

Label as 'amount A' the result of applying the first two steps (ITA 2007, s. 105(2)).

Step 4

Take the figure of the individual's total share of profits from the relevant trade, or from any other trades carried on by the firm, ignoring:

- any share that has been added to the firm's capital;
- any part of that share that the individual has received in money or money's worth; and
- the individual's share of any losses from the relevant trade (or from any other trade) that would otherwise reduce that amount.

Label this 'amount B' (ITA 2007, s. 105(6)–(10)).

Step 5

Add amounts A and B and adjust the resulting figure as required by ITA 2007, s. 113A (see ¶25-460 under the heading 'Exclusion of amounts contributed for a prohibited purpose') or by any regulations made under ITA 2007, s. 114 (power to exclude other amounts: see ¶25-500) (ITA 2007, s. 105(11)).

Legislation: ITA 2007, s. 104

25-420   Income tax restrictions on reliefs for individual members of limited liability partnerships

Loss relief is restricted where, in a given tax year ('the relevant tax year'), an individual makes a loss in a trade ('the relevant trade') that he is carrying on as a member of a limited liability partnership (ITA 2007, s. 107). The restriction applies to 'sideways relief' (against the individual's other income) and to 'capital gains relief'; see ¶25-360 for definitions of both of these terms. There is no restriction on the right to carry the loss forward and set it against future profits from the same trade.

If, however, the relevant tax year is an 'early tax year' (as defined), during which the individual carries on the trade as a 'non-active partner', then the rules of ITA 2007, s. 110 apply instead of those described in this numbered paragraph. See ¶25-460 for commentary on those rules (including definitions of the terms 'early tax year' and 'non-active partner').

The maximum amount of relief that can be claimed for the loss made by the individual can be expressed as follows:

- the individual's contribution to the LLP as at the end of the basis period for the relevant tax year; plus
- the total amount (if any) of recovered relief; less
- the total amount (if any) of all other relevant relief given.

The reference to the basis period (rather than the tax year itself) and the reference to the contribution to the firm rather than to the trade, are both minor changes to the legislation introduced as part of the tax law rewrite process that led to the enactment of the *Income Tax Act* 2007.

Relevant relief

The term 'relevant relief ' is defined (at ITA 2007, s. 107(6)) to mean sideways or capital gains relief (see, in each case, ¶25-360) that is given to the individual for a loss made in the relevant trade:

- in a tax year at a time during which the individual carries on that trade as member of an LLP; or
- in an 'early tax year' during which the individual carries on that trade as a 'non-active partner' (see, in each case, ¶25-460).

See below for cases where the firm is carrying on more than one trade.

When the legislation was rewritten into the *Income Tax Act* 2007, the inclusion of losses used as capital losses was made more explicit (*Change 13*). Transitional rules in ITA 2007, Sch. 2, para. 28 confirm that certain losses used under the pre-ITA rules are treated in the same way.

Recovered relief

This term refers to any income treated as received by the individual under ITA 2007, s. 792 (recovery of excess relief) in relation to claims for relief for losses made in the relevant trade (see ¶25-620) (ITA 2007, s. 107(7)).

See below for cases where the firm is carrying on more than one trade.

More than one trade

It is possible, of course, that the LLP will be carrying on other trades in addition to the relevant trade that has given rise to the loss claim.

In such a case, the amount of 'relevant relief' is calculated in relation to all such other trades (as well as the relevant trade), and all such amounts are aggregated. In the same way, the amount of any recovered relief is calculated by including claims for losses made by the individual in other trades, as well as in the relevant trade (ITA 2007, s. 107(8)).

Contribution to the LLP

Although the legislation does not talk of 'steps' in this context, the clearest way of showing how the 'contribution to the LLP' is to be calculated at any time ('the relevant time') for the purposes of ITA 2007, s. 107 is as follows. In each case, references to profits or losses are to such amounts as calculated in accordance with generally accepted accounting practice (before any adjustments made for tax purposes) (ITA 2007, s. 108(4)).

Step 1

Take the amount that the individual has contributed to the LLP as capital, including the individual's share of any profits of the LLP to the extent that such profit share has been added to the LLP's capital (ITA 2007, s. 108(2)–(3)).

Step 2

Deduct from the figure in Step 1 any amount that the individual:

- has previously drawn out or received back;
- draws out or receives back within five years from the relevant time;
- is or may be entitled to draw out or receive back at any time when the individual is a member of the LLP; or
- is or may be entitled to require another person to reimburse to the individual.

For these purposes, the concept of 'drawing out or receiving back' is interpreted to cover cases in which an amount is so drawn or received either directly or indirectly, but does not include any amount that is chargeable to income tax as trading profits by virtue of its being drawn out or received back (ITA 2007, s. 108(5)–(6)).

Step 3

Label as 'amount A' the result of applying the first two steps (ITA 2007, s. 108(2)).

Step 4

Label as 'amount B' the 'amount of the individual's liability on a winding up of the LLP' (so far as that amount is not included in amount A), where this term is defined (ITA 2007, s. 108(7)–(8)) as the amount that the individual is liable to contribute to the assets of the LLP in the event of its being wound up, and remains liable to contribute for the period of at least five years beginning with the relevant time (or until the LLP is wound up, if that happens before the end of that period).

Step 5

Add amounts A and B and adjust the resulting figure as required by any regulations made under ITA 2007, s. 113A (see ¶25-460 under the heading 'Exclusion of amounts contributed for a prohibited purpose') or by ITA 2007, s. 114 (power to exclude other amounts: see ¶25-500 (ITA 2007, s. 108(9)).

Legislation: ITA 2007, s. 108

25-440 Income tax unrelieved losses brought forward (individual members of LLPs)

Where relief has been restricted under the provisions of ITA 2007, s. 107 (see ¶25-420), the unrelieved loss may in certain circumstances be carried forward and treated as arising in a later year (ITA 2007, s. 109).

More specifically, later relief may be given where 'sideways relief' or 'capital gains relief ' (see ¶25-360) has been denied to an individual member of an LLP because of the provisions of ITA 2007, s. 107. A condition of relief is that the individual still carries on a trade as a member of the LLP during a later year (the 'current year').

The effect of the rule is to allow sideways or capital gains relief in the later year as if the amount previously excluded were a loss made in that later year. However, no relief will be given to the extent that:

- loss relief has already been given for years since the original year of loss, but before the current year, under ITA 2007, s. 109;
- loss relief could have been so given if a claim had been made (i.e. so that it is not possible simply to defer the relief until it is more advantageous); or
- relief for the loss has been given under some other provision, whether for an earlier year or for the current tax year.

When the legislation was rewritten into the *Income Tax Act* 2007, the inclusion of losses used as capital losses was made more explicit (*Change 13*). Transitional rules in ITA 2007, Sch. 2, para. 29 confirm that certain losses used under the pre-ITA rules are treated in the same way.

Legislation: ITA 2007, s. 109

25-460 Income tax restrictions on reliefs for non-active individual partners in early tax years

Loss relief is restricted where, in a given tax year ('the relevant tax year'), an individual makes a loss in a trade ('the relevant trade') that he is carrying on as a non-active member of a firm (ITA 2007, s. 110). The restriction applies to 'sideways relief' (against the individual's other income) and to 'capital gains relief'; see ¶25-360 for definitions of both of these terms.

There is no restriction on the right to carry the loss forward and set it against future profits from the same trade.

The restriction for non-active partners does not apply to a trade consisting of the underwriting business of a member of Lloyd's (within the meaning of FA 1993, s. 184) (ITA 2007, s. 110(8)).

The maximum amount of relief that can be claimed for the loss made by the individual can be expressed as follows:

- the individual's contribution to the firm as at the end of the basis period for the relevant tax year; plus
- the total amount (if any) of recovered relief, less
- the total amount (if any) of all other relevant relief given.

The reference to the basis period (rather than the tax year itself) and the reference to the contribution to the firm rather than to the trade are both minor changes to the legislation introduced as part of the tax law rewrite process that led to the enactment of the *Income Tax Act* 2007. See, however, ¶25-480 (under the sub-heading 'winding up') for a variation of this rule in certain cases involving the winding up of a partnership.

Relevant relief

The term 'relevant relief' is defined (at ITA 2007, s. 110(5)) to mean sideways or capital gains relief (see, in each case, ¶25-360) that is given to the individual for a loss made in the relevant trade:

- in a tax year at a time during which the individual carries on that trade as a limited partner or as a member of an LLP; or
- in an 'early tax year' during which the individual carries on that trade as a 'non-active partner' (see, in each case, below).

See below for cases where the firm is carrying on more than one trade.

When the legislation was rewritten into the *Income Tax Act* 2007, the inclusion of losses used as capital losses was made more explicit (*Change 13*). Transitional rules in ITA 2007, Sch. 2, para. 30 confirm that certain losses used under the pre-ITA rules are treated in the same way.

Recovered relief

This term refers to any income treated as received by the individual under ITA 2007, s. 792 (recovery of excess relief) in relation to claims for relief for losses made in the relevant trade (see ¶25-620) (ITA 2007, s. 110(6)).

See below for cases where the firm is carrying on more than one trade.

More than one trade

It is possible, of course, that the firm will be carrying on other trades in addition to the relevant trade that has given rise to the loss claim.

In such a case, the amount of 'relevant relief' is calculated in relation to all such other trades (as well as the relevant trade), and all such amounts are aggregated. In the same way, the amount of any recovered relief is calculated by including claims for losses made by the individual in other trades, as well as in the relevant trade (ITA 2007, s. 110(7)).

Contribution to the firm

Although the legislation does not talk of 'steps' in this context, the clearest way of showing how the 'contribution to the firm' is to be calculated at any time ('the relevant time') for the purposes of ITA 2007, s. 110 is as follows. In each case, references to profits or losses are to such amounts as calculated in accordance with generally accepted accounting practice (before any adjustments made for tax purposes) (ITA 2007, s. 111(9)).

Step 1

Take the amount that the individual has contributed to the firm as capital, including the individual's share of any profits of the firm to the extent that such profit share has been added to the firm's capital (ITA 2007, s. 111(2)–(3)).

Step 2

Deduct from the figure in Step 1 any amount that the individual:

- has previously drawn out or received back;
- draws out or receives back within five years from the relevant time;
- is or may be entitled to draw out or receive back at any time when the individual is carrying on a trade as a partner in the firm; or
- is or may be entitled to require another person to reimburse to the individual.

For these purposes, the concept of 'drawing out or receiving back' is interpreted to cover cases in which an amount is so drawn or received either directly or indirectly, but does not include any amount that is chargeable to income tax as trading profits by virtue of its being drawn out or received back (ITA 2007, s. 111(4)–(5)).

Step 3

Label as 'amount A' the result of applying the first two steps (ITA 2007, s. 111(2)).

Step 4

Take the figure of the individual's total share of profits from the relevant trade, or from any other trades carried on by the firm, ignoring:

- any share that has been added to the firm's capital;
- any part of that share that the individual has received in money or money's worth; and
- the individual's share of any losses from the relevant trade (or from any other trade) that would otherwise reduce that amount.

Label this 'amount B' (ITA 2007, s. 111(6)–(8)).

Step 5

If the firm is wound up, label as 'amount C' any amounts that the individual has contributed to the assets of the firm on its winding up, except to the extent that they are already included in amounts A or B.

Step 6

Add together amounts A, B and C and adjust the resulting figure as required by any regulations made under ITA 2007, s. 113A (see below) or ITA 2007, s. 114 (power to exclude other amounts: see ¶25-500) (ITA 2007, s. 111(1) and (12)).

Exclusion of amounts contributed for a prohibited purpose

Certain amounts contributed by individuals as capital are excluded when calculating the contribution made by the individual for the purposes of ITA 2007, s. 104 or 110. The restriction applies if the contribution was made for a 'prohibited purpose' (see below) (s. 113A(1)).

Similarly, a restriction applies if (ITA 2007, s. 113A(2)):

- an individual carries on a trade as a member of an LLP at a time in a tax year;
- the individual does not devote a significant amount of time to the trade in the relevant period for that year; and
- the individual contributes an amount to the LLP as capital at any time in that year.

In such a case, the amount in question is excluded in calculating the contribution made by the individual for the purposes of ITA 2007, s. 107 if the contribution was made for a 'prohibited purpose' (see below).

Timing of restriction

Generally, the restriction outlined immediately above has effect in relation to any amount contributed to a firm or LLP as capital on or after 2 March 2007. However, it has no effect in relation to any amount contributed by an individual on or after that date if the amount is contributed pursuant to an obligation in a contract made before that date, and the obligation may not be varied or extinguished by the exercise of any right conferred on the individual (whether or not the right arises under the contract) (FA 2007, Sch. 4, para. 2(2), (4)).

An amount of money is not treated as having been contributed as capital to a firm or LLP until the money is actually paid to the firm or LLP. Similarly, a right or other asset is not treated as having been contributed as capital to a firm or LLP until it is in fact transferred to the firm or LLP (FA 2007, Sch. 4, para. 2(3)).

Prohibited purpose

A contribution is made for a prohibited purpose 'if the main purpose, or one of the main purposes, of making the contribution is the obtaining of a reduction in tax liability by means of sideways relief or capital gains relief' (ITA 2007, s. 113A(3)).

Films

No restriction is made under ITA 2007, s. 113A in relation to a loss that derives wholly from 'qualifying film expenditure' (see ¶25-520) (s. 113A(4)).

Non-active partner

The term 'non-active partner' is now defined at ITA 2007, s. 103B, introduced by *Finance Act* 2007 but deemed always to have effect. The term is used to describe an individual (other than a limited partner – see ¶25-360 – but including a member of an LLP) who carries on a trade as a partner in a firm at any time during the tax year in question but who does not devote 'a significant amount of time' to the trade in the 'relevant period for the year'.

For these purposes, an individual is said to devote a significant amount of time to a trade if, in the relevant period, he spends an average of at least ten hours a week personally engaged in trading activities (ITA 2007, s. 103B(2)). In relation to relevant periods ending on or after 12 March 2008, the legislation (as amended by *Finance Act* 2008) specifies that the activities must be carried on on a commercial basis and 'with a view to the realisation of profits as a result of the activities'. If relief is given on the basis that the individual is expected to devote a significant amount of time to the trade in the relevant period, but he or she in the event fails to do so, then an income tax assessment is made to withdraw the relief.

The First-tier Tribunal (FTT) case of *Acornwood LLP* [2014] TC 03545 (known unofficially as Icebreaker 2) provided some guidance on the active partner test. The case involved arrangements entered into by several partnerships for the acquisition and exploitation of intellectual property rights. HMRC accepted that members of the partnerships had spent an average of ten hours a week on partnership activities, therefore the FTT concentrated on whether the activities were, in periods before 12 March 2008, 'for the purposes of the trade' and, for periods from 12 March 2008, 'carried on, on a commercial basis, and with a view to the realisation of profits'. The FTT accepted that members typically spent approximately two hours a week on 'management activities', such as attending partnership meetings, considering reports, draft resolutions and similar documents and exchanging emails. The FTT were satisfied that at least some of the activities would have met the test and without going into it in detail got the impression that an equal division would have been fair. The FTT was willing to assume that a typical member spent a further eight hours a week on 'research activities', such as listening to music, reading periodicals, and attending sports events or concerts. However, the FTT found that these activities did not advance the trade of any partnership and had no realistic prospect of ever doing so. Although the partnership agreements made it possible to acquire additional intellectual property rights, this did not seem to have been implemented and there were no examples of members identifying a new project which was then adopted. The FTT was satisfied that the partners 'spent the time because they had been told they must, and that they undertook activities such as they described, not in the expectation or even hope that anything useful might come of them, either for that reason alone or, because they happened to enjoy the particular activity for its own sake, as a pleasurable means of fulfilling a statutory requirement'. Therefore, even if the scheme had worked to secure sideways loss relief for the partnerships' members, which the FTT had already concluded it substantially did not, the individual partners would have been denied sideways loss relief by virtue of being non-active partners.

The 'relevant period for the year' is normally defined to mean the basis period for the tax year in question. However, if that basis period is less than six months, then it means:

(a)   the six-month period beginning with the date on which the individual first started to carry on the trade (if the basis period begins with that date); or

(b)   the six-month period ending with the date on which the individual permanently ceased to carry on the trade (if the basis period ends with that date) (ITA 2007, s. 103B(4)).

Early tax year

This term (referred to several times in the preceding paragraphs) denotes the tax year in which an individual first starts to carry on a trade or any of the following three tax years (ITA 2007, s. 112(6)). However, the term does not include any tax year for which the basis period ends before 10 February 2004 (ITA 2007, Sch. 2, para. 32).

Withdrawal of relief

It is possible that relief will be given on the assumption that an individual will devote a significant amount of time to the trade in the relevant period. If the individual in fact fails to do so then an assessment may be made under ITA 2007, s. 103B(5) to withdraw that relief.

Legislation: ITA 2007, 103B, 110, 111, 112, 113A

25-480   Income tax unrelieved losses brought forward (non-active individual partners)

Where relief has been restricted under the provisions of ITA 2007, s. 110 (see ¶25-460), the unrelieved loss may in certain circumstances be carried forward and treated as arising in a later year (ITA 2007, s. 113).

More specifically, later relief may be given where 'sideways relief' or 'capital gains relief' (see ¶25-360) has been denied to a non-active partner because of the provisions of ITA 2007, s. 110. A condition of relief is that, during the later year for which the claim is made (the 'current year'), the individual either still carries on a trade as a member of the firm, or makes a contribution, during the firm's winding up, to the assets of a firm in which he or she has previously carried on the trade as a partner.

The effect of the rule is to allow sideways or capital gains relief in the later year as if the amount previously excluded were a loss made in that later year. However, no relief will be given to the extent that:

- loss relief has already been given for years since the original year of loss, but before the current year, under this ITA 2007, s. 113;
- loss relief could have been so given if a claim had been made (i.e. so that it is not possible simply to defer the relief until it is more advantageous); or
- relief for the loss has been given under some other provision, whether for an earlier year or for the current tax year.

When the legislation was rewritten into the *Income Tax Act* 2007, the inclusion of losses used as capital losses was made more explicit (*Change 13*). Transitional rules in ITA 2007, Sch. 2, para. 31 confirm that certain losses used under the pre-ITA rules are treated in the same way.

The legislation contains rules allowing the restrictions for members of LLPs, or non-active partners (see, respectively, ¶25-420 and ¶25-460) to be applied in relation to losses treated under this rule as arising in the current tax year (ITA 2007, s. 113(5)):

- the individual in question is treated as having carried on the trade during the current tax year as a non-active partner in the firm; and
- the current tax year is treated as if it were an 'early tax year' (see ¶25-460) in relation to the individual's carrying on of the trade.

Winding up

As noted above, relief under this rule may be available if the claimant makes a contribution, during the firm's winding up, to the assets of a firm in which he or she has previously carried on the trade as a partner. Various special rules apply where, in such a case, the individual concerned was not carrying on the trade as a partner in the year in which such a contribution is made (ITA 2007, s. 113(5)). Those special rules apply to the amounts of the loss treated under ITA 2007, s. 113 as arising in the current year:

(a) the restrictions re relief for uncommercial trades under ITA 2007, s. 66 (relief against general income: see ¶25-020) and under ITA 2007, s. 74(1) (relief for losses in first four years: see ¶25-040) do not apply; and

(b) the rules of ITA 2007, s. 110(4) (see ¶25-460) have effect by reference to the tax year itself rather than the basis period for that year.

Legislation: ITA 2007, s. 113

25-500 Income tax exclusion of amounts in calculating contribution to the firm or LLP

Legal background

Provisions allow HMRC to set out, in regulations, certain types of contributions to a trade that may be ignored in determining the contribution made by an individual to a firm. The regulations must be approved by a House of Commons resolution but, subject to that, may be made retrospective effect (ITA 2007, s. 114). Regulations may 'contain incidental, supplemental, consequential and transitional provision and savings' and 'make different provision for different cases or purposes' (so that, for example, particular rules may apply only to film-related losses). Partners whose losses may be restricted are:

* limited partners (ITA 2007, s. 104: see ¶25-400);
* members of a limited liability partnership (ITA 2007, s. 107: see ¶25-420); and
* non-active partners (ITA 2007, s. 110: see ¶25-460).

In commenting on these powers when they were first introduced, HMRC observed that 'Some seek to avoid these restrictions by, for example, the use of limited or non-recourse loans to provide an amount which counts as capital contributed but which is not in practice at risk in the way of ordinary capital.' As such, *Finance Act* 2005 introduced further provisions to 'provide additional restrictions on the amount of trading losses that some partners can set against their other income or gains' (2004 pre-Budget report document, *Tax avoidance using film and partnership reliefs*).

The fact that the restriction is applied by reference to an individual's contribution to the *firm* (rather than to the trade) is a minor change in law introduced as part of the rewrite process. Transitional provisions in ITA 2007, Sch. 2, para. 34 ensure that the repeal of the older legislation does not prevent regulations from being made that affect years before 2007–08.

Actual restrictions

Under the provisions explained above, regulations were made by the *Partnerships (Restrictions on Contributions to a Trade) Regulations* 2005 (SI 2005/2017) with the aim of excluding certain amounts in two situations (quoting from the explanatory note to those regulations):

'The first is where the individual takes out a loan to finance a contribution to a trade, and the loan is on limited or non-recourse terms, or in the event, the cost of repaying the loan is borne, assumed or released by someone else (see Conditions 1 to 3 in regulation 4). There is a backup test whether the individual's loan repayment costs over any period of 5 years are less than they would be on arm's length commercial terms (see Condition 4 in regulation 4).

The second is where arrangements are made so that the financial cost to the individual of making a contribution to a trade can be reimbursed by someone else (see regulation 5).'.

(The regulations of SI 2005/2017 were made under the predecessor legislation in ICTA 1988, s. 118ZO, but their continued application to the rewritten rules is assured by ITA 2007, Sch. 2, para. 35.)

Loans

More specifically, the restrictions re loans apply if an individual takes out a loan in connection with his financing of the whole or part of a contribution to the relevant trade, and at least one of the following conditions applies (SI 2005/2017, reg. 4):

- there is an arrangement whereby some or all of the financial cost of repaying the loan may ultimately be borne by another person;
- some or all of the financial cost of repaying the loan is in fact ultimately borne by another person;
- the liability to repay the loan is assumed or released by another person; or
- the actual financial cost that the individual incurs in repaying the loan during a defined five-year period is either nil or is substantially less than it would have been on arm's length repayment terms (as defined for these purposes).

Reimbursements

The financial cost of making a contribution that is (or may be) directly or indirectly reimbursed by another person will be excluded when computing the amount of an individual's contribution to the relevant trade at the time in question (SI 2005/2017, reg. 5).

In the First-tier Tribunal (FTT) case of *Acornwood LLP* [2014] TC 03545 (known unofficially as Icebreaker 2), the FTT found that the aim of the Restriction Regulations in SI 2005/2017 was to remove or restrict relief in those cases in which the borrower did not truly have any liability to repay the borrowing – so the provisions were aimed at arrangements in which there was the appearance but not the substance of a borrowing, or where the borrower is in some way fully indemnified without cost to himself. Although the FTT found the borrowings in this case to be wholly unnecessary, and undertaken only in order to increase the amount of tax relief, the arrangements were not a sham. Thus the members did each borrow money, and they used it to purchase an income stream and final minimum sum which would have enabled them to repay the loans and service them in the meantime. Although the possibility that they would have to repay the borrowings from funds not within the scheme was illusory the FTT accepted that these were full recourse loans, albeit fully secured. There was no realistic prospect that the partnership would have to repay the loan; but even if there were, a partnership which pays a member's debt from the member's share of the partnership assets is not, as the conditions require, bearing or assuming the liability; in a meaningful sense it is doing no more than discharging it for the member. Therefore the restrictions in SI 2005/2017 did not apply to any of the individual partners (although the scheme did fail to secure sideways loss relief for the partners for other reasons).

Legislation: ITA 2007, s. 113A; SI 2005/2017

25-520   Income tax films

Overview

Certain restrictions apply to loss reliefs that would otherwise be available for partners carrying on a trade of 'exploiting films'. The rewritten rules relating to these restrictions are contained in ITA 2007, s. 115.

The restrictions apply where:

(1)   an individual carries on a trade as a partner in a firm at a time during a tax year;

(2)   the trade consists of or includes the exploitation of films;

(3)   the individual makes a loss in the trade in the tax year ('the affected tax year');

(4)   the individual does not devote a significant amount of time to the trade in the relevant period for the affected tax year;

(5)   the affected tax year is the one in which the individual first started to carry on the trade or is one of the next three tax years; and

(6)   a relevant agreement existed at a time during the affected tax year which guaranteed the individual an amount of income.

See below for various definitions.

Nature of restriction

The rules have the effect (ITA 2007, s. 115(2)) of denying:

- sideways relief (defined at ¶25-360), except that losses may be set against any of the individual's profits from the same trade; and
- capital gains relief (also defined at ¶25-360).

The restrictions do not apply if, or to the extent that, the loss derives from 'qualifying film expenditure'. The amount so derived is determined on a just and reasonable basis (ITA 2007, s. 103D(4)).

Qualifying film expenditure

The concept of 'qualifying film expenditure' is defined at ITA 2007, s. 103D.

The term 'film' is interpreted in accordance with the provisions of Sch. 1, para. 1 of the *Films Act* 1985 (applied by ITA 2007, s. 103D(5)). The term is thus defined to include 'any record, however made, of a sequence of visual images that is capable of being used as a means of showing that sequence as a moving picture'.

Expenditure is treated as qualifying film expenditure if:

(1)   it is deducted under ITTOIA 2005, s. 137–140 (relief for certified master versions of films) for the purposes of the calculation required by s. 849 of that Act (calculation of firm's profits or losses); or

(2) it is incidental expenditure which is *not* deducted under ITTOIA 2005, s. 137–140 but which is incurred in connection with the production of a film, or the acquisition of the original master version of a film (see ITTOIA 2005, s. 130 and 132), in relation to which expenditure is so deducted.

Incidental expenditure includes expenses of management, administration or obtaining finance, and the amount of such expenditure is to be determined on a just and reasonable basis.

Relevant agreement

Tax relief is only restricted if there was a 'relevant agreement' (see condition (6) above).

An agreement is defined as 'relevant' if (ITA 2007, s. 115(5)):

(1) it is made with a view to the individual's carrying on the trade;

(2) it is made in the course of the individual's carrying on that trade; or

(3) it is related to an agreement within (1) or (2) immediately above. Two agreements are treated as related if they are entered into under the same arrangement (irrespective of timings).

The individual may be required under the agreement to contribute an amount to the trade. That has no bearing on the question of whether or not the agreement is 'relevant' for these purposes (ITA 2007, s. 115(6)).

A relevant agreement is said to guarantee the individual an amount of income if the agreement (in whole or in part) is designed to ensure that the individual receives at least that amount of income (ITA 2007, s. 115(8)). The question of when the income is to be received (or is in fact received) is not taken into account (s. 115(9)).

Former rules

Before the enactment of the *Income Tax Act* 2007, the rules were given at ICTA 1988, s. 118ZL. The structure of that legislation was very different but the effect was broadly the same.

Unrestricted film expenditure

When originally enacted, the *Income Tax Act* 2007 contained a section (s. 116) that prevented the restrictions of s. 115 from applying in certain circumstances, whereby expenditure was said to be 'unrestricted film expenditure'. However, that relaxation was omitted and repealed by FA 2007, s. 114 and Sch. 27, Pt. 2(1), and the omission and repeal are deemed always to have had effect.

Legislation: ITA 2007, s. 115

25-540   Income tax restriction: partnerships with mixed membership

A mixed member partnership is a partnership or LLP which has both individual members and non-individual members (typically companies but can include trusts or other entities).

The allocation of the partnership's taxable profit or allowable loss for any accounting period is to be in accordance with the firm's profit-sharing arrangements for that period, subject to the provisions of s. 850A and 850B which reallocate the firm's result to ensure that no partner can have a profit or loss greater than that which accrued to the firm (see ¶19-080).

Despite those provisions, however, it was possible to manipulate the commercial allocation of profits under s. 850 by the use of a corporate partner controlled by an individual partner. Profit could be diverted to the company from the individual and thus be liable only to corporation tax, rather than the higher income tax rates. Conversely, in a loss situation, the company's share of the loss might be diverted to the individual to gain greater loss relief.

HMRC's guidance explains that:

'In a typical case, arrangements are made between a company and wealthy individuals, where the individuals will contribute funding to a business venture in return for the losses generated in the early years of the partnership, perhaps through capital allowances. The losses will be less valuable to the company than to the individuals, who are taxable at higher income tax rates. When the business becomes profitable, the individual members will have their contribution returned and they will withdraw from the partnership.'

In order to counter these tactics, legislation was brought in by *Finance Act* 2014, which operates in two ways:

(1)   profits are reallocated;

(2)   relief for losses is restricted.

The rules took effect in relation to losses made in the tax year 2014–15 and subsequent tax years.

For provisions on excess profit allocations, see ¶19-280ff.

The main provisions

The main provision for trading losses is at the *Income Tax Act* 2007, s. 116A. This rule states that if in a tax year, an individual, A, makes a loss in trade as a partner in a firm and A's loss arises wholly or partly, directly or indirectly in consequence of, or otherwise in connection with, relevant tax avoidance arrangements, then no relevant tax relief may be given for A's loss (ITA 2007, s. 116A(1) and (2)).

Definitions

Relevant tax avoidance arrangements are arrangements to which A is a party, and the main, or one of the main, purposes is to secure that the trading losses are allocated or otherwise arise in whole or in part to A, rather than to someone who is not an individual, so that A will obtain the relevant loss relief (ITA 2007, s. 116A(3)).

References to A are to include references to A and other individuals too, so it is about transferring the trading losses from a non-individual member to the individual member or members of a partnership. That said, the legislation also states that it does not matter if the non-individual is not, in fact, a partner in the firm, or indeed is an unknown person or does not exist (ITA 2007, s. 116A(5)). It is understood that this is directed at some of the more aggressive tax planning schemes.

Relevant loss relief means sideways relief, carry forward loss relief (ITA 2007, s. 83), terminal loss relief (ITA 2007, s. 89) and capital gains relief. And arrangements means any agreement, understanding, scheme, transaction or serious of transactions (whether or not legally enforceable). Both of these definitions are at s. 116A(6).

The provision applies to professions as well as to trades (s. 116A(7)).

Example and impact

HMRC's manual only has one example (example 24) explaining how the restriction might apply. The suggestion is an LLP with 100 individual members and one corporate member. The individual members each introduce £40,000 and the corporate member provides £60m, giving a total of £100m. (This is quoting directly from the example, as the arithmetic is clearly incorrect and it should probably show each individual contributing £400,000.)

The example goes on to show the LLP spending £100m on an asset that qualifies for 100% allowances in the year of acquisition, albeit with a significant income stream into the future. The partnership agreement provides that the profits or losses of the first year are all allocated to the individual members, and for subsequent years all or most of the profits or losses are allocated to the corporate member. The example suggests that this is an arrangement simply to ensure that the losses arising from the acquisition of the asset and the tax write-down are all allocated to the individuals, in which case the new legislation applies.

The effect is to deny relief for those losses for the individuals concerned.

It also appears from the way the legislation is written, and the interaction with the general rules for allocating profits and losses, that any losses that are purportedly transferred to the individual members in these circumstances are, in fact, completely lost, on the basis that the losses have been formally passed to the individuals, under the partnership agreement. So the non-individual member cannot reclaim the losses that are not to be used by the individuals and use them itself, as there is no mechanism for them to be allocated to that non-individual.

Loss allocations in property businesses

There is an identical rule preventing excess loss allocation to partners who are not individuals in a UK property business or an overseas property business in a mixed partnership. The legislation, in ITA 2007, s. 127C, is almost exactly word for word the same as ITA 2007, s. 116A, apart from replacing references to trading losses, etc. with references to losses in a UK property business or an overseas property business.

In this provision, relevant loss relief refers to carried forward property loss relief (ITA 2007, s. 118) or property loss relief against general income (ITA 2007, s. 120).

Commencement

The legislation officially came into force on 5 December 2013, but essentially only affects tax liabilities for periods of account beginning on or after 6 April 2014, subject to the transitional provisions.

Both sets of rules apply for losses of 2014–15 and later years. Where a period of account straddles 6 April 2014, the losses of that period are to be apportioned on a time basis and the Excess Loss Allocation Rules will apply to that proportion of the loss arising on or after 6 April 2014. If this method of apportionment gives an unjust and unreasonable result, another method that provides a just and reasonable result can be used, instead (*Finance Act* 2014, Sch. 17, para. 14).

Legislation: ITA 2007, s. 116A

25-560 Corporation tax restriction on reliefs for company limited partners

As noted at ¶25-340, relief for its share of partnership trading losses may be restricted for an accounting period of a company if the company is a limited partner.

For these purposes, a limited partner is a company carrying on a trade:

- as a limited partner in a limited partnership registered under the *Limited Partnership Act* 1907;
- as a general partner with no management entitlement and restricted liability; or
- as a joint owner under foreign law with no management entitlement and restricted liability,

(CTA 2010, s. 58).

The reliefs to which these provisions apply are as follows:

- offset of the partnership trading losses against total profits under CTA 2010, s. 37; and
- group relief under CTA 2010, Pt. 5.

The restriction does not extend to relief against future profits from the same trade under CTA 2010, s. 45.

Relief will be restricted to the extent that the cumulative relief allowed for any accounting periods during which the company has been a limited partner exceeds its 'contribution to the firm' (CTA 2010, s. 56). In other words, a comparison must be made, at the end of the company's own accounting period, between the total amount of relief already allowed together with the relief sought for the accounting period in question (or for the part of that period up to cessation of the limited partnership trade, if earlier), and the company's contribution to the firm at the end of the loss-making accounting period (or, if the company ceases to carry on the trade during the period, at the time it does so).

Contribution to the firm

Contribution to the firm is defined as the sum of amounts A and B with:

- Amount A being the amount the company has contributed to the firm as capital (including the company's share of any profits so far as it has been added to the firm's capital) and that the company has not received back, directly or indirectly, and that the company is not entitled to withdraw or have reimbursed to it; and
- Amount B is the amount of any profits from the limited partnership trade to which the company is entitled but has not received in money or in money's worth and that has not been added to the firm's capital.

(CTA 2010, s. 57).

Prior to the enactment of CTA 2010, relief for limited partners was restricted by reference to the company's contribution to the *trade* as opposed to contribution to the *firm*. Explanatory notes to the rewrite clarify that the change is to bring the wording in relation to limited partners in line with the wording relating to LLPs, in respect of which the source legislation referred to *contribution to the limited liability partnership*. This relaxation allows for total profit relief or group relief to be obtained by reference to a larger amount than would otherwise be the case as contributions to the partnership itself may be applied in a number of different ways, to fund various activities including investments, etc. and not just a particular trade.

A number of other minor changes to the law were also made in order to clarify what is included in a company's contribution, in particular, capitalised profits (CTA 2010, s. 57(3)); trading profits not drawn (CTA 2010, s. 57(8)) and that profits for these purposes are to be calculated in accordance with UK GAAP rather than as adjusted for tax purposes (CTA 2010, s. 57(9)).

When tests applied

HMRC's manuals at BIM82105 gives the following guidance on timing of the calculation and evidence supporting any claim for relief:

'For corporate partners these tests should be applied at the end of the limited partner company's own accounting period.

Where these dates coincide with the accounting date of the partnership, the partnership balance sheet can be used to compute the company's contribution to the firm but in other cases a separate computation must be called for in support of any claim to relief. However, a balance sheet at say 31 March, may be taken as proxy for a computation as at 5 April.'.

Calculation of restriction of relief

Example

On 1 May 2014, a limited partnership is formed. Company A (limited partner) contributes £1,000 as capital. Accounts are drawn up to 30 April 2015 showing a £10,000 loss of which one-third is allocated to Company A. During the year to 30 April 2016, Company A contributes a further £4,000 as capital and the accounts show a loss of £16,000 of which one-third is allocated to Company A.

	30 Apr 15 £	30 Apr 16 £
Loss per partnership accounts	(10,000)	(16,000)
Capital allowances	(8,000)	(4,000)
Total loss	(18,000)	(20,000)
Allocated to company A	(6,000)	(6,667)
Contribution to the firm at 30 April 2015–16	1,000	5,000
Relief already given	–	(1,000)
Loss available for relief	1,000	4,000
Balance of loss carried forward	(5,000)	(7,667)

Legislation: CTA 2010, s. 56–58

25-580 Corporation tax restriction on relief for company members of LLPs

The restrictions noted at ¶25-400 that apply to restrict loss relief for limited partners are largely mirrored in respect of corporate members of LLP in CTA 2010, s. 59–61.

The reliefs to which these provisions apply are as follows:

- offset of the partnership trading losses against total profits under CTA 2010, s. 37; and
- group relief under CTA 2010, Pt. 5.

Relief will be restricted to the extent that the cumulative relief allowed for any accounting periods during which the company has been a member of the LLP exceeds its 'contribution to the LLP' (CTA 2010, s. 59).

Contribution to the LLP

A slightly different definition of 'contribution to the LLP' applies to the definition that applies for a limited partnership. Contribution to the LLP is the sum of amounts A and B, with:

(a)   amount A being the amount which the company has contributed to the LLP as capital less deductions for amounts which the company:

    (i)   has previously directly or indirectly drawn out or received back;

    (ii)   draws out or receives back during the period of five years beginning with the 'relevant time';

    (iii) is or may be entitled so to draw out or receive back at any time when it is a member of the LLP; or

    (iv) is or may be entitled to require another person to reimburse to it,

(CTA 2010, s. 60(2), (3) and (5)); and

(b)   amount B being the amount of the member's liability on a winding up (so far as not included within amount A). This is specifically defined as the amount which:

    (i)   the company is liable to contribute to the assets of the LLP in the event of its being wound up; and

    (ii)   the company remains liable to contribute for the period of at least five years beginning with the relevant time (or until the LLP is wound up, if that happens before the end of that period),

(CTA 2010, s. 60(7) and (8)).

The undrawn profits of a member of an LLP are not normally added to their 'capital contribution' unless the terms of the agreement between the members specifically provide that the undrawn profit stands as part of a member's capital contribution and the agreement is unconditional. Otherwise, a member's undrawn profit is normally regarded as a debt of the LLP with the member ranking alongside the other creditors in the event of liquidation.

Where relief has been restricted under CTA 2010, s. 59 (i.e. where the company is a member of an LLP), relief may be due in a later accounting period if certain conditions are met (CTA 2010, s. 61).

In *R & C Commrs v Hamilton & Kinneil (Archerfield Ltd)* [2015] BTC 512 the corporate LLP member argued that under the former provisions in ICTA 1988, s. 118ZC (now CTA 2010, s. 60), its 'capital contribution' included an amount credited to its capital account in the accounts of the LLP. The company itself had not paid in any cash nor transferred any other assets to the LLP but had been credited with a share of the cash contribution of the other member in accordance with the capital sharing ratio under the LLP agreement. The FTT were unanimous that the company had made no contribution under former s. 118ZC(3) (now CTA 2010, s. 60(3)), but split in its opinion on the amount the company was liable to contribute upon a winding up under former s. 118ZC(4) (now CTA 2010, s. 60(7)). The dissenting view was that this was also zero because the company had contributed no money or other property, however, the casting vote exercised by Judge Raghavan had ruled that the company's capital account constituted the amount it was liable to contribute on a winding up. The FTT, however, reversed the decision finding that the dissenting view of the FTT was correct.

Legislation: CTA 2010, s. 59, 60, 61

Case: *R & C Commrs v Hamilton & Kinneil (Archerfield Ltd)* [2015] BTC 512

INCOME TAX AVOIDANCE INVOLVING TRADE LOSSES

25-600   Income tax avoidance involving trade losses overview

Imposition of tax charge

In certain circumstances, an income tax charge is imposed on individuals who have obtained tax relief for losses incurred. The charges are imposed on:

- partners claiming 'excess relief' (ITA 2007, s. 791ff.: see ¶25-620ff.);
- individuals claiming relief for film-related trading losses (ITA 2007, s. 796ff.: see ¶25-700ff.); and
- partners claiming relief for licence-related trading losses (ITA 2007, s. 804ff.: see ¶25-820ff.).

Denial of tax relief

These anti-avoidance rules, imposing a tax charge after the event, may be seen as complementary to the provisions of ITA 2007, Pt. 4, Ch. 3 ('restrictions on trade loss relief for certain partners': see ¶25-320ff.), which restrict the amount of relief that can be given in the first place.

Legislation: ITA 2007, Pt. 13, Ch. 5

25-620 Individuals in partnership: recovery of excess relief – overview

If a partner claims loss relief but subsequently has his partnership contribution reduced, an income tax charge is made to recover the 'excess relief' (ITA 2007, s. 791ff.). The individual partner is taxed on the amount of income he is treated as receiving under these anti-avoidance provisions.

The charge arises where partners (who must have been limited partners, members of an LLP or non-active partners) have claimed relief for trading losses. The individual is treated as receiving non-trading income every time a 'chargeable event' occurs (ITA 2007, s. 792(4)).

See:

- ¶25-640 for details of the conditions applying;
- ¶25-660 for details of how the amount of taxable income is calculated; and
- ¶25-680 for the definition of the amount of trade losses claimed and certain other key concepts.

Legislation: ITA 2007, s. 791, 792

25-640 Individuals in partnership: recovery of excess relief – conditions

Overview

As noted at ¶25-620, an income tax charge is in certain circumstances imposed on a partner who has claimed tax relief. For these purposes, a partner includes a limited partner as defined at ITA 2007, s. 103A (in accordance with s. 103A(1)(c)), and in such a case the concept of 'firm' is adapted accordingly (ITA 2007, s. 792(7), (8)).

The conditions for imposing this charge are as follows (ITA 2007, s. 792):

(1) An individual must be carrying on a trade 'the relevant trade' as a partner.

(2) The individual claims certain loss relief (see below) for trading losses sustained in periods beginning on or after 2 December 2004.

(3) One of the following provisions applies (whether or not relief has been restricted under any of these provisions):

    (a) the individual is carrying on a trade as a limited partner (as defined at ITA 2007, s. 104);

    (b) the individual is carrying on a trade as a member of a limited liability partnership (as defined at ITA 2007, s. 107); or

(c)   the individual is carrying on a trade as a non-active partner (as defined at ITA 2007, s. 110).

(4)   A 'chargeable event' occurs after the individual has claimed tax relief for the loss.

Types of loss relief affected

These provisions only apply where the relief is one of the following:

- sideways relief (defined at ¶25-360) claimed against income other than profits of the same trade; or
- capital gains relief (defined at ¶25-360).

When the legislation was rewritten into the *Income Tax Act* 2007, the inclusion of losses used as capital losses was made more explicit (*Change 13*).

Chargeable events

Provisions allow HMRC to set out, in regulations, certain types of contributions to a trade that may be ignored in determining the contribution made by an individual to a firm. The regulations must be approved by a House of Commons resolution but, subject to that, may be made retrospective in their effect (ITA 2007, s. 114). This is explained in more detail at ¶25-500.

A chargeable event occurs if (but only if) the individual's contribution to the firm is reduced as a result of the application of regulations made under s. 114 (s. 792(3)). That reduction must immediately have the effect that:

- the total trade losses for which relief is claimed (see ¶25-680), less any relief that has been reclaimed, start to exceed the contribution; or
- there is an increase in the amount by which that net relief exceeds the contribution.

An example of a chargeable event might be the release of a loan that was taken out to finance the individual partner's contribution to the partnership.

More than one trade

If the firm carries on more than one trade, those trades are taken together when determining whether or not there has been a chargeable event, and the amount of any income tax charge arising (s. 792(6)). This is a change (*Change 16*) introduced when the *Income Tax Act* 2007 was enacted. The effect is primarily achieved by referring to the contribution made to the firm rather than to the trade.

Special provisions apply in these circumstances with regard to the amount of trade losses claimed: see ¶25-680.

Legislation: ITA 2007, s. 792

25-660   Individuals in partnership: recovery of excess relief – amount of income treated as received

As noted at ¶25-640, an income tax charge is imposed on a partner who has claimed tax relief, if there is subsequently a chargeable event. The amount of income charged to tax in these circumstances is broadly the reduction in the individual's contribution, as resulting from the regulations, but capped by reference to the amount of losses claimed and not reclaimed. More specifically, the income treated as received is the lowest of Amounts A to C, as follows (ITA 2007, s. 793):

Amount A

This is the amount by which the individual's contribution to the firm is reduced as a result of the application of regulations made under s. 114 (explained under 'chargeable events' at ¶25-640).

Amount B

This is calculated immediately after the chargeable event and is then calculated by taking the total amount of post-1 December 2004 losses, and reducing that amount by any reclaimed relief (but not so as to take the figure below zero).

Amount C

Again, this is calculated immediately after the chargeable event. It is calculated by taking the amount by which, at that time, the total amount of trade losses claimed exceeds the individual's contribution to the firm, and then deducting any reclaimed relief (but not so as to take the figure below zero).

Legislation: ITA 2007, s. 793

25-680   Individuals in partnership: recovery of excess relief – key definitions

Meaning of 'amount of trade losses claimed'

As noted at ¶25-620, an income tax charge is in certain circumstances imposed on a partner who has claimed tax relief. The charge is imposed when, broadly, a reduction in the individual's contribution to the firm means that the contribution is less than 'the total amount of trade losses claimed'.

The expression 'the total amount of trade losses claimed' is defined to cover losses for which sideways relief or capital gains relief have been claimed (see ¶25-360) but only if the losses were made by the individual in the relevant trade:

- in a tax year during which the individual was carrying on the relevant trade as either a limited partner or as a member of an LLP; or
- in an 'early tax year' during which the individual was carrying on the relevant trade as a 'non-active partner' (see, in each case, ¶25-460),

(ITA 2007, s. 794).

If the firm is carrying on more than one trade then these provisions are applied to each trade separately, and the results are then aggregated (ITA 2007, s. 794(6)(a)).

Reclaimed relief

This concept prevents a tax charge from being imposed twice.

The term is defined to mean the amount of income that has already been treated as received by the individual under these provisions as a result of an earlier application of s. 792 in relation to claims for relief for losses made by the individual in the relevant trade (ITA 2007, s. 794(3)).

If the firm is carrying on more than one trade then these provisions are applied as if references to the relevant trade include any of the trades carried on by the firm (ITA 2007, s. 794(6)(b)).

Individual's contribution to the firm

As noted at ¶25-620, the imposition of an income tax charge arises if the following provisions applies (whether or not relief has been restricted under any of these provisions):

(1)   the individual is carrying on a trade as a limited partner (as defined at ITA 2007, s. 104);

(2)   the individual is carrying on a trade as a member of a limited liability partnership (as defined at ITA 2007, s. 107), or

(3)   the individual is carrying on a trade as a non-active partner (as defined at ITA 2007, s. 110).

The individual's contribution to the firm is defined as his contribution to the firm (or, as the case may be, to the LLP) at the time in question, as calculated for the purposes of the relevant provision (s. 794(4)). If more than one of those sections applies, the relevant provision is the one applying to the relief available for the individual's most recent loss in the relevant trade. If the firm is carrying on more than one trade then these provisions are applied as if references to the relevant trade include any of the trades carried on by the firm (ITA 2007, s. 794(6)(b)).

For the purposes of:

- s. 104 (restriction on reliefs for limited partners), the term 'contribution to the firm' is defined at s. 105: see ¶25-400;
- s. 107 (restriction on reliefs for members of LLPs), the term 'contribution to the LLP' is defined at s. 108: see ¶25-420; and
- s. 110 (restriction on reliefs for certain non-active partners), the term 'contribution to the firm' is defined at s. 111: see ¶25-460.

Legislation: ITA 2007, s. 794

25-700 Individuals claiming relief for film-related losses: introduction

If an individual claims certain types of loss relief for film-related losses, an income tax charge is made if there is a 'chargeable event' (ITA 2007, s. 796ff.). The individual is taxed on the amount of income he is treated as receiving under these anti-avoidance provisions.

The structure of the legislation at ITA 2007, Pt. 13, Ch. 5 is as follows:

- charge to tax on certain income (ITA 2007, s. 796);
- individuals claiming sideways or capital gains relief for film-related losses (s. 797);
- meaning of non-taxable consideration (s. 798);
- meaning of disposal of individual's right to profits (s. 799);
- meaning of film-related losses (s. 800);
- meaning of capital contribution (s. 801–802); and
- prohibition against double counting (s. 803).

Legislation: ITA 2007, s. 796

25-720 Individuals claiming relief for film-related losses: detailed conditions

Overview

An income tax charge is imposed in certain circumstances on an individual who has claimed film-related losses. Three key conditions need to be met if the charge is to be imposed:

(1) First, these provisions only apply where one of the following types of relief is claimed for a film-related loss (as defined below):

    (a) sideways relief (defined at ¶25-360); or

    (b) capital gains relief (defined at ¶25-360).

The term 'relevant claim' is given to such a claim.

(2)   The second condition is that there is a disposal (a 'relevant disposal') of the individual's right to trading profits.

(3)   Thirdly, an exit event must occur.

Exit events

As just noted, there can only be a charge under these provisions if there is an exit event.

An exit event occurs in either of two ways (s. 797(2)):

(1)   If the individual receives any 'non-taxable consideration' (i.e. consideration that is not otherwise chargeable to income tax) for a relevant disposal. (Care is thus needed with the heading given to s. 798: it is not a relieving provision!) If consideration is received after deduction of any costs relating to the disposal, or exit event, then the gross amount is treated as the non-taxable consideration.

(2)   If there is either:

    (a)   an increase in the individual's claimed film-related losses; or
    (b)   a decrease in the individual's capital contribution,

as a result of which the losses exceed (or further exceed) the contribution.

The occasion of charge to tax: chargeable events

The individual is treated as receiving taxable income (but not trading profits) whenever there is a 'chargeable event'. A chargeable event occurs whenever any of the following applies (ITA 2007, s. 797(4)):

'(a)   the individual makes a relevant claim (if by that time a relevant disposal and an exit event have occurred),

(b)   a relevant disposal occurs (if by that time an exit event has occurred and the individual has made a relevant claim), or

(c)   an exit event occurs (if by that time a relevant disposal has occurred and the individual has made a relevant claim).'.

The question of whether the trade is still carried on at the time of the chargeable event (whether by the individual or by anybody else) is not relevant for these purposes. Similarly, no account is taken of whether the individual receives both taxable and non-taxable consideration (ITA 2007, s. 797(6)).

The amount of the tax charge

On the occurrence of a chargeable event, the individual is treated as receiving the amount (or value) of any non-taxable consideration received by the individual for relevant disposals, plus the amount (if any) by which the individual's claimed film-related losses exceed his capital contribution (ITA 2007, s. 797(5)). The calculation is to be made immediately after the chargeable event has occurred.

Rules (at ITA 2007, s. 800) prevent double counting: see ¶25-800.

Legislation: ITA 2007, s. 796

25-740 Individuals claiming relief for film-related losses: disposal of a right to profits

The legislation states that any reference to a disposal of a right of an individual to trading profits includes 'in particular' any of events A to D, as listed below. The inclusion of the words 'in particular' implies that there are other circumstances that could also be caught.

Event A

Event A is when the individual, or the firm (partnership) in which he is a partner, disposes or gives up or loses 'a right arising from the trade to income (or any part of any income)'. For these purposes, the question of whether the disposal, giving up or loss is part of a larger disposal, etc. is irrelevant.

Event B

Event B is the disposal, giving up or loss of the individual's interest in a firm that carries on the trade. This is specifically defined to include a dissolution of the firm.

Event C

Event C is a default in the payment of income to which the individual (or his firm) has a right arising from the trade.

Event D

Event D has a more complex definition.

Initially, it covers any change in the individual's entitlement to trading profits or losses if the effect is that either the individual's share of any profits is reduced (including to nil), or the individual becomes entitled to a share (or greater share) of any losses without becoming entitled to a corresponding share of profits.

The changes include cases where there is an agreement under which the individual is entitled to a particular share of any profits or losses arising from the trade in a period (including a nil share), but to a different share of any such profits or losses in a succeeding period (again, including a nil share). In these cases the change is treated as occurring at the beginning of the succeeding period.

Legislation: ITA 2007, s. 799

25-760 Individuals claiming relief for film-related losses: key definitions

Film-related loss

A tax loss is described as 'film-related' if (ITA 2007, s. 800(2)) the profits or losses in question are calculated in accordance with any provision of ITTOIA 2005, Pt. 2, Ch. 9 (Trade profits: sound recordings). This is still the statutory definition, even though most of that chapter has been repealed.

Claimed losses

The concept of the 'individual's claimed film-related losses' is defined to mean the individual's total film-related losses in the trade to the extent that the individual has made a relevant claim for them, less the amount of any 'relevant recovered relief' (ITA 2007, s. 800(4)). If the firm carries on more than one trade then the amounts for each trade are calculated separately and then aggregated (ITA 2007, s. 800(10)(a)). The concept of 'relevant recovered relief' is defined as the lower of Amounts A or B where:

(1) Amount A is the amount of income treated as received by the individual under ITA 2007, s. 792 (recovery of excess relief: see ¶25-620) in relation to claims for relief for losses made by the individual in the trade. If the firm carries on more than one trade then the reference to the trade is read as a reference to any of those trades (ITA 2007, s. 800(10)(b)).

(2) Amount B relates to a loss made by the individual in the trade in a tax year during which the individual carries on the trade as a member of an LLP or as a limited partner, or in an 'early tax year' during which the individual carries on the trade as a 'non-active partner'. Amount B is then the total amount of such film-related losses for which the individual has made a relevant claim. If the firm carries on more than one trade then the amounts for each trade are calculated separately and then aggregated (ITA 2007, s. 800(10)(c)). As regards the meaning of 'early tax year' and 'non-active partner', see ¶25-460.

Legislation: ITA 2007, s. 800

25-780 Individuals claiming relief for film-related losses: capital contribution

As noted at ¶25-720, a tax charge can arise under these rules if film losses for which an individual is claiming relief exceed that person's capital contribution.

Essentially, but subject to complications considered below, the individual's capital contribution is defined (ITA 2007, s. 801) as the amount he has contributed to the trade as capital, less any amounts that the individual:

(1)   has previously drawn out or received back;

(2)   is entitled to draw out or receive back;

(3)   has received by way of reimbursement from another person; or

(4)   is entitled to require another person to reimburse to him.

References to drawing out, receiving back or reimbursing an amount include indirect as well as direct instances of so doing. But references to drawing out or receiving back an amount are not counted for these purposes if that amount is thereby chargeable to income tax as trading profits. The concept of reimbursement includes the discharging or assuming of any part of an individual's liability, but this provision 'does not affect what counts as the receipt back or reimbursement of an amount' (ITA 2007, s. 801(8)).

Modification for previous claim

The definition is modified if the individual has already made a 'relevant claim' (see ¶25-720) for a 'film-related loss' (see ¶25-760) that he made in the trade as a partner. In this case, the starting point is the amount the individual has contributed to the *firm* rather than just to the trade. This specifically includes any part of the individual's share of the firm's profits to the extent that that share has been added to the firm's capital (and such profits are as calculated for accounting purposes – in accordance with GAAP – rather than as adjusted for the tax computation) (ITA 2007, s. 801(3)–(5)).

Modification for chargeable event

The rules are further modified where there is a chargeable event (see ¶25-720). In such a case, it is necessary to identify amounts within ITA 2007, s. 797(5)(a) ('the total amount or value of all non-taxable consideration received by the individual for relevant disposals'). Such an amount, treated as consideration received by the individual for a relevant disposal, is *not* treated as capital in calculating the individual's capital contribution for the purposes of ITA 2007, s. 797(5)(b).

Statutory exclusions

Regulations may be made, and may have retrospective effect, to exclude certain amounts from the calculation of an individual's capital contributions. Such regulations are subject to the 'affirmative resolution procedure', which requires them to be approved by a resolution of the House of Commons.

Regulations made in SI 2006/1639, enacted under FA 2004, s. 122A ('the *Partnership (Restrictions on Contributions to a Trade) Regulations* 2006') have effect for these purposes, but subject to modifications made by ITA 2007, Sch. 2, Pt. 14, para. 148. Those regulations (as modified) apply where:

- a relevant individual disposes of his right to profits arising from a firm's trade (within the meaning of ITA 2007, s. 799);
- as a result, his share of all or part of the profits arising from the trade is reduced or extinguished, or his share of all or part of the losses arising from the trade is increased;

- another person becomes a partner in the firm; and
- the new partner contributes or agrees to contribute an amount as capital to the partnership.

An apportionment is then made between the partners to recalculate the amount of the capital contribution.

Legislation: ITA 2007, s. 801; SI 2006/1639

25-800 Individuals claiming relief for film-related losses: prevention of double counting

Consideration is only brought into account once (ITA 2007, s. 803). More specifically, the calculation of income received under ITA 2007, s. 797 (see ¶25-720) is modified if chargeable events have previously occurred in respect of the individual and the trade. In such a case:

- any consideration taken into account in calculating the amount of income received on an earlier chargeable event is left out of account; and
- the amount of income received as a result of ITA 2007, s. 797(5)(b) is reduced (but not below nil) by the total amount of income received on earlier chargeable events as a result of that provision.

If the firm carries on (or has carried on) more than one trade then references for these purposes to 'the trade' are taken to include references to any of those trades. It may be that chargeable events in respect of the individual and any of the firm's trades occur at the same time. In this case, the total amount of income received under ITA 2007, s. 797 is calculated separately on each chargeable event (ignoring the other chargeable events) and is then aggregated; the result is then reduced as appropriate to avoid any double counting.

Legislation: ITA 2007, s. 803

25-820 Individuals in partnership claiming relief for licence-related trading losses: overview

If an individual claims certain types of loss relief for 'licence-related losses', an income tax charge is made if there is a 'relevant disposal' (ITA 2007, s. 804ff.). The individual is taxed on the amount of income he is treated as receiving under these anti-avoidance provisions. The income is not treated as trading profits for tax purposes.

The tax charge arises (ITA 2007, s. 805) if:

- the individual carries on a trade as a 'non-active partner' during an 'early tax year';
- he makes a loss in the trade in that tax year;
- he claims 'sideways relief' or 'capital gains relief' (see ¶25-360) (a 'relevant claim');

- the loss derives to any extent from expenditure incurred in the trade in exploiting a licence acquired in carrying on the trade; and
- there is a relevant disposal of the licence.

The individual is then treated as receiving an amount of income if there is at least one chargeable event in the year.

Relevant disposal

There is a relevant disposal of a licence whenever the individual receives non-taxable consideration for a disposal of either the licence or a right to income under an agreement related to or containing the licence (ITA 2007, s. 805(2)).

For these purposes, consideration is said to be non-taxable if it is not otherwise chargeable to income tax and if its receipt is not an exit event for the purposes of ITA 2007, s. 797 (see ¶25-720).

Chargeable event

A chargeable event occurs if (ITA 2007, s. 805(4)–(6)):

(1) there is a relevant disposal of the licence (if by that time the individual has made a relevant claim); or

(2) the individual makes a relevant claim (if by that time there has been a relevant disposal of the licence).

It does not matter whether or not the trade is still being carried on when a chargeable event occurs. Nor does it matter whether or not the disposal is part of a larger disposal or whether the individual receives both taxable and non-taxable consideration for a relevant disposal of the licence.

Legislation: ITA 2007, s. 805

25-840 Individuals in partnership claiming relief for licence-related trading losses: calculation of income chargeable to tax

The income treated as received by the individual under the anti-avoidance provisions of ITA 2007, s. 805 is calculated by using five statutory steps, as follows (s. 806). If the result is a negative figure, the income is nil.

Step 1

At the end of the tax year, calculate the amount of claimed losses (so far as relating to the licence) made by the individual in the trade in any 'early tax year' during which the individual carried on the trade as a 'non-active partner'. See ¶25-460 for definitions of these terms.

For the purposes of this Step, the amount of a loss made in a tax year that relates to the licence is so much of the loss in the tax year as derives from expenditure incurred in the trade in exploiting the licence. The amount of the loss that derives from such expenditure is to be determined on a just and reasonable basis (s. 807(2), (3)).

For the purposes of this Step, a loss is treated as a claimed loss if the individual has claimed sideways or capital gains relief for the loss (see ¶25-360 for the meaning of these terms) (s. 807(4)).

Step 2

At the end of the tax year, calculate the amount of the profits (so far as relating to the licence) made by the individual in the trade in any tax year.

For the purposes of this Step, the amount of profits made in a tax year that relates to the licence is so much of the individual's profits from the trade in the tax year as derives from income arising from an agreement related to or containing the licence. The amount of the profits that derives from such income is to be determined on a just and reasonable basis (s. 807(5), (6)).

Step 3

Deduct the total calculated at Step 2 from the total calculated at Step 1 to give 'the net licence-related loss'. If this figure is nil or negative then no income is treated as received in the tax year and the next two steps are ignored.

Step 4

At the end of the tax year, calculate the amount or value of all non-taxable consideration received by the individual for relevant disposals. In principle, this includes any consideration received in previous tax years but non-taxable consideration received before 10 February 2004 is excluded (ITA 2007, Sch. 2, para. 151(1)).

Step 5

Take the lower of the net licence-related loss, and the result of Step 4, and deduct from that lower figure the amount of all income treated under s. 805 as received by the individual in previous tax years as a result of chargeable events. For these purposes, the reference to s. 805 includes a reference to former FA 2004, s. 127 and reference to chargeable events includes reference to chargeable events for the purposes of that section (ITA 2007, Sch. 2, para. 151(2)).

Trade carried on before 26 March 2004

If the individual carried on trade at any time before 26 March 2004, any reference to expenditure incurred in the trade in exploiting the licence excludes expenditure incurred before 10 February 2004 (ITA 2007, Sch. 2, para. 152).

Legislation: ITA 2007, s. 806, 807

25-860   Individuals in partnership claiming relief for licence-related trading losses: key definitions

Disposal of the licence

The statute provides a number of situations that are within the rules. Any reference in ITA 2007, s. 805 to the disposal of a licence acquired in carrying on a trade (or to a disposal of a right to income under an agreement related to or containing a licence acquired in carrying on a trade ('a licence-related agreement')) specifically includes the following events (ITA 2007, s. 808):

Event A

The revocation of the licence.

Event B

The disposal, giving-up or loss of a right under the licence, or a right to income (or any part of any income) under a licence-related agreement, whether by the individual or by a firm in which the individual is a partner. It does not matter whether or not the right is disposed of, given up or lost as part of a larger disposal, giving-up or loss.

Event C

The disposal, giving-up or loss of the individual's interest in a firm that has the licence or a right to income under a licence-related agreement. This is specifically defined to include the dissolution of the firm.

Event D

A default in the payment of income to which either the individual, or a firm in which the individual is a partner, has a right under a licence-related agreement.

Event E

A change in the individual's entitlement to any profits or losses relating to the licence, if that change has the effect that:

(1)   the individual's share of any profits is reduced (whether or not to nil); or

(2)   the individual becomes entitled to a share (or greater share) of any losses without becoming entitled to a corresponding share of profits.

This includes cases where there is an agreement under which the individual is entitled to a particular share (including a nil share) of any profits or losses relating to the licence in one period but to a different share of any such profits or losses (once more, including a nil share) in a succeeding period. In these cases the change in the individual's entitlement is treated for the purposes of ITA 2007, s. 805 as occurring at the beginning of the succeeding period (ITA 2007, s. 808(8)).

Profits relating to the licence

For these purposes, profits relating to the licence are defined to mean any profits that derive to any extent from income to which the individual has a right under a licence-related agreement. Similarly, references to any losses relating to the licence are to losses that derive to any extent from expenditure incurred in exploiting the licence (ITA 2007, s. 808(9)).

Non-active partner

For the purposes of the rules governing licence-related losses, the term 'non-active partner' is interpreted in accordance with ITA 2007, s. 103B, except that the requirement that the individual does not carry on the trade as a limited partner at any time during the tax year is omitted (ITA 2007, s. 809).

Related to the licence

For the purposes of the rules governing licence-related losses, an agreement is related to a licence if the agreement and licence are entered into under the same arrangement (regardless of when the agreement or licence is entered into) (ITA 2007, s. 809(3)).

Licence

For the purposes of the rules governing licence-related losses, an agreement (or part of an agreement) is not prevented from being a licence merely because it imposes an obligation to do a thing (rather than merely gives authority to do it). References to exploiting a licence are interpreted accordingly (ITA 2007, s. 809(4)).

Legislation: ITA 2007, s. 808–809

PART 3: OTHER ISSUES

Chapter 17: Alternative investment funds

26-000 Background

An Alternative Investment Fund ('AIF') is a collective investment scheme dealing in any form of investments other than cash, bonds or shares. For the purposes of investor protection, EU Directive 2011/61/EU provides that firms which act as managers of AIFs must make the remuneration of their key individuals subject to performance and deferral conditions. Where the AIF manager is a partnership (including an LLP), this creates a position where a partner's share of profit is taxed as it is earned (rather than when it is received) but that partner may not be able to access those profits for some time, if at all.

To alleviate this situation, FA 2014 introduced a 'special mechanism' whereby profits due to a partner, which cannot be immediately accessed, may be taxed on the partnership itself rather than on the individual partner (see ¶26-040). Thus, the partnership is treated as a taxpayer in its own right, contrary to the 'tax transparency' it normally enjoys. Once the partner becomes entitled to these 'restricted profits', they become his income for the tax year of entitlement and he is given credit for the tax paid by the partnership.

Legislation: ITTOIA 2005, s. 863H–863L

26-020 The election for the 'special mechanism'

The special mechanism (see ¶26-040) is only available once an election is made by an 'AIFM firm', one whose regular business is the management of one or more alternative investment funds either in its own right or as a delegate of such a firm, or indeed the sub-delegate of such a delegate. The election only has effect in respect of the 'AIFM trade' of the AIFM firm and must be made within six months after the end of the first period of account for which it is to have effect (ITTOIA 2005, s. 863H).

A form of election is available to download from the GOV.UK website *www.gov. uk/government/uploads/system/uploads/attachment_data/file/404999/electionForm_ v6_clean.pdf*. This should be returned to HMRC AIFMD Team – S1278 PO Box 202 Bootle L69 9AL.

As the mechanism is available for tax years 2014–15 onwards, this means that the first possible election was for the period of account forming the basis period for 2014–15. Although not specifically stated in the legislation, the election continues in force until revoked. It should be noted that this is merely a preparatory step to enable the partners to take advantage of the mechanism, if they choose, by allocating relevant restricted profits to the partnership (see ¶26-040).

Legislation: ITTOIA 2005, s. 863H–863L

26-040   The 'special mechanism'

If the partnership has a valid election in force and a partner is allocated a share of profit under s. 850, 850A or 850C (see ¶19-020ff., ¶19-080 and ¶19-280ff.) which includes, in whole or in part, 'relevant restricted profit', the partner may allocate any part of that restricted profit to the partnership (ITTOIA 2005, s. 863I(1), (2)).

The method of allocating profits to the firm is by means of self-assessment returns. The partner is not required to make a return of those profits which he has allocated to the firm. These are to be shown in the partnership statement forming part of the partnership return.

'Relevant restricted profits' are profits determined under s. 850, 850A or 850C so far as they represent variable remuneration and are awarded to the partner as either:

- 'deferred remuneration' (including remuneration which will be in the form of 'instruments', i.e. units or shares of the AIF managed by the AIFM firm or equivalent ownership interests); or
- 'upfront remuneration' in the form of instruments which the partner must retain for a period of at least 6 months before they can be sold

(ITTOIA 2005, s. 863I(6)).

For any variable remuneration to count as relevant restricted profit, it must have been awarded in accordance with arrangements which are consistent with the *Guidelines on Sound Remuneration Policies under the AIFMD* (ESMA/2013/232; see *www. esma.europa.eu/sites/default/files/library/2015/11/2013-232_aifmd_guidelines_on_ remuneration_-_en.pdf*) issued by the European Securities and Markets Authority (ITTOIA 2005, s. 863I(7), 863L).

Where a firm is an 'AIFM firm' only by reason of being a delegate or a sub-delegate of an AIF manager, the right to allocate relevant restricted profit to the firm only applies to partners who are classified as 'identified staff' in accordance with the ESMA Guidelines on Remuneration (ITTOIA 2005, s. 863I(8)).

Legislation: ITTOIA 2005, s. 863I

Other material: FCA guidance at *www.fca.org.uk/static/documents/finalised-guidance/ fg14-02.pdf*;

ESMA guidance at *www.esma.europa.eu/sites/default/files/library/2015/11/2013-232_ aifmd_guidelines_on_remuneration_-_en.pdf*

26-060   Consequences of allocating profits

Where a partner allocates the whole or part of the relevant restricted profit (see ¶26-040) to the firm:

- that allocation is to be excluded from his share of the profit as determined under s. 850, 850A or 850C (see ¶19-020ff., ¶19-080 or ¶19-280ff., respectively); and
- the firm is to be treated as if it was itself a partner and its profit share under s. 850 is an amount equal to the allocated profit. It is chargeable to income tax at the additional rate for the tax year in which the period of account ends

(ITTOIA 2005, s. 863I(3), (4)).

HMRC have the power to make regulations in connection with the charge on AIFM firms modifying existing income tax provisions relating to reporting obligations, the assessment and collection of the tax, appeals procedures and penalties (ITTOIA 2005, s. 863(5)).

Legislation: ITTOIA 2005, s. 863I

26-080 Vesting of previously allocated profits

Where a partner has allocated the whole or part of his relevant restricted profit to the AIFM firm and the deferred remuneration or the upfront remuneration (in the form of instruments) (see ¶26-040) represented by that allocation subsequently becomes vested in him at a time when he is still carrying on the trade of managing an AIF (either as a partner in that firm or otherwise), an amount is treated as the partner's profit for the 'relevant tax year' from that trade (ITTOIA 2005, s. 863J(1), (2)). The relevant tax year in the case of deferred remuneration, is the year in which vesting occurs, or, in the case of upfront remuneration, the tax year for which the allocated profit would have been chargeable on the partner (ITTOIA 2005, s. 863J(7)(a)).

If, at the time of vesting, the individual is no longer carrying on a trade of managing an AIF, he is treated as receiving an amount of income and subject to a stand-alone charge to income tax (ITTOIA 2005, s. 863(4)). HMRC's *Revised Technical Note and Guidance* published on 27 March 2014 state that such income is not eligible for treatment as post-cessation receipts (under ITTOIA 2005, Pt. 2, Ch. 18) and will not be liable to Class 4 National Insurance contributions; this is on the grounds that it is not trading income.

The amount to be treated as trading profits or income (as the case may be) is:

(a) that part of the allocated profit which has now vested, net of the income tax chargeable on the AIFM firm; plus
(b) the income tax actually paid by the firm on that allocated profit by the date of vesting, or, where vesting occurs in the same tax year for which the allocated profit is chargeable on the firm, the income tax paid in respect of that year, even if paid after the vesting date,

(ITTOIA 2005, s. 863J(5)).

In addition, the individual is treated as having paid an amount of income tax equal to the amount in (b) above which is to be taken into account in determining his liability for that tax year (ITTOIA 2005, s. 863J(6)).

Legislation: ITTOIA 2005, s. 863J

Other material: HMRC Guidance Partnerships: A review of two aspects of the tax rules Revised Technical Note and Guidance: – Alternative Investment Fund Managers at *www.gov.uk/government/uploads/system/uploads/attachment_data/file/298736/ Partnerships_Mixed_membership_partnerships__Alternative_investment_fund_ managers__Transfer_of_assets___income_Streams_through_partnerships.pdf.*

26-100   Vesting statements

Where all or part of variable remuneration has been allocated to the AIFM firm and subsequently vests in the partner, the firm must provide him with a statement showing:

- the gross amount of the allocated profit;
- the amount of income tax for which the firm is liable; and
- the amount of that tax which has been paid by the vesting date (or, where vesting occurs in the same tax year as the allocated profit is chargeable on the firm, the amount of tax due for that year whether or not it was paid by the vesting date),

(ITTOIA 2005, s. 863K).

Legislation: ITTOIA 2005, s. 863K

26-120   Capital gains consequences

Where the partner's relevant restricted profits are in the form of instruments (i.e. deferred remuneration which, if it vests, will vest in the form of instruments or upfront remuneration which vests in the form of instruments with retention period of at least six months), special rules apply to cover the acquisition and disposal of those instruments.

The partner

Where a partner has allocated an amount of profit, which, if it vests in him, will vest in the form of instruments, on vesting there will be a disposal by the AIFM firm and an acquisition by the partner. His base cost for any future disposal of those instruments is to be the amount of the allocated profit, less the income tax which the firm has paid on that profit (TCGA 1992, s. 59B).

The firm

Where the remuneration allocated by the partner is represented by instruments, the AIFM firm will, at some point, have to acquire those instruments in order to satisfy its obligation to the partner. Those instruments will be partnership assets and each partner will be regarded as owning a proportionate share (see ¶12-040). If the remuneration vests, then there will be a disposal to the partner concerned by the other partners. The partner in whom the remuneration vests will, of course, already own a proportion of the instruments and cannot make a disposal to himself.

Where the instruments vest in the partner, the other partners are to be treated as having disposed of their proportionate shares for a consideration equal to the vesting partner's base cost as above (amount of the allocated profit net of income tax paid by the firm). Depending on the actual cost to them of the instruments, this may give rise to a chargeable gain or allowable loss for the other partners. A similar rule applies in cases where the disposal of the instruments to the partner is by a company which is a partner in the AIFM firm (TCGA 1992, s. 59B, 59C).

The following example is a simplified version of that contained in HMRC's Guidance:

'An AIFM firm has three partners sharing profits equally. On 1 May 2015 Partner A becomes entitled to variable remuneration of £500,000 in respect of the calendar year 2014. This remuneration is to be payable on 30 April 2018 in the form of units in a hedge fund. None of the other partners is entitled to variable remuneration.

The firm has made the election necessary to apply the "special mechanism" and A allocates the whole of the variable remuneration to the firm. The firm pays £225,000 income tax in respect of the allocated profit so that A's entitlement becomes 275,000 units in the hedge fund (fixed by reference to their market value at 1 May 2015).

The units are worth £1 each on 1 May 2015. However, the firm does not acquire units to meet its obligations until 1 May 2016 when the units cost £1.50 each. It then acquires 275,000 units costing a total of £412,500. Each partner is treated as having acquired a one-third share at a cost of £137,500.

If the remuneration does in fact vest on 1 May 2018, the other partners, B and C, will each make a disposal of their one-third shares in the hedge fund units for a consideration equal to one-third of £275,000 (the amount of the allocated profit net of the additional rate income tax paid by the firm), i.e. £91,666. Thus, they will have an allowable loss of £45,834 each.

A's base cost for any future disposal of the units will be the sum of the cost of his actual acquisition in the market of his one-third share (£137,500) and the deemed acquisition cost of the remaining two-thirds from B and C (£91,666 × 2), i.e. £320,832.

Of course, if in that example, the remuneration fails to vest, e.g because performance targets are not met, A will still own one-third of the units, but the cost will have been charged to his capital account with the firm.

In cases where the partner does not allocate any part of the remuneration to the AIFM firm, the normal rules relating to partnership assets will apply.'

Legislation: TCGA 1992, s. 59B, 59C

Chapter 18:   Inheritance tax

27-000   Overview

In line with other direct taxes, partnerships are treated as 'transparent' for the purposes of inheritance tax (IHT).

Although an LLP is a corporate body and therefore a legal persona distinct from its members, it is treated as transparent for inheritance tax purposes (IHTA 1984, s. 267A). The members of an LLP are consequently treated as partners in a 'traditional' partnership.

An interest in an LLP is however treated as an interest in each and every asset (IHTA 1984, s. 267A(a)), whereas a traditional partnership interest is a 'chose in action' and an asset in its own right.

Legislation: IHTA 1984, s. 267A

27-020   Transfer of partnership assets

The measure of liability to inheritance tax, including tax on lifetime gifts, is the 'value transferred' by a transfer, i.e. the amount by which the transferor's estate is less than it otherwise would have been (IHTA 1984, s. 3(1)).

In England, a partnership has no legal persona of its own, and so is incapable of making a transfer of value. Any transfer of partnership property will thus be a transfer of value by such of the individual partners who are beneficially entitled to shares of the partnership assets.

In Scotland, a partnership is a separate legal person (*Partnership Act* 1890, s. 4(2)) and as such is capable of making a transfer of value. However, although a Scottish partnership can make a transfer of value, it is not an individual and so cannot make a chargeable transfer. It might therefore appear that no tax can be charged where a partnership makes a transfer which results in a diminution of the partnership capital. However, any such diminution must necessarily be the result of an act or omission by the individual partners, resulting in a reduction in the value of their share in the partnership. Any such act, or omission to prevent such a reduction, will constitute a transfer of value in itself, whether chargeable or exempt, by each partner.

A transfer of all or part of an interest in a partnership will constitute a transfer of value for inheritance tax purposes.

By virtue of IHTA 1984, s. 10, a disposition is not a transfer of value if it is shown:

(1) that it was not *intended*, and was not made in a *transaction* intended to confer any *gratuitous benefit* on *any person*; and

(2) either:
   (a) that it was made in a transaction *at arm's length* between persons *not connected* with each other; or
   (b) that it was such as might be expected to be made in a transaction at arm's length between persons not connected with each other.

The inheritance tax charge on death is contained in IHTA 1984, s. 4(1) which provides:

> 'On the death of any person tax shall be charged as if, immediately before his death, he had made a transfer of value and the value transferred by it had been equal to the value of his estate immediately before his death.'

In relation to partnerships, therefore, transfers of value could occur if a partners gifts all or part of his share in a partnership to another person (which could be another person) or may occur on the death of a partner.

Usually, the partnership agreement will determine what will happen to a partner's interest in the partnership on the event of the partner's death (e.g. the agreement may stipulate that the executors must sell the deceased partner's interest to the remaining partners, or there may be a cross option arrangement with the executors having an option to require the remaining partners to buy the interest and the remaining partners having the option to purchase the deceased partner's interest).

As the legislation contains no specific provisions regarding partnership shares or assets, a disposition of such an interest will be dealt with under the normal rules. Most of the difficulties regarding such transfers are concerned (especially when subject to an option or accruer in favour of the other partners) with:

(1) the valuation of the interest; and
(2) the question of sufficiency of consideration where HMRC claim that a gift has been made.

Excluded property

Being situated outside the UK may result in partnership property being excluded property if the partner is also non-UK domiciled. A partnership interest will normally be situated in the jurisdiction in which the overall management and control is exercised.

Legislation: IHTA 1984, s. 3, 4, 10

27-040   Transfers to partnerships

A transfer of value that falls within IHTA 1984, s. 3A is a potentially exempt transfer. A potentially exempt transfer has no immediate tax consequences as it is assumed that it will prove to be exempt (i.e. it is assumed that the transferor will survive for seven years).

The assumption that the transfer will prove to be exempt is maintained until either:

(1)   the seventh anniversary of the transfer; or
(2)   the earlier death of the transferor (IHTA 1984, s. 3A(5)).

Whenever one of these occurs, the transfer is determined either (if (1)) as an exempt transfer; or (if (2)) as a chargeable transfer (IHTA 1984, s. 3A(4)).

Under IHTA 1984, s. 3A(1)(c), only gifts made before 22 March 2006 to individuals or to the two types of trust mentioned are potentially exempt and under s. 3A(1A)(c) gifts made on or after 22 March 2006 to individuals or the two types of trust mentioned are potentially exempt.

Accordingly, transfers to a Scottish partnership cannot be potentially exempt. At first sight s. 3A(2)(b) comes to the rescue here in providing that a transfer can be potentially exempt to the extent that it increases the value of an individual's estate. However, this only applies where the value transferred is not attributable to property which becomes comprised in another person's estate. For those purposes a Scottish partnership is a person in whose estate the property becomes comprised, and so s. 3A(2)(b) is of no assistance. As regards English partnerships, there is no difficulty as the partnership has no separate personality and the property would be transferred to the partners as joint tenants or tenants in common.

Legislation: IHTA 1984, s. 3A

27-060   Agricultural property relief

Under IHTA 1984, s. 115(2), 'agricultural property' means:

- agricultural land or pasture;
- woodland ancillary to agricultural land or pasture occupied with it;
- buildings used in connection with the intensive rearing of livestock or fish, provided such a building is ancillary to agricultural land or pasture occupied with it;
- cottages, farm buildings and farmhouses, together with land occupied with them, provided they are of a 'character appropriate to the property'.

Agricultural property relief is given on the agricultural value of the property in question (i.e. its value if its use for any other purpose was prohibited) (IHTA 1984, s. 115).

Once it has been established that the property transferred qualifies for agricultural property relief, it must also be established that the transferor satisfies the requirements of IHTA 1984, s. 117–121.

This section examines the requirements as they apply where the property belongs to the partners in a partnership. It will be kept in mind that what we are concerned with here is the land itself, and not the value of the partner's respective interests in the business (for which business and not agricultural relief is relevant). Two questions must be answered:

(1) Does the property fulfil either or both of the conditions in IHTA 1984, s. 117 (two-year occupation; seven-year ownership)?

(2) At what rate is relief given?

Legislation: IHTA 1984, Pt. V, Ch. 2

27-080 Qualification for APR relief

Qualification by occupation for two years

Under English law, a partnership has no legal personality; accordingly occupation by a partnership is equivalent to occupation by all the partners. Therefore, the occupation requirement may be fulfilled. Under Scots law, a partnership is a distinct legal person (*Partnership Act* 1890, s. 4(2)). However, IHTA 1984, s. 119(2) provides that occupation by a Scottish partnership is treated as occupation by the partners. Therefore the occupation requirement may be fulfilled, as in England.

Qualification by ownership for seven years

The legislation provides no definition of ownership, nor any indication of why this expression is used in preference to the more common 'beneficial entitlement'. HMRC regard ownership as covering both the legal owner and the beneficial owner. In England, the legal title is normally held by some or all of the partners as joint tenants, with the equitable interest belonging to the partners (in terms of the partnership deed) as tenants in common. Thus, on the basis of the HMRC statement, it seems that each partner who is beneficially entitled as a tenant in common may be regarded as an owner for the purposes of s. 117(b). Therefore, the ownership requirement may be fulfilled.

In Scotland, title to partnership property is held by some or all of the partners as trustees for the partnership. It is accordingly the partnership which owns the property, and not the partners, who merely have a *jus crediti* in the firm's property.

Therefore, where land is held in the firm's name, there is no question of an individual partner making a transfer of anything other than a share in the firm's property, in respect of which agricultural property relief is not relevant.

Example 1

Alexander, Bruce and Charles are the partners in an English farming business. The partnership assets include a farm whose legal title is held by Alexander and Bruce as joint tenants. The beneficial interest is held by Alexander, Bruce and Charles as tenants in common in the proportions 50:25:25.

Charles dies, leaving his share of the business, including the land, to his son David. Agricultural property relief is available if either:

(1)   the partnership (with Charles as a partner) has occupied the land for two years; or

(2)   Charles has owned his share for seven years and someone has occupied the land for agricultural purposes during that time.

Example 2

The facts are as in Example 1, except that the partnership is Scottish, and the land is held by Alexander and Bruce as trustees for the firm. Partnership capital is held for the partners in the proportions above.

The transfer on Charles's death will not attract agricultural property relief. It may, however, attract business property relief (see ¶27-140).

Legislation: IHTA 1984, s. 117, 119

27-100   Rate of APR relief

The question to be answered in determining the rate of relief is: does the interest of the transferor carry the right to vacant possession?

If land is owned by one or more of the partners as individuals, and occupied by the partnership (without a formal lease) the answer is clearly yes, and relief is at 100%.

In England a tenancy cannot be granted in favour of a partnership as such, and is therefore granted in favour of the partners as joint tenants in respect of the legal title and as tenants in common in respect of the beneficial title. The rate of relief on the death of the partner who is the landlord will depend upon whether the lease terminates as a result of the death.

If the land is owned by the partners as joint tenants with the equitable interest belonging to some or all of the partners as tenants in common, s. 116(6) is relevant. This provides that if the interest of all together carries the right to vacant possession, then the interest of each partner is taken to carry such a right. Accordingly, if the land is not subject to a tenancy, a transfer by any of the equitable owners will obtain relief at 100%. If the land is subject to a tenancy continuing after the transfer, relief is at 50%.

> ### *Example 1*
>
> The facts are as in Example 1 (¶27-080) above. Provided the interest of Alexander, Bruce and Charles together carries the right to vacant possession, relief at 100% is available.

> ### *Example 2*
>
> The facts are as in Example 1 (¶27-080), except that Alexander, Bruce and Charles's business consists of leasing land for agricultural purposes. The land has been farmed by a tenant, Thomas, for more than seven years.
>
> On the assumption that Thomas's lease continues after the transfer by Charles to David, relief at 50% is available.

Scotland

If in Scotland the partnership occupies the land by virtue of a formal lease, the rate of relief will depend upon whether the lease terminates as a result of the transfer of value. The partnership agreement may provide that the partnership is not to terminate on the death of a partner, in which case the lease may continue after the death of one of the partners who own the land. In such a case, the land is valued subject to tenancy and relief is at 50%. Where there are only two partners, the death of either automatically terminates the partnership. The land is then valued with vacant possession (*IR Commrs v Graham's Trustees* 1971 SLT 46), and relief is at 100%.

It has been suggested that land let to a partnership in Scotland could be valued in certain circumstances with vacant possession, but with relief restricted to 50%. The argument is that where A lets land to a partnership including himself, his right to obtain vacant possession stems not from his interest in the land but from his right to terminate the partnership. There may be some merit in this argument, which is dependent upon the strict wording of IHTA 1984, s. 116(2), but it is understood that HMRC are not taking the point in what is meant to be a relieving provision.

Legislation: IHTA 1984, s. 116

Cases: *IR Commrs v Graham's Trustees* 1971 SLT 46

27-120 Availability of APR relief – limited partnerships

Property owned by one of the partners of a limited partnership is capable of qualifying for relief in the same way as an ordinary partnership. Where, for example, property is let to a partnership consisting of the landlord (L) and the tenant (T), a transfer by L may qualify on the basis of either the partnership's occupation or L's ownership. If the transfer is on L's death, the partnership and the lease will terminate. Thus, the property will be valued with vacant possession, and will attract relief at 100%.

Legislation: IHTA 1984, Pt. V, Ch. II

27-140   Business property relief

Relief under IHTA 1984, s. 104 is given where value transferred by a transfer of value is attributable to 'relevant business property'. There are six types of relevant business property, attracting relief at the following rates:

(1)   a business or an interest in a business (100%);

(2)   a controlling shareholding in an unquoted company (100%);

(3)   a minority shareholding of shares in an unquoted company (100%);

(4)   a controlling shareholding in a quoted company (50%);

(5)   land, buildings, machinery or plant used in a business carried on by a company controlled by the transferor or by a partnership of which he is a partner (50%); and

(6)   land, buildings, machinery or plant in which the transferor was beneficially entitled to an interest in possession and which is used in his business (100% if transferred with the business; 50% if not).

Relief is not available:

(1)   where the business consists of dealing in securities, stocks or shares, land or buildings, or making or holding investments;

(2)   where the property transferred is subject to a binding contract for sale;

(3)   in respect of shares in a company in liquidation;

(4)   in respect of assets not used wholly or mainly for business purposes.

As a general rule, the transferor must have owned the property for at least two years before the transfer. This requirement is adapted where, within the two-year period, the property has replaced other business property, or there have been two transfers, one of which was on death. Where a traditional partnership incorporates itself as an LLP, a partner's period of ownership for the purposes of qualifying for BPR is not interrupted.

The only guidance given by the legislation as to the meaning of 'business' is that it includes a business carried on in the exercise of a profession or vocation, but does not include a business carried on otherwise than for gain (IHTA 1984, s. 103(3)). This at least indicates that the word is treated as having a wide meaning: wider, for example, than the word 'trade'. It includes farming, commercial management of woodlands, and other activities charged to tax under ICTA 1988, s. 55 and ITTOIA 2005, s. 12.

The interest of a partner, or other joint owner, qualifies as an 'interest in a business', however, the interest of a loan creditor does not qualify.

In *Beckman v IR Commrs* (2000) Sp C 226, the deceased had carried on business in a partnership until four years before her death. Her capital account as a partner was derived from the capital which she introduced into the business and from accumulated profits which had not been withdrawn. At the time of her death, the sum of £112,800 was standing to the credit of her capital account. The special commissioner held that this was not an 'interest in a business': after her retirement her rights were simply those of a creditor of the business.

Property letting

The issue of whether the letting of property of itself constitutes a business qualifying for business property relief is one which recurs regularly.

In *Hall v IR Commrs* (1997) Sp C 114, the deceased owned and ran a caravan site in partnership with her son. The caravans were static and were purchased from the site owners by their respective occupiers, who paid rent for the summer season. In accordance with the terms of their licence from the local authority, the site owners provided facilities such as toilets and showers, telephone, electricity, fire-fighting equipment, space for children's games, and refuse disposal. The special commissioners held that their business consisted mainly of making or holding investments. Since the caravan occupiers did not come to the site to enjoy the facilities provided but to use it as a base from which to enjoy a holiday, the owners' rental income was income from holding an investment.

Assets

A distinction must be drawn between a business or interest in a business on the one hand, and the assets of a business on the other. The latter do not qualify under IHTA 1984, s. 105(1)(a), although they are likely to qualify under s. 105(1)(d) at a lower rate.

Land or buildings and machinery or plant owned by the transferor qualify for relief at 50% if, immediately before the transfer, they were used wholly or mainly for the purposes of a business carried on by:

(1)   a company controlled by the transferor; or

(2)   a partnership of which the transferor was then a partner (IHTA 1984, s. 105(1)(d)).

Where the transfer concerned is of land, buildings, machinery or plant used by the transferor's partnership or controlled company (i.e. an asset qualifying for 50% relief under IHTA 1984, s. 105(1)(d)), the rules are slightly different from those for an interest in a business itself. An asset in this category is not relevant business property unless either:

(1)   it was used wholly or mainly for the purposes of the business carried on by the partnership or company throughout the last two years; or

(2)   it replaced another asset so used, and it and the other asset and any asset replaced in turn by the other asset were together so used for two out of the last five years (IHTA 1984, s. 112(3)).

It will be noted that an asset in this category cannot qualify on the basis of requirement for future business use.

Difficulties sometimes arise with regard to sums of money held in a partner's current account with the firm. In certain cases, HMRC will argue that such sums are not used wholly or mainly for the purposes of the business. Much will depend upon the facts of each case, but it is considered that relief ought to be granted except where it is clear that the sum in question has effectively been withdrawn from the business and that there is no intention of reinvesting it in non-liquid business property.

In the case of a transfer falling within IHTA 1984, s. 109 (successive transfers within two years), the condition in s. 112(3) is satisfied if the asset (and any other asset it replaced) was so used throughout the period between the transfers, or throughout the part of that period during which it was owned by the transferor or his spouse.

Example

Dennis and Eric carry on business in partnership, in an office owned by Dennis. On 1 June 2007, Dennis dies, leaving the office to Eric and his interest in the business to his son Fred. On 1 May 2010, Eric sells the office to a third party, and two months later purchases new premises with the proceeds of sale. On 1 October 2010, Eric makes a gift of one-half share of the new office to Fred. Eric dies in 2013, and it is necessary to determine whether business relief is available in respect of the gift by Eric to Fred.

By virtue of s. 109, the 'ownership' requirement of s. 106 is satisfied. By virtue of the proviso to s. 112(3), the 'business use' requirement is also satisfied and the office qualifies for relief.

Legislation: IHTA 1984, Pt. V, Ch. I

Cases: *Beckman v IR Commrs* (2000) Sp C 226; *Hall v IR Commrs* (1997) Sp C 114

Chapter 19:   Value added tax

REGISTRATION

28-000   Introduction to registration of partnerships

A partnership can be:

(1)   a 'normal' partnership of individuals or companies (¶10-020ff.);

(2)   a limited liability partnership (LLP) (¶10-280ff.); or

(3)   a limited partnership (LP) (¶10-260).

Most businesses can now register for VAT online, including partnerships.

Paper registration applications are by means of form VAT 1. In the case of a partnership, not only must Form VAT 1 be completed to notify a liability to register, but also Form VAT 2 should be submitted to HMRC (*Value Added Tax Regulations 1995* (SI 1995/2518), reg. 5(1) and 4B being a 'specified communication').

Form VAT 2 is available at *www.gov.uk/government/publications/vat-partnership-details-vat2* and form VAT 1 at *www.gov.uk/government/publications/vat-application-for-registration-vat1*.

Form VAT 1 must be signed by one of the partners. However, HMRC cannot insist that the partners complete Form VAT 2. The *Value Added Tax Regulations* 1995 (SI 1995/2518), reg. 5 is drafted so that although HMRC can require that partnerships applying for registration or notifying changes in the composition of the firm provide all the information required on Form VAT 2 (i.e. name, address, work telephone number, home telephone number and signature), HMRC cannot insist that they use Form VAT 2.

Although a partnership (outside Scotland) is not a legal person distinct from the persons constituting the partnership, VAT law effectively treats a partnership as a person.

In *Yasin* [1999] BVC 4,031, HMRC compulsorily registered only some of the partners and assessed the registered persons. The tribunal rejected the assessments because, although the wives had little involvement in running the business, the wives should be on the list of registered partners. HMRC held signed accounts showing the appellants and their wives as partners and such accounts should have put HMRC on notice. Thus, the assessments were invalid even without considering whether the threshold for registration had been exceeded.

If the partners are the same in each partnership (whether or not the profit/loss sharing ratios are identical), the partnerships are treated as a single entity for VAT purposes (*C & E Commrs v Glassborow* (1974) 1 BVC 4). There is a single VAT registration and the results of all the offices are consolidated into a single VAT return.

HMRC *VAT – Registration Manual* at VATREG08250 covers registration by partners: *www.hmrc.gov.uk/manuals/vatregmanual/VATREG08250.htm*.

Legislation: SI 1995/2518, reg. 5, 7

Cases: *Yasin* [1999] BVC 4,031; *C & E Commrs v Glassborow* (1974) 1 BVC 4

Other material: HMRC VAT Registration Manual VATREG08250ff.

28-020   Partnership as a separate person

Following *C & E Commrs v Glassborow* (1974) 1 BVC 4, it was generally thought that a partnership had, for VAT purposes, assumed a legal 'persona' similar to the legal persona of a partnership under Scottish law. The case established that a partnership was a 'single entity' for the purposes of VAT registration.

However, the position was complicated by *C & E Commrs v Evans (t/a the Grape Escape Wine Bar)* (1981) 1 BVC 455. The result was that the law relating to the registration of partners for VAT was changed. A registration does not now automatically continue when a sole trader takes a partner into his business or when a business previously carried on by a partnership is continued by a former partner trading on his own account (VATA 1994, s. 45(1)). Thus, unless an application is made to transfer the VAT registration number, either change results in de-registration of the partnership or sole trader and registration of the sole trader or the partnership.

In *Beaton, Snelling & Co* (1986) 2 BVC 208,116, two sole practitioner chartered accountants, each of whom was registered, merged their practices and incurred a penalty for not notifying HMRC that each needed to de-register and the new partnership needed to register.

In *Chiplen* [1995] BVC 1,519, Mr C ran a property development business in partnership with his wife and they were VAT-registered. As a sole trader, he also ran a technical drawing business, but he was unregistered. In 1992, Mr C telephoned his local VAT office and was told that if (1) the partnership ceased and (2) he continued the property development business as a sole trader, this would not affect the VAT treatment of his technical drawing business. The partnership ceased and he continued the property business as a sole trader. Later HMRC assessed Mr C for output tax on the supplies made in relation to the technical drawing business. He unsuccessfully appealed. The tribunal decided that there was insufficient evidence that HMRC had misled him.

For an example of a case where HMRC unsuccessfully claimed that one partnership carried on two businesses, see *Summers* [2012] TC 02267. As neither partnership exceeded the VAT registration threshold, the liability to register and account for VAT was not triggered.

Example 1: Partnership registration

John and Jill traded as partners until last May when Jack joined them as a third partner. The business was not transferred last May.

However, within 30 days of the change they should notify HMRC by submitting Form VAT 2.

Example 2: Partnership registration

Tom and Tim were VAT-registered and they traded as partners until last June when Tim retired and Tom continued the business as a sole trader.

The business was transferred last July, because there was a partnership before, but not after, the change. Tom and Tim must de-register for VAT. Tom must register if he satisfies the conditions in VATA 1994, Sch. 1, para. 1.

Later if Tom takes in another partner, Tom must de-register. The new partnership must register, if it satisfies the conditions in VATA 1994, Sch. 1, para. 1. There have been instances when a sole proprietor took his wife into partnership and failed to advise HMRC for many months, but declared all output tax on the VAT returns which he received as a sole trader. Once HMRC are satisfied that all the output tax was so declared, they have been known to resist the opportunity to assess a penalty for late notification of the partnership's liability to register unless they feel that the proprietor should have known better.

Example 3: Partnership registration

If a VAT-registered partnership of Alan, Brian and Colin demerges, so that then all three practice independently, the partnership must de-register and the sole practitioners must, subject to the usual rules, register.

However, if only Colin leaves the partnership, then the partnership need not de-register, because there was a partnership both before and after the change. They should notify HMRC of the partner's departure within 30 days of that event (*Value Added Tax Regulations* 1995 (SI 1995/2518), reg. 5(2)). A departing partner remains liable for the firm's VAT until HMRC receive notification (VATA 1994, s. 45(2)).

Legislation: VATA 1994, s. 45 and Sch. 1, para. 1; SI 1995/2518, reg. 5, 7

Cases: *C & E Commrs v Glassborow* (1974) 1 BVC 4; *C & E Commrs v Evans (t/a the Grape Escape Wine Bar)* (1981) 1 BVC 455; *Beaton, Snelling & Co* (1986) 2 BVC 208,116; *Chiplen* [1995] BVC 1,519; *Summers* [2012] TC 02267

28-040 Registration in the name of the firm: liability for VAT

Although under VATA 1994, s. 45(1) the registration of partners may be in the name of the firm, this is merely procedural, so it does not establish a legal or taxable personality for VAT purposes separate from the individual partners. Thus, in *Scrace v R & C Commrs* [2007] BVC 791, the High Court held on 14 July 2006 that taxpayers who carried on business in partnership were jointly and severally liable for VAT under an assessment issued in the name of the partnership, although the partnership name had changed during the relevant years of assessment from 'Gloria Hair Fashions' to 'The Cutting Edge'. Whether the persons carrying on the partnership or the firm itself had been VAT-registered is irrelevant because the partners, rather than the partnership, as taxable persons are liable to make VAT returns.

Legislation: VATA 1994, s. 45(1)

Case: *Scrace v R & C Commrs* [2007] BVC 791

28-060 Notices served on a partnership

Any notice, whether of assessment or otherwise, which is served on a partnership and relates to, or to any matter arising in, a period where a person was a member of the partnership, may be served on the partnership and is *deemed* to have been served on *all* partners (VATA 1994, s. 45(4)). A penalty assessment can be made against persons who comprise a partnership even if any dishonesty is not that of all the partners.

Legislation: VATA 1994, s. 45(4)

28-080 Change in circumstances: notifying HMRC

Changes in the membership of a continuing partnership must be notified to HMRC. A new partner should send HMRC a supplementary Form VAT 2. A retiring partner should advise HMRC.

Where any notice is required to be given by a partnership, it is the joint and several liability of all the partners to give such notice, but notice given by one partner is sufficient. In Scotland, a notice can be signed by an authorised person, who need not be one of the partners. (*Value Added Tax Regulations* 1995 (SI 1995/2518, reg. 7.)

Legislation: SI 1995/2518, reg. 7

28-100   Partner's VAT liability

A retiring partner *remains* jointly liable for the firm's VAT liability for the period up to the date when the partnership change is *notified* to HMRC even if he ceased to be a partner years before the notification (VATA 1994, s. 45(2); *C & E Commrs v Jamieson* [2002] BVC 354 where a married couple traded as partners until the marriage broke down and the wife left her husband and the partnership).

This provision is without prejudice to *Partnership Act* 1890, s. 36 which provides, inter alia 'The estate of a partner who dies ... is not liable for partnership debts contracted after the date of death ...'. However, subject to any agreement between partners, every partnership is dissolved as regards all partners by the death of any partner (*Partnership Act* 1890, s. 33(1)). Thus, VATA 1994 does not change the liability of the estate of a partner who dies.

The following is a suggested letter advising HMRC that a partner has retired:

(Date)

Registration Section

HM Revenue and Customs VAT Office

Dear Sir

VAT registration number

......

Name of partnership:...............

I write to notify you that I shall cease to be a member of the above partnership with effect from (date).

Please acknowledge receipt of this letter and confirm that your records have been amended to reflect this change.

Yours faithfully

(Name of retiring partner)

Where a person is a partner during *part* only of a prescribed accounting period his liability for the firm's VAT is 'such proportion ... as may be just' (VATA 1994, s. 45(5)).

429

A partner's incapacity may have prevented him from promptly notifying his retirement from a partnership. However, should enforcement of a debt against a partner be necessary HMRC might take into account the partner's incapacity under their general powers of management (VATA 1994, Sch. 11, para. 1(1)).

Legislation: VATA 1994, s. 45 and Sch. 11, para. 1

Case: *C & E Commrs v Jamieson* [2002] BVC 354

28-120   Partners' entitlement to repayments

In *Hawthorn v Smallcorn* [1998] BVC 101, a retired partner successfully claimed against his former partner a share of a VAT repayment arising due to a change in the law following his retirement. The plaintiff ('H') was a member of a partnership of opticians. In November 1992, H assigned his share in the partnership to a third party. The deed of retirement provided that H was to be paid:

(1)   for his share of the fixed assets of the partnership by the continuing partner; and

(2)   the balance of his share of current assets less liabilities as at the date of the deed.

H had to indemnify the continuing partner against taxes which might be assessed on the partnership properly attributable to his share in the profit or losses of the partnership while he was a member. Following *C & E Commrs v Leightons Ltd* [1995] BVC 192, the dispensing element in the supply of spectacles was exempt. The defendant received a VAT repayment. H claimed that in so far as VAT repaid represented overpayments made in respect of a period when he was still a partner, he was due an appropriate part. H contended that the effect of the VAT registration of a partnership was as though the names of the partners were recorded as registered. Subject to the deed of retirement, H ought to receive such overpaid VAT as were attributable to H's share of the partnership. The defendant contended that the deed entitled H only to his share of current assets at the date of the deed. The VAT repayment arising after that date was excluded in the deed. Laws J held that the parties' intention should be inferred from the whole of the deed. The provision regarding the potential liability of H for his share of any tax arising after the date of the deed, but in respect of a period when he was still a partner, showed that they had not drawn a line as at the date of the deed. Since H would have been liable for his share of any underpayment, it could not be inferred that any overpayment later recovered would be lost to him. Such an unjust contrast could not have represented the parties' intentions.

Cases: *Hawthorn v Smallcorn* [1998] BVC 101; *C & E Commrs v Leightons Ltd* [1995] BVC 192

28-140   Consideration for VATable services or distribution of partners' funds?

Private and Confidential Ltd [2009] TC 00038 unsuccessfully contested HMRC's decision to register it for VAT as a result of the payments received from Oakmall concerning a building development. It claimed that it had acted in partnership with Oakmall and that the payments from Oakmall were a distribution of partnership funds, which is outside the scope of VAT, rather than payment for its supply of property consultancy services. The First-tier Tribunal decided that there was insufficient evidence to show that a partnership had been formed with Oakmall. Thus, the appellant company was liable to VAT register and account for VAT on the payments received.

Case: *Private and Confidential Ltd* [2009] TC 00038

28-160   Partnerships and VAT groups

A partnership cannot under UK law form a VAT group with a limited company.

However, two or more companies (i.e. 'bodies corporate') that are controlled by individuals in partnership can be members of a group. The conditions for VAT grouping require each company to be established or have a fixed establishment in the UK, and the companies to be under common control such that:

(1)   one of them 'controls' each of the others; or

(2)   one person, whether a body corporate or an individual, controls all of them; or

(3)   two or more individuals carrying on a business in partnership control all of them, (VATA 1994, s. 43A; Notice 700/2).

Legislation: VATA 1994, s. 43–43D

Other material: VAT Notice 700/2

28-180   Capital paid on joining partnership

In *KapHag Renditefonds v Finanzamt Charlottenburg* (Case C-442/01) [2005] BVC 566, the court held that the admission of a partner into a partnership in consideration for a payment does not constitute an economic activity by the partner. It was irrelevant whether the admission of a partner was the act of the partnership or the other partners, since the admission of a partner does not constitute a supply of services for consideration.

KapHag has been cited as authority for the view that an issue of shares by a company (as opposed to a sale) is similarly not a supply. However, HMRC argue that the formation or variation of a partnership is distinguishable from a company issuing shares in return for consideration. *KapHag* concerned solely the issues surrounding a partnership. In *Trinity Mirror plc v C & E Commrs* [2001] BVC 167, the Court of Appeal held that an issue of shares by a company was a supply of services and exempt under VATA 1994, Sch. 9, Grp. 5, item 6. Usually, there is a restriction of input tax under the partial exemption rules.

In *KapHag*, the incoming partner contributed cash in return for admission into the partnership, but sometimes the contribution is in the form of other assets. For example, a new partner's contribution may comprise land or interests in land. The ECJ's decision tacitly accepted the Advocate-General's opinion that the same principles would apply whether the contribution consisted of cash or other assets. Whatever the nature of the assets comprising the contribution, there is no reciprocal supply from the partnership. However, where the assets are not cash, the making of the partnership contribution may have other VAT consequences.

The Advocate-General was satisfied that there was 'no doubt that the new partner is effecting an act of disposal of his assets, for which the admission to the partnership is not the consideration' (para. 33 of the opinion). Such a disposal can therefore have VAT consequences when the partner contributing the assets is VAT-registered. These consequences vary depending on the nature of the assets being contributed.

KapHag establishes that nothing is provided by the partnership in return for the assets contributed, therefore any such disposal by the incoming partner is made for no consideration. The *Value Added Tax Act* 1994 provides that certain things are VATable even when they are provided or done for no consideration. HMRC's view is that all those provisions still apply where there is no consideration when there is a contribution to partnership assets. A VAT-registered person may therefore have to account for VAT if he contributes assets to the partnership in the circumstances described in the Act. The VAT consequences can be considered under several main heads:

(1)   contribution to partnership comprising services;

(2)   contribution to partnership comprising goods other than land;

(3)   contribution to partnership comprising land or interests in land;

(4)   whether contribution to partnership can constitute the transfer of a going concern (TOGC);

(5)   how the partnership can reclaim the output tax accounted for by an incoming partner on his contribution as its input tax;

(6)   capital goods scheme consequences; and

(7)   transfer of assets out of a partnership.

Business Brief 21/2004 (10 August 2004), which is reproduced below, has much detail under each heading.

'VAT POSITION OF SHARE ISSUES AND PARTNERSHIP CONTRIBUTIONS FOLLOWING THE EUROPEAN COURT OF JUSTICE DECISION IN KAPHAG RENDITEFONDS

This Business Brief clarifies Customs' position on two issues arising from the decision of the European Court of Justice in the German case of KapHag Renditefonds v Finanzamt Charlottenburg (Case C-442/01):

A – Whether the issue of shares constitutes a supply for VAT purposes; and

B – The VAT position of contributions to partnerships.

The case of KapHag concerned the admission of a new partner into a partnership on payment of a capital contribution. The European Court held that no supply was being made by either the individual partners or the partnership to the incoming partner in return for the capital contribution.

A – Whether the issue of shares constitutes a supply

The KapHag decision has been cited as authority for the view that an issue of shares by a company is similarly not a supply for VAT purposes. It is claimed that an issue of shares therefore falls outside the terms of Item 6 of Grp. 5 of Sch. 9 to the *Value Added Tax Act* 1994. That Item exempts from VAT:

"The issue, transfer or receipt of, or any dealing with, any security or secondary security ..."

It is Customs' view that the formation or variation of a partnership arrangement is wholly distinguishable from the position where a company issues shares in return for consideration. KapHag was concerned solely with the issues surrounding a partnership. The VAT treatment of share issues has been considered by the Court of Appeal in Trinity Mirror plc above where it was held that an issue of shares by a company did constitute a supply of services for VAT purposes and these fall to be exempt under Item 6 of Grp. 5 of Sch. 9 to the Act. In most circumstances there will then be a restriction of input tax under the partial exemption rules. Further information is available from VAT Notice 706 "Partial Exemption" available online at www.gov.uk/government/publications/vat-notice-706-partial-exemption

B – Contributions to partnerships

Partnerships to which this section applies include "normal" partnerships of individuals or corporate bodies, limited partnerships whose members are individuals or corporate bodies, overseas limited partnerships that are registered as "normal" partnerships or corporate bodies and limited liability partnerships.

Background

In KapHag, the incoming partner was contributing cash in return for admission into the partnership but it will often be the case that the contribution is in the form of other assets. For example, a new partner's contribution may comprise land or interests in land. The European Court's decision tacitly accepted the Advocate-General's Opinion that the same principles would apply whether the contribution consisted of cash or other assets. Whatever the nature of the assets comprising the contribution, there is no reciprocal supply from the partnership. However, where the assets are not cash, the making of the partnership contribution may have other VAT consequences.

The Advocate-General was satisfied that there was "no doubt that the new partner is effecting an act of disposal of his assets, for which the admission to the partnership is not the consideration" (Paragraph 33 of the Opinion). Such a disposal can therefore have VAT consequences when the partner contributing the assets is a VAT registered person. These consequences will vary depending on the nature of the assets being contributed.

KapHag establishes that nothing is provided by the partnership in return for the assets contributed, therefore any such disposal by the incoming partner is made for no consideration. The VAT Act provides that certain things are subject to VAT even when they are provided or done for no consideration. Customs' view is that all those provisions will still apply where there is no consideration when there is a contribution to partnership assets. A VAT registered person may therefore have to account for tax if he contributes assets to the partnership in the circumstances described in the Act. The VAT consequences can be considered under several main heads:

(i)   Contribution to partnership comprising services;
(ii)   Contribution to partnership comprising goods other than land;
(iii) Contribution to partnership comprising land or interests in land;
(iv)   Whether contribution to partnership can constitute the transfer of a going concern;
(v)   How the partnership can reclaim the output tax accounted for by an incoming partner on his contribution as its input tax;
(vi)   Capital Goods Scheme consequences; and
(vii) Transfer of assets out of a partnership.

(i)   Contribution to partnership comprising services

A partnership contribution may comprise services rather than goods – examples of this could be a trademark or trading logo or the use of an asset the ownership of which is retained by the incoming partner. Two legislative provisions set out the circumstances in which such a contribution may be regarded as a taxable supply, paragraph 5(4) of Schedule 4 to the VAT Act and the Value Added Tax (Supply of Services) Order 1993 (SI 1993/1507).

A supply can arise under paragraph 5(4) where a taxable person applies business goods to private use or makes them available for purposes other than those of his business. The taxable person or his predecessor must have been entitled to input tax under sections 25 and 26 on the supply of those goods (or anything comprised in them) to him.

The Supply of Services Order similarly provides that a supply arises where a taxable person applies bought-in services to private or non-business use for no consideration where he has been entitled to input tax credit under sections 25 and 26. The value of such a supply cannot exceed the taxable person's input tax entitlement.

Where the above criteria are satisfied, a VAT registered incoming partner will have to account for tax on the supply of services that he is regarded as making in the disposal of the services from his existing business. The partnership may be able to recover this as its input tax where the contributed services are to be used for its business. The procedure for doing this is described at (v) below.

(ii)   Contribution to partnership comprising goods other than land

If a partnership contribution comprises goods other than land that a taxable person (the transferor) held as assets, then a deemed supply will be generated as a result of Paragraph

5(1) of Schedule 4 to the VAT Act. This deemed supply does not require there to be consideration when the goods are transferred. It does however only apply where the taxable person disposing of the goods, or their predecessor, if for example they obtained the goods by way of a TOGC, was entitled to full or partial credit for the VAT charged when the goods were supplied to him. Where such a deemed supply arises, the incoming partner will have to account for VAT. The partnership may be able to recover this as its input tax where the contributed assets are to be used for its business. The procedure for doing this is described at (v) below.

(iii)   Contribution to partnership comprising land or interests in land

The VAT treatment of land or interests in land also depends upon whether the incoming partner or his predecessor was entitled to deduct input tax in relation to the property that he is contributing to the partnership. For example, if he had opted to tax the property, or it was inherently taxable like new freehold commercial property, there may be a deemed supply as described at (ii) above. The incoming partner will then have to account for VAT on this supply. As with other contributed goods, the partnership may be entitled to recover this as input tax where the property is to be used for the partnership's business. The procedure for doing this is described at (v) below.

Please note all submitted notifications of an option to tax need to be signed by "an authorised signatory" as described in paragraph 7.1 of VAT Notice 742A – "Opting to tax Land & Buildings" available online at: www.gov.uk/government/publications/vat-notice-742a-opting-to-tax-land-and-buildings

(iv)   Whether contribution to partnership can constitute the transfer of a going concern

It is possible that when assets are transferred by way of a partnership contribution that this could qualify to be treated as a transfer of a going concern (Section 49 and Article 5 of the VAT (Special Provisions) Order 1995 (SI 1995/1268)). If the contribution meets the conditions to be treated as a transfer of a going concern no VAT will be due from the transferor.

(v)   How the partnership can reclaim the output tax accounted for by an incoming partner on his contribution as its input tax

When an incoming partner contributes goods and/or services (on which VAT is due as described above) and the partnership uses them for its business purposes, the partnership can recover the VAT as input tax subject to the normal rules. The incoming partner cannot issue a tax invoice, but in order to provide the partnership with acceptable evidence to support a claim for recovery of input tax, he may use his normal invoicing documentation overwritten with the following statement:

> "Certificate for Tax on Partnership Contribution No payment is necessary for these goods/services. Output tax has been accounted for on the supply."

The incoming partner must show full details of the goods and/or services on the documentation and the amount of VAT shown must be the amount of output tax accounted for to Customs and Excise.

(vi)   Capital Goods Scheme consequences

Where the capital contribution is in the form of an interest in land or a computer, it may be an existing capital item of the incoming partner under the Capital Goods Scheme (CGS).

If the transfer to the partnership constitutes a supply which is a disposal of an existing CGS item, then this will wind up the existing CGS item and a disposal adjustment may be due. If the transfer constitutes a TOGC then this will end the current interval for the incoming partner and the partnership will then be responsible for making adjustments for any remaining intervals.

As transfers of assets capital contributions will always constitute either a supply or a TOGC, any existing CGS items will always either be subject to a disposal adjustment or continuing CGS adjustments. Even if the asset transferred as a capital contribution is not a CGS item in the hands of the incoming partner, it may create a new CGS item for the partnership when its transfer constitutes a supply. If this happens the partnership will need to make adjustments in subsequent intervals in the normal way.

The CGS is further explained in VAT Notice 706/2 "Capital Goods Scheme" available online at: https://www.gov.uk/government/publications/vat-notice-7062-capital-goods-scheme

(vii) Transfer of assets out of a partnership

KapHag was only concerned with assets moving into a partnership in the form of a partnership contribution. It did not cover the reverse situation, where partnership assets are paid out to an outgoing partner or otherwise disposed of by the partnership for no consideration. Where a transfer of assets out of a partnership for no consideration occurs, one of the following sets of circumstances will apply.

(1)   If the incoming partner accounted for output tax when he contributed the assets to the partnership and the partnership was entitled to recover all or part of this as its input tax, there will be a subsequent supply by the partnership when the same assets are transferred out unless the transfer out now satisfies the TOGC criteria.

(2)   If no output tax was accounted for when the assets were contributed to the partnership because they constituted a TOGC, the transfer out of the same assets will be a deemed supply upon which the partnership will have to account for tax unless the TOGC criteria are again satisfied.

(3)   The partnership may be transferring out more assets than those originally contributed to it. Although the original contribution to the partnership may not have been a TOGC, the subsequent transfer out may now satisfy the TOGC criteria. If it does, no VAT will be due from the partnership.

(4)   The original contribution to the partnership may have been a TOGC but the partnership may now be transferring out less of the assets than were originally contributed. Unless the assets being transferred out still meet the TOGC criteria in their own right, there may be a deemed supply upon which the partnership will have to account for the appropriate tax. As explained at (ii) and (iii) above, the entitlement of the partnership or its predecessor to deduct input tax in relation to the items that are the subject of the transfer out will determine whether or not there is a supply.

Application of section 45 of the VAT Act 1994

In the past, there was uncertainty as to whether it was section 45(1) of the VAT Act that led to there being no supply from a partnership to an incoming partner. That section provides for the registration of partnerships in the following terms:

"45(1)   The registration under this Act of persons–

(a)   carrying on a business in partnership, or

(b)   carrying on in partnership any other activities in the course or furtherance of which they acquire goods from other member States,

may be in the name of the firm; and no account shall be taken, in determining for any purpose of this Act whether goods or services are supplied to or by such persons or are acquired by such persons from another member State, of any change in the partnership."

Partnerships in England and Wales have no legal identity. A new partner joining a partnership, or old one leaving it, would result in a new partnership rather than change the composition of the existing one. Without s. 45(1), deregistration and registration would be necessary every time a partner joined or left. The purpose of s. 45(1) is to ensure continuity by providing that a business carried on in a firm's name is treated as a continuing business irrespective of changes in its composition. The situation addressed by s. 45(1) is therefore entirely different to that considered in KapHag.'

Legislation: VATA 1994, s. 45

Cases: *KapHag Renditefonds v Finanzamt Charlottenburg* (Case C-442/01) [2005] BVC 566; *Trinity Mirror plc v C & E Commrs* [2001] BVC 167

Other material: Business Brief 21/2004 (10 August 2004)

28-200   Transfers of partnership interests

After Business Brief 21/2004 (10 August 2004) was issued stating HMRC's policy on share issues and partnership contributions, Business Brief 30/2004 (19 November 2004) explained HMRC's position on transfers of partnership interests ('shares').

KapHag established that a partnership entity or the existing partners are making no supply when a new partner is admitted in return for making a capital contribution. The question arises whether the subsequent disposal by the partner of that 'share' in the partnership is a supply. This 'share' is distinct from the assets that were contributed by the partners when they joined the partnership. Therefore, even though the selling price of the 'share' may be determined by the value of those assets, they are not the subject of the later sale, which has its own liability for VAT purposes.

Although the ECJ has not considered this type of transaction with respect to partnership 'shares', there have been cases where it considered transactions involving shares in companies. *Polysar Investments Netherlands BV v Inspecteur der Invoerrechten en Accijnzen, Arnhem* (Case C-60/90) [1993] BVC 88, *Harnas & Helm v Staatssecretaris van Financiën* (Case C-80/95) [1997] BVC 358, *Wellcome Trust Ltd v C & E Commrs* (Case C-155/94) [1996] BVC 377 and *Régie Dauphinoise – Cabinet A Forest SARL v Ministre du Budget* (Case C-306/94) [1996] BVC 447 established that the mere acquisition and holding of shares in a company is not an economic activity. However, the ECJ has stated that transactions in shares or interests in companies and associations may constitute economic activity in three situations:

(1)   where the transactions constitute the direct, permanent and necessary extension of an economic activity;

(2)   where the transactions are effected in order to secure a direct or indirect involvement in the management of a company in which the holding is acquired; and

(3)   where the transactions are effected as part of a commercial share-dealing activity.

HMRC argue that the same principles apply to transactions involving partnership 'shares'. Thus, in some cases the disposal of a partnership 'share' does not constitute a supply, but in other cases it does.

Non-supplies in relation to a partnership 'share'

The following list of circumstances in which the disposal of a partnership 'share' does not constitute a supply is not exhaustive, but the most common situations in which the disposal of a partnership 'share' by a partner is not a supply are:

(1)   *the 'share' is disposed of for no consideration* – a 'share' in a partnership comprises services, rather than goods. When services are transferred, assigned or otherwise disposed of for no consideration, they do not constitute a supply;

(2)   *the 'share' being sold was acquired simply as an investment* – where a partner has acquired his 'share' merely to secure a share in any future profits and has had no involvement in running the partnership, the subsequent sale or assignment of that 'share' for consideration is not an economic activity. This does not constitute a supply.

Supplies of a partnership 'share'

The most common situations where the disposal of a partnership 'share' by a partner is a supply are:

(1)   *where the partnership 'share' was acquired and disposed of as a direct extension of the partner's economic activities* – where a partner is a taxable person in his own right, the partnership 'share' may have been acquired in the course or furtherance of his own economic activities. If that is the case, the subsequent transfer or assignment of that 'share' for a consideration is also economic activity of that taxable person. For example, the partner may have a business asset to be sold and, rather than selling the asset directly, may have contributed that asset to a partnership and sold the resultant partnership 'share' instead. The sale of that partnership 'share' constitutes a supply;

(2)   *where the partnership 'share' was acquired in order to obtain an active role in the business of the partnership* – where a partner is a taxable person in their own right and had acquired the partnership 'share' in order to actively participate in,

or control, the business of the partnership, then the sale of that 'share' can be economic activity by the partner. The sale of the 'share' constitutes a supply;

(3)   *where the partnership 'share' was acquired as part of a commercial partnership 'share-dealing' activity* – a partner who is a taxable person may have a business of dealing in partnership 'shares'. This is economic activity on the partner's part. Sales or assignments of the partnership 'shares' that were acquired in the course of this activity that are for a consideration constitute supplies.

For the avoidance of any doubt, HMRC note that supplies of partnership 'shares' in the above circumstances cannot be disregarded under VATA 1994, s. 45(1). As Business Brief 21/2004 states, VATA 1994, s. 45(1) aims to ensure continuity by providing that changes in the composition of a partnership do not create the need for a partnership to de-register and re-register for VAT every time the partners change. It also makes it unnecessary to take account of changes in the composition of the partnership when determining what supplies have been made or received by the partnership. The section has no effect on any supply that one of the partners may be making as a taxable person in his own right.

If the disposal of a partnership 'share' is a supply, that supply is an exempt financial service.

Where the disposal of an existing partnership 'share' is not a supply, the VAT incurred in connection with the disposal is normally not input tax. Where the disposal is a supply, the related VAT is input tax, but recovery is normally fully restricted under the partial exemption rules as the supply is exempt. This is subject to the de minimis provisions.

Business Brief 30/2004 (19 November 2004) is reproduced below.

'VAT AND PARTNERSHIP "SHARES"

Background

Business Brief 21/04 clarified Customs' policy on share issues and partnership contributions following the European Court of Justice (ECJ) decision in KapHag Renditefonds (C-442/01). That Business Brief did not deal with the VAT position of transfers of partnership interests ("shares"). This Business Brief explains the VAT treatment of transactions involving the transfer of a partner's "share".

Is the disposal of a "share" in a partnership a supply?

KapHag established that a partnership entity or the existing partners are making no supply when a new partner is admitted in return for making a capital contribution. The question arises whether the subsequent disposal by the partner of that "share" in the partnership is a supply for VAT purposes. It is important to bear in mind that this "share" is distinct from the assets that were contributed by the partner when they joined the partnership. Therefore, even though the selling price of the "share" may be determined by the value of those assets, they are not the subject of the later sale, which has its own liability for VAT purposes.

Although the ECJ has not considered this type of transaction with respect to partnership "shares", there have been a number of cases where it has given a decision in respect of transactions involving shares in companies. The cases of *Polysar* (C-60/90), *Harnas and Helm* (C-80/95), *Wellcome Trust* (C-155/94) and *Regie Dauphinoise* (C-306/94) have established that the mere acquisition and holding of shares in a company is not to be regarded as an economic activity. However, it has stated that transactions in shares or interests in companies and associations may constitute economic activity in three situations:

(a) Where the transactions constitute the direct, permanent and necessary extension of an economic activity.

(b) Where the transactions are effected in order to secure a direct or indirect involvement in the management of a company in which the holding is acquired.

(c) Where the transactions are effected as part of a commercial share-dealing activity.

Customs considers that the same principles apply to transactions involving partnership "shares". This means that in some circumstances the disposal of a partnership "share" will not constitute a supply and in others it will .

Circumstances in which the disposal of a partnership "share" will not constitute a supply

This list is not exhaustive. The most common situations in which the disposal of a partnership "share" by a partner will not be a supply are likely to be:

(1) *The "share" is disposed of for no consideration* – A "share" in a partnership comprises services rather than goods. When services are transferred, assigned or otherwise disposed of for no consideration, they do not constitute any supply for VAT purposes.

(2) *The "share" being sold was acquired simply as an investment* – Where a partner has acquired his "share" merely to secure a share in any future profits and has had no involvement in running the partnership, the subsequent sale or assignment of that "share" for consideration will not be an economic activity. This will not constitute any supply for VAT purposes.

Circumstances in which the disposal of a partnership "share" will constitute a supply.

Again, this list is not exhaustive. The most common situations in which the disposal of a partnership "share" by a partner will be a supply are likely to be:

(1) *Where the partnership "share" was acquired and disposed of as a direct extension of the partner's economic activities* – Where a partner is a taxable person in their own right, the partnership "share" may have been acquired in the course or furtherance of their own economic activities. If that is the case, the subsequent transfer or assignment of that "share" for a consideration will also be economic activity of that taxable person. For example, the partner may have a business asset to be sold and, rather than selling the asset directly, may have contributed that asset into a partnership and sold the resultant partnership 'share' instead. The sale of that partnership "share" will constitute a supply for VAT purposes.

(2) *Where the partnership "share" was acquired in order to obtain an active role in the business of the partnership* – Where a partner is a taxable person in their own right and had acquired the partnership "share" in order to actively participate in, or control, the business of the partnership, then the sale of that "share" can be economic activity on the partner's part. The sale of the "share" will constitute a supply for VAT purposes.

(3) *Where the partnership 'share' was acquired as part of a commercial partnership "share-dealing" activity* – A partner who is a taxable person may have a business of dealing in partnership "shares". This will be economic activity on the partner's part. Sales or assignments of the partnership "shares" that were acquired in the course of this activity that are for a consideration will constitute supplies for VAT purposes.

For the avoidance of any doubt, you should note that supplies of partnership "shares" in the above circumstances cannot be disregarded by virtue of section 45(1) of the VAT Act 1994. As Business Brief 21/04 explained, the purpose of s. 45(1) is to ensure continuity by providing that changes in the composition of a partnership do not create the need for a partnership to deregister and re-register for VAT every time the partners change. It also makes it unnecessary to take account of any changes in the composition of the partnership when determining what supplies have been made or received by the partnership business. The section has no effect upon any supply that one of the partners may be making as a taxable person in their own right.

Liability of supplies of partnership shares

In those circumstances where the disposal of a partnership "share" is a supply, that supply will be an exempt financial service.

Treatment of VAT on associated purchases

Where the disposal of an existing partnership "share" is not a supply, the VAT incurred in connection with the disposal will normally not be input tax. Where the disposal is a supply, the related VAT will be input tax, but recovery will normally be fully restricted under the partial exemption rules as the supply is exempt. This is subject to the de minimis provisions (see VAT Notice 706 *"Partial Exemption"*).

Application to past transactions

This Business Brief clarifies existing policy and the above principles will be applied to all future transactions. Where a past transaction has been treated differently from the above and resulted in an underdeclaration Customs will take no further action. If a past transaction has been treated differently and resulted in an overdeclaration, businesses may use the voluntary disclosure procedure to reclaim the VAT. Any such claims will be subject to the "three-year [now four-year] capping rules" and rules relating to the payment of statutory interest.'

Legislation: VATA 1994, s. 45

Case: *KapHag Renditefonds v Finanzamt Charlottenburg* (Case C-442/01) [2005] BVC 566

Other material: Business Brief 30/2004 (19 November 2004)

28-220   Registration of limited liability partnerships

Limited liability partnerships can be formed from 6 April 2001. For VAT purposes:

(1)   an LLP is a body corporate which is a separate legal entity and, subject to the normal rules, the LLP rather than its partners is liable to register (*Limited Liability Partnership Act* 2000, s. 1(2));

(2)   converting an ordinary partnership into an LLP is a transfer of a going concern (TOGC); and

(3)   a LLP as a body corporate can join a VAT group (subject to the usual conditions) (HMRC *VAT – Registration Manual* at VATREG 09600 at *www.hmrc.gov.uk/manuals/vatregmanual/VATREG09600.htm*).

Business Brief 3/2001 (20 February 2001) is reproduced below.

'LIMITED LIABILITY PARTNERSHIPS AND VAT

This Business Brief is to help businesses who are considering forming Limited Liability Partnership (LLPs) and outlines Customs' views on the VAT position of such partnerships. The contents of this Business Brief have been agreed with the Association of Partnership Practitioners and other interested parties.

What is a limited liability partnership?

The *Limited Liability Partnership Act* 2000 received Royal Assent on 20 July 2000. LLPs can be formed with effect from 6 April 2001.

A LLP will have a legal status distinct from its members, and will be able to enter into contracts in its own right. This means that individual members of the LLP will be protected from debts or liabilities arising from negligence, wrongful acts or misconduct of another member, employee or agent of the LLP.

Limited liability partnerships and VAT

The members of the LLP must prepare an incorporation document for the Registrar of Companies who, on acceptance, will issue a certificate of incorporation. This means that the LLP will be a corporate body, and that it, rather than the members will be the legal entity for VAT purposes. The LLP itself then becomes liable for VAT registration, subject to the normal registration rules.

As with unlimited partnerships this does not normally mean that the members will be seen as supplying their services to the LLPs and they therefore will not normally have to register for VAT.

VAT liability if an existing partnership changes to a limited liability partnership

As the legal entity has changed from that of a partnership to a corporate body, the LLP may have to apply for VAT registration, subject to the normal rules. The normal Transfer of a

Going Concern (TOGC) rules will then also apply, including those relating to any option to tax. If the general partnership ceases to exist, it may be possible for the VAT number to be transferred to the LLP (Notice 700/9, Transfer of a Going Concern, gives full details).

Membership of a VAT group

A LLP will be able to join a VAT group provided it meets the control conditions in section 43A of the Value Added Tax Act 1994. This section allows two or more corporate bodies to apply for VAT grouping if each is established or has a fixed establishment in the UK and one of them controls the others; or one person controls all of them; or two or more individuals carrying on a business in partnership control all of them.

A corporate body is "controlled" by its "holding company". Individuals can fulfil the definition of a "holding company" without actually being a corporate body themselves. So, for VAT grouping purposes, individuals can "control" a corporate body. The terms "control" and "holding company" are defined in section 736 of the Companies Act 1985 [now Companies Act 2006, s. 1159 and Sch. 6].

Thus, if the LLP fulfils these control conditions with a number of subsidiary companies, it may form a VAT group with them. It is also possible that a group could be formed by two or more eligible companies and a LLP, where those eligible companies are controlling partners in the LLP.

Customs will also see the third of the above control conditions, i.e. two or more individuals carrying on a business in partnership control all of them – being met when the members of a LLP control all of the corporate bodies to be grouped.'

Other material: Business Brief 3/2001 (20 February 2001)

28-240   Registration of limited partnerships

Ordinary partnerships are 'persons' for VAT registration purposes. One partnership only has one registration regardless of how many businesses it runs. However, the position is different for limited partnerships (LPs). A limited partnership has at least one general partner and at least one limited partner. Form VAT 2 is only completed by general partners. A limited partner (*Limited Partnerships Act* 1907, s. 4(2)):

'... shall at the time of entering into such partnership contribute thereto a sum or sums as capital or property valued at a stated amount, and ... shall not be liable for the debts or obligations of the firm beyond the amount so contributed.'

Section 6 of the Act provides:

'(1) A limited partner shall not take part in the management of the partnership business, and shall not have power to bind the firm:

Provided that a limited partner may by himself or his agent at any time inspect the books of the firm and examine into the state and prospects of the partnership business, and may advise with the partners thereon.

If a limited partner takes part in the management of the partnership business he shall be liable for all debts and obligations of the firm incurred while he so takes part in the management as though he were a general partner.'

In *Saunders and Sorrell* (1980) 1 BVC 1,133, HMRC had decided that the appellants, who were both registered patent agents, were entitled to only one registration as they were carrying on business in partnership. Before 10 April 1972, Mr Saunders carried on his practice as a patent agent under the name of 'Saunders & Dolleymore' and Mr Sorrell carried on his practice as a patent agent under the name of 'Sorrell & Son'. The two appellants were friends and both were concerned with the position which would arise in relation to their respective practices in the event of accident or illness.

An individual may not practice as a patent agent unless he and all his partners are registered. If, therefore, Mr Saunders had suffered an accident or been incapacitated by illness, difficulty would have arisen over the continuation of his practice as 'Saunders & Dolleymore'. A similar difficulty would have arisen if Mr Sorrell suffered an accident or illness in relation to his practice as 'Sorrell & Son'. To minimise such possible difficulties they devised a limited partnership scheme. By an agreement in writing Mr Saunders agreed to admit Mr Sorrell into partnership with him in the practice of Saunders & Dolleymore ('the first firm') but only as a limited partner. This agreement expressly provided that Mr Sorrell (the limited partner) should take no part in the management of the 'first firm's' practice or purport or have power to bind the first firm. But he could inspect the books and examine the state and prospects of the practice and advise Mr Saunders (the general partner) thereon. Mr Sorrell contributed £250 by way of capital to the first firm and, under this first agreement, became entitled to receive as his share of the profits a sum equal to 2% p.a. on such capital. The balance of the capital of profits belonged to Mr Saunders. There was a provision in the agreement to the effect that, if Mr Saunders became incapacitated, the limited partner would, for a period not exceeding six months, make his services available to the general partner or his personal representatives for such working time as he was able and upon such terms as might be mutually agreed with the object of preserving the goodwill of the practice until sale.

A similar agreement in writing made on the same date admitted Mr Saunders into partnership in the practice of 'Sorrell & Son' ('the second firm'). The terms of this second agreement were similar to those of the first agreement but Mr Saunders was the limited partner and Mr Sorrell the general partner.

When VAT was introduced Mr Saunders was registered as a taxable person and so was Mr Sorrell. Having discovered the existence of the limited partnership agreements, HMRC in 1979 decided that, because of the limited partnership agreements, one of the registrations should be cancelled. The appellants successfully appealed to a tribunal contending that they were entitled to separate registrations. The tribunal said at p. 1,135:

'... the facts on this appeal are clearly distinguishable from those in the *Glassborow* case.

On this appeal I am concerned with two limited partnerships, not two general partnerships as in the *Glassborow* case. Mr. Sorrell is not liable for any of the debts or obligations of the First Firm, and Mr. Saunders is not liable to any of the debts or obligations of the Second Firm. This is so provided by the *Limited Partnerships Act* 1907. I take the view that the statutory provisions to that effect were not intended to be affected in any way by the or the regulations made thereunder. In my view, as Mr. Sorrell takes no part in the management of the First Firm, the supplies made in the course of the business of the First Firm are not supplies made by Mr. Sorrell "in the course of a business carried on by him" for the purposes of s. 2 of the Act [of 1972; now VATA 1994, s. 4(1)].

Therefore, not only is Mr. Sorrell under no liability to the Commissioners for tax on supplies made by Mr. Saunders in the course of the business of the First Firm, but he is under no obligation to the Commissioners in relation to the submission of returns to them in respect of such supplies. Similar considerations apply to Mr. Saunders in relation to the Second Firm. Yet the decision of the Commissioners would require one of the appellants to undertake the obligation to account for tax in respect of both businesses.

... The power in s. 22(1) [of FA 1972; now VATA 1994, s. 45(1)] to register two or more persons in the name of a firm arises where the persons are "carrying on a business in partnership". In my view, having regard to the restrictions on the management of a business by a limited partner imposed by s. 6 of the Limited Partnerships Act 1907, Mr. Sorrell is not carrying on the business of the First Firm in partnership with Mr. Saunders, and Mr. Saunders is not carrying on the business of the Second Firm in partnership with Mr. Sorrell, within the meaning and intent of FA 1972, s. 22(1).'

Legislation: VATA 1994, s. 45

Cases: *Saunders and Sorrell* (1980) 1 BVC 1,133

28-260   VAT assessments

An assessment must be 'notified' to the person who is assessed (VATA 1994, s. 73(1) and 76(1)). Thus, an assessment is invalid if it is addressed to the wrong person or shows an incorrect address.

Assessment of a partnership

A VAT assessment can be 'addressed to a partnership by the name in which it is registered' under the VAT Act (VATA 1994, s. 45(4); *The Bengal Brasserie* [1991] BVC 1,363).

As a partnership is a collection of persons with joint liability, an assessment can be made on the individual partners (*C & E Commrs v Evans (t/a The Grape Escape Wine Bar)* (1981) 1 BVC 455).

A separate assessment must be made for each period during which there was a different collection of partners (*Ahmed* (1987) 3 BVC 1,349).

A person who has left a partnership is treated as continuing to be a partner until the date on which a change in the partnership is notified to HMRC (VATA 1994, s. 45(2)). In *Hussein (t/a Pressing Dry Cleaners)* [2004] BVC 4,028, the tribunal decided that such notification need not be in writing and could be when a VAT officer visited the partnership and learnt that a partner had retired. However, strictly such notification should be in writing under *Value Added Tax Regulations* 1995 (SI 1995/2518), reg. 5(3)).

Example: Assessment of partnership with changing partners

Ann and Beryl started to practise as accountants on 1 January 2010 under the style of 'AB accountants and advisers'.

Carol was admitted as a partner on 1 January 2012.

Ann retired from the firm on 31 December 2013.

If there is underdeclared output tax for the five years to 31 December 2015, three separate assessments must be made, i.e. one for each of the following periods:

(1)　1 January 2010 to 31 December 2011 and addressed to either 'AB accountants and advisers' or to Ann and Beryl;

(2)　1 January 2012 to 31 December 2013 and addressed to either 'AB accountants and advisers' or to Ann, Beryl and Carol;

(3)　1 January 2014 to 31 December 2014 and addressed to either 'AB accountants and advisers' or to Beryl and Carol.

However, if notification under *Value Added Tax Regulations* 1995, reg. 5(3) of Ann's retirement was only made on 11 April 2014, then the assessments must be made for these periods:

(1)　1 January 2010 to 31 December 2011 and addressed to either 'AB accountants and advisers' or to Ann and Beryl, i.e. as above;

(2)　1 January 2012 to 11 April 2014 and addressed to either 'AB accountants and advisers' or to Ann, Beryl and Carol, i.e. Ann is also liable for any underdeclared output tax for the period from 1 January 2014 to 11 April 2014;

(3)　12 April 2014 to 31 December 2014 and addressed to either 'AB accountants and advisers' or to Beryl and Carol.

In *R & C Commrs v Pal* [2008] BVC 3, the High Court held that a VAT assessment had failed to impose a liability on two out of four taxpayers who had signed Form VAT 2 purporting to register a partnership for VAT where, on the evidence, they were not partners. Two of the four signatories on Form VAT 2 had apparently signed in their capacity as tenants only to avoid difficulties with the landlord of the property from which the partnership operated. Only a 'person' who made taxable supplies might be VAT-registered and the inclusion of non-partners on Form VAT 2 has no effect. However, the assessment was enforceable against the other two signatories because the tribunal found that they were in partnership during the period to which the assessment related.

Any notice, whether of assessment or otherwise, which is addressed to a partnership by the name in which it is registered is treated as served on the partnership (VATA 1994, s. 45(4)).

In *Yarl Wines* [2003] BVC 4,045, the tribunal held that a letter addressed to only one partner amounted to notification of an assessment.

Legislation: VATA 1994, s. 45, 73(1); SI 1995/2518, reg. 5

Cases: *The Bengal Brasserie* [1991] BVC 1,363; *C & E Commrs v Evans (t/a The Grape Escape Wine Bar)* (1981) 1 BVC 455; *Ahmed* (1987) 3 BVC 1,349; *Hussein (t/a Pressing Dry Cleaners)* [2004] BVC 4,028; *R & C Commrs v Pal* [2008] BVC 3; *Yarl Wines* [2003] BVC 4,045

28-280   Insolvency returns

Period of return for an insolvent person

If a VAT-registered trader is declared bankrupt or a liquidator or receiver is appointed, the return period in which such an event occurs is divided into two parts:

(1)   up to the end of the day before the order was made; and

(2)   from that date to the end of the return period.

A separate return is due for both period (1) and (2) (*Value Added Tax Regulations* 1995, reg. 30 and 25(3); Notice 700/56/2015, para. 5.4).

Until the insolvent trader's affairs are finalised, the 'person in charge', i.e. the trustee in bankruptcy, receiver, liquidator or Official Receiver, must make further returns in accordance with the trader's return periods.

Partnerships and insolvency

As regards a partnership, if one or more of the partners remain solvent, the solvent partner(s) must submit returns and pay any VAT liability (Notice 700/56/2015, para. 16.3).

Legislation: SI 1995/2518, reg. 25(3) and 30

Other material: HMRC VAT Notice 700/56/2015, para. 5.4 and 16.3

VAT PENALTIES

28-300   Civil fraud penalty for partners

A penalty notice can be issued to a partnership, without the need for separate notices.

In *Akbar (t/a Mumtaz Paan House)* [1998] BVC 2,157, the tribunal decided that an assessment under VATA 1994, s. 76(1) of a civil fraud penalty under VATA 1994, s. 60 could be made against a firm, i.e. against partners together, as opposed to each member of the firm. HMRC's statement of case alleged dishonest conduct on the part of the appellants, but only named one of them. Since all the dishonest conduct alleged occurred in the ordinary course of the business of the firm, the partners were jointly liable and each of them was severally liable for the dishonest conduct on the part of one or more of them (*Partnership Act* 1890, s. 10 and 12). A penalty assessment under VATA 1994, s. 60 could be validly made against several persons together, whether the dishonest conduct alleged was alleged to have been that of all of them together or was alleged to have been that of one or more of them in circumstances where the liability for the penalty was imposed on all of them.

A dishonest act can be made by an individual or by a taxable person, such as a partnership (*Islam & Goodwest Ltd* [2003] BVC 4,043).

In *Yarl Wines* [2003] BVC 4,045, a penalty notice sent to one partner was held to constitute sufficient notification of the penalty.

Legislation: VATA 1994, s. 60 and 76(1)

Cases: *Akbar (t/a Mumtaz Paan House)* [1998] BVC 2,157; *Islam & Goodwest Ltd* [2003] BVC 4,043; *Yarl Wines* [2003] BVC 4,045

28-320   Penalty for inaccurate information

Incorrect returns or claims may result in a penalty under FA 2007, Sch. 24, para. 1 depending on the behaviour of the taxpayer.

A penalty under Sch. 24, para. 1 can be assessed on a partner or the firm (Sch. 24, para. 20).

An inaccuracy made by P in a document may be:

(1)   a mistake made despite the person taking reasonable care (no penalty); or

(2)   careless (lowest penalty); or

(3)   deliberate but not concealed; or

(4)   deliberate and concealed (maximum penalty).

Legislation: FA 2007, Sch. 24, para. 1 and 20

VAT ON PARTNERSHIP TRANSACTIONS

28-340   Capital introduced

When capital is introduced into a partnership or a sole trader business by a partner or sole proprietor, this does not represent consideration for a supply by the business (*KapHag Renditefonds v Finanzamt Charlottenburg* (Case C-442/01) [2005] BVC 566; Business Brief 21/2004 (20 August 2004)), see ¶28-180.

In *Maritsan Developments Ltd* [2012] TC 01971, two individuals contributed their skills, talents, abilities and business connections in pursuit of the common goal of acquiring a property and selling it at profit with the benefit of planning permission. That was their capital contribution to the joint venture. As such, that was not the supply of services for a consideration and so was outside the scope of VAT.

Cases: *KapHag Renditefonds v Finanzamt Charlottenburg* (Case C-442/01) [2005] BVC 566; *Maritsan Developments* Ltd [2012] TC 01971

Other material: Business Brief 21/2004 (20 August 2004)

28-360   Partnership interest: purchase and disposal

When a new partner is admitted for a consideration, there is no supply by the existing partners to the new partner (*KapHag Renditefonds v Finanzamt Charlottenburg* (Case C-442/01) [2005] BVC 566; Business Brief 21/2004 (20 August 2004)), see ¶28-180.

If the new partner disposes of the acquired interest, there may or may not be a supply. There is no supply when the 'share' is disposed of for no consideration or the new partner was an investor who had 'no involvement in the running of a partnership'. There may be other circumstances when the disposal of such a 'share' is not a supply (Business Brief 30/2004 (22 November 2004) see ¶28-200).

Cases: *KapHag Renditefonds v Finanzamt Charlottenburg* (Case C-442/01) [2005] BVC 566

Other material: Business Brief 21/2004 (20 August 2004); Business Brief 30/2004 (22 November 2004)

28-380 De-registration

When a person ceases to be registered, any goods, which form part of the assets of the business carried on by him, are deemed to be supplied in the course of the business before de-registration, unless (VATA 1994, Sch. 4, para. 8(1)):

(1) the business is transferred as a going concern to another taxable person;

(2) the taxable person has died or become bankrupt, or incapacitated in some other way and the business is carried on by some other person on his behalf; or

(3) the VAT on the deemed supply would not be more than £1,000 (before 1 April 2000 the limit was £250; VATA 1994, Sch. 4, para. 8).

The deemed supply is not treated as made *to* any person.

For the purposes of these provisions, 'goods' mean tangible items such as unsold stock, plant, vehicles and fixtures and fittings. Business assets consisting of land are also treated as goods. Intangible goods, such as goodwill, copyrights, and patents do not count.

If a trader ceases registration in the UK, because his country of registration becomes the Isle of Man, there is no resulting deemed supply of the goods forming part of the assets of his business (*Value Added Tax (Isle of Man) Order* 1982 (SI 1982/1067), art. 11(8)).

No output tax is due if HMRC are satisfied that the trader did not claim credit for input tax on the supply, acquisition or importation of the goods. The lack of input tax recovery might have been because the trader was not a taxable person when the supply was made to him, and he did not recover it when he registered for VAT, nor acquire the goods from another taxable person as part of the assets of a business transferred to him on a 'going concern' basis (VATA 1994, Sch. 4, para. 8(2)).

There is also no deemed supply where a person ceases to be a taxable person by virtue of joining the agricultural flat-rate scheme (VATA 1994, Sch. 4, para. 8(3)).

VAT registered persons with substantial assets should be careful when changing from sole trader to partnership or vice versa and de-registering. Two examples below show where problems can arise.

Example 1: Deemed supply on de-registration

Paul and his wife, Paula, traded as retailers in equal partnership. They VAT-registered in the UK in 2005. In late 2012, the partnership purchased the freehold of a shop just built in the UK for £300,000 plus £52,500 VAT which was reclaimed.

In 2014, Paula retired from the partnership which de-registered. Paul immediately registered as a sole trader and continued to run the business. The shop remained in their joint ownership VATA 1994, s. 45(1) and Sch. 1, para. 1(2)). Is there a problem?

In 2015, a VAT officer at a control visit decided that the partnership transferred the business to Paul as a going concern, but without the shop. Thus, output tax was due on the deemed supply of the shop on de-registration by the partnership (VATA 1994, Sch. 4, para. 8 and Sch. 6, para. 6). That supply was standard-rated because the shop was owned by the partnership and was still 'new' – within three years of its construction in 2012 – when the partnership de-registered: its construction was completed in 2012, less than three years before the deemed supply in 2014 (VATA 1994, Sch. 9, Grp. 1, Note (4)).

In 2014, if Paul and Paula had remained registered in the partnership, opted to tax the shop and charged a commercial rent to Paul as a sole trader, that would have avoided the VAT due on de-registration.

Paul and Paula could not have reregistered in 2014 as a different type of business. Once persons are registered, the registration covers all of their business activities.

Example 2: De-registration deemed costs VAT – but irrecoverable if re-register

After de-registering on 8 January 1994 and accounting on his final VAT return for £893 of output tax on the deemed supply of the equipment on hand, *Haugh* [1997] BVC 2,525 re-registered on 1 September 1994, his business having recovered (VATA 1994, Sch. 4, para. 8).

The tribunal decided that the deemed supply on de-registration was not to himself or to anyone else. Yet a person's input tax is defined as 'VAT on the supply to him of any goods or services' (VATA 1994, s. 24(1)). Unfortunately, the situation was not covered by *Value Added Tax Regulations* 1995 (SI 1995/2518), reg. 111, which concerned purchases when a trader was unregistered.

The tribunal commented that HMRC's powers of care and management should permit them to allow the claim by concession (CRCA 2005, s. 5).

Capital goods scheme: final adjustment at de-registration

If, on cancellation of the registration, there is a capital item covered by the capital goods scheme, which is still within its adjustment period and VAT has to be accounted for on the business assets, then a final CGS adjustment must be made (*Value Added Tax Regulations* 1995 (SI 1995/2518), reg. 115(3), (3A) and (3B)).

Even if VAT is not required to be accounted for on the business assets because the value falls below the specified monetary limit relating to assets on hand at de-registration, there is still a deemed disposal of the capital item and a final adjustment must be made. This also applies if the supply is exempt or zero-rated.

The final adjustment should be made in the same way as for the disposal of a capital item within the adjustment period, except that any adjustment for the remainder of the adjustment period is included on the final VAT return (Notice 706/2/2011, para. 9.6).

Legislation: VATA 1994, s. 45, Sch. 1, para. 1, Sch. 4, para. 8, Sch. 6, para. 6, Sch. 9, Grp. 1; CRCA 2005, s. 5; SI 1995/2518, reg. 111 and 115

Other material: HMRC VAT Notice 706/2/2011, para. 9.6

INPUT TAX RECOVERY

28-400   Tripartite transactions

There is a myth that input tax can be claimed only by the person who pays for the supply. However, a key word in VAT is 'supply', rather than 'payment'. Generally, VAT on a supply is only reclaimable if it was charged on a supply *to* the claimant and not to another person (VATA 1994, s. 24(1)). Although the recipient of a supply is usually either the person with whom the supplier contracted or the person that pays for the service, this is not always true. Where three persons are involved in a transaction (a 'tripartite transaction'), there can be problems identifying the recipient of a supply who may reclaim any VAT charged on that supply.

In *Lester Aldridge (a firm)* [2005] BVC 2,231, HMRC unsuccessfully tried to stop a firm of solicitors from recovering VAT paid on rent where the lease was granted to a nominee of the firm. The firm negotiated a lease of premises for 25 years. As a partnership, the firm could take the lease in the names of no more than four of the partners or procure another entity to hold the lease for its benefit. The firm chose to acquire the lease in the name of a nominee company, Lester Aldridge Nominees Ltd, which allowed the firm to occupy the premises. The firm was a guarantor for the nominee company and undertook to pay the rent. Since the landlord had opted to tax the premises, VAT was charged on the rent. The firm recovered the VAT as input tax. The tribunal viewed the arrangements in their entirety and decided that the firm could be regarded as receiving for VAT purposes a taxable supply for which it made payment, and the supply was used for the purposes of its business.

In *Finanzamt Saarlouis v Malburg* (Case C-204/13) [2014] BVC 12, the ECJ held that a partnership could not reclaim VAT paid by one of its partners (Mr Malburg) in acquiring part of a client base of a dissolved partnership. The client base did not become part of the capital assets of the new partnership. When Mr Malburg provided the client base free of charge for use by the new partnership, this did not amount to an economic activity.

Legislation: VATA 1994, s. 24

Cases: *Lester Aldridge (a firm)* [2005] BVC 2,231; *Finanzamt Saarlouis v Malburg* (Case C-204/13) [2014] BVC 12

28-420   Business purpose test

Input tax is defined as VAT incurred on goods or services which are used or to be used for the purposes of the business (VATA 1994, s. 24(1) and Directive 2006/112, art. 168). Thus, VAT incurred on expenditure which is not for the purposes of the business is not input tax and is not recoverable.

Hartridge (t/a Hartridge Consultancy) [1998] BVC 2,281 was in dispute with his former partners and spent £100,000 in professional fees to protect his business interest, which would continue under a new entity. He successfully claimed input tax relating to the fees on the first return of the new entity. The tribunal decided that as a direct result of pursuing the dispute, he continued working with clients who might otherwise be lost during the dispute and that there was a sufficient link between the former partnership and the subsequent new business entity. In *Hartridge*, the services were supplied to Mr Hartridge, who was both a sole proprietor and the client of the solicitors.

In contrast, in the anonymised case *A Partnership* [2015] TC 04358, the First-tier Tribunal (FTT) held that one set of solicitors supplied their services only to Messrs A and B; another set supplied their services only to Mr C. However, the continuing business was carried on by a partnership of Messrs A, B and C. The services of neither firm of solicitors were supplied to the partnership of Messrs A, B and C. They were supplied only to certain persons within that partnership. The FTT held that, had the legal expenses been incurred on behalf of the partnership, it would have found that they were directly and immediately linked to the business of that partnership. However, this part of the FTT's decision proceeded only on the assumption that the supply was 'to' the partnership. Although the taxpayers won on this point, their appeal still failed (para. 73 of the decision).

Legislation: VATA 1994, s. 24

Cases: *(Hartridge t/a Hartridge Consultancy)* [1998] BVC 2,281; *A Partnership* [2015] TC 04358

28-440   Other legal services and fees

Usually, the unsuccessful party in litigation must pay the legal costs of the successful party. However, only the person to whom the legal services were supplied can make a valid input tax claim. The identity of the person making the payment is irrelevant, since that person cannot reclaim the VAT if he is not the recipient of the supply. The solicitor should address the invoice to his client, so the third party paying the costs should not, in any event, hold a VAT invoice to substantiate a claim to input tax.

In *Nye Saunders & Partners* [1995] BVC 1,339, a firm of architects which took action against a client, was ordered to pay the client's costs of more than £60,000. It deducted VAT on the costs, but the tribunal held that the legal services had been supplied to the client and there was no right of deduction by the architects.

Sometimes it is unclear to whom the legal services were provided. For example, generally a VAT-registered partnership cannot recover the VAT on fees incurred by one partner acting in his own capacity. Considering the engagement letter may resolve the issue. Ideally, the VAT invoices should be worded clearly enough to establish what they cover. Some suppliers of professional services seem deliberately to put as little detail in their VAT invoices on the basis that this gives the client little information to challenge the invoice. Other suppliers believe in listing in detail on the invoice the full range of work done.

Cases: *Nye Saunders & Partners* [1995] BVC 1,339

28-460   Accountancy fees

In *Mundays LLP* [2012] TC 02374, the partnership commissioned accountants to undertake accounting and tax compliance work. VAT was correctly charged by the accountants.

The nominated partner is liable to file a partnership tax return setting out the profits of the partnership. The partners individually are liable to file personal tax returns and to pay the tax arising in respect of them. The figures for each partner's personal return in respect of their income from the partnership is copied from the partnership return.

Under the partnership agreement, the partnership could deduct from a partner's current share of the partnership profits an amount estimated to represent that partner's future tax liability on his share of the current partnership profits. The money, although credited to each partner's tax reserve account, was cash available to be used by the partnership. It could be seen as a short-term interest-free loan from the individual partners to the partnership as a whole.

Each partner probably wishes to ensure that his partners put aside sufficient to pay their tax liabilities because it might reflect badly on the partnership if a partner became insolvent due to being unable to pay his income tax bill.

The partnership argued that 82% of the charge by the accountants was input tax of the partnership and the remaining amount of £170 per partner was 'small' and, in accordance with the HMRC Manual, should be recoverable.

HMRC accepted that tax advice on the submission of the partnership tax return was input tax of the partnership. However, HMRC argued that all of the charge per partner related to personal liabilities of the partners and had been incorrectly reclaimed. Also, the amount of £170 was not 'small' and in any event the tribunal had no jurisdiction in respect of the concessionary treatment set out in the Manual.

The First-tier Tribunal held that preparing a partnership tax return was an inevitable consequence of carrying on a business in partnership. It was part of the general overheads of the partnership's business and it was all recoverable by a fully taxable business.

It was clearly of benefit to the partnership that the partners properly filed their tax returns and on time, but benefit is not the test. The test is whether it was for the purpose of the business, i.e. it must have a direct and immediate link with the business.

Although virtually all of the partners' tax liabilities arose directly out of being partners, filing personal tax returns of its partners was not a business purpose of the partnership, nor even a consequential business expense. The expense was not incurred in order to carry out the business of practising as solicitors nor did it arise out of the partnership's business as solicitors. Tax on the individual partners' share in the profits is merely an inevitable consequence of being in a profitable partnership, but it is not a liability of the business: therefore expenses incurred in making the necessary returns and payments in respect of it are not business expenses.

Keeping the tax reserves as working capital was a purpose of the business but ensuring the partners could pay their tax was merely a benefit to the business, not a purpose of the business. In these circumstances, a single payment with both a business purpose and a business benefit is entirely input tax.

The tribunal also held that the concession in the HMRC Manual was not intended to cover invoices of the size issued and the partnership could not rely on it.

Cases: *Mundays LLP* [2012] TC 02374

28-480   Partnership – cost of raising capital

In *Rock Lambert* [1992] BVC 536, the issue was whether VAT incurred on realisation of assets owned by partners who sold property to reduce debts owed by the appellant partnership was reclaimable as input tax by the partnership (VATA 1994, s. 24(1)).

The appellant partnership was in severe financial difficulties and cash was injected into the business by the realisation of assets belonging to the partners. The majority of the money raised by that realisation was used to pay off debts due from the partnership. The partnership had no lease or other proprietary right in a property known as the 'Old Rectory', but occupied a room there from which it carried on its business. The freehold of the Old Rectory and some adjoining land was owned by a partner, and that property was sold subject to a buy-back option. The partnership continued to occupy its rooms in the Old Rectory after the sale.

The VAT on various invoices for services connected with this sale was reclaimed by the appellant as the partnership's input tax. This reclaim was disallowed by HMRC on the grounds that the supplies were neither to the partnership nor for the purposes of its business but related solely to private transactions of the partners.

The partnership contended that the VAT was reclaimable and that it was in a similar position to a company raising capital in a similar way.

The tribunal dismissed the partners' appeal. The VAT charged was not reclaimable by the partnership because the partnership had no interest in the assets whose realisation gave rise to the VAT charge. A company which raised capital through agents was a different case because the partnership was not a separate legal person and the partnership per se had not incurred any of the costs of raising the capital. The partners who owned the Old Rectory had disposed of it as individuals. The partnership was at all times one step removed from being the supplier. The input tax was, therefore, not reclaimable.

Legislation: VATA 1994, s. 24

Cases: *Rock Lambert* [1992] BVC 536

PROPERTY OWNERSHIP

28-500   Ownership of property: introduction

Sometimes the premises of a practising partnership are owned by only some of the partners. The VAT position and treatment depends on the facts. Some possibilities are considered in the following paragraphs, but each case should be considered on its merits. It is often desirable to agree the treatment with HMRC in writing.

28-520   Property owned as 'ordinary' partnership asset

If the partnership premises, whether freehold or leasehold (or Scottish near equivalents), are owned as a partnership asset in which all partners have an interest, the position is fairly straightforward. Input tax on repairs, refurbishment, extensions, etc. is recoverable subject to the ordinary rules as to evidence and partial exemption. Disposal, subletting, etc. are subject to the ordinary VAT rules, but particular attention should be given to the partial exemption implications for the practice.

Re-examine the position if the ownership changes on, say, a partnership change. If a partner retires from the partnership while retaining an interest in the property, or a new partner is admitted who does not acquire an interest in the property, then the position may change (see ¶28-540ff.).

28-540   Property owned by some partners and included in balance sheet

If only some partners have an interest in the partnership premises but, nevertheless, the premises are included in the partnership balance sheet, the VAT position is unclear. The question is whether the property is a partnership asset. If it is not, then the position is as described in ¶28-560 for property owned by some of the partners outside of the partnership.

If it is a partnership asset, there seems to be no reason why the VAT treatment is not as described in ¶28-520 for property in which all the partners have an interest. Although following a sale of the property any profit is likely, in the ordinary course of events, to accrue to those partners who have an interest in it, the property must be held, in the first instance, for the benefit of the partnership (*Partnership Act* 1890, s. 20(1)). As a matter of prudence, and bearing in mind that this is an uncertain area, the treatment should be agreed with HMRC in writing.

28-560   Property owned by some partners outside the partnership

Where the partnership premises are owned by some of the partners, but outside of the partnership and not owned as a partnership asset, the position is much the same as if the property was held by third parties having no connection with the partnership. The joint owners are regarded as making supplies to the partnership of the lease, tenancy or licence under which the partnership occupies the premises. This involves the joint owners in making exempt supplies unless they opt to tax, in which case the supplies are normally standard-rated.

If the joint owners carry out works on a non-opted property, they cannot recover VAT on the costs as input tax, since this is attributable to the exempt supplies of letting. If the joint owners opt to tax, and the option is effective, they can register for VAT and recover the tax, but they must charge and account for VAT on the rents. The VAT registration is a separate partnership registration if a partnership exists between the joint owners. If there is no partnership, the joint owners are registered as a single taxable person with joint and several liability. The charging of VAT on the rents is normally acceptable, since the practice occupying the premises can generally recover the tax. However, VAT is also due on all future supplies of the property, including possible sale or letting to a purchaser or tenant unable to recover VAT.

If the landlords do not wish to opt to tax, it makes sense from a VAT viewpoint (although other factors must be considered as well) to frame the lease in such a way as to maximise the responsibility of the practice partnership, as opposed to the property owners, for the upkeep and maintenance of the building, and fix the rent at a level which reflects the tenant's responsibilities.

Input tax incurred by the practice partnership on expenses which are its responsibility is generally recoverable in the ordinary way (subject to the partial exemption rules, etc.). However, this does not enable the practising partnership to undertake works which are the responsibility of the landlords (possibly adjusting profit shares to compensate the partners who do not have an interest in the property) and recover the VAT on these costs. In such a case, the likelihood is that either the inputs are seen by HMRC as being used for the benefit of the business of the property owners (and not recoverable by the practising partnership), or the practising partnership is seen as making a supply to the landlords.

Changes of the partners in the practising partnership and the landlords of the property should be monitored to identify the situation if the position is reached where the identities of the joint property owners and those of the partners in the practice are the same. In this situation, HMRC may contend that there is a single entity for VAT purposes. HMRC are correct in this if the relationship of the joint property owners, acting as such, is such that they amount to a partnership. If the property owners are not in partnership in respect of this activity, the position is far from clear (¶28-360).

28-580   Property owned by nominee company

The position where partnership premises are owned by a nominee company is the same as if it was held directly by the persons for whom the company is nominee (*Lester Aldridge* [2005] BVC 2,231; *Bird Semple & Crawford Herron* (1986) 2 BVC 205,488).

Cases: *Lester Aldridge* [2005] BVC 2,231; *Bird Semple & Crawford Herron* (1986) 2 BVC 205,488

28-600   Property owned by service company

When the partnership premises are owned by a service company (or some other associated company) acting in its own right rather than as nominee, the position is much the same as if it was owned by some third party landlord. It is generally as described in ¶28-560 for a property owned by some of the partners outside of the practice partnership (but there is no question, in this case, of changes in the partnership resulting in the property entity coming to be regarded as identical with the practising firm).

28-620   Interest in property retained by outgoing partner

The VAT treatment where a property is held as a partnership asset in which all of the partners have an interest is reasonably straightforward. However, the treatment which applies if a retiring partner retains an interest in the property (but not in the partnership as a whole) is unclear, and much depends on the terms under which this takes place. Arguably, for such circumstances to arise, there normally must have been a departure from the ordinary partnership agreement (or the *Partnership Act* 1890) provisions dealing with the retirement of partners. The effect in VAT terms is that the partnership supplies the property to a separate entity consisting of the joint owners (i.e. the continuing partners and the retiring partner).

Such a supply cannot be treated as a 'going concern' transfer since the partnership will not have used the asset in carrying on the same kind of business as that to be carried on by the joint owners (i.e. letting the property). The supply will be exempt or standard-rated depending on the age and tenure of the property and on whether the partnership has opted to tax in respect of it. An exempt supply of the property in these circumstances has partial exemption implications for the practising firm.

28-640   Ownership of property: summary

It can be seen from the outline at ¶28-500ff. that the position regarding the partnership premises, while usually readily manageable from day-to-day, can change considerably on partnership changes and, because of uncertainties in the legislation relating to joint property ownership, can itself be uncertain.

Until the legal position is clarified and to protect against the uncertainty it is advisable to obtain written agreement from HMRC as to the treatment. If the proper treatment ever becomes clear, it will still be necessary to be watchful, and ensure that the VAT implications are taken into account before changes affecting the property are implemented.

28-660   Property letting

Joint venture by partners

HMRC say that if persons intend to co-operate in making supplies as a joint venture, but have not formed a company or entered into a formal partnership agreement, this may nevertheless amount to a partnership which should be registered as such for VAT (Notice 700, para. 6.8 (2015 edn)).

Other material: HMRC VAT Notice 700

Joint owners letting land and buildings

Persons are jointly registrable in respect of the total value of supplies made by them as joint owners, as there is no basis for dividing the value of the supply between them.

Green [1993] BVC 628 is an example of this. Briefly, the facts were that a married couple purchased garages and let them to tenants. The tribunal held that the letting of the garages was a business activity, carried on by the couple together, and that they were liable to be registered together. The liability to register jointly arises even if the joint owners are not a partnership although, as there is no separate category of joint ownership for registration, HMRC register the joint owners as a partnership.

Cases: *Green* [1993] BVC 628

28-680   Partnership interests

The VAT aspects of transactions involving transfers of partnership interests or the contribution of property to a newly formed partnership have never been entirely clear. It was common, before the introduction of anti-avoidance rules in stamp duty land tax (SDLT) legislation, for property to be transferred to third parties by transferring interests first into a partnership and then by transferring the partnership interests to the third party. Historically, stamp duty land tax at 4% could be avoided in these circumstances.

Until recently, it was always assumed that contributions of properties to a partnership did not create a supply, or that the contribution itself was a transfer of a going concern (assuming the relevant conditions were met). Similarly, it was assumed that the sale of an interest in a partnership did not create a supply on the basis that VATA 1994, s. 45 says 'no account shall be taken, in determining [whether] goods or services are supplied to or by [partners in a partnership], of any change in the partnership'.

In 2004, HMRC appeared to change their position on the VAT treatment of partnerships, but shortly after *KapHag Renditefonds v Finanzamt Charlottenburg* (Case C-442/01) [2005] BVC 566, HMRC published Business Briefs 21/2004 (10 August 2004) and 30/2004 (19 November 2004) (see ¶28-180 and ¶28-200). In summary, HMRC consider:

(1)   that in certain circumstances a transfer of a partnership share can create a supply (e.g. dealing) and in others it does not (pure investment);

(2)   subject to (3) below, a partnership contribution does not create a supply;

(3)   however, if the partner held the asset to be contributed as a business asset, there is the potential for a supply, and

(4)   transfer as a going concern treatment could apply in appropriate cases to the contribution of business assets to a partnership.

Legislation: VATA 1994, s. 45

Case: *KapHag Renditefonds v Finanzamt Charlottenburg* (Case C-442/01) [2005] BVC 566

Other material: HMRC Business Briefs 21/2004 (10 August 2004) and 30/2004 (19 November 2004)

28-700   Opting to tax

Opting to tax land and buildings consists of:

(1)   deciding to opt; and

(2)   giving written notice to HMRC within the time-limit.

Persons authorised to opt on behalf of a body

In *Staatssecretaris van Financiën v Heerma* (Case C-23/98) [2003] BVC 97, the court held that the letting of property by a partner to a partnership of which he was a member was an independent activity. This enabled the partner to be a taxable person and to opt to tax the property.

In *DS Talafair & Sons* [1999] BVC 4,115, the tribunal decided that a partnership had only opted in respect of one property which it owned. A letter apparently opting in respect of the other properties had been sent by a relation who was not a partner, and so it did not bind the partnership.

Cases: *Staatssecretaris van Financiën v Heerma* (Case C-23/98) [2003] BVC 97; *DS Talafair & Sons* [1999] BVC 4,115

SPECIAL CIRCUMSTANCES

28-720   Partners providing professional services

Extract from HMRC VAT Notice 700/34: Staff (June 2012):

'3.4 *Sole proprietors and partnerships providing professional services*

This applies to sole proprietors or partnerships in business providing professional services (for example as a solicitor or accountant). If you take up an appointment as a company director or other paid office holder (such as a secretary or treasurer) the business must account for VAT on any payment received if all the following apply:

- the appointment results from the professional expertise which you exercise in your business or in the partnership business;
- your duties as a director or other office-holder involve, at least in part, the use of that expertise; and
- you are a partner and the payments accrue to the partnership and are not retained by you personally.

However, if you take up an appointment as an office holder and the terms under which you are appointed treat you as an employee of the person making the appointment, then any fees or payments made to you personally are outside the scope of VAT.'

Other material: HMRC VAT Notice 700/34

28-740   Private tuition by partnership

Following *C Clarke deceased* [1998] BVC 2,036, supplies of educational or vocational training made by partnerships may also be exempt (VATA 1994, Sch. 9, Grp. 6, item 2). For further details, see Business Brief 1/1998 (7 January 1998), which is reproduced below.

'PRIVATE TUITION BY PARTNERSHIPS BECOMES VAT EXEMPT

Partnerships should note that, with immediate effect, any supplies of education or vocational training they make may qualify for exemption as private tuition under item 2 of VATA 1994, Sch. 9, Grp. 6.

This follows C Clarke Deceased .... Customs previously argued that instruction could qualify as private tuition only when provided by a sole proprietor.

The exemption for private tuition applies only where all partners are jointly responsible for giving the instruction as individual teachers and on their own behalf in a subject ordinarily taught in a school or university. The supply is not one of private tuition if one or more of the partners takes no part in giving instruction or if the partnership employs or engages anyone else to provide any form of tuition on its behalf.

On the other hand, there is no requirement that the instruction should be delivered one-to-one. Neither is exemption ruled out merely because the supply is made to an organisation rather than to private individuals or because the partnership employs others for non-teaching purposes.'

Legislation: VATA 1994, Sch. 9, Grp. 6, item 2

Case: *C Clarke deceased* [1998] BVC 2,036

Other material: Business Brief 1/1998 (7 January 1998)

28-760 Transfer of a 'Going concern'

Subject to the conditions which are summarised below, a transfer of a business (or of part of a business) as a 'going concern' is not a supply for VAT purposes, so no VAT is due (*Value Added Tax (Special Provisions) Order* 1995 (SI 1995/1268), art. 5; Directive 2006/112, art. 19 and 29).

One key matter concerning a TOGC is that there must be a genuine sale of a business or part of a business, i.e. there is no TOGC if the transaction concerns only certain assets, such as the business premises.

A TOGC can be to a person with no previous interest in the business, e.g. a third-party purchaser, or it can be a change of legal entity, e.g. when a sole trader incorporates his business or takes a person into partnership with him.

The conditions that must be met for a transfer (a sale or a gift) of a business (or part of it) to be a non-supply for VAT purposes under the *Value Added Tax (Special Provisions) Order* 1995 (SI 1995/1268), art. 5(1) are:

(1)   if only part of a business is transferred as a going concern, that part must be capable of 'separate operation' (art. 5(1)(b)(i)). This is a question of fact;

(2)   the assets transferred as a going concern are intended to be used by the transferee (purchaser) 'in carrying on the same kind of business, whether or not as part of any existing business, as that carried on by the transferor' (art. 5(1)(a)(i) and (b)(ii)). If the transfer is of part of a business, the test applies to the kind of business carried on by the transferor in relation to that part. This is another question of fact;

(3)   if the transferor (vendor) is a 'taxable person', the transferee (purchaser) is already a taxable person or immediately becomes a taxable person as a result of the transfer (art. 5(1)(a)(ii) and (b)(iii)).

A person is a 'taxable person' while he is or is required to be VAT-registered (VATA 1994, s. 3(1)).

If the transferor is not a taxable person, there is no requirement that the transferee be, or become one, for non-supply treatment to apply; and

(4)   if the special provision relating to land and buildings applies (the building is new commercial or already opted), to that extent there is a standard-rated supply.

Legislation: SI 1995/1268, art. 5

Chapter 20:   Anti-avoidance: overview

29-000   Introduction

There are a number of areas of anti-avoidance legislation aimed directly at partnerships:

(1)   Disposals through partnerships of:

    (i)   income streams (ITA 2007, Pt. 13, Ch. 5AA and CTA 2010, Pt. 16, Ch. 1A); and

    (ii)   assets (ITA 2007, Pt. 13, Ch. 5D and CTA 2010, Pt. 16, Ch. 4);

(2)   Disguised investment management fees and carried interest:

    (i)   disguised investment management fees (ITA 2007, Pt. 13, Ch. 5E);

    (ii)   carried interest: computation of chargeable gains (TCGA 1992, Pt. III, Ch. V);

    (iii)   income-based carried interest (ITA 2007, Pt. 13, Ch. 5F); and

(3)   Limited liability partnerships: salaried members (ITTOIA 2005, s. 863–863G; CTA 2010, s. 1273, 1273A).

Disposals through partnerships

These rules are directed at avoidance where assets or income streams are effectively disposed of tax free by the use of partnerships. There are rules applying to disposals of income streams and to disposals of assets, see ¶30-000ff.

Disguised investment management fees and carried interest

These rules were introduced to ensure that sums which arise to investment fund managers for their services would be charged to income tax, to stop investment fund managers from using tax loopholes to avoid paying the correct amount of capital gains tax (CGT) on the profits of the fund payable to them, known as 'carried interest', and to ensure that a carried interest structure will only attract CGT treatment in relation to funds which carry on long-term investment activity, see ¶31-000ff.

Salaried members

These rules were introduced to remove the presumption of self-employment for some members of limited liability partnerships (LLPs) to tackle the disguising of employment relationships through LLPs in order to facilitate the avoidance of PAYE obligations, see ¶32-000ff.

Legislation: TCGA 1992, Pt. III, Ch. V; ITTOIA 2005, s. 863–863G; ITA 2007, Pt. 13, Ch. 5A, 5AA, 5D, 5E and 5F; CTA 2009, s. 1273, 1273A; CTA 2010, Pt. 16, Ch. 1A and 4

Chapter 21: Disposals through partnerships

30-000　Background

In 2009, legislation was introduced to counter attempts to convert income into capital by selling the rights to future income (termed 'relevant receipts') derived from an asset without disposing of the asset itself. The provisions (ITA 2007, Pt. 13, Ch. 5A and CTA 2010, Pt. 16, Ch. 1) impose a charge to income tax (or corporation tax) on the transferor of the right.

However, schemes to circumvent these provisions evolved using partnerships and exploiting an exemption whereby a disposal of a share of partnership profits was to be regarded as the transfer of an asset rather than a right to relevant receipts (ITA 2007, s. 809AZF, prior to amendment by FA 2014).

In a simple case, an individual member of a partnership would sell a share of his future partnership profits for a specified period to a corporate member for a lump sum. As this was not treated as the disposal of relevant receipts, the individual was only liable to capital gains tax, and probably benefitted from entrepreneurs' relief. As a result of the transfer, the corporate partner would receive an increased profit share liable only to corporation tax, which would provide it with a return on its investment. At the end of the specified period, the individual's profit share would be restored. The overall effect would have been the conversion of a number of years of income into a capital sum taxed at only 10%.

FA 2014 removed the exemption for partnership interests in respect of transfers on or after 6 April 2014 and introduced further provisions applicable where the substance of the transaction is the disposal of relevant receipts (see ¶30-020ff.) or the disposal of an asset (see ¶30-080ff.), in both cases involving the use of partnership interests.

Legislation: ITA 2007, s. 809AAZA–809AAZB, s. 809DZA–809DZB; CTA 2010, s. 757A and 757B, s. 779A and 779B;

30-020　Disposals of income streams: overview

The rules are in ITA 2007, s. 809AAZA and 809AAZB for income tax payers and apply to arrangements made on or after 6 April 2014. For corporation tax payers, the rules are in CTA 2010, s. 757A and 757B, and apply where arrangements are made on or after 1 April 2014. The two sets of rules are essentially identical and are similar to the existing rules for the disposals of income streams by individuals.

The income tax rules apply if:

- there are arrangements involving a person who is within the charge to income tax (the transferor) and another person (the transferee);
- there is a disposal of a right to relevant receipts by the transferor to the transferee;
- that transfer is wholly or partly by or through a partnership;
- at any time the transferor is a member of the relevant partnership or of a partnership associated with it, and the transferee is a member of the relevant partnership or of a partnership associated with it (although they do not have to be members of those partnerships at the same time).

There must also be a main purpose behind at least one of the steps effecting the disposal that is the obtaining of a tax advantage for any person. These provisions do not apply, however, if the transferor is the spouse, civil partner, brother, sister, ancestor or lineal descendant of the transferee. However, the spouse/civil partner exemption only applies if they are living together.

A partnership is associated with another partnership if it is a member of that partnership or a member of a partnership associated with that partnership and references to transferor and transferee include persons connected to either of these.

If the disposal of relevant receipts by the transferor satisfies all these conditions, then the relevant amount is treated as income of the transferor and is charged to income tax in the same way as the relevant receipts would have been chargeable to income tax or brought into account as income, but for the disposal.

As noted, the corporation tax rules are more or less identical, applying to persons within the charge to corporation tax on income, and so on (see ¶30-060).

Legislation: ITA 2007, s. 809AAZA and 809AAZB; CTA 2010, s. 757A and 757B

30-040   Disposals of income streams: income tax provisions

As mentioned in ¶30-040, a transfer of a 'right to relevant receipts' will give rise to an income tax charge on the transferor where this occurs on or after 6 April 2014.

For the charge to apply the following conditions must be satisfied:

- arrangements exist involving a person within the charge to income tax (termed the 'transferor') and another person (the 'transferee'; who may, or may not, be liable to income tax);
- directly or indirectly as a consequence of, or in connection with, those arrangements, there is disposal (either actual or in substance) of a 'right to relevant receipts' by the transferor to the transferee (including anything which would constitute a disposal for capital gains purposes);

- that disposal is effected in whole or in part through a 'relevant partnership'. In particular, a disposal can be effected by changes in an interest in the relevant partnership, including a share of profits or assets;
- at any time the transferor and the transferee have been members of the relevant partnership or of a partnership associated with that relevant partnership, though not necessarily concurrently (for these purposes the terms 'transferor' and 'transferee' include a person connected to those persons; ITA 2007, s. 809AAZA(7)); and
- the main purpose (or one of the main purposes) of any of the steps taken in effecting the disposal is to obtain a tax advantage for any person (not, therefore, necessarily the transferor nor the transferee).

(ITA 2007, s. 809AAZA(1), (3)–(5).)

Relevant partnership

A relevant partnership is the partnership through which the disposal is effected and, for these purposes, a partnership includes a limited liability partnership regardless of whether it has tax transparency (see ¶10-480). A partnership is associated with a relevant partnership if it is itself a member of that relevant partnership or is a member of a partnership that is itself associated with the relevant partnership (ITA 2007, s. 809AAZA(6), (8)).

Relevant receipts

This terms covers any income which, apart from the disposal, would be either:

- charged to income tax on the transferor (either directly or as a member of a partnership); or
- brought into account in calculating profits of the transferor (again, either directly or as a member of a partnership.

(ITA 2007, s. 809AAZA(8).)

Arrangements

As always with anti-avoidance legislation, arrangements are widely defined to include agreements, understandings, schemes and transactions regardless of whether they are legally enforceable (ITA 2007, s. 809AAZA(8)).

Tax advantage

This has the same meaning as for corporation tax purposes, being the securing of:

- relief, or increased relief, from tax;
- repayment, or increased repayment, of tax; and
- the avoidance or reduction of a charge to tax, an assessment to tax or a potential assessment to tax.

(CTA 2010, s. 1139, applied by ITA 2007, s. 809AAAZA(8).)

Consequences

Where the conditions mentioned above are satisfied, the transferor is to be charged to tax on the 'relevant amount' in the same way that he would have been had the disposal not occurred. In other words, he will be charged to income tax on deemed income equal to the relevant amount or a deemed receipt will enter into the computation of his profits. The intention being to put him back in the position which would have existed if the disposal had not occurred (ITA 2007, s. 809AAZB(1)).

The 'relevant amount' is either the amount of the consideration for the disposal of the right to relevant receipts or, where that consideration is substantially less than the market value of the right at the date of disposal, that market value (ITA 2007, s. 809AZB(2), applied by ITA 2007, s. 809AAZB(2)).

The charge to tax will normally arise in the transferor's chargeable period in which the disposal takes place. However, where any part of the relevant receipts would have entered into the computation of trading income or property income and, in accordance with generally accepted accounting practice ('GAAP'), would not have been wholly recognised in the chargeable period in which the disposal occurred, then:

- to the extent that it does not exceed the consideration for the disposal, it is treated as income for the chargeable periods in which it is recognised under GAAP; and
- otherwise, in the chargeable periods in which it would be so recognised if it were an amount equal to the market value of the right at the date of disposal.

(ITA 2007, s. 809AZB(3)–(5), applied by s. 809AAZB(2).)

However, if the transferor is a company and it becomes reasonable to assume that, under GAAP, any part of the income would not be recognised in any accounting period, that part is to be treated as arising immediately before that assumption (ITA 2007, s. 809AZB(6), applied by s. 809AAZB(2)).

Exemptions

The charge does not apply where the transferor is the spouse or civil partner of the transferee (and they are living together), or a sibling, ancestor or lineal descendant of the transferee (ITA 2007, s. 809AAZA(2)).

Furthermore, this charge will not apply if a charge would also arise under the provisions relating to disposals of assets through partnerships (see ¶30-100) and those provisions would result in a greater charge (ITA 2007, s. 809AAZB(4)).

Legislation: ITA 2007, s. 809AAZA and 809AAZB

30-060 Disposals of income streams: corporation tax provisions

The provisions apply where a company (the 'transferor') disposes of a right to *relevant receipts* to another person (the 'transferee') by or through a partnership (the relevant partnership) and the company and the transferee are members of the relevant partnership, or are members of partnerships associated with the relevant partnership. Where obtaining a tax advantage is a main purpose of any step of the arrangements directly or indirectly involving the disposal, the *relevant amount* is chargeable to corporation tax in the hands of the transferor (CTA 2010, s. 757A(1)).

Commencement

This rule applies for cases where the arrangements are made on or after 1 April 2014 (*Finance Act* 2014, Sch. 17, para. 28(2)).

Scope and limitations

The provisions also affect arrangements where there is a disposal in substance only, and where the disposal is only partly effected by or though a partnership. The transferor and transferee need not be members of the partnership (or associated partnerships) at the same time (CTA 2010, s. 757A(4)).

These rules apply in priority to the *disposals of assets through partnerships* rules (CTA 2010, Pt. 16, Ch. 4) where the result is that a greater amount would be charged to corporation tax in which case the Chapter 4 rules do not apply (CTA 2010, s. 797B(3)).

Disposal

Disposal includes anything constituting a disposal of such a right for the purposes of TCGA 1992 (CTA 2010, s. 757A(2)) and might in particular be effected by an acquisition or disposal of, or an increase or decrease in, an interest in the relevant partnership (CTA 2010, s. 757A(3)).

Definitions

- *Associated partnership* – an associated partnership is a partnership which is a member of the relevant partnership or is a member of a partnership which is associated with the relevant partnership (CTA 2010, s. 757A(5)).
- *Arrangements* includes any agreement, understanding, scheme, transaction or series of transactions whether or not legally enforceable (CTA 2010, s. 757A(7)).
- *Partnership* includes a limited liability partnership whether or not CTA 2009, s. 1273(1) (trade or business carried on by limited liability partnership, etc.) applies to it (CTA 2010, s. 757A(7)).
- The *relevant amount* is such amount that ensures that the transferor is chargeable to corporation tax in the same way and to the same extent as if the relevant receipts had been chargeable to corporation tax as income of the transferor or

had been brought into account as income in calculating profits of the transferor for corporation tax purposes. For the purposes of determining when income arises the relevant amount is to be read in accordance with CTA 2010, s. 753 (CTA 2010, s. 757B(1)).

- *Relevant receipts* means any income which (but for the disposal) would be charged to corporation tax as income of the transferor (whether directly or as a member of a partnership), or which (but for the disposal) would be brought into account as income in calculating profits of the transferor (whether directly or as a member of a partnership) for corporation tax purposes (CTA 2010, s. 757A(7)).
- *Tax advantage* means a tax advantage as defined in CTA 2010, s. 1139 in relation to income tax or the charge to corporation tax on income (CTA 2010, s. 757A(7)).

Example

The following example was published by HMRC on 27 March 2014 in a Revised Technical Note and Guidance:

Example 42 (Transfer of income streams)

C Ltd contributes an income producing asset to a partnership. C Ltd would otherwise be chargeable to corporation tax on that income. A new partner, D Ltd, joins the partnership and contributes capital equal to the present value of the income stream. The partnership's profit-sharing arrangement provides that the profits arising from the income stream will be allocated to D Ltd until such time that the value of its contribution has been repaid, along with a lending return. The arrangement allows C Ltd the right to the capital of the partnership, including D Ltd's contribution and the ownership of the underlying asset.

In effect, there has been a sale of an income stream for an upfront lump sum, i.e. D Ltd's capital contribution. Assuming that a main purpose of this arrangement was to obtain a tax advantage, C Ltd will be charged to tax as income on the lump sum payment.

Legislation: CTA 2010, s. 757A, 757B

30-080 Disposals of assets: overview

The rules are in ITA 2007, s. 809DZA and 809DZB for income tax payers and apply to arrangements made on or after 6 April 2014. For corporation tax payers the rules are in CTA 2010, s. 779A and 779B and apply where arrangements are made on or after 1 April 2014. The two sets of rules are essentially identical.

The income tax rules apply if Conditions A and B are met. Condition A is that in consequence of or in connection with arrangements involving a person within the charge to income tax (the transferor) and another person (the transferee) there is, in substance, a disposal of an asset by the transferor to the transferee, by or through a partnership. Again, the transferee and the transferor must both be members of a relevant partnership or a partnership associated with it, although not necessarily at the same time. Again, there has to be a main purpose of obtaining a tax advantage and there is the same exception for spouses, civil partners and other relatives.

Condition B is that it is reasonable to assume that, had the transferor disposed of the asset directly to the transferee, the relevant amount would have been chargeable to income tax as income of the transferor or brought into account in calculating their profits for income tax purposes.

If these conditions are satisfied, then, once again, the relevant amount is treated as income of the transferor, chargeable to income tax or brought into account as income in calculating their profits as they would have been had the disposal not occurred.

As noted, the corporation tax rules are more or less identical, applying to persons within the charge to corporation tax on income, and so on (see ¶30-120).

30-100   Disposals of assets: income tax provisions

Also as mentioned in ¶30-000, a transfer of an income-producing asset will give rise to an income tax charge where this occurs on or after 6 April 2014. This charge is almost identical in its conditions to that described in ¶30-040.

The charge will arise where the following conditions are met:

Condition A:

- arrangements exist involving a person within the charge to income tax (termed the 'transferor') and another person (the 'transferee'; who may or may not be liable to income tax);
- directly or indirectly as a consequence of, or in connection with, those arrangements, there is disposal of an asset, including anything which would constitute a disposal for capital gains purposes (contrast this with ¶30-040, where the disposal had to be of 'a right to relevant receipts');
- that disposal is effected in whole or in part through a 'relevant partnership'. In particular, a disposal can be effected by changes in an interest in the relevant partnership, including a share of profits or assets;
- at any time the transferor and the transferee have been members of the relevant partnership or of a partnership associated with that relevant partnership, though not necessarily at the same time (for these purposes the terms 'transferor' and 'transferee' include a person connected to those persons; ITA 2007, s. 809DZA(8)); and
- the main purpose (or one of the main purposes) of any of the steps taken in effecting the disposal is to obtain a tax advantage for any person (not, therefore, necessarily the transferor or the transferee).

(ITA 2007, s. 809DZA(1)–(2), (4)–(6).)

Condition B:

It is reasonable to assume that, had the disposal been directly between the transferor and transferee, the amount of the consideration for that disposal would either have been charged to income tax on the transferor or brought into account in calculating his profits for income tax purposes. Where the consideration received is less that the market value of the asset at the date of disposal, the consideration is assumed to be equal to that market value (ITA 2007, s. 809DZA(9)–(12)).

Consequences

Where the conditions mentioned above are satisfied, the transferor is to be charged to tax on the 'relevant amount' in the same way that he would have been had the disposal taken place directly with the transferee. In other words, he will be charged to income tax on deemed income equal to the relevant amount or a deemed receipt will enter into the computation of his profits to put him back in the position which would have existed if the disposal had occured directly (ITA 2007, s. 809DZB(1)).

The charge to tax will normally arise in the transferor's chargeable period in which the disposal takes place. However, where any part of the relevant amount would have entered into the computation of trading income or property income and, in accordance with generally accepted accounting practice ('GAAP'), would not have been wholly recognised in the chargeable period in which the disposal occurred, then:

- to the extent that it does not exceed the consideration for the disposal, it is treated as income for the chargeable periods in which it is recognised under GAAP; and
- otherwise, in the chargeable periods in which it would be so recognised if it were an amount equal to the market value of the right at the date of disposal.

(ITA 2007, s. 809AZB(3)–(5), applied by s. 809DZB(2).).

However, if the transferor is a company and it becomes reasonable to assume that, under GAAP, any part of the income would not be recognised in an accounting period, that part is to be treated as arising immediately before that assumption (ITA 2007, s. 809AZB(6), applied by s. 809DZB(2)).

Exemptions

The charge does not apply where the transferor is the spouse or civil partner of the transferee (and they are living together), or a sibling, ancestor or lineal descendant of the transferee (ITA 2007, s. 809DZA(3)).

Furthermore, this charge will not apply if a charge would also arise under the provisions relating to disposals income streams by means of partnerships (see ¶30-040) and those provisions would result in a charge of the same amount or greater (ITA 2007, s. 809DZB(3)).

Legislation: ITA 2007, s. 809DZA, 809DZB

30-120   Disposals of assets: corporation tax provisions

These rules are, in most cases, the mirror image of the *disposal of income streams through partnerships rules* outlined at ¶30-060 except that references to the disposal of income streams are replaced with references to the disposal of an asset with consequential amendments as appropriate.

The provisions apply where a company (the 'transferor') disposes of an asset (the *transferred asset*) to another person (the 'transferee') by or through a partnership (the relevant partnership) and the company and the transferee are members of the relevant partnership, or are members of partnerships associated with the relevant partnership (references to transferor and transferee include connected persons (CTA 20101, s. 779A(7)). Where obtaining a tax advantage is a main purpose of any step of the arrangements directly or indirectly involving the disposal, and it is reasonable to assume that had the transferred asset been disposed of directly by the transferor to the transferee it would have been chargeable to income tax as income of the transferor (or would have been brought into account as income in calculating profits of the transferor for corporation tax purposes CTA 2010, s. 779A(8)), the *relevant amount* is chargeable to corporation tax in the hands of the transferor (CTA 2010, s. 779A(2) and (8)).

Commencement

This rule applies for cases where the arrangements are made on or after 1 April 2014 (FA 2014, Sch. 17, para. 29(2)).

Scope and limitations

The provisions also affect arrangements where there is a disposal in substance only (CTA 2010, s. 779A(2)(a)), and where the disposal is only partly effected by or though a partnership (CTA 2010, s. 779A(2)(b)). The transferor and transferee (or their connected persons) need not be members of the partnership (or associated partnerships) at the same time (CTA 2010, s. 779A(5)).

These rules apply in priority to the *disposals of income streams through partnerships* rules (CTA 2010, Pt. 16, Ch. 1A) where the result is that a greater amount would be charged to corporation tax in which case the Chapter 1A rules do not apply (CTA 2010, s. 757B(4)).

Disposal

Disposal of an asset includes anything constituting a disposal of an asset for the purposes of TCGA 1992 (CTA 2010, s. 779A(3)) and might in particular be effected by an acquisition or disposal of, or an increase or decrease in, an interest in the relevant partnership (CTA 2010, s. 779A(4)).

Definitions

- *Associated partnership* – an associated partnership is a partnership which is a member of the relevant partnership or is a member of a partnership which is associated with the relevant partnership (CTA 2010, s. 779A(6)).
- *Arrangements* includes any agreement, understanding, scheme, transaction or series of transactions whether or not legally enforceable (CTA 2010, s. 779A(12)).
- *Partnership* includes a limited liability partnership whether or not CTA 2009, s. 1273(1) (trade or business carried on by limited liability partnership, etc.) applies to it (CTA 2010, s. 779A(12)).
- The *relevant amount* is the amount of the consideration received by the transferor for the disposal (CTA 2010, s. 779A(9)) and a market value consideration (at the time of the disposal) is to be assumed where no consideration is received or where the consideration is substantially less than the market value of the transferred asset (CTA 2010, s. 779A(10)). The relevant amount is to be treated as income of the transferor chargeable to corporation tax in the same way and to the same extent that it would have been chargeable to corporation tax as income of the transferor CTA 2010, s. 779B(1).
- *Tax advantage* means a tax advantage as defined in CTA 2010, s. 1139 in relation to income tax or the charge to corporation tax on income (CTA 2010, s. 779A(12)).

Example

The following example was published by HMRC on 27 March 2014 in a Revised Technical Note and Guidance:

Example 43 (Transfer of assets)

A company, J Ltd, contributes an asset with an unrealised gain (of a type which if realised would give rise to a charge to tax on income), such as an intangible fixed asset, to a partnership on a tax neutral basis. A new partner, K Ltd, joins the partnership, making a capital contribution equal to the value of the asset.

The partnership sharing arrangements are manipulated so that K Ltd had nearly all rights to capital or income until the asset is disposed of, whilst J Ltd has the right to all other partnership assets.

The substance of the arrangements is that there has been a 'disguised disposal' of the asset for the amount contributed by K Ltd in order to avoid the tax charge that would have otherwise arisen. The amount of K's contribution will be treated as income of J Ltd.

Legislation: CTA 2010, s. 779A, 779B

Chapter 22: Disguised investment management fees and carried interest

31-000 Background

Disguised investment management fees

At Autumn Statement 2014, the Government announced that legislation would be introduced from 6 April 2015 to ensure that sums which arise to investment fund managers for their services would be charged to income tax. Accordingly, ITA 2007, Pt. 13, Ch. 5E was introduced by FA 2015, s. 21 and applies to sums which arise to managers who have entered into arrangements involving partnerships or other transparent vehicles, but not to sums linked to performance, often described as 'carried interest', or returns which are exclusively from investments by partners.

Finance (No. 2) Act 2015 expanded the 'disguised investment management fees' provisions in ITA 2007, Pt. 13, Ch. 5E to clarify the meaning of 'reasonably comparable' in ITA 2007, s. 809EZB(2)(b) (see ¶31-060), with effect in relation to sums arising on or after 8 July 2015 and to insert new s. 809EZDA and 809EZDB which are designed to establish a comprehensive definition of when sums arise for income tax purposes under ITA 2007, Pt. 13, Ch. 5E where the sum is received 'indirectly' by a person or company connected with the individual or an unconnected person, and which apply in relation to sums arising on or after 22 October 2015.

Finance Act 2016 extends the provisions further (see ¶31-040), with effect in relation to sums arising on or after 6 April 2016, to:

(1) make it clear that the DMF rules apply to an individual who has performed or will, in the future, perform investment management services (i.e. there is no requirement that the individual performs investment management services in the year in which the sums arise);
(2) remove the requirement that the arrangements involve a partnership (e.g. to be present in the investment scheme or management structure); and
(3) make clear that the rules apply to sums arising to an investment manager from any investment scheme.

Carried interest

At Summer Budget 2015, the Government further announced that it intended to stop investment fund managers from using tax loopholes to avoid paying the correct amount of capital gains tax (CGT) on the profits of the fund payable to them (known as 'carried interest'). TCGA 1992, Pt. III, Ch. 5 was consequently introduced by

F(No. 2)A 2015, s. 43, with immediate effect (in relation to carried interest arising on or after 8 July 2015 under any arrangements, unless the carried interest arises in connection with the disposal of an asset or assets of a partnership or partnerships before that date). TCGA 1992, Pt. III, Ch. 5 changes the way that investment fund managers who receive carried interest compute their chargeable gains. When carried interest arises on or after 8 July 2015, the gain will normally be equal to the sum received and deductions will be allowed only for actual acquisition costs paid in the form of money (and not as money's worth) and for amounts previously taxed as earnings or as income.

For commentary on the charge to capital gains tax on carried interest, see ¶31-120ff.

Income-based carried interest (performance-based rewards)

Alongside the changes announced at Summer Budget 2015, the Government launched a consultation on the circumstances in which fund managers' performance-related returns could benefit from capital gains tax treatment as the rules for management fees introduced by *Finance Act* 2015 did not determine the tax treatment for the performance element of a fund manager's reward. This could be subject to income tax or capital gains tax depending on how the reward was structured and the Government stated that it believed that investment managers should not be able to automatically access capital gains tax treatment on the performance linked reward but that capital gains tax treatment should depend upon the their fund's activities clearly being of an investing nature.

Accordingly, following consultation, legislation was introduced by *Finance Act* 2016 to ensure that a carried interest structure will only attract CGT treatment in relation to funds which carry on long-term investment activity.

Finance Act 2016 inserts new ITA 2007, Pt. 13, Ch. 5F (see ¶31-320ff.) to replace the existing case law test based around the 'badges of trade', which mainly considered trades connected with areas such as manufacturing and retail and was, therefore, more difficult to apply to a business such as asset management.

Finance Act 2016 introduces an objective, legislative test to determine whether carried interest should be taxed as capital gains or income which depends upon the average period for which the fund holds assets. All returns which are not subject to capital gains tax will be chargeable to income tax and Class 4 National Insurance contributions as trading profits. The provisions apply to sums of carried interest arising on or after 6 April 2016.

Legislation: TCGA 1992, Pt. III, Ch. 5; ITA 2007, Pt. 13, Ch. 5E and 5F

DISGUISED INVESTMENT MANAGEMENT FEES (DMF)

31-020   Introduction

ITA 2007, Pt. 13, Ch. 5E was introduced by *Finance Act* 2015 to put beyond doubt that the 'management fee' remuneration received by investment fund managers is always subject to income tax because it is a fee calculated on the value of the assets under management and bears no risk related to the performance of the fund.

The measures were brought in specifically to counter structures that were increasingly used by private equity firms in which annual fees were paid as priority partnership shares so as to avoid an income tax charge on the fees. However, the provisions are extended by *Finance Act* 2016 which removes the requirement that the arrangements involve a partnership, with effect in relation to sums arising on or after 6 April 2016.

The income tax charge applies from 6 April 2015, in respect of disguised fees arising on or after that date, whenever the arrangements were entered into and applies to certain fees or other sums paid to investment managers and to sums paid through structures involving partnerships, unless they are already charged to income tax as employment income or brought into account in calculating profits.

'Carried interest', which is a form of performance linked reward, contingent upon the assets in the fund making a specified level of return over the life of the fund is specifically excluded from the charge. Sums allocated to an individual in satisfaction of carried interest are treated, for tax purposes, as though the individual had carried out the transactions which gave rise to the sums. Where the fund partnership is investing rather than trading for tax purposes, those sums will be treated as capital gains or income by reference to a new legislative based test from 6 April 2016, which replaces the former test based on case law (see ¶31-320ff.).

For the charge to capital gains tax on 'carried interest', see ¶31-120ff.

HMRC's guidance note '*Investment Managers: Disguised Fee Income*', issued on 29 March 2015, is available at *www.gov.uk/government/uploads/system/uploads/attachment_data/file/417049/Disguised_Investment_Management_Fees_Guidance.pdf* and provides background to the introduction of the rules and commentary on the operation of the rules per the draft legislation as was proposed at that date.

Legislation: ITA 2007, Pt. 13, Ch. 5E

Other material: HMRC's guidance at *www.gov.uk/government/uploads/system/uploads/attachment_data/file/417049/Disguised_Investment_Management_Fees_Guidance.pdf*

31-040   Charge to income tax

When a disguised fee arises to an individual from an investment scheme, the individual is liable to income tax in respect of the disguised fees as if the individual were carrying on a trade and the disguised fees were the profits from the trade (ITA 2007, s. 809EZA(1)).

Where the trade is treated as being carried on depends upon where the 'relevant services' (the investment management services giving rise to the fees) are carried on. If any of the services are performed in the UK, then the trade is treated as carried on in the UK to the extent that the services are carried on in the UK. Where services are performed outside the UK, then the trade is treated as carried on outside the UK to the extent that the services are performed by the individual outside the UK (ITA 2007, s. 809EZA(2)).

Where an individual performs investment management services before coming to the UK, the profits from any 'pre-arrival services' are similarly treated as profits of a trade carried on by the individual but where the pre-arrival services were performed outside the UK, the profits arising from those services are treated as profits from a separate and distinct trade from the trade relating to 'pre-arrival services' that were performed by the individual in the UK (ITA 2007, s. 809EZA(2A)–(2C)) (as inserted by FA 2016, s. 38, with effect in relation to sums of carried interest arising on or after 6 April 2016). The significance of this distinction is that if the manager is domiciled outside the UK, he or she will be fully chargeable to income tax on pre-arrival profits relating to services performed in the UK (the first trade), but will be potentially able to access the remittance basis in relation to pre-arrival profits in relation to services performed overseas (and of the second trade).

A disguised fee arises to an individual in a tax year from an investment scheme where:

(i)   an individual at any time performs or is to perform investment management services directly or indirectly under any arrangements;

(ii) a 'management fee' 'arises' to the individual from an investment scheme in the tax year; and

(iii) the management fee is untaxed to any extent.

(ITA 2007, s. 809EZA(3), as amended by FA 2016, s. 36(2)).

For the meaning of 'arise' in respect of sums not received directly by the individual, see ¶31-100.

The amendments by *Finance Act* 2016, which take effect in relation to all sums of carried interest arising on or after 6 April 2016):

(1)   make it clear that the DMF rules apply to an individual who has performed or will, in the future, perform investment management services (i.e. there is no requirement that the individual performs investment management services in the year in which the sums arise);

(2) remove the requirement that the arrangements involve a partnership (e.g. to be present in the investment scheme or management structure); and

(3) make clear that the rules apply to sums arising to an investment manager from any investment scheme.

The amount of the disguised fee is the amount of the fee that is 'untaxed'. That is neither charged to tax under ITEPA 2003 as employment income nor brought into account in calculating the taxable profits of a trade (including profession or vocation) of the individual for income tax purposes (ITA 2007, s. 809EZA(4)).

Anti-avoidance

Arrangements the main purpose, or one of the main purposes, of which is to secure that s. 809EZA does not apply in relation to the individual either alone or together with one or more other individuals, are disregarded (ITA 2007, s. 809EZF).

Avoidance of double taxation

When income tax is charged on an individual in respect of a disguised fee under s. 809EZA and at any time income tax or another tax is charged on the individual or another person under another section in respect of that disguised fee, or when a charge has arisen under s. 809EZA in respect of a loan and tax arises under another section on an amount which must be used to repay that loan, in order to avoid a double charge to tax, the individual may claim a consequential adjustment be made in respect of the other tax charge arising (ITA 2007, s. 809EZG(1)–(3)).

The amount of the consequential adjustment is limited to the lesser of the income tax charged under s. 809EZA and the other tax charged or the charge in respect of the amount of the loan repaid. The adjustment is to be made by HMRC (on a claim being made) and may be made in respect of any period, by way of an assessment, modification of an assessment, by amending a claim, or otherwise. The adjustment may also be made despite any time limit imposed by or under any enactment (ITA 2007, s. 809EZG(4)–(6)).

Legislation: ITA 2007, s. 809EZA, 809EZF, 809EZG

31-060   Meaning of management fee

The conditions for a sum to be a management fee are that it arises from an investment scheme and is not:

(a) the repayment of capital invested by the individual;

(b) an arm's length return on that capital; or

(c) carried interest which is not 'income-based carried interest' (with the meaning of 'carried interest' provided by ITA 2007, s. 809EZC and the meaning of 'income-based carried interest' provided by ITA 2007, Pt. 13, Ch. 5F)

(ITA 2007, s. 809EZB(1).)

Finance Act 2016 amended s. 809EZB(1)(c) so that the exclusion from the 'disguised management fee' rules for carried interest does not apply where the carried interest is 'income-based carried interest', as defined by new ITA 2007, Pt. 13, Ch. 5F (as inserted by FA 2016, s. 37(2)). The intended effect is to ensure that carried interest which does not arise from long-term investment activity will be charged to income tax under the DMF rules (where it is not already charged to tax as trading or employment income of the relevant individual).

Arm's length return

An 'arm's length return' is a return:

(a)   on an investment of the same kind as investments made by external investors;
(b)   that is reasonably comparable to the return received by external investors on comparable investments; and
(c)   on such terms as are reasonably comparable to the terms governing returns to external investors.

(ITA 2007, s. 809EZB(2).)

Reasonably comparable

The phrase 'reasonably comparable' in s. 809EZB(2)(b) is explained by s. 809EZB(2A) (as inserted by F(No. 2)A 2015, s. 44, with effect in relation to sums arising on or after 8 July 2015).

Section 809EZB(2A) provides that the return on the investment is reasonably comparable to the return to external investors on the investments referred to in s. 809EZB(2)(a) if (and only if):

(1)   the rate of return on the investment is reasonably comparable to the rate of return to external investors on those investments; and
(2)   any other factors relevant to determining the size of the return on the investment are reasonably comparable to the factors determining the size of the return to external investors on those investments.

Legislation: ITA 2007, s. 809EZB

31-080   Carried interest

Carried interest is defined as a sum arising to an individual by way of a 'profit-related return' (ITA 2007, s. 809EZC(1)).

A sum arises by way of a 'profit-related return' if:

(1)   it is dependent upon profits arising from the investments or a disposal of the investments;
(2)   it is variable by reference to the profits on the investments; and

(3) the profits are the same as those on which returns to external investors are determined.

Where any part of the sum does not meet these conditions, it is not a profit-related return (ITA 2007, s. 809EZC(2)).

Where sums arise to an individual as a profit-related return but there was no significant risk that at least a certain amount would not arise (termed the 'minimum return'), that minimum amount is not carried interest (ITA 2007, s. 809EZC(3)).

The minimum amount is calculated by taking into account the actual sum which arises, and any other sums which might have arisen under the arrangements as profit-related returns, looking at both individual sums and also at all sums arising in the tax year as a whole (ITA 2007, s. 809EZC(4)). Where there is more than one actual sum arising (by way of a profit-related return), the minimum amounts (i.e. the amounts to be treated as not being carried interest) are to be apportioned (ITA 2007, s. 809EZC(7), (8)).

The 'risk' of an amount not arising is to be assessed at the latest of:

(1) the time when the individual became party to the arrangements;
(2) the time when the individual starts to perform investment management services in respect of the arrangements; or
(3) the date of any material change to the arrangements.

The material changes to be taken into account are those which relate to the sums which may arise to the individual by way of profit-related return.

(ITA 2007, s. 809EZC(5).)

Any risk that a sum will be prevented from arising to an individual, e.g. by insolvency or otherwise, must be ignored (ITA 2007, s. 809EZC(6)).

Additionally, certain sums are treated as carried interest. These are sums paid to an individual from scheme investment profits or a particular scheme investment, after all, or substantially all, of the investments or relevant investments have been repaid, and any preferred return (defined as a return equivalent to at least compound interest calculated at the rate of 6% per annum on the sum invested) has been paid to external participants in the scheme (ITA 2007, s. 809EZD).

Legislation: ITA 2007, s. 809EZC

31-100   Carried interest and disguised investment management fees: 'arise'

ITA 2007, s. 809EZDA and 809EZDB were inserted by F(No. 2)A 2015, s. 45.

One of the conditions for a management fee to be charged under ITA 2007, Pt. 13, Ch. 5E is that the sum 'arises to the individual from the scheme in the tax year'

(s. 809EZA(3)(c)). In its original form, as inserted by FA 2015, the wording of s. 809EZA(3)(c) read 'arises to the individual **directly or indirectly** from the scheme in the tax year' but there was no further guidance in relation to situations where the sums arose indirectly. Sections 809EZDA and 809EZDB were, therefore, designed to establish a comprehensive definition of when sums arise for the purposes of ITA 2007, Pt. 13, Ch. 5E where the sum is received by a person or company other than the individual and, accordingly, the words 'directly or indirectly' became otiose and were omitted from s. 809EZA(3)(c).

Broadly, s. 809EZDA and 809EZDB provide that where the sum is received by a connected person, connected company or unconnected person, it is treated as arising to the individual when it arises to that other person or company, but in the cases of sums received by a connected company or unconnected person, only where certain enjoyment conditions are met.

The new definitions apply in relation to sums other than 'carried interest' arising on or after 22 October 2015 (whenever the arrangements under which the sums arise were made) and in relation to 'carried interest' arising on or after 22 October 2015 under any arrangements, unless the carried interest arises in connection with the disposal of an asset or assets of a partnership or partnerships before that date.

Sums arising to connected persons other than companies

Where a sum in relation to an individual arises to a person who is connected with the individual and neither income tax nor capital gains tax (under TCGA 1992, Pt. 3, Ch. 5 (see ¶31-120ff.)) is charged in respect of the sum, it is treated as arising to the individual at the time it arises to the connected person, to the extent that it would not otherwise 'arise' to the individual (ITA 2007, s. 809EZDA(1)–(3)).

Sums arising to connected company or unconnected person

Where a sum arises to a company connected with the individual or any person not connected with the individual *and* any of the enjoyment conditions is met, the sum (or part thereof) is treated as arising to the individual at the time it arises to the connected company or unconnected person, to the extent that it would not otherwise 'arise' to the individual (whether the enjoyment conditions are met at that time or at a later date) (ITA 2007, s. 809EZDB(1), (3), (4)).

Amount treated as arising

The amount treated as arising to the individual is either:

(a) the sum arising to the connected company or unconnected person; or
(b) the part of the sum to which the enjoyment condition in (a), (c), (d) or (e) below relates; or
(c) the part of the sum as is equal to the amount by which the value of the assets referred to in (b) below is increased.

(ITA 2007, s. 809EZDB(3).)

The enjoyment conditions

The enjoyment conditions are:

(a) the sum, or part thereof, is so dealt with by any person as to be calculated at some time to enure for the benefit of the individual or a person connected with the individual;

(b) the arising of the sum increases the value to the individual or any person connected with the individual of any assets which the individual (or connected person) holds or are held for the benefit of the individual (or connected person);

(c) the individual or a person connected with the individual receives or is entitled to receive at any time any benefit provided or to be provided out of the sum or part thereof;

(d) the individual or a person connected with the individual may become entitled to the beneficial enjoyment of the sum or part thereof if one or more powers are exercised or successively exercise (irrespective of who may exercise the powers or whether they are exercisable with or without the consent of another person);

(e) the individual or a person connected with the individual is able in any manner to control directly or indirectly the application of the sum or part thereof.

(ITA 2007, s. 809EZDB(2).)

In determining whether any of the enjoyment conditions is met in relation to a sum or part of a sum:

(a) regard must be had to the substantial result and effect of all the relevant circumstances; and

(b) all benefits which may at any time accrue to a person as a result of the sum arising must be taken into account, irrespective of:

    (i) the nature or form of the benefits; or

    (ii) whether the person has legal or equitable rights in respect of the benefits.

(ITA 2007, s. 809EZDB(5).)

If the only reason the enjoyment condition in (b), (c) or (d) above are met is by reason of the individual holding shares or an interest in shares in a company, the enjoyment condition is treated as not met (ITA 2007, s. 809EZDB(6)).

The enjoyment condition in (a) or (e) is also treated as not met if the sum arises to a company connected with the individual and the sum is included in the profits of the company that are charged to corporation tax unless:

(i) the company is a CFC and the exemption in TIOPA 2010, Pt. 9A, Ch. 14 applies for the accounting period in which the sum arises; or

(ii) the company is not a CFC but the exemption would apply if it were.

(ITA 2007, s. 809EZDB(7).)

Anti-avoidance

The enjoyment conditions will be treated as applying where the sum arises to a connected company or unconnected individual as part of arrangements, in respect of which it is reasonable to assume that the main purpose (or one of the main purposes) of the arrangements is the avoidance of liability to income tax, capital gains tax, inheritance tax or corporation tax, and without which arrangements it is reasonable to assume the sum would have arisen to the individual (or a connected individual) (ITA 2007, s. 809EZDB(8)).

Where the sum is applied directly or indirectly as an investment in a collective investment scheme, it is regarded as arising under arrangements the main purpose, or one of the main purposes of which, is the avoidance of income tax, capital gains tax, inheritance tax or corporation tax (ITA 2007, s. 809EZDB(9)).

Modified meaning of 'connected'

For the purposes of ITA 2007, s. 809EZDA and 809EZDB, the meaning of connected is as provided by ITA 2007, s. 993 but subject to two modifications:

(1)   connections an individual has as a partner in a partnership with other partners (and their spouse/civil partner) are ignored; and
(2)   partners in a partnership in which the individual is also a partner are not treated as 'associates' of the individual for the purposes of determining whether the individual has control over a company.

(ITA 2007, s. 809EZDA(4), 809EZDB(10).)

The definition of connected persons is therefore limited to:

- certain relatives including:
    - the individual's spouse or civil partner;
    - a relative of the individual;
    - the spouse or civil partner of a relative of the individual;
    - a relative of the individual's spouse or civil partner;
    - the spouse or civil partner of a relative of the individual's spouse or civil partner;
- certain trustees; and
- certain companies.

'Relative' means a brother, sister, ancestor or lineal descendant but excludes nephews, nieces, uncles and aunts.

A company is connected with another person if that person has control of it or that person and persons connected with him together have control of it. Any two or more persons acting together to secure or exercise control of a company are to be treated in relation to that company as connected with one another and with any person acting on the directions of any of them to secure or exercise control of the company.

'Control' is determined by CTA 2010, s. 450 and 451 which provide that a person shall be taken to have control of a company if he exercises, or is able to exercise or is entitled to acquire, direct or indirect control over the company's affairs, and in particular if he possesses or is entitled to acquire the greater part of: the company's share capital or voting power, income on a distribution, or assets on a winding up. Where two or more persons together satisfy any of these conditions they shall be taken to have control of the company. A person is treated as entitled to acquire anything which he is entitled to acquire at a future date or will at a future date be entitled to acquire and all rights and powers of any company or companies of which the individual has control (alone or together with his associates) and all rights and powers of any associates (but not associates of associates) are to be attributed to the individual for the purposes of the test.

Legislation: ITA 2007, s. 809EZDA and 809EZDB

CARRIED INTEREST: CHARGE TO CAPITAL GAINS TAX

31-120 Background

Fees or other sums for investment management paid to managers of funds are charged to income tax. From 6 April 2015, service based rewards will always be subject to income tax. For detailed commentary see ¶31-020ff.

Performance-based rewards (known as 'carried interest') are subject to either income tax or capital gains tax. Currently the test to determine which is based on case law, however, from 6 April 2016, a new legislative based test will be introduced, see ¶31-320ff.

At Summer Budget 2015, the Government announced that it intended to stop investment fund managers from using tax loopholes to avoid paying the correct amount of capital gains tax (CGT) on the profits of the fund payable to them (known as 'carried interest'). TCGA 1992, Pt. III, Ch. 5 was accordingly introduced by F(No. 2)A 2015, s. 43, with immediate effect (in relation to carried interest arising on or after 8 July 2015 under any arrangements, unless the carried interest arises in connection with the disposal of an asset or assets of a partnership or partnerships before that date). TCGA 1992, Pt. III, Ch. 5 changes the way that investment fund managers who receive carried interest compute their chargeable gains. When carried interest arises on or after 8 July 2015 the gain will normally be equal to the sum received and deductions will be allowed only for actual acquisition costs paid in the form of money (and not as money's worth) and for amounts previously taxed as earnings.

Performance-based reward

Alongside the changes announced at Summer Budget 2015, the Government launched a consultation on the circumstances in which fund managers' performance-related returns could benefit from capital gains tax treatment as the rules for management fees introduced by *Finance Act* 2015 did not determine the tax treatment for the performance element of a fund manager's reward. This could be subject to income tax or capital gains tax depending on how the reward was structured and the Government stated that it believed that investment managers should not be able to automatically access capital gains tax treatment on the performance linked reward but that capital gains tax treatment should depend upon the their fund's activities clearly being of an investing nature.

Accordingly, following consultation which ran from 8 July 2015 to 30 September 2015, legislation was introduced by *Finance Act* 2016 to ensure that a carried interest structure will only attract capital gains tax treatment in relation to funds which carry on long-term investment activity.

For detailed commentary, see ¶31-320ff.

Legislation: TCGA 1992, Pt. III, Ch. 5

31-140 Overview

Finance (No. 2) Act 2015 introduced TCGA 1992, Pt. III, Ch. 5, with effect in relation to carried interest arising on or after 8 July 2015 under any arrangements, unless the carried interest arises in connection with the disposal of an asset or assets of a partnership or partnerships before that date (see further commencement provisions below).

TCGA 1992, Pt. III, Ch. 5 changes the way that investment fund managers who receive carried interest compute their chargeable gains. When carried interest arises on or after 8 July 2015, the gain will normally be equal to the sum received. Deductions will be allowed only for actual acquisition costs paid in the form of money (and not as money's worth) and for amounts previously taxed as earnings.

Commencement provisions

TCGA 1992, Pt. III, Ch. 5 has effect in relation to carried interest arising on or after 8 July 2015, subject to the following exceptions:

(1) TCGA 1992, s. 103KB(1) (see ¶31-240) does not have effect in relation to a variation of a right to carried interest occurring on or after 8 July 2015 and before 22 October 2015;

(2) TCGA 1992, s. 103KG(2)–(15) (see ¶31-300) has effect in relation to carried interest arising on or after 22 October 2015 under any arrangements, unless the

carried interest arises in connection with the disposal of an asset or assets of a partnership or partnerships before that date.

(F(No. 2)A 2015, s. 43(3)–(4).)

Legislation: TCGA 1992, Pt. III, Ch. 5; F(No. 2)A 2015, s. 43(3)–(4)

31-160   Charge to capital gains tax

TCGA 1992, s. 103KA applies where:

(a)   an individual performs investment management services directly or indirectly in respect of an investment scheme under arrangements involving at least one partnership; and

(b)   carried interest arises to the individual under the arrangements.

When the carried interest which arises is derived directly or indirectly from a disposal of assets held by a partnership within an investment fund structure, the chargeable gain accruing on that disposal is calculated as the amount equal to the carried interest arising, less certain specific deductions. The chargeable gain is treated as accruing when the carried interest arises and no other chargeable gain is to be treated as accruing on the disposal (TCGA 1992, s. 103KA(2)).

When carried interest arises in any other circumstances, the chargeable gain is calculated as the amount equal to the carried interest arising, less similar specific deductions. The chargeable gain is treated as accruing at the time the carried interest arises (TCGA 1992, s. 103KA(3)).

Definitions

'carried interest', in relation to arrangements referred to in s. 103KA(1)(a), has the same meaning as in ITA 2007, s. 809EZB (see ¶31-080);

'arrangements' has the same meaning as in ITA 2007, Pt. 13, Ch. 5E (see s. 809EZE);

'investment scheme', 'investment management services' and 'external investor' have the same meanings as in ITA 2007, Pt. 13, Ch. 5E (see s. 809EZA(6) and 809EZE).

(TCGA 1992, s. 103KH.)

Anti-avoidance

Arrangements which are intended to ensure that the rules in TCGA 1992, s. 103KA do not apply to an individual or individuals, or to the whole of an amount of carried interest arising to an individual, are ignored (TCGA 1992, s. 103KD).

Legislation: TCGA 1992, s. 103KA, 103KD, 103KH

31-180   Permitted deductions

The permitted deductions are just and reasonable apportionments of:

(a)   money (but not money's worth) given to the investment scheme by the individual for being admitted into the arrangements under which the individual provides management services (but money given for 'co-investments' (see below) is excluded (TCGA 1992, s. 103KA(6)(a));

(b)   amounts which have been taxed as income on the individual when he or she acquired the right to the carried interest by entering into the arrangements (but amounts treated as earnings in respect of co-investments and 'exempt income' within ITEPA 2003, s. 7 are excluded (s. 103KA(6)(b)); and

(c)   other amounts which have been taxed as income on the individual in connection with his or her participation in the arrangements under which the individual provides management services and the carried interest arises, up to the time it arises (under s. 103KA(6)(c)).

No other deduction is permitted.

(TCGA 1992, s. 103KA(5), (6).)

The meaning of 'just and reasonable' is not defined, but in order to be allowed as a deduction, an amount must be closely associated with the acquisition of the right to the carried interest which has arisen, or with the arising of the carried interest itself.

When carried interest arises to an individual who acquired the right to it from another individual, the person to whom the carried interest ultimately arises may make a claim to HM Revenue & Customs (HMRC) for their gain to be reduced by an amount equal to the money they gave as consideration for the right. No deduction is due automatically: a claim must be made and the normal rules which govern time limits, the method by which the claim is made and the other relevant conditions also apply (TCGA 1992, s. 103KA(7)).

A 'co-investment' is an investment which yields an arm's length return, and no other return.

'Arm's length return' is defined in ITA 2007, s. 809EZB(2) (see ¶31-060) (TCGA 1992, s. 103KA(8)).

Legislation: TCGA 1992, s. 103KA

31-200   Exclusions from the capital gains tax charge

Excluded from the charge to capital gains tax are:

(a) amounts brought into account in calculating A's profits from a trade, profession or vocation; and

(b) amounts which constitute repayment of principal or 'return' on a co-investment (see ¶31-180). In this context, a return will by definition be an arm's length return.

(TCGA 1992, s. 103KA(4).)

'trade' includes profession or vocation (TCGA 1992, s. 103KA(8)).

Legislation: TCGA 1992, s. 103KA

31-220   Avoidance of double taxation

In order to ensure that any gain charged as a result of TCGA 1992, s. 103KA (see ¶31-160) is not actually or effectively taxed a second time on the same individual, where there is such a double charge, and tax other than capital gains tax under TCGA 1992, s. 103KA has actually been paid by the individual to whom the carried interest arose, that individual may make a claim to HMRC to eliminate the double charge (TCGA 1992, s. 103KE(1)–(4)).

The claim must be for adjustment of the capital gains tax charged, and HMRC will make just and reasonable adjustments which do not exceed the lesser of the capital gains tax charged under TCGA 1992, s. 103KA and the amount of 'other' tax (TCGA 1992, s. 103KE(5)–(6)).

Other tax charges which arise before the capital gains tax charge will generally be deductible under s. 103KA(5) (see ¶31-180), therefore, TCGA 1992, s. 103KE applies principally where other tax charges arise after that time.

Legislation: TCGA 1992, s. 103KE

31-240   Carried interest: consideration on disposal, etc. of right

When an individual disposes of his or her right to carried interest, either by selling it, surrendering it, allowing it to lapse or in any other way apart from the carried interest actually arising, consideration receivable for the disposal is treated as carried interest in the hands of the recipient arising at the time of the disposal, whatever form that consideration takes and whenever it is actually received (TCGA 1992, s. 103KB(1)).

However, this rule does not apply if the consideration is a disguised fee for the purposes of the disguised management fee rules in ITA 2007, s. 809EZA (see ¶31-040) (TCGA 1992, s. 103KB(2)).

TCGA 1992, s. 103KB(1) does not have effect in relation to a variation of a right to carried interest occurring on or after 8 July 2015 and before 22 October 2015 (F(No. 2)A 2015, s. 43(3)).

Legislation: TCGA 1992, s. 103KB

31-260 Carried interest: foreign chargeable gains

Where the individual to whom the gain arises is taxed on the remittance basis, a foreign chargeable gain will arise if any of the management services performed under the arrangements under which the carried interest arises were performed outside the United Kingdom. In these cases, the chargeable gain which accrues under TCGA 1992, s. 103KA(2) or (3) (see ¶31-160) is apportioned by reference to the services performed outside the UK expressed as a fraction of all the services the individual performed. The normal rule at TCGA 1992, s. 12(4) (meaning of 'foreign chargeable gains') does not apply, and the remittance basis rules apply to foreign chargeable gains determined under this rule, as they apply to foreign chargeable gains determined under TCGA 1992, s. 12(4) (TCGA 1992, s. 103KC).

Legislation: TCGA 1992, s. 103KC

31-280 Relief for external investors on disposal of partnership asset

Where a chargeable gain accrues to an external investment in an investment scheme on the disposal of one or more partnership assets, the external investor may make a claim for relief to reduce the chargeable gain by amount equal to:

$$I - C$$

where–

I   is an amount equal to such part of the sum invested in the fund by the external investor which on a just and reasonable basis is referable to the asset or assets disposed of, and

C   is the amount deducted under TCGA 1992, s. 38(1)(a) in respect of consideration given wholly and exclusively for the acquisition of the asset or assets.

(TCGA 1992, s. 103KF.)

Legislation: TCGA 1992, s. 103KF

31-300   Meaning of 'arise': deferred carried interest

Carried interest 'arises' to an individual if, and only if, it arises to him or her for the purposes of ITA 2007, Pt. 13, Ch. 5E (see ¶31-100) (TCGA 1992, s. 103KG(1)).

Broadly, s. 809EZDA and 809EZDB provide that where the sum is received by a connected person, connected company or unconnected person, it is treated as arising to the individual when it arises to that other person or company, but in the cases of sums received by a connected company or unconnected person, only where certain enjoyment conditions are met.

These definitions apply to sums other than carried interest and sums of carried interest for the purposes of the charge to income tax and (by TCGA 1992, s. 103KG(1)) also for the purposes of the charge to capital gains tax on carried interest.

However, TCGA 1992, s. 103KG provides that where the sum of carried interest is received by either a connected company or unconnected person, the rule (under ITA 2007, s. 809EZDB) which treats the sum as arising to the individual when it arises to the connected company or unconnected person does not apply if the sum is 'deferred carried interest'. Where the sum is 'deferred carried interest', it is treated as arising at the later date of when the sum ceases to be deferred unless the individual does not and will not derive benefit from it (satisfy the enjoyment conditions).

TCGA 1992, s. 103KG(2)–(15) has effect in relation to carried interest arising on or after 22 October 2015 under any arrangements, unless the carried interest arises in connection with the disposal of an asset or assets of a partnership or partnerships before that date (F(No. 2)A 2015, s. 43(4)).

Deferred carried interest

ITA 2007, s. 809EZDB (sums arising to connected company or unconnected person, see ¶31-100) does not apply in relation to a sum of carried interest arising to:

(1)   a company connected with the individual; or

(2)   a person not connected with the individual

where the sum is 'deferred carried interest' in relation to the individual (TCGA 1992, s. 103KG(2)).

Sums to which the condition in ITA 2007, s. 809EZDB(8)(b) applies (by virtue of s. 809EZDB(9)) (enjoyment conditions treated as met in relation to sums arising under avoidance arrangements, see ¶31-100) are not treated as 'deferred carried interest' (TCGA 1992, s. 103KG(12)). Neither are sums which are deferred under arrangements which are either not genuine commercial arrangements, or are arrangements, the main purpose of which (or one of the main purposes of which) is the avoidance of liability to income tax, capital gains tax, corporation tax or inheritance tax (TCGA 1992, s. 103KG(13)). Genuine commercial arrangements in this context means arrangements involving the individual (alone or jointly with others performing investment management services) and external investors in the investment scheme (TCGA 1992, s. 103KG(14)).

'Deferred carried interest' is:

(a) a sum of carried interest, the provision of which (to either the individual or a person connected with the individual) is deferred (whether pending the meeting of any conditions (including conditions which may never be met) or otherwise; and

(b) includes the individual's share (determined on a just and reasonable basis) of any carried interest, the provision of which to the individual and another person or persons, taken together, has been deferred (whether pending the meeting of any conditions (including conditions which may never be met) or otherwise).

(TCGA 1992, s. 103KG(3).)

Where ITA 2007, s. 809EZDB (see ¶31-100) is disapplied in relation to a sum of deferred carried interest, the sum is treated as arising to the individual when it ceases to be deferred if it would not otherwise 'arise' to the individual, unless:

(1) none of the enjoyment conditions is met when the sum ceases to be deferred carried interest; and

(2) there is no reasonable likelihood that any of those conditions will ever be met in relation to the sum.

(TCGA 1992, s. 103KG(4)–(5).)

The enjoyment conditions

The enjoyment conditions are:

(a) the sum, or part of the sum, is in fact so dealt with by any person as to be calculated at some time to enure for the benefit of the individual or a person connected with the individual;

(b) the sum's ceasing to be deferred carried interest in relation to the individual operates to increase the value to the individual (or any connected person) of any assets which:

   (i) the individual (or connected person) holds; or
   (ii) are held for the benefit of the individual (or connected person);

(c) the individual (or any connected person) receives or is entitled to receive at any time any benefit provided or to be provided out of the sum or part of the sum;

(d) the individual (or any connected person) may become entitled to the beneficial enjoyment of the sum or part of the sum if one or more powers are exercised or successively exercised (and for these purposes it does not matter who may exercise the powers or whether they are exercisable with or without the consent of another person);

(e)   the individual (or any connected person) is able in any manner to control directly or indirectly the application of the sum or part of the sum.

(TCGA 1992, s. 103KG(4)–(6).)

In determining whether any of the enjoyment conditions is met in relation to a sum or part of a sum:

(a)   regard must be had to the substantial result and effect of all the relevant circumstances; and

(b)   all benefits which may at any time accrue to a person as a result of the sum ceasing to be deferred carried interest in relation to A must be taken into account, irrespective of:

　　(i)   the nature or form of the benefits; or

　　(ii)   whether the person has legal or equitable rights in respect of the benefits.

(TCGA 1992, s. 103KG(7).)

If the only reason the enjoyment conditions are met is by reason of the individual holding shares or an interest in shares in a company, they are treated as not met (TCGA 1992, s. 103KG(8)).

The enjoyment conditions are also treated as not met if the sum arises to a company connected with the individual and the sum is included in the profits of the company that are charged to corporation tax unless:

(1)   the company is a CFC and the exemption in TIOPA 2010, Pt. 9A, Ch. 14 applies for the accounting period in which the sum arises; or

(2)   the company is not a CFC but the exemption would apply if it were.

(TCGA 1992, s. 103KG(9).)

Anti-avoidance

The enjoyment conditions will be treated as applying where the sum arises to either a company connected with the individual or an unconnected individual as part of arrangements, in respect of which it is reasonable to assume that the main purpose (or one of the main purposes) of the arrangements is the avoidance of liability to income tax, capital gains tax, inheritance tax or corporation tax, and without which arrangements it is reasonable to assume the sum would have arisen to the individual (or a connected individual) (TCGA 1992, s. 103KG(10)).

Where the sum is applied directly or indirectly as an investment in a collective investment scheme, it is regarded as arising under arrangements the main purpose, or one of the main purposes of which, is the avoidance of income tax, capital gains tax, inheritance tax or corporation tax (TCGA 1992, s. 103KG(11)).

Modified meaning of 'connected'

The same modified definition of 'connected' applies for the purposes of the charge to capital gains tax, as applies for the purposes of the charge to income tax under ITA 2007, Pt. 13, Ch. 5E.

For the purposes of TCGA 1992, s. 103KG, the meaning of 'connected' is as provided by ITA 2007, s. 993 but subject to two modifications:

(1) connections an individual has as a partner in a partnership with other partners (and their spouse/civil partner) are ignored; and

(2) partners in a partnership in which the individual is also a partner are not treated as 'associates' of the individual for the purposes of determining whether the individual has control over a company,

(TCGA 1992, s. 103KG(15)).

Legislation: TCGA 1992, s. 103KG

INCOME-BASED CARRIED INTEREST

31-320   Introduction

Carried interest arises to investment managers as a performance-based reward for managing the funds of an investment vehicle, typically a partnership. Sums allocated to an individual in satisfaction of carried interest are treated, for tax purposes, as though the individual had carried out the transactions which gave rise to the sums. Where the fund is investing rather than trading for tax purposes, those sums will be treated as capital gains or income by reference to case law.

Finance Act 2016 inserts ITA 2007, Pt. 13, Ch. 5F (see ¶31-340) to replace the case law tests based around the 'badges of trade'. This is because the case law underlying the test had mainly considered trades connected with areas such as manufacturing and retail and the test was, therefore, more difficult to apply to a business such as asset management.

31-340 Income-based carried interest

Finance Act 2016 inserts ITA 2007, Pt. 13, Ch. 5F which provides a legislative test to determine whether carried interest should be taxed as capital gains or income. Treatment under the new rules will be determined by testing the average period for which the fund holds assets. All returns which are not subject to capital gains tax will be chargeable to income tax and Class 4 National Insurance contributions as trading profits.

ITA 2007, Pt. 13, Ch. 5F provides, broadly, that where an individual performs investment management services for a collective investment scheme, then any sum of carried interest arising from that fund will only be eligible for capital gains tax treatment if the fund holds investments, on average, for at least four years. Partial capital gains tax treatment will be available where the average holding period is between three and four years. Where the average hold period is below three years all sums of carried interest arising to the individual – however structured – will be charged to tax and NICs as trading profits.

The provisions will apply to sums of carried interest arising on or after 6 April 2016.

See ¶31-120ff. for the charge to capital gains tax on 'carried interest'.

ITA 2007, Pt. 13, Ch. 5F

(1) Overview

Chapter 5F determines when carried interest arising to an individual from an investment scheme is 'income-based carried interest' for the purposes of ITA 2007, Pt. 13, Ch. 5E (and the charge to income tax under the 'disguised investment management' fee rules) and in particular, s. 809EZB(1)(c) (as amended by *Finance Act* 2016), see ¶31-060.

The provisions will not apply in relation to carried interest arising to an individual in respect of an employment-related security (as defined by ITEPA 2003, s. 421B(8)) (s. 809FZU) and the Chapter further does not affect the liability to any tax of either the investment scheme or external investors in the scheme (ITA 2007, s. 809FZA(7)).

(2) Income-based carried interest: general rule

Section 809FZB contains the general rule, under which the extent to which carried interest is income-based carried interest depends on the average holding period of the investment scheme.

Section 809FZB also introduces the concept of the 'relevant proportion' of a sum of carried interest being classified as 'income-based carried interest'. The 'relevant proportion' is determined by the average time for which the fund giving rise to the carried interest holds its investments. It is then applied to the carried interest to determine what proportion is taxable as income.

Average holding period	Relevant proportion
Less than 36 months	100%
At least 36 months but less than 37 months	80%
At least 37 months but less than 38 months	60%
At least 38 months but less than 39 months	40%
At least 39 months but less than 40 months	20%
40 months or more	0%

(3) Average holding period

Sections 809FZC – 809FZJ contain further provision relating to average holding periods.

Average holding period

Section 809FZC explains how to calculate the average holding period for the purposes of the Chapter. Only those investments by reference to which the carried interest arises are included when determining the average holding period (see subs. (2)(b)). Where carried interest is calculated by reference to the 'fund as a whole', this will include all investments made by the fund. Where carried interest is calculated by reference to the performance of a portfolio over a given period, the relevant investments will be those disposed of during that period and those which remain held at the close of the period.

Disposals

Section 809FZD determines when an investment is disposed of. The starting point is that there will be a disposal of an investment if there is a disposal for the purposes of TCGA 1992 (s. 809FZD(1)), or a deemed disposal (s. 809FZD(2)).

Part disposals

Section 809FZE sets out the rules governing part disposals. The part disposed of and the part retained are treated as two separate assets (subs. (1)). The value of each part is calculated in accordance with s. 809FZE(2) and (3).

Unwanted short-term investments

Section 809FZF makes provision for excluding the making and disposal of certain short-term investments.

Derivatives

Section 809FZG sets out the treatment of derivative contracts. The value invested for the purposes of the weighted average holding period is determined by s. 809FZG(2) depending on the type of derivative contract in question. A substantial alteration to the terms of a derivative is treated as a disposal and new acquisition at the time of the alteration (s. 809FZG(5)).

Hedging: exchange gains and losses

Section 809FZH sets out the treatment of instruments that hedge exchange gains and losses, defined in s. 809FZH(2). Such instruments are not treated as investments for the purpose of this legislation (s. 809FZH(4)), and entering into such an instrument is not treated as a deemed disposal of the hedged asset(s) for those purposes (s. 809FZH(3)).

Hedging: interest rates

Section 809FZI sets out the treatment of instruments that hedge interest rates, defined in s. 809FZI(2). Such instruments are not treated as investments for the purpose of this legislation (s. 809FZI(4)), and entering into such an instrument is not treated as a deemed disposal of the hedged asset(s) for those purposes (s. 809FZI(3)).

Significant interests

Section 809FZJ applies where an investment scheme holds a controlling interest in a company and makes a further investment in that company. Where the conditions apply, any further investment by the scheme in the company is treated as made at the time that it met the conditions for holding a 'controlling interest' (s. 809FZJ(1)).

Section 809FZJ also sets out when any disposal in a company in which the investment scheme holds a controlling interest is made. Any disposals are treated as not being made until such time as a relevant disposal is made. A relevant disposal is a disposal which has the effect that the investment scheme ceases to have a 40% interest in the company.

Venture capital funds

Section 809FZK applies where a venture capital fund has a relevant interest in a company and makes a further investment or disposal. Any investment is treated as being made at the time the relevant interest was acquired and any disposal is treated as not being made until either a relevant disposal is made or the scheme director condition ceases to be met. A relevant interest is at least 5% interest interest or investments valued at more than £1m. A relevant disposal is a disposal which has the effect that the venture capital fund has disposed of more than 80% of its greatest holding at any one time.

S. 809FZK also defines 'venture capital fund', 'venture capital investment' and the 'scheme director condition'.

Significant equity stake funds

Section 809FZL applies where a significant equity stake fund has a significant equity stake investment in a company and a further investment is made or a disposal is made. Any further investment is treated as made at the time the significant equity stake was acquired and any disposal is regarded as not being made until either a relevant disposal is made or the scheme director condition ceases to be met. A relevant disposal is a disposal which has the effect that the significant equity stake fund ceases to have a 15% interest in the company. Section 809FZL also defines 'significant equity fund' and 'significant equity stake investment'.

Controlling equity stake fund

Section 809FZM applies where a controlling equity stake fund has a 25% interest in a company and a further investment or disposal is made. Any further investment is treated as made at the time the 25% interest was acquired and any disposal is regarded as not being made until a relevant disposal is made. A relevant disposal is a disposal which has the effect that the controlling equity stake fund ceases to have a 25% interest in the company. Section 809FZM also defines 'controlling equity stake fund'.

Real estate funds

Section 809FZN applies where a real estate fund has a major interest in any land and a further investment or disposal is made. Any further investment is treated as made at the time the major interest was acquired and any disposal is regarded as not being made until a relevant disposal is made. A relevant disposal is a disposal which has the effect that the real estate fund has disposed of more than 50% of the greatest amount invested at any one time in the land. Additionally, any major interest acquired in adjacent land is treated as an investment in the original land. Section 809FZN also defines 'real estate fund'.

Funds of funds

Section 809FZO disapplies s. 809FC(5) (disregard of intermediate holding structures) in respect of a fund of funds in a collective investment scheme and accordingly, the investment is regarded as an investment in the collective investment scheme itself unless a reduction in the proportion of carried interest arising to any person that is income-based carried interest is not the main purpose or one of the main purposes of making the investment in the collective investment scheme. Where a fund of funds has a significant investment in a collective investment scheme, any further investment is treated as made at the time the significant investment was made and any disposal is regarded as not being made until a relevant disposal is made. A relevant disposal is a disposal which has the effect that the fund of funds has disposed of at least 50% of the greatest amount invested for its purpose in the underlying scheme at any one time or the value of the funds investment becomes worth less than the greater of £1 million or 5% of the total value of investments before the disposal. Section 809FZO also defines 'fund of funds', 'significant investment' and 'qualifying investment'.

Secondary funds

Section 809FZP disapplies s. 809FZC(5) (disregard of intermediate holding structures) in respect of a secondary fund in a collective investment scheme and accordingly, the investment is regarded as an investment in the collective investment scheme itself unless a reduction in the proportion of carried interest arising to any person which is income-based carried interest was not the main purpose or one of the main purposes for making the investment in the collective investment scheme. Where a secondary fund has a significant investment in a collective investment scheme, any qualifying investment acquired is treated as acquired at the time the significant investment was acquired and any disposal is regarded as not being made until a relevant disposal is made. A relevant disposal is a disposal which has the effect that the secondary fund has disposed of at least 50% of the greatest amount invested in the underlying scheme at any one time or results in the secondary fund's investment in the underlying scheme becoming worth less than the greater of £1 million or 5% of the total value of investments held before the disposal. Section 809FZP also defines 'secondary fund', 'significant interest' and 'qualifying investment'.

(4) Direct lending funds

Sections 809FZQ and 809FZR contain a particular rule for direct lending funds.

Direct lending funds

Section 809FZQ treats carried interest arising from direct lending funds as chargeable to income tax in its entirety, unless s. 809FZR applies.

Direct lending funds: exception

Section 809FZR exempts certain direct lending funds from the scope of s. 809FZQ, where the fund is a limited partnership, the carried interest falls within s. 809EZD(2) or (3) (sums treated as carried interest, see ¶31-080) and it is reasonable to suppose that when investments cease to be made for the purposes of the fund, at least 75% of loans made by the fund will have been qualifying loans. Qualifying loans are defined by s. 809FZR(2) as broadly, genuine, arm's length loans to unconnected borrowers on fixed repayment terms and for a minimum four-year term. Where those conditions apply, the general rules of Ch. 5F will apply to the carried interest instead of s. 809FZQ, although certain loans repaid before maturity will be treated as held for four years.

(5)   Conditionally exempt carried interest

Sections 809FZS and 809FZT contain an exception to the general rule for carried interest which is conditionally exempt from income tax.

Conditionally exempt carried interest

Section 809FZS sets out the treatment of 'conditionally exempt carried interest'. Where certain conditions are met, that carried interest is conditionally taxed under the chargeable gains rules and not as income (s. 809FZS(1)). This prevents carried interest being charged to income tax under these rules in the early years of a fund's existence (when the calculation required by s. 809FZC will necessarily produce an average holding period of below 40 months) when the fund expects to hold the relevant investments for a period which would exceed four years.

Carried interest which ceases to be conditionally exempt

Section 809FZT sets out how 'conditionally exempt carried interest' is subsequently to be treated.

(6)   Supplementary and interpretative provisions

Sections 809FZU–809FZZ contain supplementary and interpretative provision.

Supplementary

Employment related securities

Section 809FZU disapplies the provisions in Ch. 5F to carried interest arising to an individual in respect of employment related securities.

'Loan to own' investments

Section 809FZV provides that impaired secured debts acquired at a discount and assets acquired within three months in settlement of the debt are to be treated as a single investment valued at the amount paid for the debt.

Anti-avoidance

Section 809FZW puts in place an anti-avoidance rule to prevent manipulation of average holding periods or whether a scheme is a 'controlling equity stake fund'.

Treasury regulations

Section 809FZX provides a regulation making power to vary how the average holding period is calculated.

'Reasonable to suppose'

Section 809FZY defines what is meant by 'reasonable to suppose' for the purposes of Ch. 5F.

Interpretation

Section 809FZZ provides definitions of various terms used in Ch. 5F.

Legislation: ITA 2007, Pt. 13, Ch. 5F as inserted by *Finance Act* 2016

Chapter 23:   LLPs: Salaried members

32-000   Background

A major change to partnership tax legislation in *Finance Act* 2014 was the introduction of rules relating to 'salaried members' of LLPs. The rules are relevant to LLPs only and are necessitated by the fact that a person who is a member of an LLP cannot also be an employee of that LLP (*Limited Liability Partnerships Act* 2000, s. 4(4)). In HMRC's view, this position was abused at 'both ends of the spectrum'.

At one end, it is understood that large numbers of low paid employees, such as the office cleaning staff of a large office cleaning company, might have formed themselves into LLPs. This absolves the main company from the responsibility of having large numbers of employees, of being required to operate PAYE, etc. At the same time, those members of the LLP were being hired by the company to do exactly the same work and being paid in exactly the same way at the same hourly rate. So there was very little economic difference in their positions.

The main difference as far as the cleaners were concerned was that no tax was deducted from their pay, their National Insurance contributions were lower as self-employed people, and they only had to account for tax and National Insurance contributions twice a year. The company, of course, did not have to account for employer's National Insurance contributions, as well as not having to operate the PAYE system. So there was not just a deferral of income tax, but an absolute loss of tax in the reduced National Insurance contributions. Furthermore, in this scenario it seems highly likely that a proportion of these low paid workers would not, in fact, have saved sufficient funds to pay the tax bills twice a year, so there was probably a further absolute loss of tax through that lack of funds.

At the other end of the spectrum, HMRC were concerned that the high paid partners in many larger partnerships, and HMRC specifically pointed to professional partnerships, such as accountants and lawyers, were effectively highly paid employees and not partners on any sensible economic analysis. At first glance, one might ask why this is any different from a general partnership (i.e. a partnership that is governed by the 1890 Partnership Act). But the partners in a general partnership have unlimited liability for the losses of the partnership. So if HMRC challenge the status of a partner in a partnership that is not an LLP, regardless of how much that person might look like they are in fact an employee of the partnership, their legal relationship with the partnership and the other members is that all of their personal assets are at risk if anything goes wrong with the partnership as a whole. This is such a fundamental difference from the relationship between an employer and an employee, that HMRC were not generally able to assert that a partner in a general partnership person should be treated as an employee.

In contrast, of course, the whole point of an LLP is that the partners have limited liability in respect of the debts or losses of the firm, limited generally to the amount of capital they have contributed to the partnership or any amounts they have promised to contribute in a winding up. Generally speaking, that contribution does not extend to being the whole of their personal assets, so the major distinguishing feature between being an employee and being a partner is not, generally speaking, present in LLPs.

HMRC also point out that the 1890 Partnership Act has the effect of requiring the relationship between the parties to be considered in determining whether or not there is a partnership. Specifically, s. 1(1) of that Act states that a partnership is the relation that subsists between persons carrying on a business in common with a view to profit. In contrast, to become a member of an LLP, you merely have to subscribe to membership with a view to carrying on a lawful trade. That is, none of the 'normal' characteristics of partnership need to be present.

Overall, these reasons combine to explain the rationale behind the enactment of the legislation.

HMRC Guidance

HMRC published guidance on the rules on 27 March 2014, which can be found at *www. gov.uk/government/uploads/system/uploads/attachment_data/file/298724/Partnerships_ Salaried_member_rules.pdf.* This guidance supersedes the version originally published with the draft Finance Bill clauses in December 2014, but does not yet appear to have been incorporated into any of the HMRC Manuals.

The guidance contains HMRC's views of the way the legislation is intended to operate and has many examples, some of which are used in this book. However, HMRC's views of the meaning and operation of the legislation may not always be correct and practitioners should not be afraid to view the guidance critically and to challenge HMRC's approach, where necessary.

Legislation: ITTOIA 2005, s. 863A–863G

32-020   Structure of the legislation

The structure of the new legislation is conceptually simple. There are three Conditions, A, B and C, which must be met by an individual, M, who is a member of a limited liability partnership that carries on a trade, profession or business with a view to profit (ITTOIA 2005, s. 863A(1)). If that person, M, satisfies all three conditions, they are to be treated as being an employee of the LLP under a contract of service, and any rights or duties as a member of the LLP are to be treated as rights or duties under that contract of service (ITTOIA 2005, s. 863A(2)).

The corporation tax legislation is also amended (by the insertion of CTA 2009, s. 1273A) to ensure that, for corporation tax purposes as well, the salaried member is treated as being employed by the LLP under a contract of service, and his rights and duties as a member of the LLP are treated as rights and duties under that contract.

Although straightforward in application, these provisions are not obviously fair. As these are purely tax provisions, this means whilst a partner in an LLP may be taxed as if they were an employee, they are still actually a member of an LLP and subject to the terms of the LLP agreement which means they do not therefore have any of the normal protections afforded by law to employees.

In practice, relatively few people are actually affected by this legislation at the professional services end of the spectrum, and those who have been caught by this legislation are known to have resigned from the LLP of which they were members, in order to become employees again, so as to access to the legal protections available to employees.

Legislation: ITTOIA 2005, s. 863A–863G

32-040   Condition A

Condition A is met if, at the relevant time, it is reasonable to expect that at least 80% of the amount payable to M during the 'relevant period' under 'relevant arrangements' in respect of their performance of services in their capacity as a member of the LLP will be 'disguised salary'.

Disguised salary

Disguised salary is defined as being amounts which are fixed, or which are variable but not by reference to the overall profits or losses of the LLP, or which are not, in practice, affected by the overall amounts of those profits or losses (ITTOIA 2005, s. 863B(3), step 2).

In other words, in order to avoid satisfying Condition A, it is important that the individual concerned should expect to receive remuneration as a member of the LLP calculated so that more than 20% of their income could reasonably be expected to be based on those overall profits. At first glance, a test applied by reference to the overall profits of a partnership looks like a reasonable measure of whether somebody has a relationship that looks like a partnership, taking a share of the risks and rewards of that partnership business. Indeed, being remunerated according to a share of the profits of a partnership is a *prima facie* indication of being in partnership under the *Partnership Act* 1890, s. 2(3).

But it is not clear why HMRC insist that the test can only be failed by reference to the overall profits of the partnership, and not by reference to profits of various divisions of the partnership. For example, the remuneration of a partner in a national firm in, say, the Leicester office may all be calculated by reference to shares of profits, but there may be components made up of a share of the overall profits of the Leicester office, a share of the Midlands regional profits, a share of the profits of, say, the tax discipline regionally and/or nationally, and a final component that may be related to the overall profits of the partnership. In this case, even though the person is remunerated only by reference to the profits of various parts of the business, it is only the component related to the overall profits of the business nationally that counts towards the more than 20% required to fail Condition A.

Case Study 1

A national firm awards its partners points for their various roles within the firm, and for their performances within those roles. The total profits for a year are then divided by the total number of points that have been issued to the partners to come up with the partner remuneration in the form of pounds per point. For example, if Partner A holds 150 points and the profits of the firm are such that each partner receives £2,000 per point, Partner A will receive £300,000. In this case, it is clear that every partner is remunerated by reference to the overall profits of the firm. (This is similar to HMRC's examples 10 and 12.)

HMRC Example 27

In contrast, HMRC's example 27 involves W LLP, which operates sites offering 'hand car washes'. The individuals who wash the cars are members of the LLP, not employees. Member D washes cars at one of these sites. Member D is paid on a piece work basis, so that the more cars washed, the more he receives. His income is based on his work, not on the success of the business as a whole, so Member D receives a disguised salary and Condition A is satisfied.

HMRC Example 28

In HMRC's example 28, XYZ LLP decides to expand into a new business area. A new member, P, is recruited to run the new business area. As it is expected that the new business area will initially make a loss, P will receive a guaranteed profit share of £100,000 plus a percentage of the turnover of the new business area.

Neither the guaranteed payments (which may be called 'guaranteed profit share') nor the payment based on a percentage of the turnover of that business area is based on the profits of the LLP as a whole. Condition A is satisfied for the duration of the remuneration arrangements, whatever level of income he receives.

HMRC also provide a number of examples to demonstrate other aspects of disguised salary, such as payments based purely on personal performance, guaranteed payments, and so on.

Relevant arrangements and the capacity test

The disguised salary must be paid under relevant arrangements, being arrangements for payments to be made to M by the LLP in respect of M's performance in their capacity as a member of the LLP (ITTOIA 2005, s. 863B(2)). In other words, the disguised salary must be part of M's remuneration for being a member of the LLP, which imposes a capacity test. Thus, a person must fail Condition A, and cannot be a salaried member, if they are receiving remuneration but are not providing services to the LLP, and are not expected to, or where remuneration is paid by the LLP to them in a capacity other than that of a member.

'Arrangements' includes any agreement, understanding, scheme, transaction or series of transactions (whether or not legally enforceable) (ITTOIA 2005, s. 863B(5)).

HMRC Example 5

In HMRC's example 5, X used to be an active member of JKL LLP but effectively retired a number of years ago. In recognition of his contribution, however, he remains a member of the LLP and is allocated a profit share annually. Since this is not amounts paid in respect of his services as a member of the LLP, because he is not providing any services, he necessarily fails Condition A.

HMRC Example 6

Similarly, HMRC's example 6 shows how the same argument applies to somebody who is paid to commute a period of garden leave. Once again, such a payment would clearly not relate to the provision of services as a member of the LLP, so Condition A is failed.

HMRC Example 7

HMRC's example 7 demonstrates the necessity for the remuneration to derive from the services provided to the LLP. An LLP is formed between a family and a local developer to develop some land. Kate is a member of the family, and also a member of the LLP, but the LLP agreement does not require her to do any work for the LLP. Her profession is as an architect, and the LLP engages her to provide professional services as an architect to draw up plans for the LLP, for which she charges an arm's length fee under her normal professional terms of engagement. Whilst she is providing services to the LLP, she is clearly not providing services as a member of that LLP. Therefore, Condition A is not engaged.

> ### HMRC Example 8
> Similarly, HMRC's example 8 has an individual renting land to a farming LLP of which he is a member. The LLP pays an arm's length rent to him for the use of the land. These amounts are not paid in respect of any services he provides to the partnership as a member of the partnership, and Condition A is, once again, not engaged.

Furthermore, HMRC also highlight that, were that person to otherwise be determined to be salaried member, the rental income would also not comprise part of their earnings from the employment, as it arises from the entirely separate source of renting the land.

Benefits

The condition specifically refers to amounts to be paid to the member of the LLP. HMRC state in their guidance that this means that any benefits provided by the partnership to the members of the LLP will be disregarded in this respect. However, if the person concerned is determined to be a salaried partner, any benefits supplied will be taxed as the benefits of an employee, in the normal way.

Relevant time and relevant period

Condition A is a forward-looking test, as is clear from the phrase 'reasonable to expect' in the description of the condition. Expectation clearly implies that one looks at the beginning of a period and asks what the likely outcome is during that period.

Initially, this requires consideration of Condition A at the following times (each of which is, accordingly, a relevant time (ITTOIA 2005, s. 863B(3)):

- if relevant arrangements are in place, on 6 April 2014 or at the later date when the individual concerned becomes a member of the LLP (ITTOIA 2005, s. 863B(1)(a));
- at any later time when relevant arrangements are put in place or modified (ITTOIA 2005, s. 863B(1)(b));
- where Condition A has previously been considered and the relevant arrangements do not end and are not modified by the end of the relevant period, we must also revisit the position at the end of the relevant period.

Condition A then requires determination of the relevant period, which is the period from the relevant time to the time when it is reasonable to expect that the relevant arrangements will end or be modified (ITTOIA 2005, s. 863B(3), at step 1).

It is then necessary to look at the level of disguised salary that it would be reasonable to expect, under the relevant arrangements, during the relevant period.

Simplifying this slightly, a determination in respect of Condition A when a person becomes a partner (assuming this is after 6 April 2014), when the remuneration arrangements for that partner are put in place or modified or when it might reasonably be anticipated that the existing arrangements would expire, and a reasonable prediction of how that member will be remunerated over the relevant period will need to be made.

HMRC's guidance is helpful in explaining that this means that the 'relevant period' can be more than a year (and, by inference, presumably can be less than a year, too).

HMRC Example 2

HMRC's example 2 has John being a member of an LLP which entered into an agreement to develop a property over three years. John will receive a fixed profit share of £100,000 for each of the first two years and be paid 50% of the profit from the development, when it matures in year 3. This latter amount is expected to be £500,000.

The relevant period is therefore the 3 years during which these relevant arrangements subsist. Clearly, looking forward from the beginning of this agreement, the fixed element of John's remuneration is only £200,000 out of an anticipated £700,000, which is much less than 80%, so Condition A is failed.

The forward looking nature of the test is also emphasised by the fact that the position is not affected if, in the event, the development project fails and, for example, John receives nothing in year 3. Despite the fact that he only received the fixed elements in years 1 and 2, Condition A is failed by virtue of what it was reasonable to expect at the beginning of the relevant period, and not with hindsight during or at the end of the relevant period.

The concept of the relevant period ending when it is reasonable to expect that the relevant arrangements will end or be modified (in ITTOIA 2005, s. 863B(c)) is also illustrated by this example. While there is no reference to any subsequent amendment of the agreement, or any new partnership agreement, clearly the relevant arrangements will expire at the end of the development, so this must also be the end of the relevant period, as defined.

Legislation: ITTOIA 2005, s. 863B

32-060 Condition B

Condition B requires that the mutual rights and duties of the members of the LLP, and of the partnership and its members, do not give the member significant influence over the affairs of the partnership (ITTOIA 2005, s. 863C). This is interpreted by HMRC as meaning significant influence over the affairs of the partnership as a whole and HMRC expected this to be a condition that would be satisfied by the vast majority of partners in large professional services firms and that they would only expect a relatively small number of people on the national executives of such firms to fail this condition. Conversely, it is probably reasonable to assume that most small partnerships would easily fail this condition, on the basis that it would be very hard for HMRC to argue that, say, all five members of an LLP did not have significant influence over the affairs of that LLP.

It is clear from HMRC's guidance that they consider that a partnership requires a group of people to be carrying on a business in common with a view to profit, referencing the *Partnership Act* 1890, s. 1(1), despite the fact that this is clearly not a requirement of LLPA 2000. Nevertheless, one might argue that it is a reasonable indicium of partnership and one relevant to the current test.

HMRC Example 32

HMRC's example 32 has a mother and father carrying on a farming business in partnership, to which they admit their son. However, they omit to amend the partnership agreement, so one has to look at the actual facts of the case to determine whether the son has significant influence over the affairs of the partnership, too.

HMRC Example 33

In example 33, they propose a partnership of ten members, all of whom have equal rights and responsibilities, and accept that all ten of those partners are likely to fail Condition B.

Case Study 2

Three individuals had been friends for many years and had always met for breakfast one day a week at a cafe down the road from the offices where they worked. They eventually set up their own accountancy practice together, as the three founding partners, but continued to meet for breakfast once a week, as they always had. Now that they were running a business together, they tended to discuss business strategy at these weekly breakfasts.

Over a number of years they invited two other people to join the partnership. They were considered equal partners in most respects but they were never invited to join the weekly breakfasts, as this was largely a matter between friends. Advice was sought regarding Condition B (although it was not clear that either Conditions A or C were a problem, in any case), and it was suggested that they could do one of two things: they could either invite the two new partners to join them for their weekly breakfast, or they could instigate a more formal weekly partners' meeting to which all five partners were invited, in order to demonstrate, in either case, that Condition B was failed for all five partners and not just the three founding partners.

HMRC's guidance gives some helpful indicia as to the sort of decisions that partners would be involved with if they have significant influence over the affairs of the business. These include matters such as:

- appointment of new partners;
- deciding the firm's areas of business;
- strategic decisions;
- business acquisitions or disposals.

There are several more but HMRC also make the point that these are merely indicia, just some guidance of aspects that HMRC consider to be appropriately significant.

Since the test requires somebody to have significant influence, HMRC also accept the possibility that somebody might, *prima facie*, have no official role but might still have considerable influence. They give the example of a semi-retired person who founded the firm and whose views are frequently, or even invariably, followed by the current partners, notwithstanding that person's lack of any official standing.

HMRC also accept that it is the real influence that must be considered, not merely what is stated to occur in the partnership agreement or similar documents. They give a number of examples where the underlying facts are at odds with the legal documentation, and stress that it is the actual position that must be considered in the context of Condition B, not merely the formal legal agreements or status of partners.

Condition B is silent as to when the test needs to be applied. HMRC's guidance suggests that this matter must be considered either on 6 April 2014, when the legislation came into force, or at the date that a person becomes a partner, and then again when the arrangements change. But this is not a legislative provision, which is not entirely satisfactory.

Consider, for example, the fact that it does not say that the person has to have significant influence throughout a particular period. So it is unclear what happens if a person who is, for example, on the management board of the firm, therefore fails Condition B at a particular point in time, but later in the year decides to step down, such that they no longer fail Condition B. In the absence of specific legislation on this point, one can only infer that HMRC would expect (assuming that that person satisfies Conditions A and C), that the moment the person starts to satisfy Condition B, they become a salaried member and must be remunerated accordingly.

Legislation: ITTOIA 2005, s. 863C

32-080   Condition C

Condition C measures the partner's capital at risk in the partnership and compares it to the likely disguised salary in a period. Specifically, Condition C is satisfied if at the relevant time, M's contribution to the LLP is less than 25% of the disguised salary which it would be reasonable to expect the LLP to pay to M for M's performance during the relevant tax year of services in M's capacity as a member of the partnership (ITTOIA 2005, s. 863D(1) and (2)).

Disguised salary takes the same definition as it does for Condition A (ITTOIA 2005, s. 863D(2)).

Essentially, therefore, a person will be treated as a partner for tax purposes, even if they have substantial disguised salary for a period, so long as the amount of capital they have at stake is at least 25% of the reasonably expected amount of disguised salary for the tax year. This flows from HMRC's perception that one of the indicia of partnership is that one has some permanent financial stake in the business, which is not entirely a commercial view of the way partnerships operate. Many partnerships will extract as much cash as possible, as early as possible, without jeopardising cash flow requirements, commercial needs, etc., as it is generally considered prudent to extract the cash as quickly as possible to protect against any future problems that may occur within the business.

Contribution to the LLP (i.e. capital at risk)

M's contribution is any amount of capital contributed to the LLP, as well as any share of the LLP's profits (calculated in accordance with generally accepted accounting practice) that is added to the partnership capital (ITTOIA 2005, s. 863E(2)–(4)).

From this amount, it is necessary to deduct any amounts that M has previously drawn out or received back, any amount that M may be entitled to draw out or receive back when a member of the LLP, or any amount that M may be entitled to require another person to reimburse to them (ITTOIA 2005, s. 863E(6)), and references to drawing amounts out or receiving them back are to be taken as references to doing so directly or indirectly (ITTOIA 2005, s. 863E(7)).

Given the distinction between amounts contributed as capital and amounts which can be drawn upon, etc., it is clear that this provision will require the relevant members to hold separate capital and current accounts, so as to distinguish between the two.

HMRC Example 42

HMRC's example 42 is helpful. This shows a sum of £10,000 contributed as capital in accordance with the LLP agreement and £50,000 described as a long-term loan, carrying interest, but otherwise held on identical terms to the capital contribution, so that the money cannot be drawn upon unless and until the partner retires from the business. There are also sums of £30,000 described as a short-term loan, £25,000 undrawn profits and £25,000 as a tax reserve account. The guidance states that the first two of these, being held on very similar terms, are clearly capital as defined, and the other sums are not. Therefore, the individual concerned has £60,000 as their contribution to the LLP.

We note that many LLP agreements provide for sums to be contributed as capital by members when they join the LLP, and also potentially for members to be liable for certain sums in the event of the LLP being wound up. However, there is no reference in Condition C to any amounts to which the member might become liable when the LLP is wound up. This may be because HMRC have deliberately chosen to arrange for the condition to refer to sums actually contributed to the LLP, not sums which might be contributed to the LLP.

When is Condition C determined

The question of whether Condition C applies is to be determined (ITTOIA 2005, s. 863D(3) and (4)):

- on 6 April 2014 (when the legislation came into force) or at any later time at which the person becomes a member of the LLP;
- at the beginning of each tax year;
- if there is a change in the person's contribution to the LLP during a tax year;
- if there is some other change of circumstances which might affect whether Condition C is satisfied.

Once Condition C is determined to be satisfied, or not, it is to be treated as being satisfied or not satisfied until the subsequent time at which it is to be re-determined (ITTOIA 2005, s. 863D(5)).

Anti-avoidance

There is an anti-avoidance provision, so that a member cannot temporarily increase their capital contribution at, say, the beginning of the tax year, in order to fail Condition C. If this is done, it must also be reasonable to expect that the condition will not be met for the remainder of the tax year, in order to fail Condition C (ITTOIA 2005, s. 863D(6) and (7)).

An increase in the contribution includes the initial contribution or any deemed contribution that is to be made within two months of joining the partnership (ITTOIA 2005, s. 863D(12)).

It is quite hard to see how this could arise. If an amount contributed on, say, 6 April does fall within the definition of capital, then it cannot be withdrawn. Alternatively, if it can be withdrawn then, surely, it does not fit within the definition of M's contribution?

Joining leaving LLPs

There is a further provision to ensure that the amount of capital taken into account is reduced in accordance with the proportion of any given tax year during which the person concerned is not a member of the LLP. This is most likely to arise in the year in which a person either joins or retires from the LLP. The essence is to reduce the amount of the contribution taken into account in determining whether Condition C is met. For example, if a person joins a firm halfway through a tax year, then only half of their capital contribution would be taken into account in considering Condition C and comparing that capital contribution to their disguised salary for the year.

If there are excluded days in a tax year, the contribution to the LLP is multiplied by the fraction $(D-E)/D$, where D is the number of days in a relevant tax year and E is the number of excluded days (ITTOIA 2005, s. 863D(8)).

In the year that a person joins an LLP, excluded days are the days in the tax year before that person joins the LLP (ITTOIA 2005, s. 863D(9)). If a person leaves an LLP during the tax year ('if … it is reasonable to expect that M will not be a member of the LLP for the remainder of the relevant tax year'), any day after the person leaves the LLP is an excluded day (ITTOIA 2005, s. 863D(10)). And if the person's contribution increases during the tax year, so that they newly fail Condition C, the excluded days are the period before Condition C ceases to be met (ITTOIA 2005, s. 863D(11)).

As noted above, an increase in the contribution includes the initial contribution or any deemed contribution that is to be made within two months of joining the partnership (ITTOIA 2005, s. 863D(12).

Legislation: ITTOIA 2005, s. 863D–863E

32-100   Date of contribution

The legislation came into force from 6 April 2014, despite still being debated by Parliament and not having been granted Royal Assent, which caused certain commercial difficulties. While this was, obviously, a one-off problem, HMRC accepted that it might take a short period of time for newly-appointed partners to arrange appropriate borrowing in order that they could make adequate capital contributions. As a result, the legislation permitted a three-month delay, so that contributions had to be made by 5 July 2014 (effectively a three-month transitional period).

For future contributions, Condition C takes into account contributions that will be made within two months of being appointed a member of the LLP. To qualify for this favourable treatment, the member must have given an undertaking (although not necessarily a legally enforceable one) to make the contribution (ITTOIA 2005, s. 863F(1)). In such cases, that person is effectively treated as having made the contribution for the purposes of Condition C, even if they have not. But this treatment only subsists during that two-month period (ITTOIA 2005, s. 863F(2)).

If the person makes the contribution during the relevant period, Condition C does not have to be reconsidered (ITTOIA 2005, s. 863F(3)). If the whole or any part of the contribution is not made within the relevant period, Condition C is to be reviewed, from the beginning of the relevant time, i.e. the tax year or from when the person became a member, on the basis that the contribution has not been made, or has only been partly made.

This could therefore lead to the position that, the person intended to make a contribution but was unable to do so, so that Condition C is retrospectively seen to have been met. It is to be hoped that this situation does not occur in practice, as it would presumably mean that, for example, if Conditions A and B were also met, it would be the case that the company should, retrospectively, have been operating

PAYE for that two-month period. This might be relatively easily rectified but could give rise to penalties on the company.

Legislation: ITTOIA 2005, s. 863F

32-120 Anti-avoidance

There are three anti-avoidance rules within the salaried members legislation. Each of them refers to arrangements of one type or another. In each case, the word arrangements includes any agreement, understanding, scheme, transaction or series of transactions (whether or not legally enforceable) (ITTOIA 2005, s. 863G(5)).

General anti-avoidance provision

The first anti-avoidance rule is to disregard any arrangements which have their main purpose, or one of their main purposes, securing that the salaried members rules do not apply to one or more individuals who are members of the LLP (ITTOIA 2005, s. 863G(1)). This is a very sweeping anti-avoidance rule, but HMRC accept that arrangements intended to ensure that the individual or individuals become, in effect, genuine partners, will not trigger the anti-avoidance legislation. In other words, if people change their behaviours in a way which HMRC consider to be appropriate, this will be accepted. What HMRC are concerned with is artificial arrangements designed to get around the legislation, without changing the partner's commercial or financial status vis-à-vis the LLP itself or the other members.

Anti-avoidance for non-individual members

This legislation only applies to individuals who are members of an LLP. So there is another anti-avoidance provision, similar to that for the mixed member partnership rules, to prevent a person sidestepping the salaried member rules by operating through a corporate or other non-individual member of the partnership, and not being a member of the partnership themselves (ITTOIA 2005, s. 863G(2)–(4)).

Essentially, this rule applies if an individual performs services for an LLP but is not a member of that LLP, and the arrangements under which the services are performed involve a member of the LLP that is not an individual, with the intention (i.e. the main purpose or one of the main purposes) of ensuring that the salaried member rules do not apply, then this rule takes effect. There must also be a sum of money arising to the non individual which would have arisen directly to the individual, had that person been a member of the partnership, and would then have been treated as employment income under the main rule.

If this rule applies, then the amounts concerned are deemed to arise directly to the individual as employment income under the main rule, and is not to be treated as the income of the individual on any other income tax basis (for example, as distributions from a corporate member).

Precedence of mixed membership rules

The salaried member legislation does not apply where an individual would otherwise be a salaried member because of arrangements that have a main purpose of securing that the mixed membership partnership legislation does not apply (ITTOIA 2005, s. 863G(4A)). In essence, this seems to prioritise the mixed membership rules. HMRC's guidance does not provide any examples.

Example 1

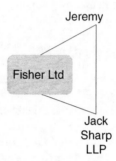

Jeremy

Fisher Ltd

Jack
Sharp
LLP

Example 1

Suppose Jeremy were to fix his profit share at £200,000, at a time when Jack Sharp LLP is making £500,000 a year profit. This would *prima facie* bring him into the salaried members regime, and the LLP would have to treat him as an employee. But in that case, he cannot be treated as an individual who is a member of a mixed membership partnership, because he cannot be both an employee and a partner. So the other £300,000 profits would flow to Fisher Ltd and the mixed member rules would not apply.

Thus ITTOIA 2005, s. 863G(4A) prevents the salaried members regime from applying, so that the mixed member rules can apply, instead.

Legislation: ITTOIA 2005, s. 863G

32-140   Consequential provisions

Deductions

The relevant rules for deductions are amended to permit deductions for the expenses paid by the partnership in respect of a salaried member's deemed employment under these rules. In other words, if a statutory deduction in respect of deemed salary, income and NICs was not available, the rules have been changed to make sure that those amounts are deductible.

For trading profits, the new rules are at ITTOIA 2005, s. 94AA, for income tax payers and at CTA 2009, s. 92A, for corporation tax payers (see ¶18-460). For the profits of a property business, there are appropriate amendments to ITTOIA 2005, s. 272, for income tax payers, and to CTA 2009, s. 210, for corporation tax payers.

Finally, the rules for companies with an investment business, are amended in relation to their management expenses by the insertion of CTA 2009, s. 1227A, so that the management expenses are treated as referable to the accounting period in which they are paid.

Returns

A salaried member is treated as an employee of the partnership, not as a member, so they are not included in the partnership return. Obviously, if they become a salaried member during a period, or cease to be one, their details will need to be included in the return, as if they had joined or left the partnership, as appropriate.

Commencement

The rules apply from 6 April 2014, except for ITTOIA 2005, s. 863G(4A) (see ¶32-120), which came into force on 13 July 2014, when *Finance Act* 2014 received Royal Assent.

Legislation: ITTOIA 2005, s. 94AA, 272; CTA 2009, s. 92A, 210, 1227A

32-160   Solutions

In smaller partnerships it might well be possible to adjust the profit-sharing arrangements within a partnership, particularly in marginal cases. So if a member of an LLP was likely to receive fixed remuneration as, say 85% of her total package, this figure could be adjusted down to, say, 75%, with 25% based on the total partnership profits. This level of restructuring would probably be more difficult with larger partnerships. Having said that, it is understood that one of the larger accountancy firms did, in fact, completely change its remuneration structure in order to ensure that all of its partners failed condition A!

In general terms, HMRC will accept that a small- to medium-sized partnership will fail Condition B in respect of all of its members. Conversely, it is understood that they consider the majority of partners in the larger professional partnership to satisfy Condition B and it would be virtually impossible to change that. The difficulty, of course, lies in understanding where the dividing line is between HMRC's example with ten partners, and a partnership with, say, 100 partners. The important issue will be to ensure that, if the members of the LLP genuinely all have the appropriate level of influence, that this is properly documented, both in terms of their contractual arrangements with the LLP and in terms of their actually being able to wield that influence, where appropriate. It will only be in relatively marginal cases where the partnership governance arrangements will be such that they can be changed in order to fail Condition B.

It is understood that Condition C has been the area of most activity, particularly with the larger professional partnerships. It is further a 'well known fact' that those LLPs have required their more junior members, i.e. the non-equity partners who do not share in the overall profits of the firm sufficiently, to make a greater permanent contribution to the partnership, in order to fail Condition C. This would also be a perfectly feasible solution for smaller partnerships, of course, although, practically, the majority of smaller partnerships are likely to fail Condition A and so are far less likely to be the target of these new rules.

APPENDICES

Appendix 1: SP D11 Partnership: assets owned by a partner

[British Tax Review 1974, p. 409]

Provided the other conditions of Sections 152–158 TCGA 1992 (Sections 115–121 CGTA 1979) are satisfied, relief is available to the owner of assets which are let to a trading or professional partnership of which he is a member and which are used for the purposes of the partnership trade or profession.

Notes

The text of SP D11 above is as it appears in HMRC's Statements of Practice as published on 30 January 2012.

Appendix 2: SP D12 Partnerships

[14 September 2015]

This statement of practice was originally issued by HM Revenue and Customs (HMRC) (previously Inland Revenue) on 17 January 1975 following discussions with the Law Society and the Allied Accountancy Bodies on the Capital Gains Tax (CGT) treatment of partnerships. This statement sets out a number of points of general practice which have been agreed in respect of partnerships to which TCGA92/S59 applies.

The enactment of the Limited Liability Partnership Act 2000 created, from April 2001, the concept of limited liability partnerships (as bodies corporate) in UK law. In conjunction with this, new CGT provisions dealing with such partnerships were introduced through TCGA92/S59A. TCGA92/S59A(1) complements TCGA92/S59 in treating any dealings in chargeable assets by a limited liability partnership as dealings by the individual members, as partners, for CGT purposes. Each member of a limited liability partnership to which TCGA92/S59A(1) applies has therefore to be regarded, like a partner in any other (non-corporate) partnership, as owning a fractional share of each of the partnership assets and not an interest in the partnership itself.

This statement of practice was therefore extended to limited liability partnerships which meet the requirements of TCGA92/S59A(1), so that capital gains of a limited liability partnership fall to be charged on its members as partners. Accordingly, in the text of the statement of practice, all references to a "partnership" or "firm" include reference to limited liability partnerships to which TCGA92/S59A(1) applies, and all references to «partner" include reference to a member of a limited liability partnership to which TCGA92/S59A(1) applies.

For the avoidance of doubt, this statement of practice does not apply to the members of a limited liability partnership which ceases to be "fiscally transparent" by reason of its not being, or it no longer being, within TCGA92/S59A(1).

In Budget 2013 the Government asked the Office of Tax Simplification (OTS) to carry out a review of ways to simplify the taxation of partnerships. The OTS published its interim report in January 2014 and its final report in January 2015. OTS concluded that as Statement of Practice D12 provides a reasonable result in most circumstances, it should be left essentially as it is, but that some text should be rewritten to replace out of date language and to replace some content which was obsolete. The recommendations made by OTS have been implemented in this revision of the statement of practice.

1. Valuation of a partner's share in a partnership asset

1.1.   Where it is necessary to determine the market value of a partner's share in a partnership asset for CGT purposes, it will be taken as a fraction of the value of the total partnership interest in the asset without any discount for the size of his share. If, for example, a partnership owned all the issued shares in a company, the value of the interest in that holding of a partner with a one-tenth share would be one-tenth of the value of the partnership's 100% holding.

1.2.   Guidance and an example concerning section 1 are available in HMRC's Capital Gains Manual at CG27250 (http://www.hmrc.gov.uk/manuals/cgmanual/cg27250. htm).

2. Disposals of assets by a partnership

2.1.   Where an asset is disposed of by a partnership to an outside party, each of the partners will be treated as disposing of his fractional share of the asset. In computing gains or losses the proceeds of disposal will be allocated between the partners in the ratio of their share in asset surpluses at the time of disposal. Where this is not specifically laid down, the allocation will follow the actual destination of the surplus as shown in the partnership accounts; regard will of course have to be paid to any agreement outside the accounts.

2.2.   If the surplus is not allocated among the partners but, for example, put to a common reserve, regard will be had to the ordinary profit sharing ratio, which is likely to be indicative in the absence of a specified asset-surplus-sharing ratio.

2.3.   Expenditure on the acquisition of assets by a partnership will be allocated between the partners according to the same principles at the time of the acquisition. This allocation may require adjustment if there is a subsequent change in the partnership sharing ratios see (section 4).

2.4.   Guidance and an example concerning section 2 are available in HMRC's Capital Gains Manual at CG27350 (http://www.hmrc.gov.uk/manuals/cgmanual/ CG27350.htm).

3. Partnership assets divided in kind among the partners

3.1.   Where a partnership distributes an asset in kind to one or more of the partners, for example on dissolution, a partner who receives the asset will not be regarded as disposing of his fractional share in it. A computation will first be necessary of the gains which would be chargeable on the individual partners if the asset had been disposed of at its current market value.

3.2. Where this results in a gain being attributed to a partner not receiving the asset, the gain will be charged at the time of the distribution of the asset. Where, however, a gain is attributed to a partner receiving the asset concerned there will be no charge on distribution. Instead, the gain is effectively deferred by reducing his CGT cost by the amount of his gain: the cost to be carried forward will be the market value of the asset at the date of distribution less the amount of gain attributed to him. The same principles will be applied where the computation results in a loss.

3.3. Guidance and an example concerning section 3 are available in HMRC's Capital Gains Manual at CG27400 (http://www.hmrc.gov.uk/manuals/cgmanual/CG27400.htm).

4. Changes in partnership sharing ratios

4.1. An occasion of charge also arises when there is a change in partnership sharing ratios, including changes arising from a partner joining or leaving the partnership. In these circumstances a partner who reduces or gives up his share in asset surpluses will be treated as disposing of part of the whole of his share in each of the partnership assets and a partner who increases his share will be treated as making a similar acquisition. Subject to the qualifications mentioned at sections 7] and section 8 below, the disposal consideration will be a fraction (equal to the fractional share changing hands) of the current balance sheet value of each chargeable asset, provided there is no direct payment of consideration outside the partnership.

4.2. In certain circumstances the calculation of the disposal consideration by reference to the current balance sheet value of the asset will produce neither a gain nor a loss. This will occur where the disposal consideration is equal to the allowable acquisition costs and is likely to arise where the partners' Capital Gains (CG) base costs are based on an amount equal to the balance sheet value of the asset. However, this outcome is unlikely to arise on a change in sharing ratios where, for example, an asset has been revalued in the partnership accounts, or where a partner transferred an asset to the partnership for an amount that is not equivalent to the CG base cost, or where the partners' CG base costs were determined in accordance with S171 TCGA 1992, rather than on the cost of the asset to the partnership.

4.3. A partner whose share in a partnership asset reduces will carry forward a smaller proportion of cost to set against a subsequent disposal of his share in the asset and a partner whose share increases will carry forward a larger proportion of cost.

4.4. The general rules in TCGA92/S42 for apportioning the total acquisition cost on a part-disposal of an asset will not be applied in the case of a partner reducing his asset-surplus share. Instead, the cost of the part disposed of will be calculated on a fractional basis.

4.5. Guidance and an example concerning section 4 are available in HMRC's Capital Gains Manual at CG27500 (http://www.hmrc.gov.uk/manuals/cgmanual/CG27500.htm) and CG27540 (http://www.hmrc.gov.uk/manuals/cgmanual/CG27540.htm).

5. Contribution of an asset to a partnership

5.1. When this statement of practice was published in 1975 it did not address the situation where a partner contributes an asset to a partnership by means of a capital contribution. HMRC clarified its approach to this in Revenue & Customs Brief 03/08. OTS asked HMRC to include this clarification in the statement of practice.

5.2. Where an asset is transferred to a partnership by means of a capital contribution, the partner in question has made a part disposal of the asset equal to the fractional share that passes to the other partners. The market value rule applies if the transfer is between connected persons or is other than by a bargain at arm's length. Otherwise the consideration for the part disposal will be a proportion of the total amount given by the partnership for the asset. That proportion equals the fractional share of the asset passing to the other partners.

5.3. A sum credited to the partner's capital account represents consideration for the disposal of the asset to the partnership. Although this is similar to a change in partnership sharing ratios, it is not possible to calculate the disposal consideration on a capital contribution by reference to section 4, as the asset does not have a balance sheet value in the partnership accounts. In these circumstances HMRC accepts the apportionment of allowable costs on a fractional basis as provided for in section 4, rather than by reference to the statutory A/A+B formula.

5.4. A gain arises on a contribution of an asset where the disposal consideration, calculated according to the fractional proportion of the total consideration or, in appropriate cases, a proportion of the market value of the asset, exceeds the allowable costs, based on a fraction of the partner's capital gains base cost.

5.5. Guidance and examples concerning section 5 are available in HMRC's Capital Gains Manual at CG27900 (http://www.hmrc.gov.uk/manuals/cgmanual/CG27900.htm) onwards.

6. Adjustment through the accounts

6.1.   Where a partnership asset is revalued a partner will be credited in his current or capital account with a sum equal to his fractional share of the increase in value. An upward revaluation of chargeable assets is not itself an occasion of charge.

6.2.   If, however, there were to be a subsequent reduction in the partner's asset-surplus share, the effect would be to reduce his potential liability to CGT on the eventual disposal of the assets, without an equivalent reduction of the credit he has received in the accounts. Consequently at the time of the reduction in sharing ratio he will be regarded as disposing of the fractional share of the partnership asset, represented by the difference between his old and his new share, for a consideration equal to that fraction of the increased value at the revaluation. The partner whose share correspondingly increases will have his acquisition cost to be carried forward for the asset increased by the same amount. The same principles will be applied in the case of a downward revaluation.

6.3.   Guidance and an example concerning section 6 are available in HMRC's Capital Gains Manual at CG27500 (http://www.hmrc.gov.uk/manuals/cgmanual/CG27500.htm) and CG27550 (http://www.hmrc.gov.uk/manuals/cgmanual/CG27550.htm).

7. Payments outside the accounts

7.1.   Where on a change of partnership sharing ratios, payments are made directly between two or more partners outside the framework of the partnership accounts, the payments represent consideration for the disposal of the whole or part of a partner's share in partnership assets in addition to any consideration calculated on the basis described in section 4 and section 6 above. Often such payments will be for goodwill not included in the balance sheet.

7.2.   The partner receiving the payment will have no CGT cost to set against it, unless he made a similar payment for his share in the asset (for example, on entering the partnership).

7.3.   The partner making the payment will only be allowed to deduct the amount in computing gains or losses on a subsequent disposal of his share in the asset. He will be able to claim a loss when he finally leaves the partnership, or when his share is reduced, provided that he then receives either no consideration or a lesser consideration for his share of the asset.

7.4.   Where the payment clearly constitutes payment for a share in assets included in the partnership accounts, the partner receiving it will be able to deduct the amount of the partnership acquisition cost represented by the fraction he disposes of. Special treatment, as outlined in section 8 below, may be necessary for transfers between persons not at arm's length.

7.5. Guidance and an example concerning section 7 are available in HMRCs Capital Gains Manual at CG27500 (http://www.hmrc.gov.uk/manuals/cgmanual/CG27500.htm) and CG27560 (http://www.hmrc.gov.uk/manuals/cgmanual/CG27560.htm).

8. Transfers between persons not at arm's length

8.1. Where no payment is made either through or outside the accounts in connection with a change in partnership sharing ratio, a CGT charge will only arise if the transaction is otherwise than by way of a bargain made at arm's length and falls therefore within TCGA92/S17, extended by TCGA92/S18 for transactions between connected persons.

8.2. Under TCGA92/S286(4) transfers of partnership assets between partners are not regarded as transactions between connected persons if they are genuine commercial arrangements. This treatment will also be given to transactions between an incoming partner and the existing partners.

8.3. Where the partners (including incoming partners) are connected other than by partnership (for example, father and daughter) or are otherwise not at arm's length (for example, aunt and nephew) the transfer of a share in the partnership assets may be treated as having been made at market value. Market value will not be substituted, however, if nothing would have been paid had the parties been at arm's length.

8.4. Similarly if consideration of less than market value passes between partners connected other than by partnership or otherwise not at arm's length, the transfer will only be regarded as having been made for full market value if the consideration actually paid was less than that which would have been paid by parties at arm's length. Where a transfer has to be treated as if it had taken place for market value, the deemed disposal will fall to be treated in the same way as payments outside the accounts.

8.5. Guidance and examples concerning section 8 are available in HMRC's Capital Gains Manual at CG27800 (http://www.hmrc.gov.uk/manuals/cgmanual/CG27800.htm) and CG27840 (http://www.hmrc.gov.uk/manuals/cgmanual/CG27840.htm).

9. Annuities provided by partnerships

9.1. A lump sum which is paid to a partner on leaving the partnership or on a reduction of his share in the partnership represents consideration for the disposal by the partner concerned of the whole or part of his share in the partnership assets and will be subject to the rules in section 7 above. The same treatment will apply when a partnership buys a purchased life annuity for a partner, the measure of the consideration being the actual costs of the annuity.

9.2. Where a partnership makes annual payments to a retired partner (whether under covenant or not) the capitalised value of the annuity will only be treated as consideration for the disposal of his share in the partnership assets under TCGA92/S37(3), if it is more than can be regarded as a reasonable recognition of the past contribution of work and effort by the partner to the partnership.

9.3. Provided that the former partner had been in the partnership for at least ten years, an annuity will be regarded as reasonable for this purpose if it is no more than two-thirds of his average share of the profits in the best three of the last seven years in which he was required to devote substantially the whole of this time to acting as a partner. In arriving at a partner's share of the profits the partnership profits assessed before deduction of any capital allowances or charges will be taken into account. The ten-year period will include any period during which the partner was a member of another firm whose business has been merged with that of the present firm. For lesser periods the following fractions will be used instead of two-thirds:

Complete years in partnership	Fraction
1 – 5	1/60 for each year
6	8/60
7	16/60
8	24/60
9	32/60

9.4. Where the capitalised value of an annuity is treated as consideration received by the retired partner, it will also be regarded as allowable expenditure by the remaining partners on the acquisition of their fractional shares in partnership assets from him.

9.5. Guidance concerning section 9 is available in HMRC's Capital Gains Manual at CG28400 (http://www.hmrc.gov.uk/manuals/cgmanual/CG28400.htm).

10. Mergers

10.1. Where the members of two or more existing partnerships come together to form a new one, the CGT treatment will follow the same principles as those for changes in partnership sharing ratios. If gains arise for reasons similar to those covered in section 6 and section 7 above, it may be possible for roll-over relief under TCGA92/S152 to be claimed by any partner continuing in the partnership, insofar as he disposes of part of his share in the assets of the old firm and acquires a share in other assets put into the merged firm. Where, however, the consideration given for the shares in chargeable assets acquired is less than the consideration for those disposed of, relief will be restricted under TCGA92/S153.

10.2. Guidance and an example concerning section 10 are available in HMRC's Capital Gains Manual at CG27700 (http://www.hmrc.gov.uk/manuals/cgmanual/CG27700.htm) and CG27740 (http://www.hmrc.gov.uk/manuals/cgmanual/CG27740.htm).

11. Shares acquired in stages

11.1. Where a share in a partnership is acquired in stages wholly after 5 April 1965, the acquisition costs of the various chargeable assets will be calculated by pooling the expenditure relating to each asset. Where a share built up in stages was acquired wholly or partly before 6 April 1965 the rules in TCGA92/Sch2/Para18, will normally be followed to identify the acquisition cost of the share in each asset which is disposed of on the occasion of a reduction in the partnership's share; that is, the disposal will normally be identified with shares acquired on a "first in, first out" basis.

11.2. HMRC will be prepared to review any case in which this principle appears to produce an unreasonable result when applied to temporary changes in the shares in a partnership, for example those occurring when a partner's departure and a new partner's arrival are out of step by a few months.

11.3. Guidance and an example concerning section 11 are available in HMRC's Capital Gains Manual at CG27300 (http://www.hmrc.gov.uk/manuals/cgmanual/CG27300.htm).

12. Elections under TCGA92 Schedule 2, paragraph 4

12.1. Where the assets disposed of are quoted securities eligible for a pooling election under paragraph 4 of TCGA92/Sch2, partners will be allowed to make separate elections in respect of shares or fixed interest securities held by the partnership as distinct from shares and securities which they hold on a personal basis.

12.2. Each partner will have a separate right of election for his proportion of the partnership securities and the time limit for the purposes of Schedule 2 will run from the earlier of:

- the first relevant disposal of shares or securities by the partnership
- the first reduction of the particular partner's share in the partnership assets after 19 March 1968

13. Partnership goodwill

13.1. This paragraph applies where the value of goodwill which a partnership generates in the conduct of its business is not recognised in its balance sheet and where, as a matter of consistent practice, no value is placed on that goodwill in dealings between the partners.

13.2. On a disposal for actual consideration of a partner's interest in the goodwill of such a partnership, that interest will be treated as the same asset (or, in the case of a part disposal, a part of the same asset) as was originally acquired by that partner when first becoming entitled to a share in the goodwill of that partnership.

13.3. This treatment will also be applied to goodwill acquired for consideration by a partnership but which is not, at any time, recognised in the partnership balance sheet at a value exceeding its cost of acquisition nor otherwise taken into account in dealings between partners.

14. Entrepreneurs' relief on transfer of a business, "roll-over" relief and business asset gift relief

14.1. An individual may qualify for entrepreneurs' relief (TCGA92/S169H) when their business becomes a partnership. A partner may also qualify for entrepreneurs' relief on a disposal of part or the whole of a partnership business.

14.2. A partner may qualify for entrepreneurs' relief (subject to the normal conditions relating eg to a personal company) when he or she disposes of all or part of a fractional share in shares which are held as partnership assets.

14.3. Guidance concerning partnerships and entrepreneurs' relief is available in HMRC's Capital Gains Manual at CG64040 (http://www.hmrc.gov.uk/manuals/cgmanual/CG64040.htm).

14.4. Roll-over relief is available to individuals who are partners where the whole of the partnership business is transferred to a company as a going concern in exchange for shares.

14.5.   Guidance concerning partnerships and roll-over relief on transfer of a business is available in HMRC's Capital Gains Manual at CG65700 (http://www.hmrc. gov.uk/manuals/cgmanual/CG65700.htm).

14.6.   Roll-over relief may also be available to partners when there is a disposal of a partnership asset and the proceeds are reinvested in another asset which is also used for trade purposes. Guidance covering this business asset roll-over relief is available in HMRC's Capital Gains Manual at CG61150 (http://www.hmrc. gov.uk/manuals/cgmanual/CG61150.htm).

14.7.   Relief for gifts of business assets (TCGA92/S165) is available to individual partners in partnerships which are treated as "transparent" for tax purposes when they dispose of a share in partnership assets, subject to the normal conditions.

14.8.   Relief for gifts of business assets is also available, subject to the normal conditions, to individuals who dispose of personal assets to a partnership. For tax purposes, the transferee is treated as making disposals to each of the partners who are treated as acquiring a share in the assets.

14.9.   Guidance concerning "gift hold-over relief" is available in HMRC's Capital Gains Manual at CG66910 (http://www.hmrc.gov.uk/manuals/cgmanual/ CG66910.htm).

Appendix 3: SP 1/79 Partnerships: extension of Statement of Practice D12

[12 January 1979]

Paragraph 8 of SP/D12 explains the circumstances in which the capitalised value of an annuity paid by a partnership to a retired partner will not be treated as consideration for the disposal of his share in the partnership assets. The Commissioners for Her Majesty's Revenue and Customs have now agreed that this practice will be extended to certain cases in which a lump sum is paid in addition to an annuity. Where the aggregate of the annuity and one-ninth of the lump sum does not exceed the appropriate fraction (as indicated in the Statement) of the retired partner's average share of the profits, the capitalised value of the annuity will not be treated as consideration in the hands of the retired partner. The lump sum, however, will continue to be so treated.

This extension of the practice will be applied to all cases in which the liability has not been finally determined at the date of this Notice.

See also SP 1/89.

Cross references

SP D12: partnerships.

SP 1/89: further extension of SP D12.

Notes

The text of SP 1/79 above is as it appears in HMRC's Statements of Practice as published on 30 January 2012.

Appendix 4: SP 1/89 Partnerships: Further Extension of Statement of Practice D12

[1 February 1989]

Rebasing

The Commissioners for Her Majesty's Revenue and Customs have agreed that a disposal of a share of partnership assets to which paragraph 4 of the Statement of Practice D12 applies so that neither a chargeable gain nor an allowable loss accrues (before indexation, for disposals before 6 April 1988,) may be treated for the purposes of Section 35 and Schedule 3 TCGA 1992 (Section 96 and Schedule 8 FA 1988) as if it were a no gain/no loss disposal within paragraph 1 of that Schedule.

Deferred Charges

A disposal of a share of partnership assets to which paragraph 4 of the Statement of Practice D12 applies so that neither a chargeable gain nor an allowable loss accrues (before indexation, for disposals before 6 April 1988,) may be treated for the purposes of Section 36 and Schedule 4 TCGA 1992 (Section 97 and Schedule 9 FA 1988) as if it were a no gain/no loss disposal within paragraph 1 of Schedule 3 TCGA 1992.

Indexation

When, on or after 6 April 1988, a partner disposes of all or part of his share of partnership assets in circumstances to which paragraph 4 of the Statement of Practice D12 applies so that neither a chargeable gain nor an allowable loss accrues, the amount of the consideration will be calculated on the assumption that an unindexed gain will accrue to the transferor equal to the indexation allowance, so that after taking account of the indexation allowance, neither a gain nor a loss accrues.

Where a partner disposes on or after 6 April 1988 of all or part of his share of partnership assets, and he is treated by virtue of this Statement as having owned the share on 31 March 1982, the indexation allowance on the disposal may be computed as if he had acquired the share on 31 March 1982. A disposal of a share in a partnership asset on or after 31 March 1982 to which paragraph 4 of the Statement of Practice D12 applies so that neither a chargeable gain nor an allowable loss accrues may be treated for the purposes of Section 55(5) TCGA 1992 (Section 68(7) FA 1985) as if it were a no gain/no loss disposal within subsection 5 of that Section. A special rule will however apply where the share changed hands on or after 6 April 1985 (1 April in the case of an acquisition from a company) and before 6 April 1988:

in these circumstances the indexation allowance will be computed by reference to the 31 March 1982 value **but** from the date of the last disposal of the share before 6 April 1988.

Revenue interpretations

IRInt. 9: Capital gains tax — rebasing effect of election under TCGA 1992, s. 35(5).

Notes

The text of SP 1/89 above is as it appears in HMRC's Statements of Practice as published on 30 January 2012.

For changes to the availability of indexation allowances, see FA 1994, s. 93 and Sch. 12.

Appendix 5: HMRC Brief 03/08 Capital gains tax and corporation tax on chargeable gains: contribution of assets to a partnership

[HMRC Brief 03/08, 21 January 2008]

This Revenue and Customs Brief clarifies HMRC's practice in relation to the treatment for capital gains purposes of a contribution of an asset to a partnership.

Statement of Practice D12 (SoP D12) was published on 17 January 1975 following discussions with the Law Society and the allied accountancy bodies and sets out our understanding of how the legislation concerning the tax treatment of partnerships works in practice. It has been updated since 1975. It does not, however, deal with the situation where a partner contributes an asset to a partnership by means of a capital contribution.

We consider that, where an asset is transferred to a partnership by means of a capital contribution, the correct application of the capital gains legislation is that the partner in question has made a part disposal of the asset equal to the fractional share that passes to the other partners.

The market value rule would apply, if the transfer is between connected persons or the transaction is other than by way of a bargain made at arm's length, Otherwise, the consideration to be taken into account in computing the chargeable gain or loss on the part disposal will be a proportion of the total consideration given by the partnership for the asset. That proportion will be equal to the fractional share of the asset passing to the other partners. We take the view that a sum credited to the partner's capital account represents consideration for the disposal of the asset to the partnership.

Although the situation is similar in some respects to a change in partnership sharing ratios, it is not possible to calculate the disposal consideration on a capital contribution by reference to paragraph 4 of SoP D12, as the asset in question would not have a balance sheet value in the partnership accounts. It has been our practice, however, to accept the apportionment of allowable costs on a fractional basis as provided for in paragraph 4, rather than by reference to the statutory $A/A+B$ formula.

A gain will arise on a contribution of an asset where the disposal consideration, calculated by reference to a fractional proportion of the total consideration or, in appropriate cases, a proportion of the market value of the asset, exceeds the allowable costs based on a fraction of the partner's capital gain base costs.

It has been brought to our attention that in the past individual HMRC (previously Inland Revenue) officers may have erroneously applied paragraph 4 of SoP D12 more widely than was justified where an asset was contributed to a partnership. We apologise if this has resulted in a misunderstanding of our practice in this area. In our view these previous applications of SoP D12 were incorrect and inconsistent with statements made by other HMRC officers. We will consider ourselves bound by statements made in individual cases. In cases where we are not bound, including all future cases, the correct treatment as described above will be applied.

Appendix 6: HMRC Brief 09/09 Capital gains tax: rebasing rules Finance Act 2008 and Partnerships

[HMRC Brief 09/09, 20 March 2009]

Introduction

This Revenue & Customs Brief is about assets held by a partnership on 31 March 1982. Assets held on that date are subject to special rules (the "rebasing" rules) when working out capital gains and losses.

The changes to Capital Gains Tax in Finance Act (FA) 2008 amended the rebasing rules. The changes apply to disposals of assets from the start of the 2008–09 tax year (6 April 2008). The Brief explains how the rebasing rules apply for people who dispose of partnership assets or who change their share of partnership assets from 2008–09 onwards.

The Brief applies only to partners whose capital gains are subject to Capital Gains Tax. The changes in FA 2008 do not apply to Corporation Tax and companies liable to Corporation Tax on their gains are not affected.

Contents

The brief covers:

- Rebasing rules for disposals before 6 April 2008.
- Rebasing rules for disposals on or after 6 April 2008.
- Statement of Practice 1/89 (SP1/89).
- Appendix A: Examples for disposals before 6 April 2008.
- Appendix B: Examples for disposals on or after 6 April 2008.

Background

Partnerships, including Scottish partnerships, are treated as transparent for Capital Gains Tax purposes. This means that any gains or losses accruing on disposals of partnership assets are chargeable on the partners rather than on the partnership itself. Partners are treated for this purpose as owning fractional interests in each of the partnership's assets. Disposals occur when the partnership disposes of an asset or when a partner's interest in an asset is reduced.

Statement of Practice D12 (SP D12) explains how gains or losses accruing on disposals of interests in partnership assets are to be computed.

Section 6 and Schedule 2 FA 2008 make rebasing of cost to 31 March 1982 compulsory for assets held at that date. The changes have effect only for the purposes of Capital Gains Tax. They do not apply for the purposes of Corporation Tax on chargeable gains.

Rebasing rules for disposals before 6 April 2008

The rebasing provisions for disposals before 6 April 2008 applied in respect of disposals on or after 6 April 1988 of assets held on 31 March 1982.

Assets held at 31 March 1982 were treated as if they had been acquired at their market value on that date so that gains or losses relating to changes in value before that date were not taken into account for Capital Gains Tax purposes. This approach was modified by the kink test which allowed for a comparison of the gain or loss based on the market value of the asset on 31 March 1982 with the gain or loss based on the actual cost before 31 March 1982. The lower of the gains was chargeable to Capital Gains Tax or the lower of the losses was allowable. If one computation resulted in a gain and the other in a loss, the person making the disposal was treated as realising neither a gain nor a loss.

A person could opt out of the kink test by electing under section 35(5) Taxation of Chargeable Gains Act (TCGA) 1992 to have gains or losses computed as if all of their assets held on 31 March 1982 had been acquired at their market value on that date.

Section 35(7) TCGA 1992 required separate rebasing elections to be made by a person who held assets in more than one capacity. For example, an election made by an individual in respect of personal assets would not cover interests in partnership assets held by that individual in his or her capacity as a partner.

There were special rules for arriving at the expenditure allowable in computing the gain on the disposal of an asset which had been acquired since 31 March 1982 by way of a statutory "no gain/no loss transfer" (a disposal which is treated for Capital Gains Tax purposes as resulting in neither a gain nor a loss for the person making the disposal) or an unbroken series of such transfers. The gain was computed as if the person making the disposal had owned the asset at 31 March 1982.

Examples of how these rules applied in relation to disposals of interests in partnership assets are included in Appendix A to this Revenue & Customs Brief.

Rebasing rules for disposals on or after 6 April 2008

Section 6 and Schedule 2 FA 2008 apply in respect of disposals on or after 6 April 2008 of assets held at 31 March 1982.

Gains or losses arising on disposals on or after 6 April 2008 are computed as if the assets disposed of had been acquired at their market value on 31 March 1982. In effect, allowable expenditure is "rebased" to 31 March 1982 thus dispensing with the need for the kink test and rebasing elections.

The new section 35A TCGA 1992 applies where a person ("P") disposes of an asset on or after 6 April 2008 and:

- P acquired the asset after 31 March 1982 and before 6 April 2008 under a statutory no gain/no loss provision and
- any previous disposal and acquisition of the asset after 31 March 1982 was one to which a statutory no gain/no loss provision applied and
- rebasing under section 35(2) TCGA 1992 did not apply to the relevant disposal, that is, the disposal of the asset to P

Where these conditions are satisfied section 35A(2) TCGA 1992 provides that the allowable expenditure taken into account in computing a gain or loss when P disposes of the asset on or after 6 April 2008 includes the value of the asset at 31 March 1982 and the indexation allowance due for the period from 31 March 1982 to the month in which P acquired the asset or, if earlier, to April 1998. The previous approach of treating P as having owned the asset at 31 March 1982 with the appropriate consequences for indexation allowance no longer applies.

Examples of how these rules apply in relation to disposals of interests in partnership assets are included in Appendix B to this Revenue & Customs Brief.

Statement of Practice 1/89 (SP1/89)

SP1/89 explains HM Revenue & Customs (HMRC) practice in relation to rebasing and indexation allowance where a transfer between partners of an interest in an asset that was held by a partnership on 31 March 1982 results in neither a gain nor a loss.

It enables transfers between partners of interests in partnership assets that result in neither gains nor losses to be treated as statutory no gain/no loss transfers for the purposes of the rebasing rules in sections 35 and 36 and Schedule 4 TCGA 1992. Partners who dispose of interests in assets that had been acquired by them as a result of such transfers are treated as having held them on 31 March 1982.

SP1/89 provides that the disposal consideration for a transfer between partners of an interest in a partnership asset that results in neither a gain nor a loss may be calculated on the assumption that an unindexed gain will accrue to the transferor equal to the indexation allowance so that, after accounting for indexation allowance, neither a gain nor a loss accrues. Such a disposal may be treated as a statutory no gain/no loss disposal for the purposes of section 55(5) TCGA 1992.

For Capital Gains Tax purposes indexation allowance was frozen as at April 1998 and has been abolished for disposals on or after 6 April 2008.

For disposals of interests in partnership assets that occur on or after 6 April 2008 SP1/89 will apply only in relation to corporate partners whose capital gains are chargeable to Corporation Tax.

Disposals on or after 6 April 2008

HMRC's practice in relation to rebasing for disposals by non-corporate partners on or after 6 April 2008 will be consistent with the previous treatment under SP1/89. Transfers between partners of interests in partnership assets after 31 March 1982 and before 6 April 2008 that resulted in neither gains nor losses may be treated as statutory no gain/no loss transfers for the purposes of section 35A(1)(b) TCGA 1992.

Where section 35A(2) TCGA 1992 applies in relation to disposals on or after 6 April 2008 the allowable expenditure to be taken into consideration in the calculation of a gain or loss includes the value of the asset at 31 March 1982 and any indexation allowance for the period from 31 March 1982 to the month in which the person making the disposal acquired it or, if earlier, to April 1998.

The effect of SP1/89 in relation to disposals of interests in partnership assets before and on or after 6 April 2008 is considered in the examples in Appendices A and B.

Appendix A

Rebasing rules for disposals of interests in partnership assets before 6 April 2008

Example 1 – change in partnership sharing ratios – no rebasing election made by disposing partner

Facts

- A and B formed a partnership on 1 January 1980 sharing assets on a 50:50 basis.
- The partnership acquired an asset for use in its business on 1 March 1980 for £100,000.
- The market value of the asset on 31 March 1982 was £120,000.
- On 1 January 2000 C was admitted as a partner and the sharing ratios were changed to A 25 per cent: B 50 per cent: C 25 per cent.
- No payment was made by Partner C to Partner A in consideration for the transfer of a 25 per cent interest in the partnership asset.
- Throughout the period the asset was included in the partnership balance sheet at its original cost of £100,000.
- Partner A did not make a rebasing election in his capacity as a partner.
- Partner B has made a rebasing election in his capacity as a partner.
- The partnership disposed of the asset on 1 March 2004 for £660,000.

Analysis

1. Change in partnership sharing ratios on 1 January 2000

Partner A – capital gains computation for 1999–2000

Disposal consideration	
£100,000 × 25%	£25,000
+ Indexation allowance £120,000 × 25%	
£30,000 × 1.047	£31,410
	£56,410
Less cost £100,000 × 25%	£25,000
Unindexed gain	£31,410
Indexation allowance	£31,410
	NG/NL

Capital gain base cost for partner A

Partner A	£100,000 × 50% = £50,000 − £25,000 = £25,000

Capital gain base cost for partner B

The effect of the rebasing election made by partner B is that his Capital Gain base cost will be based on a proportion of the market value of the asset at 31 March 1982.

Partner B	£120,000 × 50% = £60,000

Partner C's acquisition cost

Partner C will be treated as having acquired his 25 per cent interest for £56,410 on 1 January 2000, a sum equal to the disposal consideration taken into account for partner A.

2. Subsequent disposal of the asset by the partnership on 1 March 2004

The partners will be treated as having disposed of their fractional interests in the asset when the partnership disposed of the asset on 1 March 2004.

In accordance with paragraph 2 of SP D12 the disposal consideration, £660,000, will be apportioned by reference to the partners' sharing ratios:

Partner A	£660,000 × 25% = £165,000
Partner B	£660,000 × 50% = £330,000
Partner C	£660,000 × 25% = £165,000

Partner A – capital gain computation for 2003–2004

Partner A did not make a rebasing election so the kink test will apply.

	Cost	market value 31.03.82
Disposal consideration	£165,000	£165,000
Less cost	£ 25,000	
Less market value 31.03.82		
£120,000 × 25%		£ 30,000
Unindexed gain	£140,000	£135,000
Indexation allowance		
£30,000 × 1.047	£ 31,410	£ 31,410
Indexed gain	£108,590	£103,590

The chargeable gain before taper relief is the lower of the two gains, £103,590.

The chargeable gain after business asset taper relief is £103,590 × 25% = £25,897.

Partners B and C – capital gain computations for 2003–2004

The effect of SP1/89 is that partner C's acquisition cost is adjusted under section 55(5) and (6) TCGA 1992 to £25,000 (£56,410 – £31,410) and he is treated as having held his interest in the partnership asset on 31 March 1982.

Partner C makes a rebasing election in his capacity as a partner.

	Partner B	Partner C
Disposal consideration	£330,000	£165,000
Less market value 31.03.82		
£120,000 × 50%/25%	£ 60,000	£ 30,000
Unindexed gain	£270,000	£135,000
Indexation allowance		
£60,000/£30,000 × 1.047	£ 62,820	£ 31,410
Indexed gain	£207,180	£103,590

Partner B's chargeable gain after business asset taper relief is £207,180 × 25% = £51,795.

Partner C's chargeable gain after taper relief is £103,590 × 25% = £25,897.

Example 2– change in partnership sharing ratios – rebasing election made by disposing partner

Facts

- A and B formed a partnership on 1 January 1980 sharing assets on a 50:50 basis.
- The partnership acquired an asset for use in its business on 1 March 1980 for £100,000.
- The market value of the asset on 31 March 1982 was £120,000.
- On 1 January 2000 C was admitted as a partner and the sharing ratios were changed to A 25 per cent: B 50 per cent: C 25 per cent.
- No payment was made by partner C to partner A in consideration for the transfer of a 25 per cent interest in the partnership asset.
- Throughout the period the asset was included in the partnership balance sheet at its original cost of £100,000.
- Partners A and B have made rebasing elections in their capacity as partners.
- The partnership disposed of the asset on 1 March 2004 for £660,000.

Analysis

1. Change in partnership sharing ratios on 1 January 2000

Partner A disposed of a 25 per cent interest in the asset to partner C on 1 January 2000.

In accordance with paragraph 4 of SP D12 the disposal consideration will be treated as 25 per cent of the current balance sheet value of the asset, £100,000 × 25 per cent = £25,000.

SP1/89 does not apply because the transfer is not one which results in neither a gain nor a loss.

Partner A – capital gain computation for 1999–2000

Disposal consideration	
£100,000 × 25%	£25,000
Less market value at 31 March 1982	
£120,000 × 25%	£30,000
Loss	£ 5,000

Capital gain base costs for partners A and B – rebasing elections apply

Partner A	£120,000 × 50% = £60,000 – £30,000 = £30,000
Partner B	£120,000 × 50% = £60,000

Partner C's acquisition cost

Partner C will be treated as having acquired his 25 per cent interest in the partnership asset for £25,000 on 1 January 2000, a sum equal to the disposal consideration taken into account for partner A.

2. Subsequent disposal of the asset by the partnership on 1 March 2004

The partners will be treated as having disposed of their fractional interests in the asset when the partnership disposed of the asset on 1 March 2004.

In accordance with paragraph 2 of SP D12 the disposal consideration, £660,000, will be apportioned by reference to the partners' sharing ratios:

Partner A	£660,000 × 25% = £165,000
Partner B	£660,000 × 50% = £330,000
Partner C	£660,000 × 25% = £165,000

Partners' capital gain computations for 2003–2004

	Partner A	Partner B	Partner C
Disposal consideration	£165,000	£330,000	£165,000
Less market value 31.03.82			
£120,000 × 25%/50%	£ 30,000	£ 60,000	
Less cost 01.01.00			£ 25,000
Unindexed gain	£135,000	£270,000	
Gain			£140,000
Indexation allowance			
£30,000/£60,000 × 1.047	£ 31,410	£ 62,820	
Indexed gain	£103,590	£207,180	

Partner C is not entitled to indexation allowance as he acquired his interest after 31 March 1998.

Chargeable gains after business asset taper relief:

Partner A	£103,590 × 25% = £25,897
Partner B	£207,180 × 25% = £51,795
Partner C	£140,000 × 25% = £35,000

Example 3 – change in partnership sharing ratios following revaluation of an asset in the partnership accounts – rebasing election made by disposing partner

Facts

- A and B formed a partnership on 1 January 1980 sharing assets on a 50:50 basis.
- The partnership acquired an asset for use in its business on 1 March 1980 for £100,000.
- The market value of the asset on 31 March 1982 was £120,000.
- On 1 December 1999 the asset was revalued in the partnership accounts to £480,000.
- On 1 January 2000 C was admitted as a partner and the sharing ratios were changed to A 25 per cent: B 50 per cent: C 25 per cent.
- No payment was made by Partner C to Partner A in consideration for the transfer of a 25 per cent interest in the partnership asset.
- Partner A and partner B have made rebasing elections in their capacity as partners.
- The partnership disposed of the asset on 1 March 2004 for £660,000.

Analysis

1. Change in partnership sharing ratios on 1 January 2000

Partner A disposed of a 25 per cent interest in the asset to partner C on 1 January 2000.

In accordance with paragraph 4 of SP D12 the disposal consideration will be treated as 25 per cent of the current balance sheet value of the asset, £480,000 × 25 per cent = £120,000.

SP1/89 does not apply because the transfer is not one which results in neither a gain nor a loss.

Partner A – capital gain computation for 1999–2000

Disposal consideration	
£480,000 × 25%	£120,000
Less market value at 31 March 1982	
£120,000 × 25%	£ 30,000

Unindexed gain	£ 90,000
Less indexation allowance	
£30,000 × 1.047	£ 31,410
Indexed gain	£ 58,590

The chargeable gain after taper relief is £58,590 × 85% = £49,801.

Capital gain base costs for partners A and B – rebasing elections apply

Partner A	£120,000 × 50% = £60,000 − £30,000 = £30,000
Partner B	£120,000 × 50% = £60,000

Partner C's acquisition cost

Partner C will be treated as having acquired his 25 per cent interest in the partnership asset for £120,000 on 1 January 2000, a sum equal to the disposal consideration taken into account for Partner A.

2. Subsequent disposal of the asset by the partnership on 1 March 2004

The partners will be treated as having disposed of their fractional interests in the asset when the partnership disposed of the asset on 1 March 2004.

In accordance with paragraph 2 of SP D12 the disposal consideration, £660,000, will be apportioned by reference to the partners' sharing ratios:

Partner A	£660,000 × 25% = £165,000
Partner B	£660,000 × 50% = £330,000
Partner C	£660,000 × 25% = £165,000

Partners' capital gain computations for 2003–2004

	Partner A	Partner B	Partner C
Disposal consideration	£165,000	£330,000	£165,000
Less market value 31.03.82			
£120,000 × 25%/50%	£ 30,000	£ 60,000	
Less cost 01.01.00			£ 120,000
Unindexed gain	£135,000	£270,000	

Gain			£45,000
Indexation allowance			
£30,000/£60,000 × 1.047	£ 31,410	£ 62,820	
Indexed gain	£103,590	£207,180	

Partner C is not entitled to indexation allowance as he acquired his interest after 31 March 1998.

Chargeable gains after business asset taper relief:

Partner A	£103,590 × 25% = £25,897
Partner B	£207,180 × 25% = £51,795
Partner C	£45,000 × 25% = £11,250

Appendix B

Rebasing rules for disposals of interests in partnership assets on or after 6 April 2008

Example 4 – change in partnership sharing ratios on or after 6 April 2008 – FA 2008 rebasing rules

Facts

- A and B formed a partnership on 1 January 1980 sharing assets on a 50:50 basis.
- The partnership acquired an asset for use in its business on 1 March 1980 for £100,000.
- The market value of the asset on 31 March 1982 was £120,000.
- On 1 June 2008 C was admitted as a partner and the sharing ratios were changed to A 25 per cent: B 50 per cent: C 25 per cent.
- No payment was made by partner C to partner A in consideration for the transfer of a 25 per cent interest in the partnership asset.
- Throughout the period the asset was included in the partnership balance sheet at its original cost of £100,000.
- The partnership disposed of the asset on 1 September 2009 for £660,000.

Analysis

1. Change in partnership sharing ratios on 1 June 2008

Partner A disposed of a 25 per cent interest in the asset to partner C on 1 June 2008.

In accordance with paragraph 4 of SP D12 the disposal consideration will be treated as 25 per cent of the current balance sheet value of the asset, £100,000 × 25 per cent = £25,000.

SP1/89 and the practice outlined in this Brief in relation to disposals on or after 6 April 2008 do not apply because the transfer is not one which results in neither a gain nor a loss.

Partner A – capital gain computation for 2008–09 – FA 2008 rebasing rules

Disposal consideration	
£100,000 × 25%	£25,000
Less market value 31.03.82	
£120,000 × 25%	£30,000
Loss	£ 5,000

Capital gain base costs for partners A and B – FA 2008 rebasing rules

Partner A	£120,000 × 50% = £60,000 – £30,000 = £30,000
Partner B	£120,000 × 50% = £60,000

Partner C's acquisition cost

Partner C will be treated as having acquired his 25 per cent interest in the partnership asset for £25,000 on 1 June 2008, a sum equal to the disposal consideration taken into account for partner A.

2. Subsequent disposal of the asset by the partnership on 1 September 2009

The partners will be treated as having disposed of their fractional interests in the asset when the partnership disposed of the asset on 1 September 2009.

In accordance with paragraph 2 of SP D12 the disposal consideration, £660,000, will be apportioned by reference to the partners' sharing ratios.

Partner A	£660,000 × 25% = £165,000
Partner B	£660,000 × 50% = £330,000
Partner C	£660,000 × 25% = £165,000

Partners' capital gain computations for 2009–2010

	Partner A	Partner B	Partner C
Disposal consideration	£165,000	£330,000	£165,000
Less market value 31.03.82			
£120,000 × 25%/50%	£ 30,000	£ 60,000	
Less cost			£ 25,000
Gains	£135,000	£270,000	£140,000

Example 5 – change in partnership sharing ratios before 6 April 2008 followed by disposal of asset on or after 6 April 2008 – s35A TCGA 1992

Facts

- A and B formed a partnership on 1 January 1980 sharing assets on a 50:50 basis.
- The partnership acquired an asset for use in its business on 1 March 1980 for £100,000.
- The market value of the asset on 31 March 1982 was £120,000.
- On 1 January 2000 C was admitted as a partner and the sharing ratios were changed to A 25 per cent: B 50 per cent: C 25 per cent.
- No payment was made by partner C to partner A in consideration for the transfer of a 25 per cent interest in the partnership asset.
- Throughout the period the asset was included in the partnership balance sheet at its original cost of £100,000.
- Partners A and B did not make rebasing elections in their capacity as partners.
- The partnership disposed of the asset on 1 March 2009 for £660,000.

Analysis

1.   Change in partnership sharing ratios on 1 January 2000

Partner A disposed of a 25 per cent interest in the asset to partner C on 1 January 2000.

In accordance with paragraph 4 of SP D12 the disposal consideration will be treated as 25 per cent of the current balance sheet value of the asset, £100,000 × 25 per cent = £25,000.

As the disposal would result in neither a gain nor a loss SP1/89 applies to treat the transfer as a statutory no gain/no loss disposal. Therefore, rebasing does not apply in accordance with section 35(3)(d) TCGA 1992.

The effect of SP1/89 is that the disposal consideration under paragraph 4 SP D12 is adjusted so that after accounting for indexation allowance neither a gain nor a loss accrues.

Partner A – capital gain computation for 1999–2000

Disposal consideration 25%	
£100,000 × 25%	£25,000
+ Indexation allowance £120,000 × 25%	
£30,000 × 1.047	£31,410
	£56,410
Less cost £100,000 × 25%	£25,000
Unindexed gain	£31,410
Indexation allowance	£31,410
	NG/NL

Capital gain base costs for partners A and B

Partner A	£100,000 × 50% = £50,000 − £25,000 = £25,000
Partner B	£100,000 × 50% = £50,000

Partner C's acquisition cost

Partner C will be treated as having acquired his 25 per cent interest in the partnership asset for £56,410 on 1 January 2000, a sum equal to the disposal consideration taken into account for partner A.

2. Subsequent disposal of the asset by the partnership on 1 March 2009

The partners will be treated as having disposed of their fractional interests in the asset when the partnership disposed of the asset on 1 March 2009.

In accordance with paragraph 2 of SP D12 the disposal consideration, £660,000, will be apportioned by reference to the partners' sharing ratios:

Partner A	£660,000 × 25% = £165,000
Partner B	£660,000 × 50% = £330,000
Partner C	£660,000 × 25% = £165,000

Partners A and B – capital gain computations for 2008–2009 – FA 2008 rebasing rules

	Partner A	Partner B
Disposal consideration	£165,000	£330,000
Less market value 31.03.82		
£120,000 × 25%/50%	£ 30,000	£ 60,000
Gains	£135,000	£270,000

Partner C – capital gain computation for 2008–09 – section 35A TCGA 1992

The effect of SP1/89 was to treat partner C as having acquired his 25 per cent interest on 1 January 2000 for £56,410, a sum based on 25 per cent of the original cost of the asset adjusted for indexation allowance.

The changes in FA 2008 which apply to disposals on or after 6 April 2008 mean that the previous rules are superseded with the result that Section 55(5) and (6) TCGA 1992 no longer apply to strip out indexation allowance from partner C's Capital Gain base cost.

Consistently with HMRC's practice as set out in SP1/89 the disposal by which partner C acquired his 25 per cent interest in the asset after 31 March 1982 and before 6 April 2008 may be treated as a statutory no gain/no loss disposal for the purposes of section 35A(1)(b) TCGA 1992.

The effect of section 35A TCGA 1992 is to treat partner C as having acquired his interest for a sum equal to 25 per cent of the market value of the asset on 31 March 1982 plus indexation allowance for the period 31 March 1982 to 1 January 2000:

£30,000 (£120,000 × 25%) + £31,410 (£30,000 × 1.047) = £61,410

	Partner C
Disposal consideration	£165,000
Less cost per s35A(2)	£ 61,410
Gain	£103,590

Example 6 – changes in partnership sharing ratios before and after 6 April 2008 followed by disposal of asset – s35A TCGA 1992

Facts

- A and B formed a partnership on 1 January 1980 sharing assets on a 50:50 basis.
- The partnership acquired an asset for use in its business on 1 March 1980 for £100,000.
- The market value of the asset on 31 March 1982 was £120,000.
- On 1 January 2000 C was admitted as a partner and the sharing ratios were changed to A 25 per cent: B 50 per cent: C 25 per cent.
- No payment was made by partner C to partner A in consideration for the transfer of a 25 per cent interest in the partnership asset.
- Throughout the period the asset was included in the partnership balance sheet at its original cost of £100,000.
- Partners A and B did not make rebasing elections in their capacity as partners.
- On 1 June 2008 D is admitted to the partnership and the sharing ratios become A 20 per cent: B 40 per cent: C 20 per cent: D 20 per cent.
- No payment was made by partner D to partners A, B and C in consideration for the transfer of a 20 per cent interest in the partnership asset.
- The partnership disposed of the asset on 1 May 2009 for £660,000.

Analysis

1. Change in partnership sharing ratios on 1 January 2000

Partner A disposed of a 25 per cent interest in the asset to partner C on 1 January 2000.

In accordance with paragraph 4 of SP D12 the disposal consideration will be treated as 25 per cent of the current balance sheet value of the asset, £100,000 × 25 per cent = £25,000.

As the disposal would result in neither a gain nor a loss SP1/89 applies to treat the transfer as a statutory no gain/no loss disposal. Therefore, rebasing does not apply in accordance with section 35(3)(d) TCGA 1992.

The effect of SP1/89 is that the disposal consideration under paragraph 4 SP D12 is adjusted so that after accounting for indexation allowance neither a gain nor a loss accrues.

Partner A – capital gain computation for 1999–2000

Disposal consideration	
£100,000 × 25%	£25,000
+ Indexation allowance £120,000 × 25%	
£30,000 × 1.047	£31,410
	£56,410
Less cost £100,000 × 25%	£25,000
Unindexed gain	£31,410
Indexation allowance	£31,410
	NG/NL

Capital gain base costs for partners A and B

Partner A	£100,000 × 50% = £50,000 − £25,000 = £25,000
Partner B	£100,000 × 50% = £50,000

Partner C's acquisition cost

Partner C will be treated as having acquired his 25 per cent interest in the partnership asset for £56,410 on 1 January 2000, a sum equal to the disposal consideration taken into account for partner A.

2. Change in partnership sharing ratios on 1 June 2008

Partners A, B and C disposed of part of their interests in the asset to partner D on 1 June 2008.

In accordance with paragraph 4 of SP D12 the disposal consideration will be treated as a proportion of the current balance sheet value of the asset.

Partner A	£100,000 × 5% = £ 5,000
Partner B	£100,000 × 10% = £10,000
Partner C	£100,000 × 5% = £ 5,000

Partners A and B – capital gain computations for 2008–2009 – FA 2008 rebasing rules

	Partner A	Partner B
Disposal consideration	£5,000	£10,000
Less market value 31.03.82		
£120,000 × 5%/10%	£6,000	£12,000
Losses	£1,000	£ 2,000

Partner C – capital gain computation for 2008–09 – section 35A TCGA 1992

The effect of SP1/89 was to treat partner C as having acquired his 25 per cent interest on 1 January 2000 for £56,410, a sum based on 25 per cent of the original cost of the asset adjusted for indexation allowance.

The changes in FA 2008 which apply to disposals on or after 6 April 2008 mean that the previous rules are superseded with the result that Section 55(5) and (6) TCGA 1992 no longer apply to strip out indexation allowance from partner C's Capital Gain base cost.

Consistently with HMRC's practice as set out in SP1/89 the disposal by which partner C acquired his 25 per cent interest in the asset after 31 March 1982 and before 6 April 2008 may be treated as a statutory no gain/no loss disposal for the purposes of section 35A(1)(b) TCGA 1992.

The effect of section 35A TCGA 1992 is to treat partner C as having acquired his interest for a sum equal to 25 per cent of the market value of the asset on 31 March 1982 plus indexation allowance for the period 31 March 1982 to 1 January 2000:

£30,000 (£120,000 × 25%) + £31,410 (£30,000 × 1.047) = £61,410

	Partner C
Disposal consideration	£5,000
Less cost per s35A(2)	
£61,410 × 5%/25%	£12,282
Loss	£ 7,282

Capital gain base costs for partners A, B and C

Partner A	£120,000 × 20% = £24,000
Partner B	£120,000 × 40% = £48,000
Partner C	£61,410 – £12,282 = £49,128

Partner D's capital gain base cost

Partner D will be treated as having acquired his 20 per cent interest in the asset for £20,000, a sum equal to the disposal consideration taken into account for partners A, B and C (£5,000 + £10,000 + £5,000).

3. Subsequent disposal of the asset by the partnership on 1 May 2009

The partners will be treated as having disposed of their fractional interests in the asset when the partnership disposed of the asset on 1 May 2009.

In accordance with paragraph 2 of SP D12 the disposal consideration will be apportioned by reference to the partners' sharing ratios:

Partner A	£660,000 × 20% = £132,000
Partner B	£660,000 × 40% = £264,000
Partner C	£660,000 × 20% = £132,000
Partner D	£660,000 × 20% = £132,000

Partners' capital gain computations for 2009–2010

	Partner A	Partner B	Partner C	Partner D
Disposal consideration	£132,000	£264,000	£132,000	£132,000
Less market value 31.03.82	£ 24,000	£ 48,000		
less cost (per s35A)			£ 49,128	
Less cost				£ 20,000
Gains	£108,000	£216,000	£ 82,872	£112,000

Appendix 7: ESC D23 Relief for the replacement of business assets: partition of land on the dissolution of a partnership

Where land used for the purposes of a trade carried on in partnership is partitioned by the partners, the land acquired is treated for the purposes of sections 152–158, TCGA 1992 as a "new asset" provided that the partnership is dissolved immediately thereafter. This concession also applies to other qualifying assets which are acquired on the partition.

Appendix 8: HMRC Salaried Member Rules

Partnerships: A review of two aspects of the tax rules

1 Overview

1.1 Tax treatment of Limited Liability Partnerships

Limited Liability Partnerships (LLPs) incorporated in the UK combine the organisational flexibility of traditional partnerships with the benefit of limited liability for their members. In law, they are corporate bodies with greater resemblance to limited companies than to traditional partnerships. Specific tax legislation exists to ensure that they are treated as partnerships for tax purposes, rather than as companies.

In particular, the rule at section 863 of Income Tax (Trading and Other Income) Act (ITTOIA) 2005 (which has been in place since 2001) provides that any individual LLP member is treated as self-employed for tax purposes, subject to income tax and Class 4 National Insurance contributions (NICs) on the partnership profit share. The rule was intended to treat LLP members in the same way as partners in traditional partnerships.

1.2 What is the issue?

In deeming all individual LLP members to be self-employed, the existing tax rules go further than simply aligning their status with that of individuals in a traditional partnership. An individual has to have the characteristics of a partner to be determined as such in a traditional partnership. However, in an LLP, an individual needs only be registered as a member.

Over the years, it has become evident that many LLPs have members who are engaged on terms similar to those of employees rather than traditional partners.

1.3 What do the new Salaried Member rules do?

Following consultation, legislation is being introduced in Finance Bill 2014 and will take effect from 6 April 2014 to address this inconsistency and to make the rules fairer across partnership types. This ensures that LLP members who are, in effect, providing services on terms similar to employment are treated as "employees" for tax purposes. The NICs Act 2014 and associated regulations provide for the changes to NICs legislation that will take effect from 6 April 2014.

1.4   *What do the new rules not do?*

The "Salaried Member" rules apply only to LLPs formed under United Kingdom legislation (the LLP Act 2000).

These rules do not apply to general partnerships or limited partnerships that are formed under Partnership Act 1890 and Limited Partnerships Act 1907 respectively.

In addition, they do not apply to entities outside the UK that have structures broadly equivalent to a UK LLP. The tax treatment in the UK of a foreign body akin to a UK LLP will depend on the nature of the entity. There are two categories for such entities:

- The first possibility is that the entity is a person distinct from the members, and that the entity rather than the individual member is liable for any debts owed. The UK model is an example of this structure. These are referred to as "*opaque*".
- The second is that the laws of the territory under which the entity is formed confer limited liability on its members if set conditions are met. These are referred to as "*transparent*".

These entities have different tax treatments:

- If the entity is *opaque,* it is treated in the same way as any other entity liable to Corporation Tax, with the members taxable as employees.
- If it is *transparent,* the first issue to consider is whether it is a partnership for the purposes of UK law. If it is, then those who are not employees on first principles will be taxable as partners on their appropriate share of the profits.

The Salaried Member rules are tax rules. They are independent of employment law and vice versa.

General partnerships, such as small husband-and-wife partnerships, are unaffected by the Salaried Member rules, which only apply to LLPs.

1.5   *The rules at a glance*

The new rules will treat an individual member (M) of an LLP as an "employee" for tax purposes **only if three conditions are all met** and M is therefore a Salaried Member.

Conditions A and C are applied prospectively. Provided that these tests are applied reasonably, they are not revisited with the benefit of hindsight if it is found that any of the assumptions were incorrect. *The exception is Condition C where a member has given an undertaking at 6 April 2014, or, if later, on becoming a member, that they will make a contribution, but fail to do so.*

The following paragraphs provide a summary of these conditions and Chapter 2 sets out the details and provides a range of examples and scenarios. .

1.5.1 Disguised Salary (Condition A)

This test is applied "looking forward" on the basis of the arrangement in force at the time that it is being determined whether the Condition is met.

Condition A is met where it is reasonable to expect that at least 80% of the total amount payable by the LLP for M's services in M's capacity as a member of the LLP will be "Disguised Salary".

An amount within the total amount is Disguised Salary if:

- it is fixed; or
- it is variable, but varied without reference to the overall amount of the profits or losses of the LLP; or
- it is not, in practice, affected by the overall profits or losses of the LLP.

A fixed amount is a predetermined sum which is not variable.

The second requirement is intended to ensure that Disguised Salary includes any reward for services determined without reference to the profits of the LLP.

The third requirement brings in potentially variable amounts that, for practical purposes, are highly unlikely to be affected by the profits of the LLP.

In some cases, LLPs pay their fixed share members though a "fixed profit share". For example, a number of junior LLP members each have a fixed profit share of £75,000 per annum. This fixed share is the first charge against profits. Based on historical and projected performance, this aggregate entitlement is a small percentage of the firm's overall profits.

The amount is not a fixed amount because, if the LLP makes insufficient profits, the junior members would receive less than £75,000. However, on the facts, absent a catastrophic event, the junior members will receive £75,000. It is therefore reasonable to expect that they will obtain a reward which will not in practice be affected by the overall level of profits.

It should be noted that HMRC does not regard payments made on account of an expected profit share as Disguised Salary. These sums are only contingently paid and will later be tallied with actual profits (so as to give rise either to a right to further profit or a debt owed to the firm). In such a case, the reward for services is a profit share (with the drawings being the means by which the profit is accessed).

1.5.2 Significant influence (Condition B)

This condition is met if the mutual rights and duties of the members and the LLP do not give M significant influence over the affairs of the LLP.

Here, the legislation is referring to those individuals who do not have significant influence, i.e. those that merely work in the business rather than carry it on. Examples of those who do have a significant influence include those who are involved in the management of the business as a whole, or senior members of a firm who may have little interest in day-to-day management which they leave to others but their roles and rights mean that they can exert significant influence over the business as a whole.

1.5.3   Capital contribution (Condition C)

This condition is met if M's contribution to the LLP is less than 25% of the Disguised Salary which, it is reasonable to expect, will be payable in a relevant tax year in respect of M's performance of services for the LLP.

The capital contribution made by any member is likely to be well documented.

For individuals who are members at 6 April 2014, an undertaking (whether or not legally enforceable) in place by 6 April 2014 to contribute capital within three months will be taken into account in determining whether Condition C is met.

Where an individual becomes a member on or after 6 April 2014, a two-month period will be allowed to provide the capital, again subject to there being an undertaking to contribute the capital from the day of becoming a member.

The proposals above are intended to ensure that members are not subject to PAYE for short periods of time while they arrange the necessary finance to make a contribution.

1.6   A common sense approach to applying the conditions

The three Salaried Member conditions are intended collectively to encapsulate what it means to be operating in a typical partnership.

Some of the tests will be more, or less, appropriate for particular LLPs, but it is only if all three conditions are met that the individual will be treated as a Salaried Member, with the income tax and NICs treatment then applying as they would to an ordinary employee.

The conditions are intended to take into account the wide variety of circumstances applicable to particular LLPs whilst minimising any risks of unintended effects. This is illustrated in the examples included in Chapter 2 Additional examples are provided in the Annex and they cover a number of points including specific issues arising from certain global structures relevant to large professional services firms.

1.7   Anti-avoidance provisions

The Salaried Member rules contain anti-avoidance provisions to counteract attempts to circumvent the new rules by means of artificial arrangements. Chapter 3 provides more details of these provisions.

1.8   Implementation matters

The legislation will not be final until Finance Bill 2014 receives Royal Assent. The non-statutory business clearance procedure[1] will apply following the enactment of the new provisions as part of Finance Act 2014. Businesses can contact their customer relationship managers or co-ordinators for advice during this interim period or send them non-statutory clearances after Royal Assent.

LLPs with Salaried Members will be required to operate Pay As You Earn (PAYE) in respect of those members from the date the legislation comes into force (6 April 2014). For this reason, although formal clearance cannot be provided in respect of draft legislation, HMRC has given businesses, in this technical note, an informal view of how it would apply to LLP members. In particular, Chapter 4 provides information about the implications of moving from the Self Assessment regime to PAYE for those LLP members who will be Salaried Members from 6 April 2014 and for their LLPs.

2   Conditions & Examples

2.1   Interpretation (for this note)

CTA 2009 means the Corporation Tax Act 2009

CTA 2010 means the Corporation Tax Act 2010

ITA 2007 means the Income Tax Act 2007.

ITEPA means the Income Tax (Earnings and Pensions) Act 2003.

ITTOIA means the Income Tax (Trading and Other Income Act) 2005. **All statutory references are to ITTOIA unless otherwise stated.**

LLP means a UK Limited Liability Partnership formed under the Limited Liability Partnerships Act 2000 and LLPA means the Act.

NICs means National Insurance contributions.

SORP means the Statement of Recommended Practice Accounting by Limited Liability Partnerships.

2.2   The Salaried Member test (new section 863A)

The Salaried Member provisions are intended to apply to those members who are more like employees than partners in a traditional partnership, in order to address the existing inconsistency in the ways that LLPs and general partnerships are treated

---

[1] Guidance on the general non-statutory clearance process is published on the HMRC website: http://www.hmrc.gov.uk/cap/nscg.htm

for tax purposes. The legislation takes a similar approach to the wide-ranging tests that would be applied in determining whether a particular person was a partner in a traditional partnership. However, these new rules provide a more certain outcome, as was requested by many respondents to the Partnerships Review consultation[2] carried out between May and August last year.

The starting point is to look at the terms and conditions for that particular member. These will normally be set out in the LLP Agreement. HMRC has explained what constitutes the LLP Agreement in the Business Income Manual at BIM82112[3]. There may, however, be other relevant documents including a specific agreement with a member, an arrangement relating to bonus or profit share, or any remuneration agreement.

The Salaried Member legislation sets out three conditions. If all three conditions are met, then the individual is treated for tax purposes as being employed under a contract of services and is not to be treated as a member of the LLP. These conditions are set out in detail in the following paragraphs with examples and scenarios (48 in total) that HMRC received during the formal consultation in 2013 and during the consultation on the draft Finance Bill 2014 legislation and the draft guidance, which was held between 5 December 2013 and 4 February 2014. This guidance has also incorporated further comments and examples received after the revised guidance was published on 21 February 2014.

2.3 Condition A — payment for provision of services (S863B(1)-(5))

Condition A is intended to identify those members who are working for the LLP on terms that are like those of employees; that is, they are paid for their services substantially without reference to the overall profitability of the firm. It requires the LLP to consider the position of members who, in their capacity as members, are remunerated for performing services for the firm, and to decide if their remuneration is, in substance, a salary rather than a profit share. The legislation sets out to identify whether 80 % or more of the remuneration which a member expects to receive is, in essence, fixed rather than profit related.

The legislation does this by applying a two step process to determine whether Condition A is met at any time (referred to as the "relevant time").

Step 1 is to identify the "relevant period" by reference to the "relevant arrangements" in place at the relevant time.

The meaning of "relevant period" is discussed in sub-section 2.3.3.

---

[2] HMRC published the consultation document for the Partnerships Review Measure and the response to the consultation on GOV.UK on 20 May and 10 December 2013 respectively: www.gov.uk/government/consultations/a-review-of-two-aspects-of-the-tax-rules-on-partnerships.

[3] See HMRC's guidance published on its website: http://www.hmrc.gov.uk/manuals/bimmanual/bim82112.htm

The "relevant arrangements" are arrangements under which amounts will or may be, payable by the LLP to the member (M), in respect of M's services for the LLP in M's capacity as a member of the LLP. (For this reason this guidance uses the expression "remuneration arrangements" interchangeably with "relevant arrangements").

What constitutes arrangements is discussed in sub-sections 2.3.1 and 2.3.2.

Step 2 is to determine whether it is reasonable to expect that the at least 80% of the total amount payable by the LLP in respect of M's performance of services during the relevant period will be Disguised Salary.

Guidance on what it is reasonable to expect is set out in sub-section 2.3.4, while the meaning of Disguised Salary is considered in section 2.4.

Example 1

This example illustrates the application of Condition A and the process of determining if the condition applies

> *M becomes a member of an LLP on 1 July 2014 and arrangements are made that in return for working for the LLP, M will receive a fixed salary for the period from 1 July 2014 to 30 June 2015. It is expected that a new annual arrangement will be put in place from 1 July 2015.*

The relevant time at which Condition A is to be determined is 1 July 2014 being the date when M became a member and the relevant arrangements were put in place.

The relevant arrangements are the remuneration arrangements for the period from 1 July 2014 to 30 June 2015.

The relevant period is from 1 July 2014 to 30 June 2015, the latter date being the date on which it is expected that the arrangements will end.

M's services are the work that M will do for the LLP in the capacity as a member in the period from 1 July 2014 to 30 June 2015.

On 1 July 2014, it is expected that M will receive a fixed salary for the period from 1 July 2014 to 30 June 2015.

It is therefore reasonable to expect that at least 80% of the amount payable for M's services under the arrangements in place for that period will be Disguised Salary and Condition A will be met.

The determination will apply until the end of the 30 June 2015 unless the relevant arrangements change during the period.

This note also covers various other points relating to Condition A:

- What is meant by "provision of services" is discussed in sub-section 2.3.5.
- The importance of the capacity in which a partner is remunerated – see sub-section 2.3.6.

2.3.1 Relevant arrangements (S863B(2))

Condition A requires there to be "relevant arrangements" in place. This means arrangements under which amounts are to be, or may be, payable by the LLP in respect of M's performance of services for the LLP in M's capacity as a member of the firm.

2.3.2 What are "arrangements"? (S863B(5))

"Arrangements" include any agreement, understanding, scheme, transaction or series of transactions (whether or not legally enforceable).

A broad and realistic view should be taken in deciding what constitutes the arrangement. This should take into account the commercial intentions and expectations of the parties, for example, the overall financial reward that the member expects to obtain when becoming a member or when negotiating terms with the LLP on how they expect to be rewarded.

Regard should be had to the financial position of the LLP and the terms and conditions under which the individual is to be remunerated, as well as any understanding between the individual and the LLP or its investors. The budget, cash flow forecast, financial projections and documentation provided to any bank may need to be considered as well as any arrangements (formal or informal) relating to the payment of bonuses or profit share allocations to the individual or others in a similar position.

As noted below, an arrangement continues until such time as the arrangement changes (at which point a new arrangement is created) or until the arrangement was expected to end or be modified.

2.3.3 How long do arrangements have to be considered and when is the test applied? (S863B(1))

The test for Condition A is first applied:

- at 6 April 2014, if M is already a member of the LLP on that date; or
- when M joins the LLP.

The test is applied looking forward over the "relevant period"; that is the period over which it is reasonable to expect that the remuneration arrangements will remain in place unchanged.

Normally, the test for Condition A is re-applied at the earlier of when:

- the remuneration arrangements are changed; or
- the relevant period, over which the test was applied, ends.

The situation where arrangements do not end and are not modified at the end of the relevant period are discussed in Example 4 below.

An important point is that Condition A is applied looking forward. The period that is taken into account is not a fixed period of time. This period depends upon the facts of the case, reflecting business variations.

However, for most LLP businesses including those within the professional services sector, the relevant period will be a year as it is customary for remuneration arrangements to be reviewed on an annual basis.

Once an arrangement is made, and a reasonable view has been taken on the basis of the arrangement as to the status of the member for tax purposes, the view remains valid until the arrangement changes with the result that a new arrangement comes into existence or the relevant period to which the test was applied comes to an end but the arrangements continue.

A change would occur when, for example, the individual's remuneration arrangement changes or the firm's remuneration policy is altered.

An extraneous event (such as a revised profit forecast) that affects the expectation of the parties to the arrangement, but which does not result in the arrangement being altered, would not result in the arrangement being revisited. This means that Condition A would not need to be retested at that point.

In addition, where the remuneration arrangement makes provision for contingent events such as sick leave or maternity pay, a change to payment terms triggered by one of these contingencies would not constitute a change to the arrangements.

By contrast, if the LLP or members reacted to such a change by altering the remuneration agreement, this would constitute a new remuneration arrangement and the test under Condition A would then have to be reassessed.

Example 1 in section 2.3 reflects a typical scenario where the member is remunerated on an annual basis. There may be some circumstances in which the relevant period will be longer, as shown in Example 2.

Example 2

This example looks at a case where the reward arrangements are based on a period longer than a year because the package is for a project that is expected to take several years.

John is a member in an LLP which has entered into an agreement on 1 January 2015 to develop a property over a three year period. The agreement provides that John will receive a fixed profit share of £100,000 per year for the first two years and then 50% of the profit from the development, expected to be £500,000 in total. This arrangement is not changed.

John is not a Salaried Member because, viewed at the outset and taking into consideration the whole three year period, the fixed amount payable to John is expected to be less than 80% of his total profit so Condition A will not be met.

If we look again at the example above and consider the position in year 3: assume that the property market slumps and the expected profit does not materialise. John leaves the LLP with nothing other than the fixed profit amounts from years 1 and 2.

Although, as events have turned out, John has received only a salary, this is only the result of an extraneous event. As the parties expected and intended for John primarily to be rewarded through a share in the overall profits of the LLP, John is not at any time a Salaried Member.

Example 3

This looks at the position where new arrangements are entered into before the end of the relevant period.

The facts are as in Example 2, but the property development is completed ahead of schedule. The LLP decides to take on a new development and as a consequence, on 1 September 2016, John agrees a new arrangement which will see him receive £100,000 in the first year, and a profit share, estimated at £150,000 in 2018.

The existing arrangements are changed so Condition A has to be re-tested on 1 September 2016, when the change occurs.

What happens if the relevant period ends and the arrangement continues?

As previously mentioned, apart from a modification to an existing remuneration arrangement or a new arrangement, the other point at which Condition A will need to be re-tested is immediately after the end of the "relevant period". This is the period which ends at the time when it was expected that the original arrangements would end or be modified. Very often, remuneration arrangements are determined annually. However, the period can be longer. And in some cases, an arrangement may continue for longer than expected without being modified. In this case, a new relevant period then begins.

> ### Example 4
>
> This looks at where the relevant period ends but the arrangements are unchanged.
>
> *The facts are as in Example 2, but the property development is delayed by bad weather. The arrangements continue unchanged, with John receiving 50% of the profits. The only difference is that the profits are spread out over a longer period. The final sale is made four months after the end of the relevant period.'*
>
> Although the arrangements continue unchanged, the relevant period has come to an end. As John is still receiving a 50% profit share, Condition A is not met.

As before, the fact that part of the profit share did not materialise in the relevant period has no relevance. The test was properly applied on the basis of the information held at that time. It is applied again immediately after the relevant period with, in this case, the same result for the extra four months.

2.3.4 "Reasonable to expect" (S863B(3))

Condition A is framed in terms of the total amount that it is reasonable to expect the LLP is to pay to the member for the performance of services. This is a question that should be answered by reference to the substance of the matter taking a realistic view of the facts. The reasonable expectations of the parties to the arrangement, inferred from their actions as well as any documented evidence, should be taken into account.

It is clearly reasonable to expect that an amount contractually due will be paid, but in many cases there will be a range of possible outcomes. Where this is the case, the legislation looks at the most realistic outcome: this is unlikely to be either the most optimistic or the most pessimistic possible result.

HMRC would expect the LLP to consider any material reasonably relevant to this question – this includes everything relevant to the individual's expectations (see, in particular, the matters referred to in section 2.3.2).

The question of whether something will in practice be affected by the profits or losses of the LLP is considered in section 2.4.11.

2.3.5 Provision of services (S863B(3))

Condition A only applies to an individual who performs services for the LLP in the individual's capacity as a member. This means that the Salaried Member provisions do not apply to:

- companies;
- individuals who do no more than invest money; or
- individuals who no longer perform services for the LLP but who continue to receive a profit share.

Example 5

This example illustrates why an LLP member who no longer provides services is not a Salaried Member.

X used to be an active member of JKL LLP but reduced his active work a number of years ago and has not provided any services to the LLP for a year. In recognition of his contribution to the LLP over his career, X remains a member of the LLP, continuing to receive a profit share.

Although X is still a member of JKL LLP and receives a share of the profits, none of this is due to him in respect of any services he continues to perform. The reason he continues to receive a profit share does not matter, but it may, for example, reflect the fact that X still has capital invested in the LLP. X reports this profit allocation on the partnership pages of his tax return and pays income tax (and Class 2 and 4 NICs) accordingly. This reward is not Disguised Salary.

Example 6

The following example looks at the case of someone on "gardening leave".

M is a member of the BYBY LLP. He has been approached by, and has accepted, a more senior role with the Hello LLP.

Under the terms of the LLP Agreement, M will leave the BYBY LLP in three months' time. The Management Board agrees to commute M's expected profit share into a fixed sum, based on profit projections, and M is placed on "gardening leave" for three months.

The arrangement under which M is receiving the fixed sum does not involve the provision of services, and accordingly, Condition A is not met.

2.3.6   Capacity (S863B(3) - Step 1)

The individual has to carry out services for the LLP as a member. The legislation does not apply to any reward that an individual member obtains for work performed for the LLP in a separate capacity, for example as part of a separate business. This income does not come from being a member of the LLP or from rights under the LLP agreement. This comes from other business dealings between the LLP and that individual and should be taxed separately based on the nature of the arrangements.

Example 7

This example illustrates how a member can carry out work for the LLP in a different capacity which is not relevant to the Salaried Member legislation.

The B LLP is formed between the B family and a local developer to develop a plot of land. Kate B is a member of the B LLP, but under the LLP agreement, she does not need to work for the B LLP.

Kate B is an architect and engaged by B LLP to draw up plans in her capacity as an architect, for which she is paid an arm's length fee under a separate contract.

In this case, Condition A is not affected by the remuneration which Kate B receives from the LLP. Whilst Kate B is a member who performs services for the LLP, she does not perform those services as a member of the LLP. The B LLP has contracted for her to provide services as part of her profession as an architect and her reward from the LLP all arises to her in that capacity. From the point of view of B LLP, paying Kate B is no different to paying any other party that has provided services to the B LLP.

Example 8

The following example looks at another common situation, where a member is receiving rent from the LLP.

S owns a farm which he lets to a farming LLP, SSS LLP, of which he is a member. This rent is a commercial sum.

Apart from his share of the profit from the farming business, S receives a rent from the LLP. The rent is not taken into account for the purposes of Condition A (and nor, if S were a Salaried Member for other reasons, would it form part of his earnings).

2.3.7 Statutory limit for Disguised Salary (S863B(3) - Step 2)

The test applied by Step 2 is whether it is reasonable to expect that at least 80% of the total amount expected to be payable by the LLP for M's services as a member will be *Disguised Salary*.

For the purposes of the test, it is the remuneration payable in accordance with the individual's arrangements with the firm (or the profits for accounts purposes attributed to him or her) which is taken into account, not the amount that would be taxable as a result of the firm's profit sharing arrangements (if different).

2.4 Condition A – Disguised Salary (S863B(3) - Step 2)

This section of the guidance explains what is meant by "Disguised Salary".

The legislation says that an amount is a Disguised Salary

"if it -

(a) *is fixed,*
(b) *if it is variable, is varied without reference to the overall amount of the profits or losses of the limited liability partnership, or*
(c) *is not, in practice, affected by the overall amount of those profits or losses."*

2.4.1 What does Disguised Salary include?

Disguised Salary comprises amounts that will not be affected by the overall profitability of the firm. It includes:

- a fixed sum such as a salary;
- payment on a piece work basis - by the number of units produced or jobs done (see sub-section 2.4.9).
- a bonus based on a member's personal performance without reference to the success of the business (see sub-section 2.4.6);
- guaranteed payments (see sub-section 2.4.7); and
- non-refundable drawings – sub-section 2.4.4 provides information on when drawings are treated as a Disguised Salary.

It does not include drawings if it is reasonable to assume that they are sums on account of a separate amount that is not itself Disguised Salary.

2.4.2 The overall profits

The legislation refers to amounts that vary or are in practice affected by the overall amounts of profits of the LLP. For this purpose, the overall profits are the profits of the LLP that are available for allocation amongst members (including any amounts which may be reflected in the income statement as members' salaries).

2.4.3 Benefits in kind etc

A reward package may include entitlement to monetary amounts and to non-monetary benefits. However, in determining whether there is Disguised Salary, the focus falls exclusively on amounts 'payable' in respect of the individual's services.

Many LLPs provide "benefits" to members, which would be taxable as benefits in kind, if the member were an employee. These "benefits" are not taken into account for the purposes of Condition A.

Although they are not taken into account in determining whether the condition is met, they will be taxable as benefits if the individual is a Salaried Member.

Example 9

The following is an example of benefits in kind.

P is a member of a large LLP. The LLP provides benefits to members, such as private health insurance and use of a car.

The value of "benefits-in-kind" received by P (i.e. the insurance and car) is not taken into account in deciding whether or not Condition A is satisfied. However, these benefits are taxable on P if P is a Salaried Member.

2.4.4 Drawings on account of profit share vs. Disguised Salary

It is common for members of LLPs to receive monthly payments on account ("drawings") of their subsequent profit share. Typically, the amount of the monthly share will reflect the expected profit share so, for example, a member who is expected to be allocated a profit of £120,000 for the period of account may be paid drawings of £8,500 a month representing 85% of the expected profit. Such drawings are, nevertheless, a payment on account of expected profit and are subject to clawback should the expected profits not materialise.

The fact that a member is paid drawings on account of profits does not necessarily convert the payments into Disguised Salary. If the member's reward is a genuine variable share of the overall profits, the manner of taking it does not convert it into something else. Genuine payments on account of a share of overall profits are not made by the payer in exchange for services, but are partial realisations of an anticipated profit based on the expectancy of a share in future profits.

On the other hand, the member may have been told that the drawings represent a priority minimum payment which could only be refunded in the event that the profits of the firm are insufficient to cover the drawings of that member and other members with the same preferential right to payment. If the reality is that the LLP always makes profits significantly greater than those minimum drawings (with that excess to be allocated to other senior members), it is reasonable to assume that the member will retain the amounts and that those amounts will not in practice be affected by the profits (and that accordingly the payments constitute a real reward for services).

The distinction between these cases is subtle and requires consideration of what the payments are referable to. Drawings would not be considered to be Disguised Salary if they are genuine payments on account of an amount that is itself not Disguised Salary. In such a case, it would not matter whether the drawings were made on a prudent or optimistic basis since in either case they would not be Disguised Salary.

Alternatively drawings may themselves either represent a fixed entitlement or be payments on account of an amount that is itself Disguised Salary.

2.4.5 Profit share (S863B(3))

Condition A is not met if it is reasonable to expect that the member has a reward package under which more than 20% of their reward for services will be a share of the overall profits.

A share of the profit of the business does not include an amount determined only by reference to the success of a particular part of the business, such as a shop or branch office, or only by reference to how well an individual's own client portfolio has performed. It must be a share of profit which varies by reference to the profits of the business as a whole.

Example 10

This example illustrates the allocation of profits among members who do not receive fixed shares.

> *A, B and C are members of ABC LLP. A is allocated 2 points and B and C are each allocated 4 points. Regardless of the level of profits, A will receive 20%, while B and C will receive 40% each.*

None of the members receive a Disguised Salary; they each have a variable interest in the overall profits of the LLP. This would be so even if the profits were highly predictable and did not vary from year to year.

There can be significant variations in the mechanism used to allocate the profits. It is important not to focus on how the mechanism is described; it may be called a percentage, worked out as points or units. If the shares or units which are awarded are amounts which might reasonably be expected to vary with the profits of the business as a whole, the individual is not receiving a Disguised Salary.

Example 11

This example illustrates the interaction between priority profit shares and the Condition A test.

> *A, B and C expect that their LLP will make a profit of about £100,000. At the start of the period, they award themselves 'salaries' of £20,000, £40,000 and £40,000 respectively and agree that the actual total profit will be shared in proportion to those "salaries". If the overall profits of the LLP are more or less than £100,000, then each partner will share in the deficit or surplus in proportion to their agreed salary.*

It is important to take a realistic view of the facts and look at the substance of the agreement. Although they describe these sums as salaries, they are not in reality fixed amounts. Instead they have a method of sharing out the anticipated profits. The amounts are simply set out as a benchmark for allocating profits. The reality is that the members will receive a share of profits that varies by reference to the overall profits of the LLP. It is not relevant that the LLP has chosen to describe this arrangement by reference to a "salary".

Example 12

This example highlights that it is important to focus on whether, on **a realistic view**, the amount represents a share of the overall profits, so that the profit share that member gets will vary on the basis of the overall profits of the LLP.

In the ABC LLP, the profits are divided on the basis of units. Each year's profits are allocated by dividing total profits by the number of units in issue to determine the value of a "unit". There are no salaries, or guaranteed profits. Each member's profit share is calculated by reference to the profits and the number of units that they hold.

A is the senior member; he has been allocated units that reflect the time that he has been a member and the fact that he has the main client portfolio for the business.

R is semi-retired but has a large number of units, reflecting her equity investment in the business

P is a junior member but has been allocated additional units because she has had an exceptionally successful year.

Q has only just joined the LLP. He has been allocated units that are expected to give him a profit of about 10% more than the salary he had been on as an employee. It is agreed that Q can draw a higher proportion of his expected profits share, in line with his "take home" as an employee, but he has no priority over the other members, and he is aware that in the event of a shortfall, he will have to repay the excess drawings.

All four are receiving profit shares, because the sum they receive is dependent upon the profits of the business. In other words, it is not:

varied without reference to the overall amount of the profits or losses of the limited liability partnership.

To illustrate this, consider how the share P receives may be affected by the profits of the LLP as a whole:

Due to a professional negligence claim, the value of a unit is much lower than last year. As a result, although P has had an exceptional year and has been allocated more points than last year, her share of the profit is £20,000 less than the previous year.

Although P may have more units than last year, what she receives is dependent upon the profits of the business as a whole. The LLP has not had a good year, so even though she has had an exceptionally good year, P actually gets less money than the previous year.

Some may find it helpful to think of the analogy of looking at the profits of the overall business as a cake.

What P receives is a slice of that cake. The proportion of that cake she receives depends on her own performance. However, the total amount of cake P receives depends both on the size of the slice and on the size of the cake.

If the firm has had a good year, then the cake is large and each slice is worth more. In this example, the firm has had a poor year, so the cake is small. P gets a bigger slice of a smaller cake. The amount she receives does vary with the profits and Condition A is not met.

Example 13

This example illustrates the position of an individual moving from Salaried Member to partner status.

Member F was a Salaried Member, with a fixed profit share of £100,000. Member F is promoted with effect from 1 April 2015. She will have a fixed profit share of £50,000 together with 10 profit units which the firm estimates will be worth an additional £75,000 based on budget. The firm has a very poor year, and as a result, she only receives £50,000, giving total profit share of £100,000.

Condition A is not met. Member F is not a Salaried Member from 1 April 2015. Member F may have had the same profit share as last year, but half of this was dependent on the overall profits of the business. Had the firm been as successful as forecast, then she would have a profit share of £125,000.

Example 14

This example illustrates the position where the outcome is not as expected at the time when Condition A was applied and this is due to events that are beyond the control of the LLP or the relevant member.

BBB LLP is a new fund management venture. The members agree to provide seed funding of £1m while new, unconnected, investors are being sought.

B is a member of BBB and is responsible for raising the funds. The LLP documentation says that he is entitled to a first preferential profit share of £100,000 each year including the first year, which will be paid irrespective of the profit and will not be refundable. He will also be entitled to a third of the total profits, which are expected to be substantial from year 3 onwards. It is agreed that the remuneration package will be reviewed at the end of year 4.

In year 3, the funds have not been raised and the LLP is dissolved.

B fails Condition A as the arrangements are not ones where, at the date when the test is carried out, it is reasonable to expect that B will be primarily rewarded by Disguised Salary over the relevant period.

The outcome was that B received purely a salary, but was not the intention and was not the outcome that was expected when the arrangement was entered into.

Example 15

This example looks at tranches of reward, where the profit sharing arrangements vary depending on the amounts of profits made.

P works for the UVW LLP. She has no salary, but has a 10% profit share for the first £1m profits, reducing to 5% above that figure. Profits may or may not exceed £1m.

P's profit share varies by reference to the actual profits. Whilst the percentage varies, it is all profit-related. P does not satisfy Condition A.

Please note that for this example it is assumed that there is practical risk that the LLP makes less than £1m of profits; if not, P will receive Disguised Salary of £100,000 plus a profit share.

Example 16

This example considers how the legislation takes account of a theoretical but practically irrelevant prospect of a profit share.

Four people decide to set up a cafe together. Members A, B & C do not have any capital to invest so only put in £100 each. The fourth, Member D, provides the funding for the venture.

They agree that Members A, B & C will each have a salary of £25,000 a year. The agreement is that these are not repayable even if the profits are under £75,000 (and as such they are Disguised Salary).

Any loss would fall to Member D, who will receive the first £125,000 of profits after payment of salaries. Profits above that limit will be divided equally.

Members A, B & C all potentially have a share of the profits, the question is how realistic is that possibility?

For Members A, B & C to receive a variable profit share based on the overall profits of the LLP, the profits need to be in excess of £200,000. For Condition A not to be met, the profits would have to exceed £250,000.

If the business plan is based on an expectation of profits of between £100,000 and £150,000, then there is no reasonable expectation that the income of Members A, B & C will, in practice, be affected by the level of profits and Condition A is satisfied.

2.4.6 Bonus

It is a characteristic of a true partner in a business that he or she receives a share in the profits of the business. However, many individuals who are employees also receive profit-related payments which may be described as bonus or by some other label. The definition of Disguised Salary is intended to draw a distinction between amounts which are realistically a share of profits and other amounts such as those which are fixed or remunerate individual performance.

Example 17

This example looks at bonuses and remuneration committees.

J works for the ABC LLP. He will receive a salary of £100,000 plus a bonus determined by a remuneration committee, at their discretion.

For the purposes of this legislation, the question is about the terms governing the remuneration committee's exercise of its discretion in determining the bonus payable. If the bonus paid is genuinely a share of the profit of the business, it will not be considered as Disguised Salary

In this case, more information is needed to determine whether or not his award is determined as an additional share of the overall profits of the firm. What are the terms of reference for the committee?

If the bonus is an additional share of the overall profit of the business, the next question is how realistic is it that any profit share will be 25% or more of the fixed salary of £100,000 (such that less than 80% of the total rewards will be Disguised Salary). As stated above, those rewards that are unrealistic and are unlikely ever to be triggered are ignored.

2.4.7   Guaranteed payments/floors

A Disguised Salary comprises fixed amounts and amounts that are determined without reference to, or are not in practice affected by, the overall level of profits or losses for the LLP as a whole.

As a result, a Disguised Salary includes any sum that the member will receive whether or not the LLP makes sufficient profits.

The clearest example of this would be where a member will receive that sum even if the LLP makes a loss. Such payments are referred to below as guaranteed payments.

Example 18

This example illustrates the treatment of guaranteed payments.

The MNS LLP makes a loss of £500,000. However, under the profit sharing arrangements, members A, B, C, D & E will all receive a profit share of £100,000 whilst F has a loss of £250,000 and K Ltd has a loss of £750,000.'

The shares payable to members A to E are not affected by the fact that the LLP has made a loss and are disguised salaries. Members A to E satisfy Condition A.

The key point is not how the payment is described; rather that it is a sum that the member expects to receive and is not, in practice, varied with reference to, or affected by, the overall profitability of the firm, even if it is expressed to be linked to profit.

Here are some examples of arrangements which will be regarded as guaranteed payments:

- *Member A is entitled to draw £10,000 a month. Under the terms of the agreement, he is not required to repay the money once drawn.*
- *Member B has a guaranteed profit of £120,000 a year.*
- *Member C has a priority draw on profits and will be paid £120,000 a year (but no more) unless profits are less than £120,000. When the arrangement is entered into, there is no practical likelihood that profits will be less than £120,000 (and the expectation of both parties is that the reward will be £120,000).*

It is reasonable to expect that the amounts payable to A, B and C for services to the LLP will be £120,000. Receipt of this sum is not in practice in doubt since only a commercially remote event could prevent such payment being made.

Their cases can be contrasted with Member D, who is simply entitled to a percentage of the profits. He has no priority entitlement to any sum. For much of the year, he draws out money from his current account (last year's undrawn profits). Towards the end of the year, it is agreed that the LLP will pay him £10,000 a month in anticipation of his profit share for the period. Member D does not have a Disguised Salary and fails Condition A.

Example 19

This example looks at an amount of profit that it is agreed that a member will receive even if the share allocated to that member would otherwise be lower.

D joins the ABC LLP. In his first year, he is guaranteed a total profit share of no less than £30,000. If his allocated share of the profits is less than this, then his share will be £30,000 and the shares of the other members reduced accordingly.

D's guaranteed profit share of £30,000 is Disguised Salary as it is fixed. Accordingly, unless it is reasonable to expect that ultimately D's share for the period will exceed £37,500, such that his overall return is not substantially wholly fixed, he will meet Condition A.

Example 20

This example illustrates a guaranteed payment for a new joiner.

S joins the K LLP. The arrangement under which she joins the LLP provides that, in her first year, she is to be awarded 20 profit sharing units at the beginning of the year, with a guaranteed minimum profit of £80,000. This is intended to reassure her that in her first year, she will be remunerated at least the amount she was paid at her previous firm. When the units are awarded, each unit is expected to give a profit share of £4,500. In the event, the profits are higher than anticipated so that each unit is worth £5,500, giving her an actual profit allocation of £110,000.

At the start of the period, S has a Disguised Salary of £80,000 and is expected to have a total profit share of £90,000, meaning that Condition A is satisfied. This is not reviewed with hindsight. Obviously, if the profits are expected to be in line with those for the current period then this is taken into account when the test is applied again.

> ## Example 21
>
> This example illustrates a bonus based on personal performance.
>
> *It is agreed between the firm and member C that she will receive £100,000 as her profit share for the year. She is allocated 20 profit sharing units at the beginning of the year, which, based on budget, will be worth £80-100,000. At the year end, in accordance with the original arrangements, she is awarded a performance based bonus to make up for any shortfall and ensure that the total is £100,000.*
>
> Condition A is satisfied. The reality is that member C's remuneration is £100,000 and the amount will not vary with firm's profits.

2.4.8   Personal performance

Condition A will be satisfied where the individual member receives a payment that is based only on their own personal performance, rather than a share of the profits of the business as a whole.

A bonus based only on the performance of the individual is not a profit share. It is variable but is:

> *"varied without reference to the overall amount of the profits or losses of the limited liability partnership".*

On the other hand, performance-linked profit sharing arrangements that are computed by reference to the firm's overall profits are not Disguised Salary.

> ## Examples 22 & 23
>
> The following two examples illustrate the distinction between rewards for personal or team success as opposed to share of a profit of the business.
>
> *The EEE LLP awards bonuses to junior members at the year end based on their personal performance, as a percentage of salary up to 25%. This amount is a bonus and is not varied according to the profits of the business.*
>
> *The FFF LLP has an arrangement under which an amount equal to 20% of profits is set aside as a bonus pool for its junior members to receive in addition to their fixed remuneration of £50,000 per year. This is allocated after the end of the year according to the personal performance of the junior members. All the members have an equal chance of getting a bonus. Typically a bonus represents 30% or so of base pay but it may be more and it may be less. In practice, because the performance system ranks the members, it is likely that some will get up to £50,000 and some will get zero.*

On the facts, the class of members concerned is to be rewarded by a Disguised Salary of £50,000 and a profit-related bonus that is, on average, 30% of that amount. Everyone has an equal chance of getting a bonus and the award system does not favour one individual over another. The arrangement in place is not one where it is reasonable to assume that a particular individual meets Condition A.

Varying the example, if the bonus pool mechanism of FFF LLP is not fixed at the beginning of the year (so no percentage of profit is earmarked), but is decided at the discretion of a remuneration committee, there is unlikely to be a reasonable expectation of the amount at the beginning of the year and Condition A is likely to be satisfied.

Example 24

This example looks at where personal performance is reflected by the way the profits are allocated.

Members are allocated profit share units at or soon after, the beginning of the year. The allocation is based on their seniority and historical performance, with an additional award of units to reward senior management roles to be held during the year.

Condition A is not satisfied. Although the profit share units are allocated partly on the basis of personal performance, all that is happening is that the proportion of the profits going to each member is being set. How much each member will receive depends upon the amount of the overall profit.

Example 25

This example looks at how a team leader can be rewarded for the results of their team by the way the profits are allocated.

Towards the end of the year, the performance of the members is assessed and additional profit share units are allocated to members based on their performance during the year. This also takes into account the performance of the team for which they are responsible.

Condition A is not satisfied. Although the profit share units are allocated partly on the basis of personal performance, all that is happening is that the proportion of the profits going to each member is being set. How much each member will receive depends upon the amount of the overall profit.

To return to the cake analogy, their performance partly determines how large the slice is, but the actual amount of money depends on the size of the cake. An individual who receives a bigger slice of a smaller cake may have less cake than an individual receiving a thinner slice of a bigger cake.

Example 26

This example looks at the "eat what you kill" model.

> *GGG LLP is a large professional LLP and operates a remuneration system under which each partner is paid a profit share according to the amount of fees he or she has brought in.*

If this is an arrangement for the partner to be paid a share of profit, it will not be Disguised Salary. If it is an arrangement under which the partner receives a cash amount (for example, a proportion of billings), the partner will be a Salaried Member.

2.4.9 Payments linked to piece work or turnover

If a member is paid on a "piece work" basis, that is, on the basis of the number of tasks they perform or pieces of work they do, Condition A is satisfied.

A payment by reference to the number of tasks performed or by reference to turnover is variable but it is:

> *"varied without reference to the overall amount of the profits or losses of the limited liability partnership"*

Example 27

This example shows the distinction between rewards based on personal efforts as opposed to the profits of the business.

> *W LLP operates sites offering "hand car washes". The individuals who wash the cars are members of the LLP rather than being given contracts of employment. Member D washes cars at one of these sites. Member D is paid on a piece work basis; the more cars washed, the more he receives.*

Member D will earn more if more cars come to be washed. However his income is based on his work, not the success of the business as a whole. Member D receives a Disguised Salary and Condition A is satisfied.

Example 28

This example looks at guaranteed payments and rewards that are not part of the overall profits.

> *The XYZ LLP decides to expand into a new business area. A new member, P, is recruited to run the new business area.*
>
> *As it is expected that the new business area will initially make a loss, P will receive a guaranteed profit share of £100,000 plus a percentage of the turnover of the new business area.*

Neither the guaranteed payments (which may be called "guaranteed profit share") nor the payment based on a percentage of the turnover of that business area is based on the profits of the LLP as a whole. Condition A is satisfied for the duration of the remuneration arrangements.

2.4.10 Divisions of a business

If a member is be rewarded by i) a fixed amount plus ii) a bonus calculated exclusively on the basis of the success of a particular branch or unit, then Condition A is satisfied.

On the other hand, if the member is to be rewarded on a basis that takes into account the overall profitability of the firm, then (assuming the 80% test is not met in respect of any fixed entitlement the member may have) Condition A will not be met even if the reward also reflects personal performance or the performance of the division in which he or she works.

Example 29

This distinction is illustrated by the example below.

ABC LLP carries on a financial services business with two divisions; tax and audit. Hank and Mitch run the audit division and Toni and Jo run the tax division. All four are members in the firm. The two divisions keep separate accounts. It is reasonable to expect both divisions to be profitable.

Whether Condition A is met depends on all the arrangements and a relevant factor will be what would happen in the event of a loss being made by either business.

If, for example, the LLP agreement provides that each division is insulated from the results of the other (profits or losses), then all the members meet Condition A.

Alternatively the remuneration package may provide that the profits and losses of each division are to be aggregated (after deduction of common overheads) so as to give a single figure of net profit for the overall business, which is then shared between the divisions, with those shares then being further allocated to the individuals in each. Such shares may take into account personal and divisional performance as well as other factors, but with none of the members having a fixed entitlement to any of the divisional shares.

In this latter case, none of the members meets Condition A. Each division receives a share of profits allocated by reference to performance and each individual then receives a share of that share. Thus the amount that each individual receives varies with reference to the overall profits of the business (and is in practice affected by the amount of those profits).

2.4.11 Caps

Sometimes a member's share of the profits may be "capped". This means that the member will receive a percentage of profits, but only so long as the profits do not exceed a certain figure.

The result is that the member's share of profits is capped at a certain monetary amount. This may mean that the member's reward is not *in practice affected by the overall amount of the firm's profits.*

Example 30

This example looks at how the legislation applies where there is a monetary maximum share or "cap" on a member's share.

E joins the DEF LLP. It agrees that her profit share will be calculated as a proportion of the total profits of the LLP, but her share cannot exceed £100,000.

If it is realistic to expect that the cap will not be engaged, then the member's reward will in practice be affected by the level of the firm's profits and will vary by reference to them. If the LLP expects that her profit share would be between £120,000 and £150,000 so realistically she will always receive £100,000, it would imply that her total reward was not, in practice, a variable share of total profit but was simply a fixed sum meeting Condition A.

Example 31

This example illustrates that a cap that limits the return for services to a payment that will, in practice, be highly likely to be paid gives rise to a Disguised Salary even though there is a theoretical risk that the payment will not be made.

AA LLP is a UK firm that has set up a business in Australia and is highly profitable. AA LLP cannot operate directly in Australia for legal reasons. Instead, the business in Australia is operated through a general partnership AA GP. The two firms work closely together.

A, B & C are individuals who are members of AA LLP. The only other member of AA LLP is Z Ltd, which is also a partner in AA GP.

A, B & C have each been told that they will receive £100,000 fixed salary, subject to there being sufficient profits. Any profits in excess of this amount are to be allocated to Z Ltd which will distribute the amounts to the AA GP in Australia, for the benefit of the Australian partners. Profit projections show that profits of AA LLP are likely to be significantly in excess of £1m per annum.

A, B and C meet condition A. Their return is to be £100,000, which will not in practice be affected by the amount of the firm's profits.

2.5   Condition B – significant influence (S863C)

The legislation states:

> *"Condition B is that the mutual rights and duties of the members of the limited liability partnership, and of the partnership and its members, do not give M significant influence over the affairs of the partnership."*

A partnership is a group of people who are carrying on a business in common with a view to profit. In short, the partners are the business.

Condition B stipulates that the mutual rights and duties of the members of the LLP, and of the LLP and its members, do not give M significant influence over the affairs of the LLP. It is, in essence, looking at the role played by the individual in the business.

As the LLP is a body corporate governed by the agreement between the members, it allows members considerable flexibility in how they organise the affairs of the LLP.

This guidance looks at the scenarios that have been put to HMRC during the consultations, but in the final analysis, the question to ask is whether the individual has a significant influence over the activities of the LLP as a whole. Put simply, can it be said that the individual is the business rather than merely working for the business?

2.5.1   Significance of size

Condition B is likely to be particularly important for the members of smaller LLPs.

Example 32

This is an example of how Condition B applies to the facts of the case, where the written agreement does not reflect the current position

> *The Family Farm LLP has as members, a couple, A & B, and their adult son, X. The LLP Agreement has not been amended since before X was admitted. The way that the LLP operates in practice is that A, B and X all have a say in the running of the business, with A having a casting vote.*

Although the written agreement was not amended when X was admitted, the implied terms of the agreement under which X was admitted was that he would have a significant say in the business. As a result, Condition B is not satisfied and X is not a Salaried Member. The fact that A has a casting vote does not mean that only he can meet condition B. More than one person can have significant influence and that influence can be exerted in different ways.

> ## Example 33
>
> This is an example of how the legislation applies to a small LLP where all the members have a say:
>
> *B LLP is a professional legal LLP with ten members. All members have equal rights and participate equally in the management of the business. They meet each month for meetings at which the major business decisions are discussed and made. All members attend these meetings and all are entitled to speak.*
>
> All of the members fail condition B as they have a significant influence over the business.
>
> It is unlikely that this condition will exclude many members of very large LLPs, since, in such cases, it is likely that only a minority of individuals have significant influence over the affairs of the whole LLP.
>
> There is no line in the sand as to the number of members which can exist consistent with all of them having significant influence – this will vary from firm to firm depending on how they conduct their business and who is influential. However, members of an LLP management committee which has influence over the affairs of the firm as a whole might be expected to fail Condition B as explained below.

2.5.2 What type of influence is relevant to the test?

The purpose of Condition B is to exclude from being Salaried Members those individuals who have a real say in the business. The test is applied on the basis of a realistic view of the facts.

All relevant information must be considered in applying this condition including agreements between the partner and the firm, the LLP Agreement and any contracts between the firm and its investors. As explained in the Business Income Manual (see footnote 3 in section 2.2), the LLP Agreement includes not only the written agreement but also verbal or implied agreements.

The following are examples of the kind of decisions which might be involved in appropriate cases. This is not intended to be a prescriptive or definitive list and it is not necessary that the same people are involved in all the decisions. Nor would having significant, or even controlling, influence over just one of them necessarily mean that the member has significant influence over the firm as a whole:

- appointment of new members
- deciding where the firm conducts its business
- deciding the firm's areas of business
- strategic decisions
- deciding on business acquisitions or disposals
- management of key contracts relating to the firm generally (e.g. with the bank)
- appointment of key personnel

- allocation of roles to key staff
- decisions on important financial commitments
- formulating the firm's business plan
- approving major new clients or investments, especially where this is a regulatory requirement (see sub-section 2.5.3 below))
- deciding the firm's marketing strategy.

As noted above, members of the board or management committee of a large professional firm are likely to have the requisite level of influence over the affairs of the business.

By contrast, merely being able to vote, or to express a view, on such matters would be unlikely, in itself, to constitute significant influence.

Sometimes, an individual who has no apparent role in the management of the business may wield considerable influence. If, on a realistic view of the facts, the members defer to the views of that individual, then the individual can fail Condition B.

Example 34

This example illustrates an influential individual who is not a manager of the business.

T was the founder of the firm. Officially she is semi-retired and plays no role in either the management or the strategy of the business. In reality, if T indicates her views on the strategy of the business, and the strategy board will almost invariably follow her guidance. T is still associated with the firm and if she was to disassociate herself from the firm, it would be catastrophic for business.

Although T officially has no role, she continues to set the direction and strategy of the firm. T continues to hold significant influence and fails Condition B.

2.5.3 Significant influence functions of financial businesses regulated by Financial Conduct Authority (FCA)

The Financial Services and Markets Act 2000 provides that a significant influence function, in relation to the carrying on of a regulated activity by a firm, means a function that is likely to enable the person responsible for its performance to exercise a significant influence on the conduct of the firm's affairs, so far as it relates to the regulated activity.

A person carrying out such a function in relation to an authorised firm must be an FCA-approved person.

The context of FCA's significant influence function test is different from that of the significant influence rule in the Salaried Member legislation. However, HMRC would accept that the following FCA functions are likely to result in the individual exercising them having significant influence for the purposes of Condition B: CF3 (chief executive function) and CF8 (apportionment and oversight function).

On the other hand, CF4 (partner function) merely means that the individual has to be FCA-approved by virtue of being a member of the LLP (and as a result of which the FCA presumes the individual to have influence). Whether this in practice results in the individual having significant influence over the affairs of the LLP as a whole is a question of fact. In cases where the firm's activities consist wholly or almost wholly of regulated activities and the individual in question significantly contributes to the firm's major decisions (management, strategic or investment-related), then it is likely that HMRC would accept that this constitutes significant influence for the purposes of Condition B

Example 35

This example looks at whether someone who fulfils a function required by a regulatory body satisfies Condition B.

X is a member of XYZ LLP, a regulated asset manager. X is a key portfolio manager, but not on the managing committee of XYZ LLP.

X is authorised by the FCA and holds Controlled Function CF4 for FCA's purposes, which is listed as a significant influence function. In addition, X makes significant investment decisions in relation to one of the funds under management.

X fails Condition B because of his significant influence over the LLP.

2.5.4   Hierarchy of members

The terms under which people become members will vary. The point was made by a number of respondents to the consultation on the draft legislation that for practical and commercial reasons, there is a point at which businesses will introduce members with different powers. Hence it is common for there to be a hierarchy of membership.

The question is: what are the terms of each class of membership? This should be shown by the LLP Agreement, including the appropriate documentation under which an individual became a partner. Under the documentation, some members may be given more influence than others to decide matters relating to the management of the business.

Example 36

This is an example of a firm with different rights given to different members.

Legal Eagles LLP is a professional legal firm with 20 members. They meet each month for meetings at which the major business decisions are discussed and made. All members attend these meetings and all are entitled to speak. Junior members are entitled to attend these meetings (though not to vote).

On the facts, the junior members satisfy Condition B.

Suppose that the way that the firm conducts its business differs from that in the written agreement:

It has become the practice of the firm that votes are never taken and all decisions are made by consensus.

The test is applied on a realistic view of the facts. In this example, the written agreement does not reflect the entire agreement, the implied agreement is now that all members have an equal say. All members fail to satisfy Condition B.

2.5.5   Delegated powers

Some LLPs delegate a role such as management to a part of the membership.

The LLP Agreement usually indicates what and how powers are so delegated.

If the members of the management committee effectively run the LLP, then Condition B will not be satisfied in respect of those members. Condition B will be satisfied for the remaining members, who are potentially Salaried Members.

Against that, if the role of the management committee or of an individual member with management responsibilities is largely administrative, then that would satisfy Condition B.

Administrative decisions might include:

- payment of and issuing invoices
- detailed HR questions and those relating to non-key staff
- completing tax returns
- dealing with suppliers
- accounting
- management of premises
- dealing with routine compliance.

Please note that this is not an exhaustive list.

Example 37

This is an example of an influential individual in the course of retiring.

Up until 1 June 2014, E was the managing partner of GH LLP, a large professional services firm. Upon reaching the age of 60, E decided that she wanted to retire. F was appointed as the new managing partner, but F and the other members were keen to retain E's experience in order to mentor F and provide a smooth transition.

E agreed to carry on as a member for a further year, becoming the firm's chairperson. She would continue to be an integral member of the management committee in this period, providing direction to F and the other members, albeit reducing her hours at work.

E would withdraw her capital from the firm over the course of the year in order to purchase a second home in the south of France. It was also agreed that her profit share would largely be fixed for this period, even though it had been entirely variable up until 1 June 2014.

Will E be a Salaried Member in her final year with the firm?

Although it seems that Conditions A and C (see sections 2.3 and 2.6) of the test could be met in light of her move from a variable to a fixed profit share and the withdrawal of her capital, the circumstances are that she will clearly have significant influence over the affairs of the LLP for the whole of this period. Therefore, Condition B will not be met, meaning that Conditions A and C will not need to be considered; E will not be treated as a Salaried Member.

Although this example looks at a management committee, there are other aspects that may be delegated. For example, a firm may delegate to a particular group of members the power to decide the strategy of the firm. This can also mean that this group has significant influence.

Example 38

This example illustrates how controlling the strategy of the business as opposed to the managing of the business can give significant influence.

The TUV LLP is an investment manager. The four senior investment managers take no part in the day to day running of the firm, but set the investment strategy, deciding which markets the firm will invest in and reviewing the performance of the various funds, and taking action where they see the firm underperforming.

The four senior investment managers control and direct the firm's activities. They have significant influence and fail Condition B.

2.5.6   Part of a business

The test applies to the business as a whole. If an individual runs part of the LLP, such as a specific branch or shop, but has no say in the business as a whole, then Condition B will be satisfied and the individual can be a Salaried Member.

2.5.7   Indirect influence?

The test is whether that member has influence. Indirect influence, such as by being a director of another member, is not taken into account. Such indirect influence does not derive from the rights or duties of the individual as a member of the LLP.

Example 39

This example illustrates the position where there is a corporate member.

T is a member of the STU LLP and also a director of STU Ltd, the corporate member. Under the LLP agreement, control of the STU LLP is vested in the corporate member.

In her own right, T does not have significant influence. STU Ltd, of which she is a director, does have significant influence but this "indirect" influence is not taken into account. T therefore satisfies Condition B.

2.5.8 LLPs that are parents of a group

Where an LLP is a parent of a company or group of companies, then the question arises as to what is significant influence over the LLP as opposed to the group.

Example 40

This example illustrates management of a group.

The four senior members of the INT LLP hold monthly meetings at which they make strategic decisions for the group as a whole.

Other members will attend to report on the performance of subsidiaries or sectors, but the four senior members each hold 24% of the vote.

The four senior members are acting as the group's head office and have significant influence over the activities of the LLP and fail Condition B.

2.5.9 LLPs that are members of a group

The test in Condition B is whether that individual, as a member, has significant influence over that LLP.

The test is applied on the basis that whilst they may take the views of a parent body into account, the members will exercise the powers and duties placed upon them under the LLP Agreement.

Example 41

This example looks at who has significant influence when the LLP is effectively a subsidiary in a group.

The FOR LLP consists of individuals A, B & C, an unconnected corporate member FOR Ltd, and individual D, an employee of FOR Ltd. The strategy of the LLP is decided by the four individuals. On issues of importance to the FOR Group, FOR Ltd will indicate its views to the individual members.

The four individuals together decide the investment strategy. Although they will take into account the views of the FOR Group, their duties to the LLP mean that they have to make the decisions. All four individuals fail Condition B and are not Salaried Members.

It is understood that D has been appointed as representative of the FOR Group.

Although representing the Group, D is not its agent and holds significant influence in his own right. This can be contrasted with the position where FOR Ltd was also a member and D used their vote in a representative capacity.

2.6 Condition C – contribution to the LLP (S863D)

2.6.1 The general rule (S863D(1) and (2))

Condition C looks at the level of investment made by a member (M) in the LLP. Has the member made a significant investment in the business so they have a real risk resting on the success or failure of the business?

The general rule is that Condition C is met if, at the relevant time, M's capital contribution to the LLP is less than 25% of the Disguised Salary expected to be payable to M in respect of M's performance during the relevant tax year

If M has contributed less than 25%, Condition C is satisfied and M may be a Salaried Member.

Sub-section 2.6.2 considers what the capital contribution is. It should be noted that the general rule requires this amount to be compared to the Disguised Salary for the relevant tax year. This may be a different figure to that determined for the purposes of Condition A, which is based on the relevant period, not the tax year.

Sub-section 2.6.3 explains when the test should be applied.

Sub-section 2.6.4 sets outs some additional rules that need to be considered.

2.6.2 What is the contribution? (S863E(2))

The amount of capital contribution is based on the amount that the individual has invested as capital at that time in accordance with the LLP Agreement.

The capital of the LLP is the amount of money or other property that all the members have contributed in accordance with the LLP Agreement, to the permanent endowment of the firm.

As part of the LLP agreement, the amount of capital contributed cannot be varied by M alone, any variation has to be by agreement of all of the LLP members.

The capital is not the same as the assets of the LLP which includes everything with a money value and varies from day to day.

In addition to their capital, M is likely to have what is sometimes called a current account. This account reflects M's day-to-day balance with the firm reflecting things such as M's entitlement to a profit share, tax account and drawings. The current account balance is not capital contributed.

An undrawn profit share is not capital, but the members can agree to convert it into capital just as they can agree to pay a further sum in as capital.

In summary, the capital does **not** take into account:

- sums that M may be called upon to pay at some future date;
- undrawn profits unless by agreement they have been converted into capital;
- sums that are held by the LLP for M, for example, sums held in a taxation account; or
- amounts of capital that are part of arrangements to enable M to "avoid" being a Salaried Member where there is no intention that they have permanent effect or otherwise give rise to no economic risk to M.

Example 42

This is an example of the treatment of some different types of "capital contribution" and their effects on Condition C.

P has:

- *£10,000 contributed as capital in accordance with the LLP Agreement;*
- *£50,000 long term "loan". Interest is paid on this, but otherwise the amount is held on terms comparable to the capital, e.g. the loan is only repayable when P resigns, or the LLP is wound up The amount is treated for tax purposes as a share of the profit;*
- *£30,000 as a short term loan for a two year term;*
- *£25,000 undrawn profits – that can be withdrawn at any time; and*
- *£25,000 in a tax reserve current account to pay the tax on P's profit share.*

P is entitled to withdraw the short term loan, undrawn profits and the sum in the tax reserve current account, whilst he remains a member. These are not part of the capital contributed. P cannot withdraw either the sum described as capital or that described as a "loan". Regardless of the terminology used in the agreement, these are both intended for the long term financing of the firm. They act as partnership capital. P has capital of £60,000.

However, giving a guarantee is not partnership capital.

2.6.3 When to apply the test? (S863D(3) and (4))

Condition C has to be determined:

- at 6 April 2014 or, if later, when M becomes a member; and
- after that, at the beginning of each tax year.

In addition, the test needs to be re-determined whenever:

- there is a change in the contribution, or
- there is, otherwise, a change in circumstances that might affect whether or not Condition C is met.

In practice, where Condition C is not met, assuming all other circumstances remain the same, an increase in the contribution will not require a re-test as, clearly, Condition C will continue to be met.

Example 43

This example shows a change in circumstances which requires Condition C to be re-determined.

MJ is a member of the SSS LLP at 6 April 2014. At that date, MJ is expected to receive a Disguised Salary of £100,000 in the 2014/15 tax year. MJ's capital contribution at that date is £30,000, which is at least 25% of his Disguised Salary. Therefore, Condition C is not met.

On 1 October 2014, MJ's remuneration arrangements are amended so that his Disguised Salary for the tax year will now be expected to be £125,000. The change was not expected prior to this date. The new arrangement represents circumstances affecting the question of whether or not Condition C so the test needs to be re-determined on 1 October 2014. Condition C will now be met as MJ's capital contribution is less that 25% of his Disguised Salary.

2.6.4 Additional rules

In addition to the general rule, there are some additional rules which take priority over the general rule and apply:

- when a member joins or is expected to leave part way through the year (see sub-section 2.6.5);
- in order to prevent flipping between Salaried Member (employee) and partner status, when there is an increase in the capital contribution (see sub-section 2.6.6); and
- when a member provides an undertaking to make a capital contribution within a specified period (see sub-section 2.6.7).

2.6.5 Becoming, or ceasing to be, a member part way through the year (S863D(8)-(10))

Condition C requires the capital contribution to be compared to the Disguised Salary for the tax year (S863D(2)). If a member joins part way through the tax year, or is expected to cease to be a member before the end of the year, the capital contribution is proportionally reduced, on a pro rata basis, before it is compared to the Disguised Salary for the tax year.

The reduction is made on the basis of the "excluded days" rule so that the contribution reflects the number of days the individual is expected to be a member of the LLP when the test is carried out. In this context, excluded days are:

- the days in the tax year prior to the member joining the LLP, and
- any days in the tax year after the date which M is expected to cease to be a member.

Example 44

This example looks at where an individual becomes a member part way through the year.

M is appointed a member three months into the tax year. His reward package means that he will be due a fixed amount of £40,000 for the rest of the tax year (this is a Disguised Salary). The terms of his membership mean that he had to make a capital contribution of £12,000.

At first sight, M's contribution may appear to be at least 25% of his Disguised Salary (12,000/40,000 × 100 = 30%).

However, he will only be a member for nine months of the current tax year. His capital contribution is, therefore, reduced to reflect the period of the year that he will be a member: 12,000 × (9/12) = £9,000.

When the test is applied using this reduced figure (9,000/40,000 × 100 = 22.5%), Condition C is satisfied.

Extrapolating the example to the subsequent tax year, assuming that all circumstances are expected to remain the same throughout, M's Disguised Salary for that tax year will be £53,333 (£40,000 × 12/9). The actual capital contribution of £12,000 is compared to this figure at the start of the tax year but, clearly, the same result as in the previous year is produced (12,000/53,333 × 100 = 22.5%).

2.6.6 A change in the contribution part way through the year

A change in the amount of the contribution requires the test to be reapplied. The test will be applied differently depending on whether the change in contribution is a reduction or an increase.

2.6.6.1   A reduction in the contribution

Where the capital contribution is reduced, Condition C will need to be re-determined. The general rule (as set out in sub-section 2.6.1) will apply.

Example 45

This example illustrates how the test is applied when the capital contribution is reduced.

A is a member of the ABC LLP. At the start of the tax year, Condition C is not met as A has Disguised Salary of £450,000 and has made a capital contribution of £120,000 in accordance with the LLP Agreement. Therefore, A's contribution is more than 25% of his Disguised Salary.

Circumstances change and the members agree that A can reduce his capital contribution to £40,000 to enable him to fund a divorce settlement.

Condition C needs to be re-determined as there has been a change in A's capital contribution.

A now has a capital contribution of less than 25% of his Disguised Salary (($£40,000/£450,000$) x 100 = 8.8%). Condition C is now satisfied. Whether A is now a Salaried Member will depend upon whether he satisfies Conditions A and B (see sections 2.3 and 2.5).

2.6.6.2   An increase in the contribution

Where Condition C is not met, strictly, an increase in the contribution requires the test to be re-determined. The general rule (see sub-section 2.6.1) will apply. In practice, where Condition C is not met and there is an increase in the contribution (without any other change in circumstances), the condition does not need to be re-determined as, clearly, the condition will continue not to be met.

Where Condition C is met, however, an increase in the contribution will require the test to be re-determined. In this case, two special rules need to be considered which take priority over the general rule. Both rules are intended to prevent individuals from flipping between Salaried Member (employee) and partner status through short-term increases in capital contribution.

(i)   The first special rule (S863D(6) and (7)) provides that any increase in contribution which would, apart from this rule, have the effect of Condition C ceasing to be met is disregarded unless it is reasonable to expect that the condition would not be met (again, ignoring this rule) for the remainder of the tax year.

This means that it must be reasonable to expect that the increase will be a permanent one that will not later be reversed in the tax year.

(ii)   The second rule (S863D(11)) provides that any days in the tax year prior to the date on which the increased contribution is made and on which Condition C is met are excluded days, and are used to proportionally reduce the amount of the increased contribution on a pro rata basis before comparing to the Disguised Salary for the tax year.

This means that an LLP member who meets Condition C will not be able to fail the condition through an increased contribution unless the increased amount (after being reduced for excluded days) is at least 25% of the Disguised Salary.

Example 46

This example illustrates how the test is applied when the capital contribution is increased by an existing LLP member who already meets Condition C

J is a member of KLM LLP. At 6 April 2014, her capital contribution is £20,000. She is expected to receive Disguised Salary of £100,000 in the 2014/15 tax year. As J's capital contribution is less than 25% of her Disguised Salary. Condition C is met.

On 6 January 2015, J increases her capital contribution to £25,000. It is expected that the contribution will remain at this level for the rest of the tax year. As there has been a change in the contribution, Condition C needs to be re-determined.

As the change is an increase in the capital contribution and the Condition is previously met, the contribution is reduced on a pro rata basis, before comparing this to J's Disguised Salary for the **whole tax year** (i.e. not just the amount for the remainder of the year).

J's capital contribution is deemed to be £6,250 (£25,000 x 3/12). As this amount is still less than 25% of her Disguised Salary, she continues to meet Condition C for the rest of the tax year.

In contrast, if J increased her capital contribution to £100,000, instead of £25,000, then the contribution would be treated as being £25,000 (£100,000 x 3/12). As this amount is equal to at least 25% of her expected Disguised Salary in the tax year, she will not meet Condition C from 6 January 2015.

It is important to remember that, in a case where Condition C continues to be met despite the increase by virtue of the special excluded days rule, this is only fixed until the end of that tax year, assuming that no further changes are made. At the start of the next tax year, Condition C will need to be re-determined and the increased capital contribution may then be sufficient to fail Condition C until such time as the Condition needs to be re-tested.

2.6.7   Deemed contributions (S863F)

To avoid the position where individuals are treated as employees for tax purposes for a short period whilst they obtain finance in order to invest capital, the legislation provides a transitional easement.

This applies where:

- the member has given an undertaking (whether or not legally enforceable) to provide a capital contribution to the LLP (but has not made the contribution); and
- the undertaking requires the member to make the contribution by:
  - 5 July 2014 if the individual is a member at 6 April 2014, or
  - the later of 5 July 2014 and two months after the date on which the individual becomes a member, if the individual joins the LLP after 6 April 2014.

If these requirements are satisfied, the amount undertaken to be provided is treated as if it is an actual contribution made on the date the undertaking is given for the purposes of determining whether or not Condition C is met.

The actual making of all or part of the contribution is ignored, meaning that the test needs not be re-determined, provided it is made within the period as undertaken.

If the individual fails to make all, or part, of the contribution within that period, then the determination of whether Condition C was met is revisited as at the time it was originally made without taking into account so much of the deemed contribution as was not in fact paid.

Example 47

This example shows how the "Deemed Contribution" rule works where the contribution is in fact made.

M is an existing member of an LLP at 6 April 2014 who has not previously contributed capital to the LLP. On 5 April 2014, M gives an undertaking to the LLP that he will make a contribution of £50,000 by 5 July 2014.

The question of whether Condition C is met is determined on 6 April 2014 and takes into account the deemed contribution of £50,000 resulting in Condition C not being met. On 30 June 2014, M contributes £50,000 to the LLP. This contribution does not trigger a re-determination and Condition C is treated as not met until the end of the 2014/15 tax year or unless there is a later change that requires a re-determination.

Example 48

This example shows how the Deemed Contribution rule works if the member does not in fact make the contribution which was expected.

M is an existing member of an LLP at 6 April 2014 who has not previously contributed capital to the LLP. On 5 April 2014, M gives an undertaking to the LLP that he will make a contribution of £50,000 on 5 July 2014.

The question whether Condition C is met is determined on 6 April 2014 and takes into account the deemed contribution of £50,000 resulting in Condition C not being met. M fails to make any of the contribution by 5 July 2014. On 6 July 2014, the question of whether Condition C was met at 6 April 2014 is revisited. M is not treated as having made a contribution so Condition C is met. If M also meets Conditions A and B (see sections 2.3 and 2.5) on 6 April 2014, then M is treated as a Salaried Member from that date.

2.7 Further examples

There are further examples in the Annex. These examples look at the way in which the Salaried Member test is applied as a whole, rather than looking at the way that the separate conditions apply to the individual, and are based upon scenarios put to HMRC during the development of the legislation. They are used to highlight a number of points. They also highlight specific issues arising from certain global structures particularly relevant to large professional services firms.

3 Anti-Avoidance Provisions

3.1 Anti-Avoidance (S863G)

The anti-avoidance legislation is intended to prevent people using artificial structures or arrangements to place members outside the scope of the Salaried Member provisions.

It is not avoidance if the terms under which an individual is a member change and they become a member on genuine terms comparable to a partner in a traditional partnership.

The legislation also prevents the misuse of the Salaried Member provisions as part of a scheme or arrangement to avoid the impact of the mixed membership partnership provisions.

3.1.1 Avoidance arrangements (S863G(1))

In deciding whether an individual is a Salaried Member, no regard is to be had to any arrangements the main purpose, or one of the main purposes of which, is to secure that the individual (or that individual and other individuals) is not a Salaried Member.

In applying this test (Targeted Anti-avoidance Rule (TAAR)), HMRC will take into account the policy intention underlying the legislation, which is to provide a series of tests that collectively encapsulate what it means to be operating in a typical partnership. HMRC would not consider that genuine and long-term restructuring that causes an individual to fail one or more of the conditions to be contrary to this policy aim.

3.1.2   Financing arrangements

An individual will fail condition C if the individual has made a contribution 25% or more of any Disguised Salary payable in the tax year.

The capital contribution requirement is fairly prescriptive and HMRC would accept that a genuine contribution made by the individual to the LLP, intended to be enduring and giving rise to real risk, will not trigger the TAAR.

Such a contribution may be obtained through a loan from a third party, typically a bank. The firm might itself arrange the loan through a partnership facility. Provided that the debt will then be that of the individual partner, this manner of obtaining the funding will not trigger the TAAR.

It would of course be a question of fact as to whether a main purpose of the arrangement was to secure that the individual was not a Salaried Member, but it is likely that HMRC would consider the TAAR to be in point if the contribution is provided as part of an arrangement where the following features are present (noting this is not an exhaustive list):

- It derives from a non-recourse or limited recourse loan.
- The LLP, or a body connected with the LLP, loans the money back to the individual.
- The firm, rather than the individual member, pays or otherwise bears the cost of the interest on the loan. HMRC would accept that the firm does not bear the cost simply because it pays the interest as agent for the member (including where that payment is from a priority profit share created for the member as a consequence of the capital contribution).
- An individual is to be brought into the LLP for a fixed term assignment and it reasonable to assume that the capital contribution has been made so that the individual fails the test for the duration of that assignment.
- The funds derive from the firm itself or from a body connected with the LLP (for example, there is a loan from the LLP to the individual or from a bank as part of an arrangement where there is to be a reduction in the firm's indebtedness to the bank).

As regards the final bullet, a member's capital contribution will in many cases necessarily end up in the firm's bank account and, if the firm is overdrawn or otherwise in debit, have the effect of reducing the firm's debt to the bank. Provided that there is no reduction to the firm's borrowing limit as a result of the partner loan the firm can redraw the relevant amount), HMRC would not seek to apply the TAAR unless there were other offending features (e.g. the partner loan was limited recourse).

On the other hand, HMRC would consider the TAAR to be relevant in the following situations:

- The LLP has borrowed up to its facility limit and a condition of the loan to the individual member is that the contribution is used to repay a portion of the drawn facility so that the overall lending is not increased (with the relevant amount not being capable of being redrawn by the firm);
- The firm has not yet borrowed up to the facility limit, but the firm's facility limit is required to be reduced as a consequence of the loan to the individual; or
- A condition of the loan being made is that the money will end up and remain with the lending bank.

3.1.3   TAAR examples (6)

Example 1

This example describes a non recourse loan.

W is a junior member of the ABC LLP and she has only invested a nominal amount of capital. Conditions A and B are satisfied. W receives a limited recourse loan to raise her capital so that Condition C is not satisfied. In reality, the money makes its way back in a circle to the lender.

The main purpose of the loan is to enable W to avoid being a Salaried Member. The additional capital is ignored, Condition C is satisfied and W is a Salaried Member.

The position would be unchanged if the arrangements were put in place for one or one hundred members. A main purpose is to enable a member, or a number of members, avoid being a Salaried Member.

Example 2

This example covers a genuine capital contribution.

P has been an employee of the DEF LLP. She has reached that point in her career where she is offered membership.

In order to become a member, P needs to invest in the LLP. She has some capital of her own, and the LLP arranges with the Bank for her to have a normal commercial loan to cover the balance. An undertaking is given that on P's retirement from DEF LLP, the firm will pay back the loan directly out of P's capital account and, if necessary, any undrawn remuneration, with full recourse against P if these amounts prove insufficient.

These arrangements have substance and will not trigger the TAAR.

They have not been put in place to enable P to avoid being a Salaried Member. P faces genuine risk, she has invested in the DEF LLP and she does owe money to the bank, which she will need to repay and, in the interim, she will have to pay interest.

Becoming a full member, on terms akin to those of a partner in a traditional partnership, is not avoiding being a Salaried Member.

The DEF LLP has organised facilities for a number of members as well as P. As part of the arrangement, DEF LLP pays the interest as agent for the members, which is treated as a priority profit share for those members.

Although for practical reasons the LLP paid the interest centrally, they have then charged it out to the members so P has paid the interest.

Example 3

This example looks at where the loan to the member affects the loan available to the LLP.

R has been an employee of the FED LLP. She has reached that point in her career where she is offered membership.

In order to become a member, R needs to invest in the LLP. She has some capital of her own, and the LLP arranges with the Bank for her to have a normal commercial loan to cover the balance.

However, the Bank facility covers both the LLP and its members. The result of the loan to R is a reduction in the amount the LLP can borrow.

In these circumstances the TAAR is triggered as all that has happened is that a part of the loan facility of the LLP has been moved to the P.

Example 4

This example looks at where a party connected to the LLP provides a loan

The USO LLC operates in the UK through UKB LLP. Individual T is appointed a member of the UKB LLP. It is agreed that T will introduce a sum as capital. USO LLC provides a loan to T to enable him to contribute the agreed sum of capital.

In this example, the parent body of the LLP provides a loan to an individual which they then introduce as capital. On the facts, HMRC would look to apply the TAAR.

Example 5

This example shows an individual joining an LLP for a short-term engagement with no intention of being a partner.

A is an associate in a US law firm Adfsf GP. He is to be seconded to the UK "subsidiary" entity Adsfg LLP for a two year period to provide general legal support. During this period, he will be rewarded almost wholly by Disguised Salary.

He and the LLP agree as part of his terms of engagement as a member that he must contribute capital of 30% of the Disguised Salary which will be repayable immediately after the end of the two years. The firm is extremely well-capitalised and there is no real prospect of the capital being at risk. He is also given voting rights on matters which are expressed to be significant, but in reality he is a junior member with no significant influence over the firm's affairs.

Neither the capital nor A's involvement with the firm is intended to be enduring. His connection with the firm is like that of an employee on secondment rather than a partner, and there are from day one arrangements for his departure after a set period. On the facts, HMRC would look to apply the TAAR.

3.1.4 Use of intermediaries (S863G(2) and (4))

If an individual works for the LLP and, to avoid being a Salaried Member, enters into arrangements so that someone else, such as a company, becomes a member and receives amounts due to the individual then:

- the individual is treated as a Salaried Member,
- the sum paid to the actual member in relation to the individual's services is treated as being paid to the individual, and
- the sum is treated as employment income of the individual.

Example 6

This example shows the circumstances where TAAR applies.

J realises that he would be a Salaried Member. With the agreement of the LLP, he introduces as a member J Ltd. J Ltd receives the reward package that had been agreed for J.

These arrangements have been entered into to avoid the impact of the Salaried Member legislation. J is deemed to be the member, with the result that the sum due to J Ltd is treated as payable to J.

The LLP must account for PAYE and NICs on the amounts paid to J Ltd for the services of J. So if £100,000 was invoiced by J Ltd, the LLP must deduct the appropriate amounts of PAYE and NICs and account for secondary NICs on that £100,000.

3.2 Interaction with mixed membership partnership legislation

The Salaried Member legislation does not apply where an individual would otherwise be a Salaried Member because of arrangements that have a main purpose of securing that the mixed membership partnership legislation does not apply (new section 850C).

4 Implementation Matters

4.1 Deductions in respect of Salaried Members (S94AA, S272, and CTA/S92A & S210)

If a member is a Salaried Member, then the costs of employing that individual are expenses of earning profits in the same way as the costs of employing any other individual.

This means that they are allowable deductions in the same way and the same period as the expenses in respect of any regular employee.

Where the costs of employing the Salaried Member would not be deducted in arriving at the profits of the LLP under the normal accounting practice (SORP), a specific statutory deduction is available for tax purposes as explained below.

4.1.1 Trades & property businesses

For a trade or property business relief is given in the period in which the sum is treated by the SORP as a deduction in arriving at the profits, and it is not otherwise disallowable under general rules.

If the sum is not treated as a deduction under the SORP, then a statutory deduction is allowed in arriving at the profits of the LLP in the period when the sum is paid.

This is subject to a number of restrictions. No relief is available for:

- capital expenditure;
- expenditure that is not paid wholly & exclusively for the purposes of the trade;
- entertaining expenses; and
- NICs.

4.1.2 Investment companies

This section looks at the position where the profits of the LLP are calculated as for an investment company (section 1259 CTA 2009).

If costs of employing a Salaried Member would be expenses of management of a company's investment business but are not referable to an accounting period, they are treated as referable to the accounting period in which they are paid. The availability of a deduction for the payment is then subject to the normal management expenses rules.

4.1.3 Disallowable expenses

A Salaried Member is treated as an employee for tax purposes and not as a partner. Where the LLP has any expenses that are treated as disallowable for tax purposes, then these are taken into account in arriving at the taxable profit shares of those treated as partners for tax purposes.

4.2 Returns

As the Salaried Member is not treated as a partner for tax purposes, they are not included on the partnership return for a period when they are a Salaried Member.

If the circumstances of an individual changes and they are treated as a partner for part of the period, then they need to be included in the return for that part period.

This means that an individual who is determined to be a Salaried Member at 6 April 2014 when the legislation comes into effect would be included in the partnership return for the period up to 5 April 2014, and they would be treated as ceasing as a partner on that date.

Example 1

This example considers how to deal with the returns for the LLP and the effects on the individual member under the new rules.

M has been a member of ARC LLP since 1 July 2010. ARC LLP commenced trading in 2001 and has had an accounting date of 30 June throughout.

Prior to 6 April 2014, ARC LLP carries out a review of its membership as a result of the new Salaried Member rules.

The review shows that M satisfies all three conditions and so M will be a Salaried Member as of 6 April 2014.

The nominated member will include M on the partnership return as a partner for the period up to 5 April 2014. ARC LLP will then treat M as an employee and operate PAYE from 6 April 2014.

The position for M is considered in the following three sub-sections. The position for the LLP is set out at both sub-sections 4.2.3 and 4.2.4.

4.2.1 Self-employment

For tax purposes, M will cease to be a partner of ARC LLP on 5 April 2014. This means that M's basis period for the 2013/14 tax return will follow the cessation rules and run from the day after the previous basis period ends to the date M ceases to be a partner. A just and reasonable apportionment of profits earned from 1 Jul 2013 to 5 Apr 2014 should be included. M can also claim overlap relief in this final period.

M's self assessment returns will be as follows:

Tax Year	Basis period	Profits £	Overlap period	Overlap profits/relief £
2010/11	1 Jul 2010 – 5 Apr 2011	60,000		
2011/12	1 Jul 2010 – 30 Jun 2011	79,000	1 Jul 2010 – 5 Apr 2011	60,000
2012/13	1 Jul 2011 – 30 Jun 2012	81,000		
2013/14	1 Jul 2012 – 5 Apr 2014	140,000		60,000

Further information about self-employment can be obtained from HMRC's contacts: http://search2.hmrc.gov.uk/kb5/hmrc/contactus/view.page?record=fPCm_2Cccl0

4.2.2 Employment

As of 6 April 2014, M will be an employee of ARC LLP for tax purposes. M's entitlement under the LLP agreement is treated as coming from an employment. ARC LLP will need to account for PAYE on amounts paid or credited to M, including M's monthly drawings and any amounts in respect of M's variable profit share. ARC LLP will also be liable to pay employer's Class 1 NICs. M will not need to complete a tax return for 2014/15 (unless M has other income that needs to be reported through Self Assessment) as M has paid M's income tax and NICs through PAYE.

4.2.3 Implications of moving from Self Assessment to PAYE

The main implication of becoming a Salaried Member concerns the payment of NICs.

For an LLP member who is a partner, the member pays in 2014/15[4]:

---

[4] Details of NICs payments are published on the HMRC website: http://www.hmrc.gov.uk/rates/nic.htm

- Class 2 NICs on annual earnings in excess of £5,885, which is a flat rate amount of £2.75 per week;
- Class 4 NICs at 9 per cent on profits between £7,956 and £41,865; and
- Class 4 NICs at 2 per cent on any profits above this.

Any sum paid to the Salaried Member is treated as remuneration subject to deduction of PAYE and employee NICs. The LLP will be treated as the "employer" and secondary contributor for employer NICs and statutory payments. The LLP is responsible for accounting for:

- a Salaried Member's primary Class 1 NICs at 12 per cent of earnings between £153 per week and £805 per week and 2 per cent on any earnings over £805 per week; and
- secondary Class 1 NICs of 13.8 per cent due from the LLP itself on amounts over £153 per week.

4.2.4   Employment & Compliance – the LLP's Position

4.2.4.1   Operating PAYE

If the LLP currently has employees and is operating PAYE, then the following link is useful as it sets out what the LLP has to do when it is decided a member is a Salaried Member: http://www.hmrc.gov.uk/payerti/employee-starting/new-emp-info.htm

If the LLP does not currently have any employees, then it will need to set up a PAYE scheme. Please follow this link to see what is required: http://www.hmrc.gov.uk/payerti/getting-started/register.htm

Information about how to operating PAYE in real time (RTI) can be found in the following link: http://www.hmrc.gov.uk/payerti/index.htm

4.2.4.2   Benefits in kind and statutory payments

If the LLP provides a Salaried Member with a car, there will be benefits in kind implications. Benefits in kind are to be treated in the same way for employees and Salaried Members – see this link about the obligations: http://www.hmrc.gov.uk/payerti/exb/forms.htm

As the LLP is secondary contributor for NICs, they are also responsible for the operation of the regimes relating to statutory payments, statutory maternity pay, statutory sick pay, statutory adoption pay and statutory paternity pay. Details of the LLP's obligations can be found at: http://www.hmrc.gov.uk/payerti/employee/statutory-pay/index.htm

Enquiries about employment issues can be sent to HMRC's contact points: http://search2.hmrc.gov.uk/kb5/hmrc/contactus/view.page?record=yg7jCcYewik

4.2.4.3 Compliance & PAYE failure

If HMRC reviews the position and it is found that the LLP has failed to treat a member as a Salaried Member, then this would be a PAYE failure.

The result would be that the LLP, as the employer, would be liable to pay over the amount that should have been deducted from the amount that was actually paid to the employee.

For further guidance on this, please see the Compliance Operational Guidance at COG913010: http://www.hmrc.gov.uk/manuals/cogmanual/COG913010.htm

4.3 Capital assets

Where, after applying the tests in sections 863A and 863B, an individual is treated as a Salaried Member, the legislation applies to treat all amounts received by that individual as employment income subject to the applicable income tax rules under ITEPA. Class 1 and 2 NICs may also apply.

A Salaried Member is subject to the same rules on taxable benefits received as any other employee.

This treatment does not include any amounts received by a Salaried Member in respect of capital assets of the LLP that would not be taxable as employment income if received by an employee. Examples include dividends from shares held by the firm.

The interest received by a Salaried Member when becoming a member of the LLP is not itself considered to be a benefit for income tax purposes.

4.4 Further Information

This note represents an informal view of HMRC on how the legislation would apply to LLP members who are Salaried Members. Non-statutory clearances will be provided in respect of the legislation after Finance Bill 2014 receives Royal Assent (see the guidance in footnote 1 in section 1.8).

LLPs with Salaried Members will need to operate PAYE in respect of those members from 6 April 2014 when the legislation comes into force. Businesses can contact their customer relationship managers or co-ordinators for further information including how to proceed with a clearance. Additional guidance on employment taxes will be provided as appropriate.

Annex : General Examples and Global Structures

(A) General Examples

The examples in this Annex look at the way in which the Salaried Member test is applied as a whole, rather than illustrating how the separate conditions apply to the individual.

To ensure that the examples are as realistic as possible, they have been based upon scenarios put to HMRC during the consultations. They are used to highlight a number of points.

Example 1 (Condition A)

This example shows that professional qualifications are not relevant to the question whether Condition A is met.

50 people currently work for the A LLP, of whom forty-five are listed as members.

The A LLP business plan is inclusive, recognising that everyone working for the business is contributing to the success of the business; hence once it is clear that the individual is going to stay with the business, they are invited to become a member.

Of the forty-five members, 15 are professionally qualified, five of whom qualified in the last 5 years whilst 3 other members are working for their professional qualifications. The remainder have no intention of becoming professionally qualified.

The Salaried Member test is **not** concerned with experience or professional qualifications. It looks at the role that individual plays in the business.

Under the LLP agreement each member is entitled to an equivalent to statutory sick pay, maternity/paternity leave, holiday entitlement and termination rights.

Although these may make the partner look like an employee, they are **not** taken into account in the Salaried Member test.

Each member receives a profit share. The proportion varies from member to member, but everyone knows that if the business makes less profit they will have less income and if it makes a loss they get nothing.

All the members, from a secretary to the founders know that their income from year to year depends on the level of profit. If the firm makes a loss, then they have no income for the year. This means that Condition A is not satisfied. No member of the A LLP is a Salaried Member and no further action is needed.

The fact that the various members draw sums during the year does not change this, provided that the sums are simply drawings in advance of profit shares.

Example 2 (Conditions B & C)

This example looks at a similar LLP but also takes in Conditions B & C.

B LLP is similar to A LLP in the preceding example, but only the five senior members receive profit shares, the rest have non-refundable drawings and a nominal profit share, so that 90% of their income is Disguised Salary and they will meet Condition A.

The B LLP is largely a people business using rented accommodation. However, it does need capital. Each of the members has made a contribution, varying with their position in the firm, but starting at £1,000.

Whether Condition C is satisfied depends upon the amount contributed by the member. Condition C will be satisfied unless the capital is at least 25% of the expected Disguised Salary for the tax year.

If in the case of B LLP, all members satisfy Condition C.

Each of the members has a share of the proceeds in the event of winding up.

This is not a factor in the Salaried Member test.

Management of B LLP is delegated to a Management Board, consisting of 9 members who are professionally qualified (these include the 5 senior members who receive profit shares), and the Office Manager, also a member of the LLP, who has no professional qualifications. The other members have no real say in the business.

The ten members of the Management Board do not satisfy Condition B. They are not Salaried Members. The fact that the Office Manager is not professionally qualified does not matter; the key is that the role gives the individual significant control.

Example 3 (Conditions A & B)

This looks at an example of an LLP controlled by its founders and the transfer to a new generation. This results in a change in their remuneration structure and their ability to influence the firm's affairs.

C LLP was founded by two individuals, A & B. A & B are entitled to the residual profits, make all the major decisions and they have invested all but a nominal amount of the capital.

The other members receive a fixed monthly sum plus an annual discretionary bonus, typically 20% to 30% of their annual fixed compensation.

The other members are all Salaried Members, satisfying Conditions A, B & C. Whilst the bonus is sometimes more than 20% of the reward package, this is set without reference to the profits of the firm but is instead based wholly on their own fixed compensation. In addition, the individuals have no real influence and no capital contribution.

> *After a while, as had been the intention, C & D, two of the junior members, start to take on elements of the work done by A & B.*

As their terms have changed, the test needs to be applied again to C & D.

> *C & D will receive a lower monthly sum, and instead will receive a share of the profits. A reasonable estimate is that about 25 to 30% of their reward package will be in the form of a profit share. They will also take part in all major decisions.*

C & D have sacrificed an entitlement to salary in exchange for the opportunity to participate in the business in much the same way as A & B the senior members, even if as junior members they are substantially rewarded by a fixed profit share. Conditions A and B are no longer met so C & D are no longer Salaried Members.

Example 4 (Condition B)

This example looks at junior members and how one member makes the transition to a more senior position.

> *The XYZ LLP typically has about 100 members.*
>
> *Existing employees can be invited to become junior members. As a junior member, they initially introduce £4,000 as capital and receive "4 units". The unit is the measure by which residual profits are allocated. As a comparison, the senior partner has 150 units.*

The term "unit" is not material; it is simply the method of allocating the residual profits.

> *Junior members are awarded a fixed guaranteed profit share, plus the profit from their units. For a junior member, the profit share under the unit system will be no more than 5% to 10% of the total package.*
>
> *The firm's management power is centralised in a management board formed by the senior members.'*

The junior members satisfy all three conditions, they have less than 10% of their reward package as a variable profit share, nominal capital only and no real say.

> *Catherine has been a junior member but is being promoted. She will sit on the management board and have a significant influence over the running of the business. In addition, she will receive more units but it is still reasonable to expect that less than 20% of her reward package will be variable.*

Catherine has accepted an opportunity to participate in the business in much the same way as a senior member, even if, as a relatively junior member, she is still substantially rewarded by a fixed profit share. Catherine would still satisfy Condition A but she is not a Salaried Member as she now does not satisfy Condition B.

(B) Global Structures

This section looks at the position of UK LLPs that form part of structures that cross international boundaries ("global structures").

The Salaried Member legislation is applied to the individual as a member of that LLP. It does not take into account income from other parts of the global structure, influence in other parts of the global structure or capital invested in other parts of the global structure.

As the Disguised Salary test is focused on the UK LLP, it is important that the financial transactions between the UK LLP and other members of the global structure are conducted on an arm's length basis.

Example 5 (Condition A)

This example illustrates a firm doing business with an associate overseas (and the effect of the arm's length principle).

> *The members of ABC LLP are A, B and Y Ltd, a subsidiary of Swiss Co.*
>
> *The only customer of ABC LLP is Swiss Co. The profits of ABC LLP are determined on an arm's length basis reflecting its contribution to the global profits and losses of Swiss Co. As a result, ABC LLP could be profitable when Swiss Co is loss-making or vice versa.*
>
> *The profits of ABC LLP are allocated to A and B in line with variable profit sharing arrangements within ABC LLP's LLP agreement.*

A and B fail Condition A. They share only in the profits of ABC LLP which have been calculated on a normal commercial basis.

Example 6 (Condition A - no performance of services)

This example illustrates a profit share paid to a UK partner by an overseas firm.

> *ABC LLP is associated with a US partnership ABCUS LLP (formed under the law of Delaware). A B and C are members of ABC LLP and so is ABC US LLP. A B and C are members of ABC US LLP which also has a further 10 members. All profits of ABC LLP are paid to ABC US LLP and shared by its members along with the other profits of the firm. A B and C receive a share of the global profits.*

A B and C are not Salaried Members as they do not have any income in their capacity of members of ABC LLP. However, ABC LLP is a mixed membership partnership and the mixed membership partnership rules (new sections 850C to 850E) need to be considered.

1.1   Overseas members

Where a member is resident does not affect the Salaried Member legislation. If a member satisfies the three conditions then he or she is a Salaried Member.

Example 7

This example shows that residence is not a factor in deciding if someone is a Salaried Member.

D is French resident member of the UKF LLP. She works in the Paris Office and receives a salary of £75,000, has no say in the running of the LLP and has contributed no capital to the LLP.

D is a Salaried Member and treated for UK purposes as an employee. The fact that she is French resident does not alter her status for the purposes of the Salaried Member legislation. The normal employment income rules will determine to what extent she is taxable on her income in the UK. Her French tax status is a matter for the French tax authorities.

1.2   Profits from the UK LLP

The test is applied to the profit share from the UK LLP.

In some cases, it may be intended that the members of a global business are to be rewarded on the basis of global profits (this reward will reflect the contribution of local offices to the generation of those profits).

Those global profits may be the aggregate of the profits of the UK LLP plus profits earned outside the UK from a related (so-called *parallel*) partnership. The parallel partnership may exist because the laws of the relevant foreign territory will not permit the LLP to operate there.

To ensure that profits can flow between the LLP and foreign partnership, there will be at least one member common to each entity (sometimes referred to as a "valve partner"): this member may draw out profits from the foreign partnership to top up the payments to be made to the members of the UK LLP (or may receive additional amounts from the UK partnership to top up the valve partner's profit share). Amounts received from the UK LLP will fail Condition A if they are variable by reference to the profits of the UK LLP.

It should be noted that this guidance only relates to the treatment of amounts under the rules relating to treatment of Salaried Members. The tax position of this kind of arrangement generally involves other issues which are not covered in this guidance.

1.3   Global profits

Example 8

This example shows that where the size of the global profit cake varies by reference to the UK LLP's profits, then the reward derived by the members of the UK LLP may still be affected by the level of the UK LLP's profits.

Z is an Australian law firm with an LLP "subsidiary" operating in London, which is highly profitable. Z LLP cannot operate directly in Australia for legal reasons. Instead, the business in Australia is operated through a general partnership Z GP.

The two firms work closely together and the members of the Z LLP are to be rewarded by reference to the global profits of Z (including the LLP).

There is a member Y who is a member of both Z LLP and Z GP whose role is to act as valve partner.

The UK profits are expected to be a sizable proportion of the global profit, but it is highly likely that the valve partner (Y) will be used to transfer profits from the Z LLP to Z GP in Australia.

The members of Z LLP fail Condition A because:

- their reward for services is not a fixed sum;
- their reward for services is affected by the amount of the UK profits (even though it is also affected by the profits of Z in Australia); and
- their reward will in practice be affected by the amount of the Z LLP profits.

1.4   Costs plus basis

If the profits of the UK LLP are calculated on a "costs plus" basis, then Condition A is satisfied as the level of profits vary with the rewards to the members rather than the members receive a reward that varies with the profits of the LLP.

Example 9

A firm using a costs plus basis is illustrated in the following example.

P and Q are members of P&Q LLP which is a fund manager associated with a US firm. All fund management fees are paid directly to the US firm.

P and Q provide services to the US firm and agree at the end of the year that based on the profits of the US firm, £300,000 will be allocated to P&Q LLP as their remuneration, in addition to an amount equal to the costs of the business of £500,000. The LLP has agreed a 'costs plus' basis with HMRC and therefore the profit taxable in the UK will also include an additional £80,000 (i.e. a 10 per cent mark up on costs including the members' remuneration).

The £300,000 is not in practice variable by reference to the overall amount of the profits of the UK firm because it is set according to the profitability of the associated firm. Therefore it is Disguised Salary. Similarly, the additional £80,000 varies according to the members' remuneration and other costs, not the profits of P&Q LLP. P and Q meet Condition A.

Example 10

This example shows that profit shares from other members of the structure are not taken into account.

AA LLP is a UK firm that has set up a business in Australia. AA LLP cannot operate in Australia for legal reasons. Instead, the business in Australia is operated through a general partnership AA GP. The two firms work closely together. A, B & C are individuals who are members of both AA LLP and AA GP.

The Salaried Member legislation looks at the role of the member in the UK body only. In this case, only the position of the AA LLP and not the AA GP will be considered when deciding whether A, B & C are Salaried Members.

Depending upon profit levels in the two firms, A, B & C may draw profits from either body depending on the relative profits of the two firms.

How are the members to be rewarded by the UK LLP?

At the start of the year, the AA LLP must look at the individuals and decide if Condition A is going to be satisfied:

A & B work for AA LLP, they each receive a salary of £100,000 plus a proportion of the profits of AA LLP. On the basis of the business plan for the combined operation, they are expected to receive profit shares of £250,000 each from AA LLP; in addition, A is expected to receive £25,000 from AA GP.

Ignoring the share that A expects to receive from AA GP, A & B do not satisfy Condition A and are not Salaried Members.

1.5 Performance of services

C is based in Australia but she receives a profit share from the UK where AA GP makes insufficient profits. AA works full time as a member of AA GP, not for AA LLP.

In this case, C does not receive her profit share for working for AA LLP; hence she is not a Salaried Member as she does not receive a sum for working for the UK LLP.

Example 11

This example illustrates profits earned by a partner in a UK firm from an overseas firm.

Z is a member of XT UK LLP, the UK arm of a global business with its headquarters in the US. Z receives a fixed amount from XT UK LLP. Z also receives a share of the global business' profits by virtue of being a member of XT US LLP, the US parent entity.

The share of the profits she receives is expected to be more than 20% of the total amount she receives from the global business.

The Salaried Member legislation is applied at the UK LLP level. It considers the role of Z in XT UK LLP, not the global body. Z receives a fixed amount from XT UK LLP, hence she satisfies Condition A.

The amount Z receives from XT US LLP is not taken into account in deciding whether or not she is a Salaried Member. The status of Z in XT US LLP is decided under the partnership test at BIM82005[5].

1.6 Capital of the LLP

The legislation looks at the UK LLP in isolation. As a result, capital invested in another member of the structure is not taken into account, even if the UK LLP receives funding from that body.

Example 12

This example shows how HMRC would look at the LLP in isolation.

The ABC US LLP is the worldwide "parent" of the ABC firm, which operates in the UK through the ABC UK LLP and which it funds through a mixture of capital and loans.

A is a member of a US LLP, who is seconded to work in the UK, becoming a member of the UK LLP.

A has capital invested in ABS US LLP but not ABS UK LLP.

As the test applies to the UK LLP in isolation, A satisfies Condition C as he has contributed no capital to ABS UK LLP.

---

[5] See HMRC's guidance published on its website: HUhttp://www.hmrc.gov.uk/manuals/bimmanual/BIM82005.htm

1.7 Significant influence

The significant influence condition, Condition B is applied at the level of the UK LLP.

The test is applied on the basis of the rights and duties under the LLP Agreement. Whilst the board of the body at the head of the structure may express their views and it is reasonable for the members of the UK LLP to take those views into account, ultimately the influence rests with those members of the UK LLP identified in the LLP Agreement, subject to the management being carried out in accordance with the agreement.

Case Table

(References are to paragraph numbers)

Paragraph

A

A Partnership [2015] TC 04358 28-420

AB [2011] TC 01527 18-400

Acornwood LLP [2014]
TC 03545 .... 25-060; 25-460; 25-500

Ahmed (1987) 3 BVC 1,349 28-260

Akbar (t/a Mumtaz Paan House) [1998]
BVC 2,157 28-300

Alexander Bulloch & Co v IR Commrs
(1976) 51 TC 563 .... 10-120; 10-140

Ayrshire Pullman Motor Services
and DM Ritchie v IR Commrs,
(1929) 14 TC 754 .... 10-080; 10-120;
10-160; 10-200

B

Beaton, Snelling & Co
(1986) 2 BVC 208,116 28-020

Beckman v IR Commrs (2000)
Sp C 226 27-140

Bird Semple & Crawford Herron
(1986) 2 BVC 205,488 28-580

Blackpool Marton Rotary Club v
Martin [1988] BTC 442 10-080

C

C & E Commrs v Evans
(t/a The Grape Escape
Wine Bar) (1981)
1 BVC 455 .... 28-020, 28-260

C & E Commrs v
Glassborow (1974)
1 BVC 4 .... 28-000; 28-020; 28-240

C & E Commrs v Jamieson
[2002] BVC 354 28-100

C & E Commrs v Leightons Ltd
[1995] BVC 192 28-120

C & E Commrs v Lord Fisher (1981)
1 BVC 392 .... 10-080; 15-120

C Clarke deceased [1998]
BVC 2,036 28-740

Paragraph

C Connelly & Co v Wilbey
(HMIT) [1992] BTC 538 18-440

Chiplen [1995] BVC 1,519 28-020

D

Dass v Special Commissioner
[2006] BTC 866 18-380

Dickenson v Gross (1927)
11 TC 614 10-160

Dodd and Tanfield v Haddock
(1963) 42 TC 229 10-080

Dreyfus v IR Commrs (1929)
14 TC 560 10-080

DS Talafair & Sons [1999]
BVC 4,115 28-700

F

Fenston v Johnstone (1940)
23 TC 29 10-160

Finanzamt Saarlouis v Malburg
(Case C-204/13) [2014]
BVC 12 28-400

G

George Hall & Son v Platt (1954)
35 TC 440 10-080

Green [1993] BVC 628 28-660

Green v Herzog and Others [1954]
1 WLR 1309 16-900

H

Hall v IR Commrs (1997)
Sp C 114 27-140

Harnas & Helm v Staatssecretaris
van Financiën (Case C-80/95)
[1997] BVC 358 28-200

Harrison-Broadley v Smith [2008]
BTC 7,085; [1964]
1 All ER 867 16-720

Hartridge (t/a Hartridge
Consultancy) [1998]
BVC 2,281 28-420

Haugh [1997] BVC 2,525 28-380

Paragraph

Hawker v Compton (1922)
8 TC 306 10-080

Hawthorn v Smallcorn [1998]
BVC 101 28-120

Heastie v Veitch & Co (1934)
18 TC 305 18-320

Hussein (t/a Pressing Dry Cleaners)
[2004] BVC 4,028 28-260

I

IR Commrs v Gardner Mountain &
D'Ambrumenil, Ltd. (1)
(1947) 29 TC 69 19-340

IR Commrs v Gordon [1991]
BTC 130 15-140

IR Commrs v Graham's Trustees
1971 SLT 46 27-100

Islam & Goodwest Ltd [2003]
BVC 4,043 28-300

K

KapHag Renditefonds v
Finanzamt Charlottenburg
(Case C-442/01)
[2005] BVC 566 .... 28-180; 28-200;
28-340; 28-360; 28-680

L

Lawson v Brooks [1992]
BTC 53 14-060

Lester Aldridge (a firm) [2005]
BVC 2,231 .... 28-400; 28-580

London & Essex Cleaning Services
(Southern) [2010] TC 00309 10-180

M

MacKinlay (HMIT) v Arthur
Young McClelland
Moores & Co. [1989]
BTC 587 .... 10-460; 18-040; 18-260

Major (HMIT) v Brodie [1998]
BTC 141 14-200

Mann v Nash (1932) 16 TC 523 10-340

Maritsan Developments Ltd [2012]
TC 01971 28-340

Morgan; Self [2009] TC 00046 .... 18-280;
18-400

Mundays LLP [2012] TC 02374 28-460

Paragraph

N

Nationwide Building Society v
Lewis and Williams (ChD
[1997] 3 All ER 498; CA
[1998] 3 All ER 143 10-240

Nye Saunders & Partners [1995]
BVC 1,339 28-440

P

Padmore v IR Commrs [1989]
BTC 221 18-100

Parnalls Solicitors Ltd [2010]
TC 00261 18-420

PDC Copyprint (South) (1997)
Sp C 141 19-080

Phillips [2010] TC 00276 10-180

Polysar Investments Netherlands
BV v Inspecteur der
Invoerrechten en Accijnzen,
Arnhem (Case C-60/90)
[1993] BVC 88 28-200

Pooley v Driver (1876)
5 Ch D 458 10-080

Private and Confidential Ltd
[2009] TC 00038 28-140

R

R & C Commrs v Hamilton &
Kinneil (Archerfield Ltd)
[2015] BTC 512 25-580

R & C Commrs v Martin [2014]
BTC 527 19-340

R & C Commrs v Pal [2008]
BVC 3 28-260

R & C Commrs v Phillips [2010]
TC 00276 10-180

R & C Commrs v Vaines [2016]
BTC 502 .... 18-040; 18-240; 20-040

R v Income Tax General
Commissioners, ex parte
Gibbs (1942)
24 TC 221 .... 10-060; 10-460

Ramsay [2012] TC 01871 15-120

Ramsay v R & C Commrs [2013]
BTC 1,868 15-120

Reed v Young [1986] BTC 242 25-320

Paragraph

Régie Dauphinoise –Cabinet
A Forest SARL v Ministre
du Budget (Case C-306/94)
[1996] BVC 447 28-200

Richart v J Lyons & Co Ltd [1989]
BTC 337 15-440

Robinson Family Ltd [2012]
TC 02046 15-160

Rock Lambert [1992] BVC 536 28-480

Roelich [2014] TC 03704 15-160

Rolls v Miller (1884) 27 Ch D 71 10-080

S

Sadler v Whiteman [1910]
1 KB 868 10-060

Saunders and Sorrell (1980)
1 BVC 1,133 28-240

Saywell v Pope (1979)
53 TC 40 10-140

Scrace v R & C Commrs [2007]
BVC 791 28-040

Southern v AB (1933) 18 TC 59 10-340

Staatssecretaris van Financiën v
Heerma (Case C-23/98)
[2003] BVC 97 28-700

Stekel v Ellice [1973]
1 WLR 191 10-400

Paragraph

Summers [2012]
TC 02267 28-020

T

The Bengal Brasserie [1991]
BVC 1,363 28-260

Tod (HMIT) v Mudd [1987]
BTC 57 14-640

Trinity Mirror plc v C & E Commrs
[2001] BVC 167 28-180

Vaines [2013] TC 02965 .... 18-040; 18-240

Valantine [2011]
TC 01644 .... 10-080; 10-160

Waddington v O'Callaghan (1931)
16 TC 187 10-200

Walker v Hirsh (1884)
27 Ch D 460 10-240

Wellcome Trust Ltd v C & E
Commrs (Case C-155/94)
[1996] BVC 377 28-200

Yarl Wines [2003] BVC 4,045 .... 28-260;
28-300

Yasin [1999] BVC 4,031 28-000

Legislation Finding List

(References are to paragraph numbers)

Provision	Paragraph
Agricultural Holdings Act	
See generally	16-400; 16-720
Capital Allowances Act 2001	
2	22-000
3	17-100
6	22-000
15	22-040; 25-100
15(1)	22-040; 22-080
38A	22-020
38A(1)–(2)	22-020
38A(3)	22-020
38B	22-020
59	23-100
83	17-100
89	17-100
104E	22-100
108	22-100
129	17-100
131	17-100
135	17-100
163	25-200
177	17-100
183	17-100
214	22-120
215	22-120
216	22-120
217	22-120
218	22-120
218A	22-120
218ZA	22-120
225	22-120
227–228	22-120
263	22-040
260(3)	25-300
263(2)	22-040
263(3)	22-040
263(4)	22-040
263(5)	22-040
263(6)	22-040
264	14-140; 22-060
264(2)	22-060
264(3)	22-060
264(4)	22-060
265	22-080; 22-100

Provision	Paragraph
265(1)–(1B)	22-080
265(2)	22-080
265(3)	22-080
265(4)	22-080
265(5)	22-080
266	15-060; 17-100; 22-100
266(3)	22-100
266(7)	22-100
267	22-100
267(4)	22-100
267A	22-100
268	17-100
290	17-100
355	17-100
381	17-100
492	22-220
557	22-160; 22-180
557–558	22-160
558	22-160
558(3)	22-160
558(4)	22-160
558(5)	22-160
559	22-180
559(1)–(1A)	22-180
559(2)	22-180
559(3)	22-180
559(4)	22-180
559(5)	22-180
560A	22-040
561	22-040; 22-100
561A	22-040
564(2)	22-240
567	22-200; 22-220
567(1)	22-200
567(2)	22-200
567(3)	22-200
567–570	22-140
568	22-200
568–570	22-140
569	17-100; 22-220
569(1)	22-220
569(3)	22-220
570	22-220
570(1)	22-220

Capital Allowances Act 2001 — continued

Provision	Paragraph
570(2)	22-220
570(4)	22-220
570(5)	22-220
573	22-220
574	22-260
575	22-100; 22-200; 22-260
588(1)–(1A)	22-160
Pt. 2	22-200
Pt. 2, Ch. 6	22-120
Pt. 2, Ch. 6A	22-120
Pt. 2, Ch. 16A	25-260
Pt. 3A	22-200; 22-220; 23-080
Pt. 5	22-200; 22-220
Pt. 6	22-200; 22-220; 23-080
Pt. 10	22-200; 22-220
Pt. 12, Ch. 4	22-140; 22-160

Commissioners for Revenue and Customs Act 2005

Provision	Paragraph
5	28-380

Companies Act 1985

Provision	Paragraph
See generally	11-060
736	28-220

Companies Act 2006

Provision	Paragraph
See generally	10-300
603	15-040
1000	13-100
1003	13-100
1159	28-220
Sch. 6	28-220

Corporation Tax Act 2009

Provision	Paragraph
8(2)	18-160
18A	17-300
35	18-400
36	18-480
41	22-040
46	18-120; 18-160
53	18-460
54	18-320; 18-460
54(1)(a)	18-440
77(5)	21-160
80	21-160
92A	18-460; 32-140
109(1)	17-100
124(2)	17-100
127(2)	17-100
162	21-160
162(3)	21-160
178	17-100

Provision	Paragraph
180	18-560
181	18-560
182	18-560
183	18-560
184	18-560
188–196	21-160
205	18-500
206	18-520
210	32-140
261	18-560
261–262	18-560
262	18-560
262(1)	18-560
262(5)	18-560
262(6)	18-560
268	17-100
280–285	21-160
301	18-180
307	19-220
328	19-220
328(3)	19-220
328(3A)	19-220
348	19-180
349	19-180
354–357	19-180
358–360	19-180
380	18-180
380-385	19-200; 19-120
380(1)	18-180
380(2)	18-160; 18-180; 19-120; 19-200
380(3)	18-180; 19-120; 19-200
380(4)	18-180
381	19-120
381(1)	18-200
381(2)	18-200
381(2)–(4)	19-200
381(3)	18-200; 19-140
381(4)	18-200
381(5)	19-120
381(5)–(7)	18-200
381(6)	19-120
381(6)–(7)	19-200
381(7)	19-120
382	19-120; 19-200
383	19-120; 19-140; 19-160
383(2)–(4)	19-140
383(7)	19-140
383(8)	19-140

Provision	Paragraph	Provision	Paragraph
384	19-120; 19-220	1261(2)(c)	21-160; 25-220
384(2)	19-220	1261(2)(d)	21-160; 25-220
384(3)	19-220	1261(3)	21-160
385	19-120; 19-220; 19-240	1261(4)	21-160; 25-220
389	25-300	1261(5)	21-160; 25-220
407	19-240	1261(6)	18-160
459	25-300	1262	18-040; 19-100; 19-120; 19-260; 21-160
461(5)	25-240	1262(1)	18-040; 19-200
461(6)(a)	25-200	1262(2)	19-200; 19-260
462	25-200	1262(4)	19-200
463	25-200	1262–1264	19-000; 19-380; 19-420
466	19-160; 19-180	1262–1264A	19-000
466(2)	19-160	1263	19-100; 19-280
467	19-180	1264	19-100; 19-280
472	19-140; 19-180	1264A	19-000; 19-320; 19-380; 19-420; 19-480
479(1)	19-200	1264A(2)(b)	19-380; 19-420
479(2)	19-200	1265	20-200
479(3)	19-200	1265(1)	19-200
480(1)	19-200	1265(2)	19-200
481(1)	19-200	1266	18-100
481(2)	19-200	1266(1)	18-100
481(3)	19-200	1266(2)	18-100
481(4)	19-200	1266(3)	18-100
619–620	19-200	1267(3)	21-160
835	14-580	1267	18-560
857	18-060	1267(4)	21-160
912	21-180	1267–1269	18-560
913	21-180	1270(1)	18-480
914–917	21-180	1270(2)	18-500
919	21-180	1270(3)	18-520
920	21-180	1271	21-180
940A	22-040	1271(1)	21-180
948	22-040	1271(3)	21-160; 21-180
949	22-040	1271-1272	21-180
950	22-040	1272	21-180
1124(2)	19-140	1273	18-020; 29-000
1227A	32-140	1273(1)	30-060; 30-120
1257	18-060; 18-160	1273A	29-000; 32-020
1258	18-000; 18-040; 20-000	1298	18-460
1259	18-040; 18-060; 18-160; 18-460; 21-160	1302	18-460
1259(3)	18-040	1305(1)	18-160
1260	18-160	Pt. 2, Ch. 2	18-160
1260(1)	18-160	Pt. 3, Ch. 3	18-120; 18-160
1260(2)	18-160	Pt. 3, Ch. 4	18-400
1261	18-160; 21-160; 25-220	Pt. 3, Ch. 14	18-560
1261(1)	18-160; 25-220	Pt. 5	19-140; 19-160; 19-180
1261(2)(a)	18-160	Pt. 5, Ch. 5	19-120; 19-160; 19-180
1261(2)(b)	21-160		

Corporation Tax Act 2009 — continued

Provision	Paragraph	Provision	Paragraph
Pt. 5, Ch. 6	19-180	137(4)–(6)	25-300
Pt. 5, Ch. 8	19-180	137(4)(a)	25-200
Pt. 5, Ch. 9	18-180; 19-120; 19-200	137(5)	25-200
Pt. 8	12-440	137(5)(a)	25-200
Pt. 9	19-220	138	25-300
Pt. 15	25-260	152	25-300
Pt. 17	18-000; 21-000	153(1)	25-300
Pt. 22, Ch. 1	22-040	153(2)	25-300
Corporation Tax Act 2010		183	19-440
See generally	37-38; 25-000; 25-560	189(2)	25-200
4(3)	25-200	304	25-260
37	25-200; 25-240; 25-260; 25-300; 25-560; 25-580	304(1)	25-260
		387(7)	22-100
37(3)(a)	25-200	410(6)	22-100
37(3)(b)	25-200	439	24-000
37(5)	25-260	439(2)	24-000
37(6)	25-200	439(3)	24-000
39	25-220	448	24-000; 24-020
39–42	25-000	448(1)(a)	24-000; 24-020
42	25-260	448(1)(b)–(d)	24-000
44	25-260	448(1)(d)–(e)	24-000
45	25-000; 25-240; 25-260; 25-560	448(1)(f)	24-000
46	25-240	448(1)(g)	24-000
48	25-260	448(2)	24-000
52	25-260	450	31-100
53	25-260	451	31-100
54	25-260	454(1)	24-000
55	25-340	454(2)	24-000
56	25-560	455	24-000; 24-020; 24-040
56–58	25-000; 25-560	455(1)	24-000
57	25-560	455(1)(c)	24-020
57(3)	25-560	455(2)	24-000
57(8)	25-560	455(3)	24-000; 24-020
57(9)	25-560	455(4)	24-000
58	25-560	458	24-000
59–61	25-000; 25-580	458(2)	24-000
59	25-580	459	24-020
60	25-580	464A	24-040
60(2)	25-580	464A(1)	24-040
60(3)	25-580	464A(2)	24-040
60(5)	25-580	464A(3)	24-040
60(7)	25-580	464A(4)	24-040
60(8)	25-580	464A(5)	24-040
61	25-580	464A(6)	24-040
91	25-260	464A–464B	24-040
109	22-100	464B(2)	24-040
137(1)	25-300	464B(3)	24-040
137(4)	25-200	753	30-060

Provision	Paragraph
757A	29-000; 30-000; 30-020; 30-060
757A(1)	30-060
757A(2)	30-060
757A(3)	30-060
757A(4)	30-060
757A(5)	30-060
757A(7)	30-060
757B	29-000; 30-000; 30-020; 30-060
757B(1)	30-060
757B(4)	30-120
779A	29-000; 30-000; 30-080; 30-120
779A(10)	30-120
779A(12)	30-120
779A(2)	30-120
779A(2)(a)	30-120
779A(2)(b)	30-120
779A(3)	30-120
779A(4)	30-120
779A(5)	30-120
779A(6)	30-120
779A(7)	30-120
779A(8)	30-120
779A(9)	30-120
779B	29-000; 30-000; 30-080; 30-120
779B(1)	30-120
797B(3)	30-060
958–962	25-280
959	25-280
960	25-280
961(1)	25-280
961(2)	25-280
961(3)	25-280
962	25-280
1000	15-260
1000(1)	15-260
1109	17-080
1122	16-720; 16-820; 16-900
1122(6)	16-280; 16-940; 16-960; 16-995
1122(7)	16-820
1124(2)	19-140
1139	19-440; 30-040; 30-060; 30-120
1173	25-280
1273	29-000

Provision	Paragraph
1273A	29-000
Pt. 2, Ch. 4	19-200
Pt. 4	25-000
Pt. 4, Ch. 3	25-340
Pt. 4, Ch. 3	25-320
Pt. 5	25-000; 25-300; 25-560; 25-580
Pt. 9, Ch. 3	22-100
Pt. 9, Ch. 4	22-100
Pt. 14	25-260
Pt. 14A	25-260
Pt. 16, Ch. 1	29-000; 30-000
Pt. 16, Ch. 1A	29-000; 30-120
Pt. 16, Ch. 4	29-000; 30-060
Pt. 22, Ch. 3	25-280
Pt. 23, Ch. 2	18-160

Co-operative and Community Benefit Societies Act 2014

Sch. 7	10-020

Films Act 1985

Sch. 1, para. 1	25-520

Finance Act 1972

2	28-240
22(1)	28-240

Finance Act 1993

94AB(1)	19-200
94AB(2)	19-200
184	25-380; 25-460

Finance Act 1996

See generally	19-200
Sch. 9, para. 19	19-200
Sch. 9, para. 19(4)	19-200

Finance Act 1998

Sch. 18, para. 5	17-160
Sch. 18, para. 12	17-160
Sch. 18, Pt. IV	17-180
Finance Act 2002	19-200
Sch. 26, para. 49	19-200

Finance Act 2003

45	16-200
53	16-140
65	16-160
65(1)	16-040
65(2)	16-040
65(3)	16-040
65(4)	16-040
75A	16-160; 16-200
75A 1(a)–(c)	16-200
75A(1)	16-200

Finance Act 2003 — continued

Provision	Paragraph	Provision	Paragraph
75A–75C	16-120	Sch. 15, para. 29	16-660
75C	16-120	Sch. 15, para. 30	16-160; 16-480; 16-680
75C(8A)	16-200	Sch. 15, para. 31, 32, 33	16-700
Sch. 4A, para. 3	16-680	Sch. 15, para. 34	16-440; 16-620; 16-720
Sch. 4A, para. 3(B)	16-120	Sch. 15, para. 34(2)	16-240
Sch. 7, para. 3	16-640	Sch. 15, para. 35	16-740
Sch. 15	12-000; 15-060; 16-120; 16-880	Sch. 15, para. 36	16-760
Sch. 15, para. 1	16-000; 16-900	Sch. 15, para. 37	16-780
Sch. 15, para. 2	16-020; 16-920	Sch. 15, para. 38	16-800
Sch. 15, para. 3	16-020	Sch. 15, para. 39	16-820
Sch. 15, para. 4	16-020	Sch. 15, para. 40	16-160; 16-840
Sch. 15, para. 5	16-540	Sch. 15, Pt. 2	16-340; 16-540
Sch. 15, para. 5(A)	16-540	Sch. 15, Pt. 3	16-020; 16-060; 16-120; 16-140; 16-200
Sch. 15, para. 6(1)	16-060	Sch. 15, Pt. 4	16-140
Sch. 15, para. 6(2)	16-080	Sch. 16, para. 3, 4	16-860
Sch. 15, para. 7	16-100	Sch. 17A, para. 10(1)	16-800
Sch. 15, para. 8	16-080	Sch. 24, para. 10, 11, 18, 19	16-600
Sch. 15, para. 9(2)	16-220	**Finance Act 2004**	
Sch. 15, para. 9–40	16-140	See generally	16-700; 25-320
Sch. 15, para. 10	16-540; 16-600	52	19-200
Sch. 15, para. 10(1)(a), (b), (c)	16-320	74	16-990
Sch. 15, para. 10(1)(a)–(c)	16-540	122A	25-780
Sch. 15, para. 11	16-160; 16-260; 16-600	127	25-840
Sch. 15, para. 12	16-280	326	19-200
Sch. 15, para. 12A	16-340; 16-540	Pt. 2(6)	19-200
Sch. 15, para. 14	16-180; 16-380; 16-440; 16-460; 16-480	Pt. 3	16-120
Sch. 15, para. 14(3A)	16-540	Pt. 3, Ch. 3	16-380
Sch. 15, para. 14(3B)	16-540	Sch. 10, para. 35(2)	19-200
Sch. 15, para. 14(3C)	16-540	Sch. 24, para. 9	16-380
Sch. 15, para. 15	16-400; 16-540	**Finance Act 2005**	
Sch. 15, para. 16	16-410	See generally	25-500
Sch. 15, para. 17	16-160; 16-420; 16-480	**Finance (No. 2) Act 2005**	
Sch. 15, para. 17A	16-160; 16-240; 16-320; 16-620	Sch. 10, para. 10	16-320
Sch. 15, para. 18	16-560; 16-600; 16-620	Sch. 10, para. 21	16-700
		Sch. 15, para. 10	16-140; 16-240
Sch. 15, para. 18(1)	16-720	Sch. 15, para. 17A	16-140
Sch. 15, para. 19	16-160; 16-600	**Finance Act 2006**	
Sch. 15, para. 21, 22	16-160; 16-580	See generally	16-140; 16-240
Sch. 15, para. 23	16-600	75	14-260
Sch. 15, para. 24	16-560	Sch. 24, para. 3	16-260
Sch. 15, para. 25, 26, 27, 28	16-160; 16-640	Sch. 24, para. 5	16-560
		Sch. 24, para. 6	16-560
		Sch. 24, para. 7	16-560
		Sch. 24, para. 8	16-600
Sch. 15, para. 27A	16-280	Sch. 24, para. 10	16-320

Provision	Paragraph
Sch. 24, para. 14	16-320
Sch. 24, para. 17A	16-320
Finance Act 2007	
See generally	16-140; 16-180; 16-280; 16-360; 16-380; 25-360; 25-460
72(3)	16-280
72(4)	16-280; 16-560
72(7)	16-560
72(9)	16-280
72(10)	16-760
72(11)	16-820
72(12)	16-860
114	25-520
Sch. 4, para. 2(2)	25-460
Sch. 4, para. 2(3)	25-460
Sch. 4, para. 2(4)	25-460
Sch. 15, para. 36	16-520
Sch. 24, para. 1	28-320
Sch. 24, para. 20	17-260; 28-320
Sch. 27, Pt. 2(1)	25-520
Finance Act 2008	
See generally	12-220; 16-180; 16-540; 25-460
Sch. 3, para. 6	14-520
Sch. 15, para. 14	16-180
Sch. 22, para. 21	14-060
Sch. 36	17-280
Sch. 36, para. 1	17-280
Sch. 36, para. 2	17-280
Sch. 36, para. 3(1)	17-280
Sch. 36, para. 5	17-280
Sch. 36, para. 5(4)	17-280
Sch. 36, para. 5A	17-280
Sch. 36, para. 30(2)	17-280
Sch. 36, para. 37	17-280
Sch. 36, para. 37(2)	17-280
Sch. 36, para. 37(3)	17-280
Sch. 36, para. 37(4)	17-280
Sch. 36, para. 37(5)	17-280
Sch. 36, para. 37(6)	17-280
Finance Act 2009	
See generally	14-060
25	25-260
Sch. 55	17-240
Sch. 55, para. 16	17-240
Sch. 55, para. 20	17-240
Sch. 55, para. 21	17-240
Finance Act 2010	
55	16-120

Provision	Paragraph
Finance Act 2013	
See generally	14-060; 14-080; 24-020
58–61	11-020
Sch. 15	19-500
Finance Act 2014	
See generally	19-280; 19-520; 25-540; 26-000; 30-000; 31-140; 32-000; 32-140
Sch. 17, para. 12	19-480
Sch. 17, para. 12(1)	19-480
Sch. 17, para. 13	19-480
Sch. 17, para. 13(3)	19-480
Sch. 17, para. 13(4)	19-480
Sch. 17, para. 14	25-540
Sch. 17, para. 28(2)	30-060
Sch. 17, para. 29(2)	30-120
Finance Act 2015	
See generally	14-500; 14-580; 14-600; 15-020; 15-180; 15-480; 15-520; 19-500; 31-000; 31-020; 31-100; 31-120
21	31-000
25(2)(c)	19-240
25(9)–(14)	19-240
Finance (No. 2) Act 2015	
See generally	31-000; 31-140
43	31-000; 31-120
43(3)	31-240
43(3)–(4)	31-140
43(4)	31-300
44	30-060
45	31-100
Finance Act 2016	
See generally	14-500; 14-580; 14-600; 14-620; 23-440; 23-480; 31-000; 31-020; 31-060; 31-120; 31-320; 31-340
36(2)	31-040
27(2)	31-060
38	31-040
Financial Services and Markets Act 2000	
See generally	17-300
Income and Corporation Taxes Act 1970	
152	18-040
Income and Corporation Taxes Act 1988	
18	18-400
21B	21-020
55	27-140
74	18-400
111	18-040
111(1)	18-040
111(2)	18-040
111(3)	18-040

Income and Corporation
Taxes Act 1988 — continued

Provision	Paragraph
111(4)	18-040
112(4)	18-100
112(5)	18-100
113	21-020
113(1)	21-020
114	18-040; 21-160
114(1)	19-200
114(1)(a)	18-160
114(2)	19-200
114–116	21-160
115(5)	18-100
115(5A)	18-100
117	25-320
118	25-320
118ZC	25-580
118ZC(3)	25-580
118ZC(4)	25-580
118ZL	25-520
118ZO	25-500
359(1)	14-140
362	14-160; 14-200
367(4)	14-080
369	17-300
570	17-100
571(4)	17-100
787	14-120
839	16-200
839(3)	16-560

Income Tax Act 2007

Provision	Paragraph
See generally	14-140; 14-160; 14-180; 25-400; 25-420; 25-440; 25-460; 25-480; 25-520; 25-640
23	14-020; 14-240
24A	14-040; 25-020; 25-040
24A(6)(h)	14-040
26	14-240
26(1)	14-240
60(4)	25-060
64	17-320; 25-020
64–70	25-000
64(2)(a)	25-020
64(2)(b)	25-020
64(2)(c)	25-020
64(3)	25-020
64(4)	25-020
64(5)	25-020
65	25-020

Provision	Paragraph
65(1)	25-020
65(3)	25-020
66	25-020; 25-480
67–70	25-020
71	25-000; 25-020
72	17-320; 25-040
72(3)	25-040
72–74	25-000; 25-040
73	25-040
74	25-040
74(1)	25-480
74E	23-000; 23-340; 25-020; 25-040; 25-080
74ZA	25-060
74ZA(1)	25-060
74ZA(3)	25-060
74ZA(4)	25-060
74ZA(5)	25-060
74ZA–74D	25-020; 25-040
75	25-100
75(2)	25-100
75(3)	25-100
75–79	25-020; 25-040; 25-100
76	25-100
77	25-100
78	25-100
80	25-020; 25-040; 25-120
82	25-120
83	17-320; 25-140; 25-540
83–88	25-000
83(1)(b)	25-140
83(2)	25-140
83(4)	25-140
86	15-060
88	17-320
89	17-320; 25-160; 25-540
89–94	25-000; 25-160
90(1)	25-160
90(1)(a)	25-160
90(1)(b)	25-160
90(5)	25-160
90(6)	25-160
91	25-160
92	25-160
94	17-320; 25-160
95	25-020; 25-180
102	25-340
103	25-360

Provision	Paragraph	Provision	Paragraph
103(1)	25-360	110(8)	25-460
103(2)	25-360	110–114	25-000
103A	25-000; 25-360; 25-640	111	25-360; 25-460; 25-680
103A(1)(c)	25-640	111(1)	25-460
103B	25-460; 25-860	111(2)	25-460
103B–103D	25-000	111(2)–(3)	25-460
103B(2)	25-460	111(4)–(5)	25-460
103B(4)	25-460	111(6)–(8)	25-460
103B(5)	25-460	111(9)	25-460
103C	25-000; 25-380	111(12)	25-460
103C–105	25-000	112	25-460
103D	25-000; 25-380; 25-520	112(6)	25-460
103D(4)	25-520	113	25-480
103D(5)	25-520	113(5)	25-480
104	25-360; 25-400; 25-460; 25-500; 25-640; 25-680	113A	25-000; 25-400; 25-420; 25-460; 25-500
104(4)	25-400	113A(1)	25-460
104(5)	25-400	113A(2)	25-460
104(6)	25-400	113A(3)	25-460
104(7)	25-400	113A(4)	25-460
105	25-360; 25-680	114	25-000; 25-400; 25-420; 25-460; 25-500; 25-640; 25-660
105(2)	25-400		
105(2)–(3)	25-400		
105(4)–(5)	25-400	115	25-000; 25-340; 25-520
105(6)–(10)	25-400	115(2)	25-520
105(9)	25-400	115(5)	25-520
105(11)	25-400	115(6)	25-520
107	25-360; 25-420; 25-440; 25-460; 25-500; 25-640; 25-680	115(8)	25-520
		115(9)	25-520
		116	25-520
107(6)	25-420	116A	19-520; 25-000; 25-340; 25-540
107(7)	25-420		
107(8)	25-420	116A(1)	19-520; 25-540
107–109	25-000	116A(2)	19-520; 25-540
108	19-360; 25-420; 25-680	116A(3)	25-540
108(2)	25-420	116A(5)	25-540
108(2)–(3)	25-420	116A(6)	25-540
108(4)	25-420	116A(7)	25-540
108(5)–(6)	25-420	118	25-540
108(7)–(8)	25-420	120	25-540
108(9)	25-420	127C	19-520; 25-540
109	25-440	383	14-020; 17-320
110	25-360; 25-420; 25-460; 25-480; 25-500; 25-640; 25-680	383(1)	14-020; 14-240
		383(3)	14-020
		383(4)	14-020
110(4)	25-480	384	14-060
110(5)	25-460	384(1)	14-060
110(6)	25-460	384(3)	14-060
110(7)	25-460	384(4)	14-060

Income Tax Act 2007 — continued

Provision	Paragraph	Provision	Paragraph
384(5)	14-060	400(4)	14-280
384A	14-060	400(7)	14-280
384A(2)	14-060	406(1)	14-300
384B	14-060; 23-320	406(2)	14-300
384B(1)	14-060	406(3)	14-300
384B(2)	14-060	406(4)	14-300
385	14-080; 14-140	406-407	14-300
385(1)(b)	14-080	407(1)–(3)	14-300
385(2)	14-080; 14-140	407(4)	14-300
385(3)	14-080; 14-140	408	14-320
385(4)	14-080	409	14-340
386	14-080	409(1)–(2)	14-340
386(1)	14-080	410	14-340
386(2)	14-080	410(1)	14-340
386(3)	14-080	410(2)	14-340
386(4)	14-080	411	14-360
387	14-080; 14-100	411(1)	14-360
387(1)	14-100	411(2)	14-360
387(2)–(7)	14-100	411(3)	14-360
388	14-140; 23-320	411(5)	14-360
388(1)	14-140	412	14-380
388(2)(a)	14-140	448	20-180
388(2)(b)	14-140	457	17-320
388(3)	14-140	458	17-320
389	14-140	668	17-100
389(2)	14-140	669	17-100
389(3)	14-140	791	25-600; 25-620
389(4)	14-140	792	25-400; 25-420; 25-460; 25-620; 25-640; 25-680; 25-760
389(5)	14-140		
398	14-200; 23-320		
398(1)	14-160	792(3)	25-640
398(2)	14-160	792(4)	25-620
399	14-160; 14-200	792(6)	25-640
399(1)–(3)	14-160	792(7)	25-640
399(4)	14-160; 14-260	792(8)	25-640
399(5)	14-180	793	25-660
399(6)	14-160	794	25-680
399A	14-220; 14-240	794(3)	25-680
399A(1)	14-200; 14-220	794(4)	25-680
399A(2)	14-220	794(6)(a)	25-680
399A(3)-(6)	14-220	794(6)(b)	25-680
399A(7)	14-220; 14-260	796	25-600; 25-700; 25-720
399A(9)	14-220	796–803	25-120; 25-340
399B	14-240	797	25-700; 25-800; 25-820
400	14-260; 14-280	797(2)	25-720
400(1)	14-260	797(4)	25-720
400(2)	14-280	797(5)	25-720
400(3)	14-280	797(5)(a)	25-780

Provision	Paragraph
797(5)(b)	25-780; 25-800
797(6)	25-720
798	25-700; 25-720
799	25-700; 25-740; 25-780
800	25-700; 25-720; 25-760
800(2)	25-760
800(4)	25-760
800(10)(a)	25-760
800(10)(b)	25-760
800(10)(c)	25-760
801	25-780
801(3)–(5)	25-780
801(8)	25-780
801–802	25-700
803	25-700; 25-800
804	25-600; 25-820
804–809	25-340
805	25-820; 25-840; 25-860
805(2)	25-820
805(4)–(6)	25-820
806	25-840
807	25-840
807(2)	25-840
807(3)	25-840
807(4)	25-840
807(5)	25-840
807(6)	25-840
808	25-860
808(8)	25-860
808(9)	25-860
808–809	25-860
809	25-860
809(3)	25-860
809(4)	25-860
809AAZA(8)	30-040
809AAZA	30-020; 30-040
809AAZA(1)	30-040
809AAZA(2)	30-040
809AAZA(3)–(5)	30-040
809AAZA(6)	30-040
809AAZA(7)	30-040
809AAZA(8)	30-040
809AAZA–809AAZB	29-000; 30-000
809AAZB	30-020; 30-040
809AAZB(1)	30-040
809AAZB(2)	30-040
809AAZB(4)	30-040
809AZB(2)	30-040
809AZB(3)–(5)	30-040; 30-100

Provision	Paragraph
809AZB(6)	30-040; 30-100
809AZF	29-000; 30-000
809B	18-080
809D	18-080
809DZA	30-080; 30-100
809DZA(1)–(2)	30-100
809DZA(3)	30-100
809DZA(4)–(6)	30-100
809DZA(8)	30-100
809DZA(9)–(12)	30-100
809DZA–809DZB	29-000; 30-000
809DZB	30-080; 30-100
809DZB(1)	30-100
809DZB(2)	30-100
809DZB(3)	30-100
809E	18-080
809EZA	31-040; 31-240
809EZA(2)	31-040
809EZA(2A)–(2C)	31-040
809EZA(3)	31-040
809EZA(3)(c)	31-100
809EZA(4)	31-040
809EZA(6)	31-160
809EZB	31-060; 31-160
809EZB(1)	31-060
809EZB(1)(c)	31-060; 31-340
809EZB(2)	31-060; 31-180
809EZB(2)(a)	31-060
809EZB(2)(b)	31-000; 31-060
809EZB(2A)	31-060
809EZC	31-060; 31-080
809EZC(1)	31-080
809EZC(2)	31-080
809EZC(3)	31-080
809EZC(4)	31-080
809EZC(5)	31-080
809EZC(6)	31-080
809EZC(7)	31-080
809EZC(8)	31-080
809EZD	31-080
809EZD(2) or (3)	31-340
809EZDA	31-000; 31-100
809EZDA(1)–(3)	31-100
809EZDA(4)	31-100
809EZDB	31-000; 31-100; 31-300
809EZDB(1)	31-100
809EZDB(2)	31-100
809EZDB(3)	31-100
809EZDB(4)	31-100

Income Tax Act 2007 — continued

Provision	Paragraph	Provision	Paragraph
809EZDB(5)	31-100	809FZT	31-340
809EZDB(6)	31-100	809FZU–809FZZ	31-340
809EZDB(7)	31-100	809FZV	31-340
809EZDB(8)	31-100	809FZW	31-340
809EZDB(8)(b)	31-300	809FZX	31-340
809EZDB(9)	31-100; 31-300	809FZY	31-340
809EZDB(10)	31-100	809FZZ	31-340
809EZE	31-160	809ZG	14-120
809EZF	31-040	874	17-300
809EZG	31-040	874(2)	17-300
809EZG(1)–(3)	31-040	874(5A)	17-300
809EZG(4)–(6)	31-040	875	17-300
809FC(5)	31-340	876	17-300
809FZA(7)	31-340	877	17-300
809FZB	31-340	878	17-300
809FZC(5)	31-340	879	17-300
809FZC-809FZJ	31-340	880	17-300
809FZD	31-340	881	17-300
809FZD(1)	31-340	882	17-300
809FZD(2)	31-340	883	17-300
809FZE	31-340	884	17-300
809FZE(2)	31-340	885	17-300
809FZE(3)	31-340	886(1)	17-300
809FZF	31-340	886(2)	17-300
809FZG	31-340	887(1)	17-300
809FZG(2)	31-340	888	17-300
809FZG(5)	31-340	888A	17-300
809FZH	31-340	900	18-420
809FZH(2)	31-340	900(2)	17-320
809FZH(3)	31-340	903(5)	17-320
809FZH(4)	31-340	906(5)	17-320
809FZI	31-340	910	21-180
809FZI(2)	31-340	910(2)	17-320
809FZI(3)	31-340	930	17-300
809FZI(4)	31-340	944(2)	17-320
809FZJ	31-340	989	17-300
809FZJ(1)	31-340	993	16-560; 19-360; 16-720; 31-100; 31-300
809FZK	31-340	993(2)	14-280
809FZL	31-340	993(4)	19-360
809FZM	31-340	994	16-560; 16-720
809FZN	31-340	994(1)	14-280
809FZO	31-340	Pt. 3, Ch. 2	17-320
809FZP	31-340	Pt. 3, Ch. 3	17-320
809FZQ	31-340	Pt. 4	25-000
809FZR	31-340	Pt. 4, Ch. 3	19-520; 25-320; 25-340; 25-360; 25-380; 25-600
809FZR(2)	31-340		
809FZS	31-340		
809FZS(1)	31-340	Pt. 8, Ch. 1	14-040; 14-380

Provision	Paragraph
Pt. 13, Ch. 5	25-600; 25-700
Pt. 13, Ch. 5A	29-000; 30-000
Pt. 13, Ch. 5AA	29-000
Pt. 13, Ch. 5D	29-000
Pt. 13, Ch. 5E	29-000; 31-000; 31-020; 31-100; 31-160; 31-300; 31-340
Pt. 13, Ch. 5F	29-000; 31-000; 31-060; 31-320; 31-340
Pt. 15	17-300
Pt. 15, Ch. 16	17-300
Sch. 2, para. 27	25-400
Sch. 2, para. 28	25-420
Sch. 2, para. 29	25-440
Sch. 2, para. 30	25-460
Sch. 2, para. 31	25-480
Sch. 2, para. 32	25-460
Sch. 2, para. 34	25-500
Sch. 2, para. 35	25-500
Sch. 2, para. 96	14-260
Sch. 2, para. 148	25-780
Sch. 2, para. 151(1)	25-840
Sch. 2, para. 151(2)	25-840
Sch. 2, para. 152	25-840
Sch. 2, Pt. 14	25-780

Income Tax (Earnings and Pensions) Act 2003

Provision	Paragraph
See generally	31-040
7	31-180
23	25-180
62	15-260
103KA(6)(b)	31-180
103KA(6)(c)	31-180
203	15-260
355	25-180
421B(8)	31-340
575	25-180
613	25-180
615	25-180
631	25-180
635	25-180

Income Tax (Construction Industry Scheme) Regulations 2005 (SI 2005/2045)

Provision	Paragraph
See generally	17-360

Income Tax (Pay As You Earn) Regulations 2003 (SI 2003/2682)

Provision	Paragraph
reg. 102	17-340

Income Tax (Trading and Other Income) Act 2005

Provision	Paragraph
5	20-040
6(1)	20-040
7	20-040
7(2)	20-040
8	20-040
9	18-480
9(2)	21-140
12	27-140
18	22-040
25	18-120
25A	14-060; 17-100; 23-000; 23-020
31A	23-000; 23-020; 23-040; 23-060; 23-100
31B	23-000; 23-040
31C	23-000; 23-080
31D	23-000; 23-100
31E	23-120; 23-140
31E(1)	23-000
32A	23-160
33	18-460; 23-160
33A	23-160
34	18-320; 18-460
34(1)(a)	18-440
35	23-160
36	23-160
37	23-160
38(2A)	23-160
43	23-160
45	18-460
48–50B	23-160
51A(1)	23-160; 23-200
53	18-460
56A	23-200
57B	23-160
58	23-200
60–67	23-180
60–68	23-180
68	23-180
72(2A)	23-160
77	21-020
77(5)	21-080
79	21-020
79(2)	21-080
94A(4)	23-160
94AA	18-460; 32-140
94B	23-380; 23-440; 23-480
94C	23-360; 23-380;

Income Tax (Trading and Other Income)
   Act 2005 — continued

Provision	Paragraph	Provision	Paragraph
	23-440; 23-480	173	21-020
94D	23-360; 23-400; 23-420	173(3)	21-080
94D(1)	23-400	182	21-020
94D(2)	23-400	182(2)	21-080
94D(3)	23-400	185	17-100
94D(4)	23-400	194	17-100
94D(5)	23-420	197	20-080; 20-100
94E	23-400	197(2)	20-080
94E(2)	23-400	198	20-100
94E(3)	23-400	198(1)	20-040; 20-100
94F	23-420	199	20-100
94F(2)	23-420	200	20-080; 20-100
94F(6)	23-420	200(2)	20-080; 20-100
94H	23-360; 23-440; 23-460	200(3)	20-080
94H(1)	23-440	200(4)	20-080
94H(2)	23-440	202	20-080; 20-100
94H(3)	23-460	202(1)	20-100
94H(4)	23-460	202(2)	20-080
94H(6)	23-460	207	20-120
94I	23-360; 23-480; 23-500	207(1)(a)	20-120
94I(4)	23-500	207(2)	20-120
94I(5)	23-500	214(1)	20-100
94I(6)	23-500	214–218	20-100
94I(7)	23-500	215	20-100
96A	23-140	216(2)	20-100
97B	23-140	216(3)	20-100
105(2A)	23-140	216(4)	20-100
106A	23-140	217	20-100
111(1)	17-100	217(2)	20-100
111(4)	20-040	217(6)	20-100
126(2)	17-100	218	20-100
129(2)	17-100	221	20-160; 23-080
130	25-520	227	18-560
132	25-520	227A	23-220; 23-240
137–140	25-520	231	18-560
148K	23-000	232–233	18-560
149–154A	23-140	234	18-560
157	23-140	235	18-560
158	23-140	237	18-560
159	23-140	239A	23-260; 23-280
161	23-140	239B	23-280
162	23-140	240B–240D	23-300
163	23-140	246(3)(4)	21-080
164	23-140	258(1)	21-080
164A	23-140	258(2)	21-080
165–168	23-140	264	18-500
169–172ZE	23-140	265	18-520

Provision	Paragraph
272	32-140
323	15-360
326	17-100
330(1)	18-560
330(4)	18-560
333–334	18-560
353(2)	21-080
353(3)	21-080
361(1)	21-080
361(2)	21-080
362	22-040
397(1)	17-080
397A(1)	17-080
430	19-240
587	21-180
588	21-180
591(2)	21-180
592(2)	21-180
595	21-180
596	21-180
830	18-080
830(4)	18-080
832	18-080; 25-180
846	17-000
847	18-060; 19-020; 25-360
847–848	18-000
848	13-060; 13-120; 18-000; 18-040; 20-000
849	18-040; 18-060; 18-140; 18-460; 19-080; 19-320; 20-020; 20-040; 25-520
849(2)	18-040; 18-060
849(3)	18-060
849(3A)	18-060
849–856	18-080
850	18-040; 18-060; 18-140; 19-020; 19-040; 19-060; 19-080; 19-320; 20-040; 25-540; 26-040; 26-060
850(1)	18-040
850–850B	19-000; 19-380; 19-420
850A	19-080; 19-280; 19-320; 19-400; 25-540; 26-040; 26-060
850A(1)	19-080
850B	19-080; 19-280; 25-540
850C	19-280; 19-320; 19-340; 19-360; 19-380; 19-400; 19-480; 26-040; 26-060

Provision	Paragraph
850C(1)–(3)	19-320
850C(2)	19-340
850C(2)(b)	19-340
850C(3)	19-360
850C(4)	19-320; 19-340; 19-380; 19-440
850C(5)	19-320; 19-380
850C(6)	19-320
850C(8)(a)	19-340
850C(8)(b)	19-280; 19-340
850C(9)	19-340
850C(10)	19-360
850C(11)(a)	19-360
850C(12)	19-360
850C(13)	19-360
850C(15)	19-360
850C(16)	19-360
850C(17)	19-360
850C(18)	19-360
850C(18)(a)	19-360
850C(18)(b)	19-280; 19-360
850C(18)(c)	19-360
850C(19)	19-280; 19-360
850C(20)–(21)	19-360
850C(20)(b)	19-360
850C(20)(d)	19-360
850C(20)(e)	19-360
850C(21)	19-360
850C–850E	19-000
850D	19-400; 19-420
850D(1)	19-400
850D(1)–(3)	19-400
850D(1)(d)	19-400
850D(2)	19-400
850D(3)	19-400
850D(4)	19-420
850D(5)	19-420
850D(7)	19-400
850D(8)	19-400
850D(9)	19-400
850D(10)	19-400
850D(12)	19-400
850D(13)	19-400
850E	19-440; 19-480; 19-500
850E(1)–(2)	19-440
850E(3)	19-440
850E(4)	19-440
851	18-060; 18-140; 19-020

Income Tax (Trading and Other Income)
   Act 2005 — continued

Provision	Paragraph	Provision	Paragraph
852	13-060; 18-040; 20-040; 20-060	863B	32-040
852(1)	13-060	863B(1)(a)	32-040
852(2)	20-060	863B(1)(b)	32-040
852(3)	20-060	863B(2)	32-040
852(4)	20-060	863B(3)	32-040
852(5)	20-060	863B(5)	32-040
852(6)	20-060	863B(c)	32-040
852(7)	20-060	863C	32-060
852–856	21-040; 21-100; 21-120	863D(1)	32-080
853	20-020; 20-080; 20-100; 20-120; 21-020	863D(2)	32-080
853(1)	20-080	863D(3)	32-080
853(2)	20-100	863D(4)	32-080
853(3)	20-100	863D(5)	32-080
853(4)	20-120	863D(6)	32-080
853–856	20-020	863D(7)	32-080
854	21-020	863D(8)	32-080
854(1)(a)	20-140	863D(9)	32-080
854–856	20-020; 20-140	863D(10)	32-080
856	20-140	863D(11)	32-080
857	18-080	863D(12)	32-080
858	18-100	863D–863E	32-080
858(1)	18-100	863E(2)–(4)	32-080
858(2)	18-100	863E(6)	32-080
858(3)	18-100	863E(7)	32-080
859	21-140	863F	32-100
859(1)	18-480	863F(1)	32-100
859(2)	18-500	863F(2)	32-100
859(3)	18-520	863F(3)	32-100
860	18-560	863G	32-120
860(1)	21-080	863G(1)	32-120
860(2)	21-080	863G(2)–(4)	32-120
860(5)	18-560	863G(4A)	32-120; 32-140
861	21-180	863G(5)	32-120
861(1)	21-180	863H	17-180; 26-020
861(3)	21-180	863H–863L	17-180; 26-000; 26-020
862	21-180	863I	26-040; 26-060
862–862	21-180	863I(1)	26-040
863	12-040; 18-020	863I(2)	26-040
863(1)(a)	20-040	863I(3)	26-060
863(4)	26-080	863I(4)	26-060
863(5)	26-060	863I(6)	26-040
863–863G	29-000	863I(7)	26-040
863A(1)	32-020	863I(8)	26-040
863A(2)	18-460; 32-020	863J	26-080
863A–863G	32-000; 32-020	863J(1)	26-080
		863J(2)	26-080
		863J(5)	26-080

Provision	Paragraph
863J(6)	26-080
863J(7)(a)	26-080
863K	26-100
863L	26-040
Pt. 2	18-140; 23-000
Pt. 2, Ch. 2	18-400
Pt. 2, Ch. 3	18-120
Pt. 2, Ch. 4	18-400
Pt. 2, Ch. 5A	23-360
Pt. 2, Ch. 8	23-080; 23-140
Pt. 2, Ch. 9	14-260; 23-140; 25-760
Pt. 2, Ch. 10	23-140
Pt. 2, Ch. 10A	23-140
Pt. 2, Ch. 11A	23-140
Pt. 2, Ch. 13	23-140
Pt. 2, Ch. 14	23-140
Pt. 2, Ch. 15	20-040; 21-020
Pt. 2, Ch. 16	23-140
Pt. 2, Ch. 16A	23-140
Pt. 2, Ch. 16ZA	23-140
Pt. 2, Ch. 17	18-560; 23-220
Pt. 2, Ch. 18	26-080
Pt. 3, Ch. 6	14-220
Pt. 3, Ch. 7	18-560
Pt. 4, Ch. 3	18-100; 20-140
Pt. 9	17-000; 18-000; 18-040; 19-460; 20-040; 21-000; 25-360

Industrial and Provident Societies Act 1965

See generally	10-020

Inheritance Tax Act 1984

3	27-020
3(1)	27-020
3A	27-040
3A(1)(c)	27-040
3A(1A)(c)	27-040
3A(2)(b)	27-040
3A(4)	27-040
3A(5)	27-040
4	27-020
4(1)	27-020
10	27-020
103(3)	27-140
104	27-140
105(1)(a)	27-140
105(1)(d)	27-140
105(3)	16-380
106	27-140

Provision	Paragraph
109	27-140
112(3)	27-140
115	15-320; 27-060
115(2)	15-380; 27-060
116	27-100
116(2)	27-100
116(6)	27-100
117	27-060; 27-080
117(b)	27-080
117–121	27-060
119	27-080
119(2)	27-080
124A	15-380
267A	27-000
267A(a)	27-000
Pt. V, Ch. I	27-140
Pt. V, Ch. II	27-060; 27-120

Insolvency Act 1986

See generally	10-300; 13-100
87	13-100

Land and Buildings Transaction Tax (Scotland) Act 2013

Sch. 10	16-995
Sch. 10, para. 38(2)	16-995
Sch. 17	16-880; 16-995
Sch. 17, para. 1	16-880
Sch. 17, para. 2	16-900
Sch. 17, para. 3	16-920
Sch. 17, para. 4	16-920
Sch. 17, para. 5	16-920
Sch. 17, para. 6	16-920
Sch. 17, para. 7	16-920
Sch. 17, para. 7–10	16-920
Sch. 17, para. 12	16-940
Sch. 17, para. 12–22	16-900
Sch. 17, para. 13–16	16-940
Sch. 17, para. 17	16-940
Sch. 17, para. 18	16-940
Sch. 17, para. 19	16-960
Sch. 17, para. 22–26	16-960
Sch. 17, para. 27	16-960
Sch. 17, para. 28	16-960
Sch. 17, para. 29	16-980
Sch. 17, para. 31	16-990
Sch. 17, para. 32	16-990
Sch. 17, para. 33	16-990
Sch. 17, para. 34	16-990
Sch. 17, para. 35	16-940; 16-990
Sch. 17, para. 36–41	16-995

Land and Buildings Transaction
    Tax (Scotland) Act 2013 — continued

Provision	Paragraph
Sch. 17, para. 37	16-995
Sch. 17, para. 38	16-900; 16-995
Sch. 17, para. 39	16-995
Sch. 17, para. 40	16-995
Sch. 17, para. 41	16-995
Sch. 17, para. 42–50	16-900
Sch. 17, Pt. 4–7	16-920
Sch. 17, Pt. 8	16-995
Sch. 17, Pt. 9	16-900

Late Payment of Commercial
    Debts (Interest) Act 1998

Provision	Paragraph
See generally	17-300

Law of Partnership Act 1865

Provision	Paragraph
See generally	10-080

Limited Liability
    Partnership Act 2000

Provision	Paragraph
See generally	10-020; 10-300; 12-040; 12-120; 16-040; 16-900; 18-020; 19-500; 31-060
1	10-300
1(1)	32-000
1(2)	10-300; 28-220
1(5)	10-300
2	10-340
2(1)	15-040
2(1)(a)	10-340
4(4)	32-000
12	16-040
14	13-100

Limited Liability Partnership
    Regulations 2001
    (SI 2001/1090)

Provision	Paragraph
reg. 5	13-100
Sch. 3	13-100

Limited Liability Partnerships Act
    (Northern Ireland) Act 2002

Provision	Paragraph
See generally	12-040; 16-040; 16-900

Limited Liability Partnerships
    (Application of Companies Act 2006)
    Regulations 2009 (SI 2009/1804)

Provision	Paragraph
See generally	10-300

Limited Liability Partnerships
    Regulations 2001 (SI 2001/1090)

Provision	Paragraph
See generally	10-300

Limited Partnerships Act 1907

Provision	Paragraph
See generally	10-260; 10-440; 12-060; 16-900; 25-560

Provision	Paragraph
4	10-260
4(2)	10-260
4(3)	10-260
4(4)	10-260
5	10-260
6	10-260
6(1)	10-260; 14-640

Partnership Act 1865

Provision	Paragraph
See generally	10-000

Partnership Act 1890

Provision	Paragraph
See generally	10-020; 10-100; 10-120; 10-160; 10-260; 11-000; 12-020; 13-020; 13-100; 14-200; 15-000; 16-880; 24-020; 28-620
1	10-020; 10-080; 10-160; 10-220; 11-040; 13-020
1(1)	10-020; 10-080; 10-160; 10-220; 11-040; 13-020; 15-040; 17-320; 19-500; 31-000; 32-060
1(2)	10-020
2	10-000; 10-080; 10-100; 10-160
2(1)	10-100
2(2)	10-080; 10-100
2(3)	10-000; 10-080; 10-100; 10-160; 32-040
2(3)(a)–(e)	10-100
4	10-180
4(1)	10-180
4(2)	14-200; 16-880; 27-020; 27-080
5	10-180
6	10-180
9	10-180
10	28-300
11(1)	11-040
12	28-300
14	10-240
20(1)	28-540
24	12-160
24(1)	12-160
27	10-220
27(1)	10-220
27(2)	10-220
32	13-020
32(a)	13-020
32(b)	13-020
32(c)	13-020

Provision	Paragraph
33	13-020
33(1)	13-020; 28-100
33(2)	13-020
34	13-020
35	13-020
36	28-100
39	13-040
44	12-160
45	10-080

Partnerships (Restrictions on Contributions to a Trade) Regulations 2005 (SI 2005/2017)

reg. 4	25-500
reg. 5	25-500

Partnership (Restrictions on Contributions to a Trade) Regulations 2006 (SI 2006/1639)

See generally	25-780

Social Security Contributions and Benefits Act 1992

See generally	17-340
2(1)(b)	17-320
15	10-420; 17-320
15(1)	10-420
122	17-320
Sch. 2, para. 4	17-320

Stamp Duty Land Tax (Variation of the Finance Act 2003) Regulations 2006 (SI 2006/3237)

See generally	16-140
para 2(2)	16-280
para. 2(5)	16-560
Sch. 15, para. 10	16-280
Sch. 15, para. 11	16-280
Sch. 15, para. 18	16-280
Sch. 15, para. 19	16-280

Taxation of Chargeable Gains Act 1992

4A	14-600
12(4)	31-260
17	12-300; 15-300
18	12-300
24(2)	14-680
28	14-480
35	12-220
35(1)	12-220
35(2)	12-220
37	12-320

Provision	Paragraph
37(3)	12-320
38	15-420
38(1)(a)	31-280
42	12-160
59	12-020; 12-040; 12-060; 12-120; 13-080; 15-360; 19-500
59(1)	13-080
59(1)(b)	19-500
59A	12-020; 12-040; 12-060; 12-120; 13-140; 15-180; 19-500
59A(1)	12-020; 12-040; 12-120; 15-120
59A(1)(b)	19-500
59A(2)	12-040
59A(3)	12-040
59A(3)(a)	13-140
59A(3)(b)	13-140
59A(4)	12-040
59A(4)(a)	13-140
59A(4)(b)	13-140
59A(5)	12-040
59A(5)(a)	13-140
59A(5)(b)	13-140
59B	12-020; 26-120
59C	12-020; 26-120
103KA	31-160; 31-180; 31-200; 31-220
103KA(1)(a)	31-160
103KA(2)	31-160; 31-260
103KA(3)	31-160; 31-260
103KA(4)	31-200
103KA(5)	31-180; 31-220
103KA(6)	31-180
103KA(6)(a)	31-180
103KA(7)	31-180
103KA(8)	31-180; 31-200
103KB	31-240
103KB(1)	31-140; 31-240
103KB(2)	31-240
103KC	31-260
103KD	31-160
103KE	31-220
103KE(1)–(4)	31-220
103KE(5)–(6)	31-220
103KF	31-280
103KG	31-300
103KG(1)	31-300
103KG(2)	31-300
103KG(2)–(15)	31-140; 31-300

Taxation of Chargeable
  Gains Act 1992 — continued

Provision	Paragraph	Provision	Paragraph
103KG(3)	31-300	167(2)	15-400
103KG(4)–(5)	31-300	169A	12-040
103KG(4)–(6)	31-300	169H	14-420
103KG(7)	31-300	169I	14-440; 14-460; 14-480
103KG(8)	31-300	169I(2)(b)	14-480
103KG(9)	31-300	169I(3)	14-460
103KG(10)	31-300	169I(4)	14-480
103KG(11)	31-300	169I(8)(a)	14-460
103KG(12)	31-300	169I(8)(b)	14-460
103KG(13)	31-300	169I(8)(c)	14-460
103KG(14)	31-300	169J	14-540
103KG(15)	31-300	169J(1)	14-540
103KH	31-160	169J(2)	14-540
116	15-320	169J(3)	14-540
116(10)(b)	15-320	169J(5)	14-540
152	12-340; 14-640	169J(6)(b)	14-540
152–158	14-640	169K	14-500
153	12-340; 14-640	169K(1A)	14-500
156A	12-040	169K(1AA)	14-500
157	14-640	169K(1E)	14-500
158(2)	14-640	169K(3AA)	14-500
162	13-080; 15-020; 15-040; 15-080; 15-100; 15-140; 15-160; 15-180; 15-200; 15-220; 15-480; 19-500	169K(3BA)	14-500
		169K(4A)	14-500
		169K(6A)	14-500
		169K(9)	14-500
162(1)	15-100; 15-160; 15-180	169KA(1B)–(1D)	14-500
162(2)	15-200	169K(A1A)	14-500
162(3)	15-220	169L	14-560
162(3)(a)	15-220	169LA	14-580; 15-520
162(3)(b)	15-220	169LA(1)(aa)	14-580
162(4)	15-180; 15-200	169LA(1A)	14-580
162(5)	15-200	169LA(1B)	14-580
162A	15-100	169LA(1C)	14-580
162A(1)	15-100	169LA(4)	14-580
162A(2)	15-100	169LA(5)	15-520
162A(3)	15-100	169LA(6)	14-580; 15-520
162A(4)	15-100	169LA(7)	14-580; 15-520
162A(7)	15-100	169LA(8)	15-520
165	14-660; 15-020; 15-280; 15-320; 15-340; 15-360; 15-420; 15-480	169M	14-540
		169M(2)	14-540
165(1)(a)	15-320	169N	14-540
165(1)(b)	15-320; 15-340	169N(7)	14-540
165(2)	15-320; 15-360	169N(8)	14-540
165(3)	15-320	169O	14-540
165(7)	15-420	169O(1)–(3)	14-540
165(9)	15-360	169O(4)	14-540
167	15-400	169O(5)	14-540

Provision	Paragraph
169P	14-520
169P(1)–(3)	14-520
169P(4)	14-520
169P(5)	14-520
169S	14-600
169S(1)	14-460
169S(5)	14-520
171	12-200
185	15-400
216	15-080
217A	15-080
241	15-360
241(3)	15-360
241(3A)	15-360
260	15-320
261B	25-020; 25-180; 25-360
261C	25-020
286	12-300
286(4)	12-300
288	15-180; 15-360
288(1)	15-120; 15-180; 15-360
809EZDA	31-300
809EZDB	31-300
Pt. III, Ch. 5	29-000; 31-000; 31-100; 31-120; 31-140
Pt. V, Ch. 3	14-420
Sch. 2, para. 4	12-380
Sch. 2, para. 18	12-360
Sch. 7, para. 1	15-380
Sch. 7, para. 1(1)	15-380
Sch. 7, para. 1(2)	15-380
Sch. 7, para. 5	15-440
Sch. 7, para. 5(1)	15-440
Sch. 7, para. 6	15-460
Sch. 7, para. 6(1)	15-460
Sch. 7, para. 6(2)	15-460
Sch. 7ZA	14-600

Taxation (International and Other Provisions) Act 2010

Provision	Paragraph
Pt. 9A, Ch. 14	31-100; 31-300

Taxes Management Act 1970

Provision	Paragraph
8(1B)	17-160
8(1C)	17-160
9A	17-180
12(2)	17-040
12AA	12-060; 17-040; 17-060; 17-080; 17-100
12AA, 12AA(7), 12AB, 12AB(1)(b)	12-060
12AA(1)–(3)	17-040

Provision	Paragraph
12AA(2)(a)	17-240
12AA(3)	17-040
12AA(3)(a)	17-240
12AA(4)–(4E)	17-040
12AA(4A)	17-040
12AA(4B)	17-040
12AA(5)–(5E)	17-040
12AA(5A)	17-040
12AA(5B)	17-040
12AA(6)	17-040
12AA(7)	12-060; 17-040
12AA(8)	17-040
12AA(9)	17-040
12AA(10)	17-040
12AA(11)–(13)	17-040
12AB	12-060; 17-080
12AB(1)	17-080
12AB(1)(b)	12-060
12ABA	17-120
12ABB	17-120
12AC	17-180
12AD	17-180
12ADA	17-180
12B	17-220
28B	17-180
28ZA	17-180
30B	17-200
33	17-140
42	17-100; 18-120
42(6)	17-100; 18-120
42(7)	17-080; 17-100
Sch. 1A, para. 5(1)	17-180
Sch. 1AB	17-140

Value Added Tax Act 1994

Provision	Paragraph
See generally	17-280
3(1)	28-760
4(1)	28-240
24	28-400; 28-420; 28-480
24(1)	28-380; 28-400; 28-420; 28-480
43–43D	28-160
43A	28-160; 28-220
45	28-020; 28-100; 28-180; 28-200; 28-240; 28-260; 28-680
45(1)	28-020; 28-040; 28-180; 28-200; 28-240; 28-380
45(2)	28-020; 28-100; 28-260
45(4)	28-060; 28-260
45(5)	28-100
60	28-300

Value Added Tax Act 1994 — continued

Provision	Paragraph
73(1)	28-260
76(1)	28-260; 28-300
Sch. 1, para. 1	28-020; 28-380
Sch. 1, para. 1(2)	28-380
Sch. 4, para 5(1)	28-180
Sch. 4, para 5(4)	28-180
Sch. 4, para. 8	28-380
Sch. 4, para. 8(1)	28-380
Sch. 4, para. 8(2)	28-380
Sch. 4, para. 8(3)	28-380
Sch. 6, para. 6	28-380
Sch. 9, Grp. 1	28-380
Sch. 9, Grp. 1, Note (4)	28-380
Sch. 9, Grp. 5, item 6	28-180
Sch. 9, Grp. 6, item 2	28-740
Sch. 11, para. 1	28-100
Sch. 11, para. 1(1)	28-100

Value Added Tax (Isle of Man) Order 1982 (SI 1982/1067)

art. 11(8)	28-380

Value Added Tax Regulations 1995 (SI 1995/2518)

reg. 4B	28-000

Provision	Paragraph
reg. 5	28-000; 28-260
reg. 5(1)	28-000
reg. 5(2)	28-020
reg. 5(3)	28-260
reg. 7	28-000; 28-020; 28-080
reg. 25(3)	28-280
reg. 30	28-280
reg. 111	28-380
reg. 115	28-380
reg. 115(3)	28-380
reg. 115(3A)	28-380
reg. 115(3B)	28-380

Value Added Tax (Special Provisions) Order 1995 (SI 1995/1268)

art. 5	28-760
art. 5(1)	28-760
art. 5(1)(a)(i)	28-760
art. 5(1)(a)(ii)	28-760
art. 5(1)(b)(i)	28-760
art. 5(1)(b)(ii)	28-760
art. 5(1)(b)(iii)	28-760

Welfare Reform Act 2012

Pt. 1	23-040

Index

(References are to paragraph numbers)

Paragraph

Accounting periods 18-160

Allocation of firm's profits or losses

. between partners 19-000

. charitable donations 19-260

. corporate partners 19-100

. deeply discounted security,
   company partners' share 19-240

. exchange gains and losses,
   treatment of 19-220

. generally 19-000

. HMRC guidance 19-300

. income tax profits, allocation of 19-020

. loan relationships

.. allocating credits and debits to
   company partners 19-200

.. company partners and other
   connections 19-180

.. debits and credits 19-120

.. lending between partners and
   partnership 19-140

.. tax implications 19-160

. mixed member partnership 19-280

.. anti-avoidance 19-400

.. commencement 1-480

.. counteraction: reallocation of
   profits 19-380, 19-420

.. excess loss allocation 19-520

.. excess profit allocation rules,
   application of 19-460

.. practical solutions 19-500

.. preventing double taxation 19-440

. notional profit/loss, reallocation of .. 19-080

. profit sharing arrangements, changes .. 19-040

. salaries and interest on capital,
   treatment of 19-060

Alternative Investment Fund

. background 26-000

. capital gains consequences   -

.. firm 26-120

.. partner 26-120

Paragraph

. firms 17-180

. previously allocated profits,
   vesting of 26-080

. special mechanism 26-020–26-040

. vesting statements 26-100

Annual exemption 15-480

Anti-avoidance

. generally 29-000

Appropriate mileage amount 23-420

Appropriate share 19-120

Arm's length return 31-060

Business asset gift relief

. agricultural land 15-380

. claims 15-340

. conditions for relief 15-320

. effect of relief 15-300

. generally 15-280; 15-500

. incorporation for cash 15-520

. interaction with other reliefs

.. annual exemption 15-480

.. entrepreneurs' relief 15-480

.. roll-over relief 15-480

. non-qualifying use, period of 15-440

. non-resident recipients 15-400

. partial use of building 15-460

. qualifying business assets 15-360

. transfer, actual consideration for 15-420

Business entities

. deciding factors

.. commercial issues 11-020

.. regulation 11-020

.. tax issues 11-020

. forming a general partnership 11-040

. forming an LLP 11-060

. generally 11-000

Business mileage allowable 23-400

Calculation of profits and losses

. accounting period 18-160

Paragraph

. capital allowances 18-160

. corporation tax 18-160

. determination of debits and
    credits 18-200

. general 18-120

. income tax 18-140

. loan relationships 18-180

. normal practice, exceptions to 18-160

. trading profits 18-120–18-160

Capital allowances

. connected person, meaning 22-260

. market value, determination of 22-240

. other allowances 22-140–22-220

. overview 22-000

. plant and machinery allowances

.. annual investment allowance 22-020

.. anti-avoidance 22-120

.. partnership changes 22-040

.. partnership using property of
    partners 22-060

.. successions 22-080

.. successions election 22-100

Carried interest 31-020;
                     31-080; 31-120

. arise 31-100

. avoidance of double taxation 31-220

. background 31-120

. charge to capital gains tax ...31-120; 31-160

. consideration on disposal 31-240

. exclusions 31-200

. external investors on disposal of
    partnership asset 31-280

. foreign chargeable gains 31-260

. income-based 31-320

. overview 31-140

. permitted deductions 31-180

Cash basis for small businesses

. accelerate the adjustment income 23-280

. calculating profits 23-120

. capital allowances 23-300

. eligibility 23-020

. entering the cash basis 23-240

. excluded persons 23-080

Paragraph

. generally 23-000

. leaving the cash basis 23-260

. loan interest 23-200

. making an election, effect of 23-100

. partnerships, application to 23-060

. receipts and expenses

.. capital 23-140

.. cessation of profession or
    vocation 23-140

.. cessation of trade, value of
    trading stock 23-140

.. industrial development grant 23-140

.. non-commercial transactions 23-140

. relevant maximum 23-040

. restricting expenses 23-160

. tax relief on loans to buy plant or
    machinery 23-320

Chargeable event 25-640;
                    25-720; 25-820

Compliance and administration

. amendment of partnership return 17-120

. claims included in
    partnership return 17-100

. Class 2 and 4 NIC 17-320

. construction industry scheme 17-360

. discovery and partnerships 17-200

. enquiries into partnership returns

.. Alternative Investment
    Fund firms 17-180

.. amendments 17-180

.. completion 17-180

.. referral of questions to the tribunal 17-180

. generally 17-000

. income tax, deduction of

.. exceptions 17-300

.. yearly interest 17-300

. information powers 17-280

. mistakes in the partnership tax
    return, relief for 17-140

. partners' returns 17-160

. partnership statement included in
    return 17-080

. PAYE and Class 1 NIC

.. business successions 17-340

Paragraph

. penalties for failure to file
  partnership return 17-240

. penalties for inaccuracies in
  partnership return 17-260

. record-keeping 17-220

. registering partners and
  partnerships with HMRC 17-020

. returns

.. appointment of successor 17-040

.. filing deadlines 17-040

. withdrawal by HMRC a
  notice to file return 17-060

**Construction Industry
  Scheme (CIS)** 17-360

Continuity rule 16-860

Corporation tax, assessment

. return periods 20-200

Deeply discounted security 19-240

Deferred carried interest 31-300

Definitions and meanings

. affected transaction 16-340; 16-860

. agricultural property 27-060

. amount of trade losses claimed 25-680

. annual investment allowance 22-020

. appropriate notional consideration
  for services 19-360

. appropriate notional profit 19-360

. appropriate notional
  return on capital 19-360

. arrangements 15-460; 30-060; 30-120

. associate 24-000

. associated partnership 30-060; 30-120

. capital gains relief 25-360

. carried interest 31-080

. cash basis for small businesses 23-000

. close company 24-000

. co-investment 31-180

. connected persons 12-300

. connected 31-300

. deferred carried interest 31-300

. deferred profit 19-340

. disguised salary 32-040

. disposal of the licence 25-860

Paragraph

. entrepreneurs' relief 15-240

. equity partner 10-380

. excluded transaction 16-180

. excluded vehicle 23-400

. film-related loss 25-760

. firm 25-360

. 'fungible' asset 12-400

. going concern 15-120

. individual's claimed
  film-related losses 25-760

. input tax 28-420

. interest in possession 14-540

. limited liability partnership 16-040

. limited partner 10-440; 25-360

. market rent leases 16-860

. market value 12-140

. material disposal 14-440

. material time 14-540

. mixed member partnership 19-280

. money debt 18-180

. non-active partner 25-860

. number of hours worked 23-460

. ordinary partnership transaction 16-060

. participator 24-000

. partnership 16-000

. partnership property 16-860

. partnership share 16-720; 16-860

. period of account 22-000

. profits relating to the licence 25-860

. property investment
  partnership 16-540, 16-990

. qualifying beneficiary 14-540

. qualifying foreign trade income 25-180

. qualifying person 22-020

. reclaimed relief 25-680

. recovered relief 25-400; 25-460

. related to the licence 25-860

. relevant amount 30-040–30-060;
  30-120

. relevant occupant 23-500

. relevant partner 17-240

. relevant portion 14-540

Paragraph

.relevant receipts...................30-040; 30-060

.relevant relief.......................25-400; 25-460

.relevant tax amount 19-340

.relevant time 16-040

.representative partner 16-080

.responsible partners........................ 16-080

.roll-over or hold-over relief.............. 15-240

.salaried partner 10-400

.sideways relief.................................. 25-360

.sleeping partner 10-420

.tax advantage 30-060; 30-120

.trade leasing allowance.................... 25-100

.untaxed income................................ 20-140

Demergers

.income tax 21-060; 21-140

**Disguised investment
management fees**

.arise 31-100

.background 31-000

.generally 31-020

.income tax, charge to....................... 31-040

.management fee, meaning................ 31-060

Disposal

.assets after business discontinued 14-480

.assets by a partnership..................... 12-160

.associated with material disposal 14-500

.by trustees....................................... 14-540

.whole or part of a business.............. 14-460

Disposals through partnerships

.assets

..corporation tax provisions............... 30-120

..income tax provisions 30-100

..overview.. 30-080

.background 30-000

.income streams

..corporation tax provisions............... 30-060

..income tax provisions 30-040

..overview.. 30-020

Dissolution

.consequences of............................... 13-040

.limited liability partnership 13-100

.partnership....................................... 13-020

Paragraph

Dissolution of a partnership

.consequences of............................... 13-040

.generally 13-000

Double charge – see Double taxation

.removal of.. 16-320

Double taxation

.agreements....................................... 18-100

.avoidance of........... 19-380; 31-040; 31-220

Early trade losses relief...................25-040

Effect of incorporating

.general partnership 15-040

.limited liability partnership 15-040

**Film-related losses, individuals
claiming relief for**

.capital contribution.......................... 25-780

.detailed conditions........................... 25-720

.disposal of right to profit.................. 25-740

.generally 25-700

.prevention of double counting.......... 25-800

Finance Act 2004, provisions

.anti-avoidance rules......................... 16-180

.application to partnerships............... 16-200

.Finance Act 2003, Sch. 15,
Pt. 3, scope of amended 16-140

.general 16-120

.partnerships chapter......................... 16-160

**Firms' profits and losses,
computation of**

.adjustment income........................... 18-560

.calculated at a partnership level

..non-resident companies 18-060

..non-resident individual partners 18-060

..UK resident individual partners...... 18-060

.directors' fees received by
partnerships.................................. 18-220

.double taxation agreement............... 18-100

.farming and market gardening 18-480

.generally 18-000

.jointly owned property...................... 18-540

.limited liability partnerships............. 18-020

.overseas property income 18-520

.partners to whom remittance
basis applies 18-080

	Paragraph
. resident partners agreement	18-100
. specific deductions	
.. costs connected with capital structure of a business	18-440
.. deductions in relation to LLP salaried members	18-460
.. expenses incurred by partners individually	18-240
.. interest paid by partnership	18-300
.. partner recruitment costs	18-360
.. partner training costs	18-350
.. partnership annuities	18-420
.. payment to partners	18-260
.. payments to outgoing partners	18-280
.. rent	18-320
.. service companies	18-340
.. termination payments	18-400
. three-stage approach	18-040
. UK property income	18-500

Fixed rate deductions

. business mileage	23-380–23-400
. deduction amount	23-420; 23-460
. flat rate deduction: use of home for business purposes	23-440
. non-business use amount	23-500
. overview	23-360
. premises both as home and business	23-480

Group relief

. modification pertaining to calculating SLP	16-860
. modification pertaining to withdrawal provisions	16-860

Income and corporation tax, assessment to

. basis of assessment	20-020
. partnership to tax	20-000

Income tax, assessment

. claims for averaging of partnership profits	20-160
. relief for partnership annuities paid	20-180
. trading income, firms with	
.. concept of the notional trade or business	20-040

	Paragraph
.. individual partners, notional trades for	20-060
.. untaxed income or relievable losses from other sources	20-140
. trading profits, firms with	
.. investment business	20-020

Income-based carried interest

. generally	31-320
. legislation	31-340

Incorporation of partnerships

. effect of	15-040
. generally	15-000
. impact of	15-060
. mechanisms	15-020

Incorporation relief – see also Business asset gift relief

. anti-avoidance	15-260
. claims and elections	
.. disapply relief	15-100
.. limitation	15-100
. conditions	
.. assets transferred to the company	15-160
.. business must be transferred as a 'going concern'	15-140
.. consideration for the transfer is in the form of shares	15-180
.. person who is not a company transfers a business to a company	15-120
. consequences	
.. reduction in allowable cost of shares	15-220
.. reduction in net gains on old assets	15-200
. generally	15-080
. interaction with other reliefs	15-240
. legislation	15-080

Individuals claiming relief for licence-related losses

. income chargeable to tax, calculation of	25-840
. overview	25-820

Inheritance tax

. agricultural property relief	27-060
. APR relief	

	Paragraph
.. availability of	27-120
.. limited partnerships	27-120
.. qualification for	27-080
.. rate of	27-100
. business property relief	
.. assets	27-140
.. property letting	27-140
. overview	27-000
. partnership assets, transfer of	
.. excluded property	27-020

Limited liability partnerships

	Paragraph
. background, legal	10-300
. CGT provisions in detail	12-040
. corporate partners	12-440
. general partnerships, contrast with	10-340
. generally	10-280; 12-040
. intangible fixed assets	12-440
. liability, limitation of	10-320

LLPs: Salaried members

	Paragraph
. anti-avoidance rules	
.. mixed membership, precedence of	32-120
.. non-individual members	32-120
.. provisions	32-120
. background	32-000
. condition A	
.. disguised salary	32-040
. condition B	32-060
. condition C	
.. anti-avoidance	32-080
.. joining leaving LLPs	32-080
. contribution, date of	32-100
. legislation structure	32-020
. provisions	
.. deductions	32-140
.. returns	32-140
. solutions	32-160

Loan relationships 18-160

	Paragraph
. allocating credits and debits to company partner	19-200
. allocating loan relationship debits and credits	19-120
. calculation of profits and losses	18-180
. company partners and other connections	19-180
. lending between partners and partnership	19-140
.. tax implications	19-160

Loans and benefits to participators

	Paragraph
. application to partnerships	24-020
. benefits to participators	
.. background	24-040
.. FA 2013 legislation	24-040
. overview	24-000

Loans to invest in partnership 14-160

	Paragraph
. business successions	
.. between partnerships	14-340
.. incorporation	14-340
. commercial woodlands	14-360
. replacement loans	14-320
. salaried partners	14-180
. Scottish partnerships	14-200
. withdrawal of relief	14-300

Losses

	Paragraph
. corporation tax carry-forward trade loss relief	25-240
. corporation tax group loss relief	25-300
. corporation tax loss relief against total profits	25-200
. corporation tax restriction on reliefs for company limited partners	25-560
. corporation tax restriction on transferring relief	25-280
. corporation tax restrictions on use of losses	25-260
. corporation tax terminal loss relief	25-220
. early trade losses relief	25-040
. income tax against general income	25-020
. income tax avoidance involving trade losses	25-600
. income tax carry-forward loss relief	25-140

Paragraph

. income tax exclusion of amounts
in calculating contribution
.. background......................................25-500
.. restrictions.....................................25-500
. income tax films
.. overview...25-520
. income tax for non-active
individual partners 25-460
. income tax limit not to exceed
cap for tax year..............................25-380
. income tax losses from trade
carried on abroad 25-180
. income tax restriction: partnership
with mixed membership.................25-540
. income tax restrictions for
individual limited partners.............25-400
. income tax restrictions on reliefs
for individual members of
limited liability partnerships..........25-420
. income tax restrictions on
sideways relief...............................25-120
. income tax terminal trade
loss relief.......................................25-160
. income tax unrelieved losses
brought forward
.. individual members of LLPs...........25-440
.. non-active individual partners........25-480
. corporation tax restriction on
reliefs for company
members of LLPs...........................25-580
. overview 25-000
. recovery of excess relief......25-620–25-680
. sideways relief, income
tax general restrictions...................25-060
. trade loss relief for partners,
restrictions
.. background....................................25-320
.. legislation.....................................25-320
.. overview.......................................25-340
. trading losses 25-000

Management fee, meaning of 31-060

Market rent leases............................16-400
. exclusion...16-540

Mergers
. income tax 21-060

Paragraph

. old businesses cease and new
business commences......................21-080
. one business continues and the
other(s) cease 21-120
. partnerships 12-340
. previous businesses continue as
merged joint business....................21-100

Mixed member partnership 19-280;
25-540; 32-120

**Mixed partnerships:
practical solutions**
. amend partnership agreement...........19-500
. existing structure, continue with 19-500
. incorporation 19-500

Notional trade...............................20-040
. basis period....................................20-080
.. change in accounting date...............20-100
.. start-up payments 20-120
. end of..20-060
. individual partners 20-060
. start of...20-060

Ordinary partnership transactions
. liabilities for SDLT, interest or
penalties 16-100
. overview 16-060
. representative partner 16-080
. responsible partners.........................16-080

Overseas property business.............18-520

Partner, types of
. equity...10-380
. generally 10-360
. limited..10-440
. salaried...10-400
. sleeping..10-420

Partnership returns........................17-040
. amendment by taxpayer and
correction by HMRC.....................17-120
. claims to be included......................17-100
. enquiries into 17-180
. penalties for failure to file...............17-240

Partnership shares, changes in
. admission and retirement
of partners 12-080

Paragraph

. annuities provided by
partnerships.................................. 12-320

. chargeable gains 12-020

. contribution of an asset.................... 12-240

. disposals of assets by a
partnership 12-160

. distribution of partnership assets...... 12-180

. generally 12-000

. goodwill.. 12-400

. HMRC statement of practice............ 12-100

. mergers of partnerships 12-340

. partnership assets............................ 12-060

. payments between partners
outside the partnership accounts.... 12-280

. rebasing of partnership assets........... 12-220

. revaluation of partnership assets....... 12-260

. shares acquired in stages 12-360

. sharing ratios, changes in 12-200

. SP D12, application of...................... 12-120

. transfers between persons not at
arm's length.................................. 12-300

. valuation of a partnership asset 12-140

Partnership, changes

. corporation tax................................ 21-160

. generally 21-000

. income tax

.. overview.. 21-020

.. treatment 21-040

. sale of rights: effects of 21-180

Partnership, general

. agreement 10-160

. character 10-060

. consequences of............................... 10-180

. contrast with 10-340

. date exist... 10-200

. dissolution 13-020

. duration of 10-220

. employment and 10-240

. family.. 10-140

. forming 11-040

. generally 10-020

. indicia of... 10-100

. limited... 10-260

Paragraph

. partner capacity 10-120

. view of profit, persons
carrying on a business

.. activity of partners, degree of 10-080

.. business carried on in common....... 10-080

.. business in common......................... 10-080

.. business, meaning 10-080

.. no partnership 10-080

.. with a view to profit....................... 10-080

Partnerships

. 'see-through' analysis....................... 16-020

. acquisition of interest 16-860

. anti-avoidance
provisions in s. 75A...................... 16-200

. anti-avoidance rules.......................... 16-180

. chargeable interest from a
parnership, transfer of

.. application of para. 18..................... 16-620

.. basic statutory rule......................... 16-560

.. partnership share attributable to
the partner 16-580

.. partnership to partnership 16-600

. chargeable interest to a
partnership, transfer of

.. ascertaining partnership shares 16-300

.. basic statutory rule......................... 16-220

.. behind the rule 16-240

.. chargeable consideration
includes rent................................ 16-260

.. compliance issues........................... 16-480

.. existence of 'arrangements'............ 16-500

.. post-transaction consideration 16-320

.. rent 16-260

.. restrict market value charge 16-240

.. sum of the lower proportions 16-280

.. summing up..................................... 16-360

.. transfer of interest in a property
investment partnership................... 16-540

. distinction between types of............. 16-860

. land and buildings transaction tax

.. chargeable interest held by
partners, provisions....................... 16-920

.. overview.. 16-880

.. property investment partnerships 16-990

Paragraph

.. provisions on exemptions,
reliefs and notification,
application of 16-995

.. transactions of transfer from a
partnership, rules for 16-960

.. transactions of transfer to a
partnership, rules for 16-940

. meaning 16-000

. partnership interest, transfer of

.. anti-avoidance provisions 16-420

.. basic statutory rule 16-380

.. chargeable consideration 16-380

.. exchanges of land 16-410

.. income profit-sharing ratios,
changes in 16-440

.. market rent leases 16-400

. post-transaction consideration 16-320

. returns 17-040

. Schedule 15, remaining
provisions of

.. application of stamp duty on
transfers of partnership interests 16-700

.. charging provisions 16-660

.. exemptions and reliefs,
application of 16-640

.. interests held by trustees 16-680

.. interpretation 16-720–16-840

. Scottish 16-860

. SDLT manual chapter 16-160

. starting 16-040

Power to enjoy 19-360

**Property investment
partnership** 16-380; 16-540

. election by 16-340

. partnerships other than 16-380

. transfer of interest 16-540

Qualifying film expenditure 25-520

Record-keeping 17-220

Relevant agreement 25-520

Relevant loan 14-060

Relevant partnership 30-040

Roll-over relief 15-240

'See-through' analysis 16-020

Paragraph

Sum of the lower proportions 16-280

Tax adjustment 18-560

Tax reliefs available to partners

. anti-avoidance 14-120

. associated disposals, restrictions
on relief for 14-520

. business assets, material
disposal of 14-440

. commercial woodlands 14-360

. corporate partnerships 14-600

. disposal

.. assets after business discontinued 14-480

.. associated with material disposal 14-500

.. by trustees 14-540

.. whole or part of a business 14-460

. double relief exclusion 14-100

. entrepreneurs' relief 14-420; 14-600

. generally 14-000

. gifts of interests in partnership 14-660

. importance of CGT reliefs 14-400

. interest paid, relief for

.. certificates from lenders 14-380

. interest payments, general 14-020

. limit on relief 14-040

. loan to invest in a partnership

.. restriction on relief for loans to
invest in property partnership 14-220

.. tax reduction for non-deductible
loan interest 14-240

. loans to invest in partnership

.. business successions 14-340

.. replacement loans 14-320

.. salaried partners 14-180

.. Scottish partnerships 14-200

.. withdrawal of relief 14-300

. loans to buy plant and
machinery 14-140

. loans to invest in film
partnerships 14-260

. negligible value claims by
partners 14-680

. qualifying purpose

.. mixed loans 14-080

Paragraph

.relevant business assets,
    restriction to 14-560

.relevant business assets: goodwill 14-580

.replacement of business assets by
    partners.. 14-640

.restrictions on relief

..arrangements to minimise risk to
    borrower... 14-060

..cash basis applies 14-060

..interest exceeding reasonable
    amount.. 14-060

..interest on overdrafts...................... 14-060

.salaried partners............................... 14-180

.Scottish partnerships........................ 14-200

Taxation

.general partnership 10-460

.limited partnership............................ 10-460

Terminal loss..................................... 25-160

Trade leasing allowance 25-100

Unrelieved interest 14-060

Value added tax, registration

.assessments....................................... 28-260

.capital paid on joining partnership 28-180

.circumstances change: notifying
    HMRC.. 28-080

.generally 28-000

.input tax recovery

..accountancy fees 28-460

..business purpose test....................... 28-420

..cost of raising capital 28-480

..other legal services and fees 28-440

..tripartite transactions...................... 28-400

.insolvency returns............................. 28-280

.limited liability partnerships............. 28-220

.limited partnerships 28-240

.name of firm: liability for VAT........ 28-040

.notices served on partnership 28-060

.opting to tax

..person authorised on behalf
    of a body 28-700

.partner's VAT liability...................... 28-100

.partners providing professional
    services... 28-720

Paragraph

.partners' entitlement to
    repayments 28-120

.partnership 'shares' and.................... 28-200

.partnership as separate person.......... 28-020

.partnership interest, transfer of........ 28-200

..non-supplies in relation to
    partnership 'share'......................... 28-200

..supplies of a partnership 'share' 28-200

.partnership interests.......................... 28-680

.partnership transactions

..capital introduced............................ 28-340

..de-registration 28-380

..purchase and disposal 28-360

.partnerships and VAT groups............ 28-160

.penalties

..civil fraud 28-300

..inaccurate information 28-320

.private tuition by partnership............ 28-740

.property letting

..joint venture by partners 28-660

..owners letting land and buildings..... 28-660

.property ownership

..'ordinary' partnership asset............. 28-520

..generally.. 28-500

..included in the balance sheet 28-540

..interest in property retained by
    outgoing partner............................ 28-620

..nominee company 28-580

..outside the partnership 28-560

..service company............................... 28-600

..summary... 28-640

.transfer of a 'going
    concern'..............................15-140; 28-760

Winding-up a partnership

.capital gains tax 13-080

.income tax 13-060

Winding-up an LLP

.capital gains tax 13-140

.income tax 13-120

With a view to profit 10-080